LEARNING DISABILITIES
and Challenging Behaviors

SECOND
EDITION

LEARNING DISABILITIES
and Challenging Behaviors

A Guide to Intervention & Classroom Management

SECOND EDITION

by

Nancy Mather, Ph.D.
University of Arizona
Tucson

and

Sam Goldstein, Ph.D.
Neurology, Learning and Behavior Center
and University of Utah
Salt Lake City
and George Mason University
Fairfax, Virginia

·P·A·U·L·H·
BROOKES
PUBLISHING CO ®

Baltimore • London • Sydney

Paul H. Brookes Publishing Co.
Post Office Box 10624
Baltimore, Maryland 21285-0624

www.brookespublishing.com

Typeset by Spearhead Global, Inc., Bear, Delaware.
Manufactured in the United States of America by
Sheridan Books, Inc., Chelsea, Michigan.

All examples in this book are composites. Any similarity to actual individuals or circumstances is coincidental, and no implications should be inferred.

The information provided in this book is in no way meant to substitute for a medical or mental health practitioner's advice or expert opinion. Readers should consult a health or mental health professional if they are interested in more information. This book is sold without warranties of any kind, express or implied, and the publisher and authors disclaim any liability, loss, or damage caused by the contents of this book.

Library of Congress Cataloging-in-Publication Data

Mather, Nancy.
   Learning disabilities and challenging behaviors : a guide to intervention and classroom management / by Nancy Mather and Sam Goldstein — 2nd ed.
      p.   cm.
   Includes bibliographical references and index.
   ISBN-13: 978-1-55766-935-3 (pbk.)
   ISBN-10: 1-55766-935-X (pbk.)
   1. Learning disabled children—Education.   2. Behavior disorders in children.
   3. Classroom management.   I. Goldstein, Sam, 1952- II. Title.
   LC4704.M374 2008
   371.9—dc22   2008003894

British Library Cataloguing in Publication data are available from the British Library.

2012   2011   2010   2009   2008

10   9   8   7   6   5   4   3   2   1

CONTENTS

ABOUT THE AUTHORS

Nancy Mather, Ph.D., University of Arizona, College of Education, Department of Special Education, Rehabilitation, and School Psychology, Education Building 409, Tucson, Arizona 85721

Dr. Mather is a professor at the University of Arizona in the Department of Special Education, Rehabilitation, and School Psychology. She specializes in the areas of reading, writing, and learning disabilities. She received her doctorate from the University of Arizona in 1985 in learning disabilities with minor areas of study in reading and school psychology. Other professional interests include adapting special education strategies to help general education teachers accommodate student diversity. She has conducted numerous workshops nationally and internationally on assessment, instruction, and issues that affect service delivery for individuals with learning disabilities. She has written many articles on topical issues in the field of learning disabilities. Dr. Mather is a co-author of the Woodcock-Johnson III (WJ III) with Richard W. Woodcock and Kevin S. McGrew (Riverside Publishing, 2001) and has co-authored two books on interpretation and application of the WJ III: *Woodcock-Johnson III: Reports, Recommendations, and Strategies* (Wiley, 2002) and *Essentials of WJ III Tests of Achievement Assessment* (Wiley, 2001). In addition, she has co-authored *Essentials of Assessment Report Writing* (Wiley, 2004), and has co-edited, with Richard Morris, *Evidenced-Based Interventions for Students with Learning and Behavioral Challenges* (Routledge, 2008).

Sam Goldstein, Ph.D., Neurology, Learning and Behavior Center, 230 South 500 East, Suite 100, Salt Lake City, Utah 84102

Dr. Goldstein is a clinical neuropsychologist, a nationally certified school psychologist, and an assistant clinical professor of psychiatry at the University of Utah and a research professor of psychology at George Mason University in Fairfax, Virginia. He is a director at the Neurology, Learning and Behavior Center in Salt Lake City, Utah, and he is on staff at the University Neuropsychiatric Institute at the University of Utah.

He is Editor-in-Chief of the *Journal of Attention Disorders* and is on the editorial boards of six journals, including the *Journal of Learning Disabilities*. Dr. Goldstein speaks internationally on a wide range of child development topics. His publications include two dozen peer-reviewed articles, guides, 20 book chapters, and 24 texts on subjects including genetic and developmental disorders, depression, classroom consultation, learning disability, and attention-deficit/hyperactivity disorder. He co-authored *Raising a Self-Disciplined Child* with Robert Brooks (Contemporary Books, 2007).

ABOUT THE CONTRIBUTORS

Robert Brooks, Ph.D., 60 Oak Knoll Terrace, Needham, Massachusetts 02492

Dr. Brooks is a faculty member at Harvard Medical School. He also has a part-time private practice and provides consultation to several educational institutions. His major professional activity is conducting workshops and presentations nationally and internationally to groups of educators, health care professionals, business people, community organizations, and parents. His works contain a message based on encouragement, hope, and resilience, and he is renowned for the warmth and humor he uses to bring his insights and anecdotes to life. He co-authored *Raising a Self-Disciplined Child* with Sam Goldstein (Contemporary Books, 2007).

Ann M. Richards, Ph.D. West Virginia University, 508G Allen Hall, Morgantown, West Virginia 26506

Dr. Richards is an associate professor at West Virginia University, where she trains teachers of special education at both the graduate and undergraduate levels. Much of her work has been done in the areas of transition, schoolwide positive behavior support, collaboration, and learning disabilities. She has provided several professional development workshops on characteristics of special needs learners and the need for differentiated instruction within general education classrooms. She is also an active volunteer for West Virginia Special Olympics, providing preservice teachers with experiences working with individuals with disabilities.

Gretchen Schoenfield, B.S., Post Office Box 210069, College of Education, Department of Special Education, Rehabilitation, and School Psychology, University of Arizona, Tucson, Arizona 85721

Ms. Schoenfield is a doctoral student in school psychology at the University of Arizona. Her primary research interests include the neuropsychological correlates of behavior disorders and delinquency in children and adolescents.

Karyl Lynch, M.A., provided assistance on Chapters 9 and 10 on the first edition of this book.

PREFACE

Most children enter kindergarten excited, optimistic, and ready to learn. Yet, within a few years, a significant minority become disenchanted and turned off to school not because of the challenges they face, but because our educational system has failed to understand and appreciate those challenges. Most important, schools have not learned to identify children at risk before they fail. One in four children struggles with learning, behavior, or emotional problems at school. School experiences for these children further reinforce their perceptions of inadequacy. The *instinctual optimism* that children bring to life must be nurtured at school if they are to make a successful transition through their educational years.

What variables contribute to this change of heart and view of self? For example, despite failing to complete a puzzle, most first-grade students confidently report that if they were given another chance they would be able to complete the puzzle successfully. Yet by the end of elementary school, many students do not predict that they will experience future success following failure. Some would suggest that this transformation in attitude is simply a process of maturation. Young students are unable to assess their capabilities accurately and, when facing a problem, they are naive about the probability of success. Yet this very same research can be viewed from the perspective that school experiences negatively alter students' self-confidence (Goldstein & Brooks, 2007). If this is the case, we are missing a valuable opportunity to help children develop self-discipline; confidence; and a resilient, optimistic view of self, essential components for life success (Brooks & Goldstein, 2001, 2007).

Although the new millennium brings promises of an unlimited technological, scientific, and cultural future, as a society we are experiencing increasing problems preparing our youth for this future. Competency in basic academic subjects is simply not enough. Violence, vandalism, increased school dropout rates, and mental health problems among our students remind us daily of this fact. The burden of preparing children for their future has been and must be increasingly borne on the shoulders of educators. Our schools must find a way to educate all students efficiently and effectively, providing them with knowledge and instilling in them qualities of hope and resilience. These qualities will help them be confident and overcome the adversities that they will face.

To accomplish this goal, educators must begin looking at children differently. Rather than viewing the learning, emotional, and behavioral problems that some children experience as somehow making them different in a fixed and stable way, educators must view these problems as malleable and responsive to environmental manipulation. This requires a shift from a categorical model of differences to a model that acknowledges that most children's school problems result from variations in abilities and environmental influences. Children with slower learning rates, for example, learn through the same processes as others but require more time to do so. Children with attentional problems do pay attention, just not to the same degree as others. They respond to the same types of strategies and interventions that other children do but they require more assistance in developing essential self-control.

The second edition of *Learning Disabilities and Challenging Behaviors: A Guide to Intervention and Classroom Management*, marks our third collaboration in just over a decade, and is the result of a chance meeting at an educational conference in Saskatoon, Canada. We were each speaking on different but related topics concerning children's development, learning, and behavioral challenges. Although our backgrounds and training were quite different, we immediately found common ground in our conceptualization of children's development, as well as in our understanding of how to help children who struggle in the classroom.

Our first joint book, *Overcoming Underachieving* (Goldstein & Mather, 1998), was written as a guide to help parents foster their children's school success. In that volume, we took a novel approach by suggesting that an appreciation and understanding of a finite pattern of skills and abilities could help provide an explanation for children's success and failure in the classroom. Of note, these skills and abilities, which we organized into the Building Blocks of Learning model, could be used to evaluate and address children's struggles in school. A number of years later we were fortunate to meet an editor at Paul H. Brookes Publishing Co. She asked if we would be interested in creating a book for teachers based on our Building Blocks model. In 2001, we published the first edition of this volume.

In this second edition, we have revised and rewritten many chapters to include the most up-to-date information available and added more than 300 new references. We have modified the Building Blocks model to provide a better appreciation and understanding of children's learning and behavior. Our model still emphasizes the underlying behaviors and skills that contribute to efficient learning; however, it now reflects the most recent educational, psychological, and neuropsychological research. Since the publication of the first edition of this volume, for example, there has been an increased emphasis on assessing the effectiveness of schools to teach basic skills, especially in the areas of reading, writing, and mathematics. Terms such as *high-stakes testing*, *accountability*, and *merit pay* have become common terminology in the educational landscape. In an era in which educators are warned of the consequences of "leaving a child behind," it is still the case that many educational systems fail to understand and appreciate how children learn, how they differ, and what to do when they struggle.

We are confident that the revised material in this second edition enhances and expands on the first edition. It is our hope that this book will help you increase your understanding of children's learning and behavioral difficulties and of how children's abilities contribute to classroom successes and failures. We also describe and explain many common childhood problems such as anxiety, dyslexia, and attention-deficit/hyperactivity disorder (ADHD). Throughout the book we suggest many specific strategies and interventions to use with struggling students. The Additional Resources section at the end of the book provides a list of useful methods, techniques, and web sites. Application of the strategies in this book can help ensure that more students are successfully educated and prepared for their futures and, throughout this process, develop a resilient, optimistic view of themselves and their surrounding world.

REFERENCES

Brooks, R., & Goldstein, S. (2001). *Raising resilient children.* New York: Contemporary Books.

Brooks, R., & Goldstein, S. (2007). *Raising a self-disciplined child.* New York: McGraw-Hill.

Goldstein, S., & Brooks, R. (2007). *Understanding and managing children's classroom behavior.* New York: Wiley.

Mather, N., & Goldstein, S. (1998). *Overcoming underachieving: An action guide for helping your child succeed in school.* New York: Wiley.

ACKNOWLEDGMENTS

We thank Dr. Robert Brooks once again for his thoughtful contributions to Chapter 7. We also wish to thank Dr. Ann Richards and Gretchen Schoenfield for their contributions to Chapters 5, 10, and 11 and Dr. Annmarie Urso for a section in Chapter 10 and assistance in compiling the list of additional resources and web sites. Thanks also goes to our Acquisitions Editor, Sarah Shepke, at Paul H. Brookes Publishing Co., for her support, and our Senior Production Editor, Leslie K. Eckard, for her dedicated assistance and detailed editorial advice. Once again we thank Kathleen Gardner for her diligence, management, and editorial assistance with this text. Her continued dedication to our work is most appreciated. We also wish to thank and express our admiration for the many inspiring and dedicated educators who are the charismatic adults guiding children in their learning and development.

A NOTE TO TEACHERS

Your best efforts in working with challenging students will be inspiring to other teachers and parents. But your efforts will give special encouragement to the students themselves, as illustrated in this letter from Andy, a 9-year old boy, to his teacher.

Dear Ms. Caseman. Thank you for helping me with my writing this year. You listened to my ideas. Have a great summer.

*In loving memory of my parents, Chuck and Mildred,
whose love provided the foundation,
and to Michael and my sons, Benjamin and Daniel.*

—N.M.

*To my wife, Janet, and our children Allyson and Ryan.
We have witnessed the power of education in shaping your
developing minds into caring, conscientious, and accomplished young adults.*

—S.G.

*Our book is also dedicated to the memories of Drs. Sally Smith and Claire Jones.
Sally's sharp wit, creativity, colorful spirit, and tireless advocacy and
Claire's energy, enthusiasm, and care for individuals with learning and
behavioral challenges significantly touched and improved
the lives of countless families and professionals.
Although they will be missed, their numerous contributions have enriched us all.*

No one has yet fully realized the wealth of sympathy, kindness and generosity hidden in the soul of a child. The effort of every true education should be to unlock that treasure.

—*Emma Goldman*

The mediocre teacher tells. The good teacher explains. The superior teacher demonstrates. The great teacher inspires.

—*William Arthur Ward*

INTRODUCTION

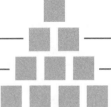

CHAPTER 1 OUTLINE

BUILDING BLOCKS OF LEARNING

The Learning Environment
Foundational Blocks
Symbolic Blocks
Conceptual Blocks
How the Blocks Work Together

COMMON PROFILES

Strengths in the Symbolic and Conceptual Blocks, Weaknesses in the
Foundational Blocks, and a Disadvantaged Environment
Strengths in the Foundational and Conceptual Blocks, Weaknesses in
the Symbolic Blocks, and a Supportive Environment
Strengths in the Foundational and Symbolic Blocks, Weaknesses in the
Conceptual Blocks
Strengths in the Conceptual Blocks, Weaknesses in the Symbolic and
Foundational Blocks
A Significant Strength or Weakness in One Block

BUILDING BLOCKS QUESTIONNAIRE

Completing the Building Blocks Questionnaire
Ryan's Profile

PURPOSE, OVERVIEW, AND AUDIENCE

APPENDIX: BUILDING BLOCKS QUESTIONNAIRE

Strategies

Language   Images

CONCEPTUAL

Phonology   Orthography   Motor

SYMBOLIC

Attention & Self-Regulation   Emotions   Behavior   Self-Esteem

FOUNDATIONAL

THE BUILDING BLOCKS OF LEARNING

A FRAMEWORK FOR UNDERSTANDING CLASSROOM LEARNING AND BEHAVIOR

The last day of school for the Harper Unified School District was a day of celebration as well as a time for reflection. Although teachers and students were looking forward to the summer break, the students were sad to leave their teachers, and the teachers had mixed feelings about the school year coming to an end, and worried about certain students. Although the teachers hoped that all of their students would be successful in school in the coming years, they were most apprehensive about the children who had learning and behavior difficulties. On some days during the past year, these students were their teachers' greatest source of fulfillment; other days, they were their teachers' greatest source of frustration.

Veteran teachers know that students with learning and behavior difficulties face a difficult journey and that their education requires constant attention and fine tuning if they are to succeed. One such teacher, Ms. Abram, considered this when working with Andy, one of her third graders. Although Andy could talk up a storm, he struggled with both fine and gross motor tasks. On the playground, balls would roll past him. He often tripped going up or down the school stairs. When the class played kickball, Andy usually wound up on the ground after attempting to kick the moving ball. Andy still could not tie his shoes, nor did he attempt to ride a bicycle. Although Ms. Abram had worked with Andy diligently all school year to improve his handwriting, he seemed to have made little progress. His spacing was still poor, and the size of his letters was inconsistent. Just that day, he had left the following note on her desk: "I'll see you later." (See Figure 1.1.)

Mr. Steen, a fourth-grade teacher, worried about Ryan. At the beginning of the year, Ryan entered his classroom with very limited reading skills. He also had difficulty completing assigned tasks and complained about how much he disliked school. He was quick to tell others that he was "dumb" and that school was "stupid." Because of the daily visits to the resource room for individualized instruction and an adapted classroom program, Ryan's reading skills, attitude, and self-confidence had improved; however, Mr. Steen was well aware that, because he was so far behind, Ryan would continue to struggle with reading and writing tasks in the years ahead.

Whenever Ms. Richards, a fourth-grade teacher, saw Stephanie on the playground, she was concerned that Stephanie did not interact with her peers appropriately. Stephanie often ran up to other children on the playground and pushed her way in between them. When they told her to stop, she would look at them and move closer. Finally, the other

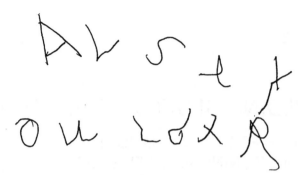

Figure 1.1. Andy's note to his third-grade teacher: "I'll see you later."

children would walk away as a group, with Stephanie lagging behind, trying to get their attention. Ms. Richards tried to create situations that would help Stephanie develop friendships, but nothing seemed to work. In the classroom, Stephanie spelled, memorized rote facts, and read words with ease. She talked quite easily about situations and information she knew well. At times, she seemed to go on and on with little point to the conversation. In contrast, when questioned about a story she had just read, Stephanie was unable to provide any answers. When she was asked to predict an answer or follow several directions, she often forgot what she was doing and was unable to complete the task at hand.

Ms. McGrew, a fifth-grade teacher, was most concerned about Katy. Unlike Stephanie, Katy had several good friends, but she also struggled to learn new concepts and vocabulary. Although she memorized her spelling words easily, she had trouble using the words in sentences. She had memorized many math facts, but, after reading a story problem, she would ask, "What am I supposed to do? Add, subtract, or times it?" She often volunteered information in class, but her answers usually missed the mark. Only last month, when Ms. McGrew asked her students what they knew about the planet Saturn, Katy raised her hand and stated, "Saturn is a car." Next year, Katy would start middle school and would work with six or more teachers each day. Ms. McGrew worried and wondered how Katy would keep up and obtain the individualized attention and support she would require in a new school environment.

Ms. Jones was thinking about Anthony, who had been in her fifth-grade class. During the year in her classroom, he had appeared withdrawn, quiet, and inattentive. Over the first few weeks of school, the quality of his work had declined and he often appeared sad. One day Ms. Jones found Anthony hiding in the coatroom. When she asked him to join the class, Anthony said he just did not feel like it.

Ms. Perry's thoughts were on Mark, a sixth-grade student. She secretly wished she could adopt Mark. She knew the boy had a lot of potential, but every afternoon when he left school, he returned to a chaotic, inconsistent home life. Mark and his two brothers and one sister were currently living in a trailer with four adults. As Ms. Perry learned more about Mark's home life, she understood why he never completed or handed in any homework or studied for the weekly quizzes. Knowing that she had no control over his home environment, she had stopped assigning Mark homework and had instead arranged a special daily study time for Mark at school. She even spent 2 days per week with Mark after school, helping him keep up with his assignments. One afternoon, Mark thanked Ms. Perry for liking him.

Mr. Chavez was thinking about Jeremy, a fifth-grade student in his class. Jeremy's first-grade teacher had described him as a "moving target who can't control his motion." Although Jeremy had been diagnosed as having attention-deficit/hyperactivity disorder (ADHD) and was receiving medical treatment and counseling, he still had trouble follow-

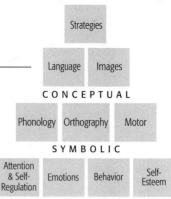

Strategies

Language | Images

CONCEPTUAL

Phonology | Orthography | Motor

SYMBOLIC

Attention & Self-Regulation | Emotions | Behavior | Self-Esteem

FOUNDATIONAL

ing directions and completing tasks. Mr. Chavez believed that Jeremy could do his school-work if he could only concentrate for longer periods of time and think through situations before he acted. Jeremy explained one day after blurting out a response in class, "I just can't keep the words in my mouth."

Ms. Rhein, a middle school English teacher, was thinking of Ben, an eighth-grade student. Ben loved physical activities and sports. He excelled in soccer, baseball, and tennis. In school he enjoyed challenging math, science, and computer activities. He loved to draw intricate sketches of machines and cars. Ben did not, however, enjoy activities involving reading and writing. Although he read fairly accurately, his reading rate was extremely slow. When most of the students had read 10 pages, Ben was just starting the second page. He often misspelled small common words, such as writing *thay* for *they.* He tried to avoid writing tasks by any means possible. Ms. Rhein wondered how Ben's high school teachers would respond to his limited writing skills as well as to his negative attitude toward writing tasks.

Mr. Arnold, a sixth-grade teacher, had recognized early in the year that Maria was having trouble with reading and spelling. When reading aloud, she skipped words that were difficult to pronounce. Some of her attempted spellings bore little resemblance to the actual sound structure of the words. Mr. Arnold had asked Maria's mother if Maria's hearing had been checked and was assured that Maria had no difficulties with hearing. Maria's mother did mention, however, that Maria had experienced many ear infections during her preschool years. Her mother also reported that they typically spent 3–4 hours each evening completing her homework. Mr. Arnold recognized how hard Maria was working and how willing she was to attempt any task, but her reading and spelling skills were far behind those of the majority of her classmates.

Ms. Handler thought about Samuel, a sixth-grade student who seemed to get in trouble for something every day. In the past, Samuel had taken jewelry from other students, lunch money, and even the door jambs from the classroom wall. Ms. Handler had to check Samuel's backpack each day to make sure that all of the contents inside were his. He had been suspended twice during the school year, once for lighting a firecracker in the school hallway and another time for bringing a pocketknife to school. Recently, when he was asked by a student teacher to remove a hat from his desk, he refused. When the request was repeated, he picked up his chair and threw it at the teacher. Last week during lunch time, he had locked two children in the art supply closet.

Dr. Mantell thought about John, a junior in her American history class. Although John was enthusiastic about learning and always completed his homework assignments, he appeared to possess very poor study skills and had trouble grasping concepts. He received As on his homework assignments but never passed in-class tests. When he volunteered a response in class, his answers revealed his limited understanding. In fact, it seemed as though he possessed "Swiss cheese" knowledge. He appeared to understand some things but lacked basic knowledge in other areas. One day in class, when he was asked to name the country that bordered the United States on the northern side, he responded, "England." When asked what material was used to make paper, he responded, "Sodium." John had extreme difficulty understanding the concepts introduced in his science class, such as the difference between meiosis and mitosis. Even with tutoring three times a week, John could not understand or retain the concepts to pass the classroom tests.

For general education teachers, special education teachers, or school psychologists who have been teaching several years or have worked with children with learning and behavior problems in some capacity, the characteristics of these various children are likely to sound familiar, and those educators in training will soon come to recognize these characteristics as well. All children possess different learning styles and abilities. The reasons why one child struggles typically differ from the reasons why another child struggles, and learning and behavior difficulties cannot be resolved quickly or easily.

This is not a typical introductory textbook about learning disabilities (LD) and classroom behavior problems. Although various learning and behavior problems are explained and informal ways to assess these difficulties are described, the main focus is on identifying the developmental, learning, and behavior skills of children and then determining the practical strategies and techniques that will be most effective for helping children to succeed in school. As illustrated by brief descriptions of the students, each child has an individual style of learning and a unique set of circumstances. Increased awareness and understanding of a child's unique profile of strengths and weaknesses can help educators improve each child's school-related outcomes.

BUILDING BLOCKS OF LEARNING

When a child struggles in school, teachers must first determine the underlying factors contributing to the learning or behavior problem because when a child acts out, the reason may not be readily apparent. Similarly, when a child fails to or refuses to complete work, it is rarely because of poor motivation. Lowered motivation in students is often a secondary symptom resulting from chronic school difficulties. Over many years of working with students, school psychologists, special and general education teachers, and parents, we have developed and revised a simple framework for explaining why children experience learning and behavior problems in the classroom. This framework is called the Building Blocks of Learning (Goldstein & Mather, 1998). Although similar in intent to our original framework, this second edition contains an updated model and a revised questionnaire.

Our efforts to develop a working model of classroom problems combined with our professional experiences led us to conclude that the classroom behavior and learning problems of children could be represented using a three-level, triangular framework reflecting foundational skills, symbolic or perceptual processing skills, and conceptual or thinking skills. The remainder of this chapter introduces the Building Blocks of Learning model. Chapter 2 reviews the theoretical foundations for the model.

Although the model has not undergone a large, research-based evaluation, we believe it is consistent with current research and with the observations and reports from parents, teachers, and specialists throughout the years. The model offers a bridge between research and educational practice. The intent is to help educators increase understanding of the various reasons why children struggle in school and, more important, the ways in which professionals can help these students.

This model, presented in Figure 1.2, contains 10 building blocks stacked into the shape of a pyramid. The base of the pyramid is the learning environment—an external variable that includes a child's home, school, and classroom environments. The 10 blocks of the pyramid are divided into three distinct groups. At the base are the four foundational blocks: *attention and self-regulation, emotions, behavior,* and *self-esteem.* The middle level contains a set of three symbolic blocks: *phonology,* for phonological processing; *orthography,* for orthographic processing; and *motor,* for and motor processing. The top level contains the three conceptual blocks: *language,* for thinking with language; *images,* for thinking with images; and *strategies,* for thinking with strategies. Although all of the blocks are the

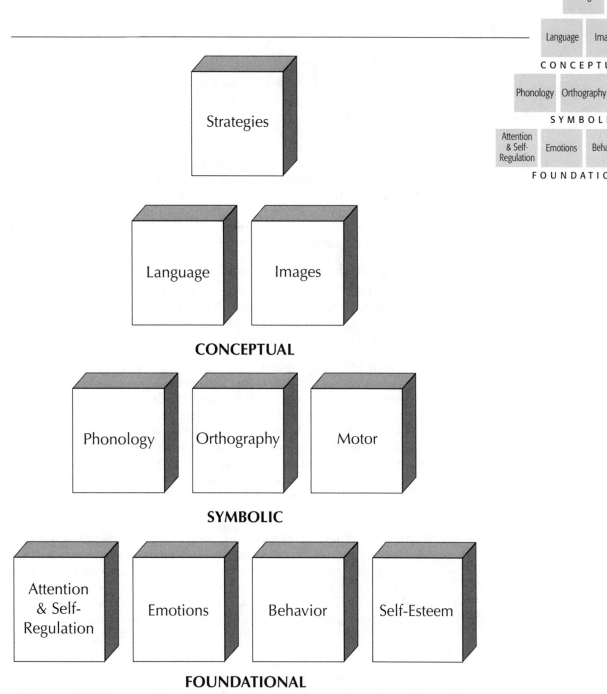

Figure 1.2. Building Blocks of Learning model.

same size, some of the blocks are more important than others for certain types of learning.

Many of the most common classroom learning and behavior problems can be represented clearly, described, and subsequently understood through the use of this model. We acknowledge that not all abilities are accounted for in this model; we also recognize that learning is an interactive process and that these blocks are not discrete units but rather encompass interrelated and interactive factors and abilities. Although learning does not consist of isolated skills, an understanding of the unique affective, behavioral, cognitive, and linguistic variables that influence development and school performance can help educators understand the various types of LD and behavior disorders and subsequently design or select appropriate behavioral and academic interventions.

The Learning Environment

Symbolically, the base of the pyramid is the learning environment. This includes the supports provided for the student in the home and school as well any special services such as speech-language or occupational therapy that the student receives. Clearly, children's learning and behavior problems can be exacerbated by factors within the home setting. For example, a lack of parental support coupled with chaos at home was having a significant effect on Mark's self-image and his emotional availability to engage in academic tasks. Despite the fact that the home environment exerts a powerful influence on school adjustment, however, our focus in this book is on the learning environment at school. Classroom teachers have the primary responsibility for creating a nurturing class environment where students feel respected, valued, and supported academically, emotionally, and socially.

Foundational Blocks

The foundational blocks provide the support system for all learning. Just as the foundation of a house must be strong enough to support the structure, these four blocks must be strong for efficient learning to occur. A brief description of the skills in the foundational blocks follows.

Attention and Self-Regulation   The building block of attention and self-regulation includes a child's ability to pay attention, self-regulate behavior, and control impulses, which are critical to all learning. Mr. Chavez knew that the basis of many of Jeremy's attention and behavior difficulties stemmed from poor self-regulation and that his problems with impulse control prevented him from focusing on the relevant requirements of classroom learning tasks. Jeremy had trouble maintaining persistent effort and was easily distracted when attempting to pursue a goal. He had difficulty sticking with a plan for completing his assignments, for example, and rarely turned in work. He also would often disturb other children.

Emotions   The building block of emotions includes a child's general temperament as well as his or her moods. This block refers to what are sometimes called *internalizing disorders*—conditions such as depression, anxiety, and poor motivation. These disorders can significantly affect a child's availability to learn. Difficulties in school also affect attitude and performance. Ben had always struggled with reading and spelling, for example. These difficulties had affected his attitude and his willingness to persevere on tasks requiring reading and writing.

Behavior   The building block of behavior includes a student's covert and overt actions, including social skills and compliance. Conduct disorder, oppositional defiant disorder, and anger control all are examples of externalizing disorders that influence interactions with teachers and peers. Samuel's behavior caused negative reactions from his peers. He would often shove another student or, without provocation, knock a student's books onto the floor. Ms. Handler had tried to implement several interventions, including moving Samuel's desk away from other students or sending him to time-out, but his disruptive behaviors continued.

Self-Esteem   The building block of self-esteem relates to how students perceive themselves and to what factors they attribute their successes and failures. These are learned attitudes, developed in part through feedback from parents, teachers, and peers. Poor academic self-esteem can affect a child's willingness to persist on difficult tasks. Maria, the sixth-grade student, wrote about this in her journal (see Figure 1.3). Clearly, her struggles with spelling and writing were

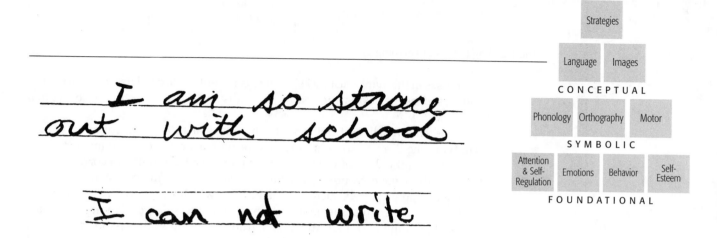

Figure 1.3. Maria's comments in her journal.

affecting her self-perception. Because of these difficulties, Maria was beginning to believe that she was not good at anything at all.

To succeed in school, a child requires a supportive classroom environment, the ability to pay attention, healthy emotions, self-discipline, and a positive view of self and school. Strengths in the foundational blocks help a student compensate for other difficulties and learn to persevere even when faced with difficult tasks. Weaknesses in the foundational blocks affect school performance, and adverse factors such as anxiety or depression reduce a child's availability for learning. Strong foundational blocks do not, however, guarantee school success. Some children have support at home and school, pay attention, and are happy and well adjusted but struggle because of specific cognitive and linguistic weaknesses in the symbolic or conceptual blocks.

Symbolic Blocks

The second level of the Building Blocks model involves the processing of information through the senses. The abilities in these blocks help children gain access to, produce, recall, and retrieve information about the symbolic aspects of language. Many terms have been applied to the deficient school achievement of this group, including LD, underachievement, learning difficulty, dyslexia, and specific developmental disorders (Hinshaw, 1992).

In general, the abilities of the symbolic blocks are conceptualized as secretarial in nature because difficulties primarily affect basic skill development or the mastery of the coding systems of language: decoding (i.e., word identification), encoding (i.e., spelling), and motor coding (i.e., handwriting). Isaacson (1989) aptly distinguished between the roles of the secretary and the author in the writing process. The secretary manages the mechanical concerns of writing, such as spelling, punctuation, and handwriting (i.e., skills affected by strengths and weaknesses in the symbolic blocks), whereas the author formulates, organizes, and expresses ideas (i.e., skills affected by strengths and weaknesses in the conceptual blocks).

Some children have trouble with phonological tasks (e.g., rhyming words, identifying the discrete sounds in words) or with aspects of verbal memory (e.g., trying to recall the days of the week or the names of the months in correct order). Other children have trouble with the orthographic or more visual aspects of learning to read and spell, such as remembering which way to write the letter *b* or how to spell the irregular element in a word. Still others do poorly with the motor aspects of learning and, like Andy, have trouble cutting with scissors or forming letters. Children with marked weaknesses in these blocks often are diagnosed as having LD. The skills in the symbolic blocks depend heavily on memory. Eventually, these abilities become increasingly more automatic (with little thinking involved) as performance becomes more effortless and efficient. A brief description of the skills represented in these blocks follows.

Phonological Processing   The main abilities of the phonological processing block are *phonological awareness* and *verbal short-term memory*. Phonological awareness is the oral language ability to understand the sound structure of speech. This awareness allows one to manipulate language sounds. As students learn an alphabetic language such as English, a critical first step is becoming aware that speech can be divided or sequenced into a series of discrete sounds, words, syllables, and phonemes, the smallest units of sound. In most instances, this awareness develops gradually during the preschool and early elementary years. Maria's difficulties with reading and spelling were caused by poor phonological awareness. She had trouble discriminating similar speech sounds and often would omit sounds when spelling a word or would confuse certain sounds, such as writing *f* for the /v/ sound.

Verbal short-term memory refers to the ability to repeat back in sequence information that has just been heard. This type of skill is needed to follow directions in a classroom or write notes during a lecture. Difficulty with memory also is associated with remembering rote information, such as learning the letter names or memorizing multiplication tables. In some cases, a student's difficulties are primarily related to memory. In other cases, problems with short-term memory tasks are more related to weaknesses in attention or language. Although Maria experienced trouble with the sounds of language, she did not have trouble listening to, repeating, or following directions.

Orthographic Processing   In a general sense, *orthography* refers to the writing system of a language, including the punctuation marks, capitalization rules, and spelling patterns. In a narrower sense, orthography refers to the perception and recall of letter strings and word forms. This ability, referred to as *orthographic awareness,* allows one to form a mental representation of the appearance of a letter or word. In addition, orthographic sensitivity helps one become aware of the common spelling patterns and word parts as well as the rules about legal letter strings or combinations that exist in a language. For example, most first-grade children quickly learn that the letters *ck* can be placed at the end of a word to make the /k/ sound but not at the start of a word.

Another part of this block involves *automatic retrieval,* or the speed of recognition of letters and words. This ability is needed to recall quickly basic sight vocabulary for both reading and spelling. A child with initial weaknesses in this block is likely to have a slow reading rate and poor spelling in later years. In fact, Ben's major problems with reading and spelling were due to his poor orthographic awareness and slow speed of word perception.

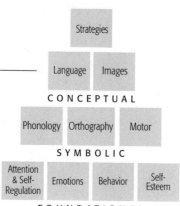

Some abilities are more complex and include aspects of two or more blocks, such as *working memory*. Working memory refers to the ability to apprehend information and then rearrange it in a specified way. A simple example would be to ask someone to listen to a series of digits and then say the digits back in a reversed order. This type of ability requires verbal short-term memory as well as the ability to visualize and rearrange the digits.

Motor Processing   The motor block consists of two types of abilities: *gross motor skills,* the skills involving large muscle movements such as those used in jumping and running, and *fine motor skills,* the skills involving small muscles such as those used in writing or drawing. A child may have a strength or weakness in one or both of these areas. For example, a child skilled in soccer may or may not possess the ability to produce neat handwriting in the classroom. In addition, fine motor skills can be broken into two types: the skills involved in symbol production (i.e., writing letters and numbers) and the skills involved in artistic expression (i.e., drawing a picture). Some children can sketch or draw wonderful illustrations but are stymied by the production of symbols. This difficulty with producing the motor patterns needed for writing is referred to as *dysgraphia.* Andy possessed weaknesses in motor planning that made it difficult to perform most types of fine and gross motor tasks. In this book, we focus on fine motor skills because they are more relevant to classroom performance.

In general, strong processing abilities make early learning easier and enable children to perform secretarial tasks such as taking notes, memorizing math facts, or acquiring accurate and fluent word identification skills. Once a child has learned a task, which may require repeated practice, these skills become increasingly automatic or *automatized* and are performed with little thought and effort. For example, when a child has learned to read a word, the word is recognized instantly when it is encountered.

Skills in these blocks help children perform various tasks, but these skills alone do not guarantee school success. Some children have no difficulty learning to read, spell, and solve math computations. These children perform automatic, symbolic tasks with ease; however, when the curriculum begins to accelerate and the children must read to learn, they may struggle because of weak conceptual and linguistic skills. They may be capable of mastering basic mathematical processes but then struggle with more complex mathematics because of difficulties with reasoning and concept formation. In our model, these types of difficulties relate to the abilities of the conceptual blocks.

Conceptual Blocks

The top of the pyramid includes the conceptual abilities: thinking with language, images, and strategies. The abilities in the conceptual blocks help children to understand meanings, comprehend relationships, visualize complex designs, and apply previously acquired knowledge as they engage in academic tasks.

Thinking with Language   Thinking with language involves tasks such as understanding what is heard, comprehending written text, expressing ideas through speaking and writing, and learning and using new vocabulary. Students with strengths in language tend to speak easily and possess an expansive vocabulary. Students with weaknesses in language often experience difficulty with tasks involving comprehension or production of text. Katy had weaknesses in language, and consequently, her answers often missed the mark. One day, Ms. McGrew showed Katy a picture of four trees and then asked her, "Half of these trees would be how many?" Katy asked as she drew a horizontal line across the trees, "You mean if you cut them this way?"

11

Thinking with Images Thinking with images involves reproducing complex visual patterns and designs as well as understanding and judging spatial relationships. Some children have more difficulty with tasks of a nonverbal nature than those involving language. These children tend to have particular difficulty grasping and acquiring mathematical concepts. They also may have trouble with developing social competence and recognizing, evaluating, and interpreting gestures and facial expressions. Stephanie had a lot of trouble interpreting facial expressions and could not readily assess how others were feeling. This block represents some problems associated with what are often referred to as *nonverbal LD*.

Thinking with Strategies Thinking with strategies involves thinking about thinking, or what is referred to as *metacognition*. This block includes the executive functions used to direct all cognitive activities and includes the abilities to plan, organize, monitor, evaluate, and reflect on one's own learning. This block is placed at the top of the model because of its importance to all learning and behavior. Strengths in this block help students to be purposeful and self-regulated and to engage in goal-directed behavior. Ultimately, if students can become strategic, goal-oriented learners, they are usually able to compensate and adjust for weaknesses in other areas.

How the Blocks Work Together

In thinking about the learning and behavior of students, one can understand the role that specific weaknesses in one or more of the building blocks can play in creating school difficulties. Ryan had weaknesses in the symbolic blocks. These contributed to his reading difficulties and consequently affected his self-esteem. Katy had weaknesses in the conceptual blocks, and she struggled to comprehend tasks that involved using language and reasoning. Jeremy struggled with weaknesses in the foundational block of attention and self-regulation. Although Ben could produce intricate sketches of machines and rebuild a motorcycle engine, he had trouble spelling even common words. Ben had trouble getting a mental image of the appearance of words. His marked difficulty with spelling contributed to a negative attitude toward all types of writing tasks. Mark came from a disadvantaged environment in which little support was provided for learning in the home.

When the blocks are stacked together as a model, one can understand how a child's unique learning and behavior characteristics, as well as the child's support system and environment, can affect school success. When considering the unique characteristics of each student, the first goal is to identify specific strengths and how these abilities can be used to enhance performance; the second is to identify the weaker areas and abilities so that appropriate accommodations and instructional plans can be developed and implemented.

COMMON PROFILES

Children's difficulties result from qualitative differences, and many different combinations of skills are possible. The slogan "One size fits all" does not apply to the learning abilities or disabilities of children. When designing academic and behavioral interventions for specific students, a more accurate adage is "One size fits one." We have, however, encountered a few frequently occurring general profiles. Five of the most common profiles are described briefly in the following sections.

Strengths in the Symbolic and Conceptual Blocks, Weaknesses in the Foundational Blocks, and a Disadvantaged Environment

Some children have the language, reasoning, and processing abilities needed for school achievement but are hampered by emotional or behavioral issues. The

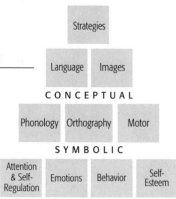

difficulties that some children experience in school can be related directly to weaknesses in the foundational blocks. Students who experience trouble with paying attention or have serious emotional or behavior problems may be unavailable for learning. Other children may return home each evening to a chaotic or extremely stressful home environment. This constant disruption at home reduces the child's ability to profit from instruction. In most instances, once their attentional, emotional, or social issues have been addressed and resolved, these children are able to succeed in school.

Strengths in the Foundational and Conceptual Blocks, Weaknesses in the Symbolic Blocks, and a Supportive Environment

Some students possess above-average language and reasoning abilities and the ability to pay attention, and they live in supportive homes and learn in nurturing school environments. In spite of their many capabilities, their marked weaknesses in the symbolic blocks affect their ability to learn and memorize specific information. Although these children may be well adjusted and highly motivated, they struggle with school tasks that require rote learning and memory, such as reading words, spelling, or calculating. They are slow to develop automaticity with word reading and spelling and may be diagnosed as having dyslexia, dyscalculia, or dysgraphia (specific reading, math, or writing disability). With understanding and systematic, intensive interventions, as well as curricular adjustments and accommodations throughout their school careers, these students can be successful.

Strengths in the Foundational and Symbolic Blocks, Weaknesses in the Conceptual Blocks

Students with weaknesses in the conceptual blocks experience difficulty with tasks involving reasoning and language. These students have particular difficulty with tasks involving comprehending and expressing ideas and problem solving. In contrast, because of strengths in the symbolic blocks, they can memorize spelling words and math facts easily but have trouble applying these skills to real-life problems. A modified and adapted curriculum coupled with direct therapy in the use of language and the application of strategies can help these students improve their chances for school success.

Strengths in the Conceptual Blocks, Weaknesses in the Symbolic and Foundational Blocks

Some children with strengths in thinking and reasoning have weaknesses in processing and attending to information. For example, some students with LD often receive the dual diagnosis of LD and ADHD. In other cases, students with LD often have low self-esteem or emotional or behavior problems. These problems contribute further to reduced motivation and school failure. With appropriate, often intensive, long-term interventions, these children can succeed in school.

A Significant Strength or Weakness in One Block

Some students excel in one area. Although Ben was having trouble with reading and writing, he was an extremely talented athlete. His success in sports helped him maintain a positive view of himself. Maria had trouble with the sounds of language but not with tasks involving thinking with language. Her strong ability to reason using language enabled her to learn through listening and compensate somewhat for her problems with phonology.

13

Other students possess a significant weakness in only one area that often results in a specific diagnosis and eligibility for special services. For example, a student with a specific weakness in phonology may be diagnosed as having dyslexia. A student with severe problems in motor skills may be classified as having a sensory motor integration disorder or dysgraphia. Similarly, a student with severe behavior problems may be classified as having a conduct disorder. A student with severe attention problems may be diagnosed as having ADHD. A student with a severe problem in language acquisition or use may be classified as having a language impairment. Students with severe weaknesses in one domain often require intensive and systematic interventions to succeed in school. Maria, Jeremy, and Andy are all examples of students with marked weaknesses in one area. To compensate, these children must learn how to rely on their strengths.

BUILDING BLOCKS QUESTIONNAIRE

The Building Blocks Questionnaire, presented in the appendix at the end of this chapter, is designed to help educators pinpoint in an informal way a student's strengths and weaknesses and to provide an overview of school-related skills and behaviors. This questionnaire has two sections: Part 1 provides 10 questions, one question for each of the 10 building blocks, which are intended to provide a general overview of a student's strengths and weaknesses. Under Foundational, for example, for the block Emotions, the general question would be, "Does the student appear to be sad or anxious more often than not during the day?" and the user would indicate whether this was true by checking the options *Rarely*, *Sometimes*, or *Frequently*. Part 2 provides an additional 10 items for each block in order to provide more in-depth information about the specifics of the behavior.

Completing the Building Blocks Questionnaire

If concerns exist about a certain student, a teacher can make a copy of the Building Blocks Questionnaire and then fill it out. A parent also can complete the questionnaire, or a teacher or school psychologist may interview a student. The purpose of completing the questionnaire is to gain a better understanding of the factors that contribute to a student's successes and struggles in school. When teachers are able to understand the reasons why a student is struggling in school, they are more efficient at determining and designing appropriate interventions. In addition, when teachers are aware of a child's strengths, they can capitalize on these abilities in designing programs and selecting interventions.

Ryan's Profile

Mr. Steen, Ryan's fourth-grade teacher, thought about Ryan as he answered the 10 questions in Part 1 of the Building Blocks Questionnaire (see Figure 1.4). He had noted that on occasion Ryan seemed inattentive, so he checked *Sometimes* for Attention and Self-Regulation. At times during the day Ryan seemed sad, so Mr. Steen checked *Sometimes* for Emotions. Ryan usually followed school rules, so Mr. Steen checked *Rarely* for Behavior. Ryan often complained about how much he disliked school and was quick to tell others that he was "dumb," so Mr. Steen checked *Frequently* for Self-Esteem. Ryan had started the year with very limited reading and spelling skills, so Mr. Steen checked *Frequently* for the Phonology and Orthography questions. Ryan's handwriting was usually legible, so Mr. Steen checked *Sometimes* for the Motor question. Ryan enjoyed science and math activities and had an adequate vocabulary, so Mr. Steen checked *Rarely* for the Thinking with Language and Images questions. Ryan was, however, inconsistent in devising and sticking with plans, so Mr. Steen checked *Sometimes* for the Strategies question. The completed questionnaire helped Mr. Steen get a sense of the kinds of tasks that would be easy and difficult for Ryan and as a result, Mr. Steen was able to develop an effective educational

Building Blocks Questionnaire

Student's name _Ryan_   Grade _4th_

Teacher's name _Mr. Steen_   Date _5/30_

PART 1

The 10 questions composing Part 1 are general and provide an overview of the student's school-related skills and behavior. For each of the Building Blocks described with questions in the left-hand column, indicate with a check mark whether the student or child exhibits the behavior *Rarely, Sometimes,* or *Frequently*. Once you have completed Part 1, for each of the questions you have answered *Frequently* or *Sometimes,* proceed to Part 2 of the questionnaire and complete the additional 10 items corresponding to that Building Block. For example, if you answer *Frequently* to "Does the student appear inattentive or impulsive?" under the Foundational/Attention and Self-Regulation item, then proceed to the first section of Part 2 and answer the additional 10 items under the category of Attention and Self-Regulation.

	Rarely	Sometimes	Frequently
FOUNDATIONAL			
1. *Attention and Self-Regulation:* Does the student appear inattentive or impulsive?		✓	
2. *Emotions:* Does the student appear to be sad or anxious more often than not during the day?		✓	
3. *Behavior:* Does the student have trouble following school rules?	✓		
4. *Self-Esteem:* Does the student appear to have a low opinion of him- or herself?			✓
SYMBOLIC			
5. *Phonological Processing:* Does the student have difficulty hearing or applying letter sounds when speaking, reading, or spelling?			✓
6. *Orthographic Processing:* Does the student have trouble reading or spelling words with irregular elements (e.g., *once*)?			✓
7. *Motor Processing:* Does the student have difficulty forming letters or writing legibly?		✓	
CONCEPTUAL			
8. *Thinking with Language:* Does the student have trouble using or understanding oral language?	✓		
9. *Thinking with Images:* Does the student have difficulty creating mental pictures?	✓		
10. *Thinking with Strategies:* Does the student have trouble forming or following a plan?		✓	

Figure 1.4. Building Blocks Questionnaire, Part 1, as completed for Ryan.

program to help Ryan improve his self-esteem and attitude as well as his basic skills in reading and spelling.

PURPOSE, OVERVIEW, AND AUDIENCE

The information in this book does not address all of the varied learning and behavior problems experienced by children. Its purpose is to help general education teachers and specialists, such as school psychologists, speech-language therapists, and special education teachers increase their knowledge of the factors that influence a student's school performance. In other words, the goal is to help professionals involved in education increase their knowledge about the ways that developmental, behavior, and academic problems influence school success and the ways in which these problems may be addressed and treated.

As we have discussed, the Building Blocks model has been developed in part through our many years of consulting, teaching, and counseling children and their families. The first requirement for helping a student is to develop a clear understanding of his or her unique characteristics by evaluating the student's strengths and weaknesses. The next step is to determine the types of educational and behavioral interventions needed and develop meaningful, realistic educational goals. A student's strengths and weaknesses in these 10 blocks can affect multiple areas of learning. Before reading further, you may find it helpful to review the complete Building Blocks Questionnaire in the chapter appendix and to complete it for one or more students. When learning and behavior are viewed within this model, it is easy to understand why children like Andy, Jeremy, Katy, Ben, and Maria are struggling in school and, more important, what we can do as professionals to mitigate their problems.

This book also is designed to serve as a text or supplement in undergraduate and graduate introductory, characteristics, and methods courses in LD and behavior problems. In addition to school psychologists, special educators, and counselors, preservice and in-service general education teachers can use this book to increase their understanding of the types of problems that their students will face and the specific teaching techniques and materials that they can use to help students overcome these difficulties. Unlike many texts and resources about behavior problems and LD, this text focuses on developing an understanding of the underlying causes of classroom problems. We stress the importance of identifying an individual's underlying strengths and weaknesses for the purpose of designing an effective intervention program.

In Section 1, the introductory section, Chapter 2 provides the theoretical rationale for the Building Blocks model. Chapter 3 discusses the importance of a positive, nurturing learning environment. The remainder of the book is divided into three sections.

Section II addresses the foundational blocks. Each chapter addresses a specific building block: attention and self-regulation, emotions, behavior, and self-esteem. If a student has problems in any of the foundational blocks, we suggest that you turn to the questionnaire, answer the 10 additional items, and then read the relevant foundational block chapter.

Section III addresses the symbolic blocks. If a student has problems in any of the symbolic blocks (phonology, orthography, or motor processing), we suggest you turn to the symbolic blocks section of the questionnaire, answer the additional items about the student's skills and abilities, and then read the most relevant chapters.

Section IV addresses the conceptual blocks. If the student has difficulty with any of the three conceptual blocks (thinking with language, images, or strategies), we suggest you turn to the conceptual blocks section in Part 2 of the questionnaire,

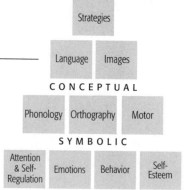

answer the additional items about the student's thinking skills, and then read the most relevant chapters. Finally, if you are in training, working as a consultant with teachers, or working in a classroom with many children, we suggest that you read through this entire text.

Many of the ideas and techniques presented in this book are ones that special educators and psychologists have used for years in working with children who are experiencing school problems. In our years of clinical work, we have used many of the described techniques at one time or another and can attest to their effectiveness with certain children. The techniques are practical, supported by evidence-based research, and relatively easy to implement.

One conclusion from research is clear: For children with learning problems, learning is hard work; for their teachers, instruction is very hard work and requires an enormous amount of training and support (Semrud-Clikeman, 2005). Effective education for students struggling with learning and behavior is dependent, however, on the individual actions of competent and caring professionals (Kauffman, 2005) and the implementation of an individualized approach that provides effective teaching strategies (Zigmond, 2004). It is our hope that all children struggling in school will receive instruction from caring, sympathetic teachers who understand learning, behavioral, and temperamental differences and know when and how to intervene to help support these children in their growth and development.

BUILDING BLOCKS QUESTIONNAIRE

Building Blocks Questionnaire

Student's name_____   Grade_____

Teacher's name_____   Date_____

PART 1

The 10 questions composing Part 1 are general and provide an overview of the student's school-related skills and behavior. For each of the Building Blocks described with questions in the left-hand column, indicate with a check mark whether the student or child exhibits the behavior *Rarely, Sometimes,* or *Frequently*. Once you have completed Part 1, for each of the questions you have answered *Frequently* or *Sometimes*, proceed to Part 2 of the questionnaire and complete the additional 10 items corresponding to that Building Block. For example, if you answer *Frequently* to "Does the student appear inattentive or impulsive?" under the Foundational/Attention and Self-Regulation item, then proceed to the first section of Part 2 and answer the additional 10 items under the category of Attention and Self-Regulation.

	Rarely	Sometimes	Frequently
FOUNDATIONAL			
1. *Attention and Self-Regulation:* Does the student appear inattentive or impulsive?			
2. *Emotions:* Does the student appear to be sad or anxious more often than not during the day?			
3. *Behavior:* Does the student have trouble following school rules?			
4. *Self-Esteem:* Does the student appear to have a low opinion of him- or herself?			
SYMBOLIC			
5. *Phonological Processing:* Does the student have difficulty hearing or applying letter sounds when speaking, reading, or spelling?			
6. *Orthographic Processing:* Does the student have trouble reading or spelling words with irregular elements (e.g., *once*)?			
7. *Motor Processing:* Does the student have difficulty forming letters or writing legibly?			
CONCEPTUAL			
8. *Thinking with Language:* Does the student have trouble using or understanding oral language?			
9. *Thinking with Images:* Does the student have difficulty creating mental pictures?			
10. *Thinking with Strategies:* Does the student have trouble forming or following a plan?			

(continued)

Building Blocks Questionnaire

PART 2

In Part 2, the Building Blocks described using the 10 questions in Part 1 are grouped according to the three tiers of the pyramid. In order to get more in-depth information about a student's strengths and weaknesses in these various areas, complete the 10 items for each corresponding block for the items for which you answered *Frequently* or *Sometimes* in Part 1.

FOUNDATIONAL			
ATTENTION AND SELF-REGULATION	**Rarely**	**Sometimes**	**Frequently**
Appears restless and fidgety			
Shows inconsistencies in behavior depending on the type of task			
Has trouble staying seated			
Seems to act before thinking			
Fails to finish tasks			
Has trouble making transitions			
Has difficulty working independently			
Has trouble persisting on routine tasks for extended periods of time			
Has difficulty listening to and following directions			
Has trouble finding and organizing tasks and materials			

EMOTIONS	**Rarely**	**Sometimes**	**Frequently**
Appears to be sad			
Changes mood quickly			
Worries excessively about school			
Complains about school tasks			
Cries			
Seems anxious			
Becomes angry quickly			
Isolates self from peers			
Seems bored or disinterested			
Puts forth little effort			

(continued)

Building Blocks Questionnaire

(continued)

FOUNDATIONAL

BEHAVIOR	Rarely	Sometimes	Frequently
Has difficulty getting along with peers			
Is frequently in trouble at school			
Lacks engagement in classroom instruction			
Does not respond to discipline as expected			
Disturbs or distracts others			
Makes inappropriate physical contacts with peers (e.g., shoving, pinching)			
Insults others verbally			
Refuses to comply when asked			
Seems argumentative			
Hurts self or others			

SELF-ESTEEM	Rarely	Sometimes	Frequently
Seems disinterested in academic tasks			
Complains about not being smart			
Complains that academic tasks are too difficult			
Has limited interactions with classmates			
Complains about not being liked			
Makes negative comments about self			
Gives up easily on tasks and assignments			
Seems overly sensitive to criticism			
Criticizes others			
Seems to lack self-confidence			

(continued)

Building Blocks Questionnaire

(continued)

SYMBOLIC

PHONOLOGICAL PROCESSING	Rarely	Sometimes	Frequently
Has trouble rhyming words			
Has difficulty pronouncing certain sounds			
Has trouble putting sounds together to pronounce words (blending) when reading			
Has difficulty breaking sounds apart in words (segmenting) when spelling			
Has trouble distinguishing letters with similar sounds (e.g., /b/ and /p/, /f/ and /v/) in speech and when spelling			
Has difficulty repeating information just heard			
Has trouble learning the days of the week and months of the year in sequence			
Has difficulty connecting sounds to letters when spelling			
Has trouble pronouncing multisyllablic words when speaking or reading			
Has difficulty pronouncing or spelling words with phonetically regular patterns			

ORTHOGRAPHIC PROCESSING	Rarely	Sometimes	Frequently
Forgets how letters look			
Confuses letters with similar appearance (e.g., *n* for *h*)			
Misreads little words in text (e.g., *were* for *where*)			
Reverses letters when spelling (e.g., *b* instead of *d*)			
Transposes letters when reading or writing (e.g., *on* instead of *no*)			
Has trouble remembering basic sight words			
Has difficulty copying from a book or chalkboard to paper			
Spells the same word in different ways			
Spells words the way they sound rather than the way they look			
Reads at a slow rate			

(continued)

Building Blocks Questionnaire

(continued)

SYMBOLIC

MOTOR PROCESSING	Rarely	Sometimes	Frequently
Draws pictures that seem immature for age			
Has difficulty with tasks involving fine motor coordination (e.g., tying shoes)			
Seems disinterested in drawing or learning to write			
Has trouble holding a crayon, pencil, or pen correctly			
Forms letters in odd ways (e.g., starts from the bottom rather than the top)			
Has poor spacing between letters and words			
Has papers that appear messy			
Has poor or sloppy handwriting			
Has difficulty learning cursive writing			
Has a slow rate of writing			

CONCEPTUAL

THINKING WITH LANGUAGE	Rarely	Sometimes	Frequently
Was slow to develop and use oral language			
Has trouble understanding directions or answering questions			
Has difficulty sustaining meaningful conversations			
Makes grammatical errors when speaking			
Has problems retrieving specific words			
Has trouble understanding what is read			
Has difficulty expressing ideas when writing			
Has trouble summarizing or drawing conclusions			
Has a limited speaking vocabulary			
Has difficulty organizing and expressing ideas			

(continued)

Building Blocks Questionnaire

(continued)

CONCEPTUAL

THINKING WITH IMAGES	Rarely	Sometimes	Frequently
Has trouble putting puzzles together			
Has difficulty constructing models or designs			
Has trouble solving math problems without counting on fingers			
Has difficulty distinguishing left from right			
Has trouble judging distances			
Has difficulty solving math problems without using paper and pencil			
Has trouble with tasks involving spatial reasoning			
Has difficulty using maps			
Has trouble understanding diagrams or graphs			
Has difficulty interpreting body language or social cues			

THINKING WITH STRATEGIES	Rarely	Sometimes	Frequently
Has trouble monitoring performance			
Has difficulty identifying the steps of a task			
Has trouble developing a plan to complete a task			
Has difficulty sustaining effort when problem solving			
Has trouble identifying and prioritizing the most relevant aspects of a task			
Has difficulty revising or generating an alternative plan			
Has trouble evaluating performance			
Has difficulty selecting and using techniques to memorize			
Has trouble selecting and using techniques to study			
Has difficulty generalizing (i.e., taking what is learned in one situation and applying it to another)			

CHAPTER 2 OUTLINE

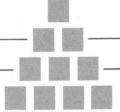

RATIONALE FOR THE LEARNING ENVIRONMENT

RATIONALE FOR THE FOUNDATIONAL BLOCKS

Attention and Self-Regulation
Emotions
Behavior
Self-Esteem

RATIONALE FOR THE SYMBOLIC AND CONCEPTUAL BLOCKS

Phonological, Orthographic, and Motor Processing
Subtypes of Reading Disabilities
Subtypes of Math Disabilities
Oral Language, Images, and Strategies

BUILDING BLOCKS MODEL AND THEORIES OF INTELLIGENCE

Planning, Attention, Simultaneous, Successive Theory
Cattell-Horn-Carroll Theory

BUILDING BLOCKS MODEL AND ACADEMIC PERFORMANCE

CONCLUSION

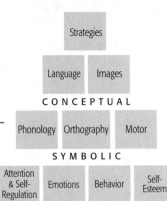

Strategies

Language | Images

CONCEPTUAL

Phonology | Orthography | Motor

SYMBOLIC

Attention & Self-Regulation | Emotions | Behavior | Self-Esteem

FOUNDATIONAL

CHAPTER 2

THEORETICAL FOUNDATIONS

This chapter provides an overview of how the theoretical framework for the Building Blocks model evolved. It begins with a brief historical overview of children's classroom problems. These include difficulties related to the environment, attention and self-regulation, emotions, behavior, and self-esteem. Next, the neurodevelopmental skills of the symbolic blocks and the linguistic, visual-spatial, and strategic abilities of the conceptual blocks are discussed. Two theories of intelligence are discussed to illustrate how they relate to the abilities included in the Building Blocks model. Throughout the chapter, relevant research is reported to substantiate the development and interpretation of the skills and abilities presented in the model. The chapter ends with a discussion of intra-individual differences and how these differences can be used to further understanding of a student's unique learning and behavior profile.

RATIONALE FOR THE LEARNING ENVIRONMENT

The learning environment provides the base for the triangle of the Building Blocks model. Both the home and school environment can support or hinder learning. Multiple environmental factors play roles in explaining school problems. Learning is affected by the complex relationships among individual characteristics as well as family- and school-based influences (Meltzer, 1994; for review, see Goldstein & Brooks, 2007). What are the factors that enable some children to achieve but cause others to fail? As Werner (1994) noted, even in the most disorganized, impoverished environments, some children still manage to develop stable, healthy personalities and function successfully in school.

Many environmental factors outside of the classroom affect children in the classroom. Nearly one in five children in the United States lives at or below the poverty level (Danziger & Danziger, 1993). In the U.S. Census Bureau (2005) (http://factfinder.census.gov/home/saff/nain.html?_ling=en), the rate of child poverty rose to 17.6%, increasing the number of poor children to 12.9 million. The poverty rate of African Americans is nearly twice that of the national rate, with nearly 25% of African Americans living below the poverty line. Children within families functioning at or below the poverty level appear to be exposed to significantly more risks than other children. The prevalence rates of physical and mental illness, child abuse, and parental problems are significantly greater in these families. Living in poverty decreases the number of protective factors a child has and increases the risk of classroom problems (Goldstein & Brooks, 2005).

The classroom is also part of a child's learning environment. Experiences at school may lessen or heighten the negative influence of family factors (Kauffman, 2005). During the school year, children spend as much time in their classrooms as they do in their homes. They also typically spend more time with their teachers than with their parents during the school year. Students with learning and behavior difficulties require extra assistance and support to succeed. In discussing the efficacy of various service delivery models, Zigmond (2004) reflects

> The accumulated experimental evidence to date produces only one unequivocal finding: Languishing in a regular education class where nothing changes and no one pays any attention to an individual is not as useful to students with learning and behavioral disorders as getting some help.... (p. 114)

Some classroom settings can foster problems, such as an inattentive class or a classroom in which too much talking is permitted. Specific class members who do not conform to generally accepted classroom rules can cause constant disruptions that interfere with academic tasks (Johnson & Bany, 1970). In addition, when the task difficulty is not controlled and students are not given work in line with their capabilities, increased behavior and attention difficulties occur in the general education classroom (Liaupsin, Umbreit, Ferro, Urso, & Upreti, 2006). Sufficient data also suggest that when teachers have too many students requiring extra attention, classrooms do not function optimally and problems often escalate. Even something as simple as the organization of desks (e.g., clusters, rows) has been found to affect classroom functioning significantly. In one elementary classroom, the frequency of disruptions was three times higher when desks were arranged in clusters than when they were arranged in rows (Wheldall & Lam, 1987). When students have an environment where they can spend time and be engaged in their work, their achievement improves. For example, the amount of time spent on task in direct and indirect reading activities predicts growth in reading for children with LD (Zigmond, 2004). Thus, one primary job of the teacher is to structure and order the learning environment "in such a way that work is accomplished, play is learned, love is felt, and fun is enjoyed—by the student and the teacher" (Kauffman, 2005, p. 441). The learning environment provides the foundation, support, and setting for students to have positive learning opportunities and experiences.

RATIONALE FOR THE FOUNDATIONAL BLOCKS

Increasingly, childhood research points to a number of areas that appear to predict school success or explain why some children experience a lack of success even when they possess adequate intellectual abilities for good school performance. The foundation of typical achievement and learning consists of children's capacity for attention and self-regulation, emotional status, behavior patterns, and self-esteem relative to school performance. These four areas form the foundational blocks, and problems in any one area can contribute to academic or social difficulties in school.

Attention and Self-Regulation

Across all grade levels, teachers' complaints about behavior most often relate to disruptive behavior. These complaints frequently contain behavior descriptions of inattention, impulsivity, hyperactivity, and poor planning, all symptoms of attention-deficit/hyperactivity disorder (ADHD). Since the 1970s, a significant issue in schools today has been providing intervention for and

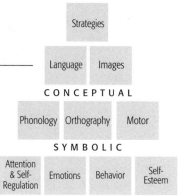

behavior management of children with ADHD (Barkley, 2005). Within class-room settings, children with ADHD symptoms experience myriad impairments. They appear to possess the kind of temperament that makes persisting with repetitive activities they may perceive to be uninteresting and that inhibit their impulses difficult for them. These children also experience difficulties as a result of their learning history—a history that often reinforces them for beginning but not completing tasks.

Frequently, teachers' efforts to manage the symptoms of ADHD result in negatively reinforcing interactions that tend to focus on the misbehavior itself rather than on the termination of the behavior. These negative interactions often further disrupt other students in the classroom. Although at one time ADHD and LD were considered to be different descriptions of the same problem, problems with attention and self-regulation really result from faulty performance, whereas problems with learning are often the result of inefficient processing, recall, or understanding of the material.

Emotions

Within the classroom, two main types of emotional problems—worry and helplessness—appear to interfere with children's ability to achieve and succeed. Symptoms of these problems form the basis of *depression* and *anxiety*. These two conditions are closely linked with a variety of other disorders and may be episodic or chronic in nature (Kauffman, 2005). These problems often are referred to as *internalizing* disorders because they are usually nondisruptive in nature. Students experiencing these problems may appear passive, withdrawn, or isolated in the classroom. Their behaviors, though not disruptive to either the teacher or nearby students, are nonetheless a cause for worry and concern. These emotional problems often interfere with a student's classroom performance and may occur along with other externalizing disorders.

Behavior

Hostile, defiant, aggressive, and antisocial behaviors involving both overt (e.g., setting fires) and covert (e.g., lying and manipulating) acts cause significant disruption in the classroom. These behaviors form two main types of behavior problems—*oppositional defiant disorder* and *conduct disorder*—both of which influence a child's chances for school success. These disorders are described as *externalizing* because they often are viewed as disruptive by teachers and intrusive by other students. A large volume of research has demonstrated that each of these two types of behavior problems may interfere with a student's classroom performance and potential for academic and vocational success.

Self-Esteem

Self-esteem encompasses children's feelings and beliefs about their competence and worth and whether they view themselves as worthy of respect. Self-esteem includes one's perceptions about one's own ability to make a difference in the world, to confront and master challenges, and to learn from successes and failures (Brooks, 1991). The attitudes, beliefs, and perceptions of potential for success that children bring to their classroom significantly affect their success, independent of other skills and abilities.

RATIONALE FOR THE SYMBOLIC AND CONCEPTUAL BLOCKS

Skill and ability weaknesses in the three areas of symbolic and conceptual learning provide an explanation for the achievement problems experienced by the majority of children struggling in the classroom. Historically, the *Illinois*

Test of Psycholinguistic Abilities (ITPA; Kirk, McCarthy, & Kirk, 1968) presented a clinical model, an adaptation of Osgood's (1957) communication model, with two levels of organization. The first level was called the *automatic level*. At this level, the individual's auditory and visual responses are less voluntary but highly integrated, such as in tasks involving rapid symbol processing, verbal short-term memory, or blending sounds together to form a word. At the second, or *representational level*, the individual engages in more complex mediating processes involved in tasks that require the comprehension of visual and auditory stimuli. Within the Building Blocks model, the automatic level is similar to the abilities of the symbolic, processing blocks, whereas the representational level encompasses the conceptual, thinking blocks. Within the adapted Osgood model, four basic processes were included: visual, auditory, vocal, and motor.

Results from factor analytic and related research on LD appear to reflect two broad groups of skills necessary for efficient learning (Ingalls, 1991):

1. *Auditory and verbal processes:* Weaknesses in these areas result in reading and writing disorders and other language-based learning problems.

2. *Visual, perceptual, and motor processes:* Weaknesses in these areas may result in reading problems but may also affect handwriting, spelling, and mathematics.

Tables 2.1 and 2.2 present a model developed by Ingalls (1991) conceptualizing these skills. Similar to the model proposed in the ITPA, this model places learning skills on rote/automatic and conceptual levels. With repeated practice, the skills in the symbolic blocks become increasingly automatic and are performed with little effort.

These levels of processing are also consistent with the distinction between automatic and conceptual processing (Schneider & Shiffrin, 1977). The automatic processes do not require attentional resources, whereas the conceptual processes are controlled and require the application of knowledge and strategies. The abilities of the symbolic blocks are related to lower order academic tasks that become automatic with repeated practice, such as memorizing multiplication facts or spelling words correctly. These abilities involve perceptual and motor processes critical for school performance. In contrast, the abilities of the conceptual blocks are related to higher order processes, such as those required in composing a letter or comprehending passages in a textbook.

Weaknesses in these cognitive and neuropsychological processes impede children's rate of learning and performing and can be used to explain LD. However, instead of the generic term *LD*, domain-specific labels, such as reading disability, math disability, and language impairment, more aptly describe the problem. As noted by Fletcher and colleagues (1998), a more appropriate approach

Table 2.1. Skills necessary for efficient learning

	Auditory/verbal	Visual/motor
Conceptual	Verbal conceptual	Visual/nonverbal conceptual
Rote/Automatic	Auditory motor	Letter perception
	Auditory perceptual	Spatial organization and nonverbal integration
	Rote auditory sequential memory	Rote visual/sequential memory and retrieval
	Rote and associated memory and retrieval	Motor sequencing/fine motor control

From Ingalls, S.I. (1991). *Skills for efficient learning* (p. 1). Salt Lake City, UT: Neurology, Learning, and Behavior Center; reprinted by permission of the author and publisher.

Table 2.2. Levels of processing related to learning disability characteristics

	Auditory/verbal	Visual/motor
Conceptual	Language semantics (word meaning, definition, vocabulary) Listening comprehension (understanding and memory of overall ideas) Reading comprehension (understanding and memory of overall ideas) Specificity and variety of verbal concepts for oral or written expression Verbal reasoning and logic	Social insight and reasoning (e.g., understanding strategies of games, jokes, motives of others, social conventions, tact) Math concepts (e.g., use of 0 in addition, subtraction, and multiplication; place value; money equivalencies; missing elements) Inferential reading comprehension and drawing conclusions Understanding relationships of historical events across time; understanding science concepts Structuring ideas hierarchically; outlining skills Generalization of abilities Integrating material into a well-organized report
Rote/automatic	Early speech (e.g., naming objects) Auditory processing (e.g., clear enunciation of speech, pronouncing sounds/syllables in correct order) Ability to name colors Ability to recall birthday, telephone number, address, and so forth Ability to say alphabet and other lists (e.g., days, months) in order Ability to easily select and sequence words with proper grammatical structure for oral or written expression Auditory "dyslexia" (i.e., no discrimination of sounds, especially vowels; auditory blend of sounds to words; no distinction of words that sound alike [e.g., *mine, mind*]) Poor phonetic spelling Poor listening or reading comprehension due to poor short-term memory, especially of rote facts Labeling and retrieving math disorder (i.e., trouble counting sequentially, mislabeling numbers, poor memory for number facts and sequence of steps for computation) Ability to recall names, dates, and historical facts Ability to learn and retain new science terminology	Ability to assemble puzzles and build with construction toys Social perception and awareness of environment Time sense (e.g., doesn't ask, "Is this the last recess?") Ability to remember and execute correct sequence for tying shoes Ability to easily negotiate stairs, climb on play equipment, learn athletic skills, and ride a bike Ability to execute daily living skills (e.g., pouring without spilling, spreading a sandwich, dressing self correctly) Ability to use the correct sequence of strokes to form manuscript or cursive letters Eye–hand coordination for drawing, assembling art projects, and handwriting Directional stability for top/bottom and left/right tracking Ability to copy from the board accurately Visual "dyslexia" (e.g., confusion when viewing visual symbols, poor visual discrimination, reversals/inversions/transpositions due to poor directionality, no recognition of shapes or forms of a word that has been seen many times before: "word-blindness") Spelling (e.g., poor visual memory for the nonphonetic elements of words)

From Ingalls, S.I. (1991). *Levels of processing in learning* (p. 1). Salt Lake City, UT: Neurology, Learning, and Behavior Center; reprinted by permission of the author and publisher.

is to describe domain-specific achievement skills and the abilities related to these skills. These domain-specific terms can occur in conjunction with other difficulties such as social, emotional, attention, or behavior problems. Part of the confusion regarding the heterogeneous term *LD* has stemmed from the misuse of the terms of *category* and *diagnosis* (Mather & Healey, 1990). In the field of LD, the term *LD* often is used erroneously to represent the category of disability as well as the causative factor. The categorical term is *LD,* whereas the diagnosis needs to be a specific type of LD such as a reading disability (e.g., caused by poor phonological awareness).

Phonological, Orthographic, and Motor Processing

The abilities in the symbolic blocks can be thought of as representing lower order functions. As noted, the symbolic blocks include phonological, orthographic, and motor processing. Problems with any one of these areas can affect performance in reading, writing, or math. Children with severe impairments in one of these domains often are identified as having LD. As Bateman (1992) observed, children with LD have more trouble acquiring, applying, and retaining information than would be predicted on the basis of other information about the child. The most common problem observed among these children is poor performance in basic reading and writing skills.

Early in the 20th century, many explanations of reading disabilities focused on the visual aspects of reading. Because the connection between the eyes and reading is obvious, the belief developed that reading disabilities are entirely a function of poor visual processing skills. Reading disorders have been attributed to faulty eye movements, problems with visual perception, slow fixations, failure of the eyes to work cooperatively, and poor scanning efficiency. In addition, many of the symptoms evidenced by poor readers also appear to be related to visual skills. Poor readers may reverse letters or transpose words when reading, such as pronouncing the word *was* as *saw.* Although various symptoms are apparent and a variety of explanations have been proposed, the exact visual mechanisms that contribute to poor reading are still not completely understood.

Although visual processes are clearly important to reading, many individuals with reading disabilities suffer from difficulty pairing the speech sounds of language (*phonemes*) with the printed letters or letter strings (*graphemes*). As Pennington (1991) eloquently wrote,

> Over and over again when we read we must translate printed letter strings into word pronunciations. To do this, we must understand that the alphabet is a code for phonemes, the individual speech sounds in a language, and we must be able to use that code quickly and automatically so that we can concentrate on the meaning of what we read. The difficulty that dyslexics have with phonics [is that] the ability to sound out words makes reading much slower and less automatic and detracts considerably from comprehension. (p. 59)

Impairments in the child's ability to learn grapheme–phoneme correspondences and then to recognize these patterns quickly impede the development of word recognition skills.

Problems with verbal short-term memory are also common among children with reading and math difficulties. Students with reading disabilities tend to perform poorly on a variety of working memory and short-term memory tasks (Mann, 2003). Students may experience difficulty with recalling letters, digits, words, phrases, or sentences. These memory difficulties can affect writing as well. The writer must not only remember a phonological code but also must

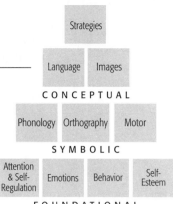

Strategies

Language   Images

CONCEPTUAL

Phonology   Orthography   Motor

SYMBOLIC

Attention & Self-Regulation   Emotions   Behavior   Self-Esteem

FOUNDATIONAL

think of the words to express meaning; organize those words according to the rules of grammar and syntax; and pay attention to the size, shape, and spacing of letters.

If the student has poor motor control, subsequent difficulty with handwriting affects written production. Although the importance of handwriting skill diminishes in adulthood, problems in motor control can affect the legibility and the speed of written production. Slow handwriting speed can then affect other aspects of writing. For example, the speed of letter writing appears to be a strong predictor of spelling outcomes for young children (Caravolas, Snowling, & Hulme, 1999).

Despite impairments in specific cognitive skills, students with LD often have intact thinking abilities. In fact, many have average or even above-average performance in oral language (Orton, 1966). Essentially, what distinguishes individuals with a reading disability from other poor readers is that their listening comprehension ability is higher than their ability to decode words (Rack, Snowling, & Olson, 1992).

Subtypes of Reading Disabilities

An understanding of the history of efforts to subtype LD can help explain why phonological, orthographic, and motor processing skills are critical for classroom success. The majority of this work has centered on individuals with specific reading disabilities. Both Boder (1973) and Bakker (1979) attempted to classify and identify subtypes of reading impairments. Boder described three subtypes of children: 1) a dysphonetic group lacking word analysis skills and having difficulty with phonics, 2) a dyseidetic group experiencing problems with whole word gestalts, and 3) a mixed dysphonetic, dyseidetic group. According to Boder's research, the dyseidetic group included 67% of those identified as having LD and the mixed group included 23%. Thus, children with visual learning problems constituted a smaller percentage of this population. Although this research was subjected to numerous criticisms, the model provided a framework for thinking about different subtypes.

Bakker (1979) described the L-type and P-type dyslexias using a theory based on the belief that the correct hemisphere of a child's brain was not emphasized at the right point during a period of early development. Bakker and Vinke (1985) attempted then to pair specific instructional methods with the type of disorder. Children with L-type dyslexia, who relied on linguistic left-hemisphere processing too early, read quickly but made errors of omission, additions, and mispronunciations. These children tried to grasp meaning directly from the word's visual appearance (Bakker, 1992). This group responded better to stimulation of the right hemisphere by flashing words on computer monitors. Children in the P-type group, who relied on perceptual right-hemisphere processing too early, tended to read slowly and to make many repetitions. These children seemed to need to use phonological recoding to pronounce words (Bakker, 1992). This group responded better to classroom methods involving left-hemisphere stimulation, such as instruction in rhyming. Although the instructional methods were too involved for most school settings, Bakker provided a clear theoretical basis, provided extensive external validation, and attempted to link this theory to instructional methods.

Among the more interesting and promising attempts to identify LD subtypes are those studies involving complex statistics such as multivariate analysis. In general, investigators concluded that several subtypes of reading problems exist. Early efforts to subtype LD using statistical analyses found that differences between good and poor readers reflected impairment in specific skills, including word rhyming, vocabulary, discrimination of reversed figures, speed of perception of visual forms, and sequential processing (Doehring, 1968). Petrauskas and Rourke (1979) used a factor-analytic method to describe the difficulties of deficient readers. The difficulties of poor readers fell into four subtypes: 1) primarily verbal problems, 2) primarily visual problems, 3) problems with conceptual flexibility, and 4) no identified specific weakness. These first two types fit into the symbolic blocks in our model. The third type fits into our conceptual blocks. The fourth type may be either a function of the measures used or a result of the inefficiencies of statistical processes, or it may constitute a group of children who do not succeed because of problems other than specific skill weaknesses. This group of children may be described as having weaknesses within the foundational blocks according to our model, such as ADHD.

A distinction concerning skill weaknesses exists between children with learning problems stemming from verbal skill weaknesses and children whose problems stem from visual weaknesses. Approximately 80% of children with a reading disability appear to experience some type of language-based impairment, with a much smaller percentage experiencing some type of visual-spatial or perceptual motor problem (Denckla, 1972; Mattis, French, & Rapin, 1975). Mattis and colleagues (1975) identified three groups of children with LD: 1) children with language problems, 2) children with articulation and graphomotor problems, and 3) children with visual-spatial perceptual disorders. Similarly, Phillips (1983) and Satz and Morris (1981) reported five distinct groups of children along the verbal–nonverbal continuum: 1) those with language impairments, 2) those with specific language problems related to naming, 3) those with mixed global language and perceptual problems, 4) those with perceptual motor impairments only, and 5) those in whom no significant skill impairments could be found. Clearly, these pioneering studies on LD support a multiple syndrome approach.

In the 1970s, the theory of a dual route model was proposed. This theory specified two interactive, yet distinctive pathways for word recognition: an indirect, sublexical phonological decoding route for pronunciation of unfamiliar words alongside a direct, lexical route for automatic recognition of high-frequency words (Coltheart, 1978). A weakness in either pathway could affect the development of reading skills and result in two different subtypes of dyslexia: phonological dyslexia (i.e., difficulty with nonword reading) and surface dyslexia (i.e., difficulty with irregular word reading) (Castles & Coltheart, 1993). An individual with phonological dyslexia experiences trouble with phonological awareness tasks and with the reading of nonwords, whereas an individual with surface dyslexia is able to read nonwords but experiences greater difficulty with exception words or words with an irregular element that do not have regular, predictable grapheme–phoneme correspondences (e.g., *once*). Although this pattern alone is insufficient to identify different subtypes, differences between performances on regular and irregular word reading and spelling may be indicative of different etiologies for reading and spelling difficulties. In addition, results from fMRI studies have indicated that children with dyslexia can have impairments that affect phonological processing in the temporoparietal cortex or orthographic processing in the word form area of the occipitoparietal regions (Shaywitz & Shaywitz, 2003; Temple et al., 2001). Findings from an fMRI study indicated that developmental dyslexia has a neural basis and is characterized by both phonological and orthographic processing deficits (Temple et al., 2001). In the study by Temple and colleagues, children with dyslexia showed less left temporoparietal activation on a phonological task (e.g., determining if two letters rhymed, such as *d* and *t*) as well as reduced extrastriate activity, especially in the occipitoparietal regions, during an orthographic task (e.g., determining if two

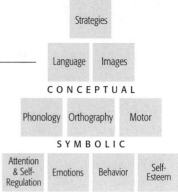

letters were visually the same). Although these skills appear to be separate components of variation in reading and spelling skill, orthographic competence may be based on already established phonological sensitivity and competence in phonological skills. Presumably, a child with limited sensitivity to speech sounds also will experience difficulty with the identification and production of orthographic patterns.

Wolf and Bowers (1999) proposed another theory referred to as the *double-deficit hypothesis,* involving phonological awareness and rapid automatized naming (RAN) speed. Both phonological awareness tasks and rapid letter naming tasks are useful predictive measures for identifying children who are at risk for reading failure (O'Connor & Jenkins, 1999). They appear to account for independent variance in later reading scores and relate to distinct aspects of reading development (Bowers, Sunseth, & Golden, 1999; Manis, Seidenberg, & Doi, 1999). This theory is discussed more thoroughly in Chapter 8.

Subtypes of Math Disabilities

Some attempts have also been made to identify specific disorders of mathematics. Some students seem to have trouble primarily with computational skills, such as adding, subtracting, and multiplying; other students have trouble with the conceptual component, such as the abilities involved in solving story problems. Novick and Arnold (1988) found that some individuals demonstrated impairments in fundamental arithmetic operations even though they demonstrated adequate reasoning, language, and visual-spatial skills. Other individuals demonstrated preserved computational skills but experienced difficulties with the production and comprehension of numbers. Novick and Arnold defined *dyscalculia* as a "developmental arithmetic disorder, which refers to the failure to develop arithmetic competence" (p. 132).

Kosc (1974) described six different subtypes of developmental dyscalculia. One type described a disorder in performing computational operations; another described a disorder in understanding mathematical concepts. Although the results of subtyping provide mixed support for the differentiation of mathematics disability subtypes, two findings are clear: 1) some students experience difficulty solely in the domain of mathematics, and 2) these children appear to show differences in neuropsychological abilities and types of arithmetic errors (Keller & Sutton, 1991).

Geary (2003) explained that many children with LD have weaknesses in the basic arithmetical competencies and have trouble retrieving basic facts from memory. Many of these students appear to have some form of working memory deficit or weak executive functioning in which they have trouble monitoring and coordinating a sequence of problem-solving steps. He describes three basic subtypes of LD in math: 1) procedural subtype, 2) semantic memory subtype, and 3) visual-spatial subtype. The procedural subtype uses developmentally immature procedures, makes frequent errors, and has trouble sequencing multiple steps; the semantic memory subtype has trouble retrieving math facts and makes frequent errors on facts; and the visual-spatial subtype misinterprets and fails to understand spatially represented information. Similarly, Montague and van Garderen (2008) described students who have serious perceptual, memory, language, and/or reasoning problems that interfere with mathematical problem solving.

In some cases, the localization of mathematics disability appears to be in the left hemisphere, causing problems in the learning and retention of facts. In other cases, dysfunction seems to be associated with the right cerebral hemisphere, causing problems in spatial organization, reasoning, and social-emotional functioning (Geary, 2003; Hale & Fiorello, 2004; Semrud-Clikeman

& Hynd, 1991; Strang & Rourke, 1985), key characteristics of a problem that often is described under the umbrella of *nonverbal learning disabilities*. Thus, the procedural and semantic memory subtypes are associated with the abilities of the symbolic blocks, whereas the visual-spatial subtype is related to the conceptual block of visual-spatial thinking.

Oral Language, Images, and Strategies

The abilities of the conceptual blocks can be thought of as representing higher order functions that support more complex learning tasks.

Oral Language At the conceptual level, thinking with language affects performance in reading comprehension, written language, and mathematical problem solving. Many of the same receptive and expressive language processes contribute to the development of these abilities. In most instances, the comprehension of spoken and written language appears to be independent of word-reading ability (Aaron & Simurdak, 1991). In the Building Blocks model, poor word-reading ability is related to the abilities in the symbolic blocks, whereas problems with the comprehension of text and the expression of ideas are related to the conceptual blocks, particularly thinking with language. Children who have difficulty understanding or using spoken language usually also have difficulty with aspects of reading, writing, and mathematics that require language-specific processes and involve higher order cognitive activities. Oral language, reading, and writing all form an integrated system with reciprocity in development: Oral language provides a knowledge base for reading and writing, and what children learn from reading and writing enhances oral language development (Lerner & Kline, 2005).

Verbal abilities and acquired knowledge have a strong and consistent relationship with reading (Evans, Floyd, McGrew, & Leforgee, 2002), mathematical problem solving (Floyd, Evans, & McGrew, 2003), and written expression (McGrew & Knopik, 1993) across the lifespan. The most substantiated relationships are between oral language abilities and reading comprehension and written expression. Both reading comprehension and written expression are dependent on background knowledge to understand and create the messages, and to provide familiarity with sentence structures, verbal reasoning abilities, and the possession of a broad and deep vocabulary (McCardle, Scarborough, & Catts, 2001). Thus, words and the concepts they represent provide the foundation for advanced literacy (Cunningham, Stanovich, & Wilson, 1990; Perfetti, Marron, & Foltz, 1996).

In the Building Blocks model, language encompasses the higher order aspects of linguistic functioning that allow students to understand what they hear and read and to express their thoughts when speaking and writing. In some cases, students with reading disabilities have underlying oral language impairments and more pervasive disturbances of reading that contribute to low scores on measures of verbal ability and reading; in other cases, students with reading disabilities have good verbal abilities but severe problems learning word recognition skills (Carlisle, 1993; Carlisle & Rice, 2002; Fletcher, Lyon, Fuchs, & Barnes, 2007).

Images As mentioned previously, problems that are not primarily language-based have been referred to collectively in the research literature as *nonverbal learning disabilities* (Johnson & Myklebust, 1971; Pennington, 1991; Rourke, 1989). Strang and Rourke (1985) suggested that children with such disabilities may experience seven areas of difficulty: 1) problems with spatial organization, 2) problems paying attention to visual detail, 3) procedural errors in mathematics, 4)

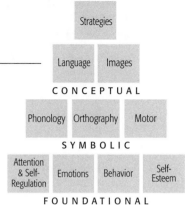

failure to shift psychological set (i.e., when two or more operations of one kind [e.g., addition] are followed by an operation of another kind [e.g., subtraction]), 5) fine motor weaknesses, 6) poor factual memory, and 7) poor judgment and reasoning. Although a number of symbolic and conceptual blocks in our model relate to these skill areas, the primary problem seems to affect spatial skills, or the ability to think with images.

Many authors (e.g., Johnson & Myklebust, 1971; Pennington, 1991; Rourke, 1989; Strang & Rourke, 1985) contend that nonverbal LD are much less common than language-based LD, occurring in only 1%–10% of children referred for learning problems. Some researchers have referred to nonverbal LD as reflecting a right-hemisphere impairment in the brain, because the right side of the brain is considered to mediate or control visual, perceptual, organizational, psychomotor coordination, and complex tactile perceptual skills (Harnadek & Rourke, 1994). At one conference, a mother informed us that her daughter had just been diagnosed as "right-brained." Although the intent of this diagnosis may be clear, it is too simplistic. The connections between the right and left hemispheres of the brain are highly complex, and it is an oversimplification to speak of one hemisphere as if it exists in isolation from the other. Nonetheless, the organization of the brain appears such that, loosely speaking, the left hemisphere processes language and is more involved with the processing of rote, detailed information, whereas the right hemisphere processes novel, holistic, and spatial information (Hale & Fiorello, 2004).

Not surprisingly, children with nonverbal weaknesses also often are described as having poorly coordinated gross and fine motor skills. They struggle with handwriting, mathematics, reading social cues, and managing emotions (Weintraub & Mesulum, 1983). Often, they also struggle with interpersonal relations—not surprising given estimates that 65% of communication is nonverbal (Mehrabian & Ferris, 1967). Nonverbal behavior appears especially important in communicating feelings, emotions, and preferences. Facial expressions, eye contact, and voice cues, such as pitch and volume, play significant roles in daily communications (Mehrabian & Ferris, 1967).

Strategies   Thinking with strategies is located at the very top of the Building Blocks model. This block contains the abilities that are needed for planning, organizing, and analyzing and solving problems, or what are sometimes referred to as metacognitive strategies. *Metacognition* has been described as knowing what one knows and knowing what needs to be known to achieve a goal (Wallach & Miller, 1988) or, more simply, the ability to think about one's own thinking. Metacognition contains two major components: knowledge about thinking and the ability to regulate one's thinking (Brown & Palinscar, 1982). Metacognitive knowledge is gained from experience and includes such things as monitoring, planning, and self-regulating (Torgesen, 1994). These variables appear to be most related to a student's ability to comprehend text, produce text, and solve problems. As an example, Baker and Brown (1980) specified some of the metacognitive behaviors involved in reading comprehension: 1) clarifying purposes, 2) identifying important aspects of a passage, 3) monitoring understanding, 4) engaging in self-questioning to determine if goals have been accomplished, and 5) taking corrective action when one fails to comprehend. Research during the 1980s and 1990s demonstrated that children with LD perform differently from others in a range of situations that involve some form of metacognitive behavior (e.g., Torgesen, 1994).

Within the neuropsychological literature, metacognition is often referred to as a part of *executive function* or *executive process* (Torgesen, 1994). Several key components of executive function include the abilities to plan, organize, and self-monitor performance (Cutting & Denckla, 2003). This awareness of "how I'm doing" is critical to the learning process (Semrud-Clikeman, 2005). Executive functioning is supported by language and spatial ability, forming the three blocks in the model that compose the conceptual abilities. Executive function has been described as the "supervisor of cognitive processing" that is capable of selecting, overseeing, and integrating information from several sources (Baddeley, 1986). These abilities apply to the awareness of how something is accomplished rather than just to what is accomplished (Semrud-Clikeman, 2005).

BUILDING BLOCKS MODEL AND THEORIES OF INTELLIGENCE

Multidimensional theories of intelligence can help us understand the cognitive processes contributing to children's learning and behavior. Two theories of intelligence are explained briefly to illustrate the relationship between these theories and how the abilities in these theories relate to the Building Blocks model.

Planning, Attention, Simultaneous, Successive Theory

The Planning, Attention, Simultaneous, Successive (PASS) theory is one view of intelligence that aims to define four basic abilities—planning, attention, simultaneous, and successive processing, termed *basic psychological processes*—that underlie performance in social, behavioral, and academic areas. This theory is rooted in the research of A.R. Luria (1966, 1973, 1980) about how the brain works (Das, Naglieri, & Kirby, 1994). Das, Naglieri, and colleagues used Luria's work as a blueprint for defining the important components of human intelligence. Their work represents an important effort to use neuropsychological theory to reconceptualize the concept of human intelligence.

Luria theorized that the four processes of the PASS theory could be conceptualized within a framework of three separate but related functional units of the brain. The three brain systems are referred to as functional units because of the unique neuropsychological mechanisms each contributes as they work in concert to achieve a specific goal. Luria (1973) stated that each form of conscious activity is always a complex functional system and takes place through the combined working of all three brain units, each of which makes its own contribution. This means that the four processes produced by the functional units form a working constellation of cognitive activity (Luria, 1966).

Each of the four PASS processes falls within one of the three functional units that can be associated with specific regions of the brain. The first functional unit, attention–arousal, provides regulation of cortical arousal and attention; the second analyzes information (using simultaneous and successive processes); and the third (planning) provides for strategy development, strategy use, self-monitoring, and control of cognitive activities.

The first of the three functional units of the brain, the attention–arousal system, is located primarily in the brainstem (Luria, 1973). This unit provides the brain with the appropriate level of alertness as well as directive and selective attention (Luria, 1973). Moreover, only when individuals are sufficiently aroused and their attention is adequately focused can they use processes in the second and third functional units. The abilities to track cues, sustain attention, choose among potential responses, and self-monitor once a commitment has been made to a particular behavior are critical for functioning effectively academically and behaviorally in the classroom. These abilities are similar to the ones in the attention/self-regulation block of the Building Blocks model.

The second functional unit is associated with the occipital, parietal, and temporal lobes of the brain. This unit is responsible for receiving, processing, and retaining information a person obtains from the external world using

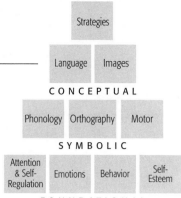

successive and simultaneous processes. *Successive processing* involves information that is linearly organized and integrated into a chain-like progression. This process is required when a child must arrange things in a strictly defined order in which each element is only related to those that precede it and the stimuli are not interrelated. For example, successive processing is involved in the decoding of unfamiliar words; the production of words in a specified order, or the *syntax* of language; and speech articulation. Following a command such as "Lilly, put your coat on the hanger, then put your book in your cubby, and then go sit in your seat" demands that the tasks and the order be remembered, which demands successive processing. Whenever information must be remembered or completed in a specific order, successive processing is involved. This process, therefore, is involved in the perception of stimuli in sequence as well as in the formation of sounds and movements in order. For this reason, successive processing is integral to activities such as phonological decoding, which involves working with sounds in sequence (Das et al., 1994). Successive processing has been conceptually and experimentally related to the concept of phonological analysis (Das et al., 1994). Successive processing is similar to the abilities involved in the phonological, orthographic, and motor blocks of the Building Blocks model.

Simultaneous processing is a mental process that requires an individual to integrate separate stimuli into a whole. It involves integrating stimuli into groups such that the interrelationships among the components can be understood. An essential feature of simultaneous processing is the organization of interrelated parts into a cohesive whole. Simultaneous processing tests have strong spatial aspects for this reason. Simultaneous processing can be used to solve tasks with both nonverbal and verbal content as long as the cognitive demand of the task requires integration of information. Simultaneous processing underlies use and comprehension of grammatical statements because they demand comprehension of word relationships, prepositions, and inflections so the person can obtain meaning based on the whole idea. For example, the use of simultaneous processing is necessary in order to follow this direction: "Get the book that is on the top shelf to the left of the door." This direction requires an understanding of the relationships among the different physical locations, the integration of the different parts of the direction into a single task, and the comprehension of logical and grammatical relationships. The images, language, and strategies blocks at the top of the Building Blocks model are similar to simultaneous processing.

The third functional unit is associated with the prefrontal areas of the frontal lobes of the brain (Luria, 1980) and provides what Naglieri and Das (1997) called *planning processing*. The prefrontal cortex plays a central role in forming goals and objectives and then in devising plans of action required to attain those goals. This functional unit selects the cognitive processes required to implement the plans, coordinates them, and applies them in a correct order. Finally, planning processing is required for evaluating one's actions as successes or failures relative to one's intentions (Goldberg, 2001) and is one of the abilities that distinguishes humans from other primates. Planning, therefore, helps an individual achieve through the use of strategies and is critical to all activities in which the individual has to determine how to solve a problem. This includes generation, evaluation, and execution of a plan as well as self-monitoring and impulse control. Thus, planning allows for the solution of problems, control of attention, and simultaneous and successive processes as well as selective use of knowledge and skills (Das, Kar, & Parrila, 1996) and provides for the most complex aspects of human behavior, including personality and consciousness (Das, 1980). Both the abilities of the thinking with strategies and the attention and self-regulation blocks

Table 2.3. Relationship of Planning, Attention, Simultaneous, Successive (PASS) processes to the Building Blocks model

PASS process	Description	Relationship to Building Blocks model
Planning	Planning is a way of thinking that a person uses to evaluate a task, select or develop a way of doing something, monitor progress, and develop new strategies when necessary.	Attention and Self-Regulation; Thinking with Strategies
Attention	Attention is a way of thinking that allows a child to focus on one thing and ignore others.	Attention and Self-Regulation
Successive	Successive processing is a way of thinking that a person uses to work with information that is arranged in order.	Phonological Processing; Orthographic Processing; Motor Processing
Simultaneous	Simultaneous processing is a way of thinking that a person uses to relate separate pieces of information to a group or to understand how parts are related to a whole.	Thinking with Language; Thinking with Images; Thinking with Strategies

of the Building Blocks model are similar to planning processes. Table 2.3 provides a comparison of the PASS processes and the Building Blocks model. As can be seen, the abilities portrayed in the PASS model incorporate in an interactive way many of the abilities represented in the Building Blocks model.

Cattell-Horn-Carroll Theory

Another theory that can be related to the Building Blocks model is the Cattell-Horn-Carroll (CHC) theory of intelligence (Carroll, 1993; Horn & Cattell, 1966; McGrew, 2005). This theory evolved from the combination of Gf-Gc theory and Carroll's three-stratum theory. Historically, Gf-Gc theory, developed from the work of Raymond Cattell and John Horn, was an acronym referring to fluid (Gf) or more innate abilities and crystallized (Gc) abilities, those more influenced by learning and experience. Carroll's three-stratum theory describes human cognitive abilities from three hierarchical stratums: Stratum I, narrow abilities; Stratum II, broad abilities; and Stratum III, general intelligence, or *g*.

CHC theory provides an empirically based description of intelligence based on the analyses of hundreds of data sets that were not restricted to a particular test battery. This theoretical framework includes several broad domains of ability as well as more than 70 narrow abilities that can be measured successfully using tests. The broad abilities are abbreviated with G, representing intellectual ability, accompanied by one or more lowercase letters that denote the specific type of ability. CHC theory includes the following cognitive abilities: Comprehension-Knowledge (Gc), Fluid Reasoning (Gf), Visual-Spatial Thinking (Gv), Long-Term Retrieval (Glr), Auditory Processing (Ga), Processing Speed (Gs), and Short-Term and Working Memory (Gsm).

Table 2.4 illustrates how the cognitive factors relate to the abilities portrayed in the Building Blocks model. In addition to the cognitive and linguistic domains, two additional CHC abilities that are typically associated with Academic Performance, Quantitative Knowledge (Gq) and Reading and Writing (Grw), are associated with Oral Language and Abilities in Numeracy (Gq) and Literacy (Grw).

As with the Building Blocks model, some students will show patterns in which certain abilities are above average and other abilities are below average. For example, Ben has well-developed visual-spatial thinking (Gv) and Reasoning Abilities (Gf) but Demonstrates Inefficiencies Associated Primarily with Orthography and Memory for Sound–Symbol Relationships (Grw). Maria has strengths in listening comprehension (an ability classified under Gc) but

Strategies

Language Images

CONCEPTUAL

Phonology Orthography Motor

SYMBOLIC

Attention & Self-Regulation | Emotions | Behavior | Self-Esteem

FOUNDATIONAL

Table 2.4. Relationship between Cattell-Horn-Carroll (CHC) abilities and the Building Blocks model

CHC Ability	Description	Relationship to Building Blocks model
Comprehension–Knowledge (Gc)	Ability to acquire general information, vocabulary, and knowledge	Oral Language
Fluid Reasoning (Gf)	Ability to reason, form concepts, and solve problems that often involves unfamiliar information or procedures	Thinking with Images; Thinking with Strategies
Visual-Spatial Thinking (Gv)	Ability to perceive, analyze, synthesize, and think with visual patterns, including the ability to store and recall visual representations	Thinking with Images
Long-Term Retrieval (Glr)	Ability to store information efficiently and retrieve it later through associations	Phonological Processing; Orthographic Processing
Auditory Processing (Ga)	Ability to analyze, synthesize, and discriminate auditory stimuli; also related to phonological awareness—the ability to analyze, synthesize, and manipulate speech sounds	Phonological Processing
Processing Speed (Gs)	Ability to perform automatic or simple cognitive tasks with speed and efficiency and ability to visually scan efficiently	Orthographic Processing
Short-Term Memory and Working Memory (Gsm)	Ability to apprehend orally presented information in immediate awareness and repeat it back within a few seconds (memory span). Ability to hold information in immediate awareness while performing a mental operation on the information (working memory).	Memory span: Phonological Processing Working memory (involves integration of several blocks): Phonological Processing; Orthographic Processing; Thinking with Images; Thinking with Strategies

weaknesses in phonological processing (an ability classified under Ga). Katy has strengths in memory (Gsm) but weakness in language (Gc) and reasoning (Gf).

CHC provides the theoretical basis for the development and interpretation of several test instruments, including the Woodcock-Johnson III Tests of Cognitive Ability (WJ III; Woodcock, McGrew, & Mather, 2001). The WJ III provides several intra-individual discrepancy procedures that allow the comparison of many domain-specific abilities. Another instrument, the Kaufman Assessment Battery for Children–II (KABC–II; Kaufman & Kaufman, 2004), uses both of these theoretical models: the CHC model of broad and narrow abilities and Luria's neuropsychological processing theory. Using a subset of subtests from the KABC–II, the evaluator can interpret the test results from two different but complementary perspectives (Kaufman & Kaufman, 2004). CHC theory places emphasis on the interpretation of specific cognitive abilities and an understanding of how these abilities are related to performance, whereas Luria's neuropsychological theory emphasizes the way children process information when solving problems.

When considering the assessment of individuals suspected of having LD, both approaches are useful for different types of referral questions. In clinical cases that involve the role of language as a factor affecting performance, application of the Luria framework de-emphasizes the role and importance of factual knowledge and allows the evaluator to consider mental processing while reducing the impact of low language performance. The authors state the following fundamental principle for understanding when to include or exclude measures of knowledge and language from an evaluation: "Measures of Gc should be excluded from any score that purports to measure a person's intelligence or overall cognitive ability whenever the measure of Gc is not likely to reflect that person's level of ability" (Kaufman & Kaufman, 2004, p. 4). In most instances, when assessing individuals suspected of having LD, the Kaufmans recommend the use of the CHC model over the Luria model because Gc is an important aspect of cognitive performance (Kaufman & Kaufman, 2004) and is often a relative strength for individuals with LD. Results from the WJ III, the KABC–II, and the Cognitive Assessment System (CAS) can help identify an individual's strengths and weaknesses in cognitive ability and mental processing, making them valuable tools for identifying basic processing disorders, a key aspect of most LD definitions. In addition, the theories of intelligence that were used to develop these instruments provide further support for the more informal methodology presented in the Building Blocks Questionnaire (see Chapter 1 Appendix). Clearly, human abilities are complex, and the completion of any task can involve the employment of numerous overlapping, interactive skills and abilities that theories of intelligence and models of performance can never fully capture. An understanding of essential abilities, however, can help us appreciate and address individual differences in learning and behavior in students.

BUILDING BLOCKS MODEL AND ACADEMIC PERFORMANCE

The Building Blocks model reflects our efforts to interpret and integrate educational research and theory into a functional framework that leads directly to intervention. It is a model that can be practically and reliably used on a daily basis by classroom teachers. Although skills and issues that cause children's classroom and achievement problems are organized into 10 blocks, multiple skills, issues, and behaviors exist within each block that either increase the probability of success or the risk of classroom problems. Table 2.5, adapted from and based on the work of developmental pediatrician Mel Levine (1990), lists basic skills necessary for achievement, beginning with the simplest and building to the more complex. These skills are hypothetically conceived as essential to the development of basic reading, writing, and mathematical abilities.

Table 2.5. Basic skills necessary for successful academic performance

Subject	Skill	Result of skill deficit
Reading	Appreciation of language sounds	Language sounds don't seem very clear.
	Remembering sound–symbol association	The sounds of combinations of letters are difficult to remember.
	Pushing together the sounds in a word	The sounds of letters are known, but it's difficult to put together the sounds in the right order to make the words during reading.
	Reading fast enough	It takes too long to pronounce or understand each word.
	Understanding sentences	The vocabulary or grammar is too difficult.
	Understanding paragraphs or passages	It's difficult to find the main ideas and the important details, or it's difficult to understand the concepts, ideas, or facts.
	Remembering while reading	Ideas don't stay in memory during reading.
	Summarizing what was read	It's too difficult to decide and remember what's important and to organize important ideas in your own words and sentences.
	Applying what was read	It's difficult to use what you've read.
	Enjoying reading	Reading is too much work; it's not automatic.
Spelling	Remembering letters and sounds	It's difficult to remember that a certain combination of letters stands for a certain language sound. It's difficult to understand how sounds are different from each other.
	Picturing words	It's difficult to remember how words look.
		It's difficult to recall and sequence the sounds of multisyllabic words.

Table 2.5. *(continued)*

Subject	Skill	Result of skill deficit
	Spelling longer words Understanding spelling rules	It's difficult to understand what combination of letters is allowed. It is also difficult to understand the vowel rules.
	Spelling consistently	It's difficult to concentrate on little details.
	Writing and spelling at the same time	It's difficult to write and spell at the same time. It's difficult to remember how to spell when writing words in sentences or paragraphs.
	Avoiding mixed spelling errors	It's difficult to distinguish word sounds, remember the rules, and picture words.
Writing	Using fine motor skills	It's difficult to keep track of just where the pencil is while writing. It's difficult to get the right muscles to work together quickly and easily. It's difficult getting finger muscles in touch with memory through many different nerve connections between the hand and the brain. It's difficult getting eyes and fingers to work together.
	Remembering and writing at the same time (i.e., mechanics)	It's difficult to remember punctuation, spelling, capitalization, grammar, vocabulary, letter formation, and ideas all at the same time.
	Thinking about ideas and writing at the same time	It's difficult to think quickly about ideas at the same time as one is writing.
	Planning and organizing	It's difficult to think up something to write about or understand what the teacher expects; decide who will read the writing; think up many good ideas and write them down; take all the ideas and put together the ones that belong together; know what ideas to put first and what ones to put second; get rid of ideas that don't fit; make sure that things make sense; and reorganize what has been written.
	Knowing how to translate ideas into language on paper	It's difficult to get ideas into good language when writing.
Mathematics	Grasping the concepts	It's difficult to understand concepts that include things such as numbers, place values, percentages, decimals, and equations.
	Remembering mathematics	Mathematics is a big memory strain. Mathematical facts need to be remembered very quickly or you may forget something you need to do. When you finish doing one part of a math problem, you need to remember what it was that you were going to do next.
	Understanding the language of mathematics	There is a lot of language (e.g., labels) in a math class, which makes it difficult to keep up with what the teacher is saying and understand certain assignments.
	Using problem-solving skills	It's difficult to think up the best way (or ways) to come up with the correct answer. It's difficult to take time to think about a solution.
	Visualizing	It's difficult to picture what you are able to describe in words.
	Remembering things in the right order	It's tricky to understand some concepts unless you can see clear pictures of images of them in your brain.
	Paying attention to detail	It's difficult to be alert and tuned in to the many little details in mathematics.
	Recognizing or admitting a lack of understanding	It's difficult to recognize or admit that you do not understand or remember basic concepts in order to understand the new ones.

Adapted from Levine, M. (1990). *Keeping ahead in school.* Cambridge, MA: Educators Publishing Service. Copyright 1990 by Educators Publishing Service. Used with permission.

Strategies

Language   Images

CONCEPTUAL

Phonology   Orthography   Motor

SYMBOLIC

Attention & Self-Regulation   Emotions   Behavior   Self-Esteem

FOUNDATIONAL

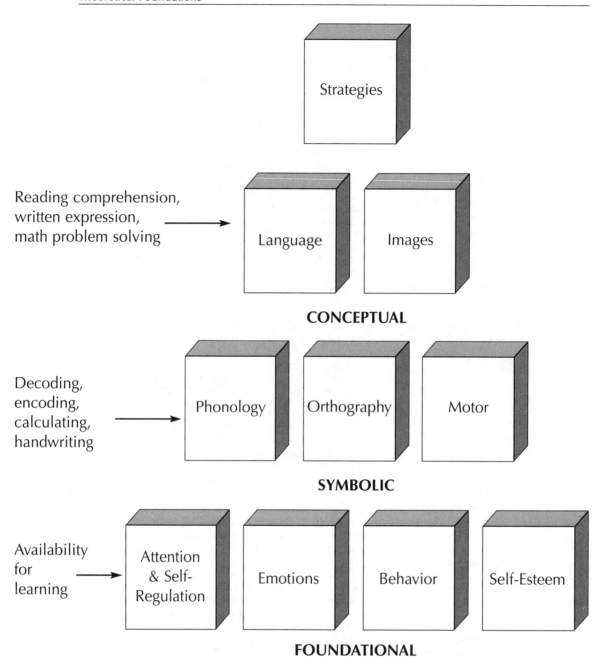

Reading comprehension, written expression, math problem solving →

CONCEPTUAL

Decoding, encoding, calculating, handwriting →

SYMBOLIC

Availability for learning →

FOUNDATIONAL

Figure 2.1. Building Blocks of Learning model that form the basis for corresponding academic skills.

CONCLUSION

The Building Blocks model is an attempt to provide a relatively simple framework for understanding intra-individual differences in learning and behavior and the elemental factors that are needed for school success (see Figure 2.1). This framework is not to be viewed as a static model of discrete elements, however, Rather, elements of each block can be viewed as involving components or elements of another block. For example, elements of a concept such as executive function, which is placed within the strategies block at the conceptual level, can also extend into the symbolic and foundational blocks. The basic level of executive function includes earlier developing abilities such as response inhibition and working memory; deficits in both of which have been associated with ADHD, whereas the higher order components are involved with organization and planning (Cutting & Denckla, 2003). Similarly, both phonology and orthography are aspects of oral and written language, but they are more central to performance and acquisition of basic learning tasks, such as spelling, than higher order tasks, such as those involved in math problem solving. *Morphology,* or the study of the meaning units in language, however, affects both spelling and vocabulary development and, thus, cannot be neatly placed beside phonology and orthography. Essentially, morphology forms a bridge between spelling and vocabulary, and an interaction exists between orthographic development and morphological knowledge (Templeton, 2004). Thus, the abilities specified in the Building Blocks model are to be viewed as interactive, overlapping, and dynamic, and the model does not cover all abilities related to effective learning.

The purpose of this multidimensional model is to represent many of the most common cognitive, motivational, environmental, and behavioral factors that may impede or enhance school performance. Once again, a multiplicity of factors and multiple developmental domains influence school success. The remainder of this book provides discussions of how problems in each of these areas can contribute to behavior and academic difficulties. In addition, specific suggestions are provided for implementing the most effective interventions and treatments.

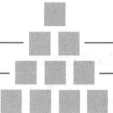

CHAPTER 3 OUTLINE

EFFECTIVE TEACHERS

CREATING OPTIMAL CLASSROOM ENVIRONMENTS

Student and Classroom Variables
Seating and Classroom Space

OUT-OF-CLASSROOM SERVICES

ALLOCATING TIME IN THE CLASSROOM

Transitions
Direct Instruction

CONDITIONS AND COMPONENTS OF THE INTERVENTIONS

Individualized and Small-Group Instruction
Relationships
Communication with Students
Communication with Parents

DIVERSE BACKGROUNDS

Economically Disadvantaged Backgrounds
Culturally and Linguistically Diverse Backgrounds

HOMEWORK

Making Assignments
Meaningfulness, Difficulty, and Assignment Length
Completing Homework
Turning in Homework

CONCLUSION

		Strategies	
	Language	Images	

CONCEPTUAL

Phonology	Orthography	Motor

SYMBOLIC

Attention & Self-Regulation	Emotions	Behavior	Self-Esteem

FOUNDATIONAL

THE LEARNING ENVIRONMENT

As a first-year, fifth-grade teacher, Ms. Perry worked diligently throughout the summer collecting interesting posters and materials for her classroom. During the days set aside before school began, Ms. Perry spent many hours preparing her classroom, deciding where to place materials and how to help students have access to activities and materials in the classroom. As a first-year teacher, Ms. Perry also attended a number of special in-service sessions. During one of these sessions, the trainer explained a method for setting up materials and learning stations in the classroom. This arrangement would allow students to move among tasks and to obtain necessary materials with some degree of autonomy. Ms. Perry was certain that she had designed her classroom for maximum efficiency and student learning. Yet within the first few days of school, she noted that students were moving around too often, and, as they moved, they often disrupted others.

Observing the increased pattern of off-task behavior in the classroom, Ms. Perry's colleague, Ms. Sammons, an experienced teacher, pointed out that sometimes too much of a good thing can turn into a bad thing. Ms. Sammons provided Ms. Perry with a set of statements to consider about her classroom environment (see Table 3.1). After reviewing the statements, Ms. Perry realized that some changes were needed in her classroom environment and management.

The performances of even the most academically advanced, well-behaved, emotionally secure students vary on the basis of environmental factors. The classroom environment includes all aspects of classroom function and structure. Such diverse factors as communication among teachers and students, issues related to discipline, size of group instruction, transition, classroom rules, and the critical link between teachers and parents can be influenced by teachers. This second edition of this book reflects our shift away from efforts to just manage classroom behavior toward the creation of a framework to develop sustainable classroom environments by shaping the mindsets of educators. Effective educators are capable of appreciating the forces that truly motivate students, even students with serious behavioral and developmental challenges. These educators are capable of recognizing that their classroom activities day in and day out do not just contribute to students' self-esteem and resilience but also they provide an essential foundation for successful transition into adult life.

This chapter provides a definition of effective teachers and explores the classroom environment. The discussion includes ways in which teachers communicate with parents about students' behavior, progress, and performance as well as the means by which homework is assigned and collected. Effective teachers create positive, nurturing classroom environments.

Table 3.1. Questions to consider about the classroom environment

Have you allocated time efficiently in the classroom?
Do you and your students get along?
When you provide directions, do students comply?
Have you developed a workable system for discipline?
Is there a workable system for seating and classroom space?
Do you have a method for providing group instruction?
Do you use a number of strategies to improve compliance?
Do you have a system for developing and implementing classroom rules?
Is a system in place to communicate effectively with parents?
Is a system in place to assign, follow up, and collect homework?

EFFECTIVE TEACHERS

More than 35 years ago, Bushell (1973) eloquently wrote that teachers are powerful change agents of student behavior. This statement remains true today. Effective teachers exert a significant impact on children's achievement, emotions, and development. Bushell described teachers as

> Purchasing agents, property clerks, and accident insurance salesmen; they are attendance monitors, playground monitors, hall monitors, lunch room monitors; they remain cheerful at faculty meetings and brave when caring for skinned knees and bloody noses; they are audio visual technicians, janitors, psychologists, revenue collectors for the lunch room, referees for athletic contests and counselors to parents. (1973, p. 1)

Effective teachers exude an aura of authority and affection. Children do not learn well from people whom they do not like or admire. A teacher's mindset about the classroom is critical in determining whether strategies, however effective in theory, work well or yield few benefits. The school environment, as the late Dr. Julius Segal (1988) reminds us, is a prime location for nurturing resilience. The mindset of effective educators provides a framework for understanding the lifelong impact adults can have on their students based on day-in and day-out classroom activities. Emphasis is placed on the importance of understanding, appreciating, and building assets and strengths as well as managing weaknesses and liabilities. An effective classroom teacher (who also can be called an *environmental engineer* [Goldstein & Jones, 1998]) must carefully select instructional goals and materials, structure and plan learning activities, involve students in the learning process, monitor students' progress closely, change and modify various interventions, and provide frequent feedback about progress and accomplishments. The teacher must organize and maintain the classroom learning environment to maximize the time spent engaged in productive activity and minimize the time lost during transitions or disruptions requiring disciplinary action. An effective teacher must develop methods to elicit achievement from students, involve students in classroom activities, and teach students a means for self-management and self-control. Effective teachers use a workable set of classroom rules and are able to respond consistently and quickly to problem situations. They have structured their classroom to minimize disruption and maximize educational experiences, and they respond to the needs of their students.

Teachers can increase the risk that all students will experience problems if they are intolerant and rigid in providing directions; aloof, distant, condescending, stiff, or formal in relationships with their students; restricted, rigid, and able to recognize only the need for academic accomplishment; or hypercritical, fault-finding, threatening, hopeless, pessimistic, unhappy, impulsive, or short tempered. In contrast, effective teachers possess the attitude that they can be and are responsive to their students' need for support and assistance and that they manage the classroom environment effectively while holding high expectations for students' achievement and behavior. Effective teachers are authentic teachers (Walker & Shea, 1991) who have chosen to work with children and know why they made this choice. They are confident, realistic, and honest when they interact with their students. They accept each student as an individual. They understand human behavior and child development and know that vast developmental differences exist in the abilities and learning rates of children. They examine their own behavior critically, learn new skills, and make changes as necessary. They are not defensive about the manner in which they deal with children in their classrooms. The mindset of effective teachers reflects a sense of patience, flexibility, and a willingness to accept that students work with rather than for them. Finally, effective teachers provide each child with a sense of security, making school a place that children desire to attend and the classroom a place where every child feels important and needed. The golden rule for being an effective teacher is to be a good human being. Strickland described a good teacher in this way:

> A good teacher should recognize that some children learn by listening, some by seeing, and some by feeling; and his classroom surely contains children with each learning style. The teacher should recognize that some children are facile with words, some with numbers, and some with neither; and that children vary widely in the amount of time needed to absorb knowledge. Most of all, an adequate teacher must realize that, if a child is doing badly in school, there is always a reason: and that reason is rarely laziness or willfulness. The child who is doing the very best she can and has no idea why she is not succeeding is depending on the teacher to find out why her struggles are in vain. If the teacher can't figure it out, then the child is in store for years of frustration. (1998, p. 132)

Some teachers blame student failure or behavior problems on internal characteristics of the student or home (Soodak & Podell, 1994), believing that a child's problems are due to something within the child or caused by the parents. They place more emphasis than consultants do on interventions aimed directly at the student, often suggesting the student needs to take ownership for the problem and solution. Athanasiou, Geil, Hazel, and Copeland (2002) noted that the internal attributional style of teachers is reflected in their beliefs about needed classroom interventions. Teachers tend to attribute lack of progress to students while crediting either themselves or students when progress is made. Yet, teachers high in efficacy tend to de-emphasize home variables in students' success and failure, pointing instead to the instructional program and teachers' roles (Hall, Hines, Bacon, & Koulianos, 1992). Teachers' stresses and their impact on withdrawal from the teaching profession have been increasingly recognized (Anderson, Levinsohn, Barker, & Kiewra, 1999). In educator surveys, teachers uniformly complain of large classrooms, discipline problems, low salaries, unsupportive parents, and the demands of state assessments and educational curriculums.

Effective teachers are an essential component of a sustainable school environment. The consensual description of the effective teacher is based on a wide variety of classrooms educating many different students. To truly understand an effective teacher and to help all educators be effective requires an appreciation of attitudes, beliefs, teacher behaviors, and instructional strategies. Though some believe characteristics of effective teachers are generic to good teaching (Kauffman & Wong, 1991), others suggest that generic skills may serve the general population but not be as effective for students with specific problems (Zabel, 1987). Yet, as noted by Hobbs in 1966, within the special education field,

Strategies

Language | Images

CONCEPTUAL

Phonology | Orthography | Motor

SYMBOLIC

Attention & Self-Regulation | Emotions | Behavior | Self-Esteem

FOUNDATIONAL

little is known about the requirements for effective teaching of students with behavior problems.

CREATING OPTIMAL CLASSROOM ENVIRONMENTS

For the purposes of this chapter, the classroom environment consists of four key areas: tasks; movement in the room; the organization of the room and related materials; and the relationships among students, peers, and teachers. The effectiveness of the classroom environment is usually measured by student behavior, student engagement, and performance. When students are actively engaged in meaningful work, following the basic classroom rules, and communicating effectively with each other and teachers, the classroom environment is effective and optimal. But optimal classroom environments do not arise spontaneously. They are not created by following a simple formula or set of guidelines. Optimal environments begin with an effective attitude and a willingness to accept a basic premise—that classroom educators should first seek to manage the learning environment rather than the student. In a synthesis of empirical investigations related to the most effective instructional conditions, Foorman (2007) noted that researchers have identified the following characteristics of schools with outstanding achievement: 1) a positive social climate, 2) strong leadership, 3) increased time spent on instruction, 4) high expectations for all students, 5) continuous monitoring of student achievement, 6) ongoing professional development, and 7) parent involvement.

Student and Classroom Variables

Since the 1970s, researchers and educators alike have recognized that student and classroom variables also play determining roles in the functioning of the classroom. Student variables such as home experiences, LD, temperament, language skills, and social and interpersonal abilities exert a significant impact on performance. A student capable of following teacher directions and rules, completing classroom work, and responding appropriately to conventional management techniques is going to experience far more success and positive feedback from teachers than a student who does not use or has not mastered these skills. Furthermore, the structure of the classroom, the number of students, the range of student abilities and achievement, the size of the room, and the manner in which work is presented also contribute to successful educational experiences. Students are nurtured by educators who are competent in behavioral and educational strategies but who are first and foremost concerned with creating a safe, accepting climate. Thus, teacher, student, and classroom variables at any given moment interact with and contribute to, in varying degrees, the manner in which the classroom operates.

Seating and Classroom Space

For children with behavior problems or LD, on-task behavior increases when conditions in the classroom change from desk clusters to rows. The rate of student disruptions has been reported to be as high as three times greater in the desk-cluster seating arrangement than it is in the row arrangement (Wheldall & Lam, 1987). Also, the greater distance between students' desks, the greater the levels of on-task behavior and the lower the levels of disruption (Weinstein, 1979). In traditional classroom settings, teachers tend to interact primarily with students in the center and in the front portion of the classroom. This area is called the *T zone.* Students seated to either side do not interact as actively. Thus, the more a teacher can circulate during direct instruction, the more likely it is that students receive equal attention. Fifer (1986) found that the more time teachers spent away from the

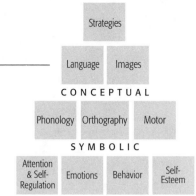

front of the classroom, the fewer the number of behavior problems. Appropriate interactions academically between teachers and students, even in secondary schools, increase as teachers move more frequently around the classroom.

The allotment of space in the classroom is also critical. Arrangement of the classroom exerts a powerful influence on teachers' abilities to praise, monitor students, and supervise effectively. Consider the following eight components concerning the allotment of classroom space (Paine, Radicchi, Rosellini, Deutchman, & Darch, 1983):

1. Placement of students' desks

2. Placement of the teacher's desk in relation to students' desks

3. Movable classroom partitions

4. Placement of teaching stations

5. The use of self-correction stations for independent work

6. Material stations

7. Activity stations

8. Bulletin boards

OUT-OF-CLASSROOM SERVICES

In a chapter about the classroom environment, it may seem odd to address out-of-classroom services, but these options are important for some students. Many students with learning, emotional, and behavior difficulties spend the majority of their time in general education classrooms. A few students with the most severe difficulties are served within self-contained classrooms and do not receive any general education services. Others receive a portion of their instruction in small-group settings or in resource rooms. Although the goals of inclusion are philosophically sound, students with severe learning, emotional, and behavior difficulties require more support and intensive individualized instruction than can be provided typically within a general education classroom.

In the late 1970s, few, if any, would argue with the spirit of the concept of the least restrictive placement. Cruickshank (1977) cautioned, however, that, for a student with LD, the least restrictive placement might often be the most restrictive academically:

> A child [who is] placed in a so-called least restrictive situation and [is] unable to achieve, who lacks an understanding teacher, who does not have appropriate learning materials, who is faced with tasks he cannot manage, whose failures result in negative comments by his classmates, and whose parents reflect frustration to him when he is at home, is indeed being restricted on all sides. (p. 194)

Given the increased responsibility and time restraints placed on classroom teachers, there is often insufficient time and resources to provide some children with the specialized help they require. Individualization in typical classrooms is simply not a reality; Lieberman pointed out, "The barrage of curriculum materials, syllabi, grade-level expectations for performance, standardized achievement tests, competency tests and so on continue to overwhelm even the most flexible teachers" (1992, p. 15).

A further concern is the lack of academic progress for some students who spend all of their time in general education environments. Even when students with LD are part of responsible inclusion programs, many do not make sufficient or acceptable academic progress in general education classrooms (Fuchs, Fuchs, &

Fernstrom, 1993; Zigmond et al., 1995). As Klingner, Vaughn, Hughes, Schumm, and Elbaum (1998) described,

> The students of greatest concern to us were those who were very poor readers at the start of the school year and as a group made no progress, despite being part of a responsible inclusion program that received substantial support. We must conclude that full-time placement in the general educational classroom with in-class support from special education teachers is not sufficient to meet the needs of these students. They require combined services that include in-class support and daily intensive one-to-one instruction from highly trained personnel. This is an expensive proposition but appears to be the only solution that will yield growth in reading for students with severe reading disabilities. (p. 159)

This level of intensive instruction is necessary for helping students with reading disabilities become competent readers.

Placement decisions should not be dictated by current political or educational trends, but rather by the needs of an individual student. Mercer (1995) noted that teachers should not be discussing the least restrictive environment but, instead, the most enabling environment. The issue to address is where the student will receive the most appropriate and effective instruction, whether in a general or special education classroom. For the majority of students, effective teachers can create an environment in which even students with weaknesses in other building blocks can function optimally and successfully.

ALLOCATING TIME IN THE CLASSROOM

Since 1975, research has documented that the proportion of time in which students are actively and productively engaged in learning best predicts their academic achievement and the overall quality of the classroom. As early as 1977, Good and Grouws reported that students make greater gains in academic achievement and like their classrooms better when minimal time is spent on discipline. When students' academic learning time is increased, achievement increases and behavior problems decrease, especially for students who typically experience low levels of achievement or who are at risk (Berliner, 1988). This is not to suggest that if students spend 100% of their time in the classroom engaged in learning that they or their teachers will be happy. Students have been reported to vary in the amount of time spent actively engaged in learning from a low of 45% to a high of 90% (Fischer et al., 1980). The amount of time appears to vary within classrooms as well as among classrooms of the same grade. A teacher's effectiveness in managing behavior and choosing instructional strategies needs to match the learning capacities of students. Though some have suggested that the nature and quality of time in the classroom may be used to create a formula to predict learning, no one has yet generated a formula that can be uniformly applied by each teacher. Productive classroom time is a function not only of students' abilities but also of the teacher's personality, teaching style, and management of the environment.

Typically, between 50% and 60% of the total school day is used for direct instruction (Strother, 1984). Time is often lost in organizing and beginning instruction, managing transitions, dealing with misbehavior, and responding to requests for assistance. Elementary school students spend more than half of their time completing individual seatwork. During these periods, researchers have suggested that students display lower engagement rates and less productive learning, likely because they are not interacting directly with their teacher (Anderson, 1985). Time can be used productively, however, if the independent student learning activities are of a high quality. Many independent student

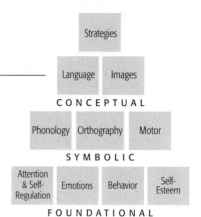

learning activities for K–3 classrooms created by the Florida Center for Reading Research can be downloaded at no cost from the following website: http://www.fcrr.org/Curriculum/studentCenterActivites.htm

Effective environments are created when teachers are interactive, fast-paced, engaging, and directive in their teaching styles. Such a style includes teacher-directed presentation of material, discussion with and review of students' work, drill with controlled practice, information assessment to observe progress, frequent opportunities for students to respond, ample opportunities for student reinforcement for success, and the close match of instructional difficulty to a student's capabilities. To increase academic learning time, teachers should focus on time allocated for instruction and student engagement (Gettinger, 1990). To increase time used for instruction, teachers should consider ways to increase school attendance and punctuality, minimize interruptions, increase nondisruptive transitions, and maintain students' academic focus.

After reviewing the basic principles of class management and organization, Ms. Sammons helped Ms. Perry reduce the number of transitions by adjusting station locations. Ms. Sammons also helped Ms. Perry with a number of other issues noted. Ms. Perry realized that even simple issues such as deciding where materials are placed in the classroom or how often students move from place to place can be powerful forces in determining student behavior, cooperation, and performance.

In regard to engaged time, teachers should clarify instructions and expectations for performance and encourage students to respond frequently. Adopting seating arrangements that maximize attention can enhance participation. Finally, with regard to productive learning time, teachers must consider the goals of seatwork and provide immediate, appropriate feedback. To do this, the teacher must diagnose, prescribe, and monitor performance actively. Teachers must also be flexible and consider that a focus on any one of these issues will likely affect other issues as well.

Mr. Chavez struggled to help Jeremy come into the classroom, settle down, and begin working. Transitions for Jeremy were particularly difficult. Because of his problems with self-control as the result of ADHD, Jeremy experienced little difficulty getting off task or moving to an enjoyable activity but experienced much more difficulty than his peers with returning to and completing a structured task. Just walking from his classroom to the resource room was a difficult transition for Jeremy. Walking through the hallway afforded Jeremy a number of interesting activities, from stopping in the bathroom to visiting with other children in the halls. Punishment for arriving late to the resource room did little to alter Jeremy's behavior. The resource teacher decided to increase Jeremy's interest in and motivation for arriving on time to his classroom, using what he had learned in a workshop about reinforcement for students with ADHD. The teacher offered an incentive for all students, including Jeremy. Students arriving early or on time were given the opportunity to stop work early and spend the last 10 minutes of class working on a group jigsaw puzzle. Once the puzzle was completed, the resource teacher had promised an ice cream party for all of his students. The solution worked effectively, and Jeremy began arriving on time to the resource classroom.

By maintaining a consistent schedule, working to minimize interruptions, and keeping time used in transitions to a minimum (i.e., no longer than 5–10 minutes), instructional time can be increased. When students understand instructions and performance expectations, engaged time also increases. Keep in mind that students appear to perform best with a slightly faster paced instructional presentation. Teachers often underestimate the amount of content they can cover with most students who learn typically (Berliner, 1988). Disruption among students is directly related to less instructional time and engaged academic time. Disruptions that interfere with others in the classroom tend to escalate and must be dealt with through warnings, reprimands, and consistency, even if the former two constitute negative feedback. By moving through the classroom during seatwork and monitoring student performance, as well as by establishing clear procedures about what students should do when their work is completed or when they have a question, the amount of engaged academic time can be increased.

Transitions

Of all the parts of the school day, transitions provide the greatest potential for disruption. The following four basic rules can decrease the number of disruptions during transitions:

1. Have students put away what they are working on and take out what they need for the move.

2. Ask students to move chairs and desks quietly when they stand up.

3. Ask students to refrain from talking to or touching each other.

4. Plan for and teach students to manage themselves during transitions.

Transitions account for close to one fifth of the time spent during the school day. Teachers can effectively manage this component of the environment by modeling appropriate behavior; signaling the beginning and ending of activities clearly; dealing with transition problems as soon as they occur; having students actually practice transitions; and providing ample reinforcement for quick, smooth transitions.

Direct Instruction

Direct instruction, or active teaching, is a proactive way of minimizing classroom disruption. The following suggested model for direct instruction has been compiled on the basis of work by Brophy and Good (1986), Rosenshine and Stevens (1986), and Morgan and Jenson (1988):

1. Involve all students in the instructional program. Do not exclude students who have low levels of achievement.

2. Provide seats for students with academic difficulties close to the teacher or to the center of active learning.

3. Present lessons in a well-organized, sequenced manner.

4. Begin lessons with a short review of previously learned skills necessary to begin the lesson.

5. Begin lessons with a short statement of goals. Provide clear, concise explanations and illustrations of what is to be learned.

6. Present new material in small steps with practice and demonstration at each step. Provide initial guidance through practice activities.

7. Provide students with frequent opportunities to practice and generalize skills.

8. Ask questions to check students' understanding and obtain responses from everyone.

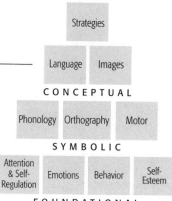

Strategies

Language | Images

CONCEPTUAL

Phonology | Orthography | Motor

SYMBOLIC

Attention & Self-Regulation | Emotions | Behavior | Self-Esteem

FOUNDATIONAL

CONDITIONS AND COMPONENTS OF THE INTERVENTIONS

The conditions and components of an intervention appear as important as the selection and use of a specific evidence-based approach. Results from intervention studies suggest that the nature of the program is less important than its comprehensiveness and intensity (Fletcher et al., 2007). For example, Torgesen and colleagues (2001) found the same positive outcomes for two different reading programs that both provided intensive, systematic, one-to-one instruction. Effective instructional elements included small-group instruction with high response rates, the provision of immediate feedback, and the sequential mastery of topics, all elements of good teaching (National Joint Committee on Learning Disabilities, 2005). In addition, several instructional principles can help inform decisions regarding diverse learners and effective early instruction: 1) Capitalize and use instructional time efficiently; 2) provide interventions early, frequently, and strategically; 3) teach less, but more thoroughly; 4) explain strategies in a clear, explicit manner to students; 5) provide teacher-directed and student-centered activities, and 6) evaluate the effectiveness of instructional materials and student progress frequently (Kame'enui, 1993). According to Hallahan, students with LD also need "intensive, relentless, iterative, and individualized instruction that depends on a viable categorical approach to special education service delivery" (2007, p. 24). In addition, many types of interventions and methodologies are needed to meet the needs of the diverse learners in any classroom.

Individualized and Small-Group Instruction

Individualized and small-group instruction are effective and necessary components for learning and are research-proven techniques to enhance student achievement. Teachers often face the dilemma, however, of working with individuals or a small group while simultaneously managing the rest of the classroom. In this circumstance, some students may be disruptive. Other students may require assistance and must wait until teachers are available, thereby wasting valuable classroom time. In some circumstances, a parent volunteer or an aide can help with this problem. In addition, periodic praise directed at the larger group can be effective in keeping students on task.

Paine and colleagues (1983) suggested the following four critical components to help teachers manage classroom instruction in groups: 1) moving consistently through the room, stopping for only 15–30 seconds at any one place while instructing or while students are working independently; 2) scanning the room to remain aware of what the entire classroom is doing; 3) praising students; and 4) following up with the groups.

A master teacher, Ms. Delphine Woods (personal communication, September 1998), advises new teachers that one of the most important ways to establish respect in the classroom is to call students by their first name and use "please" and "thank you" as many times as possible each day with students. Effective praise should follow the *if–then rule*. If a student is engaged in a behavior that a teacher wants to increase, then it should be praised. Good praise should include the student's name; a description of the behavior being praised; and a varied, convincing delivery.

Although all teachers agree that praise is important, the amount of praise that students receive for exhibiting appropriate behavior typically decreases dramatically by third grade. Concomitantly, the rate of teachers' negative attention toward students who are off task or engaged in other nonproductive activities usually increases. Praise, however, is the fuel that helps the engine of the classroom operate efficiently.

Relationships

The more positive a teacher's relationships are with students, the more likely students will want to comply when the teacher provides an instruction or directions. Unfortunately, research suggests that relative to Latino and Caucasian children, African American children and their parents appear to have less supportive relationships with teachers, and the quality of these relationships affects children's motivation, engagement, and achievement (Hughes & Kwok, 2007; see a later section of this chapter for more on cultural and ethnic backgrounds). In addition, disruptive students often develop negative relationships with their teachers. This inadvertently contributes to differences in a teacher's relationships with different students. Research has demonstrated that students whom teachers like and who are compliant are provided with more opportunities to respond academically; receive more teacher support, praise, and attention; and receive less criticism.

Unfortunately, teachers receive little professional preparation on how to build positive alliances with parents and warm relationships with students (Hughes & Kwok, 2007). To foster a positive relationship with students, teachers should consider the following:

- Avoid responding directly to student behavior that is provocative or confrontational.

- Provide genuine praise and encouragement to all students, making certain that each student experiences success every day.

- Use humor.

- Arrange opportunities for students to receive positive attention, contribute to the class, and feel that they are important classroom members.

- Work to develop positive relationships with all students in the class.

Feeling cared about by a teacher encourages students' investment and engagement in school and learning (Patrick, Ryan, & Kaplan, 2007).

Communication with Students

Teachers who rely on positive communication to interact with their students are less likely to have students who are noncompliant. In contrast, when teachers use punitive methods to discipline children, they are more likely to experience classrooms in which students resort to less acceptable forms of noncompliance, such as defiance, passivity, and oppositionality.

This chapter is in part devoted to strategies to help teachers develop effective communication with their students. The bottom line is that ineffective communication is more likely to lead to an escalating pattern of disruptive classroom behavior. As described by Forehand and McMahon (1981), when teachers provide a command directed to a student with whom they have not developed an effective means of communication, the child often interprets the command as aversive and does not comply. Teachers then give up, withdraw, or escalate coercive pressure for compliance. This may involve raising a voice, threatening, or outright intimidation. The student is then either rewarded for noncompliance by the teacher's withdrawal or termination of his or her request, or the interaction escalates, giving the student more opportunity to practice direct defiance.

Teachers usually fall into this trap with students because they themselves may have been rewarded for using coercive tactics if students eventually comply. Teachers must be sensitive to this escalating pattern of noncompliance, a pattern

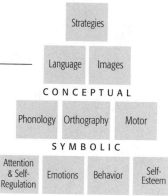

that often is driven by a negative reinforcement paradigm. To reduce risk, teachers should consider manipulating antecedent behaviors by anticipating problems and teaching students competent skills to deal with classroom issues. When a teacher acts in a reactionary manner after a problem has occurred and has begun to escalate, the probability that the classroom will be further disrupted increases. Unfortunately, most teacher interventions focus on manipulating problems after the noncompliant event occurs rather than manipulating the antecedents. Teachers use far more negative responses, such as punishment, time-out, and response cost, than positive consequences. Although antecedent manipulation is effective, most efforts to increase compliance and reduce noncompliance involve consequential events such as reward or punishment. Preventive interventions, however, are recommended because they reduce the potential number of negative interactions that arise between teachers and students. This mindset allows a teacher to act in a proactive rather than reactive fashion. Researchers on effective classrooms have suggested since the 1970s that the efficient management of antecedent events is the key to maintaining student compliance (Forehand & McMahon, 1981).

Communication with Parents

One important proactive measure for teachers to take is establishing good communication with parents. If teachers make an effort at the beginning of the school year to communicate with parents and establish a workable means by which parents can communicate with them, students are much less likely to experience problems between home and school. Parents should be encouraged to write notes, call, or e-mail with questions. Most school districts now have e-mail addresses for every teacher at the middle and high school level, and many elementary school teachers will provide them as well. This is a particularly efficient means for teachers and parents to communicate. Although a teacher's communication with many students' parents may be minimal, setting this communication system in place is invaluable as problems arise. For students with chronic or ongoing academic or behavioral challenges, a daily or weekly note is an effective means of communicating with parents. Figure 3.1 provides a sample school–home note for elementary school students.

DIVERSE BACKGROUNDS

Almost every school population consists of children from many different economic, ethnic, linguistic, and cultural backgrounds. Children who live in poverty, as well as students whose primary language is not English, face additional challenges in adapting to and being successful in the school environment.

Economically Disadvantaged Backgrounds

Although the new millennium has brought promises of unlimited technological, scientific, and cultural advances, our society is experiencing increasing problems with preparing our youth for the future. Competency in reading, writing, and mathematics is simply not enough. Violence, vandalism, increased school dropout rates, and mental health problems among our students signify this problem.

Many children do not have adequate educational opportunities prior to entering school and come from impoverished environments. Sadly, living in poverty often results in poor social and academic outcomes for children. In fact, poverty, with its many associated conditions such as inadequate food and shelter, exposure to violence and chaotic living conditions, and limited learning opportunities from nurturing adults, is the strongest predictor of school failure (Kauffman, 2005). Teachers must consider each child's living conditions. As described in Chapter 1, Mark, a fifth-grade student, lives in a crowded trailer with

Student Name _____ Date _____

Teacher directions: Please rate this student in each of the following areas, using a 1 as the best score:

Came to class prepared	5	4	3	2	1
Used class time wisely	5	4	3	2	1
Followed class rules	5	4	3	2	1
Followed recess rules	5	4	3	2	1
Respected the rights of classmates	5	4	3	2	1
Completed homework	5	4	3	2	1
Followed directions	5	4	3	2	1
Displayed a good attitude	5	4	3	2	1
Participated	5	4	3	2	1

Homework_____

_____

_____

Comments_____

_____

_____

Overall, today was a   ☐ great day

☐ good day

☐ average day

☐ mediocre day

☐ very poor day

Teacher initials _____

Figure 3.1. School–home note. A score of 1 is the best score a student can earn. (From Goldstein, S., & Goldstein, M. [1991]. *It's just attention disorder: User's manual* [p. 64]. Salt Lake City, UT: Neurology, Learning, and Behavior Center; adapted with permission.)

his three siblings and four adults. There is little room for sleeping and no room for studying. It is not reasonable to expect Mark to complete homework at night or to always come to school with clean clothes. The challenge of preparing children for the future has and must be increasingly borne on the shoulders of educators. Our schools must find a way to educate all students from all types of backgrounds efficiently and effectively by providing them with knowledge and instilling in them qualities of resilience, qualities that will help them be confident and know how to overcome the daily adversities they must face.

Culturally and Linguistically Diverse Backgrounds

An essential aspect of understanding the role of the environment on behavior and performance is consideration of the diverse cultural and linguistic backgrounds of

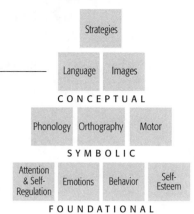

children. According to the 2000 Census, English is not the first language for about one fifth of the children enrolled in U.S. public schools (U.S. Bureau of the Census, 2005). In addition, teachers may respond and interact differently with students from different racial and ethnic backgrounds. Results from a recent meta-analysis indicated that teachers have higher expectations for Asian American and European American students than for Latino or African American students and that teachers directed more questions and encouraging remarks toward European American students than Latino and African American students (Tenenbaum & Ruck, 2007). Clearly, this reality suggests that teachers must pay attention to and develop an understanding of the unique cultural values and beliefs of each student in the classroom. Based on this individually tailored understanding of linguistic and cultural differences, a teacher can then evaluate more readily the suitability of specific behavioral and academic intervention strategies for a specific child. All teachers need to address the myriad difficulties facing students from culturally and linguistically diverse groups and select interventions that are responsive to their needs (Klingner, Sorrells, & Barrera, 2007).

For decades, concerns have been expressed regarding the fact that certain racial and ethnic groups have been and continue to be overrepresented in the LD category (Rueda & Windmueller, 2006). Many of these students may be placed in special education because they are not meeting school demands, even though they do not have a "disability" per se. Thus, the challenge becomes providing more appropriate instruction to children who speak different languages within general education settings. English immersion programs offer the least native language support, and the students enrolled in these programs are more likely to be placed in special education than students who are participating in other types of language support programs (Artiles, Rueda, Salazar, & Higareda, 2005).

School districts in California categorize English language learners into two subgroups: students with limited proficiency in English but who are proficient in their native language and students with limited proficiency in both their native language and English (Artiles et al., 2005). Clearly, as long as they receive support, students with competency in one language, even if it is not English, are better prepared to meet the academic challenges of a classroom, whereas additional supports are needed for students with global linguistic weaknesses. An understanding of each student's unique circumstances can help a teacher create a classroom atmosphere where all children feel welcome, safe, and valued as individuals. In essence, the goal for all teachers should be to learn about the cultural and linguistic backgrounds of students in the classroom and create a classroom climate where differences are respected and shared while at the same time advancing the language learning and achievement of all students (Klingner et al., 2007; Nelson & Van Meter, 2006).

HOMEWORK[1]

Successful management of homework is a key ingredient of an effective classroom environment. Children differ significantly in their attitudes about homework and the methods they use to complete homework. Teachers also differ in homework strategies, reasons for homework, and types of homework they assign. Difficulties with completing homework have been documented for more than one fourth of students in the general education classroom and for more than half of students with LD (Polloway, Epstein, & Foley, 1992). Children with weaknesses in the building blocks often consider homework another opportunity to fail, so they resist. Students with ADHD also tend to find other activities to do that are far

---

[1]The material in this section has been adapted from the text on homework by Zentall and Goldstein (1999).

more interesting than homework. They also have trouble remembering to turn in their homework even when it has been completed. Even on the days when Jeremy had his completed homework in his backpack, he rarely remembered to place it in the homework box without his teacher's prompting. Many children with weaknesses in skills and abilities struggle with the completion of homework. Andy completed his homework independently, but his teacher could not read anything he had written. Katy had difficulty because she rarely understood her assignments and could not complete them without a great deal of parental assistance. Jeremy's parents had to sit down with him in the evening or he could not accomplish anything. Even with constant nagging, Jeremy just could not sustain the attention and effort needed for homework completion. Ryan struggled with all homework involving reading and writing but completed his math assignments independently. Maria's mother spent several hours with her every evening, helping her with homework. Although Maria never had late assignments and always received high grades on homework, her mother had assumed a large role in homework completion. Ben could not keep up with the assigned readings, so he did not do any reading unless one of his parents read with him. In secondary school, John experienced problems similar to Katy's. He became overwhelmed with all of the assignments from his different classes and often did not understand what he was supposed to do. Fortunately, his father spent a lot of time helping him complete the assigned work. Samuel and Mark never turned in any homework. The purpose of homework is to promote independence, not to foster increased dependence on parents. Homework should be manageable and reasonable. For children who struggle, adjustments have to be made in the type and amount of work they receive.

In spite of these student-centered problems, some benefits can be derived from homework. Homework is a cost-effective means of delivering instruction that increases in importance as children move into junior high (middle school) and high school. Homework also can help foster positive attitudes toward school and provide an important link between home experiences and school learning. In the elementary grades, high levels of feedback and supervision are necessary so that students can practice their assignments correctly. For students in middle school and high school, homework should facilitate knowledge acquisition in specific areas. The average high school student in a class that was assigned homework outperformed almost three quarters of peers in a class without homework as measured by standardized tests, and junior high school students achieved half that gain (Cooper & Nye, 1994). Students devoting time to homework are thus likely on a path to improved achievement as well as a path of greater achievement motivation and better skill development. In general, teachers' problems with homework can be grouped into three main areas:

1. Problems making assignments

2. Problems in the meaningfulness, difficulty, and length of assignments

3. Problems getting homework returned

Making Assignments

When teachers make assignments, clear instructions are critical. A teacher should consider the purpose of the assignment; the date that it is due; the format required; the materials that are necessary; and, most important, the requirements for good performance, which may include many steps in a complex task. The majority of teachers assign homework at the end of class periods, which may penalize younger students or students with difficulties in other building block areas. The ability of these students to quickly attend at the close of the class may be compromised. Assignments with clear directions should be made early in the

Strategies

Language   Images

CONCEPTUAL

Phonology   Orthography   Motor

SYMBOLIC

Attention & Self-Regulation   Emotions   Behavior   Self-Esteem

FOUNDATIONAL

school day or lesson. Offer students the opportunity to volunteer to explain the assignment in their own words. Provide a brief time for students to begin assignments in class to make certain that they understand what they need to do. Homework assignments can be recorded in the morning on a corner of the board so students will have plenty of time to write down the tasks.

Meaningfulness, Difficulty, and Assignment Length

Assignments that are meaningful, at a moderate difficulty level, and neither too repetitive nor too long are more likely to be completed. In reality, the most frequent types of assignments are unfinished class work and practice tasks (Polloway, Epstein, Bursuck, Madhavi, & Cumblad, 1994). Boredom is a frequent complaint of students with regard to homework. Boredom results in students completing less work, less accurately. To reduce boredom, consider using homework to reinforce what has been learned, alternate math and reading homework on different nights, keep repetition to a minimum, and allow students who struggle with assignments to begin homework in class to make certain that they understand the process and task.

Motivation to complete homework can also be increased by altering the meaningfulness of assignments. If an assignment is interesting and relevant to the child's age level and if elements of choice are included in the assignment, more homework will be completed. Children who are able to understand how their schoolwork relates to their own skills and experiences have fewer homework problems (Nicholls, McKenzie, & Shufro, 1994).

Assignment difficulty is also a critical factor. For students to independently complete an assignment, they must have achieved a moderate level of understanding during class (Rosenberg, 1989). When students do not understand homework material, they become frustrated while attempting to complete homework. When assignments vary in difficulty level and students vary in ability, the teacher should consider what additional supports may be available during homework. In some schools, teachers staff telephone hotlines or schools or districts offer homework hotlines online. Helping parents understand the nature and methods for homework assignments is also critical. Homework can be reduced in length to accommodate students with slower working rates or limited attention spans without changing the purpose of homework. A teacher may also specify the amount of time that should be spent on the homework rather than specifying the amount of material to be completed. For example, a teacher may ask students to read for a half an hour rather than reading a set number of pages.

Completing Homework

Completion of homework depends in part on a teacher's ability to communicate that completed assignments are important, valued, expected, and rewarded (Rosenberg, 1989). Homework completion must provide some positive outcome for students. Positive outcomes could include feedback when homework is completed successfully and turned in for a grade. When teachers convey the significance of homework to students patiently and consistently, students eventually understand that completion of homework is important.

When students experience difficulty with one of the building blocks of learning, modifications may need to be made in homework. An assignment change involves alteration of the information, curriculum content, or lesson objective. If the lesson objective is solving math story problems, then reading the problem to the child or allowing the child to use a calculator does not represent a change of lesson objective. However, if the objective is math calculation and the child computes math problems using a calculator, then a change of lesson objective has been made. In this case, checking math calculations with a calculator would be reinforcing to the child after the completion of a certain number of problems. This would not involve changing the lesson objective. When a change in lesson objective has been made, a teacher may find it difficult to justify giving that student the same grade as others. Particularly in elementary school, grades should be based on personal accomplishments and not on peer comparison. When teachers compare students who have marked weaknesses in one or more building blocks with peers, the students' performance appears substandard and they are assigned failing grades. For a student for whom a task change has been made and who put forth reasonable effort, a grade that reflects his or her abilities and effort should be provided. Katy, one of the students mentioned earlier in this book, is several years behind most of her peers in academic performance. If adjustments are not made, Katy will receive several failing grades. This would defeat the purpose and goals of education.

Turning in Homework

When students fail to complete assignments, consider talking to them about why the assignment was not completed, and assist them in developing a system to make certain assignments are completed in the future. Also, consider whether too many assignments are being made. Assess adaptations, and actively involve parents by providing recommended homework strategies. Assignments are more likely to be completed and turned in when a routine has been established for homework, when reduced homework is offered as an incentive for completed homework, and when school privileges are used as incentives as well. As a general rule, homework assignments should not be used as punishment. When assignments become part of a behavior management system, students' attitudes toward these assignments become equally negative. Often this attitude spreads to all assignments. One of the purposes of homework is to foster an enjoyment of working during leisure time. If students find that their assignments are intended as punishment, then the proposed benefits of homework are not realized.

Increased parental involvement has also been found to increase homework completion, increase attendance rates of students who may avoid school, decrease disruptive behavior at school, improve students' attitudes toward school, and increase math and reading achievement (Bryan & Nelson, 1994). At the beginning of the school year, a teacher can meet with parents at an after-school meeting or back-to-school night and provide a brief, printed overview to parents about homework for the coming year. After the first month, a teacher can ask parents whether they are satisfied with the type and amount of homework their child receives, how much time the child is spending, how much assistance is provided, what kinds of problems are encountered, and what suggestions they could offer to improve the class's homework policies. Communication with parents is even more critical when children experience weaknesses in the building blocks that cause them behavior, emotional, or achievement problems at school.

Occasionally, it is unreasonable to expect children to complete homework. Because of limited home support, Mark, the student mentioned earlier in this chapter, never attempted homework assignments. Because Ms. Perry, his fifth-grade teacher, was aware of his circumstances, she arranged a time for Mark to complete homework during the school day. Although it involved taking the late bus home, Mark was willing to stay at school with his teacher's supervision and complete his assignments.

Figure 3.2 presents a questionnaire about effective procedures for homework. This checklist offers excellent guidelines for teachers to begin establishing policies, attitudes, and activities regarding homework. Teachers rarely take a class about homework; yet, the management of homework is a significant factor in enhancing student performance.

Strategies

Language | Images

CONCEPTUAL

Phonology | Orthography | Motor

SYMBOLIC

Attention & Self-Regulation | Emotions | Behavior | Self-Esteem

FOUNDATIONAL

Assigning Homework

☐ Yes ☐ No   1. Do you use an outline of assignments and dates?

☐ Yes ☐ No   2. Do you make sure students have assignment books, homework planners, or homework buddies?

☐ Yes ☐ No   3. Do you make daily assignments at the beginning of the class rather than at the end?

☐ Yes ☐ No   4. Do you make sure the directions given to students about homework are clear by asking a student to repeat them or checking what is written down in the assignment books?

☐ Yes ☐ No   5. Do you present instructions visually (e.g., on the overhead projector, on the board) as well as orally?

☐ Yes ☐ No   6. Do you provide assistance at the end of the period or end of the day to students who have trouble organizing their materials?

☐ Yes ☐ No   7. Do you provide assistance to students who have trouble sustaining attention by modifying the amount of work required of them?

Meaningfulness, Difficulty, and Length of Homework

☐ Yes ☐ No   1. Does the homework assignment overlap the lessons from the day?

☐ Yes ☐ No   2. Do you make homework assignments interesting to students?

☐ Yes ☐ No   3. Do you talk about the purposes of the assignment?

☐ Yes ☐ No   4. Do you communicate to parents what is being taught and explain how parents can help?

☐ Yes ☐ No   5. Do you avoid assignments that require self-teaching or new learning?

☐ Yes ☐ No   6. Do you involve parents, other family members, or community resources in homework projects?

☐ Yes ☐ No   7. Do you use in-class study periods for elementary students?

☐ Yes ☐ No   8. Do you allow students with handwriting difficulties to use adaptations such as computers, notetakers, taped reports, printing, or reduced writing and copying?

☐ Yes ☐ No   9. Do you give assignments that are active as opposed to passive (e.g., gathering resources, interviewing people)?

Collecting and Returning Homework with Feedback

☐ Yes ☐ No   1. Do you teach children who have difficulty returning homework how to graph percent of homework completed per day using colorful bars?

☐ Yes ☐ No   2. Are the rewards for completing homework as great as the consequences for not completing it?

☐ Yes ☐ No   3. Do you consistently grade homework or provide feedback to the student?

☐ Yes ☐ No   4. Do you give students incentives for completing homework, such as extra recess or class outings?

☐ Yes ☐ No   5. Do you have students turn in written excuses for missed assignments?

☐ Yes ☐ No   6. Do you allow a certain number of excused homework assignments (especially for students with special learning needs or with many after-school responsibilities)?

Figure 3.2.   Positive teacher homework practices. (From Zentall, S., & Goldstein, S. [1999]. *Seven steps to homework success* [pp. 98–99]. Plantation, FL: Specialty Press; adapted by permission.)

In the elementary grades, teachers and parents often perceive the primary role of homework as the opportunity to review and strengthen basic achievement. Homework in the elementary grades is a critical activity that assists students in developing the independent learning skills, self-management, and responsibility necessary to become independent learners. When students struggle as the result of learning, emotional, or behavior problems, these important benefits of homework are jeopardized due to the increased stress and pressure that homework places on these students and their families. Teachers not only must make adjustments in homework for these students but also attempt to locate and provide other activities and opportunities for these students to develop independent learning skills.

CONCLUSION

By understanding the powerful role of environmental factors in the classroom, teachers can enhance each child's educational success and also create an effective and efficient setting for learning. Strengthening a student's sense of self-esteem and emotional well-being is not an "extra" curriculum; if anything, a student's sense of belonging, security, and self-confidence provide the scaffolding that supports the foundation for enhanced learning, motivation, and self-discipline. The educational atmosphere must instill a resilient mindset in students (Brooks, 1991). Teachers must provide social and emotional interventions hand in hand with academic education (Merrell, 2002; Weist, 2003). In fact, a sustainable school environment must be capable of meeting the social, emotional, and academic needs of all students (Elias, Zins, Graczyk, & Weissberg, 2003; Goldstein & Brooks, 2007). All aspects of the learning environment from materials to routines and placement of furniture play a role in shaping the classroom atmosphere.

FOUNDATIONAL
BLOCKS

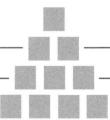

CHAPTER 4 OUTLINE

CHAPTER 4

ATTENTION AND SELF-REGULATION

UNDERSTANDING AND MANAGING STUDENTS WITH HYPERACTIVITY AND POOR ATTENTION, PLANNING, AND IMPULSE CONTROL

As a 10 ½ -year-old fifth-grade student, Jeremy had a history of impulsive, inattentive, and poorly disciplined behaviors at school. According to Jeremy's family history, his father and mother had similar problems as students. Two nephews on his mother's side of the family had been diagnosed as having attention-deficit/hyperactivity disorder (ADHD). Jeremy reached his early developmental milestones at a typical rate, and he did not experience any serious developmental problems. At home, Jeremy's parents described him as inattentive and overactive, although he enjoyed watching television. He belonged to a scout troop but did not participate in any other activities. His grades at school were adequate, but every year teachers commented about his problems with completing work without significant prompts and supports. Although his grades were average, group achievement test data reflected that Jeremy's skills were in the top 10% for his age group. Clearly, he was not performing in school at that level.

Jeremy demonstrates a fairly typical history of an elementary school child with hyperactivity and poor attention, planning, and impulse control. Together these problems constitute ADHD in the absence of other serious psychiatric or developmental problems.

The childhood cognitive and behavior problems characterized by hyperactivity and inattention, poor planning, and impulse control have long constituted the most chronic behavior problems of childhood (for a historical review, see Barkley, 2005). Since the early 1980s, these problems have composed the largest single source of referrals to child mental health centers (Barkley, 1981; Jensen et al., 1999; Medco Health Solutions, 2005). It is not surprising, therefore, that these problems also result in the most common teacher complaints and may account for as many as 40% of referrals to special education services and child guidance clinics (Barkley, 2005; Goldstein & Goldstein, 1998). Referrals of boys have consistently outnumbered referrals of girls by nearly six to one. In large-scale community-based studies—in which many of these children receive diagnoses of ADHD—the gender ratio for the diagnosis, until recently, has been closer at three to one (Barkley, 1990). The higher referral rate for boys may be a function of the greater prevalence in boys of other disruptive problems, such as oppositional defiant disorder and conduct disorder (Breen & Barkley, 1988; Goldstein & Gordon, 2003). Prevalence rates have also changed as the diagnostic criteria have changed. Although prevalence rates are now considered roughly equal, females are now *diagnosed* at a higher rate than males (Medco Health Solutions, 2005).

Because poor attention, planning, and impulse control and hyperactivity compose the core symptoms of ADHD, this chapter is organized by research related to this diagnosis.

CHARACTERISTICS OF STUDENTS WITH HYPERACTIVITY AND POOR ATTENTION, PLANNING, AND IMPULSE CONTROL

Even as educators use the current diagnostic criteria for ADHD related to symptoms of inattention, hyperactivity, and impulsivity, data are being generated to support the hypothesis that, for the majority of affected children, poor executive functioning and planning leading to poor self-discipline represent the core impairment of this disorder (Barkley, 2005; Goldstein & Goldstein, 1998; Goldstein & Naglieri, 2006). The major consequence of these neuropsychological impairments is impulsive behavior. Problems with impulsivity affect children's interactions in all areas of the environment, particularly in the classroom. Impulsivity results in a child's inability to meet situational demands in an age-appropriate fashion (Routh, 1978). Children with ADHD typically experience difficulty in educational environments. Their behavior is often described as uneven, unpredictable, and inconsistent. The elusive quality of their behavior—now you see it, now you don't—adds additional stress for educators and often leads to the erroneous belief that these problems stem from reduced motivation and limited desire rather than from neurologically based disabilities. It is easy to think that a capable student such as Jeremy could just complete his work if he really tried, but this is not the case.

School Problems

Children with ADHD present an unpredictable variety of school problems. For a significant percentage of children, problems observed in preschool progress as the child advances in school (Campbell, Endman, & Bernfeld, 1977; Schleifer et al., 1975). A review of the available literature suggests that measures of attention, activity, and inappropriate vocalization in the classroom consistently distinguish children with ADHD from groups of children without ADHD (Platzman et al., 1992). In fact, Jeremy's mother recalled the day when the kindergarten teacher asked her to come to school to get Jeremy because he was under his desk, barking like a dog.

In elementary school, school-based ADHD-associated symptoms include problems with activity level, problems with vocalization, negative peer and teacher interactions, and off-task behavior (Platzman et al., 1992). For students at the secondary and postsecondary levels, the continued problems of ADHD combine increasingly with a history of negative school experiences to exert a cumulative negative impact on behavior, achievement, emotions, and self-esteem.

When considering the chronology of problems, it is important to review a child's experiences in the early grades.

Jeremy was first diagnosed with ADHD in kindergarten. One of his teachers had a 15-year-old son with ADHD and recognized some of the symptoms in Jeremy. Somewhat reluctantly, Jeremy's parents, Mr. and Ms. Hanson, agreed to have the school conduct an evaluation. The summary from this evaluation is presented in Figure 4.1.

When the Hansons met with the school team, the psychologist noted that he had never tested a child before who had such a high intellectual level in addition to symptoms consistent with the diagnosis of ADHD. The Hansons then took Jeremy to a psychiatrist in town who specialized in ADHD. He interviewed Jeremy and his parents but did not do further testing.

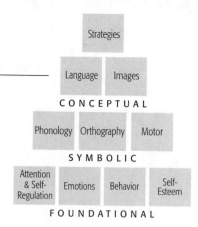

Jeremy, a child functioning in the superior range of intellectual skill, demonstrates a history of mild to moderate disruptive behaviors. This pattern of problems is chronic and has caused Jeremy school problems since his entry into kindergarten.

Jeremy struggles to attend to repetitive, effortful, uninteresting activities. He experiences difficulties with restless, hyperactive behavior and often acts impulsively. This symptom profile appears consistent with DSM-IV diagnostic criteria for attention-deficit/hyperactivity disorder. This diagnosis is deferred to Jeremy's physician.

Despite exceptional intellectual ability and advanced academic achievement, Jeremy's problems with attention, hyperactivity, and impulse control have significantly and negatively affected his ability to succeed in school and benefit from his education. He does not experience specific physical disabilities, developmental delays, social difficulties, or serious psychological or emotional problems.

Figure 4.1. Summary of Jeremy's evaluation report.

Jeremy began on a low dose of Ritalin (methylphenidate hydrochloride) in the summer before first grade. Although the medicine helped Jeremy tremendously, each year, he experienced new struggles with behavior and achievement. In fact, his school career has been marked by performance inconsistencies. Jeremy went from the honor role in third grade to getting straight Ds in fourth grade.

Attention-Deficit/Hyperactivity Disorder in Adulthood

For many individuals, ADHD represents a lifelong disorder (Goldstein, 1997; Kessler, Berglund, Demler, Jin, & Walters, 2005; Roffman, 2000). Research reflects the significant and pervasive effect that symptoms of ADHD have for the majority of children with ADHD as they enter into adulthood (Biederman et al., 1999; Hart, Lahey, Loeber, Applegate, & Frick, 1995; Lomas & Gartside, 1999). Years of ineffective interactions with parents, teachers, and peers and failure to meet the expectations of one's surroundings result in a long history of negative experiences (Leitchman, 1993). These in turn become a major force in an individual's emerging personality (Brooks, 2002; Wender, 1979). Clearly, the daily experiences of children contribute to their adult life outcomes, with even small successes building resilience and the capacity to deal with stress (Werner, 1994). Thus, educators must be concerned not only with the effect in the classroom of the core symptoms of ADHD but also with the significant secondary impact these problems will have on a child's future life and the lives of his or her family members.

Biology and Environment

Although some have argued that the problems of ADHD may in part represent a cultural phenomenon (Block, 1977; Diller, 2006a; 2006b), ADHD is a disorder in which the severity of a child's problems results from the interaction of the child's temperament and the environmental demands placed on the child. The symptoms of ADHD reflect an interaction of biology and environment. Biology appears to set the risk for problems. The type of classroom environment, however, is likely to affect the number of teacher complaints and the severity of reported problems (Goldstein & Brooks, 2007). In addition, although culture makes a difference in terms of the expectations and tasks placed on children by educational systems, children with ADHD worldwide demonstrate a fairly homogeneous set of symptoms (Baydala, Sherman, Rasmussen, Wikman, & Janzen, 2006; Bener, Al

Qahtani, & Abdelaal, 2006; Pierrehumbert, Bader, Thévoz, Kinal, & Halfon, 2006). For individuals who have ADHD or who demonstrate impairment from these skill weaknesses short of meeting full diagnostic criteria, a poor fit results between classroom expectations and the individual's abilities to meet those expectations. Fortunately, in many cases, ADHD can be reliably evaluated and effectively managed and treated.

Incidence

As the tempo of society increases, a greater incidence of ADHD may exist (Diller, 1998; McNamara, 1972). The reported incidence of diagnosis and medication treatment for ADHD has increased rapidly since 1985 (Medco Health Solutions, 2005; Safer, Zito, & Fine, 1996). However, normative data for standard educational assessment tools do not support the hypothesis that children are increasingly less attentive or more impulsive (Naglieri & Das, 2007; Spring, Yellin, & Greenberg, 1976; Wechsler, 1991). In fact, as a result of children's early exposure to the media, their capacity for sustained attention may have increased at younger ages rather than decreased. A more likely explanation for the increase in diagnosis reflects more widespread community, professional, and parental awareness of symptoms of ADHD, leading to more children being referred, correctly identified, and offered appropriate treatments and interventions (Goldstein, 1995). The consensus among researchers and professionals is that the core symptoms of ADHD affect a significant minority of the educational population, approximately 3%–5% of students. Statistics vary depending on the population studied, the thresholds, and the definitional criteria that are used (Faraone & Biederman, 2005). Recent studies suggest a conservative incidence of 4%–8% across all ages (Kessler et al., 2006; Medco Health Solutions, 2005).

Other Causes of Hyperactivity and Poor Attention, Planning, and Impulse Control

Multiple causes other than ADHD can be responsible for a child's apparent hyperactivity, inattention, and poor planning and impulse control. Depressed, anxious, and even angry children at times may be described as inattentive in the classroom. Some medical conditions can cause these behaviors. Some children may be weak in planning skills, leading to poor school performance. However, if these patterns of behavior are observed frequently in the classroom, ADHD should be considered as a causative condition.

A Cluster of Symptomatic Problems

In part, the controversy and, at times, confusion concerning various aspects of ADHD may be the result of a tendency to view this disorder as a unitary phenomenon with a single cause. The symptoms of ADHD may be conceptualized most accurately as a set of symptomatic problems rather than a single, atypical behavior (Voeller, 1991). The cluster of symptoms associated with ADHD makes it distinct from other classroom problems (Accardo, Blondis, & Whitman, 1990; Biederman, Faraone, Milberger, Curtiss, et al., 1996; Biederman, Faraone, Milberger, Jetton, et al., 1996).

Throughout his school career, Jeremy's behaviors were described in the following ways: "Jeremy fails to complete tasks," "He appears not to listen," "He loses focus easily," "Jeremy acts before thinking," "He bothers his peers when they are trying to work," and "He makes impulsive judgments." These behaviors were apparent both in school and at home. During the summer before second grade, the Hansons tried to take Jeremy off of medication. The

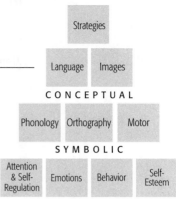

first week of summer break, Jeremy took off into the desert at dusk, chasing the family dog. The dog came back, but Jeremy did not. Several hours later, Ms. Hanson found him wandering around. The next morning, she called the doctor to renew the prescription.

Over lunch, three elementary school teachers were discussing their views about ADHD. Based on her experience, the first teacher commented that ADHD is probably best defined as difficulty listening and paying attention. The second teacher disagreed, noting that, in his experience, children with ADHD were capable of listening and paying attention but never seemed to finish what they started. The third teacher commented that, in her view, children with ADHD were not completely different from other children; rather, their problems represented an exaggeration of typical classroom problems related to general behavior, conduct, and accuracy and completion of work. In different situations, for different students, all of these perceptions are correct.

From an educational perspective, the concepts of *attention* and *planning* as executive or foundational skills required for classroom success have gained increasing popularity (for review, see Barkley, 2005; Goldstein & Naglieri, 2006; Paolito, 1999). Sustained mental effort, self-regulation, planning, execution, and task maintenance are all considered measures of executive functioning (Daigneault, Braun, & Whitaker, 1992). For children to perform competently in the classroom, to meet expectations, to manage themselves, and to interact appropriately with others, the efficient use of these executive skills is essential. Thus, not surprisingly, children who are struggling with these skills experience problems with functioning effectively in the classroom, despite the fact that they may possess adequate basic achievement skills.

In our market economy, as a particular problem becomes popular, controversy and opinion concerning that problem as well as diverse recommendations and solutions come to the forefront (Goldstein, 2006). Many more lay than clinical texts are published on the particular subject in question so that the field continues to be overrepresented by opinion. In 1992, Goodman and Poillion reviewed articles and books about ADHD and identified 69 characteristics and 38 causes. At that time there was no clear-cut pattern for identifying the condition and little agreement about its cause.

Though it is true that many symptoms of ADHD share common ground with other psychiatric and developmental conditions (Jiron, Sherrill, & Chiodo, 1995), a solid body of scientific evidence demonstrates that the cluster of symptomatic problems used to define ADHD in the early part of the 21st century clinically represents a disorder distinct from other conditions (Biederman, Faraone, Milberger, Curtiss, et al., 1996). Multiple physical and biological differences (Dickstein et al., 2005; McConville & Cornell, 2003) as well as genetic differences (Faraone, Perlis, et al., 2005; Fisher et al., 2002) have been identified. As noted, since the 1970s, however, research has increasingly suggested that the core problem for ADHD is not excessive activity but impairments in executive functioning (Douglas & Peters, 1979; for review, see Barkley, 1997a, 2005). Though the criteria for ADHD in the *Diagnostic and Statistical Manual of Mental Disorders, Fourth Edition, Text Revision (DSM-IV-TR;* American Psychiatric Association [APA], 2000*)* continue to weigh heavily toward symptoms of inattention, the emerging literature across the lifespan provides strong contrary evidence that difficulties with self-regulation and executive functioning offer a better explanation of this condition and its impairments (Barkley & Murphy, 2006). Yet the change in focus to problems of poor self-regulation and executive dysfunction (both likely driven by impulsivity) as the core symptoms of ADHD causing the most serious impairments has not come easily. Just as the lay public begins to accept that inattentiveness is a problem for some, the preponderance of the research literature since the mid 1990s suggests that in laboratory settings, the problem is not that these individuals *cannot* pay attention but that they *do not pay attention efficiently or effectively.* Their inconsistent attention occurs in repetitive, effortful situations in which inhibition, planning, and working memory are required. Converging lines of evidence including measures of physiological functioning, laboratory tests, and neuroimaging studies increasingly support disinhibition as a core impairment in ADHD (for review, see Barkley, 2005; Harrier & DeOrnellas, 2005; Wellington, Semrud-Clikeman, Gregory, Murphy, & Lancaster, 2006)

Barkley suggested that "ADHD represents a profound disturbance in self-regulation and organization behavior across time" (1994, page vii). These functions are subserved by prefrontal, midbrain, and cerebellar regions in the human brain (Fuster, 1989). ADHD appears to be a condition that affects the organism's ability to organize behavior over time and meet demands for present and future performance. To understand the condition, one has to go where it lives, at the point of performance (Ingersoll & Goldstein, 1993). ADHD is a condition best captured and understood by the observation and measurement of real-life behavior. As Barkley (1994) noted, impairments caused by ADHD are driven by the following:

- Difficulty fixing on and sustaining mental images or messages that relate to external events so that one can act or not act on them

- Problems referencing the past in relation to those events

- Difficulty imagining hypothetical futures that might result from those events

- Problems establishing goals and plans of action to implement them

- Difficulty avoiding reacting to stimuli likely to interfere with goal-directed behaviors

- Poor utilization of internal speech in the service of self-regulation and goal-directed behaviors

- Inefficient regulation of affect and motivation or response to situational demands

- Problems separating affect from information or feelings from facts

- Difficulty analyzing and synthesizing information

Thus, ADHD, a problem occurring at the point of performance, well defines a disorder of executive functioning. The problem results from being capable of learning from experiences but incapable of acting efficiently on that learning at the point of performance (Ingersoll & Goldstein, 1993). It is thus a disorder of inadequate response inhibition—a problem of performance, not skills.

A Problem of Faulty Performance

Despite the seemingly different classroom definitions of ADHD, a consensus exists that ADHD represents a problem of faulty performance rather than faulty input. It is not that children with ADHD do not know what to do in the classroom but that they do not do what they know consistently. ADHD is a problem of inconsistency rather than inability (Goldstein & Goldstein, 1992; Stein, 1997). Children with ADHD often act and then reflect on their actions.

In third grade, Jeremy pulled a switch that shut off all the power in the school. As a result, all of the people working on computers lost their work. When asked why he pulled the switch, Jeremy replied, "I just wanted to see what would happen." One afternoon, Jeremy

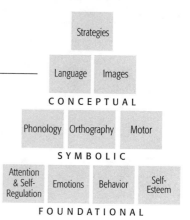

dug up all the potatoes in the family garden. Later, he asked his mother if it was time to dig up the potatoes.

All educators need to have a working understanding of the diagnostic criteria for ADHD and a practical perception of the ways in which the symptoms of ADHD affect a child's classroom functioning. The frequency and severity of symptoms fluctuate across educational environments and activities, and the perceptions of educators fluctuate also (Tarver-Behring, Barkley, & Karlsson, 1985; Zentall, 1984, 2006). Furthermore, the traditional disease model does not apply to the concept of ADHD (Ellis, 1985). ADHD is more like creativity or linguistic ability: Individuals differ not in having or not having the traits but in the degree of manifestation. ADHD symptoms are also multidimensional rather than unitary (Guevremont, DuPaul, & Barkley, 1993). Thus, interventions are needed when a child's attention skills and impulse control are markedly discrepant from those expected at a particular age (Kauffman, 2005).

Core Symptoms

Agreement regarding which dimensions represent the most distinguishing impairments of ADHD is not resolved. A general consensus exists that symptoms of ADHD fall into two broad dimensions: those related to the behavioral manifestation of faulty attention and those related to hyperactivity and impulsivity. Symptoms of hyperactivity and impulsivity appear to co-occur at such a high frequency that on a statistical basis it is difficult to separate them. However, hyperactivity reduces significantly with age (Barkley & Murphy, 2006). With regard to predicting future functioning, however, the level of impulsivity stemming from poor planning and other weak executive skills appears to correlate positively with impaired classroom performance and life outcome: The greater the degree of reported impulsive behavior, the more problems in the classroom and later life. Thus, it has been increasingly hypothesized that the core impairment in ADHD represents faulty inhibition or self-control, secondary to executive skill impairments leading to a constellation of related symptoms.

Key differences exist between the symptoms and consequences of ADHD. Symptoms represent a limited, research-based list that defines the problem and describes individuals. Consequences, however, represent an open-ended list of outcomes that can occur from living with the defined symptoms. Although the symptoms of ADHD may be powerfully influenced by heredity and minimally responsive to behavior management, the consequences of ADHD can be managed effectively in classroom environments with a variety of behavior management strategies. The first goal, then, is to describe the symptoms.

The Hansons, Jeremy's classroom teacher, his principal, and the school psychologist met to discuss Jeremy's reported problems with attention in the classroom. Jeremy's teacher, Mr. Chavez, began the meeting by explaining that Jeremy struggled to begin tasks and stick with them until they were finished effectively. He appeared to rush through his work. From a classroom perspective, his teacher could not identify a single activity to which Jeremy paid attention well. The school psychologist, however, commented that during her meeting with Jeremy, he focused on tasks reasonably well, was quite verbally engaging, and appeared to enjoy the assessment session. The principal added that he had observed Jeremy on the playground, commenting that it appeared that Jeremy did not stick with any activity or play with any group of children for more than a short period of time before moving off. Finally, the Hansons observed that at home he paid attention quite well to activities that were of interest to him, such as watching television programs about science or playing video games.

Diagnostic Criteria

The *DSM-IV-TR* (APA, 2000) defines the range of childhood developmental, emotional, and behavior problems that appear to set children apart from their peers and cause impairments in daily functioning. The *DSM-IV* diagnostic criteria made an effort to correct the mistaken course that ADHD represents a disorder of only one type (APA, 1994). The field studies for the ADHD diagnosis were more comprehensive and better structured than previous efforts. Note that, using the current criteria, three subtypes of ADHD are identified: 1) ADHD, combined type; 2) ADHD, predominantly inattentive type; and 3) ADHD, predominantly hyperactive-impulsive type. The following is a summary of the *DSM-IV-TR* criteria for ADHD (APA, 2000):

1. The child must present with at least six of nine inattentive symptoms (e.g., often fails to give close attention to details; makes careless mistakes in school work, work, or other activities), six of the six hyperactive (e.g., often fidgets with hands or feet or squirms in seat) and three impulsive (e.g., has difficulty awaiting turn) symptoms, or both.

2. Some of these symptoms that caused impairment were present before 7 years of age.

3. Some impairment is present in two or more settings (e.g., school and home).

4. There is clear evidence of clinically significant impairment in social, academic, or occupational functioning.

5. The symptoms do not occur exclusively as the result of other psychiatric conditions.

In these field studies, approximately half of the children diagnosed had the combined type, three tenths had the inattentive type, and one fifth had the hyperactive-impulsive type (Lahey et al., 1994). Children with the hyperactive-impulsive type tended to be the age at which they were just entering school. It was hypothesized that this group would ultimately receive the combined-type diagnosis when they were required to sustain mental effort in the classroom.

In classroom environments, teachers are most likely to encounter children experiencing the combined type of ADHD. Children with the inattentive type are often overlooked or described as lazy, unmotivated, or withdrawn. Some researchers have suggested that their problem reflects slow cognitive tempo (Milich, Ballentine, & Lynam, 2001). The children with inattentive-type ADHD are less easily identified because they have fewer behavior problems and are less problematic in the classroom. The child with combined-type ADHD experiences more disruptive problems in the classroom, thus increasing the risk that he or she may be labeled by teachers as defiant or purposely misbehaving.

Jeremy's difficulties are better described as impulsive rather than inattentive. When Jeremy was in second grade, he went to the gifted and talented class one day per week. After he had attended this class for several weeks, the teacher called the Hansons and informed them that he could no longer be in the class because his behavior was too distracting and he was constantly bothering other students. Jeremy was taking Ritalin at the time, so the Hansons did not know what else to do. They pulled him from the program because they were afraid that it was becoming another negative experience.

Unfortunately, the *DSM-IV-TR* criteria continue to focus on inattention as the core problem for the disorder, limiting the scope and focus on the impact of impulsivity due to poor planning and other executive skill weaknesses as the core impairment. This perpetuates a number of major misconceptions, including that

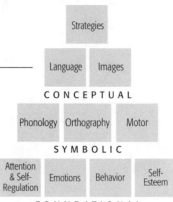

Strategies

Language | Images

CONCEPTUAL

Phonology | Orthography | Motor

SYMBOLIC

Attention & Self-Regulation | Emotions | Behavior | Self-Esteem

FOUNDATIONAL

the inattentive type of ADHD represents a subtype of the combined disorder (Anastopoulos, Barkley, & Shelton, 1994). Increasingly, research indicates that it does not (for review, see Barkley, 2005). The more likely possibility is that the inattentive type represents a distinct disorder, primarily reflecting difficulty with organization and paying attention to repetitive, effortful tasks. The problems that children in this group experience may very well be the result of faulty skills as opposed to inconsistent or inadequate use of skills. That is, children with the inattentive type of ADHD may well lack ability, whereas children with the combined type are inefficient and ineffective in using the abilities they possess.

Based on the work of Douglas and Peters (1979) and Douglas (1985), Goldstein and Goldstein (1990) first proposed a four-part practical definition of ADHD, which was later expanded to five parts (Goldstein & Goldstein, 1998). This definition, modified for this chapter, provides an educational perspective of the condition. It is offered as a way to facilitate understanding, measure impairment, and design effective intervention. As Douglas (1985) noted, those with ADHD experience a constitutional predisposition to struggle with attention, effort, inhibitory control, and fully modulated arousal and have a need to seek stimulation. They struggle with the executive processes well defined by Barkley (2005). The five components of Goldstein and Goldstein's definition include the following:

1. *Impulsivity and planning.* This group of individuals experiences difficulty with inhibition leading to problems in planning. Planning is a mental process by which an individual determines, selects, acts on, and evaluates solutions to problems (Naglieri & Das, 1997). Planning requires the efficient choice of strategies; it is the ability to self-monitor, self-correct, shift flexibly, and adjust to feedback. These students have difficulty weighing the consequences of their actions before acting and do not reasonably consider the consequences of their past behavior. They struggle with rule-governed behavior (Barkley, 1981), likely due to an inability to separate experience from response, thought from emotion, and action from reaction. Their behavior seems impetuous, and they seemingly do not appear to learn from experience. These individuals are often repeat offenders, a pattern that frustrates parents, teachers, friends, and caregivers.

   Scholnick (1995) reviewed an extensive body of literature including nearly 11,000 references concerning the development and implementation of planning. Planning requires an internal process of problem solving that precedes the external strategic action; requires the capacity to inhibit action while thinking through the best ways to obtain goals; and involves multiple stages, each of which is critical in designing, choosing, and following through with the problem-solving approach regardless of the nature of the task. Planning, first described by Luria, is an active process. Clearly this process requires selective inhibition or impulse control. Planning relies on working memory to construct and anticipate a plan and monitor its execution. Such a process requires prolongation, self-directed speech, and reconstitution at the very least (Barkley, 1997a). For example, if an individual is unable to anticipate future consequences of his actions or reflect while acting, he is likely to be accident prone. Adept planners make fast computations and think ahead several steps through the use of working memory. This skillful allocation of resources requires that attention be divided simultaneously between active construction and utilization of a plan. Planning is likely also influenced by long-term memory, motivation, personal attributes, and belief about personal capacities. Planning impairments have been repeatedly found to significantly discriminate youth with ADHD from those with other conditions and controls (Naglieri, Goldstein, Iseman, & Schwebach, 2003; Naglieri, Salter, & Edwards, 2004; Paolito, 1999).

2. *Inattention.* Individuals with ADHD have difficulty sustaining effort and functioning efficiently relative to their peers and ability. In new or novel settings and those that are less repetitive and effortful they appear to function better, suggesting that the fault lies not in failure to know what to do but from inefficient actions. This reinforces an important point: ADHD represents an exaggeration on a dimensional basis of typical problems such as too much restlessness or an inadequate investment in tasks that must be completed. On a dimensional basis, the behavior of these individuals represents the extreme of what is expected.

3. *Hyperactivity.* Individuals with ADHD often tend to be excessively restless and overactive and struggle in particular to control body movements when staying still is at a premium. Interestingly, even youth diagnosed with the inattentive type of ADHD demonstrate more restless, fidgety behavior than children in control groups (Lahey, Pelham, Loney, Lee, & Willcutt, 2005).

4. *Problems modulating gratification.* Individuals with ADHD often appear driven toward immediate, frequent, predictable, and meaningful consequences. They demonstrate less sensitivity to changing parameters of reinforcement rate, which may be secondary to problems with sustaining attention and/or faulty inhibition (Kollins, Lane, & Shapiro, 1997). These individuals demonstrate an excess or exaggeration in comparison to peers with regard to these variables. They experience greater difficulty working toward a long-term goal. They often require brief, repeated payoffs rather than a single long-term reward. They also do not appear to respond to rewards in a manner similar to others (Haenlein & Caul, 1987). Rewards do not appear to be effective in changing their behaviors on a long-term basis. They are quick to regress once the reward paradigm is removed. Impulsivity drives their behavior to remain consequentially bound. However, it also appears that, given a sufficient number of trials and opportunities for generalization—the capacity to do consistently what they know—their behavior can be shaped in a way similar to that of unaffected individuals (Shure & Aberson, 2005). In regard to consequences and behavioral development, for those with ADHD the issue is not so much behavior modification as behavior management. The provision of a sufficient number of supervised, structured, and reinforced trials for everything from daily habits to social, academic, and work skills is essential.

Individuals with ADHD also receive significantly more negative reinforcement than others. Their interactions with others are often shaped by an effort to avoid aversive consequences. Negative reinforcement offers a plausible, experiential explanation for the diverse problems individuals with ADHD develop. Efforts of helpers tend to reinforce passivity and helplessness. Eventually the avoidance of aversive consequences tends to exert greater influence over behavior than the seeking of positive consequences. Individuals with ADHD, children and adults alike, learn to respond to demands placed on them by the environment when an aversive stimulus is removed contingent on performance rather than for the promise of a positive future reward.

Strategies

Language | Images

CONCEPTUAL

Phonology | Orthography | Motor

SYMBOLIC

Attention & Self-Regulation | Emotions | Behavior | Self-Esteem

FOUNDATIONAL

5. *Emotional regulation.* Individuals with ADHD appear quicker to become aroused. Whether happy or sad, the speed and intensity at which they move to the extremes of emotion can be much greater than that of peers. This problem appears to reflect an impulsive inability to separate thought from emotion. They often appear to be on a roller coaster ride of emotions. When happy, they tend to be so happy that people are disrupted. When unhappy, they tend to be so unhappy that people are equally disrupted. Negative feedback from others and stressful relationships can exert a significant influence on the development of a sense of psychological well being, locus of control, and personality style. Problems with ADHD typically cause significant and pervasive impairments in day-to-day interactions in the environment across the lifespan. Familial, social, academic, and vocational demands of a fast-paced culture require a consistent, predictable, independent, and efficient approach to life. Failure to develop, maintain, and use these abilities efficiently leads to uneven and unpredictable behavior, characteristically a function of knowing what to do but being unable to do it in a consistent, predictable manner.

Legal Protections

Students with ADHD first were eligible to receive services through the Individuals with Disabilities Education Act (IDEA) Amendments of 1997 (PL 105-17) under the category of Other Health Impairment (OHI). This distinction was continued in the reauthorization of this legislation the Individuals with Disabilities Education Improvement Act (IDEA) of 2004 (PL 108-446, 34 CFR). The term *other health impairments* includes chronic or acute impairments that result in limited alertness that affects educational performance. If the multidisciplinary team determines that a student's heightened alertness to irrelevant or environmental stimuli results in limited alertness with regard to educational performance, the criterion of the OHI category would be satisfied. Some students with ADHD are served under IDEA because they have another disability, such as learning disabilities (LD), a language impairment, or a serious emotional disturbance. Unfortunately, specific eligibility criteria beyond receiving the ADHD diagnosis have yet to be determined.

Many students with ADHD who are not served under IDEA are eligible for legal protections under the guidelines of Section 504 (Rehabilitation Act Amendments of 1992, PL 102-569). Under this civil rights law, disability is defined as a condition that substantially limits a major life activity such as learning. Although the wording of both of these laws is broad in order to encompass a diverse group of children, the broad language also creates interpretive problems (Mercugliano, Power, & Blum, 1999).

Under Section 504, accommodation plans, reviewed on a yearly basis, specify the adaptations and adjustments that the child will need in the general education classroom. For students with ADHD, examples of the types of accommodations that may be included are 1) preferential seating; 2) extended time on examinations; 3) increased teacher monitoring; 4) modified or reduced work assignments; 5) more frequent breaks; or 6) specific test accommodations, such as a quiet environment. Figure 4.2 presents Jeremy's revised 504 accommodation plan in fifth grade.

CAUSES OF ATTENTION-DEFICIT/HYPERACTIVITY DISORDER

Several causes have been hypothesized and researched as being probable links to incidence of ADHD in individuals. These include genetics, brain function, and illness or health-related causes.

Section 504 Accommodation Plan

Name _Jeremy H._   Date _04/05/08_

Student ID# _JL9998_   Date of birth _10/20/99_

School _Hillworth Elementary_   Teacher _Mr. Glaser_   Grade _5th_

1. Describe the nature of the concern. _Inattentive, hyperactive, and impulsive symptoms_ _impair Jeremy's ability to succeed in school._

2. Describe the basis for the determination of disability (if any). _School and physician evaluation_

3. Describe how the disability affects a major life activity. _Despite excellent intelligence_ _and academic skills, Jeremy's inattentive, impulsive, and hyperactive symptoms_ _impair his ability to succeed at school._

4. The Child Study Team/Intervention Assistance Team has reviewed the files of the above named student and concludes that he or she meets the classification as a qualified individual with a disability under Section 504 of the Rehabilitation Act Amendments of 1992 (PL 102-569). In accordance with the Section 504 guidelines, the school has agreed to make reasonable accommodations and address the student's individual needs by:

PHYSICAL ARRANGEMENT OF ROOM

___ Seating student near the teacher   ✓ Seating student near a positive role model

✓ Standing near the student when giving directions or presenting lessons

___ Avoiding distracting stimuli (e.g., air conditioner, high traffic area)

___ Increasing the distance between the desks

___ Additional accommodations: _____

LESSON PRESENTATION

✓ Pairing students to check work   ✓ Providing written outline

___ Writing key points on the board   ___ Allowing student to tape record lessons

___ Providing peer tutoring   ___ Having child review key points orally

✓ Providing visual aids   ___ Teaching through multisensory modes

___ Providing peer notetaker   ✓ Using computer-assisted instruction

✓ Making sure directions are understood   ✓ Including a variety of activities during each lesson

___ Breaking longer presentations into shorter segments

___ Additional accommodations: _____

ASSIGNMENTS AND WORKSHEETS

___ Giving extra time to complete tasks   ✓ Using self-monitoring devices

✓ Simplifying complex directions   ___ Reducing homework assignments

✓ Handing worksheets out one at a time   ___ Not grading handwriting

___ Reducing the reading level of the assignments

___ Including a variety of activities during each lesson

___ Providing a structured routine in written form

✓ Providing study skills training/learning strategies

Figure 4.2. Jeremy's Section 504 Accommodation Plan.

	Strategies	
Language		Images

CONCEPTUAL

Phonology	Orthography	Motor

SYMBOLIC

Attention & Self-Regulation	Emotions	Behavior	Self-Esteem

FOUNDATIONAL

___ Requiring fewer correct responses to achieve grade

___ Allowing student to tape record assignments/homework

___ Giving frequent short quizzes and avoiding long tests

___ Shortening assignments; breaking work into smaller segments

✓ Allowing typewritten or computer printed assignments

___ Additional Accommodations: _____

TEST TAKING

___ Allowing open-book exams ___ Allowing extra time for exam

___ Giving exam orally ___ Reading test item to student

___ Giving take-home tests

___ Using more objective items (i.e., fewer essay responses)

___ Allowing student to give test answers on tape recorder

✓ Giving frequent short quizzes, not long exams

___ Additional accommodations: _____

ORGANIZATION

✓ Providing peer assistance with organizational skills

___ Assigning volunteer homework buddy

✓ Allowing student to have an extra set of books at home

✓ Sending daily/weekly progress reports home

___ Developing a reward system for in-schoolwork and homework completion

✓ Providing student with a homework assignment notebook

___ Additional accommodations: _____

BEHAVIORS

✓ Praising specific behaviors ✓ Allowing legitimate movement

✓ Using self-monitoring strategies ___ Contracting with the student

___ Giving extra privileges and rewards ___ Increasing the immediacy of rewards

✓ Keeping classroom rules simple and clear ___ Implementing time-out procedures

___ Making prudent use of negative consequences

___ Allowing for short breaks between assignments

___ Cuing student to stay on task (nonverbal signal)

___ Marking student's correct answers, not his or her mistakes

✓ Implementing a classroom behavior management system

___ Allowing student time out of seat to run errands and so forth

___ Ignoring inappropriate behaviors not drastically outside classroom limits

___ Additional accommodations: _____

MEDICATION

Physician's name _____ Telephone _____

Medication(s) _____ Schedule _____

Monitoring of medication(s) _____ daily _____ weekly _____

_____ as needed basis

Administered by _____

(continued)

Figure 4.2.   *(continued)*

SPECIAL CONSIDERATION

___ Suggesting parenting program(s)   ___ Alerting bus driver

___ Monitoring student closely on field trip   ___ Suggesting agency involvement

___ In-servicing teacher(s) on child's disability ___ Providing group/individual
                                                          counseling

___ Providing social skills group experiences

___ Developing intervention strategies for transitional periods (e.g., cafeteria, physical
      education)

___ Additional accommodations: _____

NOTES

Participants (name and title) _____

_____

_____

_____

Case manager's signature _____

Genetics

ADHD is one of the most heritable conditions (Edelbrock, Rende, Plomin, & Thompson, 1995). A number of genes and types of gene code for brain chemistry appear to place individuals at risk to receive a diagnosis of ADHD. Recent studies suggest that genes on chromosomes 4, 5, 8, 11, and 17 may combine to contribute to risk for this diagnosis (Muenke, 2006). In addition, other genes when present may act protectively to reduce risk. The hypothesis of genetics as a contribution to ADHD is powerfully reinforced through the findings of concordance for this disorder among identical twins (Edelbrock et al., 1995; Zahn-Waxler, Schmitz, Fulker, Robinson, & Ende, 1996). Genetics set the stage for risk. Life experience then determines whether an individual ultimately receives a diagnosis of ADHD (Goldstein & Goldstein, 1998; Ingersoll & Goldstein, 1995). Sometimes parents are diagnosed simultaneously with their children. Ms. Hanson, Jeremy's mother, was diagnosed for the first time when Jeremy was in kindergarten.

Brain Function

Researchers have also identified areas in the prefrontal cortex, basal ganglia, and cerebellum that are important in helping individuals with self-regulation. These structures have been described as the brain's "braking system" (Castellanos et al., 1996). A large body of research demonstrates structural, biochemical, and physiological differences in the brains of individuals with ADHD (Ernst, Cohen, Liebenauer, Jons, & Zametkin, 1997; Hynd, Hern, Novey, & Eliopulos, 1993;

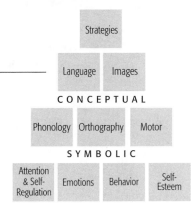

Wellington et al., 2006; Zametkin & Rapoport, 1987). Although results from these group studies have helped to develop an understanding of the causes of ADHD, these types of findings to date have not been found helpful for making the diagnosis of ADHD in individual children (Barkley, 2005; Goldstein & Goldstein, 1998).

Disease, Illness, or Other Disorder

ADHD may also be caused by a disease, illness, or other disorder. Genetic disorders such as fragile X syndrome, neurofibromatosis, Turner syndrome, Noonan syndrome, and Williams syndrome are all chromosomal and genetic disorders in which attentional problems and ADHD have been reported (Hagerman, 1991). Disorders resulting from fetal alcohol syndrome, cocaine exposure in utero, lead poisoning, vapor abuse, perinatal complications, certain medical problems (e.g., hypothyroidism, encephalitis), and radiation therapy secondary to leukemia have all been reported as responsible for creating problems with inattention and impulsivity. Cases have been reported of children experiencing specific medical conditions, such as pinworms or thyroid problems, who demonstrate a sudden onset of inattentive and hyperactive classroom behavior. In the popular press, ADHD has also been attributed in the absence of much science to a myriad of etiologies, including low birth weight, poor diet, and vitamin deficiency. These factors combined appear to account for 20% of ADHD cases (for review, see Barkley, 2005).

DEVELOPMENTAL COURSE AND COMORBIDITY

An increasing body of scientific data has been generated concerning the developmental course and adult outcome of children with ADHD. ADHD in isolation or comorbid with other conditions predicts a wide array of adversities in all major life areas. Even in isolation, ADHD is unfortunately a powerful negative force leading to increased risk for school, legal, substance, emotional, marital, and lifestyle problems (for review, see Barkley & Gordon, 2002; Goldstein & Teeter-Ellison, 2002).

Early Symptoms

Infants noted as demonstrating difficult temperaments do not handle changes in routines well and exhibit a low frustration threshold and a high intensity of response (Carey, 1970; Chess & Thomas, 1986; Thomas & Chess, 1977). In follow-up studies of such infants, as many as 70% develop school problems (Terestman, 1980). These infants appear at greater risk than others of receiving a diagnosis of ADHD and exert a significant negative impact on their developing relationships with caregivers—a relationship that is critical in predicting a child's life outcomes (Katz, 1997). Toddlers and preschoolers with ADHD often fit the description of the difficult child, having attention, impulse control, and aggression problems (Kauffman, 2005).

Although early symptoms of ADHD in children may be viewed as transient problems, research data suggest that ignoring these signs results in the loss of valuable intervention time. At least 60%–70% of children later diagnosed with ADHD could have been identified by their symptoms during the preschool years (Cohen, Sullivan, Minde, Novak, & Helwig, 1981). Young children manifesting symptoms of ADHD are more likely to have language problems (Baker & Cantwell, 1987) and to develop a wide range of behavior problems (Cantwell, Baker, & Mattison, 1981; Cohen, Davine, & Meloche-Kelly, 1989; Mathers, 2006) than are children who do not have those symptoms.

Attention-Deficit/Hyperactivity Disorder and Language Disorders

Research suggests that the comorbidity of language disorders with ADHD merits routine screening of children suspected of ADHD and language disorders, especially during their younger years. Children with ADHD relative to controls use fewer strategies of textual organization and more tangential language (Mathers, 2006). Children with both of these disorders appear to have a much poorer prognosis than those with ADHD alone (Baker & Cantwell, 1992). One may surmise that the language skills of children with ADHD may be delayed because these children do not practice or attend to their environment effectively. Or one may think that these children exhibit ADHD symptoms because they lack efficient language skills necessary for behavioral self-control. Several researchers have addressed this issue and concluded that the symptoms of ADHD and language disability develop and are maintained independently (Cantwell & Baker, 1985, 1991). Nonetheless, children who tend to act quickly without thinking and also experience a language disorder are more likely to exhibit behavior problems (Berk & Landau, 1993).

Attention-Deficit/Hyperactivity Disorder and Learning Disabilities

Depending on the diagnostic criteria, approximately 20%–50% of children with ADHD also suffer from a concomitant, often language-based, learning or reading disability (for a review, see Barkley, 2005; Goldstein, 1997). Although ADHD may prevent a child from achieving his or her academic potential (Stott, 1981), the presence of LD may make a child appear more inattentive than others (McGee & Share, 1988). Students with ADHD often experience specific weaknesses within the processing blocks that contribute to poor school performance. Both phonological and orthographic memory problems are common among these students, whereas weaknesses in motor memory are relatively rare (for a review, see Goldstein & Goldstein, 1998).

Although, in the mid-1970s, children with ADHD were described as intellectually less competent than their peers, poor performance on intellectual tasks more likely results from the impact of impulsivity and inattention on test-taking behavior rather than on an innate lack of intelligence (Barkley, 1995). In addition, because many children with ADHD also have LD, they often underperform or underachieve during the elementary years. By high school, at least 80% of these children fall behind in a basic academic subject requiring repetition and attention for competence, such as basic math knowledge, spelling, or written language (Barkley, 2005; Goldstein & Goldstein, 1998; Loney, Kramer, & Milich, 1981).

Attention-Deficit/Hyperactivity Disorder and Social Difficulties

Sociometric and play studies suggest that children with ADHD are not chosen as often by peers to be best friends or partners in activities (Pelham & Milich, 1984). An awareness of their difficulties precipitates lower self-esteem (Glow & Glow, 1980). Moreover, they appear to experience either high incidence–low impact problems that result in poor social acceptance or low incidence–high impact problems that result in social rejection (Pelham & Milich, 1984). An example of a child with low incidence–high impact problems is the intermittently aggressive child on the playground. This child does not have to strike out at others more than once or twice per day to become unpopular with peers. Jeremy's pattern of performance fit this profile. One day on the way out to the playground, he pushed a flowerpot over a ledge, and the falling pot just missed landing on a child walking down below.

Strategies

Language Images

CONCEPTUAL

Phonology Orthography Motor

SYMBOLIC

Attention & Self-Regulation Emotions Behavior Self-Esteem

FOUNDATIONAL

In contrast, the shy, socially isolated child, seemingly incapable of grasping basic interactional skills, is an example of a child with high incidence–low impact problems. This child is often isolated and alone during free time in class or on the playground. Periodically, this child is observed interacting appropriately with other children, yet he or she seems hesitant, unsure, and uncomfortable doing so.

Children with ADHD also have difficulty adapting their behavior to different situational demands (Whalen, Henker, Collins, McAuliffe, & Vaux, 1979). The impulsive behavior patterns of children with ADHD are most responsible for their social difficulty, making those with concomitant hyperactive-impulsive problems at an even greater risk of developing social difficulties (Pelham & Bender, 1982).

After just being diagnosed with ADHD, Ms. Hanson, Jeremy's mother, reflected about her early elementary years.

"I spent most of my sixth-grade year out in the hall. I remember watching through the little window of the door to see what they were doing. I felt so lonely and left out. I hated that teacher, and, by the way she treated me, I could tell she hated me, too. I was caught chewing gum once by the teacher, and she made me wear it on my nose all day. I remember holding it there because my tears had caused it to slide off. Everyone paraded by me as they went out to play, each one poking and hissing at me as they passed. I had to stay in, but that didn't matter because no one liked me anyway. Because the teacher picked on me, so did everyone else. By that point, I hated school. I didn't have any friends, and my grades were poor. I had no idea what was wrong with me. I was just a 'bad kid,' and I had learned to accept it. I did not know at the time that, because of the way I was treated, these feelings would continue to haunt me later in life."

Attention-Deficit/Hyperactivity Disorder and Behavior Problems

For some individuals, the primary symptoms of ADHD may diminish in intensity by adolescence (Bagwell, Molina, Pelham, & Hoza, 2001; Faraone, Biederman, & Mick, 2006; Weiss & Hechtman, 1979); however, most adolescents with ADHD continue to experience significant problems (for review, see Goldstein, 1997; Milich & Loney, 1979). At least 80% of adolescents with ADHD continue to manifest symptoms consistent with ADHD, and 60% develop at least one additional disruptive disorder (Barkley, Fischer, Edelbrock, & Smallish, 1990). Between 20% and 60% of adolescents with ADHD are involved in delinquent behavior, as compared with the typical occurrence of 3%–4% of adolescents without ADHD (Satterfield, Hoppe, & Schell, 1982). At least 50%–70% of these adolescents develop oppositional defiant disorder, often during younger years, and a significant number develop a conduct disorder (Barkley, Fischer, et al., 1990).

The high prevalence of delinquency issues for adolescents with ADHD most likely reflects the comorbidity of ADHD with other disruptive disorders, principally conduct disorder (Barkley, McMurray, Edelbrock, & Robbins, 1990). The preponderance of the available data suggests that, although ADHD is clearly a risk factor for the development of adolescent antisocial problems, life experience (primarily factors within families) is the most powerful factor contributing to the onset and maintenance of delinquency, conduct disorder, and subsequent antisocial problems in adulthood (Barkley, 1997a).

One third of adolescents with ADHD are suspended from school at least once (Ackerman, Dykman, & Peters, 1977), and adolescents with a history of ADHD are at greater risk of developing internalized problems, including depression (Biederman, Faraone, Mick, & Lelon, 1995) and anxiety (Pliszka, 1992). The rates of comorbidity for ADHD and internalized disorders have been estimated from 20% to 70% with a higher incidence being reported in children and adolescents also receiving a diagnosis of conduct disorder.

Adults diagnosed with ADHD as children may not appear to be at significantly greater risk for developing serious legal and substance problems in the absence of adolescent conduct disorder (for a review, see Barkley, 2005; Goldstein & Goldstein, 1998). Nevertheless, the high comorbidity of ADHD and conduct disorder raises serious concerns. Mannuzza and colleagues (1991) suggested that adults with ADHD appear at greater risk than others to receive diagnoses of antisocial and substance abuse problems. These authors found that in young adults with a history of ADHD, 43% still manifested the full symptoms of ADHD, 32% met the diagnostic criteria for antisocial personality disorder, and 10% were drug abusers. In addition, adults diagnosed with ADHD are at a greater risk for having internalizing mood, marital, and vocational problems (Barkley, 2005; Biederman et al., 1987; Weiss & Hechtman, 1993).

Newer studies reinforce the findings that ADHD can contribute to negative outcomes in adults. In a 10-year follow up study, Biederman and colleagues (2006) compared more than 100 boys between the ages of 6 and 18 with ADHD to a control group without the disorder. By the age of 21, the boys with ADHD had a much higher prevalence of antisocial, addictive, mood, and anxiety disorders even though 93% of the boys had received treatment for the disorder at some point and 86% received both medication and counseling. These longitudinal results suggest that ADHD is not just a childhood disorder and that follow-up treatment, intervention, and counseling will be needed into adulthood.

Adults with ADHD may also experience problems similar to those they experienced in childhood when they reenter an educational environment. They may have trouble keeping up with class expectations and completing assignments in a timely manner. At any level, students with ADHD need caring and understanding instructors.

Upon returning to school, Jeremy's mother, Ms. Hanson, described the following incident: "I started college at the age of 35. I had one professor who embarrassed me in front of the whole class. I raised my hand and asked a question, and she said that I needed to go back to first grade because I didn't understand the concept of something. All of a sudden, I was back in sixth grade sitting out in the hall with gum on my nose. I hadn't thought much about that for a while, but the memories all came flooding back. I ran out of the class in tears. Twenty-six years later and it still affected me like that."

THE TEACHER'S ROLE IN THE EVALUATION OF HYPERACTIVITY, ATTENTION, PLANNING, AND IMPULSE CONTROL

Due to the pervasive nature of problems and the high comorbidity for additional problems, assessment for symptoms associated with ADHD involves a thorough emotional, neuropsychological, behavioral, and medical evaluation by a team of trained professionals. Rather than label or diagnose the behavior problem, teachers must describe the behaviors they observe. Factors required for children to succeed in a classroom become the basis of teachers' reports and concerns. Coming to class with a pencil, being able to see the blackboard, remaining in one's seat, participating, and so forth are all criteria that teachers can use to define the probability of success for students with ADHD.

Once a referral is made either to school personnel or to a parent and community professional, the teacher provides both qualitative and quantitative data. Qualitative data are often provided in terms of reports, anecdotes, and work samples. The Attention and Impulse Control checklist from Part 2 of the Building Blocks Questionnaire can be used to consider symptoms consistent with the

FOUNDATIONAL			
ATTENTION AND SELF-REGULATION	Rarely	Sometimes	Frequently
Appears restless and fidgety		✓	
Shows inconsistencies in behavior depending on the type of task			✓
Has trouble staying seated			✓
Seems to act before thinking			✓
Fails to finish tasks			✓
Has trouble making transitions		✓	
Has difficulty working independently			✓
Has trouble persisting on routine tasks for extended periods of time			✓
Has difficulty listening to and following directions		✓	
Has trouble finding and organizing tasks and materials			✓

Figure 4.3. Building Blocks Questionnaire for Jeremy: Attention and self-regulation block.

diagnosis of ADHD. Using a checklist such as this can help organize a teacher's thoughts and concerns, allowing the teacher to provide a cohesive explanation to others concerning the child's attention problems.

Prior to the review of Jeremy's accommodation plan, Mr. Chavez, Jeremy's fifth-grade teacher, completed the checklist for Jeremy, presented in Figure 4.3. The Hansons, Mr. Chavez, the principal, and the school psychologist met to discuss Jeremy's problems completing classroom tasks and to revise the accommodation plan. Each person's evaluation was similar to the first evaluation. Mr. Chavez felt that Jeremy was doing a better job of following directions but that he still had difficulty completing tasks.

Quantitative data are collected through the completion of standardized questionnaires that allow evaluators to compare the referred child to a general population. In some cases, the student is administered standardized tests to help rule out other conditions such as LD. Results from both qualitative and quantitative data are then evaluated by a pediatrician or psychologist to confirm the diagnosis of ADHD. ADHD is a medical diagnosis, and, although the school provides invaluable information, the final diagnosis is made by medical personnel.

MEDICATION

Treatment and interventions for ADHD are multidisciplinary and maintained over a long period of time (Goldstein & Goldstein, 1998). By far, the most effective short-term interventions for ADHD are multimodal, reflecting the combined use of medical, behavioral, and environmental techniques. The use of medication reduces problems with impulsivity. Behavior management effectively deals with the consequences of symptoms, increasing the salience of behaving in a way that is consistent with classroom expectations. Environmental adjustments (e.g., making tasks more interesting and payoffs more valuable) reduce the risk of classroom problems. Regardless of the intervention, the basic underlying premise in managing problems of ADHD in the classroom involves increasing the child's capacity to reflect before acting.

The use of medication to treat ADHD has increased significantly since 1985 (Jensen et al., 1999; Medco Health Solutions, 2005; Safer et al., 1996). At least 3 million children receive medication for ADHD in the United States alone (Jensen, 2000). Approximately 90% of children in the United States who take medication for ADHD receive stimulants, specifically methylphenidate hydrochloride, or Ritalin. Other stimulants such as dextroamphetamine sulfate (Adderall), pemoline (Cylert), and methamphetamine hydrochloride (Desoxyn) and the tricyclic antidepressants such as imipramine (Tofranil), desipramine hydrochloride (Norpramin), and nortriptyline hydrochloride (Pamelor) have also been reported as beneficial for ADHD symptoms. Pemoline, however, is no longer recommended as a first-line treatment for ADHD due to associated liver problems. The anti-hypertensive medicines clonidine (Catapres-TTS) and guanfacine hydrochloride (Tenex) have also been suggested as beneficial for treating ADHD. Atomoxetine (Strattera), a novel antidepressant, is also approved to treat ADHD. Unlike the stimulants, however, individuals may take a longer time to adjust to atomoxetine. In contrast, the selective serotonin reuptake inhibitors (SSRIs), such as fluoxetine hydrochloride (Prozac), paroxetine hydrochloride (Paxil), and sertraline hydrochloride (Zoloft), have not demonstrated an effectiveness rate much beyond placebo (Goldstein & Goldstein, 1998). Table 4.1 contains an overview of the most common medicines and an explanation of their possible side effects.

Effects of Medication

An extensive literature attests to the benefits of medicine, specifically stimulants, in reducing key symptoms of ADHD and thus improving daily functioning (for review, see Barkley, 2005; Goldstein & Goldstein, 1998; Jenson & Cooper, 2004). Stimulants consistently have been reported to improve academic productivity and accuracy of classwork (Douglas, Barr, O'Neil, & Britton, 1986), attention span, reading comprehension, and even complex problem solving (Balthazor, Wagner, & Pelham, 1991; Pelham, 1986). Related problems including peer interactions, peer status, and relationships with family members have been reported to improve with stimulants as well (Whalen & Henker, 1991).

Because the majority of children with ADHD receive stimulants, research has focused on this class of medication. The response of children with ADHD to the administration of stimulants is remarkably positive. Placebo-controlled, double-blind trials demonstrate that 75%–80% of children with ADHD respond to stimulants, whereas only 30%–40% respond to a placebo (Barkley, 1990; Greenhill & Osman, 1991). In classroom environments, trials have resulted in increased time on task, more work completed, and dramatic improvements in general conduct and behavior. Conflicts with classmates decline. Negative interactions between parents and children decline. The effect of stimulants on academic performance has been controversial, as the quality of work may improve but the rate at which academic information is acquired may not increase dramatically. Researchers have demonstrated that for children with LD and ADHD, the degree to which the children responded to medication was a crucial factor in determining a child's response to and progress in a specialized reading program (Richardson, Kupietz, & Maitinsky, 1986).

DuPaul and Rapport (1993) examined 31 children with ADHD in a double-blind, placebo-controlled trial of four doses of stimulant medication. Ritalin exerted a significant positive effect on classroom measures of attention and academic efficiency to the point that these problems were no longer statistically deviant among those with ADHD. However, on individual examination, 25% of

Table 4.1. Chart of medications to treat attention-deficit/hyperactivity disorder

Drug	Form	Dosing	Common side effects	Duration of effects	Pros	Precautions
Methylphenidate						
Ritalin Methylin Metadate Generic MPH	Short-acting *tablet* 5 mg 10 mg 20 mg	Starting dose for children is 5 mg twice daily, 3–4 hours apart. Add third dose about 4 hours after second. Adjust timing based on duration of action. Increase by 5–10 mg incre-ments. Daily dosage above 60 mg not recom-mended. Esti-mated dose range .3–.6 mg/kg/dose	Insomnia, decreased appetite, weight loss, headache, irri-tability, stomach-ache, and rebound agitation or exag-geration of pre-medication symptoms as it is wearing off	About 3–4 hours. Most helpful when need rapid onset and short duration	Works quickly (within 30–60 minutes). Effective in more than 70% of patients	Use cautiously in patients with marked anxiety or motor tics or with family history of Tourette syndrome or history of substance abuse. Don't use if at risk for glaucoma or if taking monoamine oxidase inhibitors (MAOI)
Focalin (with isolated dextro-isomer)	Short-acting *tablet* 2.5 mg 5 mg 10 mg	Start with half the dose recom-mended for nor-mal short-acting methylphenidate above. Dose may be adjusted in 2.5 to 5 mg incre-ments to a maxi-mum of 20 mg per day (10 mg twice daily).	As above. There is suggestion that Focalin (dextro-isomer) may be less prone to causing sleep or appetite disturbance.	About 3–4 hours. Most helpful when need rapid onset and short duration. Only formulation with isolated dextro-isomer	Works quickly (within 30–60 minutes). Possibly better for use for evening needs when day's long-acting dose is wearing off	As above. Expensive compared with other short-acting prepara-tions

Treatment of ADHD usually includes medical management, behavior modification, counseling, and school or work accommodations. The medications charted above and on the following pages include: 1) stimulants, 2) the non-stimulant Strattera (atomoxetine) with effects similar to stimulants, 3) the antidepressant Wellbutrin (bupropion) and 4) two antihypertensives Catapres (clonidine) and Tenex (guanfacine). Stimulants include all formulations of methylphenidate (Ritalin, Focalin, Metadate and Methylin) and all forms of amphetamines (Dexedrine, Dextrostat and Adderall). Individuals respond in their own unique way to medication depending upon their physical make-up, severity of symptoms, associated conditions, and other factors. Careful monitoring should be done by a physician in collaboration with the teacher, therapist, parents, spouse, and patient. **Important note:** Medications to treat ADHD and related conditions should only be prescribed by a physician. Information presented here is not intended to replace the advice of a physician.

(continued)

Table 4.1. *(continued)*

Drug	Form	Dosing	Common side effects	Duration of effects	Pros	Precautions
Ritalin SR	Mid-acting *tablet* 20 mg	Start with 20 mg daily. May combine with short acting for quicker onset and/or coverage after this wears off	Insomnia, decreased appetite, weight loss, headache, irritability, stomachache	Onset delayed for 60–90 minutes. Duration supposed to be 6–8 hours, but can be quite individual and unreliable	Wears off more gradually than short acting so less risk of rebound. Lower abuse risk	As above. Note: If crushed or cut, full dose may be released at once, giving twice the intended dose in first 4 hours, none in the second 4 hours
Methylin ER Metadate ER	Mid-acting *tablet* 10 mg 20 mg					Same cautions as for immediate release
Ritalin LA *50% immediate-release beads and 50% delayed-release beads*	Mid-acting *capsule* 20 mg 30 mg 40 mg	Starting dose is 10–20 mg once daily. May be adjusted weekly in 10 mg increments to maximum of 60 mg taken once daily.	Insomnia, decreased appetite, weight loss, headache, irritability, stomachache, and rebound potential	Onset in 30–60 minutes. Duration about 8 hours	May swallow whole or sprinkle all contents on a spoonful of applesauce. Starts quickly, avoids mid-day gap unless student metabolizes medicine very rapidly	Do not chew. If beads are chewed, may release full dose at once, giving entire contents in first 4 hours
Metadate CD *30% immediate-release and 70% delayed-release beads*	Mid-acting *capsule* 10 mg 20 mg 30 mg	May add short-acting dose in morning or 8 hours later in evening if needed				
Concerta *22% immediate release and 78% gradual release*	Long-acting *tablet* 18 mg 27 mg 36 mg 54 mg	Starting dose is 18 mg or 36 mg once daily. Option to increase to 72 mg daily	Insomnia, decreased appetite, weight loss, headache, irritability, stomachache	Onset in 30–60 minutes. Duration about 10–14 hours	Works quickly (within 30–60 minutes). Given only once a day. Longest duration of MPH forms. Doesn't risk mid-day gap or rebound because medication is released gradually throughout the day. Wears off more gradually than short acting, so less rebound. Lower abuse risk	Same cautions as for immediate release. Do not cut or crush

(continued)

Table 4.1. *(continued)*

Drug	Form	Dosing	Common side effects	Duration of effects	Pros	Precautions
Dextroamphetamine						
Dextrostat	Short-acting *tablet* 5 mg 10 mg	For ages 3–5 years, starting dose is 2.5 mg of tablet. Increase by 2.5 mg at weekly intervals, increasing first dose or adding/increasing a noon dose, until effective. For ages 6 years and older, start with 5 mg once or twice daily. May increase total daily dose by 5 mg per week until reach optimal level. Tablet is given on awakening. Over age 6 years, one or two additional doses may be given at 4–6 hour intervals. Usually no more than 40 mg/day	Insomnia, decreased appetite, weight loss, headache, irritability, stomachache. Rebound agitation or exaggeration of pre-medication symptoms as it is wearing off. May also elicit psychotic symptoms	Onset in 30–60 minutes. Duration about 4–5 hours.	Approved for children under the age of 6. Good safety record. Somewhat longer action than short-acting methylphenidate	Use cautiously in patients with marked anxiety, motor tics, family history of Tourette syndrome, or history of substance abuse. Don't use if at risk for glaucoma or if taking MAOI. High abuse potential, particularly in tablet form
Dexedrine *2004 PDR does not list short-acting Dexedrine tablets*	Short-acting *tablet* 5 mg Long-acting *spansule*					
Dexedrine spansule	Long-acting *spansule* 5 mg 10 mg 15 mg	In children age 6 and older who can swallow whole capsule, morning dose of capsule equal to sum of morning and noon short acting. Increase total daily dose by 5 mg per week until reach optimal dose to maximum of 40 mg/day	Same as above	Onset in 30–60 minutes. Duration about 5–10 hours	May avoid need for noon dose, rapid onset. Good safety record	As above. Less likely to be abused intranasal or IV than short acting. Must use whole capsule
Dextroamphetamine sulfate ER	5 mg 10 mg 15 mg					
Adderall	Short-acting *tablet* 5 mg 7.5 mg 10 mg 12.5 mg 15 mg 20 mg 30 mg	Starting dose is 5 or 10 mg each morning for children age 6 and older. May be adjusted in 5–10 mg increments up to 30 mg per day	Same as above	Onset in 30–60 minutes. Duration about 4–5 hours	Wears off more gradually than dextroamphetamine alone, so rebound is less likely and more mild	Same as Dexedrine spansules except that it has documented efficacy when sprinkled on applesauce

(continued)

Table 4.1. (continued)

Drug	Form	Dosing	Common side effects	Duration of effects	Pros	Precautions
Atomoxetine Strattera	Long-acting *capsule* 10 mg 18 mg 25 mg 40 mg 60 mg	Starting dose is 0.5 mg/kg. The targeted clinical dose is approximately 1.2 mg/kg. Increase at weekly intervals. Medication must be used each day. Usually started in the morning, but may be changed to evening. It may be divided into a morning and evening dose, particularly if need higher doses	In children: decreased appetite, GI upset (can be reduced if medication taken with food), sedation (can be reduced by dosing in evening), lightheadedness. In adults: insomnia, sexual side effects, increased blood pressure	Starts working within a few days to one week, but full effect may not be evident for a month or more. Duration all day (24/7) so long as taken daily as directed	Avoids problems of rebound and gaps in coverage. Doesn't cause a "high," thus a) it does not lead to abuse, and so a) it is not a controlled drug and b) may use with history of substance abuse	Use cautiously in patients with hypertension, tachycardia, or cardiovascular or cerebrovascular disease because it can increase blood pressure and heart rate. Some drug interactions. While extensively tested, short duration of population use
Bupropion Wellbutrin IR	Short-acting *tablet* IR-75 mg 100 mg	Starting dose is 37.5 mg, increasing gradually (wait at least 3 days) to maximum of 2–3 doses, no more than 150 mg/dose	Irritability, decreased appetite, and insomnia	About 4–6 hours	Helpful for ADHD patents with comorbid depression or anxiety. May help after school	Not indicated in patients with a seizure disorder or with a current or previous diagnosis of bulimia or anorexia. May worsen tics. May cause mood deterioration at the time it wears off
Wellbutrin SR	Long-acting *tablet* SR-100 mg 150 mg 200 mg	Starting dose is 100 mg/day, increasing gradually to a maximum of 2 doses, no more than 200 mg/dose	Same as Wellbutrin IR	About 10–14 hours	Same for Wellbutrin IR. Lower seizure risk than immediate-release form. Avoids noon dose	Same as Wellbutrin IR. If a second dose is not given, may cause mood deterioration at around 10–14 hours
Wellbutrin XL	Long-acting *tablet* 150 mg 300 mg	Starting dose is 150 mg/day, increasing gradually to a maximum of 2 doses, no more than 300 mg/day	Same as Wellbutrin IR	About 24+ hours	Same for Wellbutrin IR. Single daily dose. Smooth 24-hour coverage. Lower seizure risk than immediate-release form	Same as Wellbutrin IR

(continued)

Table 4.1. (continued)

Alpha-2 Agonists

Drug	Form	Dosing	Common side effects	Duration of effects	Pros	Precautions
Catapres (Clonidine)	*Tablet* 0.1 mg 0.2 mg 0.3 mg	Starting dose is .025–.05 mg/day in evening. Increase by similar dose every 7 days, adding to morning, mid-day, possibly afternoon, and again evening doses in sequence. Total dose of 0.1–0.3 mg/day divided into 3–4 doses. Do not skip days	Sleepiness, hypotension, headache, dizziness, stomachache, nausea, dry mouth, depression, nightmares	Onset in 30–60 minutes. Duration about 3–6 hours	Helpful for ADHD patients with comorbid tic disorder or insomnia. Good for severe impulsivity, hyperactivity and/or aggression. Stimulates appetite. Especially helpful in younger children (under 6) with ADHD symptoms associated with prenatal insult or syndrome such as fragile X	Sudden discontinuation could result in rebound hypertension. Minimize daytime tiredness by starting with evening dose and increasing slowly. Avoid brand and generic formulations with red dye, which may cause hyperarousal in sensitive children
Clonidine	*Tablet* 0.1 mg 0.2 mg 0.3 mg					
Catapres patch	TTS-1 TTS-2 TTS-3	Corresponds to doses of 0.1 mg, 0.2 mg and 0.3 mg per patch. (If using .1 mg tid tablets, try TTS 2 but likely need TTS 3)	Same as Catapres tablet, but with skin patch there may be localized skin reactions	Duration 4–5 days, so avoids the vacillations in drug effect seen in tablets	Same as above	Same as above. May get rebound hypertension and return of symptoms if it isn't recognized that a patch has come off or become loose. An immature student may get excessive dose from chewing on the patch
Tenex (guanfacine)	1 mg 2 mg 3 mg	Starting dose is 0.5 mg/day in evening and increase by similar dose every 7 days as indicated. Given in divided doses 2–4 times per day. Daily dose range 0.5 - .4 mg/day. DO NOT skip days	Compared with Clonidine, lower chances/ severity of side effects, especially fatigue and depression. Also, less headache, stomachache, nausea, dry mouth. Unlike clonidine, minimal problem of rebound hypertension if doses are missed	Duration about 6–12 hours.	Can provide for 24/7 modulation of impulsivity, hyperactivity, aggression, and sensory hypersensitivity. This covers most out-of-school problems so that stimulant use can be limited to school and homework hours. Improves appetite. Less sedating than clonidine	Avoid formulations with red dye as above. Hypotension is the primary dose-limiting problem. As with clonidine, important to check blood pressures with dose increases and if symptoms suggest hypotension, such as light-headedness
guanfacine	*Tablet* 1 mg 2 mg 3 mg					

the children with ADHD failed to demonstrate normalized levels of classroom performance, suggesting that although stimulant medications are beneficial, a need for ancillary interventions remains.

Almost all children with ADHD who do not respond to one stimulant may benefit from another (Elia, Borcherding, Rapoport, & Keysor, 1991). The definition of a good response, however, is debatable. When a good response was defined as a reduction in the cardinal symptoms of ADHD and improvement in behavior and compliance at school, at least 80%–90% of children appropriately diagnosed with ADHD were viewed as responding to medication. However, when a good response was defined by performance on a cognitive task in a laboratory setting, such as a paired associate learning task, a greater number of children with ADHD were perceived as unresponsive to stimulants (Swanson, Cantwell, Lerner, McBurnett, & Hanna, 1991).

The long-term effects of stimulants have been debated. Studies have demonstrated consistent short-term benefits but not robust long-term benefits into adulthood (Goldstein, 1999; for a review, see Barkley, 2005; Goldstein, 1997). When outlook is measured in terms of socioeconomic status, vocation, marriage, drug addiction, or criminal behavior, minimal long-term positive effects of stimulants are demonstrated. However, the immediate short-term benefits of stimulant medication far outweigh the liabilities and thus appear to justify the continued use of these medications in the treatment of ADHD.

Neurotransmitters

Medications used to treat ADHD affect brain chemistry, specifically chemicals known as neurotransmitters. These chemicals help the billions of brain cells to communicate effectively. Medications used to treat ADHD appear to affect significantly the neurotransmitter called dopamine. The increased availability of dopamine allows more efficient and consistent cellular communication, particularly for messages involving self-control. This is not to suggest that ADHD results from a dopamine deficiency but rather that one link in the complex chain that leads to behaviors characteristic of ADHD may be the manner in which neurotransmitters operate. Researchers have also examined medications that affect other neurotransmitters, finding that some may yield benefits and also reduce ADHD symptoms. However, the majority of the research strongly points to dopamine as the primary neurotransmitter implicated in ADHD.

The medications used to treat ADHD have benefits as well as possible side effects. Psychostimulants such as Ritalin are often misunderstood. Take the quiz in Figure 4.4, adapted from Pancheri and Prater (1999), to check your understanding of the myths and facts surrounding Ritalin and then check your answers with the key at the bottom of the quiz.

Teachers play a critical role in monitoring the effects of medication on the behavior and schoolwork of children. An open line of communication is needed with parents and the prescribing physician. Teachers are not expected to be physicians or school nurses. When a child receiving medication for ADHD demonstrates any type of atypical behavior, physical complaints, or a change in school performance and work quality, the teacher should promptly inform the child's parents.

A CLASSROOM MODEL FOR MANAGING HYPERACTIVITY, INATTENTION, IMPULSIVITY, AND POOR PLANNING

The presence of knowledgeable, understanding teachers; the availability of appropriate support systems; and the opportunities for every student to engage successfully in a variety of classroom activities are imperative for children with

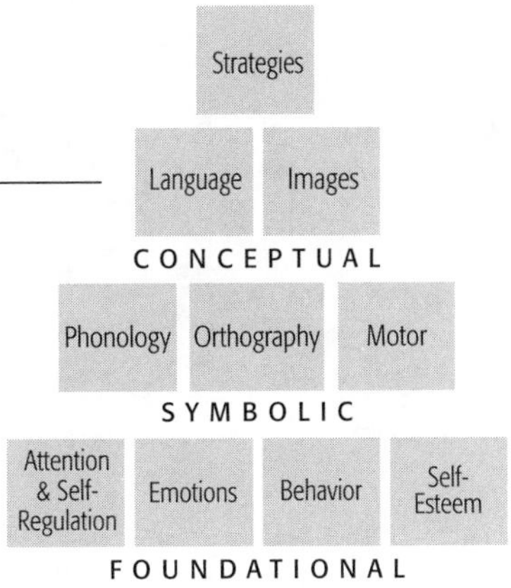

Ritalin Quiz

1. —— True   —— False   Many adolescents continue to benefit from medications such as Ritalin.

2. —— True   —— False   Dosages of medication may vary between the brandname and generic versions.

3. —— True   —— False   Ritalin use does not lead to drug abuse. Students with ADHD, however, appear to be more prone to become substance abusers under certain circumstances than their peers are.

4. —— True   —— False   Children become addicted to Ritalin.

5. —— True   —— False   Ritalin significantly affects growth rate for most children.

6. —— True   —— False   Ritalin helps teenagers control impulsive behavior.

7. —— True   —— False   Ritalin may reduce a child's appetite.

8. —— True   —— False   Ritalin helps most children with ADHD to fall asleep.

9. —— True   —— False   As Ritalin wears off, some children appear more hyperactive and irritable.

10. —— True   —— False   Headaches are rarely a side effect of Ritalin.

11. —— True   —— False   Children with ADHD taking Ritalin sometimes complain of stomachaches.

12. —— True   —— False   Ritalin does not change a child's personality.

13. —— True   —— False   Ritalin is not stored long term in any organs of the body.

14. —— True   —— False   A very small percentage of children taking Ritalin may develop tics.

15. —— True   —— False   Ritalin has been found to be a cause of serious medical problems such as seizures.

16. —— True   —— False   Ritalin may cause a slight increase in heart rate and blood pressure.

17. —— True   —— False   Long-term use of Ritalin does not cause other serious psychiatric problems such as depression and anxiety.

1. True; 2. False; 3. False; 4. False; 5. False; 6. True; 7. True; 8. False; 9. True; 10. False; 11. True; 12. True; 13. True; 14. True; 15. False; 16. True; 17. True

Strategies

Language   Images

C O N C E P T U A L

Phonology   Orthography   Motor

S Y M B O L I C

Attention & Self-Regulation   Emotions   Behavior   Self-Esteem

F O U N D A T I O N A L

Figure 4.4. Ritalin quiz. (From What teachers and parents should know about Ritalin by C. Pancheri and M.A. Prater, *Teaching Exceptional Children, 31*(4), 1999, 21. Copyright© 2001 by The Council for Exceptional Children. Reprinted with permission.)

ADHD. Teachers, particularly those at the elementary level, play a critical role in helping children with these problems. These teachers focus on academic goals, carefully select instructional materials, structure and plan learning activities, involve students in the learning process, closely monitor student progress, and provide frequent feedback on progress and accomplishments (Goldstein & Goldstein, 1990). These opportunities build self-esteem and resilience, and they contribute to future successes. Yet, as straightforward an issue as educational management appears to be, controversy follows ADHD regardless of the environment or situation in which it presents. Reid, Maag, and Vasa noted, "Not since the establishment of learning disability as a special education category has a condition so captivated both the professional community and the general public as has attention-deficit/hyperactivity disorder" (1994, p. 198). These authors questioned the validity of ADHD as a psychiatric disorder, the reliability of estimates used to justify the need for additional services, and the specificity of services offered to students with ADHD in school. Reid and colleagues (1994) concluded that all of these factors preclude ADHD from being made a specific disability category and that new categories should not be added in the absence of solid, empirical knowledge. Others have argued that children's needs should be the primary means for determining whether they qualify for assistance, rather than for a diagnosis (Stoner & Carey, 1992; Zirkel, 1992).

Despite the controversy, during the 1990s, ADHD became a widely used term in educational environments throughout the world. In 1992, the U.S. Department of Education set clear guidelines necessitating that schools identify and provide services for children with ADHD, and considerable literature has been directed at educators (Bowley & Walther, 1992; Buchoff, 1990; Burcham, Carlson, & Milich, 1993; Busch, 1993; Schwean, Parkinson, Francis, & Lee, 1993). Yet, as of 2008 when this book was published, classroom teachers continued to receive minimal direction and instruction in how to work with these children.

Students' successes may have different meanings for different teachers. For some, success for students with ADHD might mean reduced restlessness, fewer classroom disruptions, mastery of academic material, completion of assignments, the ability to follow directions the first time, improved peer relations, and even enhanced student self-esteem (Greene, 1993). The degree to which a teacher's definition of success is compatible with a student's capacity for change is critical. The teacher starts with a goal in mind, even if it is as simple as stating that he or she would like this child to function in a manner similar to the majority of children in the classroom. Historically, the majority of suggestions offered for the problems that children with ADHD experience have been directed toward specific challenging behaviors, such as those presented in Table 4.2. Although these solutions can be appropriate for a specific problem, in most instances a more comprehensive approach, such as described in the following section, is needed. This model includes a basic set of principles tied to the specific classroom problems of children with ADHD, offers a set of guidelines stemming logically from this model, and then addresses specific problems and suggestions to structure classrooms in order to facilitate success.

Classroom intervention strategies for ADHD may be categorized into two distinct sets (Goldstein & Goldstein, 1990). The first set is designed to change cognition, thoughts, and feelings with a goal of increasing skills and self-management. The second is designed to provide managed consequences and to manipulate environmental factors in order to increase the likelihood of the child's classroom success. Zentall (1995, 2005, 2006) emphasized that students with ADHD function better in classroom environments when they are allowed to move, channel activity appropriately, and talk and question actively and are provided with novel, interesting instruction.

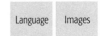

Table 4.2. Attention-deficit/hyperactivity disorder (ADHD) characteristics and remedial strategies used by resource center teachers

Characteristic	Remedial strategy
Academic difficulties	Monitor progress, assist in planning and scheduling courses/maintain communication with other teachers
Cognitive fatigue	Provide prompts, cues, encouragement/teach metacognitive strategies
Fine motor dysfunction	Promote use of computers, calculators/modify assignments
Poor quality control	Encourage self-awareness and self-management
Disorganization	Support use of acquisition outlines, structured organizers, semantic maps
Time management problems	Foster use of daily notebook/assist in short and long-term planning
Performance inconsistency	Prompt student to use compensatory, self-help, self-monitoring skills
Problem understanding directions	Persuade student to request assistance, clarification/oversee implementation of standing instructional/test modifications
Difficulty sequencing information	Teach mnemonic devices
Poor working memory	Advocate the use of study skill techniques/test-taking strategies
Inconsistent attention patterns	Maintain close supervision/provide direct instruction
Difficulty expressing needs	Coach self-advocacy skill development through role play, verbal rehearsal
Social adjustment problems	Recommend and facilitate involvement in extra-curricular activities

From *Accommodating the adolescent with attention deficit disorder: The role of the resource center teacher.* JOURNAL OF ATTENTION DISORDERS by C.G. Spinelli. Copyright 1997 by Sage Publications Inc. Journals. Reproduced with permission of Sage Publications Inc. Journals in the format Textbook via Copyright Clearance Center.

Based in part on Zentall's suggestions, Goldstein (1995) defined three key goals for children with ADHD—to start, stop, and think in a manner similar to others. As a framework for educators, these goals focus intervention on increasing a child's ability to start when everyone else starts for both academic and nonacademic tasks, to stop when everyone else stops, and to think about what the teacher is saying. Providing a conceptual framework with an understanding of the importance of making tasks interesting, making payoffs valuable, and allowing opportunities for repeated trials is the key ingredient of educational intervention for children with ADHD.

In addition to the talk, move/question, and learn model and the start/stop/think goals, a framework for implementation is suggested (Goldstein & Jones, 1998; Jones, 1989). This three-part framework focuses on

1. *Brevity:* Children with ADHD begin most tasks with less effort than is necessary. The fact that they begin with less attentional effort results in their attention more quickly falling below a threshold necessary to remain on task. Thus, the axiom that attention in classroom environments is greatest during short activities is valid for children with ADHD. Frequent, brief trials or lessons covering small chunks of information result in better classroom performance. Children with ADHD require more trials for success. The brevity concept suggests that these trials be of short duration. Furthermore, the actual pace at which tasks are presented has been found to be an instructional variable related to classroom problem behaviors (West & Sloan, 1986). Data collected with special and general education students show that relatively fast pacing within the capacity of the student's ability to learn is associated with fewer complaints about classroom misbehavior.

2. *Variety:* Children with ADHD experience "flagging attention" (Douglas, 1983). As tasks are presented repeatedly, they perform with decreasing effort and motivation. Thus, children with ADHD may be quicker to perceive tasks as repetitive or uninteresting. If they require the need for repeated trials to develop the same level of competence as their peers, the challenge for the classroom teacher is to present the same material in slightly different ways or in different applications to maximize interest. Furthermore, the availability of choice among what is to be learned is also an important variable (Dunlap, Kern-Dunlap, Clarke, & Robbins, 1991). Choice increases task interest and results in greater effort and motivation. Children with ADHD function best when various materials to enhance visual, verbal, and tactile interactions are offered. The manipulation of materials makes the task more interesting and motivating.

3. *Routine:* A consistent routine and a structured environment enhanced by a highly organized format of activities are recommended for children with ADHD. Specific daily schedules, including well-planned experiences with managed transitions, are optimal. Specific rules, expectations, and consequences need to be clearly stated. A greater number of transitions within an educational day increases the likelihood that children with ADHD will struggle (Zentall, 1988). In addition, students with ADHD have particular difficulty with days that break the familiar routine (e.g., field trips, field days, assemblies). Adolescents with ADHD often have pronounced difficulties coping with the multiple transitions required during the school day.

Elementary students with ADHD often receive negative feedback in school for their inattentive behavior and inability to perform in accordance with the teacher's directions (Bender, 1997). Difficulty with listening may then cause the child to miss out on teachers' directions. This difficulty is exacerbated in stimulating situations, such as field trips or playground games.

When Jeremy was in fourth grade, his teacher wrote the note presented in Figure 4.5 after a field trip. Although one can understand and empathize with this teacher's frustration in this situation, it is important to understand that behaviors such as ignoring directions or not listening comprise part of the core symptomatology of this disability. Jeremy understands the rules for behavior, but his impulsivity and inattention result in noncompliance that is unintentional. In other words, Jeremy is not in full control of his actions and behavior and should not be punished, because his difficulty with following directions is fairly typical and expected of a child with this disorder. Instead of insisting on parental accompaniment, a more appropriate solution would have been to provide more support and monitoring (not necessarily parental) during field trips. This may mean that one adult volunteers to supervise Jeremy for the day or that a responsible peer agrees to be a "field trip buddy."

Carefully planned daily schedules reflect strategic efforts to improve the classroom behavior and educational achievements of children with ADHD. Cooperative learning activities, such as those activities in which students work together during the learning process, can also be effective. Working with other students offers opportunities to model new behaviors and reinforce existing skills. All students learn best through a combination of watching others and having the opportunity to practice and experiment with new behaviors. Figure 4.6 provides an overview of the classroom model.

Effectiveness of Interventions

The effectiveness of classroom-based interventions depends on three factors: the characteristics of the child, the components of the intervention, and the interaction

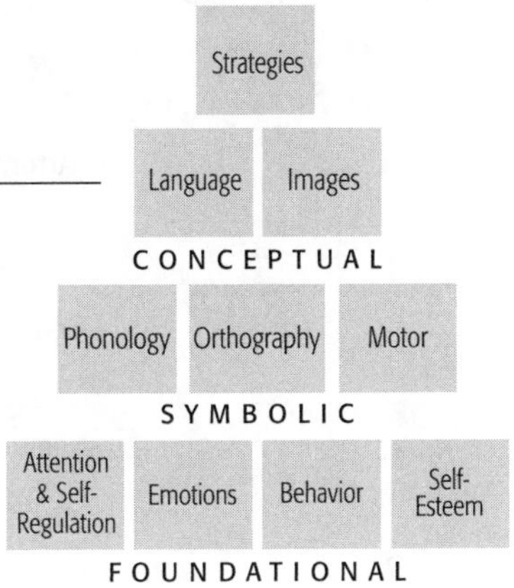
Strategies
Language
Images
CONCEPTUAL
Phonology
Orthography
Motor
SYMBOLIC
Attention & Self-Regulation
Emotions
Behavior
Self-Esteem
FOUNDATIONAL

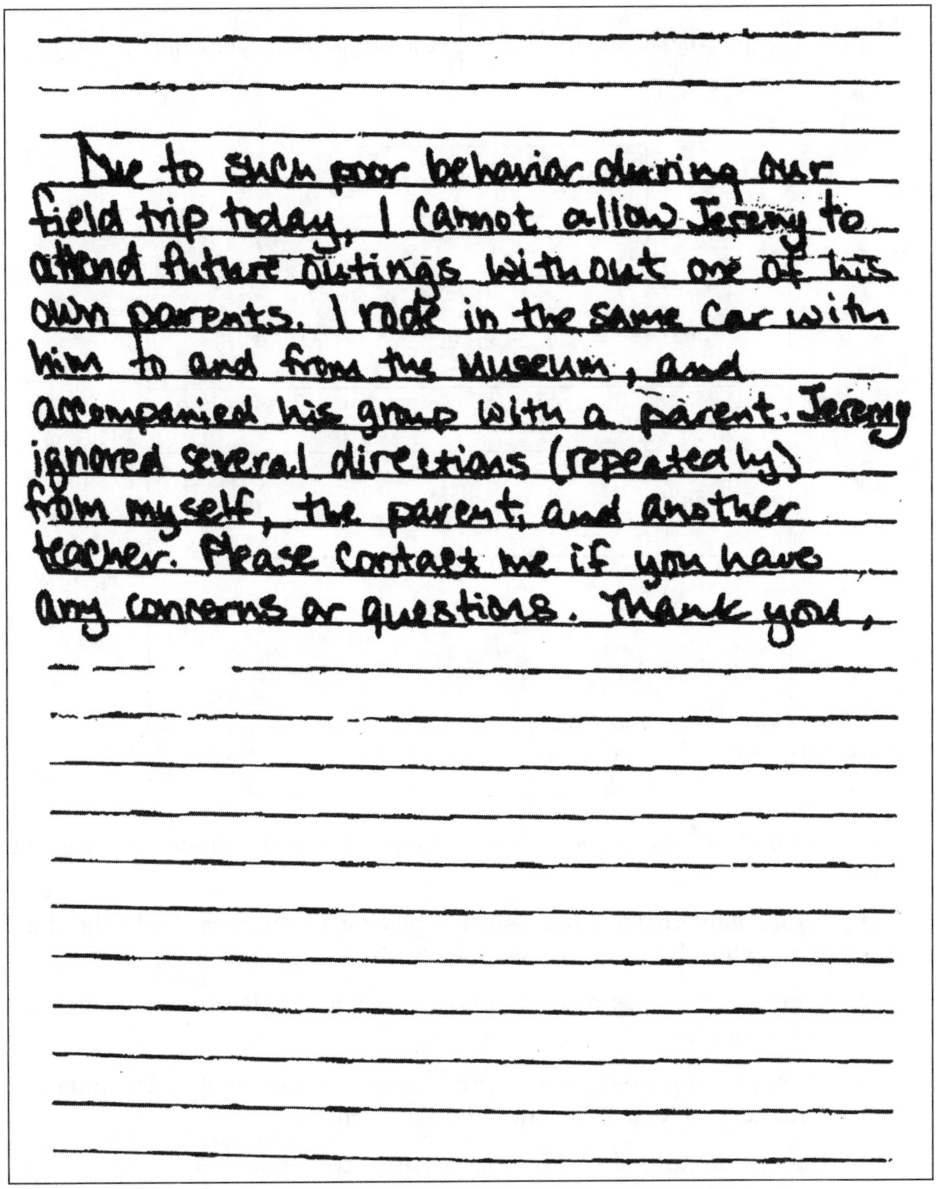

Due to such poor behavior during our field trip today, I cannot allow Jeremy to attend future outings without one of his own parents. I rode in the same car with him to and from the museum, and accompanied his group with a parent. Jeremy ignored several directions (repeatedly) from myself, the parent, and another teacher. Please contact me if you have any concerns or questions. Thank you,

Figure 4.5. Teacher's note regarding what she perceived to be poor behavior from a child with attention-deficit/hyperactivity disorder.

between the two. Rapport (1989) suggested that child characteristics include the following:

1. Breadth and severity of behavioral dysfunction
2. Intelligence
3. Presence or absence of LD
4. Gender
5. Presence of co-occurring classroom problems
6. The time interval during which adequate intervention has not been administered (e.g., birth–5, 6–9; it may be more difficult to change the behavior of a sixth grader than a kindergartner)

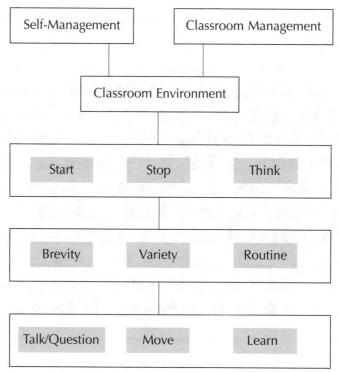

Figure 4.6. Overview of classroom model for educating children with attention-deficit/hyperactivity disorder.

Characteristics associated with behavioral interventions include the following:

1. Using nonverbal feedback, such as placing a hand on a child's shoulder, to help the child focus on what he or she is supposed to be doing

2. Limiting delays as much as possible between behavior and scheduled consequences

3. Strengthening positive and productive behavior that is incompatible with nonproductive and inappropriate behavior

4. Using a mixture of positive and negative consequences

5. Incorporating a practical feedback system that does not require a disproportionate amount of teacher time

Children with ADHD appear to function better when the following issues are considered (Rapport, 1989):

1. Limiting the number and types of distractors frequently printed in educational materials

2. Planning short versus lengthy assignments

3. Using stimulating assignments and materials whenever possible

4. Minimizing repetitive drill exercises and, when necessary, breaking them into smaller chunks

5. Making efforts to determine that a child understands assignments and prompts offered

6. Providing an opportunity to engage in a desired activity after engaging in a less-desired activity (i.e., the Premack Principle); more interesting

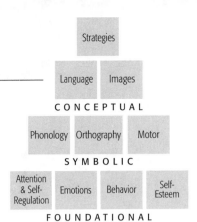

assignments and other learning activities can serve as motivational incentives (e.g., a child enjoying silent reading can be given the opportunity to have additional free time to read in school contingent on completing assigned math work)

The basic philosophy underlying these six variables involves making tasks more interesting and rewards more valuable. Understanding and maintaining this framework can help teachers choose among possible classroom interventions.

Behavior Management Strategies

Numerous studies have documented the efficacy of a wide range of behavior-based classroom interventions for students with ADHD (Abramowitz & O'Leary, 1991; DuPaul, 1991; DuPaul & Stoner, 2003). These interventions are either contingency-based (i.e., structured to provide consequences following the exhibition of desired or undesired behaviors) or they address management of antecedent behaviors. The manipulation of consequences includes contingent teacher attention, both positive and negative, and classroom token economies, including reinforcement, response cost, and contingencies arranged between home and school.

Teachers tend to manipulate consequences as a primary means of classroom intervention (Pfiffner & O'Leary, 1993) and use positive reinforcement along with mild forms of punishment. The management of consequences has become increasingly creative, ranging from the use of computers and related technology (Gordon, Thomason, Cooper, & Ivers, 1991) to the use of peers as tutors and consequence monitors (DuPaul & Henningson, 1993). Peer tutoring may be a viable addition or alternative to teacher-mediated behavioral interventions for ADHD. Children may, however, promote problem behaviors in their peers rather than encourage displays of appropriate behaviors (Solomon & Wahler, 1973). Children with ADHD may find it particularly difficult to develop positive peer interactions due to a mismatch between their need for frequent and consistent reinforcement and the typical low rates of reinforcement that children provide to one another. The success of peer-mediated programs depends on the ability and motivation of children to learn and accurately implement them (O'Leary & O'Leary, 1977). The emphasis has shifted toward preventing and managing behavior through antecedent manipulations and environmental arrangements (Sulzer-Azaroff & Mayer, 1991). In other words, the teacher attempts to predict which problems may occur so that these situations can be avoided. As an example, Jeremy's teacher would walk him each day to the bus stop. This eliminated negative confrontations with other students. A wide range of behavior management strategies are presented and reviewed in Chapter 6. The strategies are discussed from the perspective of ADHD as well as the general management of classroom behaviors.

Planning Facilitation

Good planning skills help students achieve goals for the development of strategies necessary to accomplish tasks for which a solution is required. Planning is therefore crucial to all activities that demand students to problem solve. This includes self-monitoring and impulse control as well as creation, assessment, and execution of a plan. The planning processes allow students to generate solutions, discriminate use of knowledge and skills, and manage other neuropsychological processes such as attention. Naglieri and Gottling (1995, 1997) designed a method to indirectly teach children to be more strategic and use planning in one-to-one tutoring sessions or in the classroom with the teacher. This training took place two to three times per week in half-hour blocks. Students were given a 10-minute

---

Planning Facilitation for Math Calculation

Math calculation involves recalling basic math facts, following procedures, working carefully, and checking one's work. Math calculation requires a careful—planful—approach to follow all the necessary steps.

Planning facilitation helps students develop useful strategies to carefully complete math problems through discussion and shared discovery. It encourages students to think about how they solve problems, rather than just think about whether their answer is correct. This helps them develop careful ways of doing math. Children who score low in planning are likely to improve the most from planning facilitation.

The following is an example of how parents and teachers might provide planning facilitation.

Step 1: **Provide math worksheet for a child to complete in 10 minutes.**

Step 2: **Discuss with the child how he or she completed the worksheet and how he or she will go about completing problems in the future.** Probe rather than reinforce, using questions that encourage the child to consider whether his or her strategies worked. Facilitate planning by verbalizing ideas and explaining why some strategies work better than others.

Examples of probing questions include:

How did you do the page?

What do you notice about how this page was completed?

Why did you do it that way? What did you expect to happen?

How are you going to complete the page next time so you get more correct answers?

What seemed to work well for you before, and what will you do next time?

What are some reasons why people make mistakes on problems like these?

You say these are hard. Can you think of any ways to make them easier?

There are many problems here. Can you figure out a way to do more?

Do you think you will do anything differently next time?

It is important not to say things like, "Watch me. This is how to do it." "That's right. Good, now you're getting it!" "You made a mistake. Fix it now," or "Remember to use your favorite strategy."

Step 3: **Give the child another math worksheet to complete in 10 minutes.**

Figure 4.7. Planning facilitation for math calculation. (From Naglieri, J.A., & Pickering, E.B. [2003]. *Helping children learn: Intervention handouts for use in school and at home* [pp. 109–110]. Baltimore: Paul H. Brookes Publishing Co; adapted by permission.)

period to work on a mathematics page, followed by a 10-minute period used to encourage the application of strategies, and then another 10-minute period to work on math problems. Students were encouraged to recognize the need to plan new strategies when completing mathematics problems. The teacher provided probes that facilitated discussion and encouraged the students to consider various ways to be more successful. When a student provided a response, this often became the starting point for discussion and further strategic development. This method is more fully described by Naglieri and Pickering (2003) and shown in Figure 4.7. Students exposed to this type of planning facilitation demonstrated a significant advancement in their ability to work independently and accurately. Additional information about teaching children to be more strategic is also provided by Ashman and Conway (1997) and Iseman (2005).

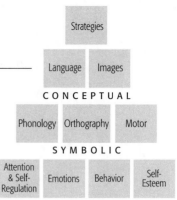

INTERACTIVE ISSUES

The following sections contain practical pointers and ideas to help students with ADHD in a variety of situations both in and out of the classroom. Teachers may find these suggestions helpful for students who have disruptive problems in addition to ADHD.

Be Positive

Students with ADHD must be told what adults want to have happen rather than what they do not want to have happen. Although this is a simple concept, it is the essence of being positive. For example, when Jeremy is exhibiting an undesirable behavior, instead of pointing out that behavior, Mr. Chavez would tell Jeremy what he wanted to see happening instead. The emphasis on what is to be done as opposed to what is to be stopped helps the student understand the task demands. This also avoids the frequent dilemma of the child following the teacher's direction to stop a particular behavior but then engaging in an alternate, nonproductive behavior. By telling students with ADHD specifically what should be happening and by making certain the child understands, the stage is set to promote desirable behavior and discipline the child for noncompliance if the student does not follow through.

Give Clear Directions

Compliance and task completion increase when teachers provide simple, single directions and seek feedback. Often teachers are unaware of the complexity of instructions they provide in the classroom and issue a sequence of directions whenever guiding their students (Goldstein, 1995). For many students with ADHD, when a teacher simplifies instructions and then requires the child to repeat the instructions, it leads to increased compliance. When group instructions are given, a teacher should then approach the child with ADHD and request the child to repeat the instruction even if the child has begun to comply.

State Rules

Compliance with instructions and classroom procedure increases when children are required to learn and follow a set of rules (Paine et al., 1983). On an intermittent basis, make certain that the child with ADHD understands the rules of specific environments. For example, before sending Jeremy out to recess, Mr. Chavez would quickly review with him the playground rules and the kind of behavior that is expected. Although this does not guarantee a reduction in impulsive behavior, it does set the stage to help the teacher understand that the child is aware of the rules even though he or she may be unable to consistently follow them.

Provide Cues

Providing the child with ADHD with external visual or auditory cues that do not directly involve teacher intervention can be beneficial in maintaining appropriate classroom behavior. External self-monitored cues help the child be an active participant in behavior change. An auditory or visual cue has been found to be as effective as direct teacher monitoring (Hayes & Nelson, 1983). Providing an auditory cue, such as running a tape on which an auditory stimulus such as a beep reminds the child to make sure that he or she is working, results in increased on-task behavior and academic performance (Blick & Test, 1987). A guideline of steps to follow to develop a self-monitoring program for improving task attention appears in Table 4.3. Figure 4.8 illustrates how to help a student begin a self-monitoring program.

Table 4.3. Self-monitoring program

1. Teacher explains to the class what on- and off-task attention/behavior is and also has class members model what it looks like to be on-task (either doing seat work, group work, or listening to teacher instruction) and off-task.

2. Teacher gives students a form for recording attention-to-task and models how the form is to be marked.

3. Teacher explains that students are to rate themselves as on- or off-task whenever they hear a tone on the audiotape the teacher will play at special times.

4. Have the students practice rating themselves for 5–10 minutes. Verbally reinforce appropriate rating behavior and verbally correct any inappropriate self-rating or behavior.

5. Show students a poster or handout that presents the standards for self-evaluation that the teacher has selected.

6. Have the children practice rating themselves for at least 20 intervals and then have them evaluate their own performance using the presented standards.

7. Explain how the children earn points, tokens, etc. for achieving the self-evaluation standards and explain how you would like them to keep track of those points, etc.

8. Explain how you will conduct honesty or accuracy checks and that, at first, children will earn bonus points for being accurate about their behavior, whether on- or off-task. Use several children to help you role-play an example of how a child can earn points for honestly rating himself on-task or off-task.

9. Conduct a trial run in which students self-monitor for 10–20 minutes, depending on their age, and then evaluate and reward their own behavior in which the teacher conducts accuracy checks.

10. After using the system in this way for a period of time, the teacher can slowly begin to raise the standards required, lengthen the period of self-monitoring, introduce point loss for students who rate themselves inaccurately, and so forth. It is recommended that one change be made at a time.

From Braswell, L., & Bloomquist, M.L. (1991). *Cognitive-behavioral therapy with ADHD children: Child, family and school interventions* (p. 210). New York: Guilford Press; reprinted by permission.

The success of such a system requires the student to be motivated and cooperative. The intervention often works best with older students. Studies have suggested that students who were more accurate in recording their behaviors were more on task than the less accurate recorders (Hallahan & Sapona, 1983). Self-management procedures such as this one have also proven effective in promoting generalization (Stokes & Baer, 1977), a frequently encountered problem in teaching attention and reflection skills.

Structure and Minimize Transitions

Children with ADHD appear to move easiest from formal to informal, focused to unfocused, or structured to unstructured environments. They are the last to begin work but the first to stop. If the teacher allows the child a few extra minutes in the morning to unwind and be off task, it will likely be more difficult to get the child to settle down and focus on task requirements. Even minor interruptions, such as someone entering the classroom, are often sufficient to take the child's attention away from a task. The child with ADHD may be the last child to settle down and return to work after a break such as recess and may have the most trouble with moving from one classroom to another efficiently. Keeping such informal transitions to a minimum, providing additional structure during transitional periods, providing positive reinforcement contingent on the child's abilities to successfully complete the transition, and helping the child with ADHD settle into a formal environment again can have a significant positive impact on overall classroom functioning.

The issue of transitions is even more important in secondary school environments in which this problem is often among the most frequently reported by teachers. Attempt to minimize as much as possible the number of transitions during the day. In some instances, teachers may assign a peer to accompany the student from class to class. For some students, it is necessary to provide a second

Strategies

Language · Images

CONCEPTUAL

Phonology · Orthography · Motor

SYMBOLIC

Attention & Self-Regulation · Emotions · Behavior · Self-Esteem

FOUNDATIONAL

Training and Implementation of Self-Monitoring Program

The following script for a teacher's introduction of self-monitoring and the implementation scenario illustrate the application of the program with Jeremy.

TEACHER: Jeremy, you know how paying attention to your work has been a problem for you. You've heard teachers tell you, "Pay attention," "Get to work," "What are you supposed to be doing?" and things like that. Well, today we're going to start something that will help you help yourself pay attention better. First, we need to make sure that you know what paying attention means. This is what I mean by paying attention. [Teacher models immediate and sustained attention to task.] And this is what I mean by not paying attention. [Teacher models inattentive behaviors such as glancing around and playing with objects.] Now you tell me if I was paying attention. [Teacher models attentive and inattentive behaviors and requires the student to categorize them.] Okay, now let me show you what we're going to do. While you're working, this tape recorder will be turned on. Every once in awhile, you'll hear a little sound like this: [Teacher plays tone on tape.] And when you hear that sound, quietly ask yourself, "Was I paying attention?" If you answer "yes," put a check in this box on your green sheet. If you answer "no," put a check in the other box. Then go right back to work. When you hear the sound again, ask the question, answer it, mark your answer, and go back to work. Now, let me show you how it works. [Teacher models entire procedure.] Now, Jeremy, I bet you can do this. Tell me what you're going to do every time you hear a tone. Let's try it. I'll start the tape and you work on these papers. [Teacher observes Jeremy's implementation of the entire procedure, praises its correct use, and gradually withdraws.]

THE NEXT DAY

A classroom of students are engaged in various activities. The teacher is walking about the room, preparing for her next activity. Some students are sitting in a semicircle facing another teacher and answering questions she poses. Other students are sitting at their desks and writing on papers or workbooks. Jeremy is working at his own desk. The teacher picks up some work pages that have green strips of paper attached to their top.

TEACHER: [Walking up to Jeremy's desk]: Jeremy, here are your seat work pages for today. I'm going to start the tape, and I want you to self-record like you have been doing. What are you going to ask yourself when you hear the beep?

JEREMY: [Taking paper]: Was I paying attention?

TEACHER: Okay, that's it. [Turning away] Will, Balin, and Anne, it's time for spelling group. [Starts a tape recorder and walks toward front of room where three students are gathering.]

JEREMY: [Begins working on his assignments; he is continuing to work when a tone comes from the tape recorder. Jeremy's lips barely move as he almost inaudibly whispers.] Was I paying attention? Yes. [He marks on the green strip of paper and returns to work. Later, another tone comes from the tape recorder. Jeremy whispers.] Was I paying attention? Yes. [He marks on the green strip of paper and returns to work. Later as the students in one group laugh, Jeremy looks up and watches them. While he is looking up, a tone occurs.] Was I paying attention? No. [He marks the strip of paper and begins working again. He continues working, questioning himself when the tone occurs, and recording his answers.]

Figure 4.8. Training and implementation of a self-monitoring program. A pre-made cuing tape is available in Harvey Parker's program *Listen, look, and think: A self-regulation program for children* (ADD Warehouse, 1-800-233-9274, http://www.addwarehouse.com). (From Lloyd, J.W., Landrum, T.J., & Hallahan, D.P. [1991]. Self-monitoring applications for classroom intervention. In H.M. Walker, M.R. Shinn, & G. Stoner [Eds.], *Interventions for achievement and behavior problems* [pp. 310–311]. Silver Spring, MD: National Association of School Psychologists; Copyright 1991 by the National Association of School Psychologists. Reprinted by permission of publisher.)

set of textbooks so that the first set is left in each class and the second set is left at home (Jones, 1994). By doing this, children always have their books when and where they need them.

Provide a Consistent Routine

Children with ADHD appear to function significantly better in a consistent environment. Varying a sequence of daily activities may be confusing, may decrease attention to task, and may hamper work completion. The impulsive, spontaneous, and randomly organized teacher may match very well with a gifted, attentive child. The child with ADHD, however, experiences problems in a classroom lacking a planned routine. Those children tend to become less cognitively efficient as the day progresses, implying that more complex problem-solving tasks should be taught in the morning, with less structured activities in the afternoon (Zagar & Bowers, 1983).

Keep Things Changing

Within the consistent routine, however, the child with ADHD functions significantly better when provided with multiple shortened work periods and opportunities for choice between work tasks and enjoyable reinforcements. Regarding reinforcements, children with ADHD respond to consequences, both positive and negative, in ways that are similar to other children; however, because of their inhibitory problems, they require more immediate, frequent, predictable, and meaningful reinforcers than other children. Reinforcement provided along this schedule does not constitute extortion or blackmail but rather better fits this child's temperament.

Allow Nondisruptive Movement

It is the impulsive, disorganized, subsequently inattentive style of the child with ADHD that primarily interferes with successful classroom performance. A teacher must prioritize classroom goals for the child with ADHD. Most teachers designate organization and work completion as priorities. The child with ADHD, even when taking medication and functioning successfully in the classroom, is likely during the course of the day to exhibit a greater degree of restless and overactive behavior than other children. This pattern of behavior needs not be seen as a detriment if the teacher is flexible and the child is completing work at a rate similar to other students.

Offer Feedback

Teachers frequently observe a direct relationship between the amount of one-to-one instruction that children with ADHD receive and their compliance and task completion. Children with ADHD function significantly better if they can be provided with immediate feedback and increased teacher attention. In some situations, moving a child's desk closer to the teacher is a positive rather than a negative way to facilitate the opportunity to provide functional feedback. In other situations, it is possible to employ adult aides or even children from upper grades as peer tutors during independent work periods.

Pair an Undesirable Task with a Desirable Task

Often students with attentional difficulties increase their on-task behavior when a task that is repetitive and uninteresting is paired with a task that is motivating. For example, Jeremy's third-grade teacher knew that he loved to draw. After he completed several math word problems from his textbook, she encouraged him to draw a picture illustrating one of the problems. This mixture of an undesirable and desirable activity helped Jeremy to complete his work.

Strategies

Language | Images

CONCEPTUAL

Phonology | Orthography | Motor

SYMBOLIC

Attention & Self-Regulation | Emotions | Behavior | Self-Esteem

FOUNDATIONAL

Build Success

Interactions with students with ADHD need to end successfully. Because of the pattern of negative reinforcement that students with ADHD frequently elicit from teachers and the multiple failures they frequently experience, they often end up being punished without being given the opportunity to succeed. Students with ADHD need opportunities to try again, succeed, and be praised. Many children with ADHD develop a view of the world as a place in which they are unable to succeed and, over time, develop feelings of helplessness and hopelessness. A teacher must develop a system to provide frequent positive reinforcement for success, no matter how minor it may be. A good rule of thumb is for teachers to note how often they reinforce all students in the classroom and then make an effort to reinforce the child with ADHD even more. The importance of success in predicting children's future life outcomes, especially those facing adversity, cannot be overstated (Werner, 1994).

Prepare for Changes

Unexpected or unexplained changes often precipitate significant behavior problems in children with ADHD because of their tendency to become overaroused easily and their difficulty in moving from one environment to another. Prepare the child with ADHD for changes by mentioning the amount of time remaining in a work period and by taking the child aside to explain any change in routine that might occur later in the day. Time countdowns and advance warnings help the child with ADHD anticipate changes and respond more appropriately.

Use Preventive Strategies

Anticipate potential problems and develop preventive rather than reactionary strategies. A thorough understanding of a child's skills and abilities facilitates the development of preventive intervention. A teacher may consider the task demands placed on the child with ADHD during a typical day and plan specific strategies for situations in which problems are anticipated. In a preventive model, the teacher intervenes by altering the demands placed on the child and by providing specific educational opportunities to increase competence. Although preventive strategies may not totally avoid problems, the old adage that an ounce of prevention is worth a pound of cure is particularly true with regard to children with ADHD. Planning ahead minimizes the severity of problems and reduces the development of secondary problems that result from repeated failures.

Use Class Time Effectively

With the increased need for structure and routine, planning for the effective use of class time is critical for students with ADHD. Unfortunately, teachers often spend a disproportionate amount of time planning for what to teach and insufficient time considering how they will teach. For example, elementary school teachers have been found to vary significantly in the actual time they use for instruction during the course of the day, from 50% to 90% of the total school time available (for review, see Goldstein, 1995). The following are some additional planning tips for teachers:

- Use an assignment notebook to be signed by the student and a parent.

- When presenting the daily planner schedule to the students, use both visual and verbal cues. Consider color coding the list for easy recall, and add verbal cues for additional support. Then select a student to come forward to orally go over the plan again for the class (Jones, 1994).

- As directions are written on the board, distinguish work by boxing it using a particular color or shape. Also, number information placed on the board and use highlighting or arrows to cue critical words (Jones, 1994).

- Teach students to highlight key directions on their own worksheet or test before they begin working so that the student with ADHD does not start before he or she clearly understands the task. When students with ADHD are required to remain on task for fixed amounts of time, they appear to manage their impulses more effectively (Jones, 1994).

- Arrange class schedules to allow specific times each day for calendar and homework recording. Encourage students to copy homework assignments together and to check on each other to make sure information has been recorded accurately (Goldstein & Goldstein, 1990).

- Provide students with advance schedules on a weekly basis of assignments, tests, and homework. Leave a copy of this advance schedule in the office for parents to check when needed or in case the student needs to see a copy (Jones, 1994). These schedules can also be posted on a teacher's or class web site.

- Post homework assignments daily on a web site so that parents can check them as needed.

Based on an in-depth review of the available literature, Lerner and Lowenthal (1992) suggested that teachers consider the following general guidelines when working with students with ADHD:

- Place the student in the least distracting location in the class. Ideally, this should be in the front of the class, away from doors, windows, air conditioners, heaters, and high-traffic areas.

- Surround the student with good role models, preferably peers that the child views as significant. Encourage peer tutoring and cooperative learning.

- Maintain a high teacher–student ratio whenever possible through the use of aides and volunteers.

- Avoid unnecessary changes in schedules and monitor transitions. When unavoidable disruptions do occur, prepare the student as much as possible by explaining the situation and describing what behaviors are appropriate.

- Maintain eye contact with the student when giving verbal instructions. Make directions clear, concise, and simple. Repeat instructions as needed in a calm voice.

- Combine visual and tactile cues with verbal instructions because, generally, multiple instructional modalities are more effective in maintaining attention and increasing learning.

- Make lists that help the student organize tasks. Have the student check off items when finished. Have students complete study guides when listening to presentations.

- Adapt worksheets so that there is less material on each page.

- Break assignments into small chunks. Provide immediate feedback on each assignment. Allow extra time if needed for the student to finish the assignment.

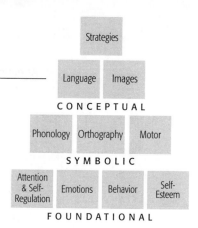

- Ensure that the student has recorded homework assignments each day before leaving school. If necessary, set up a home–school program in which the parents help the child organize and complete the homework.

- If the child has difficulty staying in one place at school, alternate sitting with standing and activities that require moving around during the day.

- Provide activities that require active participation, such as talking through problems or acting out the steps.

- Use aids such as computers, calculators, tape recorders, and DVD players.

- Provide the student with opportunities to demonstrate strengths at school.

- Set up times during which the student can assist peers or tutor younger children.

Adapt the Curriculum

Modifying a curriculum to improve behavior and increase classroom performance is a strategy that is based on an extensive research literature (Dunlap & Kern, 1996). Several chapters in this book provide specific suggestions for helping students with ADHD who also experience problems in school achievement. The following suggestions provide a limited, nonexhaustive list of practical ways to modify curriculum materials that are particularly relevant to students with ADHD. These suggestions and many more can be found in several sources (e.g., Goldstein & Jones, 1998; Jones, 1991, 1994; Mather & Jaffe, 2002; Parker, 1992; Rief, 1993).

Reading

- Break classroom assignments into shorter assignments.

- Divide worksheets and workbooks into fragments or chunks. Encourage students to work on one chunk at a time.

- Have students listen to a reading selection on a tape or CD prior to class discussions.

- Consider having students read together in teams with one reading orally while the other listens. Students may switch roles every paragraph.

- Allow students to select high-interest material for independent reading reports and projects.

- Encourage students to orally discuss what they have read and use a tape recorder to record highlights.

- Use videotapes to present information.

- Use interactive software.

Mathematics

- Encourage students to use graph paper as a way to help with organization of columns.

- Use novel strategies such as "multiplication rap CD and tape" to increase interest in exerting the effort necessary to memorize math facts (see Additional Resources).

- Place visual models of lessons on the blackboard when students are required to work independently in class.

- Consider mnemonic strategies to help students remember math facts or multiple steps in math problems.

- Offer calculators as a means for checking the accuracy of work.

- Use interesting software for math review and drill.

Written Language

- Teach students a simple system to work from a beginning idea and develop connecting thoughts to complete a structure for written projects.

- Offer untimed writing assignments. Break written assignments into parts with periodic checks to make certain that progress is being made.

- Provide a system to facilitate the organization of ideas when written assignments are required.

- Allow credit for hands-on projects and activities.

- Encourage the use of selected, high-interest software programs.

- Encourage the use of manipulatives when studying for spelling tests. Letter tiles or magnetic letters can be used to form words.

- Consider assigning two grades to written projects: one for content and one for spelling, grammar, and so forth (Jones, 1994).

Use Color Coding

The effective use of color to draw attention to relevant, discriminative stimuli has been well documented (Zentall, 1989, 1995; 2005; Zentall & Kruczek, 1988). Children with ADHD attended more readily when color was added to relevant cues on a spelling task (Zentall, 1989). Zentall (1989) demonstrated that when children with ADHD practiced a spelling assignment with all black letters first and then with color added, they outperformed other children in the study (although the converse was not found to be true). Color should be used to enhance rather than distract from tasks. Color highlights key features in repetitive tasks, perhaps increasing interest and motivation. Color cues can also be added to written work, worksheets, and study sheets. In one study, the addition of color had an immediate effect on comprehension across testing assessments with boys who experience comprehension problems as well as ADHD (Belfiore, Grskovic, Murphy, & Zentall, 1996). In the Belfiore and colleagues' study, color highlighting was added to silent reading tasks. The first paragraph appeared in black and white with subsequent paragraphs each appearing in a different color.

Teachers may find these additional tips regarding the use of color to be beneficial (Jones, 1994):

- Color code material to improve associations. For example, many students with ADHD do not remember assignments and related materials. All materials can be color coded. If the student's math book is coded in blue, a blue box can be provided in which math papers are to be placed. Students may also write their math homework with a blue pencil and place a blue dot on their daily calendars when a math test is scheduled.

- Divide weekly vocabulary lists into groups or categories (e.g., all words about animals can be placed in one group, all words that begin with *sh* in another, all words about cars in another). Each group can then be placed on its own color card.

Strategies

Language   Images

C O N C E P T U A L

Phonology   Orthography   Motor

S Y M B O L I C

Attention & Self-Regulation   Emotions   Behavior   Self-Esteem

F O U N D A T I O N A L

- Color code homework folders. Work going home goes in a green folder, work coming back in a red folder.

- When reading a literature book that may involve remembering characters and names, color code characters as they are introduced in the book by placing a removable, colorful star or dot above the character's name.

- Color code symbols when they change on worksheets. For example, make addition signs green and subtraction signs red.

- Alternate regular black markers with the use of colorful magic markers on a white board to highlight specific letter patterns.

- Use color cues on word flash cards to identify patterns with spelling words.

- When studying for a content test such as history, color code factual information. All dates to be remembered can be placed on one color card, important places on another color card, and so forth.

- When studying a foreign language and attempting to increase vocabulary recall, place all nouns on one color card, adjectives on another, and verbs on a third. Vocabulary cards can then be kept in a word box and reviewed often.[1]

CONCLUSION

Teachers play a vital role in shaping the classroom success of children with problems in planning, attention, and impulsivity and hyperactivity. Many but not all of these children qualify for a diagnosis of ADHD. Although the symptoms of ADHD can be significantly reduced with medication, the condition cannot be cured or eliminated. ADHD is a lifelong challenge that must be managed. To be an effective manager, teachers must see the world through the eyes of the student with ADHD, attempt to understand the reasons that problems occur, know specific strategies for intervention, and know how to apply these strategies effectively in the classroom.

---

[1] From Jones (1994). *Attention deficit disorder: Strategies for school-age children.* Oxford, UK: Elsevier; reprinted by permission.

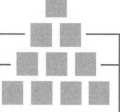

CHAPTER 5 OUTLINE

CHARACTERISTICS OF STUDENTS WITH ANXIETY AND DEPRESSION

WORRY, FEAR, AND ANXIETY

Separation Anxiety
Generalized Anxiety
Specific Phobia
Panic Disorder
Posttraumatic Stress Disorder
Social Anxiety Disorder
School Refusal

DEPRESSION

INTERNALIZING DISORDERS AND COMORBIDITY

ASSESSING ANXIETY AND DEPRESSION IN A CLASSROOM SETTING

INTERVENTIONS FOR STUDENTS WITH ANXIETY AND DEPRESSION

Participant Modeling
Reinforced Practice
Cognitive-Behavorial Interventions

CONCLUSION

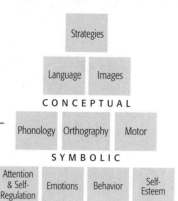

EMOTIONS

UNDERSTANDING AND MANAGING
WORRY AND HOPELESSNESS IN THE CLASSROOM

with Gretchen Schoenfield

Angela performed generally well academically and had good peer relationships. However, she became agitated and avoided situations in which she was required to read or speak aloud in class. Angela's sixth-grade class was going to be involved in a performance for parents' weekend, and all students were expected to participate. Angela's teacher reserved 30 minutes each day to rehearse. When rehearsals began, Angela became distressed each morning before attending school. Ms. Jaffe, Angela's teacher, noticed that Angela suddenly appeared to avoid participating in rehearsals. She took frequent restroom breaks and would complain of an upset stomach or a headache each day. Angela also appeared increasingly anxious, was easily agitated, and seemed to withdraw from peers. Ms. Jaffe completed the 10 items from the Emotions section of the Building Blocks Questionnaire (see Figure 5.1) and checked "Frequently" for many of the questionnaire items that corresponded to the previously described behaviors.

In contrast to Angela, whose behavior changes appeared rather swift or abrupt, Anthony was always described by his teachers as rather quiet, shy, and uninvolved. He completed classwork, but teachers commented that he was often alone on the playground. During Anthony's fifth-grade year, his mother was hospitalized for an extended period of time due to an ongoing medical condition. In class, Anthony's teacher, Ms. Jones, noticed that he became increasingly more withdrawn, quiet, and inattentive. The quality of his work declined and he often appeared sad. One day, Ms. Jones found Anthony sitting alone on the playground, crying. Though she was certain he was worried about his mother's health, he denied this concern, claiming that he did not know why he was sad. Ms. Jones completed the 10 items from the Emotions section of the Building Blocks Questionnaire (see Figure 5.2). She checked *Frequently* for many of the items related to happiness and the worsening of Anthony's mood. She felt that perhaps he was worried about school, so she answered *Sometimes* to this question. She also checked *Sometimes* for the "Cries" item, indicating that Anthony was observed to cry during the school day on occasion. She noted that although Anthony was not disruptive with friends, he seemed to be socially isolated; accordingly, she checked *Frequently* for the items about isolation from peers. She checked *Rarely* to the question about becoming angry quickly. Her main concerns were that a once quiet, somewhat shy child now appeared to be quite unhappy, disengaged, and depressed. Both Angela's and Anthony's behavior can best be characterized as internalized. In response to the stressors in their lives, they appeared to be becoming more isolated, withdrawn, and distressed.

EMOTIONS	Rarely	Sometimes	Frequently
Appears to be sad			✓
Changes mood quickly		✓	
Worries excessively about school			✓
Complains about school tasks		✓	
Cries	✓		
Seems anxious			✓
Becomes angry quickly	✓		
Isolates self from peers			✓
Seems bored or disinterested			✓
Puts forth little effort			✓

Figure 5.1. Building Blocks Questionnaire for Angela: Emotions block.

Because children spend a significant part of their waking hours in the classroom throughout the year, teachers are in an ideal position to spot the warning signs and identify children suffering from worry and feelings of hopelessness. Most teachers are very competent in identifying children who exhibit disruptive behavior problems; unfortunately, they are much less skilled at recognizing those suffering from more subtle internalizing disorders such as those related to worry and hopelessness (Layne, Bernstein, & March, 2006).

Other reasons beyond the fact that these adverse feelings are not easy to observe make it difficult for classroom educators to accurately identify children struggling from worry and hopelessness. Teachers are not in a position to observe symptoms affecting sleep, appetite, or inner thoughts. The more subtle symptoms of anxiety tend not to be disruptive; therefore, children experiencing anxiety may not be referred for help until their anxious symptoms begin to affect their schoolwork. Some of these symptoms, such as fidgeting, off-task behavior, or

EMOTIONS	Rarely	Sometimes	Frequently
Appears to be sad			✓
Changes mood quickly			✓
Worries excessively about school		✓	
Complains about school tasks		✓	
Cries		✓	
Seems anxious			✓
Becomes angry quickly	✓		
Isolates self from peers			✓
Seems bored or disinterested		✓	
Puts forth little effort			✓

Figure 5.2. Building Blocks Questionnaire for Anthony: Emotions block.

failure to complete work, initially may be interpreted as disruptive problems such as inattention or noncompliance. The teachers' misperception of the problem and subsequent attempts at punitive or even reinforcing interventions stand a significant chance of further fueling the student's anxiety.

This chapter provides an overview of internalizing problems related to worry and hopelessness, which at their extreme fall under the diagnostic categories of anxiety disorders and depression. Characteristics of various anxiety disorders and depression are discussed as well as empirically supported interventions that can be implemented within classroom settings.

CHARACTERISTICS OF STUDENTS WITH ANXIETY AND DEPRESSION

Unlike the disruptive behaviors that are usually more obvious and that lead teachers to seek consulting advice, for problems of worry and hopelessness, teachers must frequently screen students. Teachers should be aware of a set of behaviors that might indicate red flags and the need for further help. These behaviors include the following:

- *Somatic complaints*: If a student often complains of headaches, stomachaches, or other physical aches and pains, teachers should be alert to the possibility that the student may be experiencing feelings of worry or hopelessness. Frequent requests to go to the nurse's office for various ailments are clear signals that something is wrong.

- *Poor frustration tolerance*: Students suffering from hopelessness and worry often lack resilience to distress and disappointment. Some students may be perfectionistic and become tearful or angry over minor mistakes or challenges.

- *Lethargy or listlessness*: Students who fall asleep in class or appear to lack energy or enthusiasm for school activities may be suffering from depression. In teens, these symptoms may also signal drug or alcohol abuse. In either case, they are cause for concern and should be further evaluated.

- *Social isolation and/or peer problems*: Children who experience worry and hopelessness are particularly likely to have difficulty with friendships. Although some may gain peer acceptance and be well-liked, many tend to be ignored.

- *Coexisting conditions*: Children identified as having attention-deficit/hyperactivity disorder (ADHD), learning disabilities (LD), or medical problems may be at a particularly high risk for experiencing worry and hopelessness.

WORRY, FEAR, AND ANXIETY

Worry and fear are typical in childhood and adolescence and are largely considered to be an aspect of typical development. However, fear and worry that persists over time, disrupts daily functioning, and is an exaggerated reaction to situational demands may ultimately lead to impaired behavior consistent with the clinical diagnoses of anxiety and depression. Accordingly, teachers, counselors, social workers, school psychologists, and other school personnel need to be aware of some fundamental differences between those fears that are considered to be transitory and developmentally appropriate and those fears that may require clinical attention.

113

Worry, fear, and *anxiety* are terms that are often used interchangeably in the research literature. However, these three phenomena appear to be best understood as falling along a continuum, with worry reflecting the mildest problems followed by fear and finally anxiety. *Worry* reflects the inability to confidently predict a positive outcome for an upcoming event. It results from repeatedly thinking about the possible negative outcome for the prescribed event and being unable to substitute a more optimistic outlook. For some individuals, worry may not be significantly impairing or may not lead to avoidance.

Fear has been conceptualized as a developmentally appropriate reaction to an actual or perceived threat (Ollendick, King, & Muris, 2002). *Anxiety* might be best defined as a sense of apprehension or unease that is often related to the individual's expectation of some kind of threat to his or her physical or emotional well-being (Barlow, 2002). This sense of apprehension may be focused on an object, situation, or activity. For some individuals, anxiety is pervasive or free-floating and may not be tied to a specific stimulus. Anxiety disorders can greatly interfere with daily functioning, affecting academic performance and peer relationships (Last, Hanson, & Franco, 1997; McGee & Stanton, 1990). Anxiety disorders in childhood have also been associated with depression, substance abuse, and chronic anxiety in adulthood (Liebowitz, Gorman, Fyer, & Klein, 1985; Wittchen, Stein, & Kessler, 1999).

The *Diagnostic and Statistical Manual of Psychiatric Disorders, Fourth Edition, Text Revision* (*DSM-IV-TR*; American Psychiatric Association [APA], 2000) has adopted the following criteria (Marks, 1969; Miller, 1972) to differentiate between typical worries or fears and clinical anxiety. Anxiety may warrant clinical attention under the following conditions:

- It is out of proportion to the demands of the situation.

- It cannot be explained or reasoned away.

- It is beyond voluntary control.

- It leads to avoidance of the feared situation.

- It is beyond what is expected, given the child's age and developmental level.

- It disrupts the child's daily functioning.

- The child cannot quickly recover from a fearful or anxiety-provoking experience.

Anxiety can affect individuals through three different response channels: physiological, cognitive, and behavioral (Lang, 1968). Physiological or physical components are generally considered to reflect activity in the autonomic nervous system, which—among its other roles—is responsible for regulation of internal body functions. Thus, as reported by Barrios and Hartmann (1988), symptoms of perspiration, stomach pain, trembling, and even bed-wetting (enuresis) or tics can be suggestive of anxiety problems. Anxiety has been associated with headaches and fatigue as well.

A variety of cognitions may lead to anxiety in children (Kendall, Hudson, Choudhury, Webb, & Pimentel, 2005). Such cognitions, often referred to as *cognitive distortions,* reflect illogical thought processes and can lead to erroneous conclusions and fuel anxious responses. For example, Kendall, Stark, and Adam (1990) reported that depressed youngsters view themselves as less capable than nondepressed youngsters. Interestingly, this judgment is not corroborated by teachers, who tend to view both groups equally. This research indicates that children with internalizing problems tend to not only distort their capabilities but underestimate them as well.

Behavioral responses are essentially those observable behaviors that are associated with being in the presence of a feared stimulus. Examples of these responses may include avoidance of a situation associated with anxiety, overt irritability and aggression when facing a feared stimulus, or even observable symptoms attributed to physiological arousal, such as trembling.

In this section, a number of specific types of anxiety problems—separation anxiety, generalized anxiety, specific phobia, panic disorder, posttraumatic stress disorder, social anxiety disorder, and school refusal—are reviewed. Anxiety disorders fall into several diagnostic categories within the *DSM-IV-TR* (APA, 2000), described next (see Table 5.1 for a summary of anxiety disorders, according to DSM-IV-TR criteria and the common characteristics of children with fears and anxieties).

Separation Anxiety

The essential feature of this childhood problem is excessive anxiety concerning separation from a primary caregiver. Separation anxiety is a typical developmental phenomenon that occurs from approximately 7 months of age to the early preschool years. Gittelman (1984) suggested that separation anxiety may appear as panic. The child secondarily may report feeling homesick even during short separations or may worry about potential dangers that threaten the family when separated. These characteristics may occur separately or in combination (Gittelman, 1984).

To be diagnosed with separation anxiety disorder, a child must experience at least three of the following eight symptomatic problems that reflect developmentally inappropriate and excessive anxiety concerning separation from home or an attachment figure (APA, 2000):

Table 5.1.   Characteristics of anxiety disorders in children and adolescents

Anxiety disorder	Characteristics/symptoms
Panic disorder	Intense fear in the absence of an actual threat, accompanied by at least four of the following symptoms: palpitations, sweating, trembling, shortness of breath, feeling of choking, chest pain, nausea, dizziness or light-headedness, fear of losing control, fear of dying, and/or a burning or itching sensation
Specific phobia	Persistent fear of an identifiable object or situation, typically resulting in one or more of the following anxiety responses: avoidance of anticipated harm, feelings of loss of control, or a physiological response to a feared stimulus. In young or elementary school-age children, symptoms may include crying, tantrums, freezing, or clinging behaviors
Social phobia	Fearful or anxious anticipation of being negatively evaluated (such as while reading aloud in class, taking timed tests in school, or performing math problems in front of the class with the teacher watching), resulting in one or more of the following: avoidance of feared situation, headaches or stomach aches, panic attacks, and crying
Generalized anxiety disorder	Excessive anxiety and worry about several events or activities, with at least one of the following symptoms: restlessness, fatigue, difficulty concentrating, irritability, perfectionism, and seeking excessive approval
School refusal	Anxiety and avoidance due to the anticipation of attending school, excessive absences, leaving school early, refusing to attend, and occasionally somatic symptoms
Separation anxiety	Excessive anxiety due to separation from the home or from an attachment figure, social withdrawal, sadness, apathy, difficulty with concentration

Reprinted with permission from the Diagnostic and Statistical Manual of Mental Disorder, Fourth Edition, Text Revision, (Copyright 2000). American Psychiatric Association.

- Worry about losing or possible harm befalling the attachment figure

- Persistent worry that a traumatic event will lead to separation from the major attachment figure

- Refusal to attend school due to fear of separation

- Reluctance to be alone without the attachment figure

- Reluctance to go to sleep without being near the attachment figure or to sleep away from home

- Nightmares involving the theme of separation

- Complaints of physical symptoms when separation from the attachment figure is anticipated or occurs

- Excessive distress when separation from the figure occurs or is anticipated

For all of these symptoms, separation from home may provoke as much anxiety as separation from the attachment figure. These symptoms must occur for at least 4 weeks; be manifested before the child reaches the age of 18; cause distress or impaired functioning in social, academic, or other important areas of life; and not occur primarily as the result of a pervasive developmental disorder, schizophrenia, or psychotic disorder. The estimate of separation disorder within the general population of school-age children is approximately 4.1% (Shear, Jin, Ruscio, Walters, & Kessler, 2006).

Developmental differences exist in the manner in which separation anxiety is expressed. Children who are 5–8 years of age are more likely to refuse to attend school because of concern about unrealistic harm to attachment figures. Children who are 9–12 years of age frequently report distress at the time of separation. Nightmares concerning separation are commonly described by young children but are rarely reported after age 9 (Francis, Last, & Strauss, 1987). Finally, young teenagers (13–16 years of age) most commonly refuse to attend school and develop a variety of somatic complaints.

The overlap of symptoms between separation anxiety and school phobia may make distinction in diagnosis difficult. The hallmark of separation anxiety is excessive anxiety in relation to separation from a major attachment figure, whereas generalized anxiety disorder appears to be characterized by excessive anxiety about anticipated events (Foa et al., 2005; Mattison & Bagnato, 1987). In children with school phobia, anxiety appears to be focused specifically on the school environment and is usually not generalized to other settings (Last, 1989). Thus, for the child with separation anxiety, the problem that generates worrisome thoughts is not so much attending school as it is being separated from home or a parent or caregiver.

Generalized Anxiety

Children with generalized anxiety experience a sensation of anxiety or worry that is not unitarily focused on a specific object, stressor, or situation. This population of children might be best described as "worrisome." They worry about future events, past behavior, and their own competence. They frequently exhibit somatic complaints, are self-conscious, feel tense, cannot relax, and appear to need frequent reassurance.

Generalized anxiety appears to be present at an older age than separation anxiety disorder (Last, Hersen, Kazdin, Finkelstein, & Strauss, 1987). Researchers have typically thought that an equal number of boys and girls experience

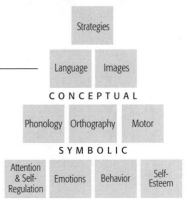

overanxious symptoms, with an overrepresentation of middle- and upper-income families. Bowen, Oxford, and Boyle (1990), however, reported a female predominance for this disorder and did not find that generalized anxiety was associated with socioeconomic class.

Overanxious children appear more aware of their symptoms than do children with separation anxiety. Older children with generalized anxiety appear to worry more about past behavior than younger children with this disorder (Strauss, Lease, Last, & Francis, 1988). Prevalence of generalized anxiety in school-age children is approximately 2%–4% (Anderson, Williams, McGee, & Silva, 1987; Bowen et al., 1990).

Specific Phobia

A specific phobia is the perceptible, isolated, and persistent fear of a particular stimulus. It is distinguished from fear of separation, humiliation, or embarrassment in social settings as well as from panic attack. The diagnosis of simple phobia is made only if the avoidant behavior interferes with typical functioning. Because of children's varied cognitive levels and development, it may be difficult to determine whether a child recognizes the irrational nature of his or her phobia (Silverman & Nelles, 1990). Temporary fears and anxieties are common in children. Many are age- or time-specific. From a developmental perspective, they may originate with startle reactions to certain stimuli during infancy or toddler years and progress to specific phobias and, in some cases, social anxiety during adolescence (Ollendick et al., 2002). Though mild fears are quite common in children of all ages, girls report fears more often than do boys (Ollendick, Yang, King, Dong, & Akande, 1996). Prevalence of specific phobia in children is approximately 4% (Essau, Conradt, & Petermann, 2000).

From the time Anthony was 2 years old to the time he reached the third grade, he was extremely afraid of dogs. His parents could not explain this fear, and it did not seem to generalize to other animals. If a dog were approaching on the sidewalk, Anthony would dart out across the street to avoid getting close to it. With increasing maturation and through a slow, gradual introduction to calm and friendly dogs, Anthony's fear was reduced.

Children's fears do appear to change as they mature cognitively and physically and as their experiences with the world increase (Muris, Merckelbach, deJong, & Ollendick, 2002). Preschoolers are usually fearful of menacing animals and the dark. Fears of imaginary characters may also occur and are typically a result of difficulty at this age in distinguishing reality from fantasy. As children mature, these fears systematically decrease (Maurer, 1965). By adolescence, anxieties tend to reflect a child's concerns about his or her competence in school and with friends and family. The sequence of these changes appears fairly constant for most children, even independent of cultural experience (Miller, 1983).

Ollendick, Matson, and Helsel (1985) described five distinct factor-generated clusters of children's fears:

1. Fear of failure and criticism from adults

2. Fear of the unknown

3. Fear of injury and small animals

4. Fear of danger and death

5. Medical fears

Table 5.2. Normative data on childhood fears and phobias

Age	Fears and phobias
0–6 months	Loss of support from caregiver, loud noises
7–12 months	Fear of strangers; sudden, unexpected, and looming objects
1 year	Separation from parent, mild injury, strangers
2 years	A multitude of fears including loud noises (e.g., sirens/alarms, ducks, thunder), animals (e.g., large dogs), dark rooms, separation from parent, scary objects (e.g., clown doll), loud machines (e.g., vacuum cleaner), change in personal environment, strangers
3 years	Masks, darkness, animals, separation from parent, being left alone
4 years	Separation from parent, animals, darkness, noises (including at night), insects
5 years	Animals, "bad" people, dark, thunder, separation from parent, bodily harm, ghosts
6 years	Supernatural beings (e.g., ghosts, witches, ghouls), bodily injuries, thunder and lightning, sleeping or staying alone, separation from parent
7–8 years	Supernatural beings, darkness, fears based on such media events as natural disasters or acts of war, staying alone, bodily injury, and school performance
9–12 years	School tests and examinations, school performance, social performance, bodily injury, terrorism, nuclear war, natural disasters, physical appearance, thunder and lightning, death

Note: From *Treating children's fears and phobias: A behavioral approach* (p. 2), by R.J. Morris & T.R. Kratochwill, 1983. Elmsford, NY: Pergamon Press; adapted by permission.

The ten most common fears of children have been reported as being hit by a car, not being able to breathe, a bombing attack, getting burned by a fire, falling from a high place, a burglar breaking into the home, an earthquake, death, getting poor grades, and snakes (Ollendick, King, & Frary, 1989). Table 5.2 provides a list of common phobias in children at various developmental levels.

Specific phobias represent a marked and persistent fear that is excessive or unreasonable and precipitated by the presence or anticipation of a specific object or situation. Exposure to the fear stimulus produces an immediate anxiety response that may be expressed in children by crying, tantrums, freezing, or clinging. The fear is often excessive and unreasonable, and the fear stimulus is avoided. Often the avoidance interferes with the child's typical routine. Specific types of phobias in the *DSM-IV-TR* (APA, 2000) include animal, natural environment, blood, injection, injury, situational, and generalized other. Generalized other phobias in children include avoidance of loud sounds or costumed characters. For example, Anthony would often cover his ears with his hands when students clapped in a school assembly.

Panic Disorder

The essential feature of panic disorder is discrete panic attacks. A panic attack is defined as an instance of intense fear in the absence of an actual threat and is associated with at least four of the following symptoms: palpitations, sweating, trembling, shortness of breath, sensation of choking, chest pain, nausea, dizziness or light-headedness, fear of losing control, fear of dying, and/or an itching or burning sensation with no apparent cause (APA, 2000). Panic disorder is characterized by recurrent panic attacks over a period of at least 1 month accompanied by excessive worry about experiencing another panic attack. At times, certain events may precipitate these attacks. More often, they occur unexpectedly for unexplained reasons. Panic disorder reportedly occurs in approximately 3% of school-age children (Goodwin & Gotlieb, 2004).

Posttraumatic Stress Disorder

Posttraumatic stress disorder (PTSD) occurs with greater frequency than first thought in children and adolescents. Nonetheless, this disorder has been studied

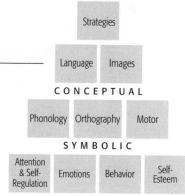

primarily among adults exposed to repeated and significant stress, such as combat veterans (Peterson, Prout, & Schwarz, 1991). Symptoms typical of depression including insomnia, poor concentration, and irritability are also characteristic of PTSD. In addition, symptoms associated with anxiety, such as nightmares, avoidance, and an exaggerated startle response often occur in PTSD as well.

Children exposed to a single violent event have been reported to develop posttraumatic symptoms (Pynoos et al., 1987). In this study, children in greater proximity to a sniper attack reported more severe symptomatic problems. Studies suggest that PTSD is common among child abuse victims. For example, among a sample of 31 sexually abused children, 48% met the criteria for PTSD (McLeer, Deblinger, Atkins, Foa, & Ralphe, 1988). Kiser and colleagues (1988) reported that symptomatic problems such as sexual acting out, developing sudden fears, and specific trauma-related fears were found among a group of young children who purportedly had been sexually abused at a child care center.

Criteria for PTSD include experiencing, witnessing, or being confronted with an event or events involving actual or threatened serious injury or death. An individual's response must involve intense fear, hopelessness, or horror. In children, this may be expressed instead by disorganized or agitated behavior. Criteria for PTSD, according to the *DSM-IV-TR* (APA, 2000), include the event being re-experienced through at least one of the following: intrusive recollections of the event, including images, thoughts, or perceptions; distressing dreams of the event; feeling as if the event is recurring; psychological distress at exposure to internal or external cues that symbolize or resemble the event; and a physiological reaction to those cues. In children, repetitive play may occur in which themes or aspects of the trauma are expressed as well as frightening dreams without recognizable content. In addition, at least three symptoms consistent with avoidance of stimuli and associated with the traumatic event must be observed, including

- Avoidance of thoughts, feelings, or conversations

- Efforts to avoid activities, places, or people

- An inability to recall important aspects of the event

- Markedly diminished interest or participation in usually enjoyable activities

- Feelings of detachment from others

- Restricted affect

- A sense of foreshortened future

In addition, at least two persistent symptoms of increased arousal must be present that were not present prior to the trauma, including difficulty falling or staying asleep, irritability or outbursts of anger, difficulty concentrating, hypervigilance, or an exaggerated startle response.

Social Anxiety Disorder

Social anxiety disorder (or social phobia) is one of the most common anxiety disorders in children, with an estimated prevalence of 5%–15% in the general population of school-age children (Kashdan & Herbert, 2001). Social anxiety is characterized by a persistent fear of embarrassment or evaluation during social, academic, or performance situations over a period of at least 6 months (APA, 2000). A child with social anxiety may experience symptoms of worry or anxious anticipation or may avoid a situation entirely. The anxiety response typically interferes with the child's daily functioning. Social anxiety also has been associated with somatic complaints such as headaches, upset stomach, and panic attacks.

Situations that commonly elicit these responses can be either academic or social. For example, a child with social anxiety may appear fearful or anxious when asked to read a report aloud; when taking a test; when asked to complete a math or other problem up at the chalkboard; or when required to participate in school activities, such as plays or skits. In some cases, the anxiety could be associated with LD or relative difficulties with certain academic skills, such as reading, math, or writing, as well as with taking examinations. In other cases, a child with social anxiety may fear or avoid social situations, such as unstructured playtime, gatherings, or classroom group activities.

Social anxiety manifested in academic skill areas may be related to a variety of circumstances. For example, math anxiety may be associated with learning difficulties, quality of instruction, and the influence of negative performance expectations (Wigfield & Meece, 1988). Research suggests that general anxiety is highly correlated with reading anxiety (Tsovili, 2004). When social anxiety is associated with a particular academic skill and the student's performance is poor, a comprehensive evaluation may be necessary to determine whether LD is present.

Social anxiety also may affect a child's performance on examinations, independent of anxiety associated with a specific academic subject. Children experiencing test anxiety may have difficulty focusing, organizing thoughts, or recalling material even when they have prepared sufficiently for the examination (Goonan, 2003). Reported prevalence of test anxiety is highly variable, ranging from 5% to 41% within the general population of school-age children (Ball, 1995; Beidel, 1991; Turner, Beidel, Hughes, & Turner, 1993).

School Refusal

Children experiencing school refusal (or school phobia) have anxiety symptoms associated with attending school. Frequent absences may occur as well as early departures and refusals to attend (Kearney & Silverman, 1996). School refusal is generally not considered to be a discrete anxiety disorder but rather a constellation of behaviors with a range of underlying causes. Separation anxiety is often associated with school refusal, especially in young children. Social anxiety is a common cause of school refusal in older children. In addition, school refusal has been associated with learning difficulties, difficulties at home, and instances of being bullied (Kearney & Albano, 2004). Estimates of school refusal are approximately 1%–5% of school-age children, occurring more commonly in children under the age of 12 (King, Heyne, Tonge, Gullone, & Ollendick, 2001).

DEPRESSION

Concerns about childhood depression have been increasingly represented in the research literature (Costello, Erklani, & Angold, 2006). Depression is best conceptualized as reflecting a continuum of mild variations in affect to severe mood swings and impairment in everyday functioning (Matson, 1989). Depressive symptoms are characterized by sadness; listlessness; a lack of energy; sleeping or eating problems; inconsistent school performance; diminished socialization; a change in attitude toward family, school, and community; physical complaints; loss of energy; and low self-esteem (Luby et al., 2002). Depression is also associated with flat affect, inability to find pleasurable activities, feelings of guilt, social isolation, impaired schoolwork, low energy level, and suicidal thoughts (Poznanski, 1982). Depressed children also often complain of somatic symptoms without an organic basis. Younger children in particular may appear irritable,

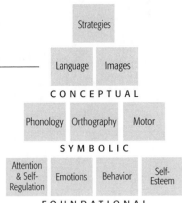

inattentive, or angry or may cry excessively. Prevalence of depressive disorders in children is approximately 2%, whereas depression in adolescents is appreciably higher at 4%–8% (Angold, Egger, Erklani, & Keeler, 2005).

Categories of depressive disorders in children according to the *DSM-IV-TR* (2000) criteria include major depressive disorder, dysthymic disorder, and depressive disorder not otherwise specified. To be diagnosed with major depressive disorder, a child must have five of the nine symptoms listed next (with at least one of those symptoms being depressed mood or loss of interest or pleasure) for a period of at least 2 weeks, and these symptoms must represent a change from the child's previous functioning (*DSM-IV-TR*, APA, 2000). The nine symptoms consist of the following:

- Depressed or irritable mood

- Markedly diminished interest or pleasure in activities

- Weight or appetite loss or gain

- Insomnia or hypersomnia

- Psychomotor agitation or retardation

- Fatigue or loss of energy

- Feelings of worthlessness or excessive guilt

- Decreased ability to think, concentrate, or make decisions

- Recurrent thoughts of death or suicide or a suicide attempt or plan

Major depressive episodes are characterized as mild, moderate, or severe, with or without psychotic features, and can occur in single or recurrent periods.

Criteria for dysthymic disorder are of particular interest for childhood educators. This disorder is defined by depressed mood or irritability for most of the day, occurring more days than not, and for children and adolescents, is indicated by subjective accounts or observations by others for at least a 1-year period. During depressed periods, at least three of the following symptoms must be reported: low self-esteem or self-confidence; feelings of inadequacy; feelings of pessimism; despair or generalized loss of interest in pleasurable activities; social withdrawal; chronic fatigue; feelings of guilt or brooding; subjective feelings of irritability or anger; decreased activity or productivity; and difficulty with concentration, memory, or indecisiveness. These symptoms should not be accounted for by major depressive episodes, and the child or adolescent should not have had a major depressive period during the year these symptoms have been observed.

Symptoms characteristic of depression may also be indicators of other childhood disorders, including anxiety and disruptive behavior. Angold, Costello, and Erklani (1999) found that nearly two thirds of children with major depressive disorder have at least one other affective disorder. Other researchers have observed this pattern, as well (Jacobson, Lahey, & Strauss, 1983; Norvell & Towle, 1986). Norvell and Towle also found several items on the Children's Depression Inventory (Kovacs, 1983) indicative of disruptive problems. Other items on this inventory, such as depressed mood, negative self-thoughts, and social withdrawal, appeared to be indicative of internalizing rather than externalizing disabilities. As Matson concluded, the "data therefore seemed to support the hypothesis that depression is a distinct disorder, although not entirely separate from other conditions" (1989, p. 9).

School performance has been suggested as a sensitive indicator of sudden onset depression in children (Tesiny, Lefkowitz, & Gordon, 1980), but consultants must be aware that the school skills of children with affective problems do not appear to differ from those of other children. Variations in intelligence or LD do not appear to be more prevalent in groups of children with or without depression (Stark, Livingston, Laurent, & Cardenas, 1993; Weinberg & Rehmet, 1983). Although nonverbal behavior among depressed adults reflects a characteristic pattern, this is not necessarily the case with children or adolescents. However, there do appear to be characteristic nonverbal signs of depression in children, such as facial expression, body movements, head and arm gestures used while speaking, head shaking, and tearfulness (Kazdin, Sherick, Esveldt-Dawson, & Rancurello, 1985). These authors found equivalent symptomatic problems in boys and girls, although boys demonstrated less eye contact, fewer smiles, and flatter intonation in speech.

Although some studies have found depressed children to be less effective social problem solvers (Marx & Schulze, 1991), other studies have failed to demonstrate social problem-solving impairments in children who are depressed when compared with their peers without depression (Joffe, Dobson, Fine, Marriage, & Haley, 1990). Marton, Connolly, Kutcher, and Cornblum (1993) found, in a population of 38 adolescent outpatients with depression, a unique impairment in social self-evaluation. These youth appeared to be excessively critical in evaluating themselves in the social realm. This tendency appeared to contribute to their problems in socialization as well as to the maintenance of a generalized state of dissatisfaction with relationships.

INTERNALIZING DISORDERS AND COMORBIDITY

Kendall and Watson (1989) described a number of overlapping symptoms in anxiety and depression, such as irritability, agitation, restlessness, concentration difficulty, insomnia, and fatigue. The 1991 normative data of the Child Behavior Checklist (Achenbach & Edelbrock, 1991) reported an internalizing factor of anxious and depressed symptoms co-occurring rather than separating out. Therefore, especially in children under the age of 12, symptoms of anxiety, worry, and depression are likely to overlap and frequently present together.

Other disorders or difficulties that are reported to commonly co-occur with depression include ADHD, relative learning difficulties or LD, and substance abuse. Pliszka (1992) evaluated 107 children meeting the criteria for ADHD. This population was subdivided into those with and without a comorbid anxiety disorder. The two groups with ADHD were then compared with each other and with a control group. The children with ADHD exhibiting anxiety problems appeared to be less impulsive and/or hyperactive than those with ADHD alone. However, they continued to be more impaired than the control group on measures of classroom observation and a continuous performance task. A trend existed in which the children with ADHD who were experiencing anxiety problems demonstrated fewer symptoms of conduct disorder than the ADHD-alone group. A recent study evaluating psychopathology among children repeatedly abused by a parent found that 35% suffered from separation anxiety disorder. Of this group, three quarters also demonstrated symptoms consistent with ADHD. These authors concluded that the relationship between ADHD and separation anxiety in this population of children warranted additional studies. They hypothesized that preexisting ADHD somehow predisposes abused children to separation anxiety or that symptoms of distractibility and poor concentration are secondary to the anxiety (Livingston, Lawson, & Jones, 1993).

More than 60% of individuals with panic disorder or agoraphobia (anxiety disorders) with panic attacks have been reported as having a history of depression (Breier, Charney, & Heninger, 1984; Evans et al., 2005). In this group, half experienced major depression prior to the onset of anxiety symptoms, a pattern

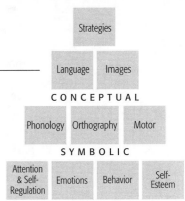

somewhat different from that reported by Kovacs, Paulauskas, Gatsonis, and Richards (1988). Puig-Antich and Rabinovich (1986) reported that 30% of children with major depression experience a concomitant anxiety disorder, most frequently separation anxiety. A comorbidity of 30% between anxiety disorders and ADHD in both epidemiological and clinic samples has been reported (Anderson et al., 1987; Last et al., 1987). In addition, higher rates of ADHD appear among high-risk children with parents experiencing anxiety disorders (Sylvester, Hyde, & Reichsler, 1987).

Interestingly, researchers have reported symptoms of agoraphobia in preschoolers with predominant anxiety symptoms (Wolfson, Fields, & Rose, 1987). Cohen and Biederman (1988) described an unusual pair of identical twins with ADHD. One developed agoraphobia without major depression; the other developed major depression without agoraphobia or other anxiety symptoms.

Eating disorders and substance abuse have been frequently reported to co-occur with depression (Attie, Brooks-Gunn, & Petersen, 1990). Extreme weight and excessive eating have been reported as covarying with depression beyond a chance level as well (Richards, Boxer, Petersen, & Albrecht, 1990). In girls, poor body image may lead to eating disorders and then to depression (Peterson et al., 1993).

The majority of suicide victims who were depressed prior to committing suicide have been reported as having experienced a primary affective disorder. More than 80% of a population of suicide victims studied by Brent and colleagues (1993) had received a diagnosis of affective disorder, and 31% of this group had been depressed for less than 3 months. Previous suicide attempts, as well as suicidal and homicidal ideation, were associated with adolescent suicide; and substance abuse and conduct disorder also appeared to increase the risk of suicide among depressed adolescents. Substance abuse was a more significant risk factor when it occurred comorbidly with an affective illness than when alone. The most significant single risk factor for suicide is major depression. The risk of anxiety disorder as predictive of suicide at this time is unclear.

Assessing Anxiety and Depression in a Classroom Setting

Because behavioral symptoms of hopelessness and worry tend to be nondisruptive, particularly in their earliest stages, teachers and other school personnel need to be well-informed about the warning signs. If a child appears to be struggling with these difficulties, a necessary first step is to record observational data. Anecdotal notes or even a daily log completed over a 1- or 2-week period can be helpful in identifying and defining the problem. Figure 5.3 illustrates the anecdotal notes Ms. Jones completed about Anthony over a week's time.

Classroom teachers are not responsible for labeling a child's behavior as being caused by depression or anxiety; they cannot and should not place themselves in the position of therapists. A teacher's role is to describe what they observe and then to organize that information to present to parents and school consultants. Moreover, teachers must view themselves as important allies in detecting problems and concerns as well as in helping students feel supported and accepted each day.

INTERVENTIONS FOR STUDENTS WITH ANXIETY AND DEPRESSION

As noted, anxiety and depression reflect a common, underlying emotional distress. Thus, certain strategies that help students who experience anxiety will likely be beneficial for students with depression (Barrett, 2004). For example, cognitive-behavioral therapy (CBT), discussed later in this chapter, has demonstrated effectiveness in treating both anxiety and depression in children.

Monday

Anthony came into school this morning and seemed unhappy and was quiet. He worked for a period of time but then put his head on his desk. I had a difficult time motivating him to work.

At recess Anthony was observed to walk alone and didn't play with anyone during lunch.

Tuesday

Anthony brought his pet turtle for Show and Tell. He seemed quite excited and the other students were interested in what he had to say. Overall, he seemed to have a good day.

Wednesday

Although I had hoped Anthony would continue to have a good week, he got into a pushing match with two other students in line. Anthony complained that they started it and seemed to have a very difficult time getting back in control of his emotions. I sent him to the office to help the secretary for the last 2 hours of the day.

Thursday

Anthony sat by himself during free time. I asked him to help me arrange the books on our library shelf. He worked diligently on this task.

Friday

Once again, Anthony looked sad all day. I asked him if he was worried about something, and he said that he wasn't. I am going to consult with the school psychologist and try to set up a meeting with Anthony's mother. We must find some ways to help Anthony feel better in school.

Figure 5.3. Daily log and anecdotal notes about Anthony as completed by Ms. Jones.

However, many of the interventions discussed in the research literature tend to be focused on a particular disorder or subset of disorders. For example, reinforced practice and participant modeling are considered to be well-established in treating specific phobias in children (Chambless & Ollendick, 2001), yet little empirical evidence suggests that these interventions are equally as effective in addressing other types of anxiety disorders or depression. Similarly, CBTs are considered to be effective in treating social anxiety disorder, separation anxiety, and generalized anxiety; however, there is less empirical support suggesting that these interventions are effective in treating specific phobias (Morris, Kratochwill, Schoenfield, & Auster, 2008).

Chapter 7 contains a set of suggestions and strategies to foster self-esteem and emotional resilience in children. These strategies are particularly valuable and important for students who are experiencing depression or anxiety. Though teacher preparation programs may not consistently include training in the implementation of depression and anxiety intervention programs, basic awareness of associated features is valuable.

Several interventions for addressing anxiety and depression in children and adolescents have been discussed in the research literature (King, Muris, & Ollendick, 2005). Three interventions have garnered considerable empirical support in treating various internalizing disorders: participant modeling and reinforced practice, both useful for treating specific phobias; and cognitive-behavioral interventions for social anxiety, separation anxiety, generalized anxiety disorder, and depression.

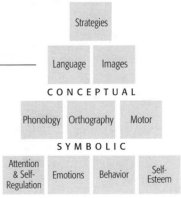

CONCEPTUAL

SYMBOLIC

FOUNDATIONAL

Participant Modeling

Participant modeling is based on the theory of observational learning (Bandura, 1969) and involves adopting behaviors or response patterns that are modeled by another individual. Within participant modeling, the child with anxiety approaches an anxiety-provoking situation in a series of graduated steps after first observing a peer approach the fear-provoking situation in a series of graduated steps.

Participant modeling has a long history of effectively addressing specific phobias in children. Ritter (1968) investigated the relative effectiveness of participant modeling compared with live modeling (a modeling procedure in which the child simply observes a peer approaching an anxiety-provoking situation rather than a gradual progression involving each step being modeled first). In addition, both groups were compared with an active intervention control group. Although both modeling conditions were more effective than the control group, significantly more children in the participant modeling group successfully completed a behavioral avoidance task versus the live modeling group. Results of the study suggest that gradually exposing the children to the anxiety-provoking stimuli—having a peer model the steps first and then guiding the child through the process—appears to be more effective than having the child simply observe a behavior and then model it afterward. To allay Anthony's fear of dogs, for example, his parents took him to a neighbor's house to watch his friend, Jimmy, interact with his new puppy.

Participant modeling is particularly conducive to the classroom environment. Plenty of familiar peers can serve as models, and there will be ample opportunities to address fears related to the academic environment (e.g., performance, peer interaction), as well.

Ms. Jaffe discussed her observations with Angela's father, who suggested that Angela be paired with one of her good friends on Monday during the next rehearsal. Angela and Jane were given similar roles in the play. Ms. Jaffe decided to break the class up into small groups and rehearse. Jane and Angela were instructed to take turns practicing their lines, beginning with only a few lines at a time. Gradually, Angela became more confident regarding her role in the class play.

Reinforced Practice

Based on the principles of behavior modification, reinforced practice is an approach that uses positive reinforcement and gradual exposure to change behaviors for a range of issues. Positive reinforcement can be construed as an event, object, or activity that follows a behavior and ultimately increases the occurrence of that behavior (Kazdin, 2000). A reinforcer in the context of therapeutic intervention for fears and anxiety may be applied as the child practices approaching the feared stimulus in a series of graduated steps. The reinforcer is then faded and eventually withdrawn once the child has successfully approached the stimulus without the fear response.

Reinforced practice has garnered considerable support in the research literature for addressing specific phobias in children (e.g., Chambless & Ollendick, 2001; Leitenberg & Callahan, 1973; Menzies & Clark, 1993; Sheslow, Bondy, & Nelson, 1983). Reinforced practice has also been applied within school settings to address school refusal (Trueman, 1984; Vaal, 1973).

The classroom environment is also conducive to implementing an intervention based on reinforced practice; teachers can systematically arrange events so that positive consequences follow and thereby strengthen the behaviors they wish to increase. Positive reinforcement techniques are commonly used in classrooms, both classroomwide and on an individual level. With regard to anxiety, reinforced practice may also be used to promote confidence and reduce avoidance behavior.

Using Angela's case as an example, Ms. Jaffe selected a few activities that Angela particularly enjoyed, such as reading and listening to music. She devised a reinforcement schedule that would permit Angela to engage in one of those activities as she participated in school play rehearsals with increasing involvement. The first step of involvement simply placed Angela within the setting, giving her tasks such as arranging the set, deciding on props, and so forth. Angela was then asked to take a small, nonspeaking part in the play. The next level of participation required Angela to recite a few lines only. Angela was reinforced after engaging in each play-related activity. Eventually, Angela was given a more prominent role in the play, which she practiced with her friend Jane. When she was able to deliver lines without an anxiety response, the reinforcement was eventually withdrawn.

Cognitive-Behavioral Interventions

Cognitive-behavioral interventions are focused not so much on consequences but on changing the way children think about themselves and the world around them. This form of intervention, also referred to as CBT, has been found to be effective in improving anxious and depressed symptoms and in helping children function more effectively on a daily basis. For example, depressed students often hold a variety of negative thoughts (e.g., "Even if I try my best, I will fail, so why bother?"). A therapist, school counselor, or school psychologist can help teachers reinforce and support these students by questioning the accuracy of these thoughts (e.g., "Has it always been the case that when you try your best, you fail? Have you ever succeeded?") and help students generate more adaptive thoughts through modeling (e.g., "If I try my best, I might fail, but I also might succeed"). Cognitive-behavioral interventions combine aspects of behavioral interventions with a focus on modifying cognitions to effect change. In the cognitive-behavioral orientation, cognitions are viewed as the mechanisms through which anxiety and depression develop. As such, managing these concerns involves replacing those cognitions with more adaptive, realistic thoughts regarding anxiety-provoking or distressing situations.

With regard to depression, CBT theorists posit that youth experiencing depressive symptoms develop a skewed perception of events and the environment, which can be caused by early adverse experiences. When the child or adolescent experiences stressful events, negative interpretations and maladaptive processing of these stressful events may cause and sustain symptoms of depression (Asarnow, Jaycox, & Tompson, 2001). As such, the aim of CBT is to alter the student's maladaptive cognitions, perceptions, and beliefs and to foster more adaptive cognitive, attributional, and behavioral styles that will lead to more adaptive behaviors (Asarnow et al., 2001; Kazdin, 2003).

Several interventions in the cognitive-behavioral orientation have been devised as structured, manual-based programs that can be easily implemented in classroom environments (Barrett, 2004, 2005; Barrett & Turner, 2001; Barrett, Webster, & Turner, 2003; Bernstein, Layne, Egan, & Tennison, 2005; Conradt & Essau, 2003; Muris & Mayer, 2000). CBT is an empirically supported intervention for generalized anxiety disorder, social anxiety, and separation anxiety (Albano & Kendall, 2002; Barrett, Duffy, Dadds, & Rapee, 2001; Kendall et al., 2005) and has also been used to address associated internalizing symptoms in children. CBT techniques can be applied at an individual level as well as within a group setting. With training, teachers and other school personnel can implement these programs to circumvent and to address anxious and depressive symptoms in children (Lowry-Webster, Barrett, & Dadds, 2001; Lowry-Webster, Barrett, & Locke, 2003).

The primary objectives of CBT are to help individuals recognize fearful/phobic feelings and physiological responses to anxiety and depressive symptoms, to identify cognitions about situations that seem to induce these responses, to develop a plan to cope with these responses, and to practice the coping strategies while gradually being exposed to situations or activities that are associated with these responses. Children learn relaxation techniques, self-reinforcement strategies, ways to identify sources of support, and constructive ways to evaluate performance.

An example of a CBT program that has been implemented successfully in a school setting with teachers as the primary facilitators is the FRIENDS program (Barrett, 2004). FRIENDS was designed as a prevention/early intervention and treatment program for anxiety symptoms and disorders in children and adolescents. FRIENDS was originally developed for children between 8 and 12 years of age but more recently has been adapted for adolescents between 13 and 16 years of age (Barrett, 2005). The program teaches children to learn to recognize signs and symptoms of their anxiety and to employ coping strategies to reduce or eliminate their symptoms. Specific techniques emphasized include relaxation, cognitive restructuring, attentional training, assisted exposure, and family and peer support. The program comprises 10 weekly sessions and two booster sessions that typically take place 1 and 3 months after the final last weekly session. The program also includes four sessions for parents, intended to provide in-depth information about the program and to discuss strategies for parenting and the use of reinforcement procedures.

Table 5.3 provides a summary of techniques teachers can use to address internalizing behaviors within the classroom.

Ms. Jones met with the school psychologist and with Anthony's parents, and they agreed to implement a classroom-based cognitive-behavioral intervention in order to address Anthony's increasing level of distress. Ms. Jones had recently attended a weekend work-

Table 5.3. What teachers can do to address internalizing behaviors in order to help reduce students' anxiety and depression

Identify any cognitive distortions that may lead to maladaptive behaviors.
Discuss any negative thought patterns, emphasizing the erroneous reasoning and thinking that elicited these thoughts.
Describe the logical consequences of various behaviors.
Help students choose alternative adaptive behaviors.
Emphasize choice within the classroom environment.
Model appropriate behaviors.
Set clear, realistic goals for students.
Provide opportunities for students to be successful.
Provide positive feedback to students.
Provide examples of constructive evaluations of behaviors.
Encourage students to provide self-reinforcement.
Create predictable environments and situations whenever possible.
Provide relaxation training.
Encourage peer interaction.
Avoid singling out individual students.

Sources: Glasser, 1965; Meichenbaum, 1977, 1986, 1990; Newcomer, 2003; Schoenfield, & Morris, 2008.

Figure 5.4. A picture from Anthony's folder that he drew at the end of the school year, which shows his growing confidence.

shop on implementing cognitive-behavioral strategies within classroom settings. Over a period of 12 weeks, Anthony was taught to examine thoughts that he had about himself, others, and distressing situations. Anthony learned to cope with his distress and sadness by replacing his negative thoughts with more positive, constructive thoughts as well as with self-reward. He was taught to identify physiological indicators of worry and to address these symptoms through deep breathing and relaxation techniques. The learning component for the intervention taught Anthony specific strategies for problem solving and self-reward. He was taught to employ these strategies while being gradually exposed to situations he found distressing. He was also taught to identify and rely on sources of support such as friends and family members. Figure 5.4 displays a picture from Anthony's folder from the end of the school year.

CONCLUSION

Students who experience affective disorders are ostensibly at risk for many negative consequences, such as academic failure, low self-esteem, difficulty with peer relationships, substance abuse, suicidal ideation, and affective disorders of adulthood. As such, there is a critical need for school-based interventions for students who are experiencing these difficulties or who are at risk for doing so. Given that students spend a significant amount of time in school and that symptoms of worry and hopelessness often are manifested in school performance and interaction with others, the classroom is an ideal environment to address such areas of concern. Clearly, not all schools have the resources to implement clinic-based interventions with all children who are at risk. However, classroom teachers and other school personnel can certainly draw on the principles of effective intervention to address students' needs.

Unlike the easily observed classroom problems caused by disruptive behavior, internalizing problems of worry, anxiety, helplessness, and hopelessness are not easily observed by teachers. Yet, these problems are just as impairing, if not more so, than the externalizing behavior problems. Although not all students experiencing difficulties in the classroom due to worry and hopelessness meet diagnostic criteria, many students may benefit from an appreciation of the challenges they face in the classroom as well as from assistance to develop more effective coping skills to manage worry and hopelessness.

129

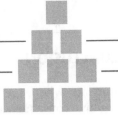

CHAPTER 6 OUTLINE

OPPOSITIONAL AND CONDUCT PROBLEMS

Causes of Oppositional and Conduct Problems
Classroom Interventions for Oppositional and Conduct Problems

BEHAVIOR MODIFICATION IN THE CLASSROOM

Reinforcement
Punishment

PREVENTIVE APPROACHES TO DISCIPLINE

Dealing with Classroom Conflicts
Classroom Rules
Ten Keys to Compliance

CONCLUSION

		Strategies	
	Language	Images	
		CONCEPTUAL	
	Phonology	Orthography	Motor
		SYMBOLIC	
Attention & Self-Regulation	Emotions	Behavior	Self-Esteem
		FOUNDATIONAL	

UNDERSTANDING AND MANAGING BEHAVIOR PROBLEMS

Children with disruptive behaviors present the most difficult challenges facing classroom teachers. A teacher's availability to other students is dramatically affected by verbal and physical aggression, tantrums, destruction of property, stealing, lying, and general noncompliance in the classroom. Disruptive students often demonstrate defiance toward authority figures and classroom rules. Some struggle academically and may also have problems with sustaining attention. Some possess the ability to complete class assignments, whereas others may have coexisting learning problems. These patterns of behavior have been found to strongly contribute to long-term risk for school failure and later serious maladjustment (Biederman, Faraone, Milberger, Curtiss, et al., 1996; Kazdin, 1987a).

When he was in third grade, Samuel would steal items from the coats of other children. He would try to leave the school grounds during recess to go and steal candy from the nearby grocery store. In fact, each day when he left the school, Ms. James, his fourth-grade teacher, had to check his pockets to see what he had acquired during the day. By sixth grade, the stealing had lessened, but every day his sixth-grade teacher, Ms. Handler, felt that much of her attention and energy were directed toward Samuel and his behavioral challenges. Samuel needed constant supervision. Ms. Handler completed the Behavior section of the Building Blocks Questionnaire, presented in Figure 6.1. Every column was checked with *Frequently* except for "Hurts self or others." Samuel was physically aggressive with his peers, but rarely did his aggression result in physical injury; more often, his actions resulted in arguments and hurt feelings.

OPPOSITIONAL AND CONDUCT PROBLEMS

Since 1980, researchers have identified a significant group of children, particularly boys beyond the preschool years, who exhibit two broad dimensions of disruptive behaviors. The first dimension, oppositionality, appears to reflect a child's primary goal of guiding his or her own behavior, independent of adult rules and limits. The second dimension appears to reflect this pattern to a more serious degree, combined with aggression in which the rights of other children, and in some cases teachers, are violated. Most researchers agree that oppositionality includes all but the most serious forms of physical aggression, which fall in the conduct realm (Achenbach, Conners, Quay, Verhulst, & Howell, 1989; Lahey et al., 1990; Loeber, Lahey, & Thomas, 1991). Some researchers have noted that children experiencing

131

FOUNDATIONAL			
BEHAVIOR	Rarely	Sometimes	Frequently
Has difficulty getting along with peers			✓
Is frequently in trouble at school			✓
Lacks engagement in classroom instruction			✓
Does not respond to discipline as expected			✓
Disturbs or distracts others			✓
Makes inappropriate physical contacts with peers (e.g., shoving, pinching)			✓
Insults others verbally			✓
Refuses to comply when asked			✓
Seems argumentative			✓
Hurts self or others		✓	

Figure 6.1. Building Blocks Questionnaire for Samuel: Behavior block.

oppositionality, particularly those who are spiteful, vindictive, and resentful in their actions, appear to have a significant risk of progressing to more serious aggressive acts (Biederman, Faraone, Milberger, Jetton, et al., 1996; Loeber et al., 1991). Unlike problems of planning, attention, and self-regulation, conditions that have a strong biological contribution, problems with oppositionality and conduct appear to be powerfully affected by three factors beyond the child's temperament: 1) the temperaments of parents, caregivers, and teachers; 2) the behavioral strategies employed by the adults; and 3) the consistency with which those strategies are used (Barkley, 1997b; Nigg & Hinshaw, 1998; Stormont, 1998).

More often than not, when children experience behavior problems at school, they also experience them at home. However, they are much more likely to "let it all hang out" at home where they feel comfortable rather than at school where a teacher might think badly of them. When called by the school to discuss their child's academic problems, some parents come away with a distinct impression that the conference was about two entirely different children: the well-behaved, cooperative student whom the teacher views and the defiant, angry, temperamental child whom the parents see at home. This is especially true of some anxious children who would never misbehave at school but then release their pent-up stress at home.

The reasons are not known why some children are much more willing to act out at school than others. Some children, in fact, may come into the world with the biological risk to be oppositional. As infants, they can be fussy or difficult to comfort. Every frustration as a toddler leads to a tantrum. As they grow older, these children continue to be quick to anger and do not appear to care about the feelings of others. When they are defiant at school, it is clear that they have brought their oppositionality to school with them. On one day, for example, Samuel was particularly frustrated about a task and jumped up on top of the table and started yelling numerous obscenities at Ms. Handler. Unsure of what to do, Ms. Handler called the principal, Mr. Alphonso, for back-up support. Mr. Alphonso then had to physically remove Samuel from the classroom.

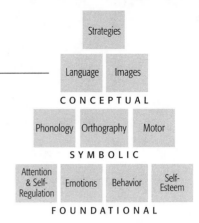

In contrast to Samuel, other children appear to be easygoing until they begin to experience problems at school. At that point, they can become angry, negative, and oppositional at home as well as at school. Many children who are struggling academically at school develop defiant patterns of behavior. Because their academic performance does not meet classroom expectations, they regularly receive huge doses of criticism. Eventually, this constant flow of negative feedback leads to frustration, and the child begins pushing back in retaliation. It is easy to appreciate how misconceptions regarding behavior occur when viewed at the beginning of a school year by a new teacher. This teacher may view the child's behaviors as simply disobedient, when closer scrutiny would reveal that the behavior has followed, rather than preceded, poor school performance.

The essential characteristics of oppositionality are negative, hostile, and defiant behaviors without more serious violations of the basic rights of others. Oppositional children are excessively argumentative with teachers; frequently lose their temper; and often appear angry, resentful, or easily annoyed with others. They tend to project the blame for their mistakes onto others. They often exhibit these behaviors to a greater degree around those whom they know well. Not surprisingly, such behaviors are rarely seen in brief interviews with school psychologists and counselors.

Problems with oppositionality usually begin by 8 years of age. When the clinical diagnosis of *oppositional defiant disorder* is made, psychologists usually look for a pattern of negative, hostile, and defiant behavior that has lasted at least 6 months. The child is usually described as quickly losing his or her temper; being argumentative with adults; defying or refusing to comply to requests to follow rules; deliberately doing things that annoy others; blaming others for mistakes or misbehavior; and being touchy and easily annoyed, angry and resentful, or spiteful and vindictive.

The more serious pattern of misbehaviors, referred to as *conduct disorder*, is considered clinically to reflect a persistent pattern of behavior in which the basic rights of others and major appropriate societal norms or rules are violated. Within this framework, conduct problems include physical aggression, cruelty, destruction of property, theft, fire setting, confrontation with a victim, and even physical violence. Older children with serious conduct problems are often truant and experiment with drugs, alcohol, and sexual behavior. For the most part, Samuel's behaviors were not intended to hurt others, but he tended to hit, push, and shove other children far more frequently than did his other classmates.

Researchers report that the incidence of oppositional and conduct disorders in children is at approximately 3% (Kazdin, 1987b; McGee, Silva, & Williams, 1984; Pelham, Gnagy, Greenslade, & Milich, 1992). Children with this pattern of disruptive behavior often have comorbid disorders of learning disabilities (LD) and attention-deficit/hyperactivity disorder. Oppositional defiant behaviors tend to decrease as children become older, but conduct disorder symptoms, which rarely occur before preschool, increase in prevalence with age for both sexes (Loeber, 1985).

Tantrums and fighting in school decline with increasing age. Stealing increases until age 10 and then declines. When Samuel was 8 years old, he was always stealing things from others such as car keys and even the stapler from the teacher's desk. Truancy and substance abuse increase through the age span of adolescence, and lying appears at all age levels (Achenbach & Edelbrock, 1981; Fergusson & Horwood, 1993). Late-onset disruptive behaviors appear to be more common in girls than in boys.

Classmates are often very sensitive to the aggressive behavior of their peers. Peer nomination has been found to correlate very well with teacher observations of aggressive children. In fact, teacher–peer agreement is even higher than teacher–parent or teacher–mental health worker ratings (Achenbach, McConaughy, & Howell, 1987). Students perceived Samuel's behaviors as being unpredictable.

Causes of Oppositional and Conduct Problems

The nature versus nurture issue concerning aggressive problems in children and adults is still unresolved. Parents may unwittingly train antisocial and inappropriate behavior at home because a child's coercive interactions and noncompliance feed parents' attempts to manage the child. In direct ways, this actually reinforces and strengthens rather than weakens the child's inappropriate behavior (Patterson, 1986). The interactional styles of both parents and teachers, as well as the disciplinary techniques used and the consistency with which those techniques are administered, can significantly contribute to problems of oppositionality and conduct. The power of teachers' words, tone of voice, and actions are still being researched and increasingly understood. For example, one study found that typical children's attention and diligence in completing work varied depending on the style in which teachers provided instructions (Bugental, Lyon, Lin, McGrath, & Binbela, 1999). Teachers providing assertive, clear, direct instructions were complied with at a much higher rate than were teachers whose style was deemed to be unassertive and less consistent.

Before children ever come to the classroom, they are significantly influenced within their homes. Preschool conduct problems have been linked to marital discord, maternal depression, and poor housing conditions (Barron & Earls, 1984). Maternal attitudes related to criticism, irritability, and coolness toward children are strongly related to the presence of behavior and conduct problems (Glasgow, Dornbusch, Troyer, Steinberg, & Ritter, 1997). These factors have been found to contribute more strongly to children's behavior than even social class or marital discord. In 1992, the preponderance of the data led Gardner to conclude, "A robust finding in this field is that children with conduct disorder are likely to come from homes with multisocial and family disadvantages" (p. 157). Yet, in 1979, Rutter, Maughan, Mortimore, and Ouston reported that good schools can reduce delinquency and disruptive behavior risks for high-risk children.

Classroom Interventions for Oppositional and Conduct Problems

Managing and modifying disruptive classroom behavior can at times overwhelm even experienced teachers. These patterns of behavior require a clear plan, an understanding of the rationale for certain interventions, the ability to apply interventions consistently, and the opportunity to troubleshoot and modify interventions as needed, often with the assistance of a classroom consultant such as a school psychologist. Often, oppositional and conduct problems are managed rather than solved. In some cases, exposure to conforming peers and parent training can have a significant, positive impact (Feldman, Caplinger, & Wodarski, 1983; Patterson, 1982). Positive daily school experiences, however, appear to be the best means of modifying and shaping this pattern of disturbing behavior (Goldstein, 1995).

Models and techniques to manage disruptive behaviors in the classroom fall into three broad areas: 1) those that focus on prevention, 2) those that focus on correction and control of misbehavior, and 3) those that focus on intervention techniques. The first set of strategies focuses on procedures that reduce the likelihood of misbehavior. The second set of strategies focuses on the modification of behavior and strategies that provide teachers with ways to model more appropriate patterns of behavior. The third set of strategies is often implemented outside of classroom settings, such as in counseling and family therapy. The

Table 6.1. Popular models and techniques for dealing with discipline referrals

Model	Techniques emphasized
	Focusing on Prevention
Preventative classroom management	Effective teaching practices, frequent monitoring, clear rules and procedures, social praise, and so forth
Prosocial behavior	Systematic reinforcement, modeling of prosocial behavior, verbal instruction, role playing
Moral education	Classroom moral discussions of real-life dilemmas, hypothetical situations, and literature; role playing; student participation in school government
Social problem solving (SPS)	Direct teaching of SPS skills (e.g., alternative thinking, means–ends thinking), self-instruction training, dialoguing
Affective and communication models	Values clarification activities, active listening, communication and interpersonal skills training for students and teachers
	Focusing on Correction and Control of Misbehavior
Behavior modification	Direct instruction; reinforcement techniques, including social praise, material reinforcers, and tokens; punishment-oriented techniques, including verbal reprimand, response cost, and time-out; group contingency techniques such as the Good Behavior Game; behavioral contracting
Assertive discipline	Teacher assertion, systematic use of behavior modification techniques, continuous monitoring
Reality therapy	Confrontation questioning, classroom meetings, classroom moral discussions, social problem solving, behavioral contracting, logical consequences, time-out, preventative techniques such as democratic governance
	Focusing on Treatment
Social skills training	Direct instruction, modeling and rehearsal, coaching, self-instruction, manipulation of antecedents and consequences
Aggression replacement training	Social skills training techniques, self-instruction (e.g., anger control training), moral discussions
Parent management training	Parent training in application of behavioral techniques
Family therapy	Variety of therapeutic and educational techniques, depending on the particular model
Behavior therapy	Variety of cognitive, behavioral, and operant techniques

From Bear, G.G. (1990). Models and techniques that focus on prevention. In A. Thomas & J. Grimes (Eds.), *Best practices in school psychology* (p. 652). Silver Spring, MD: National Association of School Psychologists; copyright 1990 by the National Association of School Psychologists. Reprinted by permission of publisher.

remainder of this chapter provides an overview of behavior modification techniques. A summary of these models and techniques appears in Table 6.1.

BEHAVIOR MODIFICATION IN THE CLASSROOM

Behavior modification assumes that observable and measurable negative behaviors are good targets for change. All behavior follows a set of consistent rules. Methods can be developed for defining, observing, and measuring behaviors as well as for designing effective interventions. Behavior modification techniques rarely ever fail. Rather, they are either applied inefficiently or inconsistently, which leads to less-than-desired change. All behavior is maintained, changed, or shaped by the consequences of that behavior. Although there are certain limits, such as temperamental or emotional influences related to ADHD or depression, all children function more effectively under the right set of consequences. *Reinforcers* are consequences that strengthen behavior. *Punishments*

135

are consequences that weaken behavior. Students' behaviors are managed and changed by the consequences of classroom behavior. The following multistep approach can be used to manage behavior through consequences:

1. Define the problem, usually by count or description.

2. Design a way to change the behavior.

3. Identify an effective reinforcer.

4. Apply the reinforcer consistently to shape or change the behavior.

Consequences of behavior are directly related to the events that either come immediately before or after them. Table 6.2 provides examples of behavioral outcomes as they relate to various behavior modifications and events.

Reinforcement and punishment follow a clear set of basic principles: 1) reinforcement or punishment always follows behavior, 2) reinforcement or punishment follows the target behavior as soon as possible, 3) reinforcement or punishment fits the target behavior and must be meaningful to the child, and 4) multiple reinforcers or punishments are likely to be more effective than single reinforcers or punishments.

Reinforcement

Although reinforcement and punishment can be equally effective in reducing specific target behaviors in the classroom, reinforcement is by far more effective in helping children develop alternative, more functional behaviors. When Jeremy was in third grade, his teacher instituted a procedure in which he would receive a tally mark if she looked over and saw that he was tipping back in his chair. She

Table 6.2. Examples of behavioral outcomes resulting from various behavior modification classifications

Classification	Exhibited behavior	Consequences	Probable future effect on behavior
Positive reinforcement	Jane cleans her room.	Jane's parents praise her.	Jane will continue to clean her room.
Positive reinforcement	Carmen brushes her teeth after meals.	Carmen receives a nickel each time.	Carmen will continue to brush her teeth after meals.
Positive reinforcement	Rob works quietly at his seat.	The teacher praises and rewards Rob.	Rob will continue to work quietly at his seat.
Negative reinforcement	Jason complains that older boys consistently beat him up, and he refuses to attend school.	Jason's parents allow him to remain at home because of his complaints.	Jason will continue to miss school.
Negative reinforcement	Balin complains of headaches when it is time to do homework.	Balin is allowed to go to bed without doing his homework.	Balin will have headaches whenever there is homework to do.
Extinction	Jim washes his father's car.	Jim's car washing behavior is ignored.	Jim will stop washing his father's car.
Extinction	Carmen puts glue on Joe's seat.	Carmen is ignored.	Carmen will stop putting glue on Joe's seat.
Punishment	Marta sits on the arm of the chair.	Marta is spanked each time she sits on the arm of the chair.	Marta will not sit on the arm of the chair.
Punishment	Takeo puts Gwen's pigtails in the paint.	The teacher administers the paddle to Takeo's posterior.	Takeo will not put Gwen's pigtail in the paint.

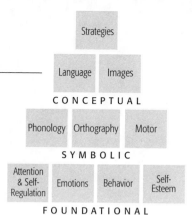

placed 4 *Xs* under each chair leg to remind him not to lean back. A more positive approach would be for the teacher to let Jeremy earn a tally mark each time she looked over and saw that all four legs of Jeremy's chair were down. This would reinforce the desired behavior. Always try a number of reinforcing strategies first before resorting to punishment as a means of reducing unwanted or aversive classroom behaviors.

Schedules   *Schedules* define and identify the amount of work required or the time that must elapse between reinforcers. Examples of schedules include continuous, fixed or variable interval (time-related), and fixed or variable ratio (related to how much work is completed). Fixed schedules result in higher rates of performance than continuous schedules. However, the drawback is that a student quickly learns that no reinforcement is going to be available until certain contingencies occur. There is less guesswork; therefore, there is likely to be a drop-off in the child's performance after earning a reward under a fixed schedule. The child works more diligently when getting closer to earning rewards and slows down after the reward is provided.

In the classroom, a variable schedule that keeps a child guessing is likely to be more effective than a fixed schedule.

In an effort to improve Samuel's classroom behavior, Mrs. Handler set up a variable interval schedule. She told Samuel that he would earn points for appropriate behavior in the classroom. However, the number of points he earned and when he earned the points changed each day. Ms. Handler explained to Samuel that each day she would roll a die. The number on the die determined how many points Samuel obtained for good behavior. She then rolled the die a second time. That determined the number of times per day she would check on Samuel's behavior. If he had been behaving appropriately in the 15 minutes before being checked, then he received points that he could trade in at the end of the week for a reinforcing activity.

Keep in mind that variable schedules are not as good for shaping new behaviors but are excellent for maintaining well-learned behaviors.

The Talking Out/Out of Seat/Attention Problem/Disruption (TOAD) system, a simple system to evaluate the most common classroom problems, appears in Figure 6.2. Information is usually obtained during 15-second observational intervals. If any of the behaviors occur, whether once or more than once, a single notation is made for that time interval.

Positive Reinforcement   The appropriate application of positive reinforcement has repeatedly been demonstrated to increase both on-task behavior and work completion (for reviews, see Barkley, 1990; DuPaul & Stoner, 2003; Goldstein & Brooks, 2007; Walker & Walker, 1991; Zentall, 2006). In the early elementary school grades, teachers provide a significant degree of positive reinforcement when desired behaviors are exhibited (White, 1975). That is, when a desired behavior is exhibited, teachers frequently respond with a consequence that is likely to increase the recurrence of that behavior. Jeremy's first-grade teacher offered frequent praise when he was sitting quietly in his seat. Samuel's second-grade teacher complimented him whenever recess occurred without some type of incident.

By middle elementary school and through secondary school, however, teachers begin paying increasingly greater attention to undesirable behaviors and less attention to appropriate behaviors. Unfortunately, paying attention to

Interval	T	O	A	D		Interval	T	O	A	D		Interval	T	O	A	D		Interval	T	O	A	D
15						15						15						15				
30						30						30						30				
45						45						45						45				
60						60						60						60				
15						15						15						15				
30						30						30						30				
45						45						45						45				
60						60						60						60				
15						15						15						15				
30						30						30						30				
45						45						45						45				
60						60						60						60				
15						15						15						15				
30						30						30						30				
45						45						45						45				
60						60						60						60				
15						15						15						15				
30						30						30						30				
45						45						45						45				
60						60						60						60				

Operational Definitions of Behaviors in the TOAD System

1. Talking Out: Spoken words, either friendly, neutral, or negative in content, are directed at either the teacher without first obtaining permission to speak or unsolicited at classmates during inappropriate times or during work periods.

2. Out of Seat: The child is not supporting his or her weight with the chair. Up on knees does not count as out-of-seat behavior.

3. Attention Problem: The child is not attending either to independent work or to a group activity. The child is therefore engaged in an activity other than that which has been directed and is clearly different from what the other children are doing. This includes the child's not following teacher directions.

4. Disruption: The child's actions result in consequences that appear to be interrupting other children's work. These behaviors might include noises or physical contact. They may be intentional or unintentional.

Figure 6.2. The Talking Out/Out of Seat/Attention Problem/Disruption (TOAD) system. (From Goldstein, S., & Goldstein, M. [1990]. *Managing attention disorders in children: A guide for practitioners* [pp. 93–94]. New York: John Wiley & Sons. This material is used by permission of John Wiley & Sons, Inc.)

Strategies

Language | Images

CONCEPTUAL

Phonology | Orthography | Motor

SYMBOLIC

Attention & Self-Regulation | Emotions | Behavior | Self-Esteem

FOUNDATIONAL

undesirable behaviors causes them to cease in the short run but occur more frequently in the long run.

Children with poor self-control may often be more interested in tasks other than those on which the teacher is focusing (Douglas, 1972). This leads to significantly more nonproductive activity and uneven, unpredictable classroom behavior. The overall rates of negative teacher–child interactions involving students whose behavior is typical, interestingly, are also higher in classrooms containing children with poor self-control (Campbell et al., 1977). According to reports, teachers are more intense and controlling when interacting with children with poor self-control. Within school settings, children with ADHD appear to experience negative consequences because of their temperament and a performance history that often involves beginning but not completing tasks. Many teachers of students with ADHD unfortunately tend to focus on the student's misbehavior rather than on the reduction or termination of the behavior.

Over the school year, Ms. Handler found that—in an effort to return Sam's behavior to normal—she paid attention to him when he was misbehaving. She realized that when he was not misbehaving, Samuel was behaving appropriately, but she was failing to reinforce or provide him with positive feedback for good behavior. Though there were times when she had to intervene because Samuel was disrupting others, there were other times when Samuel's off-task or inappropriate behavior did not disturb or disrupt other students. Ms. Handler chose to ignore the nondisruptive behaviors and use her time better in providing positive feedback to Samuel when he was behaving appropriately.

This naturally occurring pattern of teachers paying less attention to desirable behaviors and more attention to undesirable behaviors as children progress through school places children with disruptive behavior at a greater disadvantage than their classmates. In the first few grades, when teachers appear to be making a conscientious effort to positively reinforce their students, the children with disruptive behaviors often do not receive their share of positive feedback. In the later grades, as teachers exhibit less positive reinforcement, perhaps because they feel that it is not needed, these children are placed at even greater risk.

Positive reinforcement programs should begin at the level at which children can succeed. All too often, a teacher will set up a wonderful behavior program but set the initial criteria for success too high. The disruptive child in this system rarely meets with success. Problem behavior must be defined operationally, and then a level of baseline occurrence must be obtained. At first, provide reinforcement when the child is at or slightly better than baseline. For example, in first grade, Jeremy was out of his seat 10 times during a work period, so his teacher provided reinforcement when he was out of his seat no more than eight times. As Jeremy became more successful, the necessary criterion for reinforcement was gradually made stricter, allowing fewer out-of-seat behaviors during a given time period.

Response Discrepancy Observation Method   Sometimes it is important to determine the approximate amount of time a student exhibits on- and off-task behavior. One simple behavioral observation method is called *response discrepancy* because it allows you to record a discrepancy between the target student, such as Jeremy, and a typically behaving class peer (Rhode, Jenson, & Reavis, 1992). Figure 6.3 presents a form to use for this system. To begin, match the target student with a same-sex peer who exhibits typical classroom behavior. Next, check off the type of activity: class, small-group activity, or independent activity.

Student ______________ **M** ☐ **F** ☐ **Grade** ______ **Date** ____________

Observer ______________________ **Teacher** ________________

Class activity ______________________________________

Position: ☐ **Teacher-directed whole class** ☐ **Teacher-directed small group** ☐ **Independent work session**

Directions: Observe each student once at 10-second intervals, then record data. This is a partial interval recording. If possible, collect data for a full 15 minutes under teacher-directed or independent condition. If not, put a slash when classroom conditions change. Classmates observed must be the same sex as the student tested. To observe class, begin with the first same-sex student in row 1. Record each subsequent same-sex student in following intervals. Data reflect an average of classroom behavior. Skip unobservable students.

On-Task Code: E = Eye contact with teacher or task and performing the requested task.

Off-Task Codes:

T = Talking out/noise. Inappropriate verbalization or making sounds with object, mouth, or body.

O = Out of seat. Student is fully or partially out of assigned seat without teacher permission.

I = Inactive. Student not engaged with assigned task and is passively sitting.

N = Noncompliance. Breaking a classroom rule or not following teacher directions within 15 seconds.

+ = Positive teacher interaction. One-to-one positive comment, smiling, touching, or gesture.

– = Negative teacher interaction. One-to-one reprimand, implementing negative consequences, or negative gesture.

						1						2						3
Student																		
Classmate																		

						4						5						6
Student																		
Classmate																		

						7						8						9
Student																		
Classmate																		

						10						11						12
Student																		
Classmate																		

						13						14						15
Student																		
Classmate																		

Figure 6.3. Behavioral observation form. (From Rhode, G., Jenson, W.R., & Reavis, H.K. [1992]. *The tough kid book: Practical classroom management strategies* [p. 27]. Longmont, CO: Sopris West, Inc.; adapted with permission of Sopris West, Inc.)

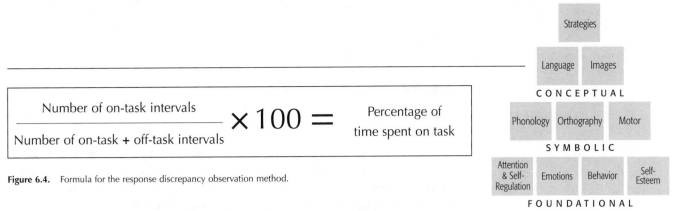

$$\frac{\text{Number of on-task intervals}}{\text{Number of on-task + off-task intervals}} \times 100 = \text{Percentage of time spent on task}$$

Figure 6.4. Formula for the response discrepancy observation method.

The observation period lasts 15 minutes, and behavior is recorded at 10-second intervals (for a total of 90 intervals). The top of the box is used for the target student and the bottom is used for the classroom peer. At the end of each 10-second interval, record a + for on-task activities or a – for off-task activities for each student. Ignore all behaviors between the recording points. At the end of the 15-minute observation period, compute the percentage of on-task behavior for both students. This may be accomplished using the formula provided in Figure 6.4 (Rhode et al., 1992).

When Jeremy was in third grade, a volunteer completed this type of observation for Jeremy and his classmate Roger while they were engaged in a small-group activity. Jeremy had been on task for 34 of the 90 intervals. He had been off task for 56 of the 90 intervals. His total time on task was 34/90 x 100, or approximately 38% of the time.

In contrast, Roger had been on task for 78 of the 90 intervals and had been off task for 12 of the intervals. His total time on task was 78/90 x 100, or approximately 87% of the time. As a general guideline, if a student is on task less than 60% of the time and the peer's average is 85% or more, the target student's attention to the task is problematic. If both students' on-task behavior is below 60%, the problem may be more related to classroom management (Rhode et al., 1992). When compared with his peer, Jeremy appears to be much more distractible and off task.

As a general rule, a student should be observed in two different settings or two different types of activities. Some students are only off task and distractible when presented with tasks they find uninteresting. Other students are distractible only during specific subjects, such as in a math class. Students' abilities to pay attention vary depending on the type of task, the difficulty of the material, the type of activity, the setting, and the teacher's classroom management skills.

Positive reinforcement should follow immediately after the good behavior. The reinforcement should be specific and initially continuous, slowly moving to an intermittent schedule. There are different types of reinforcers. Material reinforcers provide the child with something tangible; even if material reinforcers are used, however, a kind word from the teacher should always accompany them. Social reinforcers are more versatile. As a general principle, it is easier to increase behavior than decrease it. Thus, when choosing a target behavior, it is preferable to focus on behaviors to be increased rather than on those to be decreased. Shea and Bauer (1987) described the following process to apply positive reinforcements effectively:

1. Select a target behavior to increase, define the behavior, and choose a reinforcer.

2. Observe the child and watch for the behavior.

3. Reinforce the target behavior every time it is exhibited.

4. Comment in a positive way about the behavior when providing reinforcement.

141

5. Be enthusiastic and interested.

6. Offer assistance.

7. Vary the reinforcer.

Rhode and colleagues (1992) provide a well-defined model (IFEED-AV rules) for reinforcement and contingencies in the classroom, summarized in Table 6.3.

Select reinforcers that are age-appropriate and not necessarily time-limited, such as getting to participate in a popcorn party on Friday. Most important, do not deny students their basic rights (e.g., lunch, bathroom use, playground time) and then define these rights as positive reinforcers. At times, the use of a reinforcement list or menu can facilitate choosing a reinforcer that is meaningful to the child. The teacher can provide a list of enjoyable or free-time activities and ask the child to rank them by preference. The teacher can ask the child what he or she might do with free time, where he or she might like to sit, what he or she might like to learn about, and what kinds of activities make him or her feel needed, proud, and important in the classroom. Finally, one question a teacher may consider asking all students is, "What is the very best reward in this class that you could get for good work and behavior?"

Selection of Reinforcements   Some consequences that teachers provide for children are irrelevant and neither strengthen nor weaken the behavior they follow (Bushell, 1973). Many teachers believe that placing stars on a chart as a reward or providing a prize are consequences that work with all children. Some children are motivated by these consequences, whereas others are not. Furthermore, children with poor self-control may find these consequences salient one day but lose interest in them quickly the next day. Therefore, the fact that certain consequences follow a child's behavior may neither strengthen nor weaken the chances for that behavior to recur. Bushell (1973) referred to consequences that are irrelevant as *noise*—neutral consequences that have no effect on the behavior. Teachers must evaluate whether chosen consequences are positively reinforcing or simply noise. A reinforcement menu or inventory completed jointly by the teacher and the child ensures that the former rather than the latter will occur. Examples of positive reinforcement menus for varying ages appear in Table 6.4.

Ms. Adams met with Jeremy when he was in her second-grade class to select some reinforcers that would increase his time on task. Jeremy quickly offered several suggestions. He wanted time to look through books about dinosaurs, to read some joke books, and to play with blocks. He also wanted time for drawing and art projects. Ms. Adams explained that each morning they would decide what assignments needed to be completed before break. When he completed the assignments, he could choose his reward. Ms. Adams also adapted the assignments so that Jeremy would be successful. For example, Jeremy was expected to write in his journal, but he could answer questions about his reading orally.

Paine and colleagues (1983) found that the five most frequent reinforcement ideas suggested by elementary school students were additional time at recess, free time in class, material reinforcers, field trips, and class games. These ideas, perhaps with the addition of computer game time or Internet exploration, are likely equally reinforcing today. Intermediate grade students more frequently favored activities that involved interaction with teachers, including acting as an assistant in grading papers, carrying on a discussion, or playing a game on a one-to-one basis. As previously discussed, reinforcers take on different values at different ages for different students.

Strategies

Language   Images

CONCEPTUAL

Phonology   Orthography   Motor

SYMBOLIC

Attention & Self-Regulation   Emotions   Behavior   Self-Esteem

FOUNDATIONAL

Table 6.3. IFEED-AV rules

Immediately	The *I* stands for reinforcing the student immediately. The longer the teacher waits to reinforce a student, the less effective the reinforcer will be. This is particularly true of younger students or students with severe disabilities. For example, reinforcer effectiveness is limited if the student has to wait until the end of the week to receive it.
Frequently	The *F* stands for frequently reinforcing a student. It is especially important to frequently reinforce when a student is learning a new behavior or skill. If reinforcers are not given frequently enough, the student may not produce enough of a new behavior for it to become well-established. The standard rule is three or four positive reinforcers for every one negative consequence (including negative verbal comments) that the teacher delivers. If, in the beginning, there is a great deal of inappropriate behavior to which the teacher must attend, positive reinforcement and recognition of appropriate behavior must be increased accordingly to maintain the desired three or four positives to each negative. The reinforcer can be a simple social reinforcer such as, "Good job. You finished your math assignment."
Enthusiasm	The first *E* stands for enthusiasm in the delivery of the reinforcer. It is easy to simply hand an edible reinforcer to a student; it takes more effort to pair it with an enthusiastic comment. Modulation in the voice and excitement with a congratulatory air convey that the student has done something important. For most teachers, this seems artificial at first. However, with practice, enthusiasm makes the difference between a reinforcer delivered in a drab, uninteresting way and one that indicates that something important has taken place in which the teacher is interested.
Eye contact	It is also important for the teacher to look the student in the eyes when giving a reinforcer, even if the student is not looking at him or her. Like enthusiasm, eye contact suggests that a student is special and has the teacher's undivided attention. Over time, eye contact may become reinforcing in and of itself.
Describe the behavior	*D* stands for describing the behavior that is being reinforced. The younger the student or the more severe the disability, the more important it is to describe the appropriate behavior that is being reinforced. Teachers often assume that students know what it is they are doing right that has resulted in the delivery of reinforcement. However, this is often not the case. The student may not know why reinforcement is being delivered or may think that it is being delivered for some behavior other than what the teacher intended to reinforce. Even if the student does know what behavior is being reinforced, describing it is important. First, describing the behavior highlights and emphasizes the behavior the teacher wishes to reinforce. Second, if the behavior has several steps, describing it helps to review the specific expectations for the student. An example is, "Wow, you got yourself dressed—look at you! You have your socks on, your shoes are laced, your pants are on with a belt, and your shirt has all the buttons fastened and is tucked in." This is much more effective than saying, "Good job dressing."
Anticipation	Building excitement and anticipation for the earning of a reinforcer can motivate students to do their very best. The more "hype" the teacher uses, the more excited students become to earn the reinforcer. Presenting the potential reinforcer in a mysterious way also builds anticipation.
Variety	Just like adults, students get tired of the same things. A certain reinforcer may be highly desired, but, after repeated exposure, it loses its effectiveness. It is easy to get caught up in giving students the same old reinforcers time and time again. However, variety is the spice of life for everyone. Generally, when teachers are asked why they do not vary their reinforcers, they indicate that it worked very well once. It is necessary to change reinforcers frequently to make the reinforcement more effective.

From Rhode, G., Jenson, W.R., & Reavis, H.K. (1992). *The tough kid book: Practical classroom management strategies* (p. 34). Longmont, CO: Sopris West, Inc.; Reprinted with permission from Sopris West, Inc.

A teacher may develop a hierarchy of the behaviors that he or she would like to see a child exhibit. For example, in response to Jeremy's out-of-seat behavior, his teacher initiated a reinforcement system to increase in-seat behavior. However, although Jeremy may earn multiple reinforcers for remaining in his seat, this does not guarantee that he will engage in constructive or appropriate behaviors while sitting. Often, multiple reinforcers and multiple levels of reinforcement must be

Table 6.4. Examples of positive reinforcements

Type of reinforcement	Examples
Healthy edible items	Pretzels
	Fruit
	Nuts
	Juice
Tangible items	Stickers
	Pencils
	Trading cards
	Posters
	Comics
	Positive note sent home to parents
Activities	Be the line leader
	Help the teacher with a task (e.g., collecting book money, taking attendance)
	Receive a free homework pass
	Reduced assignments
	Have lunch with the teacher or principal
	Help students in other younger classes
	Be allowed to leave class early
	Have extra time for:
	playing games
	doing puzzles
	building with blocks
	coloring, painting
	playing with toys
	drawing
	art project
	recess
	library
	high-interest reading materials
	computer
	Ipods or Game Boys
	visiting with friends
	listening to music
	watching movies
	community service activities
	class project
Social	Smile
	Pat on the shoulder
	Positive comment about improved performance
	Positive feedback on the quality of assignments
	Positive feedback regarding observed behaviors

initiated. For example, Jeremy was provided with one reinforcer for sitting and a second reinforcer for working while he was sitting. Do not make reinforcers time-dependent (e.g., participating in a scheduled field trip). The student must have the opportunity to earn the reward. The variable element should be *when* Jeremy will receive the reward, not *if* he will earn it.

Token Economies Token economies are behavioral reinforcement systems used to increase the frequency with which a person demonstrates specific target behaviors. The following procedure, adapted from DuPaul and Stoner (2003), may be used:

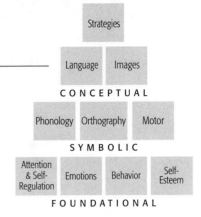

1. *Determine the behavior requiring intervention.* Using a variety of methods (e.g., teacher interviews, observations, situational rating scales), identify the student's behaviors that present the most serious challenges to learning. Jeremy's teacher wanted him to start tasks promptly and finish tasks.

2. *Identify the situation in which the problematic behavior is most likely to occur* (e.g., for Jeremy, this was independent work in reading or writing).

3. *Take baseline data.* Before initiating the intervention, take baseline data on the frequency, severity, and/or intensity of the behaviors targeted for intervention and establish a system for objectively monitoring progress. Some of the monitoring systems commonly used in schools include documenting the percentage of work completed, counting the number of times the behavior occurs in a given time period (e.g., 5 minutes), or counting the number of time periods during which the negative behavior does not occur. Jeremy typically did not begin a task until several minutes after instructions had been given. He rarely completed tasks.

4. *Select the primary and secondary reinforcers.* Token economies include primary reinforcers (i.e., the privileges, activities, and tangible items that the student is trying to earn) and secondary reinforcers (tokens that measure progress toward earning the desired reward, such as poker chips, checkmarks, or pennies). Jeremy and his teacher decided on drawing time for the primary reinforcer and tokens for the secondary reinforcer. Younger or less mature students usually require tangible items for the secondary reinforcer, whereas older students and adolescents often prefer checkmarks on a card. Students under the age of 5 generally do not understand the complexity of a two-tiered program and, consequently, need an immediate reward each time they produce the target positive behavior. Intangible and tangible reinforcers to be given on a frequent basis may include verbal praise specific to the behavior; a note to the parents; stickers on a card to bring home; or a grab bag of small, inexpensive things. Ensure that the rewards chosen are highly motivating to the student and are not easily available except within the behavior program.

5. *Assign point values to the behaviors.* Determine a point value for each demonstration of the target positive behavior or for refraining from the negative behavior. If you are targeting more than one behavior, determine and list the point value for each, assigning higher point values to more difficult tasks or behaviors. Break down complex tasks into parts, assigning a point value to each, so that the student receives credit for those parts done well. Jeremy's teacher devised a plan where he would earn two tokens each time he started to work within 10 seconds and two tokens when he completed the task.

6. *Develop a menu of privileges, activities, or tangible items for which the student can trade the tokens.* Assign a point value to each menu item according to its attraction for the student (e.g., five points for a toy from the "treasure box," 10 points for art supplies, 7 points to help deliver the school newspaper). Make sure that some rewards are valued low enough that a student could earn them in half a day or less. Initially, many students will not be able to delay gratification for more than a few hours, even with the intervening reinforcement of tokens.

7. *Explain to the student the relationship between the tokens and the primary reinforcers.* Depending on the developmental age of the student, this might include modeling the exchange of tokens for different objects. Activities and privileges on the menu can be represented by pictures.

8. *Ensure immediate success.* Initially, set the behavioral criteria for earning tokens at a level the student is already capable of meeting (e.g., writing one complete sentence in an essay, completing 50% of a worksheet, raising his or her hand even if calling out at the same time). The student must earn enough tokens to cash them in for a reward at least daily and should be encouraged to do so. Immediately, the system becomes real and the student experiences success. Remember that the tokens are only interim reinforcers. If they are not converted into rewards on a frequent and regular basis, they will lose their effectiveness as motivators.

10. *Change rewards to maintain effectiveness and interest.* Monitor the effectiveness of the behavior program on an ongoing basis. Typically, rewards have to be changed periodically so that they maintain their novelty and motivational power. Criteria for rewards may need to be lowered or altered. When the student is maintaining the target behaviors at an improved level, gradually increase the criteria for earning the same number of tokens. When the student is maintaining the behavior at a lesser level of support, substitute other problematic behaviors for intervention. Continue to reinforce previous behavior intermittently but with sufficient frequency that the student remains aware of the behavioral expectation and his or her ability to meet it.

11. *Promote generalization.* A student with behavior difficulties is unlikely to spontaneously generalize the positive behaviors developed in one situation to another situation. In all probability, the student will need guidance or direct training to do so, even in situations similar in structure and expectations. Typically, students have more difficulty maintaining behavior control in situations in which the rules, structure, and supervision are relaxed (e.g., assemblies, lunch). Although behavioral interventions in such situations are more difficult to establish, they are usually necessary.

Robinson, Newby, and Ganzell (1981) used a token reinforcement system for successful completion of four tasks, two involving learning to read and using vocabulary words and sentences and two involving teaching these tasks to other students. Tokens were exchanged for access to a pinball machine or electronic game. The token intervention program resulted in a ninefold increase in the mean number of tasks completed over the baseline level as well as significant improvements in performance on the school district's standardized weekly reading level examinations. A reduction in disruptive behavior was also anecdotally reported. This reinforcement system was managed by a single teacher working with 18 children, all of whom had received the diagnoses of ADHD. Walker and Shea (1991) also described an in-depth model of structuring a successful classroom token economy.

Negative Reinforcement   *Negative reinforcement* requires the child to work for the removal of an in-place, unpleasant consequence. The child's goal is to get rid of something that is unpleasant rather than to earn something that is desirable. In a negative reinforcement model, instead of working to earn a positive consequence, the child works to get away from an aversive consequence. Negative

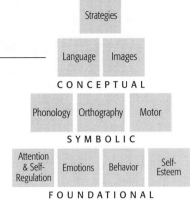

reinforcement is often used in the classroom to manage problem behaviors. Teachers inadvertently pay attention to a child who may not be complying and withdraw their attention contingent on the child's compliance. Surprisingly, this strengthens rather than weakens the noncompliant behavior. The next time a similar situation occurs, the child again will not comply until confronted with the aversive consequence (i.e., the teacher's attention). Negative reinforcement is often seductive and coercive for teachers. It works in the short run but in the long run is likely to strengthen rather than weaken the undesirable behavior.

Many of the same variables that affect positive reinforcement—immediacy, frequency, consistency—affect negative reinforcement. Behaviors that in and of themselves may not be negative become negative reinforcers when paired with certain events. For example, a teacher approaching a child who is not working quickly becomes a negative reinforcer, even though the action itself, the teacher walking up to the child, does not have a negative connotation (Favell, 1977). Clark and Elliott (1988) found that negative reinforcement was rated by teachers as the most frequently used classroom intervention. Children with disruptive behavior often experience negative reinforcement because of their temperament, which makes it difficult for them to complete tasks; their consequent learning history reinforces them for beginning but rarely for finishing a task.

A number of simple, effective ways exist to deal with this problem. If a teacher uses negative reinforcement, he or she should pay attention to the student until the assignment is completed. Although this, too, is negative reinforcement, it teaches the child that the only way to get rid of the aversive consequence (i.e., the teacher's attention) is not just to start but to complete the task at hand. As an example, the teacher may move the student's desk to a closer proximity until that particular piece of work is completed.

A second alternative involves the use of differential attention or ignoring. The term *differential attention* applies when ignoring is used as the negative consequence for exhibiting the undesirable behavior, and attention is used as a positive consequence for exhibiting the competing desirable behavior. This is an active process in which the teacher ignores the child engaged in an off-task activity but pays attention immediately when the child begins working. Many teachers avoid interaction with the child when he or she is on task for fear of interrupting the child's train of thought. It is important, however, to reinforce the child when he or she is working so that a pattern of working to earn positive reinforcement is developed rather than working to avoid negative reinforcement.

Secondary school teachers at times complain that if they ignore the adolescent exhibiting disruptive behavior, they may never have the opportunity to pay positive attention because the student may never exhibit the positive behavior during an hour-long class. Waiting for the behavior to occur, however, even if it does not occur until the next day, is more effective in the long run than paying attention to off-task behavior that does not disturb other students.

The teacher must distinguish between off-task behavior that disrupts and off-task behavior that does not disrupt. Differential attention works effectively for the latter. However, when a child is off task and disturbing others, a negative reinforcer holds an advantage in stemming the tide of an off-task behavior that involves other students as well. Differential attention alone is ineffective in maintaining high rates of on-task behavior and work productivity for students with ADHD (Rosen, O'Leary, Joyce, Conway, & Pfiffner, 1984). Many factors other than teacher attention maintain and influence student behavior.

Differential attention is a powerful intervention when used appropriately. Once the strategy of ignoring inappropriate behavior is employed, it must be continued despite escalation. If not, the teacher runs the risk of intermittently reinforcing the negative behavior, thereby strengthening its occurrence. For example, at first, Jeremy's teacher decided to use differential attention for his out-of-seat behavior, but she became sufficiently frustrated after he was out of his seat for 10 minutes. If she had responded by telling Jeremy to sit down, the behavior would have been reinforced rather than extinguished. The 10 minutes of ignoring would have been quickly lost in the one incident of negative attention. Jeremy would have received the desired attention by persisting in a negative behavior.

Madsen, Becker, and Thomas (1968) evaluated rules, praise, and ignoring for inappropriate behavior in two children in a typical second-grade classroom and in one child in a kindergarten class. The results indicated that in the absence of praise, rules and ignoring were ineffective. Inappropriate behavior decreased only after praise was added. Others have demonstrated the importance of praise in a general education classroom (Thomas, Becker, & Armstrong, 1968). Specifically, whenever teacher approval was withdrawn, disruptive behaviors increased.

Overall, however, the research on differential attention with children with poor self-control has been inconsistent. Rosen and colleagues (1984) evaluated the results of praise and reprimands in maintaining appropriate social and academic behaviors in second- and third-grade children with ADHD. Children's on-task behavior and academic performance deteriorated when negative feedback was withdrawn but not when positive feedback was omitted. Students' on-task behavior remained high, even after 9 days of no praise from the teacher. Acker and O'Leary (1988) demonstrated that the use of only reprimands for behavior management without positive consequences does not lead to dramatic improvement in on-task performance when praise is added. Dramatic deterioration in on-task behavior was observed when reprimands were subsequently withdrawn, even though the teacher was still delivering praise for appropriate behavior.

Both children with poor self-control and children who are developing typically respond better to a continuous schedule of reinforcement than to a more typical partial schedule of reinforcement in which the reinforcement is provided only sometimes (Douglas & Parry, 1983). Praise is important for the development of other attributes in human beings, such as self-esteem, school attitude, and motivation toward academics (Redd, Morris, & Martin, 1975). In addition, the opposite is also true: A large amount of punishment can negatively affect emotional development and self-esteem.

Modeling Through modeling, observation, and then imitation, children develop new behaviors. Modeling can be as simple as having a child watch another child sharpen a pencil. By watching the model, a child can learn a new behavior, inhibit a behavior, or strengthen a previously learned behavior (e.g., saying "thank you"). To use modeling effectively, a teacher must determine whether a child has the capacity to observe and then imitate the model. In classroom settings, a student's response to modeling is influenced by three factors: 1) the characteristics of the model (e.g., Is this a student whom the other students like and respect?), 2) the characteristics of the observer (e.g., Is this child capable of observing and imitating the behavior?), and 3) the positive or negative consequences associated with the behavior. Children are more likely to respond to teacher modeling when they view the teacher as competent, nurturing, supportive, fun, and interesting. Children are also more likely to imitate behaviors that result in positive consequences.

Younger children have been reported as more frequently imitating others than older children. Children consistently model someone whom they value or look up to. They also imitate the behavior of a same-sex child more often than that

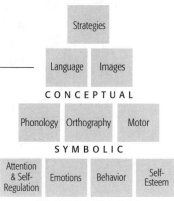

of a different-sex child. They model someone whom they perceive as successful and socially valued regardless of whether the teacher perceives that child in the same way. Finally, if a child observes a model being reinforced or punished for certain behavior, this influences the likelihood that the child will then model that behavior.

Modeling is a powerful tool, often underused by teachers. When teachers are cheerful and enthusiastic, their attitudes are contagious. When they are respectful of students, students respect each other. When teachers are patient, fair, consistent, and optimistic, their students exhibit these traits as well. Teacher behavior sets the tone for the classroom environment.

Nearly 40 years ago in 1970, Kaplan described a ripple effect in transactions between teachers and misbehaving students that affected not only those students but also the entire classroom. Teachers who were firm reduced the problem behaviors both from the first child who misbehaved and from those students who saw the initial problem behavior. When teachers enforced rules, the ripple effect worked in their favor. When they failed to follow through with rules, the ripple effect worked against them. Furthermore, the misbehaving student's social standing in the classroom was also an issue. When teachers successfully managed the behavior of high-status troublemakers, their control tended to benefit the entire classroom. Likewise, the ripple effect when high-status offenders were not managed effectively increased negative behaviors among other students.

Finally, when managing a disruptive behavior, it is important to focus on tasks and behaviors rather than on approval. In the latter situation, teachers may focus on their relationship with the disruptive student when trying to get that student to behave. This strategy, unfortunately, is usually ineffective over the long term.

Shaping   Waiting for the appropriate target behavior or something close to that behavior to occur before reinforcing the behavior is referred to as *shaping*. Shaping can be used to establish behaviors that are not routinely exhibited. Walker and Shea (1991) described the steps for effective shaping:

1. Select a target behavior and define it.

2. Observe how often the behavior is exhibited.

3. Select reinforcers.

4. Decide on close approximations and reinforce successive approximations to the target behavior each time they occur.

5. Reinforce the newly established behavior on an every-time or continuous schedule as it occurs. The key to successful shaping is to reinforce closer approximations and not reinforce lesser approximations.

Any behavior that remotely resembles the target behavior should initially be reinforced. Prompts can be used and then faded. Shaping can be used for all kinds of behaviors in the classroom, including academics. Steps toward successive approximation, however, must be carefully thought out; otherwise, behaviors that are not working toward the desired goal may inadvertently be reinforced.

Punishment

Punishment suppresses undesirable behavior but may not necessarily eliminate it (McDaniel, 1980). In some cases, the cessation may be of short duration, and when the punishment is removed, the behavior may recur. Punishment can involve presentation of an unpleasant consequence or the loss of a pleasurable consequence following the occurrence of the undesirable behavior. Punishment is designed to reduce the probability that the behavior that precedes it will recur. Although punishment is an efficient way of changing behavior, it can become seductive and reinforcing for classroom teachers and can be overused. The greatest problem with punishment is that it does not provide an appropriate model of acceptable behavior. Furthermore, in many classrooms, punishment is accompanied by an emotional response from the teacher. Although most teachers consider punishment as involving a reprimand, time-out, or loss of an activity such as recess, physical punishment is still used in some classrooms, even though it has a high emotional cost. Shea and Bauer (1987) made a strong case for minimizing the use of punishment, especially more severe punishments such as embarrassment or spanking, because these interventions are likely to erode self-esteem and further impair an already strained teacher–student relationship. When punishments are used, these guidelines should be followed:

1. All students are aware of which behaviors are punished and how they are punished.

2. Appropriate models for acceptable behavior are provided.

3. Punishments are offered immediately, consistently, and fairly.

4. Punishments are offered impersonally.

5. A natural or logical consequence should be used as often as possible.

6. The student being punished must understand the relationship between his or her behavior and the punishment.

Loss of the privilege during which the inappropriate behavior is exhibited is fair. Warning, nagging, threatening, and debating, however, should be avoided. In other words, act, don't yak. Punishment can exert a complex, negative effect in the classroom and on teacher–student relationships. Furthermore, when less punishing interventions are combined with positive reinforcers, they tend to be effective in the long run. In 1946, Anderson and Brewer reported that teachers using dominating behaviors of force, threat, shame, and blame had classrooms in which children displayed nonconforming behavior at rates higher than in classrooms in which teachers were more positive and supportive. Personal hostility from teachers and punishments in an atmosphere containing minimal positive reinforcement and emotional warmth are unproductive. To be effective, punishment must be related in form to the misbehavior. It must be consistent, fair, and just; must be delivered impersonally; and must not involve the assignment of extra work that is unrelated to the act for which the student is being punished. Opportunities must also be offered for the student to exhibit and receive reinforcement for more appropriate behavior. At times it is appropriate to allow the student to choose from several consequences (e.g., writing, talking, or drawing about an event).

Reprimands are the most frequent punishment used by teachers. Contacting parents, taking away privileges, and giving time-outs come next in frequency. Reprimands include a statement of appropriate alternative behavior. Students respond well to short reprimands followed by clear, directed statements. Effective reprimands are specific, do not humiliate the child, are provided immediately, and are given with a firm voice and controlled physical demeanor. They are often backed up with a loss of privilege, including a statement encouraging more appropriate behavior. The teacher should attempt to describe the behavior rather than how he or she feels about the behavior. Instead of telling a student that he is rude for interrupting, make a statement such as, "You have interrupted me three

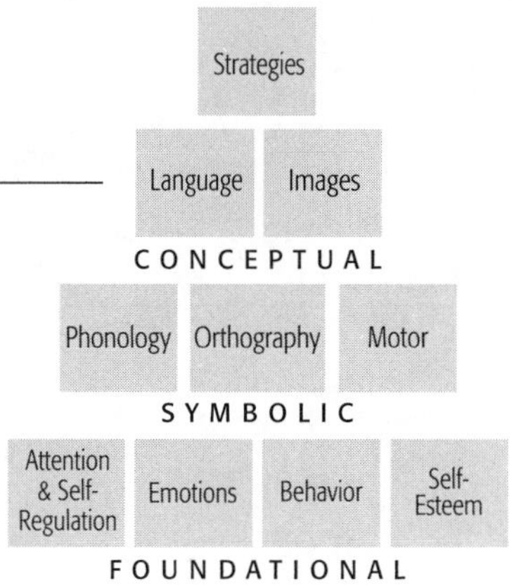

Strategies

Language | Images

CONCEPTUAL

Phonology | Orthography | Motor

SYMBOLIC

Attention & Self-Regulation | Emotions | Behavior | Self-Esteem

FOUNDATIONAL

times. I will answer your question as soon as I finish the explanation." This should be delivered in a calm way and in a way that does not embarrass the child in the presence of others. Jeremy had complained to his mother that his teacher was always yelling at him to keep still or be quiet. Feeling particularly upset one afternoon, Jeremy wrote his fifth-grade teacher the letter presented in Figure 6.5. Fortunately, after reading this letter, his teacher understood that yelling was an ineffective way to deal with Jeremy's behavior.

Abramowitz, O'Leary, and Futtersak (1988) compared the effects of short and long reprimands in an alternating treatment design. Over the course of the study, short reprimands resulted in significantly lower off-task rates than long reprimands. Prudent reprimands that are immediate, unemotional, brief, and consistently backed up with consequences are clearly preferred to lengthy reprimands that are delayed, loud, emotional, and not matched to consequences. Abramowitz and O'Leary (1991) suggested that immediate reprimands result in much lower rates of off-task interactions with peers but do not change rates of off-task behaviors that do not involve peers. The authors hypothesized that noninteractive, off-task behavior may be an avoidance response to difficult schoolwork. Interactive, off-task behaviors may be reinforced by peer attention and modified more effectively by the timing of feedback. Consistent reprimands are clearly superior to inconsistent reprimands for minimizing calling out and

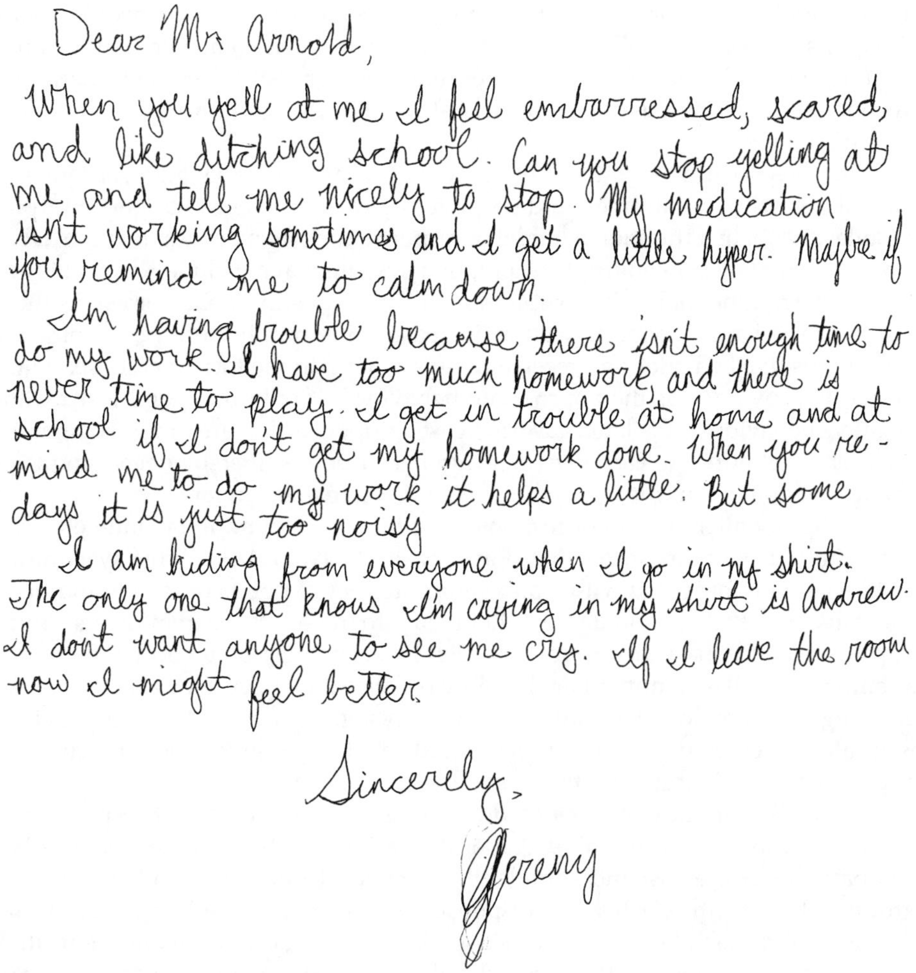

Dear Mr. Arnold,

When you yell at me I feel embarrassed, scared, and like ditching school. Can you stop yelling at me and tell me nicely to stop. My medication isn't working sometimes and I get a little hyper. Maybe if you remind me to calm down.

I'm having trouble because there isn't enough time to do my work. I have too much homework, and there is never time to play. I get in trouble at home and at school if I don't get my homework done. When you remind me to do my work it helps a little. But some days it is just too noisy

I am hiding from everyone when I go in my shirt. The only one that knows I'm crying in my shirt is Andrew. I don't want anyone to see me cry. If I leave the room now I might feel better.

Sincerely,
Jeremy

Figure 6.5. Jeremy's letter to his teacher.

other disruptive behaviors (Acker & O'Leary, 1988). When reprimands versus ignoring are evaluated as punishments for misbehaviors, however, reprimands are not particularly effective in managing off-task behavior. Reprimanding every incident of off-task behavior did not prove to be any more effective than reprimanding one quarter of misbehavior incidents. Increasing consistency in these low-rate situations does not appear to lead to significant differences (Pfiffner, O'Leary, Rosen, & Sanderson, 1985).

Furthermore, the intensity or aversiveness of the initial delivery of the reprimand may be critical for children with disruptive behavior (Futtersak, O'Leary, & Abramowitz, 1989). In this study, children were exposed to teachers who delivered either consistently strong reprimands from the outset with immediate, brief, and firm close proximity or reprimands that increased in severity over time. Results supported the hypothesis that gradually strengthening initially weak reprimands was less effective for suppressing off-task behavior than the immediate introduction and maintenance of full-strength reprimands. In addition, reprimands are more effective when delivered with eye contact and in close proximity to the child (Van Hauten, Nau, MacKenzie-Keating, Sameoto, & Colavecchia, 1982).

Response Cost *Response cost* is a punishing technique that translates to the equivalent of losing what you possess or have earned. Earned consequences are considered reinforcers. When they are lost, this is response cost. The child's inappropriate behavior places in jeopardy what he or she has earned. In many situations, response cost in the form of a penalty or fine is combined with positive reinforcement. To be effective, more reinforcers must be earned than lost. Response cost is often used to reduce off-task behavior and improve compliance with directions.

Response cost may be the most powerful means of managing consequences for children with ADHD or other disruptive behavior problems (Rapport, Murphy, & Bailey, 1982). In a traditional model of response cost, many children with ADHD may immediately go bankrupt. Alternative systems have included adjusting the ratio of the number of reinforcers provided for each positive behavior versus those lost for negative behavior as well as increasing the number of opportunities to exhibit positive behavior and receive reinforcement. In the former case, six points might be provided for the appropriate behavior but only one point lost for the negative behavior. In the latter case, increased opportunities are provided, making it easier for children to earn a greater number of points, thereby decreasing their chances of going bankrupt when they exhibit negative behavior.

A slightly altered form of response cost has been found to be quite effective with children who are impulsive (Rapport et al., 1982). Under this system, the child is initially provided with a maximum number of points or tokens and he or she must work throughout the school day to retain those reinforcers. Some impulsive children seem to work harder to keep their plates full rather than attempting to fill an empty plate. Possibly because they have a long history of not working well for positive reinforcement, a system in which they are provided with all of their reinforcement initially and must work to keep the tokens may appear more motivating or attractive to them.

A substantial body of research documents the effectiveness of response cost in the classroom (Kazdin, 1982). One of the earliest studies (Rapport et al., 1982) compared response cost and stimulant medication for task-related behavior in a group of boys with ADHD. The response cost procedure resulted in significant increases in on-task behavior and academic performance. Stimulant medication was notably less effective. Pfiffner and colleagues (1985) found that response cost in the form of lost recess was more effective than reprimands in maintaining

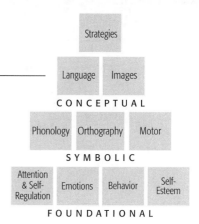

on-task behavior. Response cost has also been compared with reward alone. Both conditions resulted in a twofold increase in academic output or reduction in inappropriate classroom behavior and a corresponding increase in on-task behavior. Children often do not show a differential preference for either reward or response cost procedures (Hundert, 1976; Iwata & Bailey, 1974), but they appear to maintain intervention gains better during fading and withdrawal of response cost than they do in response to traditional rewards (Sullivan & O'Leary, 1990).

A response cost system can be as simple as chips in a cup, marks on a chart, or marbles in a jar. A more complex means of managing response cost includes electronic devices such as the Attention Training System (Gordon & Davidson, 1981; Rapport, 1987). The Attention Training System is a remote-controlled counter that sits on the student's desk. This device provides the student with a digital readout showing the number of points he or she has earned. Using a remote control device, points can be added or removed by the teacher from anywhere in the classroom, contingent on the child's on- and off-task behavior. By not having to move within physical proximity of the child, the teacher avoids becoming a negative reinforcer when the child is off task. DuPaul, Guevremont, and Barkley (1992) demonstrated the efficacy of response cost contingencies for managing classroom behavior and academic productivity using the Attention Training System. Response cost contingencies led to marked improvements on task-related attention and a reduction in ADHD symptoms during work time.

For response cost to be effective, the procedure must be used for most, if not all, of the classroom day (Morgan & Jenson, 1988). The number of students in the program must be manageable, and highly motivating rewards must be provided. If not thought out well and managed effectively, response cost can backfire and increase classroom problem behaviors (Burchard & Barrera, 1972).

Response cost can be difficult to implement. Many teachers inadvertently become negative reinforcers when they approach the child to remove a consequence, thereby building failure into a potentially useful model. When students who become bankrupt quickly or who are oppositional from the start are placed in a group contingency situation with built-in failure (e.g., everyone must earn the reinforcer or no one has access to it), the result is often increased rather than decreased classroom problems. The following guidelines suggest how to use response cost effectively in the classroom (Morgan & Jenson, 1988):

1. Use the procedure for the target behavior for most, if not all, of the classroom day.

2. Make certain the number of students using the program is manageable.

3. Make certain there are more opportunities for success than for failure.

4. Build in additional incentives, including additional reinforcers that can be earned at the end of the week by retaining a minimum number of reinforcers through the week.

5. Consider incorporating self-monitoring techniques in which students can administer response cost independently when they recognize a rule violation.

Time-Out Time-out from reinforcement excludes children from the opportunity to participate with others and receive any kind of positive reinforcement. Time-out can be effective in typical classroom settings because it restores order by removing the child who is disrupting class, by reducing the

153

opportunity for peer approval that maintains some children who disrupt, by reducing the opportunity for students to manipulate situations, and by allowing the student to demonstrate appropriate behavior before exiting time-out. Time-out is by far the best known disciplinary technique among teachers. It is also the most likely to be overused and misused in the classroom. Although a brief time-out of a few minutes duration can exert a positive influence on classroom behavior when applied appropriately, many teachers apply time-out ineffectively as often as they do effectively (Walker & Walker, 1991).

The least restrictive form of time-out consists of removal of certain reinforcing activities or objects from the misbehaving child for a short period. Time-out in a restricted environment outside of the classroom is the most extreme form of this type of discipline. The child can neither see the classroom nor interact with others.

The effectiveness of time-out is well established; however, additional research is needed to identify specific situations, parameters, and procedures associated with the success of time-out for children who are disruptive. Clearly, time-out holds a low probability of directly affecting children's symptoms for the better. Time-out can be quite effective for noncompliant children, but for children with poor self-control, which is characteristic of ADHD, the teacher must distinguish between noncompliant behaviors and behaviors resulting from ADHD.

In general, for time-out to be effective, 1) students should be separated from reinforcement, 2) the time should be short, 3) confrontation should be avoided, 4) verbal interaction should be limited, and 5) a time-contingent release should be provided (Bean & Roberts, 1981). Time-contingent release refers to the amount of time and the contingencies (e.g., sitting quietly) required to earn release. These contingencies should be explained and provided to the child prior to entering time-out. Children warned less in time-out also respond better (Roberts, 1982).

The length of time-out is also critical in determining effectiveness. A 4-minute time-out was found to be significantly better than a 10-second or 1-minute time-out among a group of elementary school students (Hobbs, Forehand, & Murray, 1978). In elementary classroom settings, time-out should be from 2 to 5 minutes. If a student is not in control, an additional minute should be added. Long periods of time-out constitute seclusion and lose their punishing value.

The time-out activity must also be less reinforcing than the setting or activity from which the child is being removed. If a particular activity the child is leaving is nonreinforcing, this child may in fact learn to misbehave as a means of going to time-out to do something else. Work should not be missed due to time-out. Time-out should be boring, uninteresting, and something the child places last on his or her list of chosen school activities. The effectiveness of time-out depends on a number of factors, including the child, the teacher's ability to apply the intervention consistently, the child's understanding of the intervention, the rules governing the intervention, characteristics of the time-out area, duration of time-out, and the ability to evaluate the effectiveness of time-out quickly. If time-out does not work in the first few interventions, an alternative strategy should be considered.

According to Scarboro and Forehand (1975), eight parameters should define the use of time-out:

1. An explanation should be provided to the child before time-out is administered.

2. A warning should be issued that time-out may be given unless the behavior is stopped.

3. The child should be consistently removed and placed in time-out when the behavior recurs.

Strategies

Language | Images

CONCEPTUAL

Phonology | Orthography | Motor

SYMBOLIC

Attention & Self-Regulation | Emotions | Behavior | Self-Esteem

FOUNDATIONAL

4. A specific location should be defined for time-out.

5. A specific duration for time-out should be set.

6. The consistent schedule for time-out use should be defined.

7. A defined behavior should lead to time-out.

8. Clear contingencies should be defined for the child to be released from time-out.

Teachers should not force resistant students into time-out but should seek help from the principal or other school personnel. Finally, as soon as possible after time-out is over, something positive in the student's behavior should be reinforced. Table 6.5 contains a list of dos and don'ts for time-out. Table 6.6 contains a thorough list of procedures for implementing seclusionary time-out.

Teachers can do many things to minimize the need to use time-out. First, classroom activities must be more reinforcing than time-out. Second, students should be given ample but not excessive opportunities to comply. Third, disruptive students can be provided with additional positive consequences for not requiring time-out in a given time span.

Consequential versus Rule-Governed Behavior   Due to their inhibitory problems, children who are impulsive may function quite well under appropriate external or environmental consequences but struggle to develop the internal self-monitoring skills to govern their own behavior. This latter issue was referred to by Barkley in 1981 as "problems following rule-governed behavior." Children who are impulsive may acquire behavior at a rate similar to others but take longer to learn to self-manage that behavior in the absence of external consequences and cues. Thus, even when appropriate reinforcers are earned, this child requires a greater number of successful trials to make the transition to self-management. In part, this speaks to the difference between behavior modification and behavior

Table 6.5.   The "dos and "don'ts of time-out

Do explain the total procedure to the child before starting time-out.	Don't start the procedure without explaining time-out to the child first in a calm setting that is not emotionally charged.
Do prepare a time-out setting for the child that is clean, well-lit, and ventilated.	Don't just pick any place. Make sure it isn't too dark, too confining, dangerous, or not ventilated.
Do pick a place or situation for time-out that is boring or less reinforcing than the classroom.	Don't pick a place that is scary or that could be more reinforcing than the classroom.
Do use a set of structured verbal requests with a child, such as the recommended precision request format.	Don't threaten a child repeatedly with a time-out.
Do remain calm, and don't talk with the child when he or she is being taken to time-out.	Don't get into a verbal exchange with the child on the way to time-out or while the child is in time-out.
Do place the child in time-out for a set period that you control.	Don't tell the child to come out of time-out when he or she is "ready to behave."
Do require the child to be quiet for 30 seconds at the end of the time-out period, before being let out.	Don't let a child out of time-out when he or she is crying, screaming, yelling, or having a tantrum.
Do use a short period of time (e.g., 5–10 minutes).	Don't use exceedingly long periods.
Do require the child to complete the request that led to time-out or missed academic work.	Don't allow the child to avoid compliance to a request or miss academic work by going to time-out.

From MORGAN, JENSON, TEACHING BEHAVIORALLY DISORDERED STUDENTS: PREFERRED PRACTICES, 1st Edition, © 1990, Pgs. 130–131. Reprinted by permission of Pearson Education, Inc. Upper Saddle River, NJ.

Table 6.6. Seclusionary time-out procedures

1. Seclusionary time-out should not be used unless all other procedures have been tried and failed. This should be a last effort technique.

2. Seclusionary time-out should never be used without a parent's written consent.

3. Seclusionary time-out should be used only if it is listed as an approved and agreed-on technique in a student's individualized education [program] (IEP) by the IEP team. The student should only be placed in time-out for approved behaviors on the IEP, such as aggression, severe noncompliance, or destructive tantrum-throwing.

4. *Seclusionary time-out* is defined as removing a student from a reinforcing classroom setting to a less reinforcing setting. This setting can be another classroom, a chair or desk outside the classroom, or a room specifically approved for time-out. If a room is used for time-out, it should be used only for time-out and no other purpose (e.g., storage, counseling students, special academic work area).

5. The time-out setting should be well-lit, well-ventilated, nonthreatening, and clean. It must also have an observation window or device. The staff member should try the technique on him- or herself before using the room with a student, and the room should be shown to the student's parents.

6. The entire time-out procedure should be explained to the student before it is implemented, prior to the occurrence of misbehavior that results in its use.

7. If misbehavior occurs, identify it. For example, tell the student in a calm, neutral manner, "That's fighting; you need to go to the time-out room." Tell the student to remove his or her jewelry, belt, and shoes. Tell the student to empty his or her pockets (in order to check for such items as pens, pencils, paper clips, knives, and so forth). The student's socks should be checked for these types of items also. If the student does not comply with these requests, call for help and then remove the items and check the pockets yourself. **No other conversation should ensue.**

8. When a student is placed in the time-out room, he or she must be constantly monitored by a staff member. The student must never be left alone.

9. When a student is placed in the time-out room, the following information should be placed in a **time-out log:**
   - Name of the student
   - Date
   - Staff member responsible for monitoring student
   - Time in and time out
   - Target behavior warranting the procedures

10. The student should be placed in the time-out room for a specific period of time. A recommended formula is 1 minute per year of age (e.g., 10 minutes for a 10-year-old child).

11. If a student is screaming, throwing a tantrum, or yelling, he or she should be quiet for 30 consecutive seconds before being released from the time-out room. This 30 seconds does not begin until the original designated time-out period has lapsed.

12. Communication between the supervising staff member and the student should not take place when the student is in the time-out room (i.e., do not talk with the student, threaten the student, or try to counsel the student at this time).

13. Do remain calm while taking a student to the time-out room. Do not argue with, threaten, or verbally reprimand the student.

14. If a student refuses to go to the time-out room, add on time to the specified time-out duration (e.g., 1 minute for each refusal, up to 5 minutes).

15. If a student refuses to come out of the time-out room, do not beg or try to remove the student. Simply wait outside, and sooner or later the student will come out on his or her own.

16. If the student makes a mess in the time-out room, require him or her to clean it up before he or she leaves.

17. Once the time-out period has ended, return the student to the ongoing classroom activity, making sure the student is required to complete the task he or she was engaged in prior to the time-out period. This ensures that students do not purposely avoid unpleasant tasks by going to the time-out room.

18. All staff members should be trained, and this training documented, before time-out procedures are started.

19. To ensure the effectiveness of time-out, the reinforcement rate for appropriate behaviors in the classroom should meet the recommended rate of three or four positive responses to each negative response (and never fewer than four positive responses per contact hour).

20. Data should be collected on target behaviors. If time-out is effective, these behaviors should decrease shortly after the technique is started. If they do not, check that the procedure is being used correctly, and the reinforcement rate for appropriate behavior in the classroom is high enough; consider another technique for possible use.

(continued)

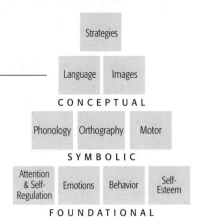

Strategies

Language Images

CONCEPTUAL

Phonology Orthography Motor

SYMBOLIC

Attention & Self-Regulation Emotions Behavior Self-Esteem

FOUNDATIONAL

Table 6.6. *(continued)*

21. The use of time-out should not be threatened (e.g., "If you do that again, I will put you in the time-out room"). Rather, the technique should be combined with a precision request, such as "I need you to stop kicking your desk." If the student persists, the time-out procedure should be used, and when the student comes out of the time-out room, the precision request should be restated ("I need you to stop kicking your desk").

22. The student should be reinforced for not needing time-out.

From Rhode, G., Jenson, W.R., & Reavis, H.K. (1992). *The tough kid book: Practical classroom management strategies* (p. 65). Longmont, CO: Sopris West; reprinted with permission of Sopris West, Inc.

management. Teachers are repeatedly taught that if they provide consequences appropriately, within a reasonable period of time, children's behavior will change. Success is usually based on the child's continuing to demonstrate the desired behavior when consequences are removed. When this model is applied to children who are impulsive, many potentially effective interventions are often deemed failures. For the child who is impulsive, demonstrating a behavior in the presence of consequences is not synonymous with having developed the self-management skills to use the behavior. For these children, it may be necessary for the teacher to shift his or her focus to behavior management. That is, the intervention may be deemed successful if the child's behavior is modified in the presence of consequences. As consequences are removed and the child's behavior regresses, this should not be interpreted as failure but rather as too quick a change in the schedule of reinforcement. The child has yet to make the transition from consequentially managed behavior to rule-governed behavior for that particular task.

Three Keys to Using Punishment Effectively Timing, intensity, and consistency are the three keys to using punishment effectively and appropriately in the classroom. The punishing procedures should be initiated as soon as possible after the aversive behavior is exhibited and should be as closely related to the misbehavior as possible. Furthermore, if punishments are too mild, they will not be effective and may slowly habituate the child to tolerate or adapt to more intensive or lengthy punishments. If too intense, however, punishments are not only abusive but likely will create other problems. Be conservative when using punishing techniques, but make certain their intensity is appropriate. To be effective, punishments must be consistent and predictable. Following punishment, the child should be allowed to return to the situation without being expected to exhibit overt guilt, and efforts should be made to reassure or reinforce the child. A consistent schedule of punishments should also be used. A continuous schedule of punishment for a specific targeted behavior is best. Finally, attempt to find out what drives the misbehavior and work toward managing the environment to minimize causative factors. As noted previously in this chapter, children who are experiencing LD may misbehave out of frustration. This may also be the case for children who are experiencing anxiety or depression. By identifying the child's goals and misbehavior, a teacher can present more appropriate opportunities and methods to reach the child's goals. When used appropriately, punishment can make a positive difference; however, punishing interventions should always follow efforts at using reinforcing interventions to model and shape appropriate classroom behavior.

PREVENTIVE APPROACHES TO DISCIPLINE

Discipline is much more than a teacher's response to students' problems in the classroom. *Discipline* is a process by which teachers help students learn from mistakes and improve their behavior and academic performance. A preventive approach to classroom discipline works best. Such an approach reduces the occurrence of common disciplinary problems and helps a teacher deal much more effectively with them when they occur. As such, preventive discipline begins by putting into place an effective learning environment, understanding each and every student in the classroom, and developing a consistent means of communicating with parents. Preventive discipline also requires that teachers do not view misconduct as a personal affront and that they avoid engaging in power struggles with students. No one wins a power struggle. When students attempt to engage teachers in a confrontation, teachers should not enter the battle. Instead, they should wait until a time when the interaction will be calmer and more positive.

Because of Samuel's disruptive behavior, his teacher, Ms. Handler, had placed him on an hourly reinforcement system. Ms. Handler had been called to the office, so the student teacher was assigned the job of designating points on the point sheet located on Samuel's desk. Samuel had his baseball cap covering the point sheet. The student teacher moved the hat just a short distance. Samuel moved the hat back and said, "Don't touch my hat." The student teacher responded, "Samuel, you need to move your hat so I can give you your hourly points. Besides, hats are not allowed on desks during class time."

"Don't tell me what to do," Samuel responded.

"Samuel, you need to move your hat so I can give you your hourly points."

"You're not the boss here, leave me alone," responded Samuel angrily.

"Samuel, you can either put your hat in the appropriate place or it will go on Ms. Handler's desk."

Samuel then responded, "Don't touch my hat. Don't tell me what to do."

After waiting 30 seconds for Samuel to move his hat, the student teacher picked up the hat and moved it to Ms. Handler's desk. Unfortunately, the student teacher did not realize that Samuel was looking for a battle and had hoped that she would remove the hat. Samuel jumped up out of his chair and approached the student teacher with his hand clenched into a fist.

"I'm going to kick your ass," Samuel yelled, drawing everyone's attention. Samuel swung at the teacher with his right hand. Fortunately, his punch did not connect. The student teacher instructed Samuel to please leave the classroom. Samuel moved backward and fell over a chair. He threw the chair that he had tripped over toward the teacher. The student teacher, the only adult in the classroom, was uncertain what to do. Again she asked Samuel to leave the room, hoping that Ms. Handler would quickly return.

"I won't," said Samuel.

By this time, all of the other students had stopped working and were watching Samuel and the student teacher. Samuel reached out for another chair and pushed it toward the teacher. At this time, Ms. Handler had just arrived back at the classroom and, hearing the altercation, called for the principal, a large but very gentle man. When the principal entered the room with Ms. Handler, he asked Samuel to please come out into the hallway.

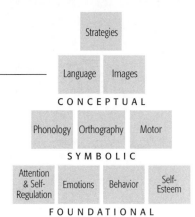

Samuel refused and appeared to be escalating out of control. The principal grabbed him by his arms and lifted Samuel up. Although Samuel was kicking and screaming, the principal carried him out into the hallway and down to the nurse's station.

The situation with Samuel could have been avoided if the student teacher had simply informed him that he would not receive points and followed through with this consequence. Instead, she wound up in a power struggle, which no one wins. Becoming an effective classroom manager requires practice and knowledge of effective approaches. Effective preventive disciplinary approaches include the following:

1. *Use group pressure.* Use subtle group pressure to enforce rules. However, do not punish the entire class because of the misbehavior of one student.

2. *When it's over, move on.* Handle problems effectively as they occur. Once consequences are administered, do not carry a grudge or embarrass students at a later point by bringing up a past infraction.

3. *Learn students' histories.* Learn as much as possible about each student, particularly if a problem arises early on in the school year. If this happens with a student, make an effort to communicate further with the child's parents and previous teachers concerning his or her history. Often, past teachers can provide valuable insights and suggestions about strategies that worked well with this student.

4. *Show respect.* Even during conflicts or difficult times, make an effort to maintain an air of professionalism and respect for all students.

5. *Model desired behaviors.* Model self-discipline and courtesy and students will be more likely to engage in appropriate behavior as well.

Dealing Positively with Classroom Conflict

Conflicts between students and teachers, as with Samuel and the student teacher, often develop from disagreements over whose concerns are more important in the classroom. Often, teachers' mindsets are that students should do what they are told, when they are told to do it. Yet, when teachers believe that they and their students can work together mutually to resolve problems, conflicts can be functional and serve useful purposes. Conflicts can be used as examples to teach conflict resolution, tolerance, and cooperation, and they can help a teacher modify ineffective classroom strategies. Conflict is dysfunctional when it establishes negative patterns of behavior among students, feeds intolerance, or results in aggression.

How should a teacher respond to conflict? Figure 6.6 contains a conflict response quiz adapted from Kreidler (1984). This quiz screens for five different but effective ways of managing classroom conflict. Effective teachers should master all five and routinely use them in their daily repertoire as appropriate.

Class meetings can be an effective means of seeking solutions when conflicts involve multiple class members. In open meetings, students can express their feelings without retribution. In problem-solving meetings, the focus is on identifying the problem, reviewing alternatives, deciding on a solution, and implementing it. Finally, in decision-making meetings, the focus can be on choosing a future program or activities for the entire classroom. This latter type of meeting is effective when teachers desire input from the class when a set of choices present themselves. Figure 6.7 contains a set of suggested steps for approaching and coping effectively with student conflicts.

How Do You Respond to Conflicts?

These exercises are designed to help you take a closer look at how you respond to classroom conflicts. There are no trick questions and no absolutely right or wrong answers. The purpose of the exercise is not to open your behavior to judgment but to make you more aware of your behavior.

Read the following statements. If a statement describes a response you usually make to a classroom conflict, write *3* in the appropriate answer blank. If it is a response that you occasionally make, write *2* in the appropriate blank, and if it is a response that you rarely or never make, write *1*.

When there is a classroom conflict, I

1. Tell the kids to knock it off
2. Try to make everyone feel at ease
3. Help the kids understand each other's point of view
4. Separate the kids, and keep them away from each other
5. Let the principal handle it
6. Decide who started it
7. Try to find out what the real problem is
8. Try to work out a compromise
9. Turn it into a joke
10. Tell them to stop making such a fuss over nothing
11. Make one kid give in and apologize
12. Encourage the kids to find alternative solutions
13. Help them decide what they can compromise on
14. Try to divert attention from the conflict
15. Let the kids fight it out, as long as no one's hurt
16. Threaten to send the kids to the principal
17. Present the kids some alternatives from which to choose
18. Help everyone feel comfortable
19. Get everyone busy doing something else
20. Tell the kids to settle it on their own time, after school

1. _____	2. _____	3. _____	4. _____	5. _____
6. _____	7. _____	8. _____	9. _____	10. _____
11. _____	12. _____	13. _____	14. _____	15. _____
16. _____	17. _____	18. _____	19. _____	20. _____
Totals _____	_____	_____	_____	_____
I	II	III	IV	V

Figure 6.6. How do you respond to conflicts? (From CREATIVE CONFLICT RESOLUTION by William J. Kreidler. Copyright © 1984 by William J. Kreidler. Used by Permission of Good Year Books, Tucson, AZ. Order online at www.goodyearbooks.com or call toll free (888) 511–1530.)

(continued)

Figure 6.6. *(continued)*

Strategies

Language | Images

CONCEPTUAL

Phonology | Orthography | Motor

SYMBOLIC

Attention & Self-Regulation | Emotions | Behavior | Self-Esteem

FOUNDATIONAL

Now add the numbers in each column. Each column reflects a particular approach and attitude toward classroom conflict. In which column did you score highest? Find the appropriate number, and see if the description corresponds to your perception of your attitudes toward conflict.

I. **The no-nonsense approach.** I don't give in. I try to be fair and honest with the kids, but they need firm guidance in learning what's acceptable behavior and what isn't.

II. **The problem-solving approach.** If there's a conflict, there's a problem. Instead of battling the kids, I try to set up a situation in which we can all solve the problem together. This produces creative ideas and stronger relationships.

III. **The compromising approach.** I listen to the kids and help them listen to each other. Then, I help them give a little. We can't all have everything we want. Half a loaf is better than none.

IV. **The smoothing approach.** I like things to stay calm and peaceful whenever possible. Most of the kids' conflicts are relatively unimportant, so I just direct attention to other things.

V. **The ignoring approach.** I point out the limits and let the kids work things out for themselves. It's good for them, and they need to learn about consequences of their behavior. There's not a lot you can do about conflict situations anyway.

At one time or another, each of these approaches is appropriate. There are times, for example, when ignoring a conflict is the best response. There are also times, particularly when a child's safety is at risk, when a very firm, no-nonsense stance is necessary and the problem-solving approach won't work.

It is useful to assess our predominant conflict resolution styles because we tend to get stuck on one or two styles and apply them inappropriately. Our emphasis, however, is not on judging our behavior but on increasing our repertoire of peacemaking skills and learning how and when to apply them most effectively. This depends in part on the type of conflict that occurs.

Teachers will also encounter conflicts between individual students. Effective strategies for dealing with these situations include cooling-off periods, mediation, reflective listening, cooperative time-out, and role playing or role reversal. When aggression breaks out between two students, the first step is to end the aggression and separate the participants until emotions have dissipated. Keep in mind that mediation strategies should be practiced and used with all students in nonconfrontational situations. This increases the probability that mediation is applied effectively in conflict situations. The following three reflective listening steps can be used when conflicts between students occur:

1. Give each student the opportunity to tell his or her side without interruption.

2. If the problem is likely to recur, have participants develop some possible solutions and choose one to actively implement.

3. If the problem is unlikely to recur, have participants discuss more effective ways of coping with the problem should it ever happen again.

Approaching Student-versus-Teacher Conflicts

Step 1: By the Rules

If you have adopted the Effective Rules approach and have established clear rules and consequences, most student-versus-teacher conflicts in your room will relate somehow to these rules. In such a case, point out how the rule was broken and the effect that breaking it has on the class. This reinforces the logical reasons for the rules. State what the consequence is. Accept no excuses. If you and the class have agreed to certain rules and consequences, then you must implement them consistently. If there are extenuating circumstances, and there frequently are, then you can take advantage of your range of options by imposing light consequences.

Step 2: One-to-One

If the child balks at the consequence or gives you a hard time, do not engage in a power struggle in front of the entire class. Instead, find a private place and confront him or her on a one-to-one basis. If appropriate, remind the student that he or she agreed to the rules and consequences. Find out why the child is resisting, and work out the details of the consequence with him or her.

Step 3: Conflict Resolution

If the student continues to resist, suggest a conflict resolution procedure. Step-by-step procedures have a calming effect because they are methodical. They allow you and the student to establish emotional distance from the problem and to focus on the problem rather than on yourselves.

Step 4: Third Party

If a conflict resolution technique fails to produce a satisfactory resolution, it may be time to call in a third party. This should be a teacher whom both you and the student trust. It is particularly important that the child not feel that the mediator is automatically on your side.

Step 5: Higher Authorities

If all else fails, your last resort is the principal or the child's parents or both. Depending on the child and his or her parents, you might want to enlist their aid right away, forgoing Step 4. As a rule, however, exhaust all other resources before appealing to higher authorities.

Always remember that, in addition to resolving a conflict, you are also serving as a model. Children watch you to see if your own conflict resolution technique is of a type that you insist they practice. Even if you are very angry, it is particularly important not to lose control of yourself. If your temper is a problem, count to 10, and, before doing anything else, ask yourself:

Is what I'm about to do going to solve the problem?

Will it affirm the children involved?

Will it build trust and community?

Remember that even as you insist that children accept responsibility for the consequences of their actions, so must you. Student-versus-teacher conflicts are an opportunity to demonstrate that conflict is a source of growth. When any conflict is resolved, ask the children:

"What have we learned from this?"

"How will it make our classroom a better place to be?"

Figure 6.7. Approaching student-versus-teacher conflicts. (From CREATIVE CONFLICT RESOLUTION by William J. Kreidler. Copyright © 1984 by William J. Kreidler. Used by Permission of Good Year Books, Tucson, AZ. Order online at www.goodyearbooks.com or call toll free (888) 511–1530.)

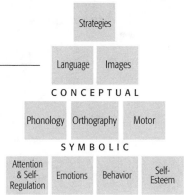

Strategies

Language | Images

CONCEPTUAL

Phonology | Orthography | Motor

SYMBOLIC

Attention & Self-Regulation | Emotions | Behavior | Self-Esteem

FOUNDATIONAL

Reflective listening involves listening actively by paraphrasing and reflecting back what is heard. This can resolve conflict or at least define a problem so that everyone can agree on what to do next. Reflective phrases such as "sounds like," "in other words," "you're saying," "sounds as if you feel," "you feel," and "he feels" can be effective in helping each student take the other's perspective. In some situations, teachers should consider minimizing a minor conflict with simply a few apologetic words and a handshake between students.

Classroom Rules

Classroom rules should clearly communicate expectations regarding academic performance and behavior. Students must understand what is expected behaviorally and academically for success. Most experts agree that classroom rules should be brief and understandable, should communicate expected behavior rather than restricted behavior, and should be developed collaboratively with students. A good set of classroom guidelines consists of no more than five rules. They should be worded simply and in a positive way and represent basic expectations; they should be specific, observable, measurable, and, most important, define consequences both for following rules and for violation of rules. Basic rules should address being punctual; moving around the classroom; following teacher directions, instructions, and commands; communicating with other students; participating in group activities; and engaging in academic work. In some circumstances, rules should be reviewed multiple times as the school year begins and, if necessary, even role-played. Examples of each rule should be developed and discussed. Rules should also be reviewed and discussed regularly with the class and modified as needed. When teachers praise students for following the rules rather than criticize students who do not, compliance with the rules increases.

At the beginning of each school year, students quickly establish an understood set of norms and accepted classroom behaviors that are strongly influenced by the teacher's efforts and attention. Therefore, at the beginning of the school year, teachers should spend the greatest amount of time on defining rules and procedures and making them an automatic part of students' mindset. Good rules are definable, reasonable, and enforceable (Smith & Smith, 1966). If a rule cannot be enforced, it will not guide behavior. If there are too many rules, students may become overwhelmed. When rules are applied inconsistently, students repeatedly test them.

In an interesting series of studies, Madsen and colleagues (1968) reported that rules alone had little effect on classroom behavior, whereas the combination of demonstrating approval for appropriate behavior and ignoring inappropriate behavior relative to rules proved most effective. Although providing approval resulted in better classroom conduct, it was not as effective as a combination of establishing rules, approving appropriate behavior, and ignoring inappropriate behavior. Thus, rules are a necessary but insufficient condition for acceptable classroom behavior.

When dealing with broken rules, the teacher must first ask, "Does the student understand the rule, and is he or she capable of complying?" If not, punishment is unlikely to modify the student's behavior. Furthermore, the teacher must question whether payoffs for following a rule are sufficient for a particular student. This method of analysis takes the emotion out of teacher–student interactions; it allows the teacher to evaluate the student's behavior objectively and make decisions based on behavior rather than on judgments about personality and attitudes. Table 6.7 offers a set of guidelines for establishing and implementing classroom rules each year.

Table 6.7. Establishing and implementing classroom rules

Before the first day of school	Decide which activities in your classroom should be covered by rules.
	Decide what kinds of rules you want to use to structure each activity in your classroom.
On the first day of school	Conduct a group discussion with the students to obtain their suggestions and additions for the set of classroom rules.
	Have the students work together in groups to make rules posters to put up before the start of the second day of school.
On the first or second day of school	Conduct rule-training sessions with students just before beginning the first activity of each type for which you have established rules.
	Try to catch the students following the rules as often as you can and praise them for doing so.
	Encourage students to support each other in rule-following by reminding each other of the rules for an activity before it begins and by thanking each other for following the rules.
On subsequent days of school	Review the rules with the students each Monday for the first few weeks of school, on the first day of school following a holiday or vacation (e.g., state education association conferences, parent–teacher conferences, Thanksgiving, Christmas) or whenever it seems necessary.
	Continue to catch your students following the rules several times each day and reward them with your attention.
	Continue to encourage students to support each other in following the rules.

From *Structuring your classroom for academic success* (p. 63). Champaign, IL: Research Press. Copyright 1983 by Paine, S.C., Radicchi, J., Rosellini, L.C., Deutchman, L., & Darch, C.B. Reprinted by permission.

TEN KEYS TO COMPLIANCE

The following ten keys, based on the work of Forehand and Scarboro (1975); Hamlet, Axelrod, and Kuerschner (1984); Morgan and Jenson (1988); and Walker and Walker (1991), can increase compliance:

Key #1: Stand close to the student when making a request. Requests made for compliance—particularly those directed at misbehaving students—from across the room stand little chance of being followed effectively.

Key #2: Maintain eye contact.

Key #3: Use a soft but firm voice.

Key #4: Make requests unemotionally. In the long run, yelling, name calling, or inducing guilt are ineffective means of increasing compliance. Students should comply because they have been told something needs to be done, not because they perceive that the teacher is upset. In reality, emotionality on the part of teachers decreases compliance and often increases situational problems.

Key #5: Use direct statements. Making requests or asking questions reduces compliance. For example, questions such as "Do you think you are ready to work yet?" or "Could you please stop teasing?" are far less effective than "Please begin working now" or "Please stop teasing."

Key #6: Provide no more than two directions at one time. Asking students to put away one book, take out another, turn to a certain page, and begin a certain task increases the likelihood that some students will become lost.

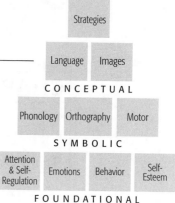

Key #7: Provide students with a reasonable amount of time to respond. Both waiting too long and responding too quickly are ineffective. When requests are made, wait 3–5 seconds before acting.

Key #8: Use start commands rather than stop commands. Stop commands tell children what not to do (e.g., "Take your feet off the desk"). They do not tell the student what to do (e.g., "Put your feet on the floor"). In the first case, the student may remove his or her feet from the desk but then place them on his or her neighbor's desk!

Key #9: Use clear commands rather than vague ones. "Pay attention" is a vague command because it does not tell the student specifically what he or she should be paying attention to. Many off-task students are paying attention to something—just not to what the teacher wants them to attend to.

Key #10: Reinforce compliance. When students comply, teachers must make an effort to acknowledge their compliance with praise.

CONCLUSION

The effective use of behavioral and cognitive strategies in the classroom may appear daunting even to experienced teachers. However, changing teacher behaviors and strategies is often the most efficient and effective means of improving all types of classroom behaviors, both disruptive and nondisruptive. Through practice comes proficiency. The building block of behavior likely contains the largest and most challenging set of problems encountered in the classroom. By first understanding these problems and attempting to see the world through the eyes of their students, and by then developing and using a set of preventive approaches to discipline and intervention strategies on a regular basis, problems of disruptive behavior can be effectively addressed and managed.

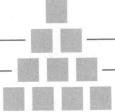

CHAPTER 7 OUTLINE

THE POWER OF MINDSETS

Components of the Mindsets of Effective Educators
Attribution Theory
Students' Basic Needs

ISLANDS OF COMPETENCE

STRATEGIES FOR FOSTERING SELF-ESTEEM, MOTIVATION, HOPE, AND RESILIENCE

The Orientation Period
Accepting Students for Who They Are
Helping Students to Develop a Sense of Responsibility
Increasing Students' Sense of Ownership
Helping Students to Establish Self-Discipline
Providing Positive Feedback and Encouragement
Teaching Students to Cope with Mistakes and Failure

CONCLUSION

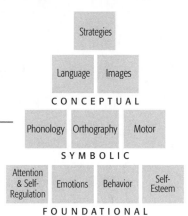

CHAPTER 7

STRATEGIES TO PROMOTE SELF-ESTEEM AND RESILIENCE

with Robert Brooks

Jeremy often had difficulty sitting still and completing his schoolwork, but it was his tendency to speak without thinking that caused frequent and sometimes amusing problems in Mr. Chavez's fifth-grade class. Jeremy and six of his classmates were supposed to be working independently on a series of math worksheets. Mr. Chavez was supervising their work and providing assistance as needed. This day, Jeremy was experiencing great difficulty keeping his mind focused on his work instead of talking to his neighbors. After multiple reminders to stay focused and quiet, out of exasperation Mr. Chavez asked Jeremy to come to the front of the room. He then explained to the other students that it was clear that Jeremy knew exactly how to complete this math because he was choosing to talk rather than do his work. Then he asked Jeremy to teach the remainder of the class. Jeremy at first looked perplexed, then became anxious as he realized that Mr. Chavez was serious.

Mr. Chavez encouraged Jeremy to teach the class. First, Jeremy said he could not do it. Mr. Chavez at this point informed Jeremy that he must. Out of frustration, Mr. Chavez had placed Jeremy in an untenable position. His unspoken intent was to embarrass Jeremy, hoping that he would then focus on his work for the remainder of the class.

Jeremy stood frozen for a few seconds. The other students in the class were clearly anxious yet relieved that they were not in the hot seat. Then, Jeremy's eyes lit up. He looked around the room. A smile came to his face. Before Mr. Chavez could say anything, Jeremy announced, "Recess!" Everyone laughed, even Mr. Chavez. Although many children in this situation might have broken down and cried or stood frozen with anxiety, Jeremy demonstrated a certain resiliency, a quality that allowed him to work through a stressful situation.

THE POWER OF MINDSETS

Mr. Chavez's beliefs about why Jeremy acted the way he did influenced the strategy he used in his attempt to lessen Jeremy's seemingly disruptive behavior. In our daily lives, we possess certain assumptions about ourselves, our children, and other people that influence our actions and interpersonal relationships. Often, we are unaware of these assumptions, although they constantly operate, directing our behavior. These assumptions may be seen as part of our mindset, affecting the ways in which we perceive and respond to people and events.

This chapter examines the components of the mindset of effective educators. These educators touch the hearts and minds of students; they appreciate the forces that truly motivate students and recognize that what they do each day in class contributes to students' self-esteem, resilience, sense of competence, and optimism. The better able teachers are to articulate these components and make them conscious guides, the more effectively they can develop and implement strategies for fostering learning.

Components of the Mindsets of Effective Educators

Effective educators focus equally on academic subjects and on the self-esteem and the social-emotional lives of students. A high school science teacher raised the following question at a workshop: "I am a science teacher. I know how to convey science facts to my students. Why should I spend time thinking about the emotional and social lives of students or about their self-esteem? With all of the material I have to cover, I don't have time to focus on other issues. If anything, this would just distract me from teaching science." Although most educators would take issue with the views expressed by this teacher, a few may concur.

Nurturing a student's emotional and social well-being is not mutually exclusive from teaching academic skills and content. Strengthening a student's self-worth is an essential part of all education. If anything, a student's feelings of belonging, security, and self-esteem in the classroom serve as the foundation for increased learning, motivation, self-discipline, responsibility, and the capacity to deal more comfortably with mistakes (Cohen, 2006). What may have contributed to this dichotomy are different perceptions of what is meant by self-esteem. Although some educators view a student's self-esteem as an integral part of the learning process, others argue that those who focus on fostering self-esteem are doing so at the expense of teaching students self-discipline, accountability, and responsibility; the latter group perceives self-esteem strategies as giving in to students and not holding them accountable for their actions (Brooks, 1999a).

One basis for the existence of the varying perspectives about the concept of self-esteem may reside in the confusion between what Lerner referred to as *feel-good-now self-esteem* versus *earned self-esteem*:

> Earned self-esteem is based on success in meeting the tests of reality—measuring up to standards at home and at school. It is necessarily hard-won and develops slowly, but it is stable and long lasting, and provides a secure foundation for further growth and development. (1996, p. 12)

In striking contrast, feel-good-now self-esteem is an approach to self-esteem that does not challenge children, set realistic expectations and goals, or teach them how to deal with frustration and mistakes.

The concept of self-esteem used in this chapter may be understood as including the feelings and thoughts that students have about their competence and worth and about their abilities to make a difference, to have control over their lives, to develop self-discipline, to confront rather than retreat from challenges, to learn from both success and failure, and to treat themselves and others with dignity and respect. Self-esteem guides and motivates one's actions, and, in turn, the outcome of these actions influences one's self-esteem, so that a dynamic, reciprocal process is constantly in force (Brooks, 1999b).

The time has come to expend less energy in debating whether educators should also focus on strengthening the self-esteem and social-emotional needs of students and spend more energy attempting to answer how to best address these needs in the classroom (Goldstein & Brooks, 2007). Effective educators recognize that students learn more comfortably in an atmosphere

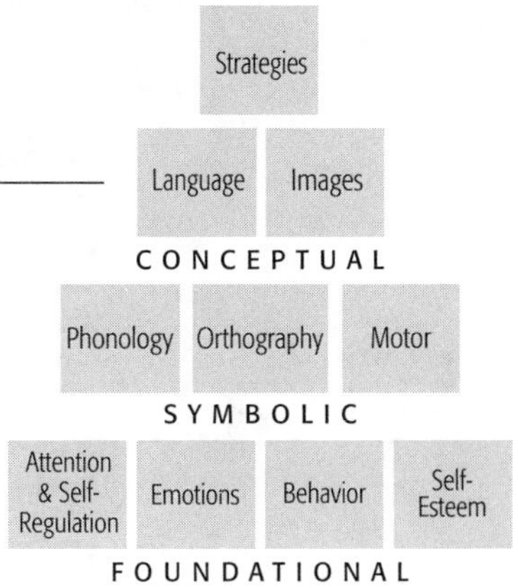

Strategies

Language Images

CONCEPTUAL

Phonology Orthography Motor

SYMBOLIC

Attention & Self-Regulation Emotions Behavior Self-Esteem

FOUNDATIONAL

in which they feel safe and secure, in which they are not haunted by fears of being ridiculed or humiliated, in which they feel challenged to develop and meet realistic goals, in which they sense that teachers genuinely care about them and respect their individuality, and in which learning is experienced as an exciting task. It is within such an atmosphere that self-esteem, motivation, hope, and resilience are nurtured.

The journal entry in Figure 7.1 was written by an 18-year-old student. This entry depicts how much pain and sadness can be experienced by students who struggle to learn to read and spell. Not only does this student feel that he does not receive any help for his problems, he also feels ridiculed by his peers because of his disabilities. All educators would agree that school experiences should not hurt children; unfortunately, for children who struggle, negative school experiences can harm self-esteem.

Effective educators recognize that a teacher has a lifelong impact on a student's capacity to be resilient (Brooks, 2004). Since the early 1980s, increased efforts have been directed to understanding not only the risk factors that contribute to the emergence and maintenance of learning, emotional, and behavior disorders but also to the protective factors that serve to buttress the resources of children to help them become more resilient (Brooks, 1999b; Katz, 1997; Rutter,

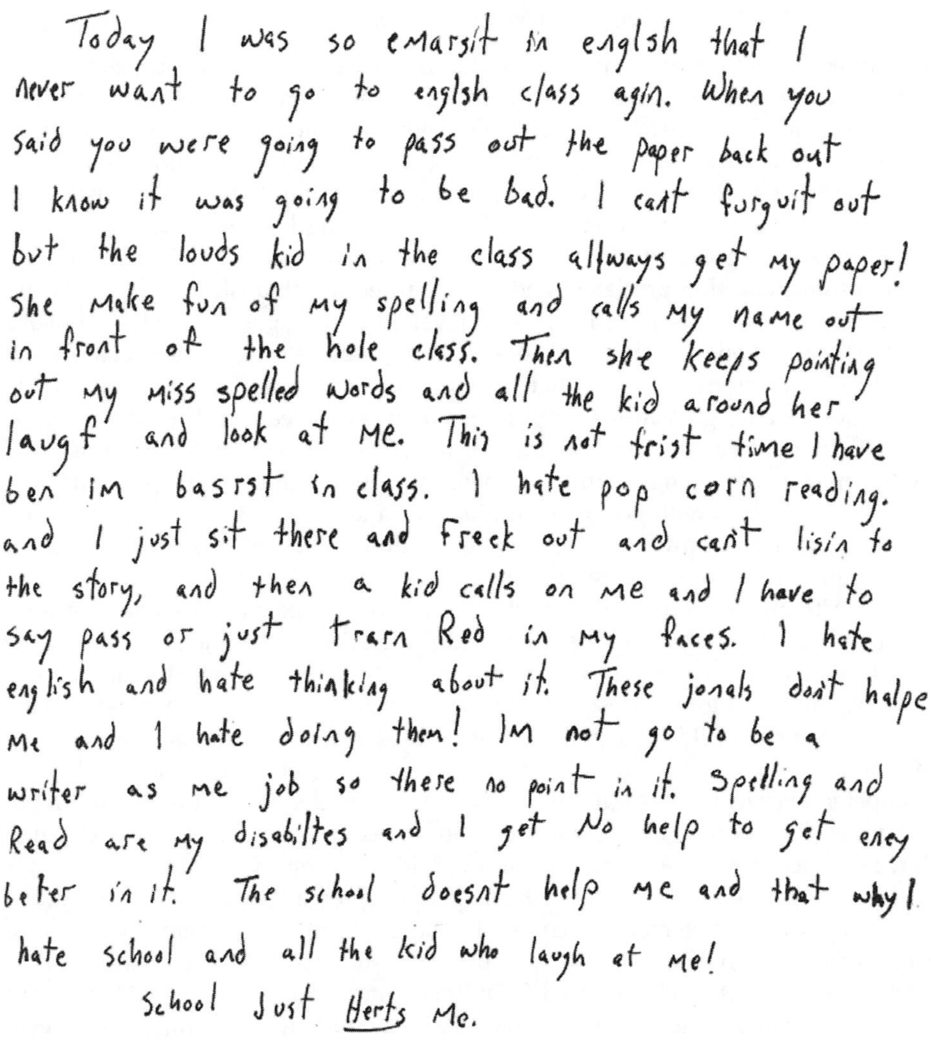

Today I was so emarsit in englsh that I never want to go to english class agin. When you said you were going to pass out the paper back out I know it was going to be bad. I cant furguit out but the louds kid in the class allways get my paper! She make fun of my spelling and calls my name out in front of the hole class. Then she keeps pointing out my miss spelled words and all the kid around her laugf and look at me. This is not frist time I have ben im basrst in class. I hate pop corn reading. and I just sit there and freck out and cant lisin to the story, and then a kid calls on me and I have to say pass or just trarn Red in my faces. I hate english and hate thinking about it. These jonals dont halpe me and I hate doing them! Im not go to be a writer as me job so these no point in it. Spelling and Read are my disabiltes and I get No help to get eney beter in it. The school doesnt help me and that why I hate school and all the kid who laugh at me!
School Just Herts Me.

Figure 7.1. School just hurts me.

169

1987; Werner & Smith, 1992). Different variables have been delineated that contribute to resilience, including a child's inborn temperament, problem-solving and interpersonal skills, self-esteem, family warmth, and support from outside the family (Hechtman, 1991).

In terms of support from outside the family, schools have been spotlighted as environments that can provide children with experiences that enhance their self-esteem and competence, thereby reinforcing resilience (Brooks, 1991; Goldstein, 1995; Goldstein & Brooks, 2007; Rutter, 1985; Thomsen, 2002). For example, Rutter noted that

> The long-term educational benefits from positive school experiences probably stem less from what children are specifically taught than from effects on children's attitude to learning, on their self-esteem, and on their task orientation and work strategies. (1985, p. 607)

The late psychologist Julius Segal wrote about resilient children:

> From studies conducted around the world, researchers have distilled a number of factors that enable such children of misfortune to beat the heavy odds against them. One factor turns out to be the presence in their lives of a charismatic adult—a person with whom they can identify and from whom they gather strength. And in a surprising number of cases, that person turns out to be a teacher. (1988, p. 2)

Effective educators understand the mindset of resilient students. They possess a sense of how resilient students perceive themselves and their world, especially in comparison with students who are not resilient. Obviously, if educators are to nurture resilience in students, they must understand the characteristics of the mindset of resilient children so that these characteristics can be reinforced in the classroom. In addition to having high self-esteem, resilient children possess good self-discipline (Goldstein & Brooks, 2007). They are hopeful and optimistic, feel appreciated, and have learned to establish realistic goals and expectations for themselves. They have developed the capacity to solve problems and make decisions and thus are more likely to perceive mistakes and obstacles as challenges to confront rather than as stressors to avoid. They rely on coping strategies that are growth-fostering rather than self-defeating. They do not deny their vulnerabilities but are cognizant of their talents. Their self-concept is filled with images of strength and competence. They have developed effective interpersonal skills with peers and adults alike and are able to seek out assistance in a comfortable, appropriate manner from adults who can provide the support they require (Brooks & Goldstein, 2001).

Effective educators are not misled by the overt negative behaviors of their students. They are aware that the wide varieties of problematic behaviors displayed by students are signals of low self-esteem and feelings of vulnerability. The indications of low self-esteem may vary considerably from one student to the next. In general, children experience low self-esteem in situations in which they do not feel successful but not in those situations in which they feel more competent. For instance, a child with LD may feel inadequate in the classroom but may engage in certain sports with self-confidence. Unfortunately, some children have such low self-esteem that they feel confident in few, if any, areas.

Some children openly convey feelings of despair, a lack of confidence, and a loss of hope with statements such as, "I'm stupid; I always do things wrong," or "I was born with half a brain." Other students do not express their low self-esteem directly. Instead, it can be inferred from the coping strategies they use to manage stress, frustration, and failure (Brooks, 1999b). Students with high self-esteem display strategies for coping that are adaptive and that nurture growth. A child

Strategies

Language | Images

CONCEPTUAL

Phonology | Orthography | Motor

SYMBOLIC

Attention & Self-Regulation | Emotions | Behavior | Self-Esteem

FOUNDATIONAL

struggling with math will ask for additional help and then spend more time practicing the new information. For example, although Maria had difficulties with reading and writing, she always talked to her teachers when she had trouble understanding or completing an assignment. She knew that they would provide additional help and explanation. She also found that asking for clarifications on tests reduced the likelihood that she would make unintended errors. Maria knew that it took her longer to complete tasks than other students so she always planned enough time for studying.

In marked contrast to Maria, students with low self-esteem frequently rely on counterproductive coping behaviors that actually intensify their difficulties. For example, although sixth-grader Samuel swaggered around the classroom and on the playground as if he possessed good self-esteem, his self-esteem appeared to be based on taking pride in doing exactly the opposite of what his teachers, fellow students, and even parents wanted him to do. Samuel's struggles in life had led him to develop a set of coping strategies that created the very antithesis of the kind of self-esteem discussed in this chapter. Samuel's strong negative feelings about himself were deeply cloaked in a pattern of disrespectful, aggressive, and defiant behavior. Ms. Handler, Samuel's teacher, felt challenged to identify strategies and activities that might help Samuel develop a resilient mindset. With Samuel in mind, Ms. Handler completed the items from the Self-Esteem section of the Building Blocks Questionnaire. Her responses appear in Figure 7.2.

The behaviors that follow are frequently used by children such as Samuel with low self-esteem to cope with the reality or the perceived possibility of failure. Although all children display some of these self-defeating behaviors at times, low self-esteem is strongly suggested when these behaviors appear with regularity. Self-defeating behaviors include the following:

- *Quitting and avoiding.* Some students may stop trying, often offering excuses such as that the work was irrelevant or stupid, when they

FOUNDATIONAL			
SELF-ESTEEM	Rarely	Sometimes	Frequently
Seems disinterested in academic tasks			✓
Complains about not being smart			✓
Complains that academic tasks are too difficult			✓
Has limited interactions with classmates	✓		
Complains about not being liked		✓	
Makes negative comments about self			✓
Gives up easily on tasks and assignments			✓
Seems overly sensitive to criticism			✓
Criticizes others		✓	
Seems to lack self-confidence			✓

Figure 7.2. Building Blocks Questionnaire for Samuel: Self-Esteem block.

become frustrated because they cannot succeed at a task or assignment. These students would rather avoid a task or refuse even to try than have anyone believe they are incapable or stupid; they seem to prefer to have the adults around them focus on their unwillingness to comply.

- *Cheating.* Students who believe that they cannot master a learning task or do well on a test are vulnerable to copying answers from others, plagiarizing materials from books or the Internet, or handing in someone else's paper.

- *Rationalizing.* Students who do not believe they are capable of succeeding frequently offer excuses for failure rather than accepting responsibility for their actions.

- *Clowning and regressing.* Some students who lack confidence consistently act silly, clown around, or behave like they are younger than they are. They resort to these ways of coping to minimize the significance of failing in certain situations, but this strategy often backfires, leading to ridicule from peers or disciplinary actions from their teachers.

- *Controlling.* Many children with low self-esteem believe they possess little control over what transpires in their lives, which contributes to a sense of helplessness. In what appears to be paradoxical behavior, they may attempt to avoid these uncomfortable feelings by pushing around others.

- *Aggressiveness and bullying.* Teasing and putdowns are common counterproductive ways of managing frustration and low self-esteem.

- *Using passive-aggressive behavior.* Some students with low self-esteem attempt to exert control by promising to meet particular responsibilities and then not meeting them. Such children are likely to be labeled oppositional.

- *Denying.* Children with low self-esteem commonly use denial as a strategy for dealing with the pain that might result if they were to acknowledge their limitations and vulnerabilities.

- *Complaining of boredom.* When frustrated, students may complain that the work they are being asked to complete is boring, uninteresting, or irrelevant. They may yawn, look tired, or put their head down on the desk to demonstrate to the teacher how uninvolved they are, when, in reality, they actually feel that the task is beyond their ability to complete.

- *Rushing.* Students with low self-esteem may rush through work as a means of contending with their difficulties. For these children, rapid completion is a higher priority than accuracy.

All of the behaviors in the previous list are self-defeating coping strategies. Their use reflects a child's vulnerable feelings, his or her wish to avoid feeling humiliated, and, in many respects, desperate attempts to maintain a sense of self-esteem and dignity. The reliance on these kinds of coping strategies exacerbates an already troubled situation. Effective educators recognize the roots of these counterproductive behaviors and ask, "What can I do to lessen this student's anxiety and vulnerability and increase his or her self-esteem and confidence?" This question prompts educators to look for frameworks for understanding the components of self-esteem and strategies that follow from these frameworks. Two frameworks have been proven to be particularly helpful to educators in guiding their interactions with students.

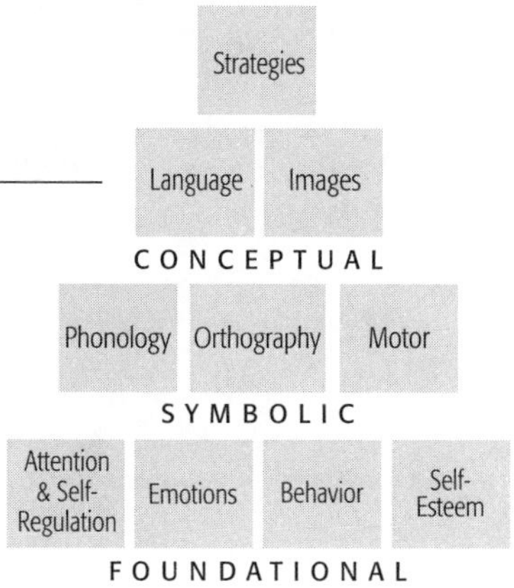

Attribution Theory

The first influential framework for examining the dimensions of self-esteem and optimism, *attribution theory*, was initially proposed by Weiner (1974) and applied by many clinicians and researchers (e.g., Brooks, 1991; Canino, 1981; Licht, 1983). Children encounter many pressures and challenges as they develop; some lead to success, others to failure. Attribution theory examines the explanations that people offer for why they think they succeeded or failed at a task or situation—explanations that have been found to be directly linked to self-esteem and the sense of hope. The appeal of this theory is that its basic premises are applicable to real-life situations, providing guideposts for interventions that foster self-esteem, motivation, and resilience.

Children with high self-esteem typically perceive their successes as based in a large part on their own efforts, resources, and abilities. These children assume realistic ownership for their accomplishments and feel a sense of personal control over what transpires in their lives.

Although Mark had little home support, he recognized that his efforts could influence results. On his social studies test, he wrote "I don't know" for most of the questions. For example, he was asked to choose three explorers from a list and then describe one important thing that each did. His answers and his note to his teacher, Ms. Perry, are presented in Figure 7.3. Mark freely admitted that he had not studied. Although he took responsibility for his behavior, Mark now needs to be helped to move to the next step of developing strategies to better prepare for tests.

In contrast, children with low self-esteem, lacking in qualities of resilience, often believe that their successes are a result of factors outside their control, such as luck or chance. Such children are quick to minimize or dismiss a high test grade with comments such as "The teacher made the test easy" or "I was lucky." Not surprisingly, such a self-perception lessens confidence about future successes.

In terms of mistakes and failures, children with high self-esteem are prone to believe that mistakes are experiences to learn from rather than to feel defeated by. Mistakes result from factors that can be changed, such as a lack of adequate effort when engaged in reaching a realistically attainable goal or the use of ineffective strategies when studying for a test. Children with low self-esteem, when faced with mistakes and failure, are susceptible to believing that they cannot correct the situation. They view mistakes as resulting from factors that cannot be modified,

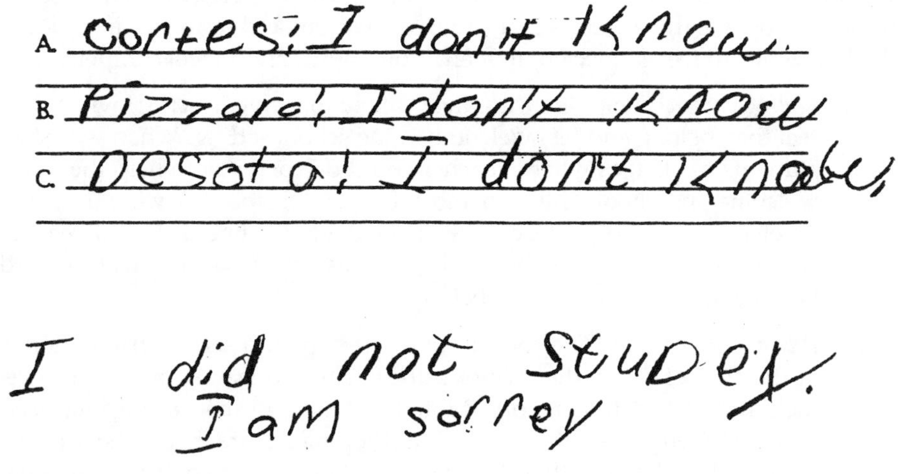

A. Cortes: I don't Know.
B. Pizzare: I don't know
C. Desoto: I don't Know,

I did not study.
I am sorry

Figure 7.3. Mark's social studies test.

173

such as a lack of ability or intelligence. This belief elicits a feeling of helplessness and hopelessness. Intensifying this negative scenario is that future success becomes less probable because these children expect to fail, and, in response, they retreat from age-expected demands and resort to self-defeating coping strategies that worsen their situation.

The mindset of effective educators recognizes that the tenets of attribution theory contain significant implications for teaching and responding to students in ways that foster their self-esteem, resilience, and motivation. It provides a blueprint for asking the following questions (Brooks, 1991, 1999b):

1. How do we create a school environment to reinforce the probability that students not only succeed but also experience their achievements as based in large part on their own abilities and efforts and not on luck or fate? Stated somewhat differently, how do we empower and reinforce a sense of personal control in children and adolescents so that they assume an increasing feeling of ownership and responsibility for their own lives? The importance of personal control and empowerment as the basic scaffolding of self-esteem, motivation, and resilience has been highlighted by a number of clinicians and researchers (e.g., Adelman & Taylor, 1983; Brendtro, Brokenleg, & Van Bockern, 1990; Curwin & Mendler, 1988; Deci & Flaste, 1995; Glasser, 1997).

2. How do we create an environment that reinforces the belief in students that mistakes and failure frequently serve as the basis for learning and are not only accepted but also expected? How do we instill in all students the conviction that their failures need not represent an albatross around their necks but rather that they can learn and succeed? How do we create safe and comfortable classroom environments that lessen or even eradicate fears of being humiliated and embarrassed for making a mistake or not understanding something the first time?

Students' Basic Needs

A second framework for examining self-esteem as well as motivation is based on the work of psychologist Edward Deci and his colleagues, who have examined self-esteem and motivation by examining the basic needs of students (Deci & Flaste, 1995). His model, which has many similarities to Glasser's (1997) *choice theory* (formerly called *control theory*) and Brendtro and colleagues' (1990) *circle of caring* philosophy, suggests that students are more willing to confront and persevere at learning tasks when educators have created a school environment in which these basic needs are satisfied. Deci and Flaste highlighted that effective educators recognize three factors that foster self-esteem and resilience in children and adolescents: to feel connected, to feel autonomous, and to feel competent.

1. *Feeling connected.* Students are more likely to thrive in school when they feel they belong and feel welcome in the school setting. When we asked students of all ages what a teacher could do each day to help them feel welcome in school, the two most frequent responses were 1) being greeted warmly by a teacher who uses your name and 2) a teacher smiling at you. Obviously, small gestures can go a long way toward helping students to feel they belong.

2. *Feeling autonomous.* The concept of ownership and self-determination is at the core of many theories of self-esteem, motivation, and resilience, including attribution theory. Motivation and resilience are increased when students feel their voice and opinions are being heard and respected and when they believe they have some control over what occurs in their lives. If children and adolescents feel that they are

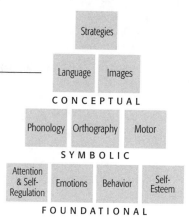

constantly being told what to do and that their lives are being dictated by others, they are less likely to be enthused about involving themselves in tasks that they feel are being imposed on them. If anything, their primary motivation may be to avoid or oppose what others wish them to do, and a power struggle is likely to ensue. The mindset of effective educators appreciates that if students are to feel a sense of self-determination and ownership, they must be taught how to 1) set realistic short- and long-term goals, 2) solve problems, 3) make wise choices and decisions to achieve their goals (this can involve academic content as well as social or interpersonal issues in a classroom, such as bullying), and 4) establish new goals when indicated.

3. *Feeling competent.* All children wish to feel successful and want to have arenas in their lives in which they feel competent and accomplished, arenas that elicit satisfaction and pride. As apparent in the journal entry in Figure 7.1, some students view school as the place in which their impairments rather than their strengths are highlighted. These feelings of incompetence prompt students to retreat from challenges and engage in self-defeating coping strategies that serve to intensify an already problematic situation. In recognizing their students' need to feel competent, effective teachers understand the importance of positive feedback and encouragement. In addition, they are aware that a focus on encouragement is not the same as giving false praise or inflated grades; students are very perceptive in knowing when they are receiving undeserved positive evaluations. Positive feedback must always be predicated on actual accomplishment and success.

ISLANDS OF COMPETENCE

Many IEPs focus only on a student's weaknesses, with strategies for fixing or addressing these weaknesses. Even when strengths are listed, little attention is directed to the ways in which these strengths might be used or nourished in the student's IEP. Effective educators appreciate the importance of identifying, reinforcing, and displaying each student's *islands of competence*—areas that are (or have the potential to be) sources of pride and accomplishment. All students have particular strengths, although not necessarily in the academic arena. Many students are confident while playing football or baseball but are ill at ease while taking a test in school or conversing with peers. Other students are self-assured in the classroom but very self-conscious while engaged in sports. Still others approach the task of fixing a car, playing the piano, or painting a picture with great confidence but are terrified by the thought of writing an essay. For example, Ben loved to play tennis, Andy loved to draw, and Maria spent each afternoon at the stables riding her horse. The effective educator discovers the strengths of each student in the classroom.

Unfortunately, some students experience self-doubt and failure in many situations. If they judge these situations to be important to significant others, their overall sense of competence suffers markedly. Given their low self-esteem, many children who are at risk seem to perceive that they are swimming or drowning in an ocean of inadequacy. To counteract this image of despair, effective teachers realize that every student possesses unique talents or islands of competence. If educators want to be charismatic adults in the lives of these students, they must assume the responsibility for identifying, reinforcing, and displaying these islands of competence; in so doing, they may create a ripple effect that provides children with the courage, strength, and motivation to venture forth and confront difficult tasks.

Researchers and clinicians have emphasized the importance of calling on selected islands of competence in building self-confidence. For instance, when discussing resilient children, Rutter observed, "Experience of success in one arena of life led to enhanced self-esteem and a feeling of self-efficacy, enabling them to cope more successfully with subsequent life challenges and adaptations" (1985, p. 604). Katz (1994) observed, "Being able to showcase our talents, and to have them valued by important people in our lives, helps us define our identities around that which we do best" (1994, p. 10). Werner (1993), describing a group of children who were at risk, wrote, "Most of the resilient children in our high-risk group were not unusually talented, but they took great pleasure in hobbies that brought them solace when things fell apart in their homes" (p. 511).

STRATEGIES FOR FOSTERING SELF-ESTEEM, MOTIVATION, HOPE, AND RESILIENCE

Effective educators develop and implement strategies for reinforcing self-esteem, motivation, hope, and resilience in students. Effective teachers recognize that a number of interventions can be used to create a positive school climate in which students' social-emotional growth is enhanced and in which students are genuinely excited and motivated about learning. If these strategies are to be effective, teachers must maintain a positive mindset—one that avoids blaming students, that focuses on and reinforces the unique gifts of each student, and that recognizes that student success has as much to do with the classroom environment as it has to do with the attitudes that students initially bring into this environment.

The Orientation Period

At the beginning of the school year, an orientation period may be used to enhance teachers' positive mindsets, although the exercises associated with this orientation may also be implemented later in the year as well. Ideally, the orientation period is divided into two parts. The first part takes place a day or so before students arrive for the new school year. During this period, teachers and school administrators as a staff reflect on and discuss why they became educators, what they perceive as their essential roles, what factors they believe are most important in creating a positive school climate, how they would describe a favorite and not-so-favorite teacher when they were students, and how they would like their students to describe them. They also consider the kinds of support they require from each other during the year to minimize cynicism and burnout.

These exercises promote staff cohesion and support and help teachers to keep in the forefront the belief that they have a lifelong effect on students. When educators are asked to recall one of their most positive and one of their most negative memories of school involving a teacher, they can be encouraged to think about how they can use these memories of their own school years to guide what they do with their students today. These exercises remind teachers of their powerful influence not only on the academic life of students but on students' social-emotional lives as well.

The second part of the orientation period occurs during the first 2 or 3 days of school, with the main focus on helping each student feel safe and secure in the school environment. During this time, teachers should not feel compelled to take out books or review academic content but instead to concentrate on creating a classroom climate in which meeting the needs of students, as outlined by Deci and Flaste (1995), is directly addressed. If a teacher attempts to engage children in academic tasks too quickly, it is often at the expense of getting to know the students, lessening their anxiety (especially students with special needs), or helping them to feel a sense of belonging in the classroom and ownership for their education.

Although some might argue that this orientation period is a waste of a few days of classroom teaching, using the first few days to meet the needs of students results in students becoming more motivated to learn, more involved in their own education, more involved as class members, more capable of dealing with frustration and mistakes, more self-disciplined, and more respectful.

Accepting Students for Who They Are

Extensive research documents the significant differences in children from birth, such as in their temperaments, learning styles, and development of language and motor abilities (Keogh, 2003, Levine, 2002). Unfortunately, people often give lip service to these differences and fail to truly accept children for who they are. Teachers may respond to students as if they were a homogeneous group and fail to establish realistic expectations, goals, and appropriate accommodations on the basis of the unique qualities of each child. One result of this mismatch between expectations and reality is that students begin to feel that they are not welcome or accepted and, in many instances, believe that they are disappointing the adults in their lives.

Some teachers still question the fairness of making accommodations for children, arguing that other students would be offended and upset by a situation that they perceive to be unfair. Although one can understand this concern, if children are different from birth, the least fair thing we can do is treat all children the same at school or at home. Although the origins of this quote are unclear, it has been said that "There is nothing as unequal as the equal treatment of unequals." Fairness should always be predicated on knowledge of the unique makeup of each child; if it is not, many children with disabilities or difficulties in the classroom will feel that they are always being criticized for things they are not capable of doing. In one fifth grade class, Katy could remember how to spell the words assigned for the spelling test but had trouble composing sentences. Maria wrote detailed sentences but had trouble spelling the words. Andy's writing was barely legible.

One of the most effective ways to address the issue of fairness is to discuss it openly with students so that the other children do not resent those students who are receiving modifications in their programs. This can be done during the second part of the orientation period. For example, to lessen the possibility of students perceiving a teacher as being unfair because of different expectations for different students, a teacher could discuss with students on the first day of school how each one of them is different and unique, how some students can run more quickly than others, how some can read more rapidly, and how some can solve math problems more efficiently. The teacher can then say that in light of these differences, there will be different expectations for the amount and kind of work that is done by each student. The teacher should then add, "One of my concerns is that because of different expectations, some of you may begin to feel that I am not being fair. If any of you begin to feel that way, please let me know so we can discuss it. This is very important because if students believe that things are not fair in a classroom, it can interfere with learning."

Feedback indicates that when a teacher introduces the issue of fairness before it becomes a problem, it basically remains a nonissue and permits a teacher to accommodate each student's unique needs without triggering negative feelings. In addition, it educates students about individual differences, resulting in an atmosphere of greater tolerance and acceptance. Teachers should also share this message about fairness with parents so that they are kept informed of what is being addressed in the classroom. Family meetings at home can be used in a similar way to discuss realistic expectations for each of the children so as to lessen sibling rivalry or jealousy.

Strategies

Language | Images

CONCEPTUAL

Phonology | Orthography | Motor

SYMBOLIC

Attention & Self-Regulation | Emotions | Behavior | Self-Esteem

FOUNDATIONAL

Many accommodations neither require major modifications in a student's program nor demand vastly different educational plans for each student. A great deal of overlap exists in the educational needs of children. All parties—students, parents, teachers, therapists—need to appreciate a child's strengths and weaknesses, develop and share common expectations and goals, and implement realistic strategies to help the child reach these goals.

Teachers must help students understand their strengths, their vulnerabilities, and the accommodations that will assist them to learn and to achieve. This task is often more difficult for children who have so-called hidden disabilities such as LD or anxiety. When done successfully, these children feel increasingly welcome in the environment, an important factor in improving their self-esteem and resilience.

Many children with learning or attentional problems expend a great deal of energy attempting to focus and learn in school. Then they are required to complete homework, which, given their learning problems, may take two or three times as long as their peers. Often they are unable to complete entire assignments. Not surprisingly, by bedtime, they are frustrated and exhausted, as are their parents. Andy remarked one night while doing math homework, "What are they trying to do? Turn me into a zombie?" Clearly, the homework involved too many problems. Katy said one evening to her mother, "I feel like they make me climb a big mountain all day long and then do it over again at night." Just as during the school day, homework assignments were often too difficult for Katy to complete without assistance. One evening, when Katy was supposed to be working on homework, she composed a paragraph instead. Figure 7.4 shows the paragraph written by Katy to explain why her homework was missing. This is the "dog ate my homework" story, Arizona-style.

Rather than continuing to engage in practices that make the learning process aversive, a more reasonable approach is to set a time limit for doing homework, regardless of how much work the child has actually accomplished. For example, if most students can complete their math homework in an hour, that should be the limit for all children, even if they complete only half of the math problems. Parents can verify that their child indeed spent a certain amount of time on homework.

Some may contend that these adjustments are unfair and represent a watering down of expectations for certain students. Continuing to provide students with the necessary assistance enables them to accomplish more and be more successful. To ask students who struggle to spend several more hours each evening on schoolwork than their peers typically proves counterproductive and turns them off to school.

In addition to taking longer to finish homework, a number of students take longer than their peers to finish tests. The logical strategy is to permit them to take untimed tests, which is becoming an increasingly common practice. This strategy

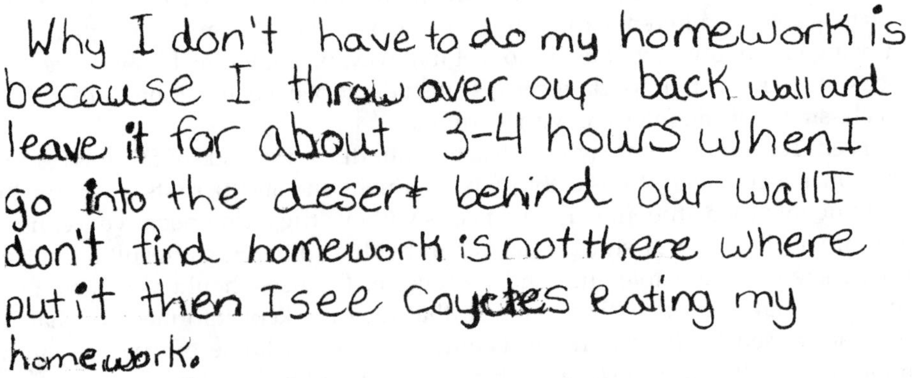

Why I don't have to do my homework is because I throw over our back wall and leave it for about 3-4 hours when I go into the desert behind our wall I don't find homework is not there where put it then I see Coyotes eating my homework.

Figure 7.4. Katy's explanation for missing homework.

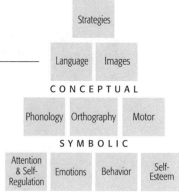

worked exceptionally well for Ben in his eighth-grade English class. Ms. Rhein took Ben aside and empathized with how hard he worked but how difficult it was for him to quickly put his ideas on paper. She offered Ben the opportunity to return at the end of the school day and use additional time to complete his English test. Ben earned a B+ on this test, an appreciable jump from previous C and D grades he had received. Without the pressure of time, Ben was relaxed and could think more clearly. Ben asked Ms. Rhein, "Who was the person who developed timed tests, and why did that person develop them?" This is an interesting question to ponder because in the larger world, although everyone confronts deadlines, adults typically possess more flexibility in getting work done than is afforded to students on tests in school.

Some students have difficulty copying homework assignments from the blackboard. Providing these students with a monthly syllabus of assignments can help to offset the possibility of assignments being copied incorrectly. College professors typically distribute a syllabus of homework and readings for the entire semester during the first class—might not the same practice be effective for students in elementary, middle, or high schools? Another possible accommodation is to assign a buddy to a student to ensure that homework assignments and due dates are accurate. Katy called her study buddy several times a week to clarify homework assignments.

Some students require more physical activity than other students or they become restless and unfocused and begin to get into trouble. These children can be provided with regular opportunities to bring messages to the office or to move around the classroom more frequently. Someone once said that an effective strategy for a student like Jeremy is to assign him two seats. That way when he is up and moving around, he is on his way to his other chair.

Although accommodations such as these communicate a sense of acceptance to children with exceptional needs, other ways also exist to help these children feel they belong and are welcome, especially in the school environment. A positive telephone call home or a note from a teacher can serve as a powerful sign of acceptance. The "Good News" postcard, shown in Figure 7.5, that Ben's teacher sent Ben's parents made him feel valued for his progress and efforts.

Helping Students to Develop a Sense of Responsibility

If children are to develop a sense of ownership and pride, they need ample opportunities for assuming responsibilities, especially those that help them feel they are making a contribution to their home, school, and community. For example, children feel a more positive attachment to school and are more motivated to learn if they are encouraged to contribute to the school milieu, an especially important tactic for students who feel alienated (Brooks, 1991; Rutter, 1980; Werner, 1993). The experience of making a positive difference in the lives of others builds self-respect, self-control, hopefulness, and resilience and serves as a powerful antidote to feelings of defeatism and despair. Several examples of this strategy follow.

Stephanie, a fourth grader, was socially isolated, and her struggle with memorization in the classroom began to take its toll on her self-esteem and resilience. Stephanie began waking up each morning with a stomachache and resisted attending school. Stephanie's parents and teacher understood the stress she was experiencing socially and academically. They decided to turn to one of Stephanie's strengths as a means of helping her gain a sense of competence at school. Stephanie spent many hours training and taking care of her dog. Stephanie's teacher recruited her as the pet monitor of the class, a position that involved taking care of the classroom fish and gerbils. On a visit to the classroom, the

179

Figure 7.5. Ben's "Good News" postcard.

principal commented that the pets in this classroom seemed to be very well taken care of. He asked Stephanie if she would be willing to train other pet monitors in other classrooms. Eventually, with the help of her teacher, Stephanie wrote a brief manual about pet care that the principal placed in the school library. Although Stephanie continued to struggle socially and academically, she was no longer sick before going to school and seemed to gather strength from her job, enabling her to persevere academically and become more accepted in the classroom.

Ms. McGrew was increasingly worried about Katy, one of her fifth-grade students. Katy was struggling to learn new concepts in the classroom. Ms. McGrew watched as Katy's academic confidence and self-esteem declined as the school year progressed. She decided to offer Katy the opportunity to teach others, recognizing that this activity often serves to boost self-confidence. Katy was asked to tutor first-grade students who were struggling with learning how to read. Learning to read had been relatively easy for Katy. The tutoring activity was so helpful that Ms. McGrew established a partnership between her class and a first-grade class so that all students could benefit from this strategy. A noticeable feeling of community began to develop. Katy approached her schoolwork diligently and with renewed effort for the remainder of the school year.

By the time Jeremy was in high school, the teachers referred to him as a "roamer." They used this term because instead of coming to his homeroom, he usually roamed the halls. In a consultation meeting with the teachers, the school psychologist asked what interventions had been attempted. The teachers listed a number of them, including a behavioral contract system. They noted that none of these interventions seemed to help. Half kidding, the school psychologist asked if perhaps Jeremy had a need to roam. At first, the teachers looked bewildered, but then they agreed and said that given his hyperactivity, perhaps he did need physical activity at the beginning of the day to become settled. They came up with the idea of implementing a physical activity that would also make him feel he was helping out. Jeremy was offered the job of attendance monitor of the school, which required him to walk through the halls during homeroom period to check that a teacher was present in each classroom and then to report back to the principal's office. With this new responsibility, Jeremy's behavior and the teachers' attitude toward him improved significantly.

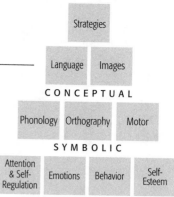

These kinds of contributory activities provide concrete evidence to students that they can be successful, that they are capable, and that they can earn respect, feelings that nurture their self-esteem and resilience. When describing the value of students helping others, Werner wrote,

> Self-esteem and self-efficacy also grew when children took on a responsible position commensurate with their ability, whether it was part-time paid work, managing the household when a parent was incapacitated, or, most often, caring for younger siblings. At some point in their young lives, usually in middle childhood and adolescence, the children who grew into resilient adults were required to carry out some socially desirable task to prevent others in their family, neighborhood, or community from experiencing distress or discomfort. (1993, p. 511)

Increasing Students' Sense of Ownership

An essential ingredient of high self-esteem and resilience is the belief that one has some control over what is occurring in one's life. To reinforce this belief in students, teachers must provide them with opportunities to learn the skills necessary for making sound decisions and solving problems and to apply and refine these skills (Adelman & Taylor, 1983; Deci & Flaste, 1995; Shure, 1994). Several examples of teaching decision making and problem solving in school follow.

Mr. Chavez recruited a group of students with special needs to conduct research about existing charities. On the basis of their research, they decided which charity to support and then decided on the most effective ways of raising money. These activities enhanced their self-esteem and reinforced the academic skills involved in the project.

Teachers can provide their students with a choice of which homework problems to do. For instance, if there are eight problems on a page, students can be permitted to choose for themselves which six of the eight to complete. In feedback we have received from teachers, they report receiving more homework on a regular basis when providing students with some choice.

Too often we attempt to solve students' daily challenges by telling them what to do, thereby robbing them of an opportunity to learn how to solve problems by themselves (Shure, 1994). Allowing children and adolescents to solve social, academic, and other problems on their own does not mean that teachers are not involved to provide guidance or should not respond to a crisis. Most problems are not crises, so teachers can allow children to derive their own solutions to problems they face.

Several steps are involved in strengthening problem-solving skills in students. A first step is for all parties to agree that a problem exists. This typically requires the students to actively consider the perspective of others. For example, Ms. Rhein, a middle-school teacher, reported an ongoing problem with students making fun of each other. This had occurred for months even though she constantly reminded them not to engage in this behavior. A more effective approach than a verbal reminder would be to 1) ask the students if they thought the teasing that was occurring in the class was a problem (if the students said that it was not a problem, Ms. Rhein could use their response to discuss why and how making fun of others interferes with a positive learning environment), 2) ask the students to consider different possible solutions to solve the problem, and 3) attempt the solution that seems most likely to be effective. Solutions that arise from children (with the necessary input of adults) are more apt to be successful than those that are handed down by adults. The active involvement of students helps them feel in control and reinforces their sense of ownership and empowerment—important ingredients in strengthening resilience and altering undesirable behaviors.

Helping Students to Establish Self-Discipline

It is difficult to conceive of children developing high self-esteem and resilience if they do not possess self-discipline, a realistic ability to stop, judge, reason, and reflect on one's behavior and its effect on others. Children are often labeled as difficult when they encounter problems in developing self-discipline. Adults describe such children as acting before they think. Unfortunately, these children, who are most in need of limits and structure, are quick to experience such limits as unfair impositions on their lives. It is often a Herculean task to establish rules in a manner that is not immediately rejected by children who feel that the rules have been proposed arbitrarily.

A major goal of discipline, in addition to establishing a safe and secure environment, is to develop self-discipline (Curwin & Mendler, 1988, 1997; Mendler, 1992; Sornson, 2005). If children are to assume ownership for their actions and not view rules as being unfairly set, they must understand the purpose of rules and contribute within reason to the formation of rules, guidelines, and consequences. Teachers and parents walk a tightrope where discipline is concerned, maintaining a delicate balance between rigidity and flexibility, striving to blend warmth, nurturance, acceptance, and humor with realistic expectations, clear-cut guidelines, and logical and natural consequences. If a child constantly challenges rules in school, teachers must strive to understand why this occurs and ask if what is being required is appropriate for this particular child. Not infrequently, children's misbehavior is rooted in demands that are perceived as unfair, elicit resentment, and lessen a sense of autonomy (Adelman & Taylor, 1990).

Also, teachers should focus on ways to prevent the emergence of misbehavior rather than expending all of their time and energy struggling with what action to take and what form of discipline to use once the misbehavior has occurred. Educators should anticipate situations that are likely to prove problematic for children and result in disruptive behaviors. Although it is often a difficult task, teachers should help students avoid these situations until they are better able to manage problems and develop realistic alternative behaviors.

During the orientation period described earlier, teachers may ask students 1) what rules they think are necessary for both students and teachers to follow for the class to run smoothly; 2) what are the best ways to remember these rules so that adults are not constantly reminding them (i.e., nagging them) and so they are not constantly reminding the teachers; and 3) what should the consequences be if someone (including the teacher) forgets a rule. Obviously, some rules related to safety are not negotiable. Students are more likely to remember and adhere to rules that they have helped to create. Skillfully involving students in this process does not result in anarchy; rather, it increases understanding of the necessity for rules and increases motivation to follow the rules (Curwin & Mendler, 1997).

One assistant principal of a middle school asked students to write or dictate a brief essay while they were serving detention. He was trying to encourage the students to reflect on their behaviors and to consider alternative ways of coping with difficulties. If they did not feel like writing, they were allowed to dictate their thoughts into a tape recorder. They were given a choice of more than 30 topics,

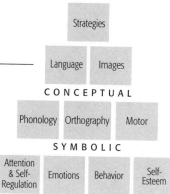

including what they would do if they ran the school, what they could do in the future to avoid detention, and what dreams they had about their futures. Many of the students were able to reflect on their lives and their behaviors and to think about alternative ways of behaving in the future.

Providing Positive Feedback and Encouragement

Positive feedback and encouragement fall under the umbrella of *discipline,* but they are listed separately to emphasize their importance. Self-esteem and resilience are nurtured when teachers and parents communicate realistic appreciation of and encouragement to children and adolescents; however, this positive communication is often limited or absent, especially when too prominent a focus is placed on a student's negative behaviors. Words and actions that help students to feel genuinely special are energizing and demonstrate to children that adults accept and believe in them. Even a small gesture of appreciation can create a lifelong impact.

John's history teacher, Dr. Mantell, had more than 150 students in her classes. She informed the students at the beginning of the year that she planned to call each of them at least twice at home during the year to find out how they were doing. On average, she spent about 7–8 minutes each evening on the telephone. Her calls had positive results. Students were more respectful and more disciplined in class and turned in assignments on a more regular basis. This teacher knew how to help students to feel welcome and appreciated.

Research indicates that when students have at least one adult in school who cares about and advocates for them, they are less likely to drop out and more likely to attend. A brief note of encouragement written by a teacher on a child's paper can be a source of positive motivation. This is especially important for students who are at risk and may feel very discouraged by their slow progress. The emotional support and encouragement offered by significant adults in a child's life are crucial for promoting self-worth and resilience. When Ben was in third grade, for example, his teacher, Ms. Chandler, realized the value of positive comments even though Ben's writing ability was quite below that of many of the other students in the class. Figure 7.6 illustrates a comment by Ms. Chandler.

Teaching Students to Cope with Mistakes and Failure

All students worry about making mistakes and appearing foolish. Given the many struggles that children with learning and attentional problems face, they are typically more anxious about making mistakes than their classmates; consequently, they retreat from challenging tasks rather than risking possible failure and humiliation. The coping strategies they employ to avoid learning tasks that they feel are beyond their skills typically prove self-defeating.

Samuel frequently gave up on classroom tasks. One day he became frustrated with a particular math assignment that he did not understand how to do. As he was going out to recess, he turned in his paper with the note presented in Figure 7.7. Samuel had decided his efforts did not pay off. As attribution theory highlights, the development of high self-esteem and resilience is intimately linked to a child's experience with and perception of failure. Consequently, efforts must be made to help students such as Samuel realize that mistakes are an important ingredient in the process of learning. Mistakes represent teachable moments.

Teachers must examine how they respond to a student's mistakes. They must have realistic expectations for students and not overreact to their mistakes. All

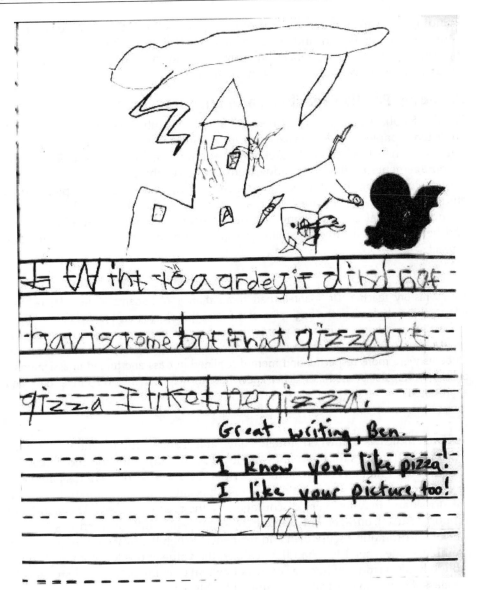

Figure 7.6. Teacher's comment on Ben's paper.

teachers become frustrated, at times, with the behavior of children, but disparaging remarks such as, "How often do I have to repeat myself?" or "Were you listening carefully in the first place?" or "You would do okay if you only tried harder" are counterproductive. For example, if a student is having difficulty listening carefully, it is far more helpful if a teacher says, "I can see that those directions were way too long. Let's try to figure out what I can do to help." Such a statement is not accusatory and also enlists the student's assistance in addressing the problem.

Teachers must also be careful of the types of comments that they write on students' papers. It is important to provide positive, encouraging remarks and to keep in mind that many students are doing the best that they can do. At the beginning of second grade, Ms. Abram would write comments such as, "Can't read," "Please try harder," and "Work more carefully, please." Figure 7.8 provides a sample of one response to Andy's paper. Andy wrote, "I had a spider in my mom's bedroom and I put him outside." Andy has severe weaknesses in motor development, and these types of comments are only discouraging.

Figure 7.7. Samuel's note.

If a student does not know an answer immediately, some teachers call on other students until the correct answer is obtained. What this practice communicates to students is that the teacher is more interested in the correct answer than in the process of solving the problem. If a child does not know the correct answer, it is far more effective for a teacher to say, "Let's review how to solve that problem." By doing so, the teacher is using the child's lack of knowledge as a teachable moment and reinforcing the message that people learn from mistakes. Such a teacher recognizes two important facts. If one student does

iLANDA SPIDRINMI
MOMSPEDROM
aNDIPotnIMAWtSID

Work more carefully please!!!
I can't read your writing.

Figure 7.8. Teacher's comment on Andy's writing.

not know an answer, there are probably other students who also do not understand the material; and if a student does not know how to solve a problem, just hearing the correct answer from another student is not helpful. Of course, additional assistance, practice, feedback, and instruction may be necessary for students who have repeated trouble grasping material.

Because the fear of failure is such a powerful classroom force, it should be addressed before students even make a mistake. This can be accomplished during the orientation period at the beginning of the school year. A teacher can ask, "Who feels that they are going to make a mistake or not understand something in class this year?" Before any of the students can respond, the teacher can raise his or her hand and begin a discussion of how the fear of making mistakes affects learning. The teacher can then involve the class in problem solving by asking what he or she can do as their teacher and what they can do as class members to minimize the fear of failing and looking foolish. Openly acknowledging the fear of failure renders it less potent and less destructive. Teachers can teach students that not comprehending material is to be expected and that the teacher's role is to help them to learn. As attribution theory has taught us, students have higher self-esteem and are more resilient when they perceive mistakes as experiences from which to learn.

CONCLUSION

A basic characteristic of resilient children is that their self-esteem and sense of academic competence have either been maintained or, if damaged, have been repaired. Resilient children possess a feeling of hope and optimism, of ownership and personal control, a feeling nurtured by charismatic adults who provide experiences that reinforce students' islands of competence and enhance their feelings of self-worth. If goals for these children are to develop self-esteem, self-respect, self-discipline, and compassion, educators must work diligently to become charismatic adults. As Segal noted, the school environment is a prime location for resilience to be nurtured. Effective educators possess a mindset enabling them to recognize the lifelong effect they have on their students.

SYMBOLIC
PROCESSING BLOCKS

CHAPTER 8 OUTLINE

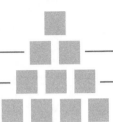

DEFINITIONS

Evolution of the Definitions of Learning
   Disability
Legal Definitions
Aptitude–Achievement Discrepancy
Individuals with Disabilities Education
   Improvement Act of 2004
Response to Intervention

THE SYMBOLIC
PROCESSING BLOCKS

PHONOLOGICAL
PROCESSING BLOCK

Phonological Processing Block
   Questionnaire
Definition of Phonological Awareness
Phonological Dyslexia
International Dyslexia Association
   Definition of Dyslexia
Brief Historical Review
Developmental Sequence
Assessment and Instructional Activities
Segmentation and Blending
Examples of Commercial Programs

ORTHOGRAPHIC
PROCESSING BLOCK

Definition of Orthographic Awareness
Characteristics of Poor Orthographic
   Awareness

Orthographic Processing Block
   Questionnaire
Brief Historical Review of Orthographic
   Dyslexia
Research on Orthographic Dyslexia
Rapid Automatized Naming
Implications for Intervention

MOTOR PROCESSING BLOCK

Motor Processing Block Questionnaire
Fine Motor Development

CLASSROOM
ACCOMMODATIONS

Copying
Timed Tests
Following Directions
Assignments

CONCLUSION

APPENDIX A: PHONOLOGICAL
AWARENESS SKILLS SCREENER

APPENDIX B: RELATIONSHIP
BETWEEN SPEECH SOUNDS
AND SPELLING DEVELOPMENT

LEARNING DISABILITIES AND THE SYMBOLIC PROCESSING BLOCKS

Strategies

Language   Images

CONCEPTUAL

Phonology   Orthography   Motor

SYMBOLIC

Attention & Self-Regulation   Emotions   Behavior   Self-Esteem

FOUNDATIONAL

A lthough the Building Blocks model can help a teacher understand both learning and behavior problems, this type of model is not used in schools to identify students as having learning disabilities (LD). Within school settings, the category of LD has traditionally been reserved for children who do not learn even though they possess a general capacity for learning (Ingersoll & Goldstein, 1993). Therefore, not all children performing poorly in school would be considered as having LD. The field has not, however, arrived at a consensus regarding how LD should be defined and identified. Before discussing the abilities in the processing blocks, a brief historical review is presented to help explain the underpinnings and evolution of the terminology in the field of LD.

DEFINITIONS

Despite continuing efforts at clarification, the ways of defining and determining which students should be identified as having LD still vary within academic, community, and even vocational settings. Some believe that the characteristics described by the term *learning disability* are so heterogeneous that the creation of a precise, clear working definition is impossible (Rutter, 1978). Others suggest that the definition of LD can be based on the existence of strengths and weaknesses within academic skills or the "variation in achievement markers" (Fletcher, Lyon, Fuchs, & Barnes, 2007, p. 4). Others stress the importance of examining intra-individual variation across cognitive, linguistic, and academic abilities (Mather & Gregg, 2006). Historically LD has been linked to the concept of "unexpected" underachievement, where some of the person's cognitive and linguistic abilities are more advanced than specific aspects of achievement would indicate. This concept can be traced back to the late 19th century and early 20th century when physicians observed children and adults who did not read as well as one would expect based on examination, consideration, and observation of their other accomplishments.

Evolution of the Definitions of Learning Disability

Beginning in the late 1880s, the concept and subsequent definitions of learning disability developed in a parallel but fairly independent manner within the fields of neurology, psychology, and education. Broca (1861) identified a neurological origin for learning problems in which otherwise intelligent individuals could have specific learning impairments. In 1922, Hohman described a group of

Table 8.1. Historical definitions of learning disorders

Year	Term
1887	Dyslexia (Berlin)
1895–1917	Congenital word blindness (Hinshelwood, Kerr, Morgan)
1922–1925	Postinfluenzal behavioral syndrome (Ebaugh, Hohman, & Stryker)
1928	Strephosymbolia (Orton)
1929	Congenital auditory imperception (Worcester-Drought & Allen)
1941	Developmental lag (Bender & Yarnell)
1943–1947	Brain-injured or brain-damaged child (Strauss & Lehtinen, Strauss & Werner)
1947	Minimally brain-damaged child (Gesell & Amatruda)
1960	Psychoneurological learning disorders (Myklebust & Boshes)
1962	Learning disabilities (Kirk)
1962–1963	Minimal brain dysfunction (MBD) (Bax & MacKeith)
1964	Developmental dyslexia (Critchley)
1967–1968	Specific learning disabilities (National Advisory Committee on Handicapped Children, U.S. Office of Education)
1969	Specific learning disabilities (Education of the Handicapped Act of 1970, PL 91-230)
1971	Psycholinguistic learning disabilities (Kirk & Kirk)
1977	Learning disabilities (Education for All Handicapped Children Act of 1975, PL 94-142)
1980	Specific developmental disorders (*Diagnostic and Statistical Manual of Mental Disorders, Third Edition*)
1987	Specific developmental disorders (*Diagnostic and Statistical Manual of Mental Disorders, Third Edition—Revised*)
1994	Learning disorders (*Diagnostic and Statistical Manual of Mental Disorders, Fourth Edition*)

From Silver, A.A., & Hagin, R.A. (1990). *Disorders of learning in childhood* (p. 51). New York: John Wiley & Sons; Copyright © 1990 by John Wiley & Sons, Inc. Reprinted by permission of John Wiley & Sons, Inc.

children with behavior problems, hyperactivity, and learning difficulty resulting from encephalitis. Subsequent research and labels for these children with impaired achievement reflected a belief that this disability was the result of some brain-based dysfunction. The term *minimal brain damage* was introduced in the 1940s by Strauss and Lehtinen (1947). A variety of other terms have also been used to describe this population of children (see Table 8.1).

In 1962/1963, Kirk and Bateman initiated an effort to define *learning disability* on the basis of objective data. The term *learning disability* was intended to mean an impairment in learning capacity and was explained as follows:

> A learning disability refers to a retardation, disorder, or delayed development in one or more of the processes of speech, language, reading, writing, arithmetic, or other school subjects resulting from a psychological handicap caused by possible cerebral dysfunction and/or emotional or behavioral disturbances. It is not the result of mental retardation, sensory deprivation, or cultural or instructional factors (p. 73).

These concepts were incorporated into the definition of *learning disability* presented to Congress by the National Advisory Committee on Handicapped Children (1968):

> Those children who have a disorder in one or more of the basic psychological processes involved in understanding or using language, spoken or written, which disorder may manifest itself in imperfect ability to listen, think, speak, read, write, spell or do mathematical calculations. Such disorders include conditions such as perceptual handicaps, brain injury, minimal brain dysfunction, dyslexia and developmental aphasia. This term does not include learning problems that are primarily the

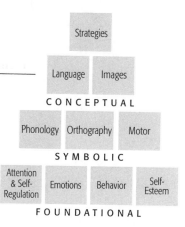

result of visual, hearing or motor handicaps, of mental retardation, of emotional disturbances or of environmental, cultural or economic disadvantage (p. 82).

This definition acknowledged that a variety of developmental and environmental factors might contribute to learning difficulties. The definition also specified that children whose faulty school performance was primarily the result of environmental influences or foundational skill impairments, such as emotional or behavior disorders, should not be considered as having LD.

Legal Definitions

In 1975, an adapted version of this basic definition was incorporated into the Education for All Handicapped Children Act of 1975 (PL 94-142), which guaranteed specialized services for children with impairments, including LD. This federal law mandating education for all children with disabilities ruled out emotional and behavioral factors as causes of LD. In such cases in which children were deemed to have impairments of a primarily emotional or behavioral nature, these children were to be referred to as having behavioral impairments rather than learning impairments.

In 1981, six professional organizations met and reached a consensus definition for learning disability. This definition refined the original concept of learning disability as a general description of children failing to learn despite apparently adequate capacity (Hammill, Leigh, McNutt, & Larsen, 1981):

> Learning disabilities is a generic term that refers to a heterogeneous group of disorders manifested by significant difficulties in the acquisition and use of listening, speaking, writing, reasoning or mathematical abilities. These disorders are intrinsic to the individual and presumed to be due to central nervous system dysfunction. Even though a learning disability may occur concomitantly with other handicapping conditions (such as sensory impairment, mental retardation), social and emotional disturbances or environmental influences (such as cultural differences, insufficient or inappropriate instruction, psychogenic factors), it is not the direct result of those conditions or influences. (p. 336)

In 1987, the Interagency Committee on Learning Disabilities maintained this basic definition and added social skills problems as potentially stemming from LD. This was the first step in recognizing that the underlying skill impairments that contributed to faulty achievement could also play a role in the development or lack thereof of other important interpersonal and behavior skills.

Within these definitions, the term *learning disability* focused on performance rather than etiology, reflecting the perception that the person with LD is unable to accomplish academic or interpersonal tasks that others can accomplish. Furthermore, this lack of accomplishment cannot be attributed to poor teaching, environmental deprivation, or limited experience but is rather the result of neurological and biological processes (Kavanagh, 1988). Unfortunately, the focus on performance facilitated the process of diagnosis but not the reasons for diagnosis, that is, the modification of the educational environment and the selection of teaching strategies to accelerate achievement. In other words, the focus on labels (e.g., reading disability) may result in overlooking the cause of the problem (e.g., poor phonological or orthographic processing) and the subsequent development of an appropriate intervention plan. Despite the well-established importance of phonological, orthographic, and morphological processes in reading, few students receive instructional interventions that are designed to address these impairments (Berninger & Abbott, 1994).

Aptitude–Achievement Discrepancy

The difficulty in developing a qualitative definition of learning disability, combined with the need to make funding decisions, prompted school districts to use statistical methods to identify children with LD (Silver & Hagin, 1990). Because of legal mandates and the definition of learning disabilities provided in the Education for All Handicapped Children Act of 1975 (PL 94-142), as well as the subsequent revisions and reauthorizations, a discrepancy model was often used, requiring a specific gap between predicted and actual school performance. In the discrepancy model, a child's actual achievement (based on measures of oral expression, listening comprehension, written expression, basic reading, reading comprehension, and mathematical calculation or mathematical problem solving) is compared with his or her predicted achievement (based on measures of intellectual functioning). This discrepancy model became the methodology then for determining the percentage of students served and the available funding for providing special help. Although some school districts still use the discrepancy criteria as one component of an evaluation, states may not now mandate its use. Thus, sole reliance on this procedure for LD identification has decreased, partially because of new legal mandates, but also because of all the associated problems with using this model as the basis for identifying LD.

Problems with the Aptitude–Achievement Discrepancy Model
Since the 1980s, the use of an aptitude–achievement discrepancy model as the sole or determining criterion for the diagnosis of dyslexia and LD has been questioned and criticized. The problems in using a formula to identify children are many, serious, and too often disregarded (Bateman, 1992). Aaron (1997) identified many of these problems in an article titled "The Impending Demise of the Discrepancy Formula." Although this criterion was used widely in schools, it was described as being both unnecessary (Mather & Healey, 1990) and invalid (Lyon, 1995). Despite a plethora of criticisms and concerns, state and district identification guidelines continued to demonstrate increased reliance on formulae (Frankenberger & Fronzaglio, 1991). To further complicate matters, state and school district guidelines varied with regard to the specific method used to define a discrepancy and the magnitude of the discrepancy required in order for a child to be deemed eligible for services. Therefore, a child could be identified as having LD in one district and then denied services in another. As Berninger (1996) described, "The criterion set for the size of discrepancy that counts as a reading or writing disability is always arbitrary and varies widely among states and among schools within states" (pp. 158–159). She further stated, "Whether a child is or is not diagnosed as learning disabled depends on the state and the local criteria in which a child lives or on the personal philosophy of an independent evaluator who assesses the child" (p. 164). Similarly, Simpson and Buckhalt (1990) stated,

> Though the formula method may have some appeal because it requires less clinical competence and judgment, the fact remains that reducing an important diagnostic decision to a mathematical equation gives a false sense of objectivity to a contrived procedure that is still essentially subjective. (p. 274)

Nonetheless, in both public school and vocational settings, the most widely accepted criterion for determination of LD called for a difference of at least 22 points or 1.5 standard deviations between intelligence test scores and achievement test scores.

Preschool Through Second Grade
For children in preschool through second grade, the criterion of an aptitude–achievement discrepancy was

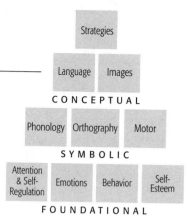

predicated on failure. Children needed to fall behind their predicted level of performance to be deemed technically eligible for services. This often resulted in services being delayed until third grade and beyond. In fact, some school districts would not even evaluate children for eligibility for services under the LD category until after first grade. Thus, children were forced to cross a threshold of severe academic failure prior to receiving help. In the interim, the children made minimal progress, and once identified, students who were struggling to keep up then faced the arduous task of catching up and keeping up simultaneously. After attending a staffing in which a student did not qualify for help, one frustrated second-grade teacher lamented, "You have to be careful of what early intervention you do for your children because it can backfire. You provide a child with help in first and second grade and then they don't have a big enough gap between scores to qualify for services."

Fletcher and colleagues (1998) described how discrepancy models prevent early intervention:

> The treatment implications of discrepancy models are perhaps the most serious limitations. The average age of identification of children with LD is about 10 years of age. This is partly an effect of the need for children who are struggling with academic skills to stay at the floor of the achievement tests as they fail to master skills to obtain a sufficiently low score to obtain a discrepancy. The use of discrepancy clearly moves the identification and intervention component to the later part of elementary school. Unfortunately, it is also clear that severe RD [reading disabilities] identified after age 8 may be more refractory to intervention, reflecting observations made many years ago. (p. 197)

Third Grade and Beyond   Students who are not identified with LD until third grade and beyond often suffer from concomitant social, behavior, and emotional problems in the foundational blocks. Their poor school performance contributes to lowered self-image and self-esteem. Attitude and motivation may become as much of a barrier to learning as the LD itself. As students progress through school, the magnitude of the discrepancy between predicted performance (based on the results of an intelligence test) and actual performance (based on the results of achievement tests) may decrease. As a result, using the discrepancy model, a student with a real LD may be excluded from services and legal protections.

One reason for the decrease in the gap is that effective interventions resulted in improved academic performance or that the person has learned to circumvent difficulties. With regard to reading, these individuals have been described as "compensated dyslexics." Difficulties in learning could also result in lowered performance on the intelligence or aptitude measure. In other words, because of limited reading experiences, the student has reduced exposure to vocabulary and knowledge that is subsequently reflected by lowered aptitude scores. A further consideration is that selected tests may be inadequate for the purpose. For example, the student who initially struggled to learn to decode may now be able to read a list of words with accurate pronunciation, thereby attaining an average score on a measure of word identification. The student's poor performance in reading, however, is now due to limitations in speed and fluency (reading abilities that were not tested) rather than poor word identification skill. Furthermore, problems related to inattentiveness or poor memory might not qualify a child for services unless a significant discrepancy could be demonstrated. Similarly, children with neuropsychological impairments that may affect their daily classroom performance, such as a slow speed of processing, would not qualify for special services unless they obtained low scores on standardized achievement tests as well (Goldstein & Goldstein, 1998).

More than 2 decades of research have undermined the practice of using aptitude–achievement discrepancy as the sole criterion for LD (Stanovich, 1994; Stanovich, 2005). Stanovich (1999) stated,

> None of the critics of discrepancy definitions are denying the existence of severe reading disability per se or the importance of remedial help. Instead, they are questioning the rationale of differential treatment and resources being allocated on the basis of IQ-achievement discrepancy. (p. 355)

Individuals with Disabilities Education Improvement Act of 2004

The recommended procedures for identifying LD have been revised with the Individuals with Disabilities Education Improvement Act (IDEA) of 2004 (PL 108-446). IDEA 2004 was signed into law on Dec. 3, 2004, by President George W. Bush; the provisions of the act became effective on July 1, 2005; and the final regulations were published on August 14, 2006. With the advent of this recent reauthorization, the definition of LD was maintained as "a disorder in one or more of the basic psychological processes involved in understanding or in using language, spoken or written, which...may manifest itself in the imperfect ability to listen, think, speak, read well, or do mathematical calculations" (20 U.S.C. §1401 [30]). In addition, IDEA 2004 specifically prohibits the use of any single assessment instrument as the sole criterion for the identification of a disability. The following information on the IDEA 2004 federal regulations and the implementation of response to intervention (RTI), described later in this chapter, can be found on the National Research Center on Learning Disabilities web site (http://www.nrcld. org), the federal web site dedicated to IDEA 2004 (http://idea.ed.gov), and LD Online (http://www.ldonline.org/article/11202).

According to IDEA 2004,

> The group...may determine that a child has a specific learning disability, as defined in 34 CFR 300.8(c)(10), if:
>
> - The child does not achieve adequately for the child's age or to meet State-approved grade-level standards in one or more of the following areas, when provided with learning experiences and instruction appropriate for the child's age or State-approved grade–level standards:
>   - Oral expression.
>   - Listening comprehension.
>   - Written expression.
>   - Basic reading skills.
>   - Reading fluency skills.
>   - Reading comprehension.
>   - Mathematics calculation.
>   - Mathematics problem solving.
> - The child does not make sufficient progress to meet age or State-approved grade-level standards in one or more of the areas identified in 34 CFR 300.309(a)(1) when using a process based on the child's response to scientific, research-based intervention; or the child exhibits a pattern of strengths and weaknesses in performance, achievement, or both, relative to age, State-approved grade-level standards, or intellectual development, that is determined by the

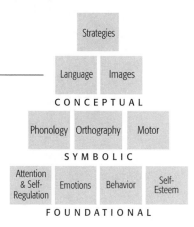

group to be relevant to the identification of a specific learning disability, using appropriate assessments, consistent with 34 CFR 300.304 and 300.305; and the group determines that its findings under 34 CFR 300.309(a)(1) and (2) are not primarily the result of:

- A visual, hearing, or motor disability;
- Mental retardation;
- Emotional disturbance;
- Cultural factors;
- Environmental or economic disadvantage; or
- Limited English proficiency.

To ensure that underachievement in a child suspected of having a specific learning disability is not due to lack of appropriate instruction in reading or math, the group must consider, as part of the evaluation described in 34 CFR 300.304 through 300.306:

- Data that demonstrate that prior to, or as a part of, the referral process, the child was provided appropriate instruction in regular education settings, delivered by qualified personnel; and
- Data-based documentation of repeated assessments of achievement at reasonable intervals, reflecting formal assessment of student progress during instruction, which was provided to the child's parents.

The central changes in the law reflect an acknowledgement that more information, such as classroom performance, information processing abilities, intellectual capacity, and qualitative information from parents and teachers, must be gathered to refute or support a diagnosis of LD. The policies and procedures, for identifying students with LD, however, have been modified so that an aptitude–achievement discrepancy is no longer a requirement. The IDEA regulations specify that

A State must adopt, consistent with 34 CFR 300.309, criteria for determining whether a child has a specific learning disability as defined in 34 CFR 300.8(c)(10). In addition, the criteria adopted by the State:

- Must not require the use of a severe discrepancy between intellectual ability and achievement for determining whether a child has a specific learning disability, as defined in 34 CFR 300.8(c)(10);
- Must permit the use of a process based on the child's response to scientific, research-based intervention; and
- May permit the use of other alternative research-based procedures for determining whether a child has a specific learning disability, as defined in 34 CFR 300.8(c)(10).

Response to Intervention

As noted above, states are no longer allowed to require the use of a severe discrepancy (IDEA 2004, 34 CFR 300.8[c][10]) and must permit other alternative research-based procedures for diagnosing LD (34 CFR 300.8[c][10]). In addition, the new language in IDEA 2004 specifies that a local educational agency may use a process that determines whether a child responds to scientific research-based intervention as *part* of the evaluation process (Sec. 614[b][6B]). This process often is referred to as RTI. Like the use of the discrepancy model, RTI is not mandated.

RTI is perhaps most accurately described as a prereferral treatment model that incorporates systematic, schoolwide reform and intervention efforts to help all students. Use of RTI can document the presence of low achievement or identify a pool of at-risk students, but it does not diagnose the existence of LD (Kavale, 2005; Kavale, Kaufman, Naglieri, & Hale, 2005; NJCLD, 2005). RTI does not take into account the various linguistic and neuropsychological functions that underlie academic performance nor does it provide clear rationales for selecting alternative types of instruction or service delivery that may be more effective with an individual student. Most of the work on implementation of RTI has focused on the early elementary years, and little empirical evidence exists that these models can be implemented effectively with children in the upper grades (Semrud-Clikeman, 2005).

The National Joint Committee on Learning Disabilities (NJCLD, 2005) specified the following core concepts of RTI: 1) use of scientific, research-based interventions in general education, 2) measurement of student response to the interventions, and 3) use of the response data to alter or increase the intensity of the interventions. RTI models use informal, curriculum-based measures to address each student's relative standing and performance in the curriculum. The goal of RTI is not to determine an aptitude–achievement discrepancy but rather to evaluate the discrepancy between a student's individual performance on particular measures as compared with the performance of his or her grade-level peers.

Although RTI approaches vary considerably, most employ a three-or four-tiered data-based model of intervention that delineates a continuum of services. The primary tier (Tier I) is general education; the secondary tier (Tier II) provides more specialized intervention and small-group instruction; and the tertiary tier (Tier III) provides more individualized and intensive services and may result in a comprehensive evaluation and consideration for special education eligibility. Repeated curriculum-based measurements are used to document the outcomes of instruction; students with the poorest response to instruction receive increased educational assistance.

The advantages of an RTI approach are clear. Prereferral interventions provide a direct focus on student learning and outcomes and increase accountability for all students regardless of whether they are eventually referred for special education (NJCLD, 2005). RTI can also result in earlier identification and intervention (Fuchs, Mock, Morgan, & Young, 2003; Fuchs & Vaughn, 2005). Clearly, implementation of RTI in the general education curriculum adds an important dimension to the screening equation for areas of basic academic skills (e.g., reading decoding, spelling, math computation) (Speece, 2005).

Much remains to be known about how RTI models will be implemented in schools. Fuchs and Deshler (2007) discussed the unknowns of RTI implementation, including 1) identifying the purpose of RTI (early intervention or disability identification); 2) identifying the conditions of successful implementation; 3) determining the nature of instruction in Tier I; 4) determining how to use problem solving to promote the academic achievement among at-risk children as well as children with severe learning problems; 5) deciding how to evaluate nonre-sponsiveness and identify the nonresponders; 6) determining the relevance for middle and high school students, 7) deciding how to apply RTI principles to other areas besides early reading; and 8) determining whether RTI implementation is successful. It is hoped that future research will enhance the knowledge base regarding effective ways to implement RTI.

Just as with the aptitude–achievement discrepancy model, the RTI model suggests that for some children, identification would not occur until after they have failed to make adequate progress; in addition, the use of the model may lead to a denial of services to children who are at risk for LD (Semrud-Clikeman, 2005). Thus, the mandated procedures for identifying children with LD within public

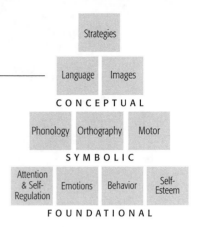

schools still focus on academic performance impairments rather than on the underlying correlates and causes of the difficulties.

Rather than wait for a child to demonstrate poor performance, attempts should be made to examine the factors and the underlying abilities related to school difficulties. As Scarborough (1991) explained,

> Instead of casting the preschool characteristics of dyslexic children as "precursors" and the reading problems of these children as "outcomes," it might be more helpful to view both as successive, observable symptoms of the same condition…. Therefore, while the education goal may be to explain reading disability for its own sake, the neuropsychological goal is to define the nature of the fundamental difficulty that manifests itself most evidently, but not solely, as underachievement in reading. (pp. 38–39)

As with the discrepancy model, RTI does not differentiate among learners with varying learning needs (Semrud-Clikeman, 2005) or help answer the question of why a certain student is struggling. Many extrinsic and intrinsic reasons exist that could explain why a student might not respond to a particular intervention. Students with a variety of conditions (e.g., attention-deficit/ hyperactivity disorder, behavior disorders, language impairments, English language learners) may show low responsiveness to intervention and, therefore, be misidentified as having LD. Furthermore, high-ability students with LD would not be identified for services because they would partially compensate for their difficulties through the use of their strengths in language and reasoning and not be the lowest performers in the classroom. Thus, they would be denied the individualized instruction that would enable them to make progress consistent with their high abilities (NJCLD, 2005). As Martin (2005) observed, it is important to keep in mind that the "evaluation for a learning disability is not triggered only by failure. It is designed to determine if the student has a learning disability no matter how well the student is currently performing" (p. 145). Highly intelligent people can have LD, and the sole use of RTI will result in these individuals being overlooked and denied needed services and accommodations. It matters *why* a student is not learning (Mather & Kaufman, 2006).

As a final point, clinical judgment is needed for accurate identification. Trained educational personnel make good decisions, and accurate diagnoses and placement decisions are made by people—not test scores or formulae. As Bateman (1992) stated,

> The key to preventing further overidentification and misidentification is to exercise trained professional judgment. Our widespread reluctance to use this essential professional judgment in determining eligibility has been due not only to the eligibility teams' lack of experience but also to a fear that courts expect objective quantification as the sole or major basis for decision making. Nothing could be further from the truth. The courts show the highest respect for professional judgment, originally of medical doctors and now of most other qualified experts, too…. First, if not foremost, it is a violation of law to rely on anything other than professional judgment. (pp. 29, 32)

Learning disabilities cannot be validly identified through the sole use of aptitude–achievement discrepancies or sole reliance on an RTI model. Skilled professionals must review a variety of factors including a student's school records, family history, performance on standardized tests, response to classroom instruction, and rate of progress. The emphasis is placed on understanding a student's unique learning abilities as well as any learning disabilities. The Building Blocks model provides a framework for thinking about and understanding a child's intra-individual strengths and weaknesses in performance, which is the essential consideration in determining whether an individual has a specific learning disability.

THE SYMBOLIC PROCESSING BLOCKS

As described in Chapter 2, the abilities in the symbolic processing blocks help children to process, produce, recall, and retrieve information. These abilities enable children to master the symbolic aspects of language (i.e., word identification, spelling, calculating, and handwriting). An ability to recognize symbolic processing problems can help educators identify a student's specific problems and then select and implement appropriate accommodations and effective interventions. This part of the chapter provides a review of the difficulties that children experience when they have weaknesses in the phonological, orthographic, and/or motor processing blocks as well as several informal assessments and interventions that can be used. The major focus of the chapter is on word identification abilities because dyslexia appears to be the most common neurobiological disorder affecting children (Shaywitz & Shaywitz, 2003).

PHONOLOGICAL PROCESSING BLOCK

The phonological processing block consists of two major abilities: phonological awareness and verbal short-term memory. *Phonological awareness* has been a major focus of reading research since the 1980s (Chard & Dickson, 1999). It is an oral language ability that refers to the ability to attend to various aspects of the sound structure of speech. This metacognitive understanding involves the realization that spoken language is made up of a series of sounds that are arranged in a particular order (Clark & Uhry, 1995).

Verbal short-term memory is the ability to repeat information immediately after hearing it. Poor verbal short-term memory is one of the most frequently reported cognitive characteristics of individuals with severe reading disabilities (Morris et al., 1998; Torgesen & Burgess, 1998). The tasks, such as repeating a series of digits in sequence or saying the months in order, require some form of processing of the phonological features of language. Weaknesses in verbal short-term memory can also affect the development of computational skill. A student may struggle to follow directions, memorize counting patterns, and keep pace with oral drills in the classroom.

Students with weaknesses in short-term memory often also have difficulty following lengthy discussions or directions and thus require specific classroom accommodations and compensations as they progress through school. Some students have weaknesses in both short-term memory and phonological awareness. Others, like Maria, only have difficulty with the phonological aspects of language. Although specific strategies and accommodations can be used to enhance memory performance, memory is a capacity that is more innate and difficult to alter. Examples of common classroom accommodations are provided at the end of the chapter.

Phonological Processing Block Questionnaire

Preschool was the first time that Maria's mother noted her difficulties with sounds. Maria would talk about the "aminals" and her favorite food, "psaghetti." Although confusions in articulation were resolved by the end of first grade, difficulties with reading and spelling persisted. In sixth grade, when she was reading a story about

SYMBOLIC			
PHONOLOGICAL PROCESSING	Rarely	Sometimes	Frequently
Has trouble rhyming words	✓		
Has difficulty pronouncing certain sounds			✓
Has trouble putting sounds together to pronounce words (blending) when reading			✓
Has difficulty breaking sounds apart in words (segmenting) when spelling			✓
Has trouble distinguishing letters with similar sounds (e.g., /b/ and /p/, /f/ and /v/) in speech and when spelling			✓
Has difficulty repeating information just heard	✓		
Has trouble learning the days of the week and months of the year in sequence	✓		
Has difficulty connecting sounds to letters when spelling			✓
Has trouble pronouncing multisyllablic words when speaking or reading			✓
Has difficulty pronouncing or spelling words with phonetically regular patterns			✓

Figure 8.1. Building Blocks Questionnaire for Maria: Phonological Processing block.

a bicycle race, Maria came to the sentence, "A foul had been made." She misread the sentence as "The fool had been mad." With a puzzled expression, she asked, "The fool?" Maria monitored her reading for understanding, but she had such difficulty identifying words accurately when reading that her comprehension was affected.

Because he was knowledgeable about Maria's reading and writing skills, Mr. Arnold, Maria's sixth-grade teacher, completed the Phonological Processing section of the Building Blocks Questionnaire with the help of Maria's mother, who could recall Maria's development in first and second grade. Many of the statements were marked with a check in the *Frequently* column (see Figure 8.1).

This section presents a description of phonological abilities, provides an explanation of phonological dyslexia, describes specific instructional activities for helping students learn to perceive and manipulate sounds, and explains the relationships between speech sounds and print. Chapter 9 presents specific strategies for helping students move from an understanding of speech sounds to print as well as examples of specific strategies for helping students improve decoding and encoding abilities.

Definition of Phonological Awareness

As students learn an alphabetic language such as English, a critical first step is becoming aware that speech can be divided or sequenced into a series of discrete sounds, words, syllables, and phonemes. English words can be divided into three main levels of analysis: syllables, onsets and rimes, and phonemes. In the English language, *syllables* are formed by single vowels or vowels with combinations of consonants. The *onset* refers to the initial part of the syllable (i.e., one or more consonants) that precedes the vowel in a monosyllabic word, and the *rime* is the ending unit. In English, every syllable has a rime, but not necessarily an onset. For example, in the word *open*, the first syllable /ō/ is considered to be a rime, but the second syllable /pĕn/ contains both the onset /p/ and the rime /ĕn/. *Phonemes* are the smallest unit of speech sounds. *Phonemic awareness* is the ability to recognize that words are composed of discrete segments of speech sounds. This awareness allows students to perceive and manipulate language sounds. The number of sounds in a word is not necessarily the same as the number of letters. For example, the word *soap* has three sounds: /s/, /ō/, /p/, whereas the word *fox* has four sounds: /f/, /ŏ/, /k/, and /s/. When children are first learning to write, they listen carefully to words and attempt to record the sounds that they hear. When Ben was in second grade, he posted the note displayed in Figure 8.2 on his bedroom door. Notice that he has attempted to capture the sounds of the letters *qu* by using *cw*.

Phonological Dyslexia

Presently, a substantial body of research supports the link between phonological processing abilities and the subsequent development of reading skill (e.g., Lyon, 1995; Perfetti, 1992; Torgesen, 1992, 1993; Wagner & Torgesen, 1987). *Phonological dyslexia* refers to a problem with the acquisition of decoding or encoding skills that is caused by difficulty with manipulating and integrating the sounds of a language effectively (Newby, Recht, & Caldwell, 1993; Richardson, 1992; Westman, 1996). In other words, poor phonological awareness impairs the ability to segment, analyze, and synthesize speech sounds (Stanovich, 1982a, 1982b). These impairments comprise the most common characteristics of individuals with dyslexia (Felton, 1993; Perfetti, 1992; Wagner & Torgesen, 1987). Students with phonologically based reading impairments perform poorly on measures of phonological awareness as well as measures involving the application of speech sounds to letters, such as reading and spelling nonsense words that conform to regular English spelling patterns (Stanovich, Siegel, & Gottardo, 1997).

Phonological processes are also critical for the development of encoding or spelling skills (Bailet, 1991) because spelling requires an awareness of the internal

Figure 8.2. "Be Quiet" note by Ben.

structure of words (Blachman, 1994). Phonological abilities are related significantly to spelling performance through high school (Calfee, Lindamood, & Lindamood, 1973). Even spelling problems in young adults often reflect specific impairments in the phonological aspects of language (Moats, 1991). For example, Bruck (1993) found that although college students with a childhood diagnosis of dyslexia attempted to preserve the phonological structure of words, their knowledge of sound–symbol associations was limited. Throughout their school careers, individuals with phonological dyslexia are often identifiable by their phonetically inaccurate misspellings (Boder, 1973; Johnson, 1995; Mather & Roberts, 1995).

The following list, adapted from Mather and Roberts (1995), summarizes several characteristics that are symptomatic of phonological dyslexia.

Early Speech/Language Difficulties

- Articulation errors
- Mispronunciations of multisyllabic words

Word Identification (Decoding)

- Trouble remembering sound–symbol relationships
- Confusion between similar-sounding sounds (e.g., /b/ and /p/)
- Overreliance on whole-word and context cues
- Difficulty sequencing sounds in words
- Trouble pronouncing multisyllabic words
- Trouble pronouncing phonically regular nonsense words
- Difficulty applying phonics to pronounce unfamiliar words
- Slow reading rate

Spelling (Encoding)

- Confusion between similar-sounding sounds (e.g., vowels, voiced and unvoiced consonant pairs)
- Difficulty sequencing sounds
- Tendency to omit some sounds
- Tendency to include a few unnecessary sounds
- Difficulty representing each syllable
- Tendency to rely on the visual appearance of words rather than on the letter–sound relationships

International Dyslexia Association Definition of Dyslexia

In April of 1994, the International Dyslexia Association (IDA; formerly called the Orton Dyslexia Society) Research Committee, a group comprised of investigators and representatives from advocacy groups, and the National Institute of Child Health and Human Development (NICHD) proposed a revised definition of dyslexia (Lyon, 1995). This definition states,

> Dyslexia is one of several distinct learning disabilities. It is a specific language-based disorder of constitutional origin characterized by difficulties in single word decoding, usually reflecting insufficient phonological processing abilities. These difficulties in single word

Strategies

Language   Images

CONCEPTUAL

Phonology   Orthography   Motor

SYMBOLIC

Attention & Self-Regulation   Emotions   Behavior   Self-Esteem

FOUNDATIONAL

> decoding are often unexpected in relation to age and other cognitive and academic abilities; they are not the result of generalized developmental delay or sensory impairment. Dyslexia is manifested by variable difficulty with different forms of language, often including, in addition to problems reading, a conspicuous problem with acquiring proficiency in writing and spelling. (p. 9)

More recently, members of the working group of IDA expanded and updated this working definition (Lyon, Shaywitz, & Shaywitz, 2003). This revised definition states,

> Dyslexia is a specific learning disability that is neurobiological in origin. It is characterized by difficulties with accurate and/or fluent word recognition and by poor spelling and decoding abilities. These difficulties typically result from a deficit in the phonological component of language that is often unexpected in relation to other cognitive abilities and the provision of effective classroom instruction. Secondary consequences may include problems in reading comprehension and reduced reading experience that can impede growth of vocabulary and background knowledge." (Lyon et al., 2003, p. 2)

This definition is an attempt to incorporate the most current evidence regarding reading development, reading disabilities, and reading instruction.

Brief Historical Review

Several decades after descriptions were written about the condition called *word blindness,* another type of reading disability was recognized. Orton (1937), one of the pioneer investigators of the developmental language disability of *word deafness,* noted that although children with this condition had adequate hearing, they had difficulties with recalling the auditory patterns of spoken words. Monroe and Backus (1937) discussed the children who lacked proper discrimination of sounds. They noted that these children exhibited some of the following characteristics in reading: 1) errors in the vowel and consonant sounds of words, 2) additions and omissions of sounds, 3) confusion of words that sound alike, and 4) poor understanding of oral directions.

In the 1970s, Bakker (1972) proposed that dyslexia may be caused by deficient word perception and verbal sequential memory. His work revived interest in phonology and helped clarify the distinction between auditory or phonological dyslexia and generalized language disorders (Vellutino, 1979). Many research studies were conducted during the early 1970s, providing support for the existence of phonological dyslexia (e.g., Bannatyne, 1971; Corkin, 1974; Downing, 1973; Elkonin, 1973; Liberman, 1973). Two researchers, Downing (1973) and Elkonin (1973), simultaneously but independently explained the intrinsic relationship between reading disorders and poor phonemic awareness.

Phonological skill impairments are often the cause of severe word identification and spelling problems (DeFries, Olson, Pennington, & Smith, 1991; Ehri, 1994; Felton & Wood, 1989; Liberman & Shankweiler, 1985; Stanovich, 1991; Vellutino & Scanlon, 1987). As Richardson observed, "Much in our medical and psycholinguistic history substantiates the proposition that developmental dyslexia is a specific developmental language disorder involving some phonological processing deficits" (1992, p. 46). The difficulties with speech sounds may be mild or very severe. In the literature, phonological dyslexia has been described by a variety of terms for more than 60 years (e.g., Geschwind, 1982; Monroe, 1932; Orton, 1925, 1937; Vellutino, 1979). This type of dyslexia has been referred to as *dysphonetic* (Boder, 1973), P-type (Bakker, 1972, 1992), and *accuracy*

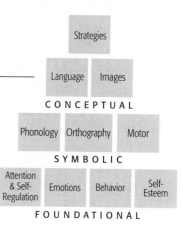

Strategies

Language | Images

CONCEPTUAL

Phonology | Orthography | Motor

SYMBOLIC

Attention & Self-Regulation | Emotions | Behavior | Self-Esteem

FOUNDATIONAL

disabled (Lovett, 1987) as well as a *specific language deficit* (Lyon & Watson, 1981) or verbal impairment (Morris, Blashfield, & Satz, 1986).

Developmental Sequence

Efficient phonological processing abilities are needed in order to learn to read and spell successfully (Felton & Wood, 1992; Rack, Snowling, & Olson, 1992). For most, children, phonological awareness and knowledge of phoneme–grapheme correspondences develop naturally over the preschool and early elementary years, progressing from the skill of rhyming words to the ability to hear and manipulate the individual sounds within words. As general guidelines, many children in preschool and most students in kindergarten are able to rhyme words. The majority of first-grade students can count syllables, delete part of a compound word, and count and blend syllables (Smith, 1997). By second grade, most children can perform all types of tasks involving phonemic manipulations, such as deleting a sound from the front, middle, or end of a word. Anthony and Francis (2005) described the two overlapping patterns of development: 1) children increase sensitivity to smaller and smaller parts of words as they grow older; and 2) children can first detect and manipulate syllables in words, then onsets and rimes, and finally phonemes.

For some children, awareness of language sounds does not come naturally or easily. In fact, children do not start school understanding the relationships between spoken and written words and their sounds and letters. Fortunately, when young children are lacking in grapheme–phoneme awareness, they may be taught these relationships directly prior to school entry or within the kindergarten and first-grade year. If students have trouble with these tasks, they need to spend time with activities that help them discover these relationships. As a general principle, they must move from easier tasks, such as rhyming, to more complex tasks, such as blending, segmenting, and manipulating phonemes (Anthony & Francis, 2005; Chard & Dickson, 1999). Unlike verbal short-term memory, phonological awareness skills can be taught. Similar tasks may be used for informal assessment and instruction in these skills.

Assessment and Instructional Activities

Students who are in kindergarten through second grade or older students having trouble learning to decode or encode need to develop knowledge of the sound structure of language. The purposes of assessing phonological abilities are twofold: 1) to identify students who are at risk for reading failure and 2) to monitor the progress of students who are receiving instruction (Chard & Dickson, 1999).

Student knowledge can be assessed using several types of tasks. Appendix A includes instructions for administration of the Phonological Awareness Skills Screener (PASS), which was originally called the Screening of Early Reading Processes (Mather, Bos, Podhajski, Babur, & Rhein, 2000). This phonological assessment was partially based on an adaptation of Sawyer's (1987) Test of Awareness of Language Segments. Administration time for the PASS is approximately 15 minutes. This assessment has been extensively field-tested and includes 10 measures of phonological awareness. Local norms can be developed by administering the test to 100 students at kindergarten, first-grade, and second-grade levels. Results would differ depending on whether the instrument was administered at the beginning or end of the school year. The important information obtained from the PASS is not quantitative but rather a determination of what types of tasks a student can and cannot do.

Phonological abilities can also be assessed in a less formal way. The following are some examples of tasks, presented from easiest to most difficult, that students can be asked to do to demonstrate their phonological abilities. If a student is unable to perform a task, instruction can be designed to teach that specific skill.

Rhyme Recognition:
"Tell me the two words that rhyme."

1. *cat, dog, hat*

2. *tree, bee, house*

3. *top, star, hop*

4. *stop, man, fan*

5. *wall, car, fall*

Rhyme Production:
"Tell me all the words you can think of that rhyme with"

1. *cat*

2. *see*

3. *log*

4. *shoe*

5. *pig*

Phoneme Matching:
"Tell me the word that starts with a different sound."

1. *ball, bat, tree*

2. *step, dog, star*

3. *boy, clock, clown*

4. *milk, man, shoe*

5. *apple, car, ax*

Word Counting:
"Clap or tap out the number of words you hear in each sentence."

1. Jim runs.

2. Pat drives a car.

3. Bill went to school.

4. Jane had a big lunch.

5. Tom likes to ride his bike.

Syllable Counting:
"Clap or tap out the number of syllables you hear in each word."

1. *maybe* (2)

2. *turtle* (2)

3. *exercise* (3)

4. *carpenter* (3)

5. *basketball* (3)

Compound Word Deletion:
"Say the word."

1. *cowboy* without *cow*

2. *cupcake* without *cup*

3. *birthday* without *birth*

4. *rainbow* without *rain*

5. *sunshine* without *shine*

Syllable Blending:
"Tell me the word I am trying to say."[Pause for about 1 second between syllables.]

1. tur•tle

2. hap•py

3. pen•cil

4. com•pu•ter

5. car•pen•ter

Sound Blending:
"Tell me the word I am trying to say." [Make the sounds of the letters as they are usually pronounced, and pause for about 1 second between parts.]

1. c•at

2. sh•oe

3. b•ir•d

4. t•a•b•le

5. h•a•m•b•ur•g•er

Sound Counting:
"How many sounds do you hear in the word"

1. *toy* (2)

2. *girl* (3)

3. *box* (4)

4. *eight* (2)

5. *rabbit* (5)

Although the word *box* is composed of three letters, there are four separate phonemes (i.e., /b/, /ŏ/, /k/, /s/). If the student is not ready to count the number of sounds, have him or her push forward a poker chip for each sound as you pronounce the word slowly.

Phoneme Deletion: Say the word:

1. *hat* without the /h/ sound

2. *ran* without the /r/ sound

3. *sold* without the /s/ sound

4. *gate* without the /g/ sound

5. *cart* without the /t/ sound

Phoneme Substitution

1. Change the /t/ in *tip* to /r/.

2. Change the /n/ in *can* to /t/.

3. Change the /ă/ in *hat* to /ĭ/.

4. Change the /s/ in *slip* to a /f/.

5. Change the /m/ in *smart* to a /t/.

Classroom activities for promoting phonological awareness are most often interactive and game-like, involving singing, rhyming, clapping, and movement. The goals of these activities are to draw students' attention to the elements of spoken speech and increase their ability to analyze speech sounds. Several carefully developed commercial programs and compilations of classroom activities are available for promoting phonological awareness (e.g., Adams, Foorman, Lundberg, & Beeler, 1998; Blachman, Ball, Black, & Tangel, 2000; see Additional Resources).

Students benefit from performing activities involving rhyming words; clapping out and counting the number of syllables in words; and pronouncing words slowly by syllables and phonemes. Activities such as reading nursery rhymes or poems or singing songs can be integrated into story time. Many books are available that emphasize rhyming words, or familiar songs can be adapted to introduce letter names and their corresponding sounds (Edelen-Smith, 1997).

Ms. Janus, a kindergarten teacher, would sing the following song to the tune of "Old Mac-Donald Had a Farm": "What is the sound that starts these words, *book* and *box* and *bear*? What is the sound that starts these words, *book* and *box* and *bear*?" She would then pause for the children to respond and then continue, "/B/ is the sound that starts these words: *book* and *box* and *bear*. /B/ is the sound that starts these words: *book* and *box* and *bear*. With a /b/ /b/ here and a /b/ /b/ there...."

Segmentation and Blending

The two most important phonological awareness abilities are blending (synthesizing sounds) and segmentation (analyzing sounds) (Ehri, 2006). For blending, children are presented with a series of sounds and then asked to push the sounds together to form a word. For segmentation, children are presented with a word and then asked to break the word apart into the individual sounds. Some students have trouble learning how to segment and then blend sounds. At first, when Maria was learning to blend, she would sound out the word, but she was not able to put it back together again. Gradually, she learned how to pronounce the word aloud, but she still had trouble with silent reading.

Both segmentation and blending can be taught using a variety of manipulatives, including plastic markers, poker chips, colored tiles, magnetic letters, and scrabble tiles. Different colored chips can represent the consonant and vowel sounds (e.g., consonant sounds are blue and vowel sounds are red). Using letters, the teacher can demonstrate how to pull the sounds of a word apart and then push the sounds back together again to form a word. Without appropriate intervention in important phonological abilities such as blending and segmentation, the reading development of children with poor phonological processing skills will be impeded (Lipka, Lesaux, & Siegel, 2006).

Teaching Segmentation   The following sequence may be used to assess or teach segmentation. Begin with tasks that require students to segment compound words (e.g., *raincoat*) and then progress to syllables. An easy way to help students

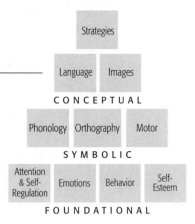

learn to count the number of syllables is to have them place their hand under their chin and then say the word aloud. The number of syllables is equal to the number of times the chin drops. When students have learned to break words into syllables, teach them how to segment short words into onsets and rimes (e.g., c-at) and then into individual phonemes.

Blending Words The purpose of teaching blending is to help young children combine letter sounds to be able to pronounce or decode words (Ehri, 2006). Chard and Osborn (1999a) recommended a three-step procedure for helping students like Maria learn to blend sounds together to pronounce words more easily:

1. Encourage students to blend sounds together as quickly as possible rather than stopping between the sounds.

2. Ask students to follow the sounding out of the word with a fast pronunciation of the word.

3. Have students move from sounding out words aloud to sounding out words in their heads.

Gradually, as skill progresses, word reading changes from an overt activity to a covert activity. At this stage, the teacher may need to model for students by mouthing the pronunciation of words, showing them how words can be sounded out silently.

The difficulty level of a blending task is affected by both the length of the pause between the sounds as well as the number of sounds that are presented in the sequence. A word that is sounded with a short pause between the sounds is much easier to blend than a word that is presented with a one-second interval between the sounds. Instruction then begins with words with two sounds (/sh/oe/), then three sounds (/c/a/t/), and finally four sounds (/s/a/n/d/) (Kirk, Kirk, Minskoff, Mather, & Roberts, 2007). In addition, speech sounds that can be prolonged and sustained (e.g., /s/, /f/, /m/, /l/, /n/, /r/, /v/, /z/) are easier to blend than those that cannot (e.g., /b/, /t/) (Carnine, Silbert, Kame'enui, & Tarver, 2004). Carnine and colleagues described a similar procedure called *telescoping sounds* in which a student transforms a series of blended sounds pronounced quickly in succession (e.g., /i/ /i/ i/ /t/ /t/ /t/) into a word (e.g., "it") said at a typical rate.

Examples of Commercial Programs

Many commercial programs are available to improve phonemic awareness and build skills in phonics. Several examples are described below.

Lindamood Phoneme Sequencing Program for Reading, Spelling, and Speech For students with more severe difficulty with sounds, a program that stresses the oral-motor characteristics of speech can be beneficial. One carefully designed, intensive program for developing phonemic awareness is the *Lindamood Phoneme Sequencing Program for Reading, Spelling, and Speech* (LiPS; Lindamood & Lindamood, 1998; see Additional Resources). This program addresses the development of phonemic awareness as a base for accurate reading and spelling and provides explicit instruction about the articulatory dimensions of speech. The program progresses from sounds in isolation, to sequences of sounds in nonwords and real words, to reading in context.

Fast ForWord *Fast ForWord* is a program developed by the Scientific Learning Corporation (see Additional Resources) to assist students who have difficulty with reading or spelling, problems understanding and using language, or difficulty remembering oral instructions. Using a CD-ROM, Fast ForWord training focuses on the general ability to attend to the sounds of language. The student learns to recognize and use sound units such as words, syllables, and phonemes through acoustically modified exercises with sounds. The intent of this program is to address a presumed cause of language problems, that is, the inability to perceive the quickly changing elements of oral language. Initially, the duration of the presented sounds is increased to make them easier to perceive. Gradually, the exercises progress to typical speech. Although initial research by the Scientific Learning Corporation supports rapid gains for students with language and reading problems, further research is needed to validate the efficacy of this training program.

Earobics Another example of a commercial program is a software product called *Earobics* (see Additional Resources). This program is aimed at helping students develop phonemic awareness skills. The program charts performance and prints progress reports for different users.

Chapter 9 describes several techniques for helping a student move from an understanding of sounds to pairing sounds with printed letters. A teacher can informally assess a student's grasp of the alphabetic principle and knowledge of phoneme–grapheme relationships by analyzing his or her attempted spellings. An understanding of how specific speech sounds relate to written language development will help the teacher pinpoint the specific difficulties and select appropriate interventions. Moats (2000) provided a comprehensive guide to help teachers understand language structure and exactly how the phonological, or speech-sound processing, system relates to print. The Florida Center for Reading Research webcast page (http://www.fcrr.org) also provides a video podcast for teachers on how to pronounce the sounds of standard English.

Figure 8.3 presents a writing sample from Maria's journal when she was in fifth grade. Write down all the misspelled words and then attempt to identify why Maria has spelled the words in these ways. Next, review the information in Appendix B, "Relationship Between Speech Sounds and Spelling Development," and then review the spellings again.

ORTHOGRAPHIC PROCESSING BLOCK

Orthographic awareness refers to the ability to form a mental image of words and specific letter sequences. This section provides a description of orthographic awareness, a review of characteristics associated with weaknesses in this ability, a brief historic account, a review of related research, and a discussion of implications for intervention.

Definition of Orthographic Awareness

Orthographic awareness is the ability to perceive and recall letters, letter strings, and words. This ability helps students to establish detailed visual or mental representations of letter strings and words and to have rapid, fluent access to these representations. Successful word identification involves the abilities to 1) identify letters in written words, word strings, or nonwords; 2) remember the position of each letter in the word; and 3) recall in sequence the letters that belong together. Vellutino, Scanlon, and Tanzman defined this process of *orthographic coding* as "the ability to represent the unique array of letters that defines a printed word, as well as general attributes of the writing system such as sequential dependencies, structural redundancies, and letter position frequencies" (1994, p. 314). This knowledge refers specifically to print (Corcos & Willows, 1993). The term *orthographic dyslexia* is used to describe students whose reading and spelling

Today is Wendnesday August 25. One tam I went to Nagales. I wet to my casens hous. We playt and playt. Ten we tog a pah. We wet op a mouten and we cot paterfles and we putem in a gor. Ten me and my cosent wet ton the mouten and we wet to bet.

The End

Figure 8.3. Writing sample from Maria's journal.

Strategies	
Language	Images

CONCEPTUAL

Phonology	Orthography	Motor

SYMBOLIC

Attention & Self-Regulation	Emotions	Behavior	Self-Esteem

FOUNDATIONAL

problems are characterized by poor memory of letter forms and letter strings (Mather & Roberts, 1995).

The following list, adapted from Mather and Roberts (1995) and Willows and Terepocki (1993), summarizes several characteristics of individuals with orthographic dyslexia.

Symbol Recognition and Recall Difficulties

- Difficulty learning how to form symbols
- Confusion of symbols similar in appearance (e.g., *b* and *d*, *n* and *u*, *2* and *5*)
- Trouble with near-point and far-point copying tasks
- Tendency to reverse letters or numbers past the age of 7

Word Identification (Decoding)

- Trouble with accurate and rapid word recognition
- Trouble reading exception or irregular words

- Trouble remembering how words look
- Trouble remembering letter sequences
- Overreliance on phonological and contextual strategies as aids in word identification
- Slow reading speed

Spelling (Encoding)

- Tendency to reverse and transpose letters (e.g., *grils* for *girls*)
- Tendency to use different spellings for the same word (e.g., *Pual* and *Paul*)
- Tendency to overrely on the phonological rather than the visual features of words
- Tendency to omit word endings

Calculating

- Tendency to reverse and transpose digits (e.g., *12* for *21*)
- Trouble learning and retaining basic math facts
- Difficulty counting in a sequence (e.g., counting by 2)
- Trouble solving multistep problems

Characteristics of Poor Orthographic Awareness

Students with poor orthographic awareness often have symbol recognition and recall difficulties at a young age and make errors in letter or number formation. For example, by the time Ben had finished kindergarten, he recognized only two letters of the alphabet, the letters *b* and *n* in his name. As Ben progressed through school, he continued to make errors in letter and number orientation past the age of 7. He had trouble copying from both textbooks and chalkboards because of his difficulty maintaining and sustaining a mental image of letter strings. As his eyes moved from one surface to another, he would lose his place. These difficulties followed Ben into adulthood.

With regard to reading performance, Ben was slow to recognize high-incidence words, exception words (e.g., words with irregular spelling patterns), and syllable units. Because he tended to overrely on phonics and contextual strategies to compensate, he frequently confused similar-looking letters or words and sometimes had more difficulty recognizing short, common words, such as *were, how,* and *said,* than he did longer, more meaningful words, such as *dinosaur* or *elevator.* Ben lost his place easily when reading and needed to use his finger to track lines of print. Even after he was taught to decode, Ben demonstrated a compromised, slow reading rate and tended to confuse words with similar appearance (e.g., *feather* and *father*).

Spelling causes students like Ben the most difficulty because successful performance depends on recall of letter–sound sequences and patterns. In eighth grade, after Ben had read *Tom Sawyer,* he spelled the name *Becky* six different ways in the first draft of his book report (*Becy, Beacey, Becky, Beacky, Beke, Beckey*). These inconsistencies, coupled with his misspellings of simple high-frequency words such as *they, was,* and *were,* illustrated that Ben did not recall spellings easily. In addition, when Ben attempted to spell a word, the spellings were reasonable in terms of the sequence of sounds but impossible in terms of English regularities and spelling rules (e.g., *egz* for *eggs*). On one paper, Ben spelled the word *exact* as *egzakt.* In most instances, the most obvious symptom of this problem in later years is spelling that is phonetically accurate but violates the rules of English spelling.

Strategies

Language | Images

CONCEPTUAL

Phonology | Orthography | Motor

SYMBOLIC

Attention & Self-Regulation | Emotions | Behavior | Self-Esteem

FOUNDATIONAL

Some students with poor orthographic awareness do not have problems learning to read but they do experience problems in learning to spell. In a synthesis of Samuel Orton's work, June Orton (1966) explained that for these students, visual memory of words is sufficient enough to recognize the printed word in reading but not strong enough to recall the image of the word to reconstruct it for spelling. In other words, for reading, one has to identify the word; but for spelling, one has to produce the entire pattern.

These types of symbolic confusions can also affect performance in computations, and these students often have trouble memorizing math facts. One day, as Ben was attempting to solve some multiplication problems, he remarked, "Ugh, multiplication—this feels just like spelling. What is this doing to me?" Even in fifth grade, Ben still reversed the number 5 and transposed numbers when working at his desk or when copying a problem from the board. By the time Ben copied the problems from the board, he was so far behind that the teacher had already changed to a new topic.

Students like Ben are likely to work slowly and lose their place often. They may confuse operation symbols (e.g., addition and multiplication signs), have trouble retaining basic facts, and reverse and transpose digits. As they progress in school, they may have difficulty learning multistep computations, such as the sequence of steps required in long division.

Orthographic Processing Block Questionnaire

Because she was knowledgeable about Ben's reading and writing skills, Ms. Rhein, Ben's eighth-grade English teacher, completed the Orthographic Processing block items on the Building Blocks Questionnaire (see Figure 8.4). If this checklist had been completed for Ben in first or second grade, all of the statements would have received a check in the "Frequently" column.

ORTHOGRAPHIC PROCESSING	Rarely	Sometimes	Frequently
Forgets how letters look	✓		
Confuses letters with similar appearance (e.g., *n* for *h*)			✓
Misreads little words in text (e.g., *were* for *where*)			✓
Reverses letters when spelling (e.g., *b* instead of *d*)		✓	
Transposes letters when reading or writing (e.g., *on* instead of *no*)		✓	
Has trouble remembering basic sight words		✓	
Has difficulty copying from a book or chalkboard to paper			✓
Spells the same word in different ways			✓
Spells words the way they sound rather than the way they look			✓
Reads at a slow rate			✓

Figure 8.4. Building Blocks Questionnaire for Ben: Orthographic Processing block.

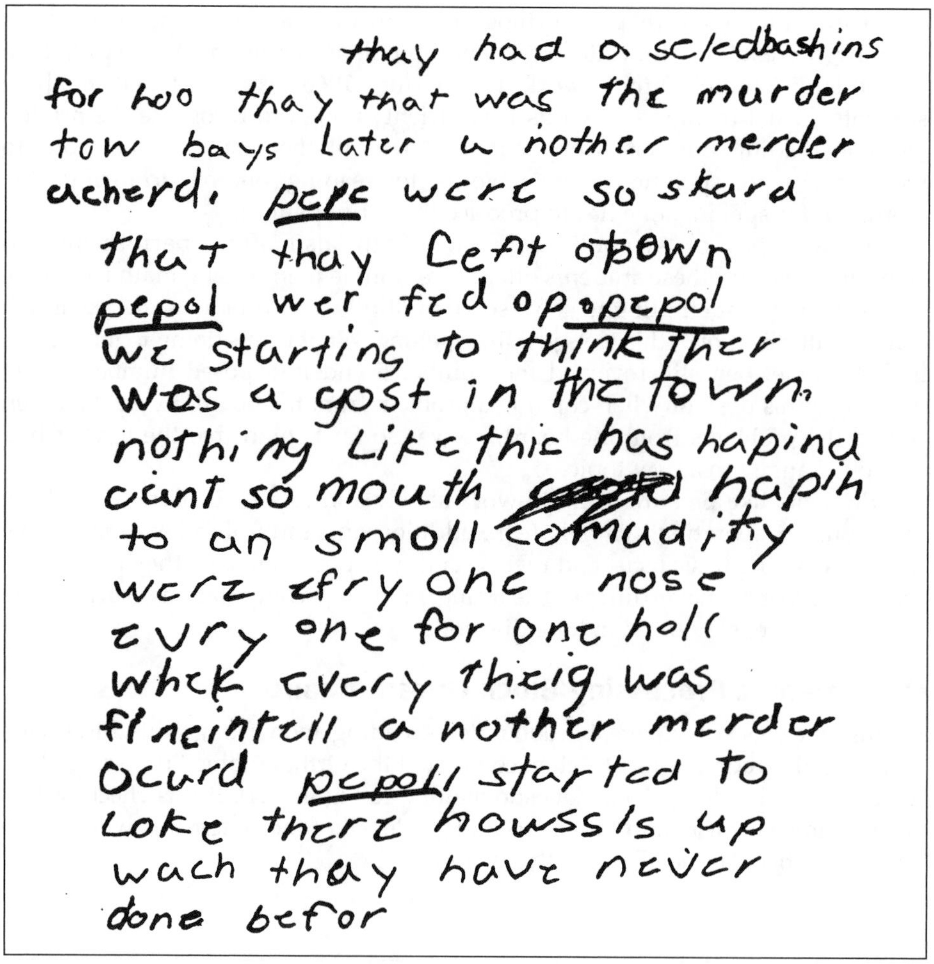
thay had a scledbashins
for too thay that was the murder
tow bays later a nother merder
acherd. pepe were so skard
that thay Left of town
pepol wer fed op pepol
we starting to think ther
was a gost in the town.
nothing Like this has hapind
cant so mouth hapin
to an smoll comudity
were efry one nose
evry one for one holl
whek every thig was
flneintell a nother merder
ocurd pepoll started to
Loke there howssls up
wach thay have never
done befor

Figure 8.5. Excerpt from a story by Ben.

Figure 8.5 presents an excerpt from a story Ben was creating for Ms. Rhein's English class. Notice the different spellings of the word *people,* the transpositions (e.g., *tow bays* for *two days*), and the reliance on sounds for spelling rather than on the visual appearance of the word (e.g., *howssis* for *houses*). Ben's weakness in forming and recalling visual images needed for accurate word pronunciation and spelling is apparent. He seems to lack sensitivity to orthographic redundancies or common English spelling patterns. Despite repeated exposures to words, mental images of common words are only partially retained. As students such as Ben progress through school, limited retention of letter strings and spelling patterns usually has a pronounced effect on the students' word identification and spelling development. These orthographic processing skills predict differences in word recognition independent of phonological factors (Cunningham & Stanovich, 1998).

Brief Historical Review of Orthographic Dyslexia

Discussion of orthographic dyslexia can be traced back to the late 1800s. In 1872, Sir William Broadbent described cortical damage present in an autopsy of an individual who had had reading disabilities (cited in Critchley, 1964; Richardson, 1992). Five years later, Kussmaul (1877a) noted that "a complete text blindness may exist although the power of sight, the intellect, and the powers of speech are intact" (p. 595). In other words, the problem does not affect the development of abilities within the conceptual blocks. In 1887, Berlin used the term *dyslexia* to

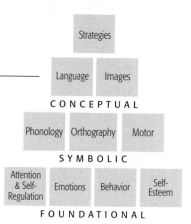

Strategies

Language | Images

CONCEPTUAL

Phonology | Orthography | Motor

SYMBOLIC

Attention & Self-Regulation | Emotions | Behavior | Self-Esteem

FOUNDATIONAL

describe a condition acquired through cerebral disease (cited in Richardson, 1992). In 1895, Hinshelwood, a surgeon at the Glasgow Eye Infirmary, wrote an article that described *acquired word blindness*. The following year, two more accounts of congenital word blindness were published.

The first account was written by James Kerr, a health officer, who described a boy of average or above-average intelligence who suffered from word blindness despite being able to spell the separate letters (cited in Critchley, 1964). The second article, written by Morgan (1896), described the characteristics of an intelligent 14-year-old boy who excelled in arithmetic but could not read:

> His greatest difficulty has been—and is now—his inability to learn to read. This inability is so remarkable, and so pronounced, that I have no doubt it is due to some congenital defect…. The following is the result of an examination I made a short time since. He knows all his letters and can write them and read them. In writing from dictation, he comes to grief over any but the simplest words. For instance, I dictated the following sentence: "Now, you watch me while I spin it." He wrote, "Now you word me wale I spin it" and again, "Carefully winding the string round the peg" was written "culfuly winder the sturng rond the pag." In writing his own name, he made a mistake, putting "Precy" for "Percy," and he did not notice the mistake until his attention was called to it more than once …. I then asked him to read me a sentence out of an easy child's book without spelling the words. The result was curious. He did not read a single word correctly, with the exception of "and," "the," "of," "that," etc.; the other words seemed to be quite unknown to him, and he could not even make an attempt to pronounce them…. He seems to have no power of preserving and storing up the visual impression produced by words—hence the words, though seen, have no significance for him. His visual memory for words is defective or absent, which is equivalent to saying that he is what Kussmaul has termed "word blind." I may add that the boy is bright and of average intelligence in conversation…his eyesight is good. The schoolmaster who has taught him for some years says that he would be the smartest lad in the school if the instruction were entirely oral. (p. 94)

It appears that the term *word blindness* was first applied to individuals with aphasia who had lost the ability to read (Kussmaul, 1877b). In 1896, Morgan described a reading difficulty that he referred to as *congenital word blindness*.

In 1902, Hinshelwood described in detail two cases of congenital word blindness in which the reading problem was attributed to a defect in the visual memory of letters and words. He reached the following conclusions, which are still pertinent today: 1) Particular areas of the brain appear to be involved; 2) the children often have average or above intelligence and good memory in other respects; 3) the problem with reading is localized, not generalized to all areas of performance; 4) the children do not learn to read with the same rapidity as other children; 5) the earlier the problem is identified, the better so as not to waste valuable time; 6) the children must be taught by special methods adapted to help them overcome their difficulties; 7) the sense of touch can help children retain visual impressions; and 8) persistent and persevering attempts will often help children improve their reading. He further noted that the diagnosis itself is easy to make because the features of the disorder are so distinct and easily understood. More than a century later, Shaywitz (2003) concurred that the diagnosis of dyslexia is as precise and accurate as any known medical condition.

Hinshelwood described a 10-year-old boy with adequate visual acuity who could not learn words by sight but, instead, spelled out words letter by letter. Regarding treatment, Hinshelwood observed that because students with word blindness had trouble learning to read by sight alone, they would benefit from a multisensory teaching method.

In 1917, Hinshelwood reviewed the articles by Kerr and Morgan in his seminal monograph titled *Congenital Word-Blindness.* Within this monograph, Hinshelwood attempted to clarify the distinction between word blindness and more generalized developmental delays:

> When I see it stated that congenital word-blindness may be combined with any amount of other mental defects from mere dullness to low-grade mental defects, imbecility, or idiocy, I can understand how confusion has arisen from the loose application of the term *congenital word-blindness* to all conditions in which there is defective development of the visual memory center, quite independently of any consideration as to whether it is a strict local defect or only a symptom of a general cerebral degeneration. It is a great injustice to the children affected with the pure type of congenital word-blindness, a strict local affection [sic], to be placed in the same category as others suffering from generalized cerebral defects, as the former can be successfully dealt with, while the latter are practically irremediable. (pp. 93–94)

The first report on word blindness to appear in the American medical literature was written by Samuel Orton (1925). Orton agreed with Hinshelwood that word blindness 1) was not related to mental retardation, 2) ranged from mild to severe, and 3) was caused by physiological deficits in the brain. One specific characteristic that Orton observed in the children he studied was the instability and poor recall of both the orientation and order of letters. He identified this intrinsic disability as *strephosymbolia,* which means twisted symbols (Orton, S.T., 1925, 1937; Orton, J., 1966). Monroe and Backus (1937) also noted that children with visual defects affecting reading tended to show the following characteristics: 1) excessive reversals, 2) line and word skipping, 3) slow reading rate, 4) errors on words with similar spelling configurations (e.g., *bread* and *beard*), and 5) complaints of eyestrain when reading.

Although the characteristics described tend to vary slightly, these types of difficulties have been identified as word blindness (Hinshelwood, 1902; Orton, 1925), visual dyslexia (Johnson & Myklebust, 1971), dyseidetic dyslexia (Boder, 1973), L-type dyslexia (Bakker, 1980, 1992), rate-disabled dyslexia (Lovett, 1987), visual-perceptual deficit (Lyon & Watson, 1981), visual-spatial impairment (Morris et al., 1986), surface dyslexia (Castles & Coltheart, 1993; Marshall & Newcombe, 1978), logographic dyslexia (Seymour & Evans, 1999), and orthographic dyslexia (Mather & Roberts, 1995). Early case studies of visually based reading problems are described in several sources (e.g., Fernald, 1943; Hinshelwood, 1917; Morgan, 1896; Orton, 1925, 1937).

Research on Orthographic Dyslexia

Within discussions of acquired dyslexia (i.e., reading problems resulting from brain injury), a similar subtype of dyslexia has been most commonly referred to as *surface dyslexia.* Surface dyslexia has a lower prevalence and is less easily identified than phonological dyslexia (Stanovich, 1999). Unlike individuals with phonologically based reading and spelling disorders, these individuals have intact phonological awareness and tend to over-rely on the use of phonology for reading and spelling (Goulandris & Snowling, 1991). Manis and colleagues (1999) indicated that surface dyslexia can be created in a computer simulation by introducing a visual processing impairment or a lack of reading experience.

The term *orthographic dyslexia* seems to describe the central difficulties involved in this condition: difficulties with whole-word identification, sight word

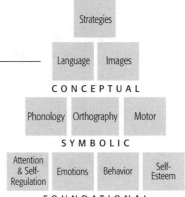

retention, and reading and spelling irregular letter strings. A common characteristic of individuals with orthographic dyslexia is that they have difficulty storing mental representations of irregular words or gestalts (Boder, 1973; Newby et al., 1993; Westman, 1996; Willows, Kruk, & Corcos, 1993). As a result, their performance reading exception words (i.e., words with irregular spelling patterns, such as *yacht*) is typically lower than their performance reading phonically regular nonsense words (e.g., *spub*).

Despite sufficient phonological awareness, students with orthographic dyslexia do have difficulty with tasks that involve the application of phonological skills, such as pronouncing phonically regular nonsense words. This is because a task like the reading of nonsense words involves both phonological abilities (i.e., application of speech sounds to print), and orthographic abilities (i.e., rapid recognition of the common letter patterns).

When Ben was in fourth grade, he scored in the superior range on several tasks measuring phonological awareness, such as the ability to blend and segment sounds. On a test of nonword reading, however, Ben scored in the low average range. Presumably, in Ben's case, his difficulties with reading nonwords stem from poor recall of orthographic representations or spelling–sound (grapheme–phoneme) correspondences rather than poor phonological awareness. In other words, a failure to internalize grapheme–phoneme correspondences affects learning to read and spell all types of letter strings, but exception words are the most difficult and vulnerable (Manis, Seidenberg, Doi, McBride-Chang, & Petersen, 1996).

Manis and colleagues (1996) suggested that phonological and orthographic subtypes may be differentiated by comparing performance on tasks that involve orthographic abilities (e.g., identifying the correct spelling of a word from several possible phonically regular spellings, such as *rain* or *rane*) with tasks that involve phonological skills (e.g., reading or spelling phonically regular nonsense words). Students with orthographic dyslexia will have low levels of orthographic knowledge relative to their phonological skill, whereas students with phonological dyslexia will be more impaired in phonological skills.

In addition, one has to consider reading development in the context of a specific language (e.g., Spanish has more regular grapheme–phoneme correspondence than English). Children learning more consistent orthographies learn to read more quickly than those learning to read and spell inconsistent orthographies. It appears that phonological development may be universal to the development of alphabetic languages, whereas the way sounds are mapped to letters may be language specific, making some languages easier to read and spell than others (Goswami, 2006). These differences in orthographies of languages should be considered when helping English language learners. In addition, the nature of orthography of the native language will influence how children attempt to spell the English words that they are learning (Joshi, Hoien, Feng, Chengappa, & Boulware-Gooden, 2006).

Table 8.2 presents two lists of words that can be used for an informal assessment. The first list consists of phonically regular nonwords that are spelled as if they were real English words. The second list contains examples of exception words that have irregular elements. Students may read or attempt to spell these words. Analysis of performance may provide some insight into the factors contributing to reading or spelling difficulties.

Students who have trouble reading exception words also have trouble spelling the irregular parts of words. Review the sample of Ben's writing presented in Figure 8.5. Notice that even simple high-frequency words such as *they* are misspelled. Although there are a few misspellings indicative of phonological confusions (e.g., *evry* and *efry* for *every*), clearly, his difficulties with spelling are more attributed to poor recall of letter strings than to weaknesses in phonology.

Table 8.2. List of regular nonwords and exception words

Regular nonwords	Exception words
barches	once
tranning	sure
straking	who
quib	laugh
smuff	island
meck	comb
widge	does
crusp	echo
gruzz	machine
bungic	tough

Misspellings by students with this difficulty often have good phonemic resemblance to the target words (Freebody & Byrne, 1988; Johnson, 1995; Westman, 1996; Willows et al., 1993). Freebody and Byrne suggested that the existence of phonetically accurate spellings in these individuals confirms that their literacy development is hindered by something other than poor phonological processing.

This type of problem persists into adulthood. Figure 8.6 depicts several sample spellings (*shout, correct, believe, suggestion, equipment, literature, precious, executive, physician*) by Ryan when he was a senior in high school. Note that Ryan was able to sequence sounds correctly but produced improbable spelling patterns and had not mastered common English spelling patterns, such as the *-tion* in the word *suggestion.* He also had not mastered English spelling rules, such as knowing that English words do not end with the letter *v.*

To quickly determine whether a student forms orthographic images with ease, show him or her a word, then cover it up and ask him or her to write the word from memory.

When Ben was in fourth grade, Mr. Steen wrote the word *game* at the top of the page. He instructed Ben to look at the word, then covered the word and asked Ben to write it without looking. Ben's attempts are presented in Figure 8.7. On the sixth trial, Ben was able to write the word correctly.

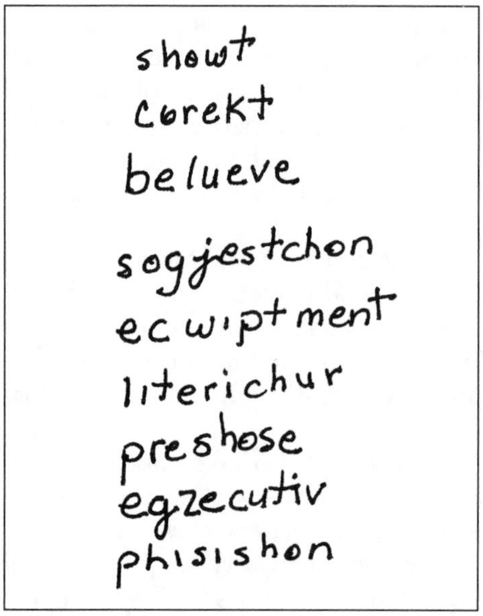

Figure 8.6. Ryan's spellings.

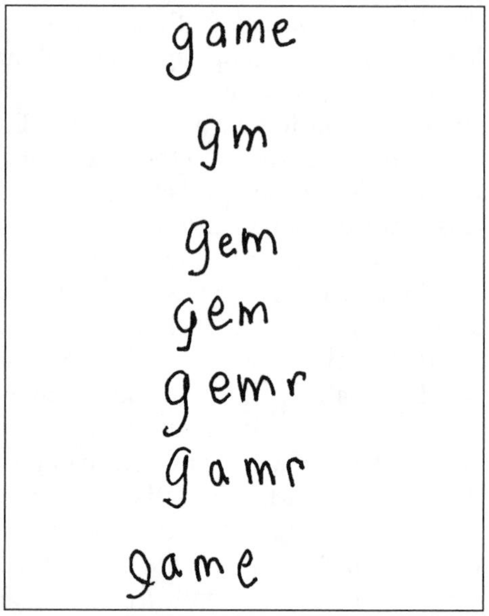

Figure 8.7. Ben's spelling of *game.*

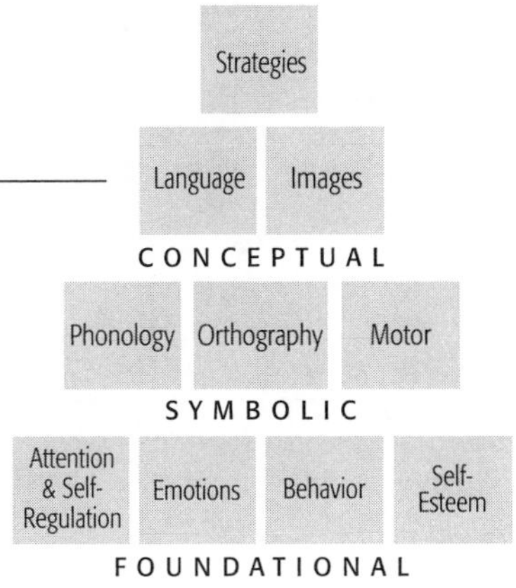

Strategies

Language Images

CONCEPTUAL

Phonology Orthography Motor

SYMBOLIC

Attention & Self-Regulation Emotions Behavior Self-Esteem

FOUNDATIONAL

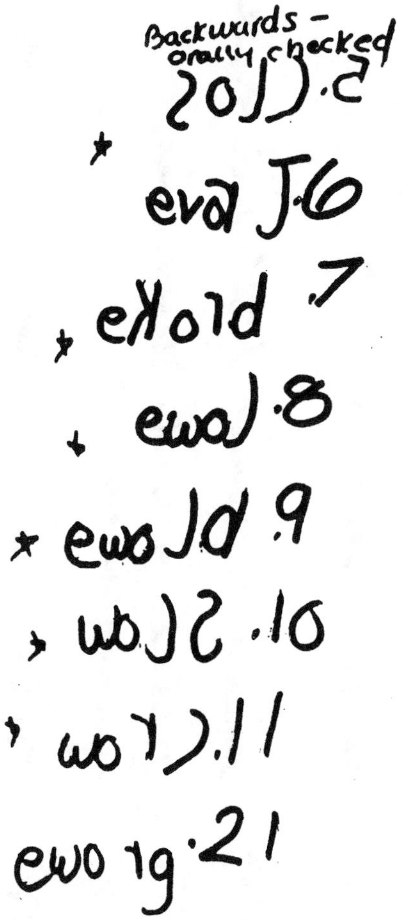

Figure 8.8. Items from Sara's spelling test with a teacher's note

A popular oversimplification of orthographic dyslexia is that it causes people to see things backwards (Richardson & DiBenedetto, 1996). It is not this simple. In extreme cases, however, students with this type of difficulty do reverse many letters and sometimes even produce mirror writing. Figure 8.8 depicts the spelling test of a third-grade girl, Sara. Notice that even though many of her letters are reversed, several of the words are spelled accurately. She had practiced the words orally with her father the prior evening.

This type of mirror writing can even persist into adulthood. Figure 8.9 presents a brief sample from Esther, a young woman enrolled in a university program for students with LD. She produced this text by writing with both hands simultaneously. Although she has learned how to write conventionally, she reports that it takes her twice as long to write if she has to concentrate on orienting the letters correctly.

Goulandris and Snowling (1991) described an undergraduate student with developmental dyslexia. Although her earlier reading difficulties were resolved by this time and her phonological reading strategies were within the normal range, she experienced serious difficulties with spelling. Her difficulties were most pronounced when she was asked to spell irregular words and homophones, words with the same sound but different spellings (e.g., *blue* and *blew*). Goulandris and Snowling suggested that this young woman's difficulties appear to be related to a problem with constructing detailed orthographic representations of words for spelling. This failure to establish images may contribute to a compromised reading rate as well. As observed by Reitsma (1989), "The ability to

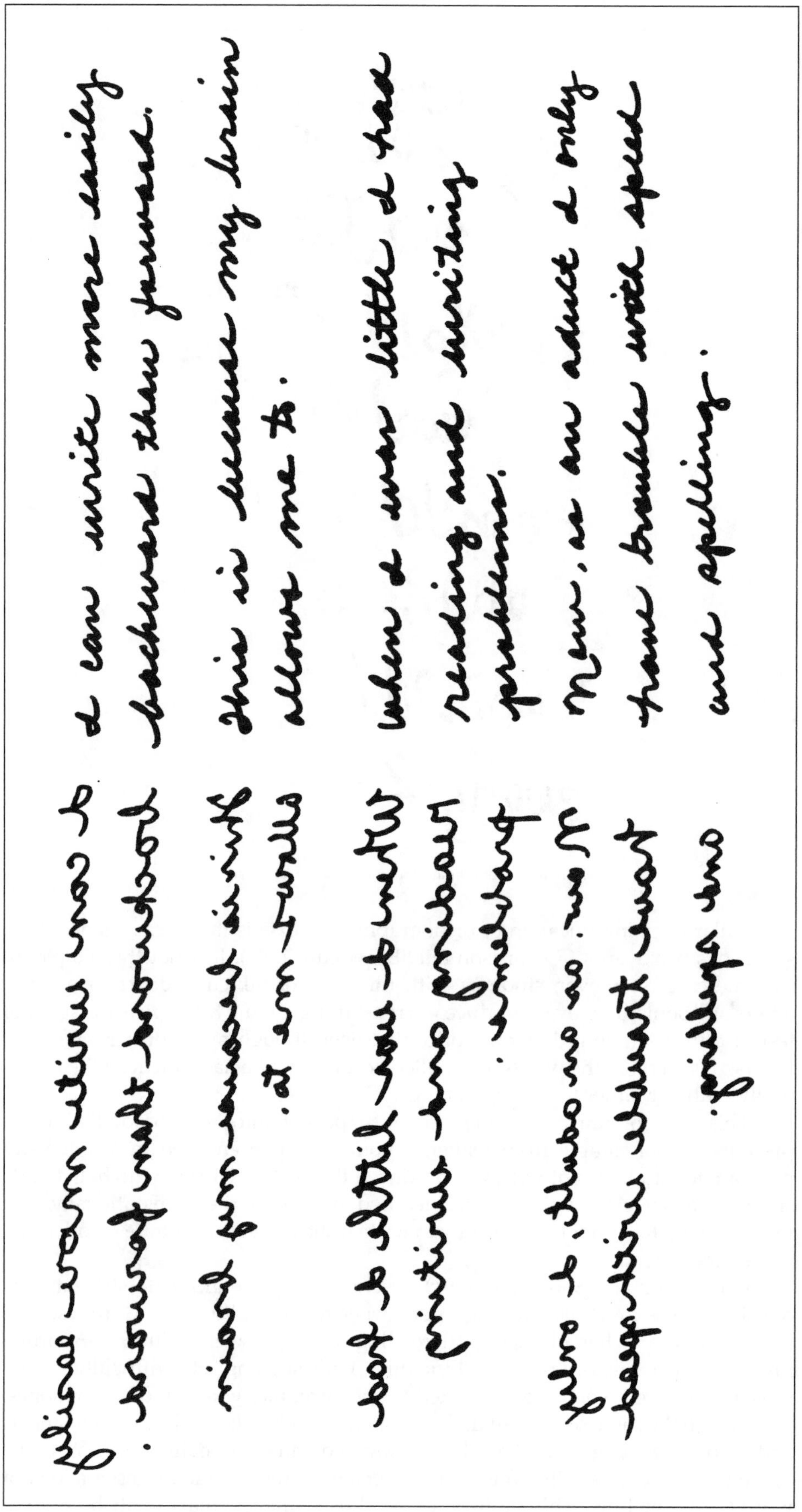

Figure 8.9. Esther's backward and forward writing.

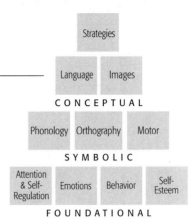

store the orthographic form of words in memory may be fundamental to attaining fluency in reading" (p. 65).

Rapid Automatized Naming

Another ability that may be particularly relevant to the orthographic processing block and to orthographic dyslexia is *rapid automatized naming* (RAN). On these types of tasks, a student is typically shown an array of objects, colors, letters, or digits that repeat in pattern (6–8 in a row, with a total of 30–50) and asked to name the symbols as quickly as possible. Although this area has been the focus of extensive research in recent years, use of this type of assessment began in the mid-1970s (Denckla & Rudel, 1974). Several RAN tests are available commercially, including the *Rapid Automatized Naming and Rapid Alternating Stimulus Tests* (Wolf & Denckla, 2006).

Although widespread agreement exists that RAN tasks are linked to reading failure, a lack of consensus exists in regard to exactly which mental operations are involved. For example, Torgesen and Burgess (1998) proposed that these tasks form a dimension of phonological processing skill and cited three reasons for this belief: 1) RAN tasks are highly correlated with other phonological skills; 2) as with phonological skills, these skills show unique causal relationships with the development of early literacy skills; and 3) no evidence exists from their longitudinal research to support the assertion that RAN ability contributes uniquely to the development of orthographic representations of words.

Others have suggested that RAN tasks are measuring processes related to visual and speed components that are particularly important for the development of orthographic representations and fluent reading (Badian, 1997, 1998; Wolf & Bowers, 1999). Bowers and Wolf (1993) hypothesized that slow RAN signifies disruption of the automatic processes that result in quick word recognition. They noted that RAN speed is determined by a complex ensemble of attentional, memory, cognitive, perceptual, motor, and linguistic processes that need to work in concert. Individuals who have difficulty rapidly retrieving and labeling visual symbols tend to perform poorly on these measures. Conceivably, their lack of automaticity affects processing speed (i.e., the ability to scan symbols rapidly) and efficiency. Morris and colleagues (1998) referred to this specific subtype as a *rate deficit*. These students with rate deficits were impaired on tasks requiring rapid serial naming but not on measures of phonological awareness.

A similar explanation is that rapid sequential processing is common to naming speed, processing speed, and reading tasks and that slow RAN reflects a global deficit in the rapid execution of a variety of cognitive processes (Kail, Hall, & Caskey, 1999). It appears that whatever RAN represents, it is partially subsumed under the rubric of processing speed (Denckla & Cutting, 1999).

Manis and colleagues (1999) summarized what the existing research suggests about RAN:

1. The RAN task appears to be independent from phonology and appears to contribute independent variance to word identification and comprehension. The independent contribution appears larger with younger children and individuals with reading disabilities.

2. RAN does not relate to the ability to read phonetically regular nonsense words.

3. RAN appears to be more related to tasks involving orthography than to tasks more dependent on phonology.

4. RAN is related to both the accuracy and speed of reading words, and the relationship with speed measures is stronger.

219

5. The relationship of RAN to reading skills past the early period of acquisition has not been resolved.

Meyer, Wood, Hart, and Felton (1998) found that RAN had predictive power for only poor readers. They suggested that this predictive power comes from the automaticity of retrieval. For a few students, slow performance on RAN tasks may be more likely linked to a slow speed of word retrieval (probably more related to the language block), whereas for others, RAN tasks appear to be tapping processes within the visual domain, primarily orthographic processing skills. If common letter patterns are not recognized easily and quickly, orthographic pattern knowledge is slow to develop (Bowers & Wolf, 1993).

In general, students with RAN impairments have less knowledge of orthographic patterns and are slower readers than students with poor phonemic awareness. In addition, orthographic pattern knowledge depends in part on the processes tapped by naming speed (Bowers, Sunseth, & Golden, 1999). Although a consensus regarding how RAN ability affects reading development has yet to be reached, one fact appears to be clear: Students with weaknesses in both phonological awareness and RAN abilities have the most pronounced reading impairments and are the most resistant to intervention (Badian, 1998; Bowers et al., 1999; Wagner, Torgesen, Laughon, Simmons, & Rashotte, 1993; Wolf & Bowers, 1999). Bowers and colleagues (1999) noted that these "double-deficit" children are clearly impaired on all reading measures. Although future research is likely to confirm the exact processes involved in RAN tasks, students with naming deficits appear to have a poorer prognosis for reading success than do other subgroups (Korhonen, 1991). Denckla (1979) described these students as a "hard-to-learn group." One can surmise that these students also require more intensive interventions that focus on the development of reading fluency. Research has also suggested that adults with weaknesses in both phonological awareness and RAN have significantly lower reading achievement than adults with no deficit or a single deficit and that these factors continue to play a role in adult reading achievement (Miller et al., 2006).

Both Maria's and Ben's problems are the result of weaknesses in one aspect of symbolic learning. For other students, however, weaknesses are found in several aspects of symbolic development.

In fourth grade, Ryan showed weaknesses in both phonology and orthography. He also evidenced low scores on tests of processing speed. He was slow on RAN tests and below average on phonological assessments. Although his reading and spelling had improved with instruction using a structured language program, his rate of word recognition was still severely compromised.

Many students with reading impairments have severe weaknesses in processing speed. In some cases, these students perform adequately on tasks involving phonological awareness and RAN. Clearly, as noted by Wolf (1999), reading difficulties are caused by a multiplicity of factors rather than simply a "double deficit" or "triple deficit":

> This new conceptualization of reading disabilities was, ironically, named too quickly. To be sure, double deficit captures the phenomenon of study—that is, the importance of understanding the separate and combined effects of two core deficits—but it fails miserably in redirecting our simultaneous attention as a field to the entire profile of strengths and limitations manifest in children with reading disabilities. Only when we develop truly

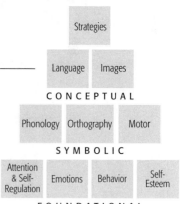

Strategies

Language | Images

CONCEPTUAL

Phonology | Orthography | Motor

SYMBOLIC

Attention & Self-Regulation | Emotions | Behavior | Self-Esteem

FOUNDATIONAL

multidimensional models of deficits and strengths will our diagnostic and remedial efforts be best matched to individual children. (p. 23)

As observed by Monroe (1932), a broad constellation of factors may affect reading and writing development.

Implications for Intervention

Unlike phonological awareness, not as much is known about how to improve the abilities related to orthographic coding. Although commercial materials designed to improve performance on RAN tasks are available, no evidence suggests that these kinds of procedures are beneficial or contribute to improved reading. For students with weaknesses in the recall of symbols, two types of intervention seem most promising. One involves the use of multisensory procedures (i.e., instruction that integrates the three symbolic processing blocks) to teach word identification, spelling, and math facts (e.g., Birsh, 2005). Tracing activities, for example, appear to 1) provide a memory trace that improves retention of letters, words, and numbers; 2) improve visual discrimination; 3) direct attention to word learning; 4) increase visual memory of words; and 5) help develop associations between spoken and written words (Hulme, 1981).

As an example, Brunsdon, Coltheart, and Nickels (2005) found that training in the spelling of irregular words could improve the quality of stored orthographic representations. In this procedure, irregular words were written on flash cards with the correct spelling. The word was read aloud, and the student was asked to copy the word. The word was then removed from view, and the student was asked to write the word after a 10-second delay. If incorrect, the student was shown the flash card again for 5 seconds and then asked again to write the word from memory. If the response was correct, he was then asked to write the word from dictation. This procedure resulted in increased reliance on orthography for spelling as opposed to an overreliance on phoneme to grapheme conversions. These types of multisensory approaches for learning the spellings of irregular words are discussed more thoroughly in Chapter 9.

The other intervention for students who have difficulty recalling symbols involves instructional techniques directed toward building rate and fluency within specific academic domains (e.g., reading fluency methods, timed writings, math fact flash cards). A new promising approach is the *Retrieval, Automaticity, Vocabulary, Elaboration, Orthography* (RAVE-O) program, a multicomponential approach to increasing fluency (Wolf, Miller, & Donnelly, 2000; Wolf & Segal, 1999; Wolf et al., 2003). (See Additional Resources). With the use of computerized games and a variety of manipulative materials, the program is designed to help develop and increase accuracy and automaticity at both the sublexical and lexical levels by helping young readers develop explicit and rapid connections among the phonological, orthographic, syntactic, semantic, and morphological systems (Wolf et al., 2003). When used as an intervention, RAVE-O is taught in conjunction with a program that teaches phonological awareness and blending. The program was developed from a strong research and theoretical base, and preliminary research results support its effectiveness (Lovett, Lacerenza, & Borden, 2000). The curriculum was originally designed to assist struggling second and third graders; however, successful results have been obtained with fourth-grade children (Wolf et al., 2003). Although RAVE-O is described as a reading fluency intervention, its goal is improvement in comprehension through use of a comprehensive, engaging, developmental approach (Wolf et al., 2003).

Students who experience difficulty with learning to read often have slow reading rates into adulthood. Chapter 9 reviews specific techniques for assessing and improving reading speed. In first and second grade, Ryan, Maria, and Ben all had difficulty learning to pronounce words because of weaknesses within the

221

symbolic blocks. Although Maria's problems were related to phonology, Ben's difficulties were related to orthography, and Ryan had weaknesses in both areas, they all had trouble reading rapidly and using reading to learn. Unfortunately, a weakness in the symbolic blocks can go on to affect performance in the conceptual blocks unless certain accommodations, such as listening to books on tape, are made.

MOTOR PROCESSING BLOCK

Andy's second-grade teacher, Ms. Abram, expressed her concerns about Andy's handwriting to the special education teacher. She described his writing in this way: "His letters are big and different sizes. Even when copying from the board or a paper right next to him, I cannot always figure out the letters. Often letters are reversed, and they are never on the line. The letters tend to drift off above and to the right of the first letter of the words so that the words seem to float on the page. In fact, his papers tend to resemble a bowl of alphabet soup."

Andy had the poorest fine motor skills of any child Ms. Abram had ever taught. Even though Andy wrote on a daily basis, his handwriting did not seem to be improving. During school, he often sat at his desk with his arms wrapped around his paper so that no one could see his writing. In fact, Andy's handwriting difficulties were beginning to affect the foundational blocks of emotions, behavior, and self-esteem. Ms. Abram placed comments on his papers, such as "Work carefully, please," or "Please form letters neatly," but this feedback did not seem to help. His most recent paper was returned with the comment, "Can't read!" Although one can empathize with her frustration, it is tempting to write back, "Can't write." Andy attempted to work carefully, but he had trouble performing the motor movements needed for letter formation. A sample of his writing and a picture are presented in Figure 8.10. The sentence reads, "Me and Sean built a fort."

Andy's school performance was becoming increasingly influenced by his difficulty with writing legibly. These difficulties stemmed from a severe weakness in the motor block—they were not the result of a poor attitude or lack of effort. Handwriting involves integration of skills within the visual and motor blocks. As illustrated in Figure 8.11, writing requires the student to retrieve a mental image of the letter form and then to produce that image on paper.

Andy had difficulty with any task involving fine motor skills. By the time he had completed kindergarten, he still could not write his name legibly or cut with scissors. His

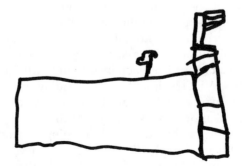

Figure 8.10. Writing sample for Andy: "Me and Sean built a fort."

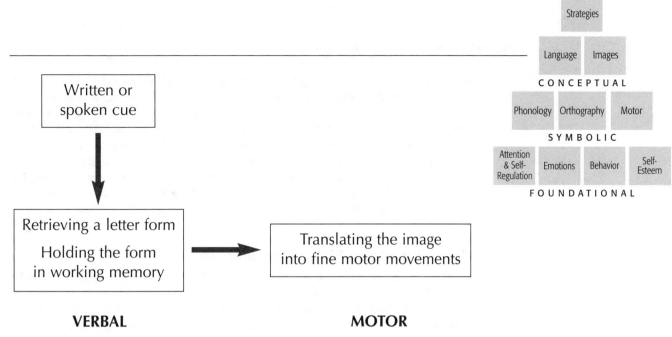

Figure 8.11. Visual and motor skills for handwriting

attempts at drawing in a coloring book consisted of scribbles and a few straight lines drawn through the pictures. He only engaged in these types of activities when required to do so by his teachers or parents. Because writing was so difficult for him, he engaged in lower levels of practice. These types of difficulties lead students to avoid writing, which further arrests writing development (Berninger, Mizokawa, & Bragg, 1991). Thus, skill development is affected by both the weaknesses in motor skills and avoidance of tasks that would actually improve skill.

In contrast to his motor skills, Andy's oral language skills were well developed. He expressed himself clearly and was quite imaginative. He loved reading books and telling stories. His strengths within the conceptual block of language were as readily apparent as his weaknesses within the motor block. In fact, Andy's oral language had always seemed advanced for his age. His parents reported that, before entering school, he would talk excessively regardless of whether anyone was around to listen.

Andy had been referred to the school occupational therapist in first grade and had been identified as having a sensory integration deficit. In her evaluation, she noted that he was well below his age level on tasks involving both visual and motor skills. His printing of uppercase letters was characterized by numerous reversals (9 of 26, or 34%), as was his printing of the numbers 1–10. She noted that on all tasks involving fine motor skill, he had a slow response speed. He was unable to stay within 1/4" of graded curved and angled lines or to color within a small given area. His grip was described as an overlapping thumb grasp and was contributing to his lack of control. In contrast, on tasks involving non–motor-visual-perceptual skills, Andy scored within the average range.

Delays were also noted in gross motor tasks. He still had difficulty with tasks such as buttoning his shirt or tying his shoes. In second grade, his parents reported that if he was not awakened midway through the night, he would still wet the bed. He walked on his toes, and, when standing, his feet seemed to be splayed in opposite directions. He often tripped when running down the hallway or coming down stairs. He seemed to lose his balance easily. Although Andy was almost 9 years old, he had not learned how to ride a bike. These are all characteristics of a medical condition referred to as a *developmental motor coordination disorder.*

Because of these developmental delays, the first-grade teacher had wondered if Andy should repeat first grade. He seemed uninterested in learning to write. Mr. and

Mrs. Parson, Andy's parents, struggled with the decision. Andy's motor skills were delayed, but they wondered if eventually he would just catch up. They finally decided against retention because of Andy's strengths in the conceptual block of language. His good oral language abilities would enable him to keep up with peers on certain activities, although he would continue to struggle with activities involving gross motor skills and fine motor skills, such as handwriting. The occupational therapist summarized, "As the academic demands increase, Andy's weakness in fine motor, gross motor, and motor planning will affect his classroom and playground performance. Occupational therapy is recommended to focus on improving these skills."

Motor Processing Block Questionnaire

Ms. Abram had contacted the school's occupational therapist to discuss ways in which she could help Andy in the classroom. Prior to the meeting, Ms. Abram completed the Motor Processing section of the Building Blocks Questionnaire. Her responses are shown in Figure 8.12. Andy was just beginning to learn cursive writing, so she left that statement blank. She checked *Sometimes* for the question about seeming disinterested in drawing and writing because Andy loved to draw but didn't like to write.

Although delayed development in either gross or fine motor skills can affect a child's school performance, weaknesses in fine motor skills pose a greater barrier to academic success. For this reason, the focus in this book is on helping a student develop fine motor skills, or what are sometimes referred to as *visual-motor skills*. As depicted in Figure 8.11, handwriting primarily involves the integration of both visual and motor skills. Chapter 9 provides specific suggestions for helping students with poor handwriting.

Fine Motor Development

Preschool children engage in many fine motor activities as they learn to build with blocks, draw, and turn the pages in a book. For most children, these skills develop

MOTOR PROCESSING	Rarely	Sometimes	Frequently
Draws pictures that seem immature for age			✓
Has difficulty with tasks involving fine motor coordination (e.g., tying shoes)			✓
Seems disinterested in drawing or learning to write		✓	
Has trouble holding a crayon, pencil, or pen correctly			✓
Forms letters in odd ways (e.g., starts from the bottom rather than the top)			✓
Has poor spacing between letters and words			✓
Has papers that appear messy			✓
Has poor or sloppy handwriting			✓
Has difficulty learning cursive writing			✓
Has a slow rate of writing			✓

Figure 8.12. Building Blocks Questionnaire for Andy: Motor Processing block.

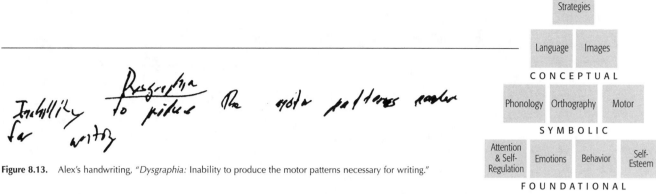

Figure 8.13. Alex's handwriting, *"Dysgraphia:* Inability to produce the motor patterns necessary for writing."

naturally because children enjoy activities involving coloring, painting, cutting, drawing, and writing. Gradually, as a child progresses in school, drawing and coloring are viewed as supplementary or optional activities, whereas writing becomes increasingly required. Some children continue to struggle to draw a straight line or a circle.

The main way that weak fine motor skills affect school performance is through handwriting. Although a child may have trouble drawing, poor artists can be highly successful in school. Failure to develop a legible writing style, however, is problematic to a child (and his or her teacher) in any grade. Figure 8.13 presents the handwriting of Alex, a student in college who was enrolled in an introductory course about LD. Note that he is defining the term *dysgraphia,* an inability to produce the motor patterns necessary for writing. His handwriting is so difficult to read that he either has to have a scribe when taking examinations or has to write his responses on a computer.

Just as with reading, some children have difficulty with producing acceptable writing, even though they have practiced and have had adequate instruction (Hamstra-Bletz & Blote, 1993). For these writers, so much energy is expended in trying to produce motor patterns that the quality and quantity of writing are often lacking. These difficulties appear in first grade and continue into higher grades. Figure 8.14 displays Andy's attempt to write the alphabet at the end of second grade. His class had spent time each day practicing writing skills, but Andy is still struggling with letter formation.

The next section presents several strategies for informally evaluating handwriting ability, specifically considering the types of errors a child might be making as well as his or her speed of writing. Specific instructional strategies for improving handwriting are presented in Chapter 9.

Legibility   Figure 8.15 provides a simple form to use for the evaluation of handwriting. By observing a student, one can ascertain quickly which aspects of handwriting need improvement.

Handwriting Rate   One characteristic of students with difficulties in motor development is slow handwriting speed. Some students do not have the expected writing speed for their grade and thus are often slow when completing writing assignments. Although writing speed increases each year, when compared with their classmates, students with LD demonstrate a relatively slower rate

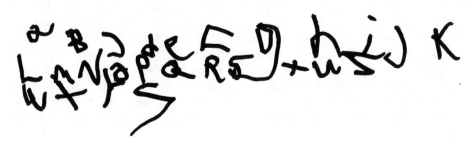

Figure 8.14. Andy's written alphabet.

Handwriting Evaluation Scale

Student _____ Date _____

Teacher _____ Grade _____

	Satisfactory	Needs Improvement
Pencil grip	☐	☐
Letter formation	☐	☐
Word formation	☐	☐
Size	☐	☐
Spacing	☐	☐
Alignment	☐	☐
Slant	☐	☐
Rate	☐	☐
Neatness	☐	☐

Specific concerns: _____

_____

_____

Figure 8.15.   Handwriting evaluation scale.

(Weintraub & Graham, 1998). As a consequence, these students often have trouble keeping up when taking notes, are slow copying off of boards or from books, and take longer to complete writing assignments. On the basis of handwriting alone, students with LD accomplish in 50 minutes what peers with average achievement can do in 30 minutes (Weintraub & Graham, 1998).

By using the Zaner-Bloser scale of handwriting proficiency (Barbe, Lucas, Wasylyk, Hackney, & Braun, 1987), one can easily determine if a student has the expected writing speed for his or her grade. To do a simple evaluation, ask the student to copy a sentence that contains most or all of the letters of the alphabet, such as "The quick brown fox jumps over the lazy dog." Have the student practice the sentence one time, and then ask him or her to copy the sentence as many times as possible in 3 minutes. Count the total number of letters that the child has written in the 3-minute period, and then divide this number by 3 to get the total letters per minute (lpm). The student's proficiency level can be compared with the following scale:

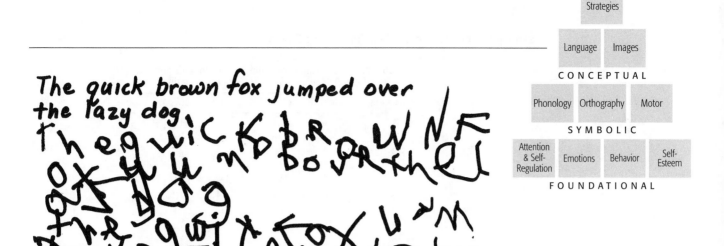

Figure 8.16. Andy's writing speed test with his teacher's writing at the top.

Grade 1: 25 lpm
Grade 2: 30 lpm
Grade 3: 38 lpm
Grade 4: 45 lpm
Grade 5: 60 lpm
Grade 6: 67 lpm
Grade 7: 74 lpm

Ms. Abram asked Andy to copy the sentence "The quick brown fox jumped over the lazy dog" in his best handwriting. She then asked Andy to write the sentence as many times as he could in 3 minutes. The results of this informal evaluation are presented in Figure 8.16. Andy wrote approximately 78 letters within the 3-minute period, so his average was 26 lpm. His speed was lower than most of his classmates, and his legibility was very poor.

Graham, Berninger, Weintraub, and Schafer (1997) provided normative data on handwriting speed for both girls and boys in Grades 1–9. In a study investigating the speed and legibility in 900 children in Grades 1–9, they found that 1) girls' handwriting was more legible than boys' handwriting; 2) although girls tend to write faster than boys overall, significant differences were noted in Grades 1, 6, and 7; and 3) right-handers were faster than left-handers, although there was no difference in legibility.

For this procedure, children were asked to copy a paragraph as quickly as possible without making any mistakes for 1.5 minutes (see Table 8.3). In general, these reported speeds are somewhat faster than the Zaner-Bloser scale. This may be because students wrote for only 1.5 minutes as opposed to 3 minutes, and handwriting speed is likely to slow down with increased time.

Graham and colleagues observed that considerable variability existed in children's handwriting speeds at each grade level tested. For example, in Grade 5, speed ranged from 43 lpm to 125 lpm. As a general principle in working with students like Andy, emphasis should be placed on legibility rather than speed (Hamstra-Bletz & Blote, 1993). Andy also had difficulty forming numbers and, as

Table 8.3 The mean handwriting speeds for girls and boys in Grades 1–9 as measured in letters per minute (lpm)

Grade	Girls	Boys
1	21	17
2	36	32
3	50	45
4	66	61
5	75	71
6	91	78
7	109	91
8	118	112
9	121	114

From *Journal of Educational Research*, 92, 42–52. Adapted by permission of the Helen Dwight Reid Educational Foundation. Published by Heldref Publications, 1319 Eighteenth St., NW, Washington, DC 20036-1802. Copyright © 19997.

a consequence, worked slowly on the timed math problems he was asked to solve in the classroom.

Students with developmental delays in visual-motor skill often require classroom accommodations throughout their school careers. The occupational therapist suggested that Ms. Abram provide the following accommodations for Andy:

1. Eliminate copying from the chalkboard or the textbook. Instead, provide Andy with prewritten notes and assignments.

2. Provide extended time on tasks involving writing.

3. Shorten writing assignments, and encourage Andy to supplement his work with illustrations, clip art, and verbal explanations.

4. Introduce keyboarding skills. As Andy's skills develop, provide him with the option of using a word processor at his desk rather than paper and pencil.

5. Use graph paper for place value or when adding and subtracting two-digit numbers.

As students progress in school, they need additional adjustments, such as photocopying another student's notes or being permitted to answer questions orally. The next section of this chapter provides additional information about the types of classroom accommodations that students with weaknesses in the symbolic blocks often require.

CLASSROOM ACCOMMODATIONS

Children with weaknesses in the abilities of the symbolic blocks often require accommodations or adjustments in the classroom so that they can be successful. They may require oral examinations, less material presented on a page, or special pencil grips. For accommodations to be effective, they must be fully supported by the student and the general education teacher. Ensuring this acceptance often requires discussion and adaptations. Children do not like to appear or feel different from other children. If an accommodation singles them out as being different, students are likely not to comply.

When Ryan was in fifth grade, he obtained low scores on the weekly spelling tests. His teacher suggested that Ryan only take the first 5 words; Ryan refused and said he wanted to do all 20 words, just like everyone else. His teacher then

Strategies

Language | Images

CONCEPTUAL

Phonology | Orthography | Motor

SYMBOLIC

Attention & Self-Regulation | Emotions | Behavior | Self-Esteem

FOUNDATIONAL

suggested that he take all 20 words but they would have a silent pact regarding which 5 words she would grade. Ryan agreed that this would be a good accommodation.

Examples of the most common accommodations for students with weaknesses in the symbolic blocks are described in the following section. Chapter 9 provides additional ideas for students who are particularly low in one subject area, such as spelling or calculating.

Copying

Students with weaknesses in the memory of forms and symbols often have difficulty copying information from chalkboards or from a textbook to a piece of paper. To circumvent this difficulty, students can be provided ahead of time with lecture notes or problems to be copied from a textbook or the chalkboard. These students are also likely to have trouble filling out bubble sheets. When Ben was in fifth grade, his teacher sent home the note in Figure 8.17. To reduce the frustration for students like Ben, provide an enlarged bubble sheet or let the student mark the answers directly on the test book.

Timed Tests

Students who have had trouble with language sounds, retention of letter strings, or production of symbols often have compromised rates and are likely to require extended time on reading, writing, and math assignments and examinations. As students with dyslexia proceed through school, they may become more accurate but still read slowly; thus, they may require the accommodation of extended time on examinations (Shaywitz & Shaywitz, 2003).

If the examination is timed, estimate the appropriate amount of time the student needs to have equal access to the test questions. If the examination is not timed, the student should have as much time as he or she needs in order to complete the test. In fact, if the purpose of an examination is to test knowledge, all students should have as much time as needed. If speed is judged to be a necessary factor for performance, then a time limit must be set. As noted by Stanovich, "In those (probably very few) cases where speed is judged to be a genuine academic virtue, no time accommodation should be given to anyone" (1999, p. 358).

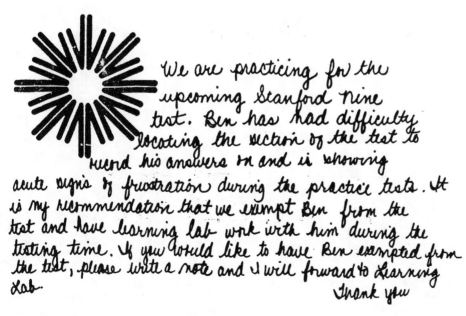

We are practicing for the upcoming Stanford Nine test. Ben has had difficulty locating the section of the test to record his answers on and is showing acute signs of frustration during the practice tests. It is my recommendation that we exempt Ben from the test and have learning lab work with him during the testing time. If you would like to have Ben exempted from the test, please write a note and I will forward to Learning Lab.

Thank you

Figure 8.17. Ben's teacher's note.

Following Directions

Students with weaknesses in verbal short-term memory may have trouble with following lengthy directions. For this type of student, the teacher may need to ask him or her to repeat instructions to ensure understanding; repeat and simplify instructions; and supplement oral instructions with visual instructions and demonstrations. Peer tutors can be enlisted to clarify assignments or in-class instructions.

Assignments

Because of the slow processing of symbols, some students need to have the amount of work they are assigned adjusted. Instead of assigning a specific amount of homework, advise students to accomplish as much as they can within a certain time frame. For example, Ms. Abram advised Andy that he should spend no more than 30 minutes on his nightly homework. Or, within the classroom, ask the student to complete as many problems as he or she can within a 15-minute period rather than assigning a specific number of problems.

CONCLUSION

Children who experience these difficulties in learning are heterogeneous in diagnosis and prognosis (Korhonen, 1991). For example, some students with reading impairments have phonological disorders, whereas others have specific orthographic impairments and are slow to recognize words and spelling patterns. Understanding the various types of reading impairments can enhance a teacher's ability to diagnose the problem accurately and develop systematic interventions (Lyon, 1995; Semrud-Clikeman, 1996).

PHONOLOGICAL AWARENESS SKILLS SCREENER (PASS)

The Phonological Awareness Skills Screener (PASS) is designed for students in kindergarten through second grade, although it may also be used with older students who are experiencing difficulty developing phonological awareness. This informal assessment is designed to help teachers detect students who are at risk for reading and spelling difficulties and to determine what type of instruction is needed in phonological awareness skills.

ADMINISTRATION INSTRUCTIONS

Materials

To administer this test, you need a set of 10 colored blocks, chips, or tiles (all the same color); a test record form (see Figure 8A.1); and these directions. The PASS has the following 10 brief sections, each of which will require 1–3 minutes to complete:

1. Word discrimination

2. Rhyme recognition

3. Rhyme production

4. Syllable blending

5. Syllable segmentation

6. Syllable deletion

7. Phoneme recognition

8. Phoneme blending

9. Phoneme segmentation

10. Phoneme deletion

This assessment tool was originally developed by N. Mather in collaboration with B. Podhajski, D. Rhein, and N. Babur. The first version was titled *Screening of Early Reading Processes* and was published in Mather and Goldstein (2001). The phonological segmentation tasks were adapted from Sawyer's (1987) *Test of Awareness of Language Segments*. The most recent edition, the PASS, was revised by N. Mather, J. Sammons, B. Podhajski, J. Kroese, and M. Varricchio.

PASS Test Record

Name _____ Grade _____ Age _____ Test date _____ Total test score, Sections 1–10 _____

1: Word Discrimination Samples: frog/frog: same; plane/bike: different	**2: Rhyme Recognition** Samples: sun: cat, run moon: car, spoon	**3: Rhyme Production** Sample: tree	**4: Syllable Blending** Samples: sail•boat, pen•cil	**5: Syllable Segmentation** Samples: foot•ball, pa•per, so•mer•sault
___ 1. bye/pie	___ 1. rat: hat, car	___ 1. bat	___ 1. snow•man	___ 1. hotdog (hot•dog)
___ 2. back/bag	___ 2. man: dog, fan	___ 2. hop	___ 2. sun•set	___ 2. baseball (base•ball)
___ 3. gum/gum	___ 3. back: sack, trip	___ 3. rag	___ 3. jump•ing	___ 3. doorbell (door•bell)
___ 4. bass/bass	___ 4. night: fan, light	___ 4. fun	___ 4. can•dle	___ 4. funny (fun•ny)
___ 5. cub/cup	___ 5. hole: pole, clock	___ 5. seat	___ 5. ho•tel	___ 5. camping (camp•ing)
___ 6. fly/fly	___ 6. street: nap, meet	___ 6. tail	___ 6. bas•ket•ball	___ 6. elbow (el•bow)
___ 7. comb/cone	___ 7. show: toe, plane	___ 7. night	___ 7. po•lice•man	___ 7. computer (com•pu•ter)
___ 8. teeth/teethe	___ 8. fast: race, last	___ 8. ringing	___ 8. kin•der•gar•ten	___ 8. radio (ra•di•o)
___ 9. pull/pull	___ 9. shark: dark, pork	___ 9. money	___ 9. hel•i•cop•ter	___ 9. transportation (trans•por•ta•tion)
___ 10. with/whiff	___ 10. mouth: north, south	___ 10. stamp	___ 10. hip•po•pot• a•mus	___ 10. vacationing (va•ca•tion•ing)
Total ___	Total ___	Total ___	Total ___	Total ___

Figure 8A.1. The Phonological Awareness Skills Screener (PASS) test record form.

232

6: Syllable Deletion

Samples: goldfish but don't say fish (gold), candle but don't say /dle/ (can)

___ 1. pancake but don't say cake (pan)

___ 2. starfish but don't say fish (star)

___ 3. haircut but don't say hair (cut)

___ 4. rainbow but don't say rain (bow)

___ 5. teacher but don't say /er/ (teach)

___ 6. slowly but don't say /ly/ (slow)

___ 7. walnut but don't say wall (nut)

___ 8. enjoy but don't say /en/ (joy)

___ 9. paperback but don't say back (paper)

___ 10. outstanding but don't say out (standing)

Total ___

7: Phoneme Recognition

Samples: cat; mother

___ 1. boy

___ 2. sun

___ 3. car

___ 4. fish

___ 5. horse

___ 6. nest

___ 7. apple

___ 8. jump

___ 9. shoe

___ 10. chop

Total ___

8: Phoneme Blending

Sample: /b/ /e/

___ 1. /sh/ /e/ (she)

___ 2. /n/ /o/ (no)

___ 3. /s/ /a/ /t/ (sat)

___ 4. /t/ /e/ /n/ (ten)

___ 5. /b/ /a/ /ke/ (bake)

___ 6. /s/ /p/ /o/ /t/ (spot)

___ 7. /f/ /i/ /n/ /d/ (fiind)

___ 8. /l/ /e/ /tt/ /er/ (letter)

___ 9. /w/ /i/ /n/ /d/ /ow/ (window)

___ 10. /b/ /a/ /s/ /k/ /e/ /t/ (basket)

Total ___

9: Phoneme Segmentation

Sample: toe: /t/ /oe/

___ 1. me: /m/ /e/ (2)

___ 2. go: /g/ /o/ (2)

___ 3. bit: /b/ /i/ /t/ (3)

___ 4. red: /r/ /e/ /d/ (3)

___ 5. food: /f/ /oo/ /d/ (3)

___ 6. skate: /s/ /k/ /a/ /te/ (4)

___ 7. rust: /r/ /u/ /s/ /t/ (4)

___ 8. grasp: /g/ /r/ /a/ /s/ /p/ (5)

___ 9. friend: /f/ /r/ /ie/ /n/ /d/ (5)

___ 10. splash: /s/ /p/ /l/ /a/ /sh/ (5)

Total ___

10: Phoneme Deletion

Sample: sat but don't say /s/ (at)

___ 1. ran but don't say /r/ (an)

___ 2. beat but don't say /b/ (eat)

___ 3. make but don't say /k/ (may)

___ 4. shown but don't say /n/ (show)

___ 5. blame but don't say /b/ (lame)

___ 6. hold but don't say /d/ (hole)

___ 7. cart but don't say /t/ (car)

___ 8. sting but don't say /t/ (sing)

___ 9. frame but don't say /r/ (fame)

___ 10. splint but don't say /n/ (split)

Total ___

Rhyming score (2 & 3) ___ Blending score (4 & 8) ___ Segmenting score (6 & 10) ___ Phoneme discrimination score (1 & 7) ___

Blending score (2 & 3) ___ Segmenting score (4 & 8) ___ Deleting score (5 & 9) ___

Instructions

Each section contains instructions and a script for the teacher that gives student directions. You may rephrase these directions as needed to ensure that the student understands the task. Once testing begins, however, do not provide extra help, supports, or additional instructions. Begin each part when the student understands the task. If the student cannot understand or perform the task, do not administer that section. Do not penalize for articulation or sound production errors. If needed, you may repeat any item. Be sure to give enough time for a response.

- **Stopping points:** For each section, discontinue the task if the student cannot perform *any* of the sample items or misses three items in a row.

- **Scoring:** Score correct responses 1; incorrect responses 0. Write in errors next to each item.

1. Word Discrimination

Say, "I'm going to say two words, and I want you to tell me whether they are the same or different. For example, if I say, *'car, car'* you would say, *'same.'* If I say, *'horse, house,'* you would say, *'different.'* Now you try one: *frog, frog.*" If the student is correct, say, "That's right. They are the same." If the student is incorrect or does not respond, say, "*Frog, frog* are the same. Here's another: *plane, bike.*" If the student is correct, say, "That's right. They are different. Here are some more." Pause about 1 second between words. If the student does not understand, practice with two or three additional examples (e.g., *blue, blue; dog, sock*). Begin each item cupping your hand over your mouth as you state the words.

2. Rhyme Recognition

Pause briefly after each word. Say, "I am going to say three words, and I want you to tell me the two words that end the same or rhyme. If I say, 'What ends the same or rhymes with *cat? Hat* or *sun?*,' you would say *hat* because *cat* and *hat* both end the same or rhyme. Now you do one. What rhymes with *sun? Cat* or *run?* What rhymes with *moon? Car* or *spoon?*" If the student does not understand, practice with two or three additional examples (e.g., "What ends the same or rhymes with *blue? New* or *tree?* What ends the same or rhymes with *ten? Step* or *men?*") Begin each item with "What rhymes with... ?"

3. Rhyme Production

Say, "I'm going to say two words that rhyme. *Cat* rhymes with *hat,* and *boat* rhymes with *coat.* Now you do one. Tell me a word that rhymes with *tree.*" If the student does not understand, practice with two or three additional examples (e.g., "What rhymes with *wall?*" "What rhymes with *ten?*"). Accept rhyming nonsense words. Begin each item by saying, "What rhymes with... ?"

4. Syllable Blending

Begin each item with "What is... ?" Say, "I am going to say the parts of a word and then say the parts together fast." Pause about 1/2 second between parts. "If I say, cup•cake fast, it would be *cupcake.* Rain•coat would be *raincoat.* Now you do one. What is sail•boat?" Pause for the student to respond. If the student does not understand, give another example (e.g., horse•shoe, sun•shine).

Say, "Here is a different one. If I say 'tur...tle' fast, it would be *turtle.* What is pen...cil?" If the student does not understand, practice with two or three additional examples (e.g., han•dle, tall•er).

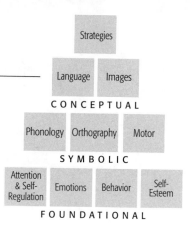

5. Syllable Segmentation

Say, "I'm going to use these blocks to break a word into parts. *Cupcake* has two parts." Push forward one block for each part as you say it. Then point to each block and say, "This block is *cup*, and this one is *cake*." After each item, push the blocks back into a group. Push the blocks in front of the student and say, "Now you do one. Use the blocks to tell and show me the two parts of *football*." If the student does not understand, practice with two or three additional examples (e.g., *raindrop, popcorn, toothbrush*). If the student is incorrect or does not respond, discontinue this section.

Say, "Here is a different one. The word *doctor* has two parts." Push forward one block as you say each part. This first block is /doc/ and this next one is /tor/. Now you do one. Use the blocks to tell and show me the word *paper*." If the student does not understand, practice with two or three additional examples (e.g., *flying, happy, running*). Say, "Here's another one. The word *somersault* has three parts." Push forward one block as you say each part. "Now you do it. Use the blocks to show me *somersault*." For a correct response, the student needs to break the words into parts orally but does not need to identify the correct number of blocks. Begin each item with, "Tell and show me the parts of… ."

6. Syllable Deletion

Say, "I'm going to say a word and leave off one part. If I say 'raincoat' but don't say 'rain,' it would be *coat*. Now you do one. Say the word 'goldfish.'" Pause for a response. "Now say the word 'goldfish' but don't say 'fish.'" If the student does not understand, practice with two or three additional examples (e.g., *raindrop, popcorn, toothbrush*).

Say, "Here is a different one. The word *turkey* has two parts. The first part is /tur/ and the second part is /key/. If I say, 'turkey' but don't say /tur/, it would be *key.* Now you do one. Say the word *candle*. Now say the word 'candle' but don't say /dle/." If the student does not understand, practice with two or three additional examples (e.g., *flying, candy, funny*). For a correct response, the student needs to delete the syllable. Begin each item with, "Say the word. . .but don't say… ."

7. Phoneme Recognition

Begin each item with, "Tell me a word that starts like… ." Say, "I'm going to say a word and then ask you to tell me another word that starts with the same sound. If I say, 'What starts like the word *bat*,' you could say, 'boy' or 'bike' or 'boat.' Tell me a word that starts like the word *cat.*" If the student is correct, say, "That's right. The word. . .starts like *cat.*" If the child says a rhyming word on any of the samples or items, say, "That word rhymes. Tell me a word that starts like… ." If the student is incorrect or does not respond, say, "You could say, 'car' or 'cake.'" Say, "Let's try another. What starts like the word *mother?*" If correct, say, "That's right. The word . . . starts like *mother.*" If the student does not understand, practice with two or three additional examples (e.g., *girl, fan, run*).

If the student responds incorrectly or does not respond, say, "Does. . .start the same as… ? Provide three samples (e.g., *girl, gate; dog, dad; hot, hid*). If the student still does not understand, discontinue this section.

8. Phoneme Blending

Say, "Now I'm going to say the sounds of a word slowly and then say the word." Pronounce each phoneme as it sounds in the word and pause about one second between sounds. "Listen. . ./s/•/oa/•/p/ is *soap*. Now you do one. What is /b/•/e/?" Begin each item with "What is… ?" If the student does not understand, practice with two or three additional items (e.g., /s/•/o/,/b/•/i/•/ke/).

235

9. Phoneme Segmentation

Say, "I'm going to use the blocks to show you all of the sounds in a word. The word *time* would be /t/ /i/ /m/." Push a block forward as you say each sound. Push the blocks back together and say, "The word *play* would be /p/ /l/ /ay/." Place the blocks in front of the student. "Now you do one. Show me the sounds in the word *toe*." Begin each item with "Tell and show me the sounds in… ." If the student does not understand, provide two or three additional examples (e.g., *row, make, boat*). For a correct response, the student needs to segment the sounds correctly but does not need to identify the correct number of blocks. After each item, push the blocks back into a group.

10. Phoneme Deletion

Say, "I'm going to say a word and leave off one sound. If I say *seat* but don't say /s/, it would be *eat*. If I say *past* but don't say /t/, it would be *pass*. Now you do one. Say, '*sat*' but don't say /s/." Begin each item with "Say. . .but don't say… ." If the student does not understand, practice with two or three additional items (e.g., say, '*pan*' but don't say /p/, say, '*rat*' but don't say /r/).

OPTIONAL LETTER–SOUND IDENTIFICATION SECTION

Figure 8A.2 includes two other Letter–Sound Identification charts and recording sheets—one for uppercase letters and one for lowercase letters. A checklist for each is included for recording purposes. Score 1 for correct; 0 for incorrect. You may ask the student to identify the letter names, the letter sounds, or both.

Say: "I want you to tell me the names [or sounds] of these letters. Start here [point to the first letter in the upper left corner] and end here." [Point to the last letter in the lower right corner.] If the student does not read across the rows, point to each letter.

Record the total number correct. If desired, record errors on specific letters on the blank next to the letter. For example, if a student identified the letter *b* as *d*, you would write a *d* next to the *b*.

Note: For the vowel sounds, if a student says the long sound or the letter name, say, "Tell me another common sound for that letter." When asking for the sounds of letters *c* and *g*, if the student says the soft sound /s/ or /j/, say, "Tell me another common sound for that letter."

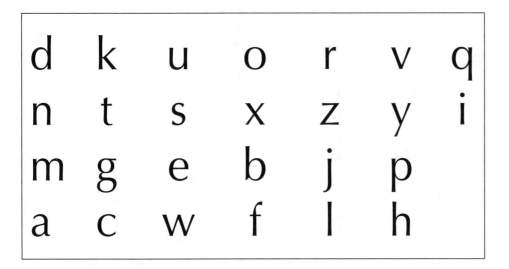

Figure 8A.2. Lettter–Sound Identification charts and recording sheets. Key: 1 = Correct response; 0 = Incorrect response. Correct responses = Short vowel sounds for vowels (*a, e, i, o, u*) and hard sounds for *c* and *g* (e.g., *cat, gate*).

(continued)

Letter–Sound Identification
Uppercase

Name _____

	Date		Date		Date		Date	
	Name	Sound	Name	Sound	Name	Sound	Name	Sound
F								
Z								
U								
V								
N								
R								
S								
D								
K								
X								
T								
B								
Y								
I								
M								
O								
J								
G								
W								
P								
C								
A								
E								
L								
H								
Q								
Totals								

(continued)

Letter–Sound Identification
Lowercase

Name _____

	Date		Date		Date		Date	
	Name	Sound	Name	Sound	Name	Sound	Name	Sound
d								
k								
u								
o								
r								
v								
q								
n								
t								
s								
x								
z								
y								
i								
m								
g								
e								
b								
j								
p								
a								
c								
w								
f								
l								
h								
Totals								

RELATIONSHIP BETWEEN SPEECH SOUNDS AND SPELLING DEVELOPMENT

C hildren's ability to spell develops through gradual refinement of their phonological knowledge. Because young children have little knowledge of how spellings are influenced by word derivations and lexical forms (e.g., *please* and *pleasant*), they spell what they see, feel, and hear. Developing writers have an unconscious knowledge of aspects of the English sound system, and their misspellings reflect their developing linguistic knowledge (Treiman, 1998).

The information in this section has been synthesized and adapted from three sources (Moats, 1995; Read, 1971; Wilde, 1997). Although this information is somewhat technical, an understanding of the English sound system can help educators understand the reasons why students spell words the way they do, as well as help one recognize linguistic difficulties with older students.

Phonemes are the smallest sound units that are represented by *graphemes* (i.e., various letter units). Although the English language has approximately 42–44 phonemes, there are approximately 250 graphemes. For example, consider the phoneme /f/. This sound can be spelled with several different graphemes: *f, ff, ph, lf* or *gh*. As a result of several alternative spelling possibilities, the process of spelling words is much more difficult than the process of reading words. Rules regarding the position of letters within words underlie the spelling system, however; for example, an English word cannot begin with the letters *ff*.

CONSONANTS AND VOWELS

The English language is composed of two types of sounds: consonants and vowels. For consonant sounds, the airflow is cut off partially or incompletely. For vowel sounds, the air flows through the mouth unobstructed.

Consonants

Consonants can be combined into blends, digraphs, and trigraphs. *Blends* are two or more consonant sounds occurring in sequence that retain their identity (e.g., *bl* or *fr*). Digraphs and trigraphs refer to two or three adjacent letters that represent one phoneme not represented by either letter alone (e.g., *sh, gh,* or *tch*). Consonants are classified by both the place of articulation and the manner of articulation. Children's substitutions are often reasonable and involve a change either in voicing (e.g., /b/ for /p/), place of articulation, or manner of articulation (e.g., a fricative for a stop). Note: Digraphs are particularly hard to spell because one cannot hear the letter names. Therefore, children may leave out one letter in a digraph, spelling /ch/ with the letter *c* or *h* or /k/ with the letter *c* or *k*.

Table 8B.1. Voiced and unvoiced consonant pairs and other sounds.

Voiced	Unvoiced
/b/	/p/
/d/	/t/
/g/	/k/
/v/	/f/
/th/	/th/
/z/	/s/
/zh/	/sh/
/j/	/ch/
/ng/	
/wh/	

Other sounds
/m/, /n/
/w/, /h/
/l/, /r/
/k/, /s/
/z/, /ks/
/qu/, (/kw/)
/y/ (e, i)

Place of Articulation Different sounds are pronounced using different parts of the mouth.

1. Labial: sounds made with lips
2. Dental: sounds made with teeth
3. Alveolar: sounds made that contact the ridge behind the teeth
4. Palatal: sounds made that use the roof of the mouth
5. Velar: sounds made that use the soft palate at the back of the mouth cavity
6. Glottal: sounds made at the vocal folds

Manner of Articulation Consonants are divided into five groups based on how the air stream is affected as it travels through the mouth: 1) stops, 2) fricatives and affricates, 3) nasals, 4) liquids, and 5) glides. Some are *voiced* (i.e., vocal cords vibrate), whereas others are *unvoiced* (i.e., vocal cords do not vibrate). The English language has eight pairs of voiced and unvoiced consonants. Table 8B.1 lists the eight pairs of voiced and unvoiced consonants. The LiPS program (Lindamood and Lindamood, 1998) has child-friendly terminology for introducing these sounds, such as referring to /p/ and /b/ as *lip poppers*, and /t/ and /d/ as *tip tappers*. In the program, the unvoiced sounds are referred to as *quiet sounds*, whereas the voiced sounds are labeled as *noisy*.

Stops Stops are formed by closing off the stream of the breath (see Table 8B.2). Medial /t/ and /d/ phonemes are often reduced to a tongue flap and are hard to distinguish (e.g., *ladder* and *latter*), so a child may spell *lidl* for *little* or *spitr* for *spider*.

Table 8B.2 Examples of stops

	Voiced	Unvoiced
Lips (bilabial)	/b/	/p/
	big	pig
Front of mouth (alveolar)	/d/	/t/
	dip	tip
Back of mouth (velar)	/g/	/k/
	got	cot

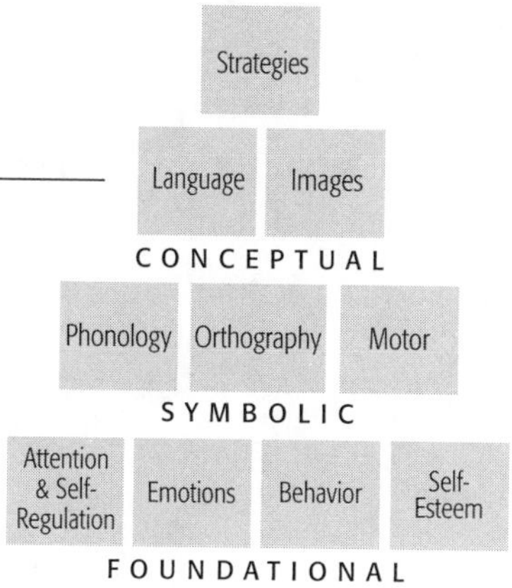
Strategies
Language
Images
CONCEPTUAL
Phonology
Orthography
Motor
SYMBOLIC
Attention & Self-Regulation
Emotions
Behavior
Self-Esteem
FOUNDATIONAL

Table 8B.3 Examples of fricatives

	Voiced	Unvoiced
Lips/teeth (labiodental)	/v/ *vine*	/f/ *fine*
Teeth (dental)	/th/ *thy*	/th/ *thigh*
Front of mouth (alveolar)	/z/ *zip*	/s/ *sip*
Roof of mouth (palatal)	/zh/ *genre*	/sh/ *ship*

Fricatives Fricatives are formed with friction in the mouth and a slight hissing sound (see Table 8B.3). When writing /s/ or /z/, children often do not make a distinction between voiced and unvoiced variants. In most instances, they choose to represent either sound with the letter *s*.

Affricates Affricates are a stop followed by a fricative (Table 8B.4). Examples include *chill, chip,* and *gypsy.* In certain contexts, /t/ and /d/ are articulated much like affricates (e.g., *dress, trash*). Before the letter *r,* the sounds /t/ and /d/ are affricated (i.e., released slowly with a resulting /sh/ sound). The affrication of stops before an /r/ is common for young children. Often, children notice this and thus produce the following types of spellings: *chran* for train or *jragn* or *jragin* for *dragon.* Particularly before the letter *r,* children are likely to spell the /t/ sound as /ch/ and the /d/ sound as /j/. The affrication of stops before an *r* in English continues until children learn that this pronunciation is predictable.

Table 8B.4 Examples of affricates

	Voiced	Unvoiced
Roof of mouth (palatal)	/j/ *jar*	/ch/ *char*

Nasals are formed by air going through the nose (see Table 8B.5). These consonant sounds are acquired later in development than are other consonant sounds. When a nasal or liquid occurs before a voiceless stop consonant (e.g., /t/, /p/, /k/), children often omit the letter because it is not pronounced as strongly (e.g., *wet* for *went*). There is no tongue movement between a nasal and a following consonant, thus making it more difficult to hear. Children can learn how to detect words with nasals by having them hold their nose and pronounce the words (e.g., *wet* and *went*). It is easy to identify the nosy word. Children may overgeneralize the spelling of the /ng/ sound (e.g., *thingk* for *think*). Or they may use the letter *g* to represent the /ng/ sound, such as in spelling the word *finger* as *fegr.* They also tend to spell *-ing* endings as *eg* or *ig.*

Liquids are formed when the air stream is interrupted but with no real friction (see Table 8B.6). Both liquids and nasals have an apparent vocalic quality. When the letters *r, l, m,* or *n* come between two consonants or at the end of a word after a consonant, children perceive and write it as a separate syllable. Children

Table 8B.5 Examples of nasals

Lips (bilabial)	/m/ *mice*
Front of mouth (alveolar)	/n/ *nice*
Back of mouth (velar)	/ng/ *sing, sink*

Table 8B.6	Examples of liquids	
Tip of tongue curls up	/r/	
	rap	
Sides of tongue curl in	/l/	
	lap	

Table 8B.7	Examples of semivowels	
Mouth moves from one vowel-like position to another	/w/ wet /y/ yet	
Air pushed through nonvibrating vocal cords (glottal)	/h/ hike	

thus often omit vowels with liquids and nasals. Although the vowel is usually an *e*, children rarely represent such a vowel in early writing, writing *tigr* for *tiger* or *tabl* for *table*. This omission of vowels with liquids and nasals applies to medial consonants as well (e.g., *hrd* for *heard*, *grl* for *girl*). Omissions of liquids and nasals from consonant blends account for a large proportion of spelling errors through sixth grade. When liquids and nasals are not involved, children are more likely to include a vowel in the syllable.

Glides are considered semivowels (see Table 8B.7). Sometimes diphthongs or glided vowels sound like /w/ or /y/, so children spell them that way.

Vowels

Children spell vowel sounds according to certain articulatory properties. The sound of a vowel is determined by where it occurs in the mouth. Vowels are described in terms of the position of the tongue during articulation: front or back, high, mid, or low. English has about 16 vowel sounds, 13 simple sounds, and 2–3 diphthongs (i.e., sounds made by gliding one vowel sound to another within the same syllable, such as oi in coin). Pronunciation of vowel sounds varies in different parts of the country.

Long and Short Vowel Sounds   Long (or tense) vowel sounds are often used to represent their own names in words. So a child may write *da* for *day* or *lade* for *lady*. Short (or lax) vowel sounds are often substituted by long vowels that are most similar in sound. So a child might spell *igloo* as *egloo* or *fell* as *fall*. Vowel sounds are often distorted when followed by an /r/, making them harder to spell than other vowels.

Diphthongs   A diphthong is a vowel that has two distinct parts that glide from one location in the mouth to another (*oi, oy, ou, ow*). In certain positions, vowels are elongated. For example, the /i/ vowel sound in the word *ride* is held out longer than in the word *write*. Children may represent this with a diphthong, especially in words in which the vowel is followed by a voiced consonant such as /d/ (e.g., writing *raed* or *riyd* for *ride* or spelling the word *fly* as *fliy* and *try* and *triy*). Vowels with back glides as in *boat* or *boot* are often spelled by children using *ow*.

Digraph   A digraph is one sound represented by two vowels. Children often omit one vowel from a digraph, representing the most salient sound (e.g., *fet* for *feet*, *bot* for *boat*).

Schwa   A schwa sound is a weak mid-central vowel sound in an unaccented syllable (e.g., the first syllable in *about* and *upon*). This sound is represented by an upside-down lowercase *e*(ə). The schwa sound is the most likely vowel sound to be misspelled because one cannot hear which letter to use. The spelling of the unstressed schwa sound becomes particularly problematic in third grade and beyond.

Moats (1995) explained how vowels are classified by whether the tongue is high or low in the mouth and according to which part of the tongue is used—front or back. Pronounce the following sequence of words while exaggerating the vowel sound: *beet, bit, bait, bet, bat, butt, body, bore, boat, book, boot.* Notice how your mouth moves from a closed, smiley position to a rounded, closed position. Vowel substitutions tend to be made with vowels that are adjacent in articulation, particularly short /e/ and /i/ sounds. Most children do not master vowel spellings until fourth grade.

As children practice applying their knowledge of phonology to their temporary spellings, their proficiency increases. Through repeated exposures to phonological, orthographic, and morphological patterns, most children gradually come to master conventional spellings. Children with weaknesses in phonology, however, often continue to make these types of errors. After reading this Appendix, reanalyze Maria's spelling in Figure 8.3. Maria makes several spelling errors on vowel sounds, nasals, and voiced and unvoiced consonant pairs.

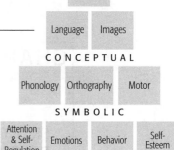

CHAPTER 9 OUTLINE

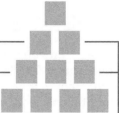

SKILL DEVELOPMENT IN DECODING AND ENCODING

Stage Theories and the Strategy
   Approach
Spelling Assessment and Instruction
From Phonological Awareness to Print

PHONICS

Synthetic Phonics
Analytic Phonics

TYPE OF TEXT

Instructional Level
Decodable Text
High-Frequency Words
Multisensory Procedures

READING FLUENCY

Determining a Student's Reading Rate
Adjusting Reading Rate
Instructional Activities for Increasing
   Reading Rate

CALCULATING

Early Concepts
Multisensory Procedures
Calculators
Error Analysis
Modeling

HANDWRITING

Readiness
Fundamentals
Developmental Stages
General Principles
Choosing a Style
Letter Formation
Strategies to Build Writing Speed

CONCLUSION

APPENDIX: FRY'S 300 INSTANT WORD LIST

CHAPTER **9**

INSTRUCTION FOR THE SYMBOLIC PROCESSING BLOCKS

DECODING, ENCODING, READING FLUENCY, CALCULATING, AND HANDWRITING

"Failure to learn to read as others do is a major catastrophe in a child's life"
—Dolch, 1939, p.1

Decoding (i.e., identifying printed words) and encoding (i.e., spelling words) involve similar processes, including knowledge of grapheme–phoneme relationships and the ability to recall letter strings and words. To identify a printed word, a student needs to know how to break apart the sounds and then how to blend the sounds back together to make a word; for spelling, a student needs to be able to break pronunciations into the component sounds. As teachers work with students who are struggling to learn to decode, they will also want to concentrate on helping them improve their spelling skills. Students with word recognition and spelling problems require explicit instruction and practice in reading and spelling single words (Berninger et al., 2000).

Dyslexia, which has a locus in neurobiological factors, is the most common form of learning disability (LD); and word reading and spelling problems are the primary academic skill impairments (Fletcher et al., 2007). Although the environment influences the development of readings skills, the contribution of genetic factors is greater (Fletcher et al., 2007). As noted in Chapter 8, dyslexia causes a breakdown in the acquisition and application of alphabet knowledge (i.e., phonology, orthography, or both), which results in slow, labored reading development; delayed automaticity; and poor spelling. Intervention requires direct, intensive instruction in the alphabetic system, followed by methods to build rate and fluency.

In relation to the symbolic processing blocks, decoding involves primarily phonology and orthography. An individual may attempt to sound out a word by breaking it into its constituent elements or may recognize a word by sight. With encoding, the writer must begin with sounds and images and then represent these patterns in writing. Learning to encode is far more difficult than learning to decode because to decode, one produces single pronunciations and meanings for written words, whereas to encode, one must produce multiple letters in correct sequence (Ehri, 2000). Figure 9.1 illustrates the relationship between decoding and encoding and phonological, orthographic, and motor abilities. As described by Berninger and colleagues, "Learning to spell requires that the mind's eye, ear, mouth, and hand learn to communicate in processing and producing spoken words" (2000, p. 118).

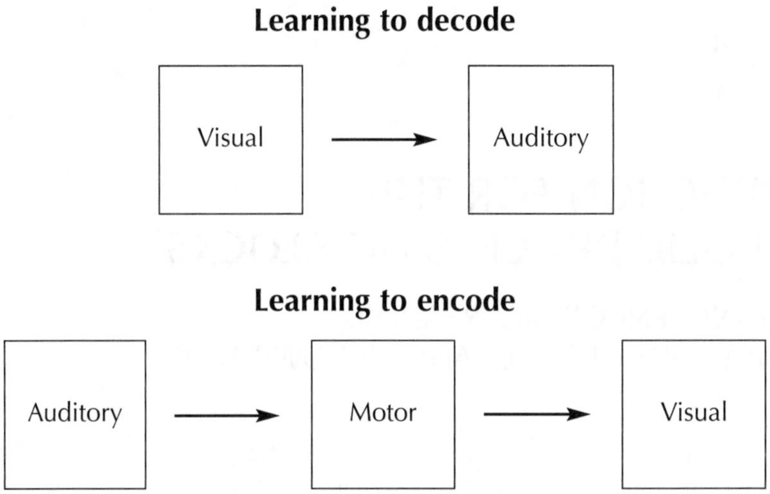

Learning to decode

Visual → Auditory

Learning to encode

Auditory → Motor → Visual

Figure 9.1. Relationship between decoding and encoding.

Students who have weaknesses in symbolic learning require more repetition, more practice, and more review to acquire basic skills than children without these weaknesses. Instruction needs to be highly systematic and carefully designed, aimed at improving the overall level of skill and efficiency of the learner. In fact, comparisons of results in intervention studies suggest that the nature of the program is less important than its comprehensiveness and intensity (Fletcher et al., 2007). Effective strategies include the following components: 1) drills and probes, 2) provision of immediate feedback, 3) rapid pacing of instruction, and 4) carefully sequenced instruction (Swanson & Hoskyn, 1998). In addition, instruction needs to be adapted to the level of skill development.

SKILL DEVELOPMENT IN DECODING AND ENCODING

As students learn to read, they progress naturally through various stages. As noted in Chapter 8, phonological awareness provides support for decoding and encoding development. When young children are first introduced to reading, they often memorize words as whole units. With more exposure to print, they develop the knowledge that, in an alphabetic language such as English, printed letters represent speech sounds (i.e., the alphabetic principle). Students start observing the details and differences among words. They then begin to notice that words are formed of common parts and units. Soon their attempts to decode new words are based on letter groupings and orthographic patterns as opposed to single letters and sounds. The more they engage in reading, the more rapidly they recognize words and the more fluent their reading becomes. Skilled word identification then provides the reader with the opportunity to comprehend. As we discuss in Chapters 10 and 11, as long as a student has developed skilled word identification, comprehension of text is related to the abilities in the conceptual blocks: acquired knowledge, vocabulary, and reasoning.

For many students, learning to read follows a natural progression, but for children with severe weaknesses in symbolic learning, it does not. Spear-Swerling and Sternberg (1996) discussed what happens when poor readers go "off track" on the road to reading success or fail to progress typically in skill acquisition. In addition to struggling with reading, they descend into the "swamp of reading disability" (Spear-Swerling & Sternberg, 1996, p. 134). This swamp is characterized by lowered expectations from teachers, lowered levels of practice, and lowered levels of motivation. Once a student is entangled in the swamp, it is difficult to get

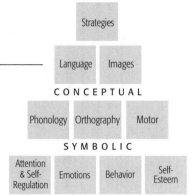

back on track. For example, even as early as middle school, neither Ryan nor Ben spent time reading unless an adult sat and read along with them.

Students with weaknesses in symbolic learning often experience difficulty during a stage of reading development or when developing strategies for word identification. Ehri (1998) explained that skilled readers can identify different words when reading in at least five different ways:

1. By blending the sounds of letters into words

2. By pronouncing and blending spelling patterns

3. By retrieving sight words from memory

4. By making analogies to words already known by sight

5. By using context clues to predict words

A central goal of instruction is to ensure that students can use all of the strategies for word identification and that they do not have to overrely on one strategy, such as guessing at the words solely on the basis of context. As Ehri noted, however, skilled reading is based on retrieving sight words rapidly and easily from memory because all of the other cueing systems require attention and disrupt the reading process.

When Maria was in first grade, her teacher observed that she seemed to rely primarily on context clues. She would look at the picture, think of words that made sense, and make up the text. She showed limited ability to use graphophonic (i.e., letter–sound) clues to check her semantic predictions. She also seemed unaware of where word breaks were in the text and how these breaks might relate to the space breaks on the page. For example, where the text said, "The hand," Maria ran her finger underneath the text and read, "The hand is coming out." When asked to point to a particular word on the page, she was unable to do so. Fortunately, her teacher could see that Maria needed to acquire specific concepts about grapheme–phoneme relationships before she would develop a sight vocabulary.

Stage Theories and the Strategy Approach

As with reading, students progress in learning to spell. Two theoretical approaches have been proposed to explain spelling development: stage theories and the strategy approach. The stage theorists propose that children appear to progress through several developmental stages or phases when learning to spell (Ehri, 1986, 1989; Gentry, 1982, 1984, 1987; Henderson, 1990; Reid, 1988; Weiner, 1994). For example, Henderson (1990) outlined five development stages: 1) scribbles and pictures (i.e., the preliterate stage), 2) letter–name representation (i.e., letters are used to represent sounds), 3) recognition of within-word patterns (i.e., orthographic and morphological patterns are observed), 4) syllable juncture (i.e., consonants are doubled and patterns present in syllables are observed), and 5) derivational constancy (i.e., roots and derivations are used).

The strategy approach depicts spelling development as being more continuous, suggesting that children incorporate a variety of spelling strategies from the very beginning of their acquisition of writing skills (Treiman, 1998). Although they help depict spelling development, stage theories, unlike the strategy approach, do not capture fully the complexities of the phonological, orthographic, and morphological representations that are related to spelling (Treiman & Bourassa, 2000). However, even though many children do incorporate varied aspects of linguistic knowledge in their initial spellings and reveal sensitivity to orthographic and morphological influences, the proposed stages of development help explain how reading and spelling abilities evolve.

Ehri's Phases Ehri (2005) preferred the term *phase theory* to stage theory, suggesting that phase theory provides a more accurate description of the course of development because the stages of spelling are not qualitatively distinct. Ehri (1998, 2000, 2005) described four phases that underlie the development of both a sight vocabulary and spelling: prealphabetic, partial alphabetic, full alphabetic, and consolidated alphabetic. During the prealphabetic phase, readers recognize words by selected visual attributes that are not connected to grapheme–phoneme relationships. They remember words by configuration or general visual appearance, and their spellings are often a string of letters in random order (Moats, 2000). In kindergarten, Maria knew the word *look* because her teacher had drawn eyes into the two *Os*. Once students begin to use alphabetic processes, the subsequent phases emerge successively (Ehri, 2005). In the partial alphabetic phase, readers discover the alphabetic principle and make connections between some of the letters and sounds in written words. In the full alphabetic phase, students make complete connections between letters and sounds, and they are able to pronounce phonically regular words. In the consolidated alphabetic phase, letter patterns that occur across many words are retained. These larger units consist of morphemes, syllables, or onsets and rimes.

Similar Theories of Spelling Development Other researchers in addition to Ehri (1998) have developed similar theories that focus primarily on spelling development (Gentry, 1984; Henderson, 1990). Although the stages or phases described vary somewhat in enumeration and description from Ehri's, they typically include five stages: prephonetic, semiphonetic, phonetic, transitional, and conventional. Students with spelling difficulties appear to progress through similar stages as their peers, but their development is slower. Often, their difficulties appear indicative of arrest in one of the stages in spelling development (Moats, 1991). Even though learning to read and learning to spell involve almost identical processes, spelling is much more difficult (Ehri, 1997). Children with dyslexia require substantially more practice to learn to spell. Moats (1995) indicated that before children with dyslexia can memorize a word, they require as many as 40 opportunities to write it correctly. The following sections describe the five different stages of spelling.

Prephonetic or Prephonemic In the initial and earliest phases of learning to spell, a child combines a string of unrelated letters to communicate a message. When first writing, many children are not aware of the alphabetic principle and simply write known letters. Figure 9.2 presents a story written by Maria in kindergarten. The first line contains both letters and numbers. At the bottom of the page, she wrote wavy lines as she made the comment, "I think I'll just write the rest in cursive." At this phase, the child knows little about the alphabetic system and recognizes words through memory of selected visual features (Ehri, 2005).

Semiphonetic or Partial Alphabetic In the semiphonetic phase, letters are used to represent sounds, but only a few sounds in words are represented. Children recognize some of the letters and sounds in words, such as the first and last letter sounds in the word. In some instances, students may use the names of letters rather than the letter sounds (Adams, 1990). For example, the word *while* may be written as *yl*. They may spell by writing a few consonants that are the most salient in speech, such as spelling the word *happy* as *hp* (Moats, 2000). During this phase, although spellings may follow logical linguistic patterns, children know very few correct spellings. A student may know consonant sounds, long vowel sounds, and an occasional sight word. Figure 9.3 illustrates Ryan's writing when he was in third grade. He is giving advice to Winnie the Pooh about when he

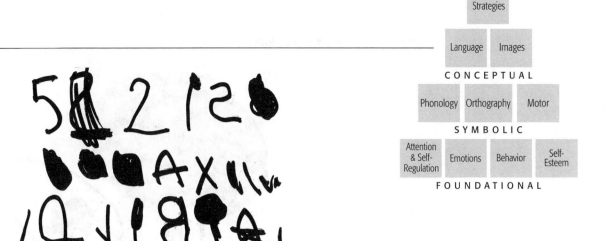

Figure 9.2. Maria's kindergarten story.

should climb trees to avoid the bees. As can be seen, some of his attempted spellings are semiphonetic (e.g., *wn*), whereas others are phonetic (e.g., *clim*).

Some students are not able to decode words in a complete and accurate manner even in middle school and secondary school.

When Ben's reading and spelling development were reviewed in eighth grade, it became apparent that he went off track in second grade. In second grade, Ben had trouble memorizing words and building a sight vocabulary. He hesitated before pronouncing common words such as *of*. His oral reading was characterized by numerous pauses and repetitions. He also did not analyze words carefully when trying to pronounce them. When reading a short passage from an informal reading inventory in third grade, he identified the word *penny* as *party* and then in the next line he read it as *pretty*. In spelling, he had difficulty with producing letter sequences and spelling irregular words. Ben made many reading and spelling errors that suggested that he was still in a partial alphabetic phase. He tended to misread words that were similar in appearance. For example, he misread the word *experiment* as *experience*. This weakness appears to be most related to insufficient formation of orthographic images in memory and failure to note all of the features in the word (see Chapter 8).

Many older children with reading disabilities would be identified as partial alphabetic phase readers (Ehri, 2005). Ehri suggested that partial alphabetic phase readers do not store sight words in memory in sufficient letter detail to recognize how they are similar yet different from other words.

Phonetic or Full Alphabetic In the phonetic phase, students produce spellings that demonstrate grapheme–phoneme correspondence. When writing, they attempt to record all of the sounds within a word and present them in the

Figure 9.3. Ryan's Story about Winnie the Pooh: "He should climb when the bees are gone."

correct sound sequence. Students with weaknesses in the orthographic block often overrely on sounds as a strategy for spelling (see Chapter 8). Even in eighth grade, Ben's attempted spellings revealed too much reliance on sounds. Individuals like Ben who have weaknesses in orthographic processing continue to produce phonetic spellings into adulthood.

Transitional or Consolidated Alphabetic In the transitional phase, the writer demonstrates awareness of many of the conventions of English orthography. For example, the student spells the ending of the past tense of a verb as -ed even when the ending sounds like a /t/, such as in the word trapped. Operating with chunks of words makes it easier for the student to decode and encode multisyllabic words (Ehri, 2000; 2005).

Conventional In this phase, the writer possesses multiple strategies for determining standard spelling. Although not all words are spelled correctly, the writer regularly employs information from all sources, sounds, sight, and meaning as an aid to English spelling.

Spelling Assessment and Instruction

As a general rule, teachers should not give students lists of words to memorize for a spelling test until the students understand how the spelling system works (Ehri, 1998). Ehri indicated that children should be able to generate spellings that are phonetically complete and graphemically possible before they should be expected to memorize a list of words for a spelling test. She stated,

> Learning the spellings of specific words by memorizing word lists should
> not begin until students understand how the conventional system works

graphophonically. Once this point is reached, remembering the spellings of specific words will be much easier, so spelling instruction can shift to this learning activity. (p. 34)

Selecting Spelling Words   A serious mismatch is often found between a child's level of spelling development and the words that the student is assigned to memorize for a Friday spelling test. When Ryan was in third grade, he did not know how to spell many simple words, such as *they* and *was*. Despite this, his Friday spelling test contained the words *Chinese* and *chopsticks*. Ben was given lists of words to memorize that he could not even read in sixth grade. His average spelling score every Friday was 0%. When selecting words for spelling practice, make sure that the child knows how to read the word, understands the meaning of the word, and uses the word in speaking and writing.

Scott (2000) suggested several ideas for selecting and using word lists for students having difficulty with spelling:

- Use high-frequency words.
- Use self-selected words.
- Use some irregular words.
- Use multisensory study techniques.
- Practice fewer words, more often, over longer time periods.
- Use computers to practice words.
- Use computer programs that allow teacher input of word lists.

Using the Spelling Rating Scale   When evaluating a student's spelling development, a spelling rating scale is more sensitive to measuring growth than the use of dichotomous scoring (i.e., correct or incorrect). The following scale, adapted from Tangel and Blachman (1992) and Kroese, Hynd, Knight, Hiemenz, and Hall (2000), can be used to evaluate performance on spelling tests.

0 points: Random letters
1 point: One phonetically related letter
2 points: Correct initial phoneme
3 points: Two correct phonemes (does not have to be correct grapheme)
4 points: Correct number of syllables represented (only used for multisyllabic words)
5 points: All phonemes in the word are represented
6 points: All phonemes in the word are represented with possible English spellings (e.g., *rane* for *rain*).
7 points: Correct spelling

This type of scoring system can help a teacher monitor a student's progress in sequencing sounds correctly. Several instructional activities are described in the next section that can help students increase their knowledge of word spellings.

From Phonological Awareness to Print

For students with weaknesses in phonology, explicit instruction in phonemic awareness should be coupled with instruction in grapheme–phoneme relationships (Calfee, 1998). By the end of kindergarten, children should be able to blend and segment sounds and use sounds to spell simple words (Chard & Dickson, 1999). As a first step, students must grasp the alphabetic principle. This principle has been defined simply as the understanding that the discrete letters of the alphabet represent the discrete sounds of speech (Liberman, Shankweiler, &

Strategies

Language   Images

CONCEPTUAL

Phonology   Orthography   Motor

SYMBOLIC

Attention & Self-Regulation   Emotions   Behavior   Self-Esteem

FOUNDATIONAL

Liberman, 1989). In other words, the beginning reader must discover that words have an internal phonemic structure that is represented by letters, and then they must be able to use and apply this knowledge. Several training programs are available that are designed to help teachers increase their abilities to teach and understand language structure, including the *Language Essentials for Teachers of Reading and Spelling* (LETRS®). (See Additional Resources for more information.)

Invented or Temporary Spelling One way to help students increase phonological awareness is to encourage the use of invented spelling. Invented spelling does not mean that the word bears no resemblance to the correct spelling or that students simply make up the spellings of a word. Instead, invented spelling means that students listen carefully to the sounds in a word and then write the sounds in the correct order. Encouraging children to produce their own spellings requires them to think about the ways that words are written. Many teachers now refer to invented spelling as *temporary spelling*. The concept of temporary spelling communicates to parents that this type of spelling is only a stage in the developmental process and that it is important to teach correct spelling once students understand how to sequence the sounds in a word.

When children are first learning to spell, they often pronounce the word and then attempt to write the sequence of sounds in order (phoneme to grapheme conversion). As skill progresses in spelling, children begin to incorporate orthographic and morphological strategies. They record memorized combinations of letter sequences, such as the *-ight* pattern in the word *night*. After writing a word, they may analyze the word to see if the sequence of letters looks right. They may also think that even though a word sounds like it ends in a /t/ (e.g., *jumped*), the spelling is likely to be *-ed* because *-ed* signifies past tense.

Because invented spelling reduces reliance on memory of how words appear, children who have difficulty picturing the visual appearance of words can increase their knowledge of sounds by writing words according to the way that they sound. When students are attempting to spell an unknown word, encourage them to pronounce the word slowly aloud while they attempt to sequence the sounds in the correct order.

For students who enter school with poor phonological awareness, more than just writing with invented spelling is needed to help them grasp grapheme–phoneme associations (Treiman, 1998). These students require instruction that is more explicit and intense. Liberman and colleagues (1989) noted that approximately 75% of students gain an understanding of the connection between spoken and written words without much explicit instruction but that the other 25% of the children require explicit instruction or they remain locked into a sight word stage of reading. These children require direct, intensive, and systematic training in how phonological structure relates to reading and spelling. The earlier in a child's school career these difficulties are addressed, the better.

Many of the activities designed to build this knowledge involve moving around letters to form words by using letter cards, alphabet blocks, Scrabble tiles, or magnetic letters. In addition, words can be constructed by using a small pocket chart. Specific examples of activities used to help students increase their knowledge of grapheme–phoneme relationships are described in the following sections.

Analyzing Word Structure Teaching students about the regularities that exist in the language is more important than asking them to memorize phonic or spelling rules (Ehri, 2000). Teachers can foster linguistic awareness by engaging children in activities that involve active word study. Once students can sequence sounds, in-depth instruction in word structure is appropriate. The goal of this instruction is to help children understand (as much as possible) why English words are spelled the way that they are spelled.

Talk-to-Yourself Chart   Gaskins (1998) described a procedure called a Talk-to-Yourself Chart that is used at the Benchmark school to help students learn common English spelling patterns. The purpose is to teach students to fully analyze key words, or words that contain high-frequency spelling patterns. This procedure is based on the premise that it is easier for students to segment a word into sounds if they do not already have a visual image.

The teacher introduces a key word such as the word *right* and then asks students to stretch out the sounds and raise a finger for each sound that they hear. After the students respond by raising three fingers, the teacher places the word card up on the board and asks the students to count the number of letters that they see. Next, the students are asked to attempt to match the letters they hear with the letters that they see: The letters *r* and *t* each represent one sound and the three letters *igh* represent the vowel sound. The Talk-to-Yourself Chart, adapted from this program (Gaskins, 1998), is placed on the board to remind the students of the steps involved:

1. The word is _____.

2. When I stretch the word, I hear _____ sounds.

3. There are _____ letters because _____.

4. The spelling pattern is _____.

5. This is what I know about the vowel: _____

6. Another word I know with the same vowel sound is _____.

7. Other words that share this same spelling pattern are: _____

Using the example of the word *right*, students would say

1. The word is *right*.

2. When I stretch the word, I hear 3 sounds.

3. There are 5 letters because it takes *igh* to represent the /i/ sound.

4. The spelling pattern is *ight*.

5. This is what I know about the vowel: The vowel is the only vowel in the word, and it says its own name.

6. Another word that I know with the same vowel sound is *ride*.

7. Other words that share this same spelling pattern are: *night, might, fight, tight, sight, right, plight,* and *fright*.

This type of procedure can also help students such as Ryan, Maria, and Ben with spelling. The emphasis is not placed on teaching specific rules but rather on making explicit the connection between phonemes and graphemes. For instruction in both decoding and encoding, it is best to help children recognize and then internalize common English spelling patterns. Memorized rules do not improve spelling performance. A student must develop a working knowledge of the alphabetic system that he or she can apply to decoding or encoding (Ehri, 2000).

Adapted Elkonin Procedure   Elkonin (1973), a Russian psychologist, developed several simple procedures for explaining to students the relationship between speech sounds and printed letters. The following procedure, adapted from Elkonin, moves the student gradually from counting speech sounds to translating these sounds into letters.

1. Select a simple line drawing.

2. Place a rectangle for a word related to the drawing under the drawing. Divide the rectangle into squares equal to the number of phonemes. Begin with words in which the number of phonemes matches the number of graphemes. In other words, the number of sounds should match the number of letters.

3. Ask the student to say the word slowly and push a marker forward for each sound. You can use poker chips or colored tiles. Once a student is able to perform Step 3 with confidence, progress to Step 4.

4. In Step 4, color-code markers for vowels and consonants, such as making consonant sounds be represented by blue poker chips and vowel sounds by red poker chips. Have the student push forward the blue chips for the consonant sounds and the red chips for the vowel sounds in the word. Once a student can identify and differentiate vowel and consonant sounds, proceed to Step 5.

5. In Step 5, use letter tiles, magnetic letters, or letter cards. At first, use words in which single phonemes are represented by single graphemes. Once a student is able to spell words with predictable spelling patterns, introduce additional graphemes. For example, demonstrate how the word *came* has three speech sounds but four letters. In these examples, the number of boxes does not match the number of speech sounds, so make larger squares for the speech sounds that can be heard and smaller boxes for the letters that are silent. The word *came* would have three large boxes (*c, a, m,*) and one small box for the silent *e*. Write consonant and vowel digraphs (i.e., one speech sound spelled with two letters) in one box. For example, when writing the word *boat*, make three boxes, placing the *oa* into the middle box. Discuss with the student the difference between how a word is written and what you hear. This type of instruction can improve both decoding and encoding ability because the emphasis is placed on segmenting and blending sounds. The following web site allows teachers to create worksheets with pictures and Elkonin boxes with ease: http://www.bogglesworldesl.com

Auditory Sequencing Bannatyne (1971) discussed a similar procedure for helping students attend to the sequence of sounds when spelling.

1. Make small letter cards or use Scrabble tiles.

2. Sound out a word slowly and have the student attempt to place the letter tiles in correct sequence from left to right. When necessary, provide demonstrations on how to arrange the tiles before the child attempts to build the word.

3. After building the word, encourage the student to trace and then print the word.

4. As skill increases, use individual letter tiles to break words into syllables or to build several words around a root.

Teachers can also put dots under each letter or an arrow under the word to reinforce the concept of blending the sounds together. As skill develops, teachers can begin using an activity such as *Making Words* (Cunningham & Cunningham, 1992; Cunningham & Hall, 1994) to help students learn to sequence sounds in longer words.

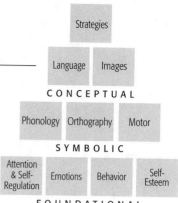

Making Words   The purpose of Making Words, a guided invented spelling task, is to help students develop phonemic awareness and discover how the alphabetic system works by increasing their understanding of grapheme–phoneme relationships. This strategy should be used along with typical writing activities. In this 15-minute activity, students are individually given letters that they will use to make 12–15 words. The activities begin with short easy words and end with a big word that uses all of the letters. For the first lessons, students are given only one vowel letter, which is written in red, and several consonants. Later, students may be given two or more vowels. The patterns begin with two-letter words and increase in length. The final word, a six-, seven-, or eight-letter word, includes all of the letters that the students have. In all activities, emphasis is placed on how the pronunciation of words changes when letters are moved and added.

Cunningham and Hall have presented lessons for this activity in several books (see Additional Resources). In addition, Lynch (1998) developed a book about making word-type activities targeted to the beginning reader from kindergarten to second grade. This program has also been included in a literacy model for classroom instruction called the *Four-Blocks Way* (Cunningham, Hall, & Cunningham, 2000). The four blocks include guided reading, self-selected reading, writing, and working with words.

Road to the Code   Blachman and colleagues (2000) prepared *Road to the Code: A Phonological Awareness Program for Young Children,* a research-based manual to help teachers incorporate phonological awareness and early literacy activities into the classroom. (See Additional Resources.) One activity, Say-It-and-Move-It, is used each day during this 11-week program. This activity is followed by instruction in letter names and sounds. The lessons are carefully sequenced and take 15–20 minutes a day. A newer work, *Road to Reading: A Program for Preventing and Remediating Reading Difficulties,* includes many more activities (Blachman & Tangel, 2008).

Phonics and Spelling through Phoneme-Grapheme Mapping   Grace (2007) provided a sequential, systematic, explicit program for teaching students the relationships between letters and sounds. (See Additional Resources for more information.) The procedure is designed to be used three times a week for about 20 minutes. Six to ten colored tiles and phoneme-grapheme mapping paper (similar to graph paper) are used to teach students phonemes and graphemes. Lessons are organized around the six syllable types of English (i.e., closed syllables, syllables with vowels and the silent *e,* open syllables, syllables ending in a consonant with -*le, r*-controlled syllables, and diphthong syllables). For the mapping procedure, students are instructed to

1. Say each phoneme and place one tile in each grid square for each sound

2. Point to the first tile and say the sound and then move the tile up and write the grapheme in the square

3. Continue with each tile until the exact spelling of the word is represented in the boxes based on phoneme-grapheme correspondences, not the number of letters in the word. For example, the digraph /sh/ would be written in one box because it only makes one sound.

Poor word recognition is a stumbling block for many young readers:

When Maria was in preschool, she had trouble pronouncing words. In second grade, she memorized many words. By the time Maria was in sixth grade, however, her word identification and spelling skills were several years below grade level. Her word reading was nonautomatic, and she did not understand how to pronounce common clusters in words. For example, when attempting to pronounce the word *wrestle*, Maria first made the /w/ sound and then the /r/ sound. When she came to the letters *le*, she attempted to pronounce the letters independently, producing two syllables. After repeated attempts, she commented, "Oh, the *e* doesn't make a sound." She still could not, however, produce the correct sound for this pattern. Maria knew individual letters and their corresponding sounds and could be described as fully alphabetic but had yet to master common syllable units and spelling patterns in the English language.

Reading Pen One example of technology that may help a student such as Maria with word pronunciation is a talking or reading pen. The user scans the pen over a word, and it reads the word aloud. The Reading Pen (see Additional Resources) scans any word from printed text, displays a word in large characters, reads the word aloud through a built-in speaker or earphones, and defines the word. In addition, the pen can display syllable units and spell words out loud. Ben found that use of this pen enabled him to complete his assigned readings in a shorter amount of time because he no longer needed to rely on other people for help pronouncing certain words. John, a high school student, used the pen as an aid to understanding vocabulary.

PHONICS

Some children easily intuit phonics skills by being readers and writers and do not need to be taught the rules and principles of grapheme–phoneme relationships. For these children, a teacher may model and provide guided practice in word instruction within the context of connected text (Allen, 1998). Students with marked weaknesses in phonology or orthography, however, typically require more explicit instruction to learn to read and spell. Ryan, Ben, and Maria are all examples of students who need more intensive, systematic instruction. Chard and Osborn (1999b) discussed the following five essential components of word recognition: letter–sound correspondences, regular word reading, story reading, irregular word reading, and advanced word analysis. Chard and Osborn (1999a, 1999b) provided a comprehensive set of guidelines to follow when providing word recognition instruction to children with reading disabilities, such as Maria. Essentially, two broad categories of phonics methods exist: synthetic and analytic.

Synthetic Phonics

With synthetic phonics instruction, a student is explicitly taught the relationships between letters and sounds using a part-to-whole approach. Sounds initially are taught in isolation, and then the student is taught how to blend the phonemes together to pronounce words (Ehri, 2006). Once the student can blend single phonemes, additional graphemes are introduced and emphasis is placed on learning to break words into their basic parts.

Two widely used synthetic phonics approaches are Orton-Gillingham (Gillingham & Stillman, 1973) and Slingerland (Slingerland, 1981). These methods provide instruction aimed at strengthening visual and auditory associations through tracing. Although both of these approaches are highly effective for students with reading disabilities, they require intensive teacher training. In lieu of these methods, several other easy-to-use synthetic phonics programs are described in the following sections. Information for ordering these programs is presented in Additional Resources.

The Reading Lesson *The Reading Lesson* (Levin & Langton, 1998) is a practical, structured approach designed for teaching young children ages 4–7 years

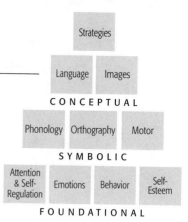

how to read. Although the program is designed for parents, the format is easy to use with a young child who is struggling with decoding. The program is divided into 20 easy-to-follow lessons. The method begins with the most common letters and sounds and teaches children how to put the sounds together to read simple words. The program gradually progresses to longer words. After completing the last book in the series, a child can read with ease at the second-grade level.

Reading Reflex The *Reading Reflex* (McGuinness & McGuinness, 1998) program was designed for young children and elementary-age children who are struggling to learn to read. The program, which may be used by reading teachers or parents, provides a child with systematic instruction in the alphabetic code. The book includes simple diagnostic tests, lesson plans, word exercises, and games. Additional support materials are available that can be used in conjunction with the book.

Phonic Reading Lessons The *Phonic Reading Lessons* (Kirk et al., 2007; Roberts & Mather, 2007) consist of two volumes: Skills and Practice. This systematic method is easy for teachers to learn to use and provides a step-by-step procedure for teaching phonics and reinforcing grapheme–phoneme relationships. No rules are taught. Instead, sounds are introduced one at a time in the Skills volume using a variety of words so that the student develops an automatic response to each symbol. The Practice volume supports and reinforces the lessons from Skills through the use of story reading and spelling practice. As a supplement to the program, the child is asked to write words while carefully pronouncing each sound. In its third revision, this program has been used successfully with individuals of all ages.

Spalding Method The *Spalding Method*, described in the book *The Writing Road to Reading* (Spalding & Spalding, 1990), is a language arts program that integrates handwriting, spelling, reading, speaking, and writing. Children are taught to recognize and write 70 common phonograms, which include single letters and sounds. The text includes a complete list of the rules to be taught and the individual phonograms. Phonogram cards are used to present the sounds. After the child has learned 54 phonograms, he or she receives instruction in spelling. To help with spelling, children learn to master the 70 phonograms and 29 spelling rules. The Spaldings claimed that, armed with sounds and rules, a child can spell about 80% of English words correctly. This method has been used successfully with students from first grade through college.

Other programs are designed to be more appealing to older students. Two examples of structured reading programs that are appropriate for upper elementary or secondary students are described briefly in the following sections.

Language! *Language! The Comprehensive Literacy Curriculum* program, now in its second edition (Greene, 2005), is designed for students ranging from third grade through adulthood. The curriculum is designed for students who are not fluent readers, writers, and spellers and who are not making adequate gains with conventional methods. Effective use of the program requires background in structured language teaching. The program is based on building students' knowledge and mastery of phonological and linguistic awareness; decoding and encoding isolated words; and reading sentences, paragraphs, and passages for meaning. The curriculum contains instruction on reading, spelling, composition, comprehension, vocabulary, grammar, and usage, and it is designed to assist teachers in providing individualized instruction. The content is presented sequentially, and progress is based on each student's mastery of concepts. A supplementary reading series matches the language concepts that have been taught.

Specialized Program Individualizing Reading Excellence® *Specialized Program Individualizing Reading Excellence*® (S.P.I.R.E.) is another example of a comprehensive multisensory program for struggling readers in kindergarten through eighth grade. (See Additional Resources.) Based on Orton-Gillingham methodologies, S.P.I.R.E. focuses on instruction in phonological awareness, phonics, fluency, comprehension, spelling, and handwriting. The integrated curriculum is designed to be used for 1 hour each day. Using magnetic boards, students engage in daily word-building activities. Decodable word cards are provided in the three colors of a stoplight: green (Go ahead, you know the sounds); yellow (Slow down because a part of the word has a less common pronunciation); and red (Stop, think, and remember because you cannot use the sounds to decode this word). Decodable texts and workbooks accompany the program to reinforce learning and provide additional practice in decoding, fluency, and comprehension.

Wilson Reading System® The *Wilson Reading System*® (WRS) is based on Orton-Gillingham principles and is a multisensory, synthetic approach to teaching reading and writing (Wilson, 2004). The program was originally designed for older students in Grades 4–12, but adaptations have been made for younger students. *Fundations*® (Wilson Language Training, 2002) is now available for students in K–3 in general education classrooms. Teachers can incorporate a 30-minute daily *Fundations*® lesson into their language arts classroom instruction with lessons that focus on carefully sequenced skills including print knowledge, alphabetic awareness, phonological awareness, phonemic awareness, and decoding.

The WRS is a research-based complete curriculum for teaching decoding and encoding beginning with phoneme segmentation. The program directly teaches the structure of English words so that students master the coding system for reading and spelling in a systematic and cumulative manner. This program uses multisensory structured language that is designed to teach specific strategies for decoding and encoding in a step-by-step fashion. The English language is studied as a system with dependable rules. This program was designed with 10 underlying principles in mind:

1. Teach sounds to automaticity.

2. Teach total word structure—not just sounds.

3. Present concepts within context-controlled, written text.

4. Present the structure of language in a systematic, cumulative manner.

5. Teach all principles of English language structure directly.

6. Teach and reinforce concepts with visual-auditory-kinesthetic-tactile methods.

7. Teach phonemic and syllabic segmentation.

8. Include constant review and repetition.

9. Use questioning techniques for reinforcement and feedback.

10. Use diagnostic teaching to monitor progress.

In the beginning steps, phonological awareness, segmenting, and blending are stressed. Students use sound cards to learn and practice sounds and then to manipulate them to make words. Word cards are then used to present and practice words using the sounds on the sound cards. Students then read words from lists, and their progress is charted. Students read decodable text; practice spelling using sound, syllable, and suffix cards; and write dictated words and sentences in a dictation book.

The program is sequenced in 12 steps that are based on six syllable types (closed syllables, syllables with vowels and the silent *e*, open syllables, syllables ending in a consonant with *-le*, *r*-controlled syllables, and diphthong syllables). Lessons are taught using the same basic structure. In Steps 1–6, the students learn to rely on the syllable rules; in Steps 7–12, students learn rules for adding suffixes to change base words. Examples of these six syllable types are provided:

Closed syllable: *cat*
Silent *e*: *bike*
Open syllable: *motion*
Consonant *-le*: *turtle*
R-controlled: *car*
Diphthong syllable: *out*

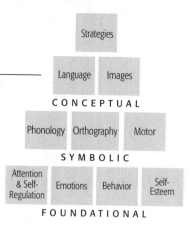

A simple syllable marking is used to code for each of these syllable types. Using a left-to-right movement, a student draws a curved or straight line under each syllable. He or she then identifies the type of syllable, codes the vowels with a long or short marking, puts a slash through the *e* if it is a silent *e* or consonant *-le* syllable, and draws a circle around the vowels. Instruction in syllable types may also facilitate spelling, particularly mastery of words with a final silent *e*.

The WRS is one of the few structured reading methods that was originally designed for use with older students and adults, and the stories are written with the interests of older readers in mind. All of the materials used in the program are carefully sequenced and color coded for each step. In fifth grade, Ryan was taught using the WRS in the resource room. Instruction in the six syllable types helped Ryan to understand how to pronounce vowel sounds in unfamiliar words. The careful sequence of the program helped improve both his decoding and encoding skills.

If Maria had been provided with this type of program in sixth grade, her decoding and encoding skills would have improved. Unfortunately, this type of teaching was not available in her school. Students with severe weaknesses within the symbolic blocks need to be provided with specifically designed and carefully sequenced reading programs. Although students with the most severe difficulties usually require a synthetic phonics approach, students with more moderate weaknesses can learn to read with an analytic phonics approach.

Analytic Phonics

Analytic phonics approaches use a whole-to-part approach that teaches children to analyze letter–sound patterns once the word has been identified as a whole (Ehri, 2006). Instruction begins with common words or word families. A student is shown the word *cat* and taught that *a* and *t* say /ăt/ and then is taught to read the many words in the /ăt/ family (e.g., *bat, cat, fat, hat, mat, pat, rat, sat, brat, chat, drat, flat, splat*). The student then practices reading these words in short, controlled stories.

Analogy Strategy The basic idea of the analogy approach is that beginning readers can recognize unfamiliar words through knowledge of the letter patterns of similar, known words (Allen, 1998). This type of approach has also been referred to as a word family or linguistic approach. Teaching students to read and spell words by analogy includes instruction in the use of onsets (i.e., initial consonants and consonant clusters) and rimes (i.e., the ending portion of the syllable). As described in Chapter 8, in the word *hat*, the /h/ is the onset and the /ăt/ is the rime. Wylie and Durrell (1970) indicated that nearly 500 primary-grade words can be derived from a set of 37 rimes (see Figure 9.4).

-ack	-ain	-ake	-ale	-all	-ame	-an
-ank	-ap	-ash	-at	-ate	-aw	-ay
-eat	-ell	-est	-ice	-ick	-ide	-ight
-ill	-in	-ine	-ing	-ink	-ip	-ir
-ock	-oke	-op	-or	-ore	-uck	-ug
-ump	-unk					

Figure 9.4. Set of 37 rimes from which 500 primary words can be taught. (*Source:* Wylie & Durrell [1970]).

To help children start to appreciate the relationship between spoken rhymes and written rimes, after reading a story, discuss the rhyming words. Write the words on the board and show students how the spellings of the words are similar. For example, after reading a story that had the sentence, "He turned off the light and said good night," Maria's first-grade teacher wrote the words *light* and *night* on the board and then discussed the shared spelling pattern.

Rhyming words that have the same rime can be placed on one side of a classroom word wall and words that rhyme but differ in spelling patterns can be placed on the other side for further study and review. Pinnell and Fountas (1998) presented a thorough reference for helping children learn about letters, sounds, and words, including a comprehensive list of phonograms.

Instruction with analogies focuses on both reading and spelling words. Englert, Hiebert, and Stewart (1985) presented an analogy strategy to help students notice orthographic similarities among words and then to generalize this information to the spelling of new words. The following procedure is used:

1. Identify the words that a student misspelled on a pretest.

2. Develop a spelling bank of 15 words. Select words for the spelling bank by their similarity to the misspelled words. For example, the word *other* may be selected if the student misspelled the word *brother*.

3. Explain that the last parts of rhyming words are often spelled the same.

4. Present a list of words. Say one word and ask the student to identify the word in the spelling bank that rhymes with the stimulus word.

5. Using the rhyming rule, have the student identify which letters of the printed and orally presented words would be spelled the same.

6. Have the student practice the words by spelling them orally from memory.

7. Have the student write the words twice from memory.

8. Have the student write the words from memory in a test of delayed recall.

After developing the spelling bank, have students practice the transfer words in a cloze passage. Encourage students to fill in the missing words without looking at the analogous words. Ask students to think of the word from the spelling bank that rhymes with the transfer word.

The analogy strategy may also be used to teach words that have the same letter patterns but do not rhyme (e.g., *have, gave*) (Gerber, 1993). Point out the similar spelling patterns and then discuss the exception to the spelling rules. Effective spelling instruction provides focus on different language units: 1) phonemes to graphemes, 2) spoken words to whole written words, and 3) spoken and written onsets and rimes (Berninger et al., 2000).

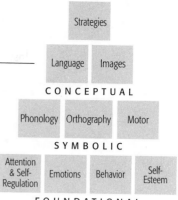

Glass Analysis Method for Decoding Only Although she had full alphabetic knowledge, Maria did not know how to break words into parts to aid in pronunciation. In light of Ehri's (1998) framework, Maria needed to move from the full alphabetic to the consolidated alphabetic phase. To do this, she required a reading method that would help her learn to group or chunk common word parts as an aid to pronunciation.

It is important to note that interventions for spelling and reading must address the morphophonemic principle in English. A constant trade-off exists in written English between representation of the sounds of the letters and preservation of the morphological roots of the words.

Another easy-to-use method for helping students learn to recognize and pronounce common spelling units and to pronounce words with more than one syllable is the Glass Analysis Method for Decoding Only (Glass, 1973). To begin, write several multisyllabic words on index cards. For practice, you may select words from the class reading material. Do not cover up parts of the word or present clusters separately from the word. Teach students only common letter clusters that can be generalized to new words. If possible, practice with this technique 10–15 minutes daily. Use these five general steps to present each word:

1. Identify the whole word. For example, present the word *carpenter* on an index card and say, "This word is *carpenter*."

2. Pronounce a sound in the word and ask students to name the letter or letters that make that sound. Say, "In the word *carpenter*, what letters make the /ar/ sound? What letters make the /pĕn/ sound?" and so forth. (For this step, say the letter sounds, not the letter names.)

3. Ask for the sound that certain letters or letter combinations make. Say, "What sound do the letters *er* make? What sound do the letters *ter* make?" and so forth. (For this step, say the letter names, not the letter sounds.)

4. Take away letters (auditorily, not visually) and ask for the remaining sound. Say, "In the word *carpenter*, if I took off /car/, how would you pronounce the word? If I took off /ter/, how would you pronounce the word? If I took off /pĕnter/, how would you say the word?" Think of as many combinations as you can.

5. Ask students to say the whole word.

Although the Glass Analysis Method was developed primarily for teaching decoding skills, it can be modified easily to work on encoding skills (Mather, 1991). For example, if students were learning to spell the word *consideration*, you could use these steps:

1. Identify and discuss the visual and auditory clusters in the word.

2. Ask students to write the letters that make the /cŭn/ sound, then the /sid/ sound, then the /er/ sound, then the /ā/ sound, and finally the /shŭn/ or -tion sound.

3. Have students write the word *consideration* while pronouncing each part slowly: "con•sid•er•a•tion."

4. Have students turn their papers over and write the word *consideration* from memory while saying the word as it is written.

5. Have students write the word from memory two more times.

When using this adapted method for spelling, emphasize ordering the sounds of a word in the correct sequence. This can be accomplished by presenting and

Write the word	Say the word	Write the # of syllables	Write each syllable				Write and say the word
			1	2	3	4	

Figure 9.5. Sample spelling grid (Source: Wong, 1986).

practicing the visual and auditory clusters of a word in the order in which they appear. Other remedial spelling techniques encourage students to listen carefully to the sequence of sounds.

Spelling Grid Just as chunking strategies are needed for reading, as skill progresses, the focus of spelling instruction should be directed to the correct spelling of word parts and syllable units. Some students can improve their spellings of multisyllabic words through the use of a spelling grid (Wong, 1986; see Figure 9.5 for an example). The purpose of a spelling grid is to promote structural analysis of words. Wong recommended the following steps:

1. Write the spelling word in column one, and then pronounce the word and discuss its meanings.

2. Have the student say the word in column two.

3. In column three, have the student write the number of syllables in the word.

4. In column four, have the student divide the word into syllables and then write each syllable.

5. In column five, have the student write and say the word.

6. As a final step, have the student turn over the paper and write the word from memory.

Reading Excellence: Word Attack and Rate Development Strategies

Archer, Gleason, and Vachon (2000) developed a program called *Reading*

Excellence: Word Attack and Rate Development Strategies (REWARDS®) that is designed to teach upper elementary and secondary school students the pronunciation of multisyllabic words. This specialized reading program teaches students the use of a flexible strategy for decoding multisyllabic words. The aim is to increase comprehension by increasing oral and silent reading fluency. Using REWARDS®, readers are taught an overt and a covert strategy. The overt strategy involves circling the prefixes, circling the suffixes, and underlining the vowel sound in the root word. The teacher then says, "What part? What part? What part?" while drawing scoops under the segments or decodable "chunks." Then, students are instructed to say the words quickly. Eventually, the steps of underlining the vowel and circling the word parts are eliminated, leaving the student with the covert strategy of looking for the word parts and vowel sounds and saying the parts quickly to form a real word.

TYPE OF TEXT

A critical factor for improving reading performance is time spent reading.

Ryan would often sit in his fourth-grade class with a book placed in front of him that was too difficult to read. On occasion, he would turn a page, look at the pictures on the new page, and then glance around the room. The books used in the classroom were too difficult for Ryan to read independently. Although he sat quietly during reading time, the books he was given to read were inhibiting his reading development.

Instructional Level

An element of effective instruction in both decoding and encoding is to provide students with books that they are able to read independently and words that they are able to learn for spelling. Betts (1946) described three levels of reading material: 1) the independent level (99% accuracy), 2) the instructional level (95% accuracy), and 3) the frustration level (below 90% accuracy). In other words, out of 100 words, a student should mispronounce only 1 to be at the independent level and no more than 5 to be at the instructional level. This procedure has sometimes been referred to as the rule of thumb for choosing student texts. The teacher counts out a 100-word passage. As the child reads, the teacher presses down a finger each time that an error is made, starting with the little finger and moving toward the thumb. If the thumb is reached before the passage has been completed, the material is too difficult for the student. Although motivation and interest also play a major role in students' willingness to read, these high values indicate that readers must be familiar with the majority of words for a text to be at an appropriate level.

Many students with reading disabilities spend the entire school day facing text that is at their frustration level. If teachers give all children in the classroom the same textbook, it is invariably too easy for some and too difficult for others. Betts (1946) provided the following description of rigid and prescriptive instruction:

> Once upon a time there was a third-grade teacher who was proud of the fact that she knew third-grade work and little about the nature of the experiences which came before or after. Now this teacher was immensely proud to be a specialist—she also might have been elated to be one of the three blind men who so surely described the elephant. Having some

doubt in her mind regarding certain children in the room, she called in the researchers. By using a graded series of readers, these scientists found some children who could read with understanding nothing above a preprimer, the other pupils ranging from first- to average sixth-grade ability.

When the evidence was placed before this teacher, she irately exclaimed to the principal, "See I knew that Miss So-and-So, the second-grade teacher, was sending me some children who were not ready for my third-grade work." During the ensuing conversation, it was explained that she had a somewhat typical third grade, composed of children who varied above as well as below the ability of the average third-grade child.

But the conversation did not end here…. After some explanation, she understood that because she only knew how to teach one third of the pupils, perhaps she should return $800 of her $1,200 salary to the school and that she should pay also an additional $800 for confusing the lower third of the class with third-grade materials and for failing to challenge the upper third with materials at their level. It took no specialist in mathematics to prove to this able teacher that she really owed the community $400 per year for the privilege of teaching in the school. (pp. 542–543)

For both home and school reading, consider each student's reading level when you attempt to match books to his or her present skill level. Fountas and Pinnell (1999) provided a list of books for use in kindergarten through third grade organized by level of difficulty. Word counts are presented for most books. Although students with severe reading disabilities need to engage in authentic reading activities as part of their reading program, they also need to practice their developing skills using decodable text.

Decodable Text

Students with reading disabilities need extensive practice in applying their knowledge of grapheme–phoneme relationships to the task of reading (Grossen, 1997). The examples of programs described previously all include what is referred to as decodable text. When students are learning to read using a synthetic or analytic phonics approach, they need to practice the skills being taught in short passages that are controlled, or easily decodable. Decodable text consists primarily of words with regular grapheme–phoneme relationships and a few sight words that have been taught systematically. This type of text allows beginning readers to integrate their knowledge in the context of connected reading and to practice and apply their developing knowledge of grapheme–phoneme correspondences to text. These materials are not to be viewed as a replacement for authentic, high-interest text but rather as a component of decoding instruction for reinforcing instruction in grapheme–phoneme relationships. One example of a set of decodable texts that teachers can copy and that students can color are EZ2 Read Decodable Books. (See Additional Resources.)

Read Well   One example of a research-based primary reading program that uses decodable text is *Read Well* (Sprick, Howard, & Fidanque, 1998). This program provides systematic phonics instruction and fully decodable text and integrates reading and writing, including oral and written comprehension activities. The program provides expanded units for students who perform at a lower level and procedures for ongoing assessment for guiding instructional decisions. One of the nice features of this program is that decodable words are presented in large print, whereas words that are more difficult to pronounce are written in small print to be read by the teacher.

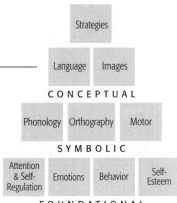

High-Frequency Words

One way to help students with reading and spelling is to focus on high-frequency words, the words that are most commonly used in writing. Some people refer to these words as sight words because they are supposed to be recognized instantly and easily without an analysis of sounds. As noted by Ehri (1998), with sufficient practice, all words acquire the status of sight words.

Instant Words The most systematic way to work on high-frequency words is to provide practice with a carefully developed list of words. Edward Fry's list of 300 Instant Words (Fry, 1977) makes up about 60% of the words used in written material (see the appendix to this chapter). This list may be used to teach students high-frequency words for reading and spelling.

As an informal assessment, a teacher may ask a student to read the words starting at the beginning of the list and to continue reading until an error is made. Instruction then begins at the point where the student does not immediately recognize or does not know how to spell a word. Next, the teacher can establish a program to help the student master the unknown words. This type of program does not need to be time consuming. An effective program can be conducted using only 10 minutes daily. The student starts at the beginning of the list and reads as many words as he or she can within 1 minute. After the minute, the teacher records the number of words read and then reviews any words that were not recognized instantly. A graph may be used to monitor progress. For the next few minutes, the student can practice spelling several of the unknown words and then review these words the following day. The teacher or student then checks off each word after the student has learned to read and spell it.

Flashcards Students who have difficulty with memorizing benefit from rehearsal, review, and repetition as well as from immediate feedback. Some students benefit from creating flashcards, particularly when extensive memorization is required. These cards should be viewed frequently for short periods of time. Several types of memorization software programs that may be used to create either virtual or printed flashcards with questions and answers are reviewed at http://www.quingle.com/softarea/flash.htm

Flow List One way to orchestrate an individualized spelling program is to use a flow list, or a list that changes as a student learns to spell words. This is a different procedure than using a fixed list, such as the kind that many teachers use for the weekly spelling test. The purpose of using a spelling flow list is to provide systematic instruction and review to promote mastery of spelling words. This type of procedure, adapted from McCoy and Prehm (1987), was used to help Ben improve his spelling skills when he was in fifth grade.

Ben was still misspelling basic common words, such as *they.* His teacher used the following steps:

1. Ben would identify six words that he uses in his writing but spells incorrectly. He could select the words either from his writing or from a high-frequency word list, such as the list presented in the appendix to this chapter.

2. The selected words were placed on the spelling flow list form.

3. Ben would study the words and then his teacher would test him daily on the words.

4. Ben's teacher marked each correctly spelled word with a *C* and each incorrect word with a check.

Spelling Flow List

Name: <u>Ben</u>   Starting Date: <u>11/12</u>

Study word	M	T	W	TH	F	M	T	W	TH	F	M	T	W	TH	F
they	C	C	C				C								
said	C	√	√	C	C	C						√			
people	√	C	C	C					√						
would	√	C	√	C	C	C						√			
could	√	C	C	C				C						C	
should	√	C	C	C				C						C	
were			√	C	C	C						C			√
any				C	√	√	C	C	C						C
people										√	C	C	√	√	C
said											C	√	C		C
would											C	C	C		
every											C	C	C		
busy														√	√
because															√
any															C
friend															C

C = Correct

√ = Incorrect

Figure 9.6. Sample spelling flow list.

5. When a word was spelled correctly 3 days in a row, it would be crossed off the list, and a new word would be added. Ben would file all correct words alphabetically into a word bank.

6. One week later, Ben's teacher would check to make sure that he still knew how to spell words added to the bank. If a word was incorrect, Ben would add the word back on his list. A sample form is presented in Figure 9.6.

Struthers, Bartlamay, Dell, and McLaughlin (1994) investigated the use of an Add-A-Word spelling program for students with spelling difficulties. In this program, students had individualized words presented on a flow list instead of a fixed spelling list. When the spelling of a word was correct on three consecutive daily tests, the word was replaced by another. The dropped words were retested at a later date. When mastery was demonstrated, they were removed from the list. The results of the study indicated that this type of procedure was more effective for struggling students than having traditional weekly spelling tests.

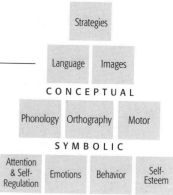

This procedure could also be adapted to learning sight words. Write or have the students write high-frequency words on cards. Have the students practice these words and then test the students on them daily. When a student identifies word 3 days in a row correctly, file the word or have the student file the word in the student's word bank. A week later, review the word and replace it on the list for additional review, if needed.

Personalized Dictionary Some students with spelling difficulties can benefit from keeping an individualized spelling dictionary that contains their own frequently misspelled words. Each letter of the alphabet is written in order on a separate page. In their dictionary, students then write words that they use in their writing but have difficulty spelling. They may then consult their dictionaries when writing or when editing.

Scheuermann, Jacobs, McCall, and Knies (1994) described the following process for making and using a personal spelling dictionary: 1) obtain a pocketsize notebook, 2) tab the pages in alphabetical order, and 3) if desired, laminate each page. Students may then write words on file folder labels to allow for easy removal once the words have been learned. As an alternative, students can use *A Spelling Dictionary for Beginning Writers* (Hurray, 1993). This dictionary contains the words most commonly used by novice writers. Another example is *Quick Word* (Sitton & Forest, 1994). This dictionary includes preprinted high-frequency words and provides blank spaces so that students can add words. Ben found that the easiest and quickest way to locate and correct misspelled words was to use his personalized dictionary.

Backward Spelling Another activity that may help students such as Ben learn to form more complete orthographic images is backward spelling (Glenn & Hurley, 1993). For this procedure, a word is presented on a card and the student is asked to look at the word, look away from the card and attempt to visualize the word, and then check back and forth to confirm that the visualization is correct. Next, the card is turned over, and the student is asked to visualize the word and then spell the word forward and then backward. Backward spelling involves working memory and is only possible if the student forms a complete image of all of the graphemes in the word (Apel & Swank, 1999). In turn, the ability to form a complete mental image of a word promotes the development of a sight vocabulary and reading fluency.

Self-Monitoring Students should also be encouraged to monitor their own spelling development. If spelling tests are used, students can examine any missed words to determine what part of the word is incorrect. Were letters omitted or extra letters added? Misspelled words may also be taken from writing assignments and analyzed. Figure 9.7 depicts a sample self-monitoring form. By analyzing the parts of the words they are misspelling, students can focus on the specific orthographic patterns that occur within high frequency words, such as the -*dge* or -*tch* spelling pattern.

Multisensory Procedures

Many of the programs designed for helping students with reading and writing problems are multisensory in nature. This means that the type of instruction incorporates abilities from all three symbolic blocks: phonological, orthographic, and motor. The student is encouraged to look at the word, say the word, and trace the word. This type of procedure helps students with weaknesses in one or more of these blocks. Naming letters and words while tracing binds the orthographic, motor, and phonological images of the letter together at once (Adams, 1990). When Ryan traced each spelling word several times and then practiced writing

Spelling Self-Monitoring Form

Name _____   Spelling self-analysis score _____   Pretest score _____   Posttest score _____

List word	Attempted spelling	Missing letters	Extra letters	Letters in wrong order	Cover list word and rewrite correct spelling

Figure 9.7.   Sample spelling self-monitoring form.

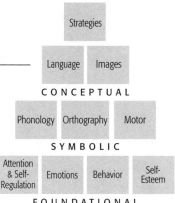

the word from memory, he was able to recall the words on his spelling flow list more easily. The majority of these techniques involve three components: 1) multisensory word study, 2) emphasis on visual imagery, and 3) writing the word from memory.

Fernald Method One example of a multisensory technique is called the Fernald Method (Fernald, 1943). Fernald stressed the importance of providing children with meaningful reading and writing activities. As she so aptly observed, "The child is much more interested in writing and reading fairly difficult material that is on the level of his understanding than simpler material which is below his mental age level" (p. 44). The method she created has been used effectively to teach struggling readers of all ages. The Fernald Method provides instruction aimed simultaneously at the phonological, orthographic, and motor blocks. Because the method involves tracing, it can actually help children increase their abilities to picture words using the skills of the orthographic block. The technique ensures that the student pays attention to the details of the word.

The Fernald Method is appropriate for students who have failed to learn to read with other instructional methods. This method consists of four stages through which students progress as their skill increases. Before starting, explain to the student that he or she will be shown a new way to learn words that has been successful with other learners.

In the first stage, the student selects a word that he or she cannot read but would like to learn. Discuss the meaning of the word with the student and then use the following steps to teach the word:

1. Write the word. Sit beside the student and ask the student to watch and listen while you 1) say the word, 2) use a crayon to write the word in large print in manuscript or cursive (depending on which writing style the child uses) on an index card, and 3) say the word again while running a finger underneath the word.

2. Model word tracing. Say, "Watch what I do and listen to what I say." Use the following steps: 1) say the word; 2) trace the word using one or two fingers, saying each part of the word while tracing it; and 3) say the word again while running a finger underneath the word. Have the student practice tracing the word using these steps.

3. Have the student continue tracing the word until he or she can write the word from memory. Remind the student to say each part of the word while tracing it.

4. Have the student attempt to write the word from memory. When the student feels ready, remove the model and ask the student to write the word from memory. Make sure the student says the word while writing. If at any point the student makes an error, stop him or her immediately, cover the error, and model the tracing procedure again before proceeding.

5. File the word. After the student writes the word correctly three times without the model, have the student file the word in a word bank alphabetically to practice on a later date.

Although a few students continue to need tracing for word learning, most individuals progress through three more stages when using this method. By the second stage, the student no longer needs to trace words and can learn a word by looking at the word after you write it, saying the word, and then writing it. By the third stage, the student is able to learn new words directly from printed words without having them written. When reading with the student, tell him or her any unknown words. After reading, have the student review and write the unknown words. By the fourth stage, most students begin to notice similarities between unknown and known words and can recognize many new words without being told what they are.

A helpful technique is to ask the student to glance over a paragraph and underline any unknown words before reading. Tell the student how to pronounce the words and then ask the student to trace the words and then write the words from memory. This type of tracing technique is particularly useful for students such as Ryan and Ben, who have weaknesses in orthography and difficulty remembering how to spell commonly used words. Words may be selected from a high-frequency list or an assigned spelling list. Use the following procedures, adapted from Fernald (1943), for spelling:

1. Have the student select the word to learn.

2. Write the word on a card.

3. Pronounce the word clearly and distinctly. Ask the student to repeat the pronunciation while looking at the word.

4. Provide the student with time to develop a visual image of the word. A student who learns visually is encouraged to form a mental picture of the word; a student who learns auditorally is encouraged to say the word slowly; and a student with motor strengths is encouraged to trace the word with his or her finger.

5. When the student says that the word is known, erase or cover the word and have the student attempt to write the word from memory. If the word is incorrect, return to Step 3. If the word is correct, cover it and have the student write the word another time from memory.

Cover–Write Methods   Other remedial spelling methods use similar multisensory techniques to help students with word learning. As noted previously, these cover–write methods are most useful for students such as Ryan and Ben who have difficulty with forming and retrieving word images. Most of these methods include some variation of the following steps:

1. Select a word for the student to learn. Write the word on a card and pronounce it.

2. Have the student look at the word and then pronounce it.

3. Have the student say the letter sounds while tracing each letter.

4. Have the student continue to pronounce the word while tracing it several times.

5. Have the student turn over the word and then pronounce the word while writing it on paper. If the word is spelled incorrectly, repeat Step 4.

Continue the process until the student can write the word correctly three times.

READING FLUENCY

Reading fluency encompasses the speed or rate of reading as well as the ability to read materials with expression. Meyer and Felton (1999) defined fluency as "the ability to read connected text rapidly, smoothly, effortlessly, and automatically with little conscious attention to the mechanics of reading, such as decoding" (p.

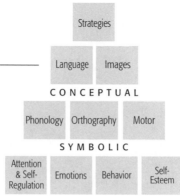

284). The core cognitive correlates of reading fluency involve rapid automatized naming, orthographic processing, attention, and lexical retrieval (Fletcher et al., 2007). Children are successful with decoding when the process used to identify words is fast and nearly effortless or automatic. As noted, the concept of automaticity refers to a student's ability to recognize words rapidly with little attention required to the word's appearance. The ability to read words by sight automatically is the key to skilled reading (Ehri, 1998).

Some children have developed accurate word pronunciation skills but read slowly. For these children, decoding is not automatic or fluent, and their limited fluency may affect performance in the following ways: 1) they read less text than peers and have less time to remember, review, or comprehend the text; 2) they expend more cognitive energy than peers trying to identify individual words; and 3) they may be less able to retain text in their memories and less likely to integrate those segments with other parts of the text (Mastropieri, Leinart, & Scruggs, 1999).

When Maria was in sixth grade, she still read very slowly. Although she pronounced most words correctly, she read with little expression. She complained that because she read so slowly, she could not understand what she was reading. She usually had to read materials several times in order to comprehend them. Students such as Maria, Ryan, and Ben require more exposures and more practice to recognize individual words easily and automatically. Even into middle school, these students often devote an inordinate amount of energy to word identification.

Determining a Student's Reading Rate

A student's reading rate may be calculated by dividing the number of words read correctly by the total amount of reading time. Count out 100 words in a passage and then time the student as he or she reads the passage. In the fall of sixth grade, Maria was given a passage to read with 100 words. She read 92 words correctly in 1.5 minutes, or 61 words per minute (wpm). Hasbrouck and Tindal (2005) completed an extensive study of oral reading fluency in 2004. The results of their study are published in a technical report titled, "Oral Reading Fluency: 90 Years of Measurement," which is available on the University of Oregon's web site(http://www.brtprojects.org/tech_reports.htm).

Table 9.1 shows the oral reading fluency rates for students in the fall, winter, and spring of Grades 1–8 as determined by Hasbrouck and Tindal's (2005) study. The information in this table can be used to draw conclusions and make decisions about the oral reading fluency of students. Students scoring below the 50th percentile using the average score of two unpracticed readings from grade-level materials need a fluency-building program. In addition, teachers can use the table to set the long-term fluency goals for their students who are struggling with reading.

In Table 9.1, average weekly improvement is shown by the average growth per week in words that can be expected from a student. It was calculated by subtracting the fall score from the spring score and dividing the difference by 32, the typical number of weeks between the fall and spring assessments. For Grade 1, because there is no fall assessment, the average weekly improvement was calculated by subtracting the winter score from the spring score and dividing the difference by 16, the typical number of weeks between the winter and spring assessments. Analysis of the Hasbrouck and Tindal table reveals that Maria is reading at much slower rate than many of her peers.

Adjusting Reading Rate

Most people have a constant rate when reading. This rate is the fastest pace at which a person can understand complete thoughts in successive sentences of

Table 9.1. Hasbrouck and Tindal (2005) Oral Reading Fluency data

Grade	Percentile	Fall WCPM*	Winter WCPM*	Spring WCPM*	Average weekly improvement**
	90	–	81	111	1.9
	75	–	47	82	2.2
1	50	–	23	53	1.9
	25	–	12	28	1.0
	10	–	6	15	0.6
2	90	106	125	142	1.1
	75	79	100	117	1.2
	50	51	72	89	1.2
	25	25	42	61	1.1
	10	11	18	31	0.6
3	90	128	146	162	1.1
	75	99	120	137	1.2
	50	71	92	107	1.1
	25	44	62	78	1.1
	10	21	36	48	0.8
4	90	145	166	180	1.1
	75	119	139	152	1.0
	50	94	112	123	0.9
	25	68	87	98	0.9
	10	45	61	72	0.8
5	90	166	182	194	0.9
	75	139	156	168	0.9
	50	110	127	139	0.9
	25	85	99	109	0.8
	10	61	74	83	0.7
6	90	177	195	204	0.8
	75	153	167	177	0.8
	50	127	140	150	0.7
	25	98	111	122	0.8
	10	68	82	93	0.8
7	90	180	192	202	0.7
	75	156	165	177	0.7
	50	128	136	150	0.7
	25	102	109	123	0.7
	10	79	88	98	0.6
8	90	185	199	199	0.4
	75	161	173	177	0.5
	50	133	146	151	0.6
	25	106	115	124	0.6
	10	77	84	97	0.6

From: Hasbrouck, J., & Tindal, G. (2005). *Oral reading fluency: 90 years of measurement* (Tech. Rep. No. 33). Eugene, Oregon: University of Oregon, College of Education, Behavioral Research and Teaching; reprinted with permission.

*WCPM = Words Correct per Minute.

**Average words per week improvement. Average weekly improvement is the average words per week growth you can expect from a student. It was calculated by subtracting the fall score from the spring score and dividing the difference by 32, the typical number of weeks between the fall and spring assessments. For grade 1, because there is no fall assessment, the average weekly improvement was calculated by subtracting the winter score from the spring score and dividing the difference by 16, the typical number of weeks between the winter and spring assessments.

relatively easy material. As long as the material is relatively easy to read, a person's rate stays constant. For different types of tasks, however, readers often alter their rate. Students with slow reading rates are often not aware that good readers adjust their rate depending on the purpose of reading. Making these types of adjustments is particularly important for a student with poor reading skills

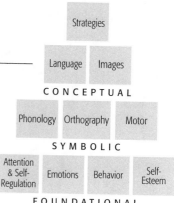

when studying or completing assigned readings because otherwise he or she will struggle to complete lengthy reading assignments.

Carver (1990) used the analogy of adjusting reading speed to the shifting of gears in a car. First and second gears are the slowest, most powerful gears. First gear is used to memorize material. Second gear is used to learn material. Third gear is the typical reading rate. The fourth gear, skimming, and the fifth gear, scanning, are the fastest but least powerful gears. These gears are useful for locating a specific piece of information or trying to get the general sense of a passage without reading every word.

Adult readers monitor their reading pace and shift gears depending on the goals. If one is trying to memorize material for a test, the reading pace is slow and reflective, characterized by stopping and reviewing the material. If one is reading a novel for pleasure, the pace is steady and fluent. If one is searching for information in a catalog, the pace is rapid. Skilled readers know how to adjust the gears of their reading rate based on the purpose for reading.

Some children have not learned how to adjust their reading rates; they attempt to read information in an encyclopedia at the same pace that they read a novel. To help develop increased reading speed, encourage students to adjust their rate depending on the purpose of reading. Students can practice skimming through a chapter to get a sense of the information and then moving through the chapter more slowly to study for the weekly test. Model for the students how to change one's rate of reading for different types of materials.

Instructional Activities for Increasing Reading Rate

Teachers often describe students who would benefit from methods to increase reading speed as slow, laborious readers who read word-by-word with limited expression. Instructional activities for increasing reading rate are most useful with students who have acquired some proficiency in decoding skill but whose level of decoding skill is lower than their oral language abilities. Methods for increasing reading rate have several common features: 1) students listen to text as they follow along with the book, 2) students follow the print using their fingers as guides, and 3) reading materials are used that students would be unable to read independently. In addition, most of the fluency procedures involve repeated exposures to words with material at the student's instructional reading level (Fletcher et al., 2007). Chard and Osborn (1999a) suggested that a beginning reading program should provide opportunities for partner reading, practice reading difficult words prior to reading the text, timings for accuracy and rate, opportunities to hear books read, and opportunities to read to others. The following methods for increasing fluency are easy to use.

Speed Drills   For reading lists of words with a speed drill and a 1-minute timing, Fischer (1999) suggested using the following general guidelines: 30 correct wpm for first- and second-grade children; 40 correct wpm for beginning third-grade children; 60 correct wpm for mid–third grade; and 80 wpm for students in fourth grade and higher. To conduct a speed drill, the student reads a list of words for 1 minute as the number of errors is recorded. The list may be a high-frequency word list or the sample speed drills provided in Fischer's program, Concept Phonics (see Additional Resources). These drills are designed to develop automatic sight recognition of words.

Rapid Word Recognition Chart   An easy way to improve speed of recognition for words with an irregular element is the use of a rapid word recognition chart (Carreker, 2005). The chart is similar to a rapid serial naming task. It is a matrix that contains five rows of six exception words (e.g., *who, said*), with each row containing the same six words in a different order. After a brief review of the words and a warm-up during which the teacher points randomly to 8 to 10 words on the chart, students are timed for 1 minute as they read the words in the squares aloud. Students can then count and record the number of words they have read correctly. This type of procedure can help students such as Ben recognize words with irregular orthographic patterns more quickly.

Great Leaps Reading Program   *Great Leaps Reading Program* (Campbell, 1998, 2005) was designed to help students build reading speed. One-minute timings employ three stimuli: phonics, sight phrases, and reading short stories. Before beginning this program, teachers assess the student's present reading level. Instruction begins at the level within the program at which reading speed is slow and the student makes several errors. After recording the time, the teacher reviews the errors with the student and discusses strategies that they can use to improve performance. Performance is charted on graphs so that both students and teachers can keep track of progress. The program takes approximately 10 minutes per day. A K–2 version of this program provides a phonological awareness instruction component (Mercer & Campbell, 1998). Results from one study indicate that daily application of this program with middle school students with LD contributed to growth in reading and an improvement in reading rate (Mercer, Campbell, Miller, Mercer, & Lane, 2000).

Wilson Reading Fluency/Basic   *Wilson Fluency/Basic*™ (Wilson Language Training, 2006) is a supplemental fluency program for students in early grades who are learning to read as well as older students who are struggling to learn to read. Wilson Fluency/Basic provides students with practice reading connected text so that they can develop rate-appropriate independent reading with ease and expression. The program includes four readers that focus on short vowel words with several 200–250 word passages composed of 90% decodable text.

Choral Reading or Neurological Impress Method   The neurological impress method (Heckelman, 1969, 1986) is a method for choral or concert reading. In this method, a teacher and student read aloud together for 10–15 minutes daily. To begin, select a high-interest book or a content-area textbook from the classroom. Sit next to the student and read aloud as you point to the words with your index finger. Read at a slightly faster pace than the student and encourage him or her to try and keep up with you. When necessary, remind the student to keep his or her eyes on the words. Successful decoding requires the reader to connect the flow of spoken language with the flow of text (Carreker, 2005). Reading aloud with students can help them to practice phrasing and intonation.

Repeated Reading   The repeated reading technique is designed for children who read slowly despite adequate word recognition (Samuels, 1979). For this procedure, a child reads the same passage over and over again until a desired level of fluency is attained. To begin, the teacher may select an interesting passage that is 50–100 words long from a book that is slightly above the student's independent reading level. The teacher has the student read the selection orally while he or she times the reading and counts the number of words that are pronounced incorrectly. The teacher then records the reading time and the number of words pronounced incorrectly. If desired, the teacher and student can set a realistic goal for speed and number of errors.

Figure 9.8 presents a sample recording form to use for repeated reading. The teacher may use two different color pencils for recording time and errors or a circle to indicate points on the line for time and an X or a square to indicate

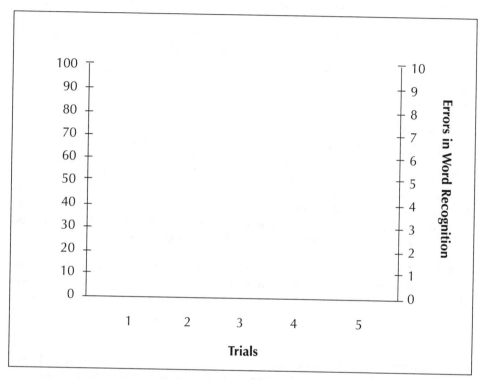

Repeated Reading Graph

Name: _____

Book: _____

Date: _____

Strategies

Language   Images

C O N C E P T U A L

Phonology   Orthography   Motor

S Y M B O L I C

Attention & Self-Regulation   Emotions   Behavior   Self-Esteem

F O U N D A T I O N A L

Errors in Word Recognition

Trials

Figure 9.8.   Sample repeated reading graph.

points on the line for errors. Between timings, the teacher may ask the student to look over the selection, reread it, and practice words that caused difficulty in the initial reading. When the student is ready, he or she rereads the same passage. Once again, the teacher times the reading, and records the time and number of errors. The student repeatedly practices reading the selection as the teacher charts progress after each trial until a predetermined goal is reached or until the student is able to read the passage fluently with few mistakes. Research on repeated reading suggests that fluency can be improved as long as students are provided with specific instructions and procedures are used to monitor their progress (Mastropieri et al., 1999). An easy way to monitor student performance using this chart is for the teacher to keep a log of the dated charts. To control for a similar readability level, the teacher may select the passages to read from the same book. As performance improves, the time to perform the initial reading should decrease.

Repeated reading has also been used as a component of classwide peer tutoring (Mathes & Fuchs, 1993). In a study of this intervention, pairs of students in one group read continuously over a 10-minute period, whereas pairs of students in the other group read a passage together three times before going on to the next passage. Although both experimental conditions produced higher results than the typical reading instruction, no difference existed between the procedures, suggesting that the main benefit of the intervention is the student reading involvement and the increased time spent in reading (Mastropieri et al., 1999).

In a review of the effectiveness of repeated reading, Meyer and Felton (1999) concluded that the method of repeated reading improves reading speed for a wide variety of readers. They made the following recommendations for helping students to improve fluency: 1) have students engage in multiple readings (three to four times); 2) use instructional level text; 3) use decodable text with struggling readers; 4) provide short, frequent periods of fluency practice; and 5) provide concrete measures of progress. Base the amount of teacher guidance on each individual's characteristics. With students with poor reading skills, modeling and practicing of words between readings improve student performance and reduce frustration.

Previewing   Previewing is a technique similar to repeated reading, involving preexposure to materials before they are formally read (Rose, 1984). For this type of procedure, a student can preview the material silently, or you may read the passage aloud as the student follows along, or the student may first listen to the recorded passage on tape. Rose and Sherry (1984) found that both silent previewing and teacher-directed previewing were more effective than no previewing. Maria found that, by hearing the passage before she was asked to read it, she made fewer errors and was more successful reading the text.

Taped Books   Another way to help students practice reading is to use audiorecorded books. Have the student listen to the reading while he or she follows along with an unabridged copy of the book. Most public libraries provide a wide selection of recorded books for loan.

When Maria was in fifth grade, she was interested in horses. Her mother would take her to the library, and they would check out books and the corresponding CDs. Each evening, she would listen to classic stories about horses as she followed along with the text.

If a student has been identified as having LD or dyslexia, taped books are available from Recording for the Blind & Dyslexic® (RFB&D). This national, nonprofit organization provides textbooks for individuals who are unable to read standard print because of visual, physical, or perceptual disabilities. The extensive tape library has educational books that range from upper-elementary to postgraduate level. If a book is unavailable, an individual may request that it be recorded, and, if it fits within the scope of the collection, the book will be recorded. (Information for contacting RFB&D is provided in Additional Resources.)

Some commercial recordings, such as those obtained at the public library, go too fast for individuals with reading disabilities. In addition, because younger and struggling readers lose their place quite frequently, it is important to have a procedure for relocating the place at the top of each page. Many teachers prefer to make their own recordings of books so that they can select materials that are of high interest to students and control the rate of delivery.

Carbo Method   Carbo (1989) developed procedures for recording books to achieve maximum gains in fluency. A brief description of how to record books using this method is described:

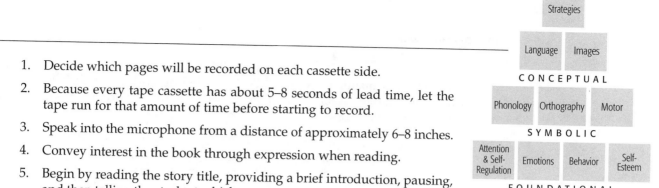

1. Decide which pages will be recorded on each cassette side.

2. Because every tape cassette has about 5–8 seconds of lead time, let the tape run for that amount of time before starting to record.

3. Speak into the microphone from a distance of approximately 6–8 inches.

4. Convey interest in the book through expression when reading.

5. Begin by reading the story title, providing a brief introduction, pausing, and then telling the student which page to turn to. Pause long enough so that the reader has enough time to turn pages and look at pictures.

6. Tell the student when to turn the page. In order not to distract from the content, soften your voice slightly when stating a page number.

7. Read the story in logical phrases, slowly enough so that most students can follow along but not so slowly that they become bored.

8. End each tape with, "Please rewind the tape for the next listener. This ends this recording."

As general guidelines, record 5–15 minutes at a typical pace for instructional level material and have the student listen to the tape once. For difficult material, record no more than 2 minutes at a slow pace with good expression and have the student listen to the passage two or three times. After listening, have the student read the passage aloud.

Read Naturally Another program designed to build fluency in students from mid–first through sixth grade is called *Read Naturally* (see Additional Resources). Instruction is individualized and involves three main steps: 1) reading along with an audiorecording of a story that provides a model of fluent reading; 2) intensive, repeated practice to build speed and accuracy; and 3) monitoring and evaluating performance through graphing. To use the program, students are placed into an appropriate level on the basis of their oral reading fluency. The sequenced reading levels range from beginning reading to sixth-grade level with 24 stories available for each level. In addition, the lower level materials have been translated into Spanish.

Fluency methods are designed to increase rate and automaticity. They should be taught as a part of an effective reading program along with instruction in phonological awareness and decoding in the younger grades and vocabulary and comprehension in all grades (Stahl & Stahl, 2004). Methods to increase rate are particularly beneficial for students such as Maria and Ben who have strong conceptual abilities but poor automaticity because of weaknesses within their phonological or orthographic abilities. These repeated readings of words and text provide repeated exposures that facilitate word mastery and automaticity. They can help a student move from Ehri's (1998) full alphabetic stage to the consolidated alphabetic stage, in which word learning is accomplished more easily.

CALCULATING

Parallels can be drawn among the developments of decoding, encoding, and calculating skills. Acquisition of basic math skills may be affected by problems similar to those that affect decoding and encoding. A student who has trouble with memorizing basic math facts and developing numerical facility often has trouble solving mathematical problems. Students with math disabilities tend to have trouble retrieving basic math facts from memory, use procedures that are more commonly used by younger children, and tend to make more procedural errors (Geary, 2003).

More advanced levels of mathematics require rapid and accurate handling of numerical quantities (Carroll, 1993). Carroll defined *numerical facility*, which he identifies as *Factor N*, and explained the importance of this ability to mathematical thinking:

> Factor N refers simply to the degree to which the individual has developed skills in dealing with numbers, from the most elementary skills of counting objects and recognizing written numbers and their order, to the more advanced skills of correctly adding, subtracting, multiplying, and dividing numbers with an increasing number of digits, or with fractions and decimals. These are skills that are learned through experiences in the home, school, or even in the workplace. (p. 469)

Carroll also explained the importance of this facility:

> In the early years, skills deal with simple numbers and operations, and the important object is to be able to deal with number problems correctly, at whatever speed. In later years, practice is aimed at handling computations with greater speed as well as accuracy. More complex problems can be dealt with effectively and efficiently only if skills with simple problems are increasingly automatized. (p. 469)

Just as with decoding and encoding, the lower level skills of calculating must become increasingly automatized so that one may devote attention to problem solving.

Ryan's confusion with symbols extended into mathematics. He often reversed or transposed numbers (e.g., writing 12 for 21). He had trouble with memorizing multiplication facts. He confused the directionality of symbols (e.g., the symbol for less than [<] and the symbol for greater than [>]), and he had trouble recalling the procedures for multiple steps, such as the steps required for long division. As with instruction in decoding and encoding, Ryan needed math instruction that was sequential, systematic, and multisensory in nature.

Failure in computation first occurs when the instruction is inappropriate or too limited to develop the skill being taught. Even though Ryan had only scored 30% correct on the chapter review, he was assigned problems from the next chapter along with his classmates. Unfortunately, Ryan was not experiencing immediate and continual success in his math program. With every chapter, he fell further behind. Ideally, a student should master concepts and skills before moving on to new information or the next chapter. This is not, however, always the case. When a teacher tries to keep all children in a classroom on the same page of a textbook, the pace becomes too fast for some and too slow for others.

Early Concepts

Just as the beginning reader/writer needs to acquire alphabetic knowledge, the beginning math student needs to acquire basic concepts for numeracy development. Some children acquire fundamental math skills in the preschool years. Maria always excelled in math, and, by the time she entered kindergarten, she could count from 1 to 100 and add and subtract using objects. Learning number concepts was easy for Maria.

One-to-One Correspondence   Accurate counting is based on the concept of one-to-one correspondence. This means that one object in a group is

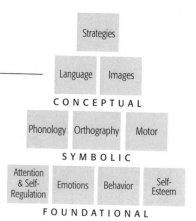

Strategies

Language | Images

CONCEPTUAL

Phonology | Orthography | Motor

SYMBOLIC

Attention & Self-Regulation | Emotions | Behavior | Self-Esteem

FOUNDATIONAL

represented by one number and that two sets of objects with the same number can be matched. In other words, two cookies can be matched to two glasses of milk. Children soon begin to realize that as each object is added to a set, the number increases by one. Most children master this concept between the ages of 4 and 5.

When Stephanie was in first grade, she was still having trouble with accurate counting. When given 10 objects to count, she would go around in a circle and count each object several times. She had trouble with remembering which ones she had already counted. Her teacher decided to line up the objects horizontally and have her count slowly as she pointed to each object in the line. Gradually, she moved objects more and more away from a straight line. She encouraged Stephanie to touch each object as she counted it and to push it slightly away from the group.

An abacus can also be used for additional practice. Touching and moving the beads reinforces the concept of one-to-one correspondence and helps a student develop an initial understanding of place value.

Drill For cases in which a student has trouble with memory, daily trials may increase the speed and accuracy of recall. One way to help the student become more automatic with math facts is to practice with flashcards. First, identify the facts that the student does not know. Then practice three unknown facts at a time. Present the card and ask the student to respond. If the response takes longer than 2 seconds, tell the student the answer and move on to the next card. Once the student has mastered these three facts, place them in a pile for review on the following day. As an alternative to requiring an oral response, place three answers on the table and have the student point to the correct response. Once he or she can do this successfully, present the cards one at a time. When working with a student with weaknesses in memory, you may need to reduce the number of facts the student is expected to learn at any one time and repeat and practice the facts more often. Make a math flow list, similar to the spelling flow list, and do daily testing of a few facts. When the student remembers the fact correctly 3 days in a row, the fact can be removed from the list and then reviewed 1 week later. Research results support the importance of ongoing monitoring of performance coupled with student goal setting and feedback on fact retrieval (Fletcher et al., 2007).

The use of 1-Minute Timings is another evidence-based practice for increasing fluency with math computations (Miller & Hudson, 2007). Miller and Hudson describe the following procedure:

1. Provide students with a worksheet of problems that cannot typically be completed within 1 minute.

2. Tell students to begin and complete as many problems as they can within the minute.

3. Tell students to stop after 1 minute.

4. Score the sheet by counting the number of correct and incorrect digits written.

5. Plot the total number of correct digits on a graph.

Students may then review errors with the teacher or a peer or correct errors with a calculator.

Peer tutoring has also been used to help students improve math computation skill. In a meta-analysis of peer-mediated interventions, Kunsch, Jitendra, and Sood (2007) found that peer-mediated interventions were most effective for helping elementary-age students at risk for math failure improve computation skill in general education classrooms. Interventions were not as effective for addressing higher order mathematical skills.

Fact Charts A pocket-sized fact chart can also help students overcome computational weaknesses. Unlike a calculator, in which only one fact is viewed at a time, the chart allows students to view a full set of facts. Finding the same fact in the same location reinforces learning of the math fact. When facts have been mastered, they may be blackened over or removed from the pocket chart. Remember that the difference between students with weaknesses in memory and other learners is not the process by which they learn but rather the number of trials necessary for mastery. Patience, persistence, and frequent praise are essential in helping to motivate students to stick with it even though mastery may seem to be a slow, laborious process.

Software Many software programs are available to help students practice and master basic math facts. Some provide an engaging game format. Some students are more willing to practice with computers than with teachers. One nice thing about the computer is that it has unlimited patience.

One example is Math Flash (Fuchs, Hamlett, & Powell, 2003). In this program, the computer briefly displays a math fact, such as $8 \times 7 = 56$; then, after the prompt disappears, the student types the fact into the computer. If the fact is correct, it remains on the screen, the computer says the fact aloud, and the student receives points and prizes. If the response is incorrect, the student's response disappears and the computer says and shows the correct fact for the student to attempt again. The duration of the flash is increased or decreased depending on a student's performance during the session.

Multisensory Procedures

As with decoding and encoding, children with weaknesses in the processing blocks often benefit from a multisensory approach to learning math facts. Similar to teaching reading and spelling, the abilities of the symbolic blocks are used to aid memorization. Students may need different approaches depending on their learning styles. Maria found it easiest to learn math facts if she would say the fact aloud while looking at it; Ben needed to look at the fact, say it, trace it, and then write it.

For many children, the act of saying the facts and then trying to write them from memory enhances learning. As with teaching spelling, encourage students to write answers from memory rather than simply copying. Use this simple procedure:

1. Have the student look at a fact with the answer.

2. Have the student say the fact. (Have the student say and trace the fact, if needed.)

3. Remove the fact.

4. Ask the student to say and write the fact and the answer.

5. Hold up the fact, and have the student check it.

Touch Points For students who make frequent errors in computation but understand the basic operations, the teacher may place dot patterns on numbers (e.g., place four dots on the number 4) to help improve accuracy in addition and subtraction. As proficiency increases, students may just tap their pencils on each number as they count and perform simple addition and subtraction facts.

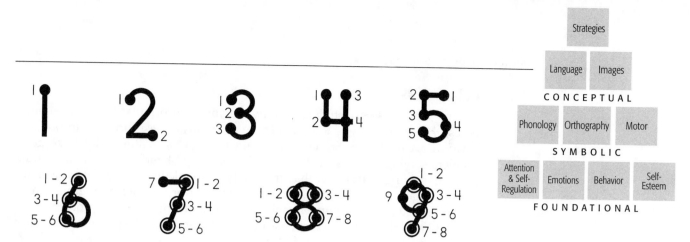

Figure 9.9. TouchMath touch points. (From *TouchMath: The Touchpoint Approach for Teaching Basic Math Computation* [4th. ed.], revised and enlarged. By permission of J. Bullock and Innovative Learning Concepts, Inc. Copyright © 1984, 1986, 1992, by Innovation Learning Concepts, Inc., Colorado Springs. All rights reserved.)

TouchMath A multisensory approach for teaching four basic computational skills that uses touch points is called TouchMath (Bullock, 1991). (See Additional Resources.) For this approach, students are taught to touch the dots on each of the numbers when counting. Several steps are included in the process. To add a series of numbers, students touch the dots on the numbers and count forward. To subtract, students say the name of the larger number and then touch the dots while counting backward. Many first- and second-grade teachers use this type of method in conjunction with existing math programs to help children improve their accuracy in addition and subtraction and to aid with memorization of basic facts. Children are encouraged to eliminate touching the points as they become more proficient. Specific classroom sets are available for first and second grade. Figure 9.9 illustrates the touch points for the numbers.

Structural Arithmetic Structural arithmetic is another multisensory teaching approach that helps children learn number concepts (Stern & Stern, 1971). This program encourages the use of manipulatives and exploration so that children can discover the basic principles underlying the arithmetic processes. Many sequenced activities and games are available. Stern (2005) provided a comprehensive overview of the basic features of this program.

For students whose problems are caused or compounded by poor handwriting, difficulty aligning figures, errors in transposing figures, or crowding figures on the page, the use of paper with boxes or columns marked on it may reduce problems. When Andy used graph paper with large boxes, he was able to align his numbers more accurately.

Mnemonics Students who have difficulty with memorizing math facts may memorize facts more easily if instruction is linked with other stronger abilities. Greene (1999) found that students with LD learned multiplication facts more easily with mnemonic instruction. Students were taught facts associated with a pegword phrase for each number (e.g., 6 = sticks, 7 = heaven, 42 = warty shoe) and an associated picture (e.g., 6 × 7 = 42; sticks in heaven with a warty shoe).

If a student has strengths in the conceptual block of language, facts may be learned most easily with the use of music or rhyme. Rap tapes are available that review multiplication facts. Inexpensive commercial rhyme cards, such as Times Tables the Fun Way and Addition the Fun Way, are also available. Rhymes for facts with associated picture cards are available from City Creek Press (see Additional Resources). An example from these cards is "6 × 6 are very thirsty sixes" with a picture to reinforce the fact.

Calculators

In some math classes, a student's ability to remember formulas is critical; at other times, the student needs to demonstrate an ability to use formulas in order to perform a calculation. Students who are poor at calculating may have good problem-solving abilities. If the goal of a test or problem set is to demonstrate problem-solving skills rather than the ability to do calculations, use of a calculator is appropriate. Although tools such as a calculator or a software program can be helpful, students need to understand how to use the tools to solve problems.

A few teachers may feel that use of a calculator should be prohibited because it may inhibit learning of math facts.

Stephanie's individualized education program (IEP) stated that she should be encouraged to use a calculator for all math activities so that she could focus her attention on problem solving. She asked Ms. Richards, her fourth-grade teacher, if she could use her calculator on her homework that evening. Ms. Richards replied, "Yes, if you show your work." Stephanie said that she would and the next day she turned in the drawing shown in Figure 9.10.

Error Analysis

One of the most effective ways to help resolve a student's errors is to analyze any mistakes he or she makes on school papers or homework assignments. Attempt to

Figure 9.10. Stephanie's calculator drawing.

determine exactly why the student has missed certain problems. The important point to realize is that students will continue to make the same type of errors unless intervention occurs. When you cannot determine why a student has missed a problem, ask the student to say aloud step-by-step what he or she was doing when attempting to solve the problem. Listen carefully to the student's explanation and ask questions as needed to discover why the student is making errors.

When Stephanie would add or subtract problems with a zero, she would always obtain a wrong answer. She would answer $7 + 0 = 0$. When asked to explain what she was doing, Stephanie reported, "Zero means that there is nothing there so you can't have anything when there is a zero." Using manipulatives, her teacher then showed her that when you add or subtract zero, the number of objects in the set remains the same.

Modeling

When introducing new concepts and skills, use modeling and demonstrations. Have students watch how you perform a task as you talk yourself through it. Then students can perform the task as you talk the students through it. Finally, students can perform the tasks as they talk themselves through it. This procedure focuses on the conceptual block of strategies and helps students understand the basic process involved in computations.

In fourth grade, Stephanie was having trouble understanding how to do division problems. Ms. Richards, her teacher, showed her step-by-step how to solve 25 divided by 3:

1. Ask yourself, "Does 3 go into 2?" Because the answer is no, ask yourself if 3 goes into 25. Because the answer is yes, count how many times.

2. Record 8 on the top of the line.

3. Multiply 8×3 and record 24 below 25.

4. Subtract.

5. Check to make sure all the 3s are out.

6. Record the remainder.

After they had talked through several different examples, Ms. Richards summarized the steps of division on an index card.

1. Ask.

2. Write the number.

3. Multiply and write.

4. Subtract.

5. Check.

6. Bring down.

Stephanie then used this card to talk herself through the steps of the division problems that she was attempting to solve.

As described in Chapters 10 and 11, to increase understanding, students need to see, hear, perform, and talk about what they are learning. One fact is clear: A student's later mathematics achievement is compromised if he or she fails to acquire sufficient skill in performing basic operations with or without a calculator. In other words, limited fluency with the recall of basic facts hinders the development of higher level math skills. Although increasing a student's problem-solving skills is of the utmost importance, the student must also master basic math skills. When facts are mastered, the student is able to direct attention to the skills of the conceptual blocks required for effective math problem solving.

HANDWRITING

Students with weaknesses in the motor block require specific instruction in handwriting. The basic goals of this instruction are to help students develop legible writing styles and be able to write quickly and easily without devoting conscious attention to letter formation (Graham, 1999). In addition to motor skills, handwriting involves knowledge of orthography and planning ability (Fletcher et al., 2007). Early intervention with students with handwriting difficulties should focus on forming letters automatically and retrieving them quickly from memory; this type of intervention can help prevent more serious writing problems later in school (e.g., Berninger & Amtmann, 2003).

Readiness

Some children begin attempting to write letters as young as age 2. They enjoy activities that involve small muscle control.

When Stephanie was 2 years old, she announced that she was writing a story. She had watched her older sister, Haley, who was in kindergarten, and wanted to engage in similar tasks. She informed her mother that she was going to sign her name. Stephanie's story is shown in Figure 9.11. Notice her attempt to write a small *HA* at the bottom of the page. Stephanie had watched her sister write her name enough times that she was trying to produce the first two letters.

Vast differences exist in the development of children's motor skills. By the time Stephanie entered kindergarten, her motor skills were well developed because she was already drawing and attempting to write at the age of 2. Other children pick up a pencil for the first time when they enter a kindergarten classroom. Figure 9.12 shows a class of kindergarten children writing or attempting to write their names. Notice the difference in motor control between Kenneth and Dominic and Tony and Sarah. Kenneth and Dominic already write stories. Clearly, Tony and Sarah are not ready to start writing letters.

Prior to handwriting instruction, children such as Tony and Sarah need to increase their fine motor coordination because forming letters requires controlled motor skill. Activities such as digging in the sand and playing with clay increase muscle tone. Encourage children to color and draw because these activities also help them strengthen their hands. As children begin using a crayon, encourage scribbling. Scribbling builds strength and helps prepare children for the more precise motor movements that are needed for handwriting.

Figure 9.11. Stephanie's writing.

As a child's skill increases, you may provide him or her with more specific readiness activities, such as tracing and copying shapes and lines, completing dot-to-dot activity books, and drawing lines and circles. Unfortunately, children such as Tony and Sarah often do not like to color or draw, so extra time must be provided to develop readiness skills.

Letter formation requires the use of circles, lines, and curves. Sample prewriting activities include

1. Producing scribbles

2. Drawing a horizontal line

3. Drawing a circle

4. Drawing a cross, square, and rectangle

5. Drawing lines that slant to the left and lines that slant to the right

Teachers can encourage students to use these lines and shapes when drawing. For example, ask a child to draw a windy road, a long fence, a group of balls, some valleys and mountains, and a curvy snake. These forms can be drawn or painted on sheets of old newspaper.

Fundamentals

Prior to formal handwriting instruction, a few children need assistance with establishing hand preference. If a child has not developed a preferred hand by kindergarten, attempt to determine which hand is used more often and appears more coordinated. Although a child may switch back and forth, in most cases, he or she uses one hand more than the other. Through careful observation, a child's natural hand preference is likely to become apparent.

Andy tended to perform most activities with his right hand, although when he was using a pencil, he would sometimes pass the pencil from one hand to the other, depending on which side of the paper he was drawing on. Andy found it uncomfortable to cross the midline of his body so his simple solution was to switch hands instead. Once his first-grade teacher decided that Andy should use his right hand for writing, Andy was not sure which hand was the right one. For a few weeks, he wore a ring on his hand as a reminder.

Some children have ineffective pencil grips. Most people hold the pencil between the thumb and index finger with the pencil resting on the middle finger. Andy also seemed to squeeze the pencil with an uncomfortable grip. After writing for a few minutes, he always complained that his hand was tired. Several options are available for students such as Andy. Some students benefit from triangular pencil grips, available at most teaching supply stores. This type of rubber grip helps position the fingers around the pencil. As an alternative, rubber bands can also be wrapped around the pencil at the place where the middle finger rests. In addition,

Figure 9.12. Name writing of kindergarten students.

Figure 9.12.   *(continued)*

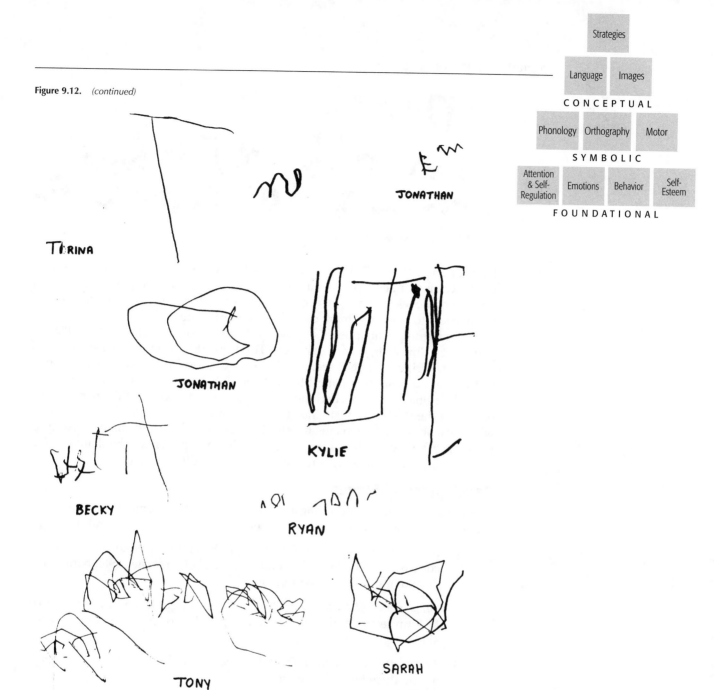

Pencil Grip manufactures special grips that position the hand so that the pencil rests on the first joint of the middle finger and the thumb and index fingers hold the pencil in place (see Additional Resources).

When a child is writing, he or she should be able to move his or her writing arm smoothly and easily across the paper. If the student is printing, the writing paper is usually positioned straight up and down in front of the body. When writing in manu-cursive or cursive style, right-handed students typically slant the paper to the left, whereas left-handed students slant the paper to the right. Some students have difficulty with keeping the writing paper positioned correctly on the table and find it easier to write if papers are attached to a clipboard.

Even though many children have trouble developing legible handwriting, some children receive very little instruction on how to form letters. As you can see from the sample in Figure 9.13, the size and shape of Andy's letters are inconsistent, and many of the words are hard to discern. He tried to form letters, but he had trouble controlling the pencil. He was trying to write a note to his

Figure 9.13. Andy's writing: "Dan. I'm sorry that I made you mad."

friend, Dan, that said, "I'm sorry that I made you mad." Ms. Abram, his second-grade teacher, understands his difficulties and provides a supportive classroom for writing development; however, as Andy gets older, his teachers are likely to become less tolerant and more critical of his poor writing.

Handwriting that appears sloppy affects how people react to a paper. Picture yourself grading a large stack of papers. Think about how you feel when you look at a neatly written paper. It seems to invite you to read it. Think about how you feel when you come to a paper that is filled with smudge marks or seems only partially legible. Your eyes become tired, and you may even put the paper at the bottom of the stack and delay the grading. A neatly written paper implies effort, whereas a sloppy paper seems to reflect a lack of effort. Unfortunately, Andy is more likely to receive lower grades on writing assignments if his handwriting does not improve or if he does not develop keyboarding skill.

Developmental Stages

Like the development of decoding and encoding, the development of handwriting proficiency can be described by stages. Levine (1987) described several stages:

1. *Imitation:* From preschool to first grade, children pretend to write by copying others (e.g., by imitating her older sister, Stephanie was developing skill in letter formation).

2. *Graphic presentation:* During first and second grade, children learn how to form letters and to write on a line with proper spacing. Fine motor skills become better developed.

3. *Progressive incorporation:* From late second grade to fourth grade, letters are produced with less effort.

4. *Automatization:* In fourth through seventh grade, children write rapidly and efficiently.

In the final stages, children develop personalized styles and increase proficiency in writing. As with other instruction in basic skills, the goal is to establish automaticity, or rapid and easy production of letter forms.

General Principles

Graham and Madan (1981) noted that an effective program for teaching letter formation is based on the following four principles: 1) overlearning letters in isolation and then applying them in a written context; 2) forming letters with external cues, such as verbalizing and tracing until they become automatic; 3) encouraging students to evaluate their own handwriting; and 4) providing students with assistance in maintaining a consistent and legible writing style.

Important elements of handwriting instruction, therefore, include modeling and describing letter formation, discussing critical attributes, giving feedback and reinforcement, and having students practice tracing, self-verbalizing, and writing

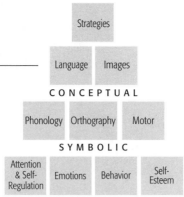

from memory (Graham & Madan, 1981; Graham & Miller, 1980). Many students require explicit and direct help to establish the patterns needed for legible, fluent writing (Graham, 1983). Skills are overlearned in isolation and then applied in meaningful assignments (Graham & Madan, 1981; Graham & Miller, 1980). In general, students benefit from supervised practice with immediate reinforcement and correction (Meese, 1994). As skill progresses, students can improve their handwriting as they write meaningful text, such as copying the final drafts of their own compositions. McCarney and Cummins (1988) summarized several general principles teachers should follow when helping students develop their handwriting skills:

1. Provide the student with ample opportunities to practice handwriting skill.

2. Model neat and correct handwriting at all times.

3. Have the student trace over model handwriting. As skill develops, slowly fade the model to promote independence.

4. Initially, provide the student with primary paper with a middle line in order to foster the correct size of letters. As skill develops, have the student use standard paper.

5. Provide the student with wide-ruled paper. As skill improves, gradually reduce the width of the lines.

6. If the student is having difficulty with spacing, provide the student with paper that has both horizontal and vertical lines. Teach the student to write one symbol in each box and to leave one box empty after a comma and two empty boxes after a period.

7. If the student's handwriting is affected by poor positioning of the pencil, provide the student with a triangular pencil grip.

8. When teaching handwriting to older students, provide them with functional opportunities to practice handwriting (e.g., filling out a job application or bank forms).

9. Recognize and reinforce improvement.

Choosing a Style

Students may be taught several styles of script. The three most widely used writing styles are manuscript, manu-cursive, and cursive writing. Although most school districts adopt a certain approach to teaching handwriting, research has not demonstrated a clear advantage of one style over another (Graham, 1999; Graham & Miller, 1980). Traditionally, instruction in manuscript is provided in first and second grade, and then cursive instruction begins in second or third grade. Increasingly, schools are turning more to a manu-cursive method because it avoids devoting instructional time to a new writing style and eliminates the later transition from manuscript to cursive. In addition, improved technology has resulted in alternatives to handwriting: keyboarding and voice-activated word processing.

In a traditional manuscript instructional program, children are taught that letter forms are composed of simple sticks and circles. They are then taught how to make various combinations of circles and sticks to form the letters of the alphabet. This style is sometimes referred to as the ball-stick method.

Manu-cursive is a writing style that combines manuscript and cursive letter formation. The most widely used manu-cursive writing style is D'Nealian

(Thurber, 1983). In this method, the majority of letters are formed using a continuous stroke motion. This provides a natural progression from manuscript to cursive letter formation because the letters are connected by adding joining strokes. In addition, D'Nealian offers visual, auditory, and tactile-kinesthetic clues to help children remember how the letters are formed. Figure 9.14a and b presents D'Nealian number descriptions and lowercase manuscript letters with the suggested oral directions to use when teaching the letters. For cursive writing, all letters are formed with a continuous motion, and words are written as units.

Some individuals believe that manuscript is an easier style and the preferred method for young children to learn. Manuscript letters may be easier to form than cursive letters and are similar to the print that children see in books. In addition, cursive writing can pose problems for some children with motor weaknesses because they lack the fine motor coordination needed to sustain a rhythmic motion and make the required continuous strokes. Even after students have been taught cursive writing, they should not be discouraged from continuing to write in manuscript (Graham, 1999).

Other individuals believe that children should begin with manu-cursive or cursive writing styles. Manu-cursive and cursive approaches appear to be effective for some children with fine motor weaknesses for several reasons. First,

Number Descriptions

 Start at the top, slant down to the bottom.
[Top start; slant down.]

Start a little below the top; curve up right to the top; curve down right to the middle; slant down left to the bottom; make a bar to the right.
[Start below the top; curve up, around; slant down left; and over right.]

 Start a little below the top; curve up right to the top; curve down right to the middle; curve down right again to the bottom; curve up left, and stop.
[Start below the top; curve up, around halfway; around again, up, and stop.]

Start at the top; slant down to the middle; make a bar to the right. Start again at the top, to the right of the first start; slant down through the bar to the bottom.
[Top start; down halfway; over right. Another top start, to the right; slant down, and through.]

 Start at the top; make a bar to the left; slant down to the middle; curve down right to the bottom; curve up left, and stop.
[Top start; over left; slant down halfway; curve around, down, up, and stop.]

 Start at the top; slant down left to the middle; curve down left to the bottom; curve up right to the middle; curve left, and close.
[Top start; slant down and curve around; up, and close.]

 Start at the top; make a bar to the right; slant down left to the bottom.
[Top start; over right; slant down left.]

Start a little below the top; curve up left to the top and down left to the middle; curve down right to the bottom; curve up left; slant up right, through the middle, to the beginning, and touch.
[Start below the top; curve up, around, down; a snake tail; slant up right; through, and touch.]

 Start at the top; curve down left to the middle; curve up right to the beginning, and close; slant down to the bottom.
[Top start; curve down, around, close; slant down.]

 Start at the top; slant down to the bottom. Start again at the top, to the right of the first start; curve down left to the bottom; curve up right to the top, and close.
[Top start; slant down. Another top start, to the right; curve down, around, and close.]

Figure 9.14a. D'Nealian script: Number descriptions. (From Manuscript and Cursive Alphabets and Number Descriptions from D'NEALIAN HANDWRITING Book 4, 3rd ed. by Donald Neal Thurber. Copyright © 1993 by Scott, Foresman and Company. Reprinted by permission of Pearson Education, Inc.)

Lowercase Manuscript Letter Descriptions

a Start at the middle line; curve down left to the bottom line; curve up right to the beginning, and close; retrace down, and swing up.
[Middle start; around down, close up, down, and a monkey tail.]

b Start at the top line; slant down to the bottom line; curve up right to the middle line; curve left, and close.
[Top start; slant down, around, up, and a tummy.]

c Start a little below the middle line; curve up left to the middle line; curve down left to the bottom line; curve up right, and stop.
[Start below the middle; curve up, around, down, up, and stop.]

d Start at the middle line; curve down left to the bottom line; curve up right to the beginning; touch, and keep going up to the top line; retrace down and swing up.
[Middle start; around down, touch up high, down, and a monkey tail.]

e Start between the middle line and the bottom line; curve up right to the middle line; curve down left; touch, and keep going down to the bottom line; curve up right, and stop.
[Start between the middle and bottom; curve up, around, touch, down, up, and stop.]

f Start a little below the top line; curve up left to the top line; slant down to the bottom line. Make a crossbar on the middle line.
[Start below the top; curve up, around, and slant down. Cross.]

g Start at the middle line; curve down left to the bottom line; curve up right to the beginning, and close; retrace down to halfway below the bottom line, and hook left.
[Middle start; around down, close up, down under water, and a fishhook.]

h Start at the top line; slant down to the bottom line; retrace up halfway; make a hill to the right, and swing up.
[Top start; slant down, up over the hill, and a monkey tail.]

i Start at the middle line; slant down to the bottom line, and swing up. Make a dot above the letter.
[Middle start; slant down, and a monkey tail. Add a dot.]

j Start at the middle line; slant down to halfway below the bottom line, and hook left. Make a dot above the letter.
[Middle start; slant down under water, and a fishhook. Add a dot.]

k Start at the top line; slant down to the bottom line; retrace up halfway; curve right; make a small loop left, and close; slant down right to the bottom line, and swing up.
[Top start; slant down, up into a little tummy, and a monkey tail.]

l Start at the top line; slant down to the bottom line, and swing up.
[Top start; slant down, and a monkey tail.]

m Start at the middle line; slant down to the bottom line; retrace up, and make a hill to the right; retrace up; make another hill to the right; and swing up.
[Middle start; slant down, up over the hill, up over the hill again, and a monkey tail.]

n Start at the middle line; slant down to the bottom line; retrace up; make a hill to the right, and swing up.
[Middle start; slant down, up over he hill, and a monkey tail.]

o Start at the middle line; curve down left to the bottom line; curve up right to the beginning, and close.
[Middle start; around down, and close up.]

p Start at the middle line; slant down to halfway below the bottom line; retrace up; curve down right to the bottom line; curve left, and close.
[Middle start; slant down under water, up, around, and a tummy.]

q Start at the middle line; curve down left to the bottom line; curve up right to the beginning, and close; retrace down to halfway below the bottom line, and hook right.
[Middle start; around down, close up, down under water, and a backwards fishhook.]

r Start at the middle line; slant down to the bottom line; retrace up; curve right, and stop.
[Middle start; slant down, up, and a roof.]

Figure 9.14b. D'Nealian script: Lowercase manuscript letter descriptions. (From Manuscript and Cursive Alphabets and Number Descriptions from D'NEALIAN HANDWRITING Book 4, 3rd ed. by Donald Neal Thurber. Copyright © 1993 by Scott, Foresman and Company. Reprinted by permission of Pearson Education, Inc.)

Strategies

Language   Images

CONCEPTUAL

Phonology   Orthography   Motor

SYMBOLIC

Attention & Self-Regulation   Emotions   Behavior   Self-Esteem

FOUNDATIONAL

Figure 9.14b. *(continued)*

Lowercase Manuscript Letter Descriptions

 Start a little below the middle line; curve up left to the middle line and down left halfway; curve down right to the bottom line; curve up left, and stop.
[Start below the middle; curve up, around, down, and a snake tail.]

 Start at the top line; slant down to the bottom line, and swing up. Make a crossbar on the middle line.
[Top start; slant down, and a monkey tail. Cross.]

 Start at the middle line; slant down to the bottom line, and curve right; slant up to the middle line; retrace down, and swing up.
[Middle start; down, around, up, down, and a monkey tail.]

 Start at the middle line; slant down right to the bottom line; slant up right to the middle line.
[Middle start; slant down right, and slant up right.]

 Start at the middle line; slant down to the bottom line, and curve right; slant up to the middle line; retrace down, and curve right; slant up to the middle line. [Middle start; down, around, up, and down, around, up again.]

 Start at the middle line; slant down right to the bottom line, and swing up. Cross through the letter with a slant down left.
[Middle start; down, around, up, and down, around, up again.]

 Start at the middle line; slant down to the bottom line, and curve right; slant up to the middle line; retrace down to halfway below the bottom line, and hook left.
[Middle start; down, around, up, down under water, and a fishhook.]

 Start at the middle line; make a bar to the right; slant down left to the bottom line; make a bar to the right.
[Middle start; over right, slant down left, and over right.]

in using these writing styles, children make fewer reversals because the letters are formed differently and are easier to discriminate. Second, they do not need to learn two different patterns of letter formation. Third, the continuous motion and rhythm can help a child with spacing and speed. Fourth, cursive writing can help reduce inconsistencies in the size and shape of letters.

Although Andy had problems with fine motor coordination, the occupational therapist recommended that he be taught cursive writing. She felt that cursive writing would help Andy keep the words together as a unit, so that the individual letters did not land above or below the writing line. In other words, cursive writing would eliminate having to pick up the pencil and replace it somewhere on the page. This method would reduce the frequency of letter reversals as well as the requirements for motor planning. Because cursive words are written as a unit, Andy would not have to relocate the line with formation of each letter. After 2 months of instruction, the legibility of Andy's writing improved. Figure 9.15 provides an illustration of his cursive writing: "I had camp today."

In general, as indicated by these various theories, there is a lack of evidence and consensus regarding what type of script to teach (Graham, 1999). Depending on a child's characteristics, one writing style may be easier than another. Some children learn to print easily but struggle to learn cursive. Others have tremendous difficulty learning to print and then experience similar difficulties in learning to write in cursive. In these cases, too much time can be wasted on developing an alternative writing style. The major goal of handwriting instruction is legibility, not proficiency or mastery of a certain style. For a child with weaknesses in motor

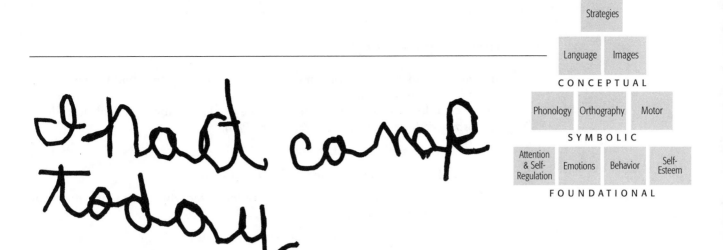

Figure 9.15. Andy's cursive writing.

skill, it is better to teach one system well than to insist on mastery of both manuscript and cursive writing.

Ultimately, handwriting is idiosyncratic: Each writer develops his or her own personal style that may sometimes involve a blending of different scripts. In fact, Graham, Weintraub, and Berninger (1998) found that students who used a mixed style received higher ratings for legibility than students who used either manuscript or cursive exclusively.

Letter Formation

Most children require some guidance as they are beginning to learn how to form letters. In these initial stages of learning, you may need to guide a child's hand physically as you say the letter name. This type of demonstration and practice can be provided easily on a chalkboard. As a general rule, teach the child how to form letters beginning at the top of the stroke. Although their first independent attempts at letter formation appear awkward, most children soon learn to form letters easily from memory.

When practicing letter formation with a student, begin with practice writing letters in isolation. After the student has mastered the basic forms of the letters, progress to practicing letters within words and then within sentences. The following activities can be used to help students acquire legible, fluent writing.

Multisensory Instruction As with teaching spelling, instruction in handwriting for students with weaknesses in orthographic and motor blocks needs to be multisensory. Tracing exercises are critical for children who have severe weaknesses in fine motor skills. One of the most important ways to help a child who struggles with letter formation is to have him or her practice tracing letters until the motor movement becomes easy and automatic. Encourage younger children to trace letters made from sandpaper or felt.

One easy multisensory way to make letters or numbers with a raised surface is to write letters on index cards in different colors. Draw the outline on top of the letter with Elmer's glue. Let the letters dry, and then have the child use the raised surface for tracing. At first, you may need to guide the child's index finger over the letter. When the child is able to trace the letter easily, he or she can then trace the letter with a marking pen. Once the child is able to trace the letter successfully on paper, he or she can try to reproduce the letter on paper. Older children may use tracing paper or go over letters with a crayon or marking pen.

Many multisensory teaching techniques provide children with extensive practice in letter and number formation through repetitive tracings. This muscle

295

movement and the development of motor memory help the child remember the specific patterns for letter formation.

The following simple procedure may be used for helping students learn how to form specific letters (Graham & Miller, 1980):

1. Write the letter with a crayon while the student observes.

2. Say the name of the letter with the student.

3. Have the student say the name of the letter while tracing it with his or her index finger.

4. Repeat Step 3 until the student is successful on five consecutive trials.

5. Have the student write the letter while looking at the model.

6. Repeat Step 5 until the student copies the letter successfully three times.

7. Have the student say the name of the letter while writing it from memory.

8. Repeat Step 7 until the student has written the letter successfully three times.

As another example of a multisensory procedure, Thurber (1983) described a six-step process for teaching letter formation that incorporates visual, auditory, and motor abilities using D'Nealian print.

Step 1: Tell the student which letter will be formed (e.g., "Now, we will make the letter *a*").

Step 2: First, make eye contact with the student. Second, orally state the directions (e.g., up, around, down) for writing the letter while simultaneously writing the letter in the air. If facing the student, write the letter backwards so that the child can see the correct formation.

Step 3: Have the student repeat the directions with you as you trace the letter in the air.

Step 4: When the student has mastered the letter formation, have him or her practice writing the letter on paper with a marker or pencil. Next, have the student write the letter with a few other letters in groups of three; two or three different groups may be needed for learning the correct formation. Then, have the student repeat the directions for the letter when writing. At this point, do not allow the student to erase; have him or her simply cross out errors and practice again so that he or she may gauge his or her progress.

Step 5: Trace the letter on the student's arm, hand, or back with a finger while saying the directions. Repeat this step if necessary.

Step 6: Have the student trace the letter on your hand and say the directions. When the student succeeds, check to see if he or she has memorized the letter's formation. Do this by saying the directions and tracing the letter inaccurately on the child's hand. Encourage the student to indicate the error.

Directional Arrows   Placing numbered arrow cues on letters can increase automaticity of production (Brooks, Vaughan, & Berninger, 1999). Brooks and colleagues employed a procedure in which students were asked to look closely at the number arrow cues, cover the letter, and write the letter from memory. The interval of time for covering the letter before writing was increased systematically from 1 second (for the first four lessons) to 3 seconds (for the next four lessons) to 6 seconds (for the third set of four lessons), and so forth. This type of procedure is similar to the cover–write techniques discussed in the spelling section but

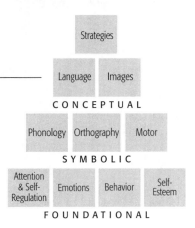

includes the addition of numbered arrow cues to remind the student of how to form the letter. Berninger and colleagues (2006) found that direct instruction in letter writing that included following numbered arrow cues and writing letters from memory improved automaticity of legible letter writing.

Oral Descriptions   Another effective way to help a child with poor handwriting is to use the skills of the conceptual blocks of language and images to reinforce weaknesses in the symbolic blocks of motor or visual processing. Some children experiencing problems with letter formation have trouble getting a mental picture of a letter. As a child is tracing a letter or number, describe aloud the movement needed to form the symbol correctly. For example, when teaching a child to form the printed letter *a*, you may say, "Start up at the top and then swing around to the left in a circle and then come down." This verbal description helps the student remember the sequence of movements. Gradually, encourage the child to say the verbal prompts.

In the Spalding method (Spalding & Spalding, 1990), children are prompted to visualize a clock face with all of the numbers. Using a clock as a guide to teach formation of the letter *c*, you may say, "Start at 2:00 and drive back all the way around to 4:00." Or to teach the letter *a* with a clock you may say, "Start at 2:00 and swing all the way back around to 2:00 and then draw a straight line down."

If the student is learning a manu-cursive writing style, the teacher may use the oral descriptions provided with the D'Nealian letters (Thurber, 1983). Gradually, students can describe the movements themselves as they write letters. For example, when printing the letter *n*, the student may say, "Down and then up. Make one hump."

Self-Guided Symbol Formation Strategy   Graham and colleagues (1998) examined the handwriting of 300 children in Grades 1–3. They found that the following six lowercase letters accounted for 48% of the omissions, miscues, and illegibilities: *q, j, z, u, n, k*. When only illegibilities were considered, five letters accounted for 54% of the errors. Thus, handwriting instruction may focus on mastery of specific letters.

Graham and Madan (1981) described an intensive remedial method for helping a student master the formation of a particular letter. The procedure is practiced on lined paper and can be used with either cursive or manuscript writing. The strategy consists of the following five steps.

1. Identify the letter that the student typically forms incorrectly. Ask the student to write a sample sentence that contains all of the letters, such as "The quick brown fox jumps over the lazy dog."

2. Select one letter that the student has trouble forming. Model the correct letter formation with a crayon, marker, or chalk. Write the letter again while verbally describing the process. Continue until the student can repeat the verbal description with the teacher.

3. Have the student trace the letter until he or she can verbalize the steps alone. If needed, guide the student's tracing through the use of arrows or colored dots. Encourage the student to act as his or her own instructor by defining the task, correcting errors, and praising accurate letter formation. Continue with Step 3 until the student can copy the letter correctly five times.

4. Describe the formation of the target letter while the student attempts to visualize and write the letter. Provide corrective feedback. Continue until the student can write the letter five times from memory.

5. Have the student practice the target letter in meaningful contexts. Begin with practice of single words, phrases, and then sentences.

Persistent Reversals A few students continue to reverse or invert letters and numbers past the age of 7. Even in eighth grade, Ben sometimes confused the letters *b* and *d*. Students who continue to reverse and invert letters often have weaknesses in the orthographic block, the phonological block, or both. They may have trouble recalling a mental image of a letter, forming letter images, or hearing subtle differences in sounds. Some types of errors (e.g., *b* and *d*) are more indicative of a weakness with orthographic images; other types (e.g., *b* and *p*) are more related to sound confusions (e.g., voiced and unvoiced consonant pairs).

The following simple suggestions can help a student reduce the frequency of reversed letters or numbers:

1. Have a student describe the movements for forming the letter. For example, if using the image of a clock face, the student can say for the letter *d*, "I begin at 2:00, swing back around, go up, and then go down."

2. Have the student associate a problematic letter with another letter that does not cause confusion. The lowercase *b* can be related to the uppercase *B*, or a lowercase *a* can be associated as the beginning movement for making a lowercase *d*. The student may say, "I start the letter *d* just like the letter *a*."

3. Use tracing to overteach a simple, common word beginning with one of the problematic letters. For example, if the student reverses the letters *b* and *d*, teach the word *dad* and point out that all three letters are formed in the same way. Encourage the student to think of the word *dad* when uncertain of orientation.

4. Use a cue word, such as the word *bed*, which contains the two problematic letters. Draw a line across the word to show how the word looks like a bed. Encourage the student to think of the word *bed* when checking whether the letter is *b* or *d*.

5. Encourage the student to use cursive writing rather than manuscript because reversals appear less frequently in cursive writing.

Strategies to Build Writing Speed

As increased writing demands are placed on students, handwriting fluency increases in importance (Larsen, 1987). One instructional goal, therefore, is to help students develop a fluid, rapid style. Just as with decoding, encoding, and calculating, practice contributes to automaticity as the motor patterns needed for legible writing become more firmly established.

Timed Writing One technique that may be used to improve writing rate and fluency and to encourage reluctant writers to increase their productivity is daily timed writings. Several variations are described briefly. The first variation, adapted from Houten, Morrison, Jarvis, and MacDonald (1974), uses the following steps:

1. Write a topic on the board.

2. Have students write about the topic for 10 minutes, trying to write more words than they did on the previous day.

3. At the end of the time period, have students count the number of words and record the word count on the top of the paper. Do not count words from repetitious or incomplete sentences.

4. Verify the scores and record the word count on a chart.

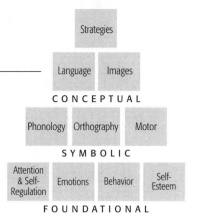

In a second variation, adapted from Alvarez (1983), students select their own topics. Sufficient knowledge of the topic helps students feel more comfortable in writing. For this procedure, use the following steps:

1. Have students select their own topics (although the teacher may choose to select the topic occasionally as a variation).

2. Have students write about their topics for 6 minutes during which time the teacher spells words as requested.

3. At the end of the time period, have the student count the number of words.

4. Have the student record the number of words on the top of the paper and on individual graphs.

In another variation, suggested by Douglass (1984), the teacher writes along with the students. Teacher participation may increase the motivation of some individuals. Use the following procedure:

1. Have students select their own topics.

2. Spend 5 minutes writing about a topic of your choice while the students do the same.

3. Encourage the students to share their writing.

The fourth variation, adapted from several sources (Brigham, Graubard, & Stans, 1972; Rumsey & Ballard, 1985; Seabaugh & Schumaker, 1981), incorporates some reinforcement. For this procedure, use the following steps:

1. Have students write daily for an assigned time.

2. Have them count and record the number of letters, words, or sentences.

3. Provide individual reinforcements contingent on performance, such as points for an assigned number of letters, words, or sentences.

4. Provide students with opportunities to trade the reinforcements for various predetermined privileges.

By the time Ryan was in sixth grade, his cursive writing was neat and legible. Two years of instruction with a multisensory approach had helped him master the movements needed for writing. Although his difficulties with spelling were still apparent, he was clearly working carefully and taking pride in his writing. In his paragraph presented in Figure 9.16, he recounted one of his favorite jokes about a man going to visit a psychiatrist because his wife thinks that she is a chicken.

Computers

Computers can also be used to generate practice worksheets for handwriting, or as an accommodation for poor handwriting. Many students complete the majority of their writing assignments on computer. Students can also learn to use voice-activated software as an aid to writing.

Software Two examples of flexible software programs for working on legibility and production speed are Start Write and Fonts4Teachers (see Additional Resources). These programs allow teachers to develop their own worksheets for handwriting practice. The teacher may select the style of writing: manuscript, modern manuscript (manu-cursive), or cursive and can specify the font size, add directional arrows, and have letters presented with faded dots or

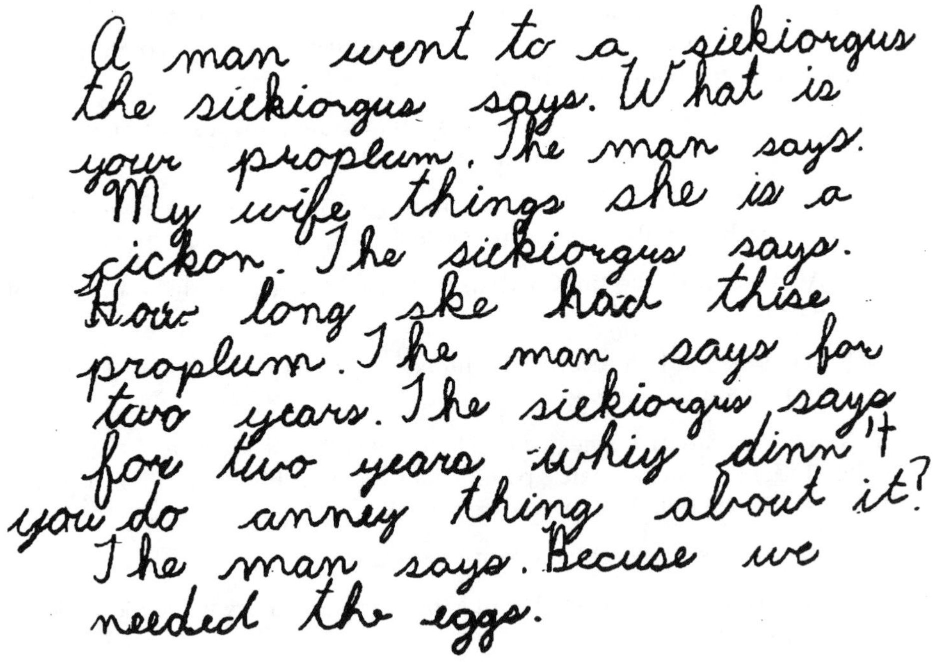

Figure 9.16. Ryan's cursive writing.

light lines. In this way, students can practice handwriting on meaningful, individualized materials.

Andy's second-grade teacher, Ms. Abram, prepared daily individualized worksheets for him to provide supplemental handwriting practice. On occasion, she had him write his spelling words. At other times, she had him dictate a story that she had typed and then he had traced. The addition of the directional arrows reminded Andy of how to form letters properly.

Keyboarding To compensate for severe fine motor difficulties, students such as Andy need to begin keyboarding instruction as early as possible. Several software programs are available that are designed to teach young children how to type. One interactive, carefully developed program called Read, Write, and Type is designed to increase beginning reading, writing, and keyboarding skills (see Additional Resources).

Voice-Activated Software Older students with poor handwriting or spelling difficulties can be taught to use voice-activated word processing programs or voice recognition software (VRS). The student speaks into a microphone, and the text is then translated into a word processing format on the computer. Although this procedure is not error-free, it can significantly reduce the demands on a student's secretarial skills, allowing a student to concentrate more fully on expressing and organizing ideas. These types of systems may allow students with LD to transcribe at rates closer to the speed of speech (de la Paz, 1999).

Sanderson (1999), however, described the frustration experienced by older students with reading impairments in training VRS systems. Common difficulties these students experience center around reading difficulties (the student must read phrases on the screen correctly on the first attempt), mispronunciations of known and unknown words, and lack of confidence while completing the training task.

300

Using a VRS system, Ben was able to complete the training session (independent reading of text for 30 minutes) with the assistance of a tutor over four short sessions. Prior to reading the paragraph, Ben would turn off the microphone and practice reading the passage with the tutor's assistance several times. The program would save the portion of the training that had been completed, and Ben could resume the training a few days later. Unfortunately for Ben, the program worked well for several months but then his voice changed and he had to complete the training sessions all over again.

Fortunately, several of the newer programs do not require training. Examples include Dragon Naturally Speaking and SpeakQ™, which was designed specifically for students who cannot dictate at a fast rate, get through the training, or remember verbal commands with ease. (See Additional Resources for more information about these programs.)

Even when individuals have been trained on the system, individuals with reading and spelling difficulties are likely to have difficulties correcting material that has not been transcribed accurately. Despite the limitations, VRS is likely to benefit many individuals with dyslexia or dysgraphia. As noted by de la Paz, "In an age where electronic products rapidly become smaller and more sophisticated, we may all soon prefer to talk to our computers instead of struggling with keyboards or handwritten forms of composing" (1999, p. 181).

CONCLUSION

The basic skill areas are linked to the acquisition and mastery of symbols. Students with weaknesses in symbolic learning struggle with the acquisition and mastery of basic reading, writing, and numeracy skills. As noted in Chapter 8, students with weaknesses in basic skills often require more time, shortened assignments, and specialized instruction. A teacher may need to manipulate other variables, such as the size of print, the color of the materials, or the kind of type or writing used. Ryan could not read the worksheets distributed in class; Ben complained that he had trouble reading cursive writing from the board; Maria rarely completed in-class reading assignments; Andy rarely finished writing assignments. For students with weaknesses in basic skills, selecting and implementing accommodations and instructional strategies requires flexibility, adaptability, and patience. Some students with weaknesses in basic skills have strengths in conceptual abilities, and intervention plans should also include activities that focus on strong areas of performance in addition to weak areas of performance.

With all of the skill areas, however, the most effective programs are explicit and directed to academic content, teach to mastery, provide scaffolding and emotional support, and monitor student progress (Fletcher et al., 2007). Students with LD require intensive, structured teaching that includes multisensory instruction, review, practice, and feedback as well as opportunities to apply these skills in meaningful contexts. In addition, these students often require specific classroom accommodations and adjustments to promote classroom success. Several advances in technology can also be used to benefit students with weaknesses in the symbolic blocks.

FRY'S 300 INSTANT WORD LIST

First Hundred

____ 1.	the	____ 26.	or	____ 51.	will	____ 76.	number
____ 2.	of	____ 27.	one	____ 52.	up	____ 77.	no
____ 3.	and	____ 28.	had	____ 53.	other	____ 78.	way
____ 4.	a	____ 29.	by	____ 54.	about	____ 79.	could
____ 5.	to	____ 30.	word	____ 55.	out	____ 80.	people
____ 6.	in	____ 31.	but	____ 56.	many	____ 81.	my
____ 7.	is	____ 32.	not	____ 57.	then	____ 82.	than
____ 8.	you	____ 33.	what	____ 58.	them	____ 83.	first
____ 9.	that	____ 34.	all	____ 59.	these	____ 84.	water
____ 10.	it	____ 35.	were	____ 60.	so	____ 85.	been
____ 11.	he	____ 36.	we	____ 61.	some	____ 86.	call
____ 12.	was	____ 37.	when	____ 62.	her	____ 87.	who
____ 13.	for	____ 38.	your	____ 63.	would	____ 88.	oil
____ 14.	on	____ 39.	can	____ 64.	make	____ 89.	now
____ 15.	are	____ 40.	said	____ 65.	like	____ 90.	find
____ 16.	as	____ 41.	there	____ 66.	him	____ 91.	long
____ 17.	with	____ 42.	use	____ 67.	into	____ 92.	down
____ 18.	his	____ 43.	an	____ 68.	time	____ 93.	day
____ 19.	they	____ 44.	each	____ 69.	has	____ 94.	did
____ 20.	I	____ 45.	which	____ 70.	look	____ 95.	get
____ 21.	at	____ 46.	she	____ 71.	two	____ 96.	come
____ 22.	be	____ 47.	do	____ 72.	more	____ 97.	made
____ 23.	this	____ 48.	how	____ 73.	write	____ 98.	may
____ 24.	have	____ 49.	their	____ 74.	go	____ 99.	part
____ 25.	from	____ 50.	if	____ 75.	see	____ 100.	over

Common suffixes: ____ -s, ____ -ing, ____ -ed

Second Hundred

____ 101.	new	____ 126.	great	____ 151.	put	____ 176.	kind
____ 102.	sound	____ 127.	where	____ 152.	end	____ 177.	hand
____ 103.	take	____ 128.	help	____ 153.	does	____ 178.	picture
____ 104.	only	____ 129.	through	____ 154.	another	____ 179.	again
____ 105.	little	____ 130.	much	____ 155.	well	____ 180.	change
____ 106.	work	____ 131.	before	____ 156.	large	____ 181.	off

____ 107. know	____ 132. line	____ 157. must	____ 182. play
____ 108. place	____ 133. right	____ 158. big	____ 183. spell
____ 109. year	____ 134. too	____ 159. even	____ 184. air
____ 110. live	____ 135. mean	____ 160. such	____ 185. away
____ 111. me	____ 136. old	____ 161. because	____ 186. animal
____ 112. back	____ 137. any	____ 162. turned	____ 187. house
____ 113. give	____ 138. same	____ 163. here	____ 188. point
____ 114. most	____ 139. tell	____ 164. why	____ 189. page
____ 115. very	____ 140. boy	____ 165. ask	____ 190. letter
____ 116. after	____ 141. follow	____ 166. went	____ 191. mother
____ 117. thing	____ 142. came	____ 167. men	____ 192. answer
____ 118. our	____ 143. want	____ 168. read	____ 193. found
____ 119. just	____ 144. show	____ 169. need	____ 194. study
____ 120. name	____ 145. also	____ 170. land	____ 195. still
____ 121. good	____ 146. around	____ 171. different	____ 196. learn
____ 122. sentence	____ 147. form	____ 172. home	____ 197. should
____ 123. man	____ 148. three	____ 173. us	____ 198. America
____ 124. think	____ 149. small	____ 174. move	____ 199. world
____ 125. say	____ 150. set	____ 175. try	____ 200. high

Common Suffixes: ____ -s, ____ -ing, ____ -ed, ____ -er, ____ -ly, ____ -est

Third Hundred

____ 201. every	____ 226. left	____ 251. until	____ 276. idea
____ 202. near	____ 227. don't	____ 252. children	____ 277. enough
____ 203. add	____ 228. few	____ 253. side	____ 278. eat
____ 204. food	____ 229. while	____ 254. feet	____ 279. face
____ 205. between	____ 230. along	____ 255. car	____ 280. watch
____ 206. own	____ 231. might	____ 256. mile	____ 281. far
____ 207. below	____ 232. close	____ 257. night	____ 282. Indian
____ 208. country	____ 233. something	____ 258. walk	____ 283. real
____ 209. plant	____ 234. seem	____ 259. white	____ 284. almost
____ 210. last	____ 235. next	____ 260. sea	____ 285. let
____ 211. school	____ 236. hard	____ 261. began	____ 286. above
____ 212. father	____ 237. open	____ 262. grow	____ 287. girl
____ 213. keep	____ 238. example	____ 263. took	____ 288. sometimes
____ 214. tree	____ 239. beginning	____ 264. river	____ 289. mountain
____ 215. never	____ 240. life	____ 265. four	____ 290. cut
____ 216. start	____ 241. always	____ 266. carry	____ 291. young
____ 217. city	____ 242. those	____ 267. state	____ 292. talk
____ 218. earth	____ 243. both	____ 268. once	____ 293. soon
____ 219. eye	____ 244. paper	____ 269. book	____ 294. list
____ 220. light	____ 245. together	____ 270. hear	____ 295. song
____ 221. thought	____ 246. got	____ 271. stop	____ 296. leave
____ 222. head	____ 247. group	____ 272. without	____ 297. family
____ 223. under	____ 248. often	____ 273. second	____ 298. body
____ 224. story	____ 249. run	____ 274. late	____ 299. music
____ 225. saw	____ 250. important	____ 275. miss	____ 300. color

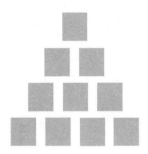

CONCEPTUAL BLOCKS

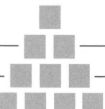

CHAPTER 10 OUTLINE

THINKING WITH LANGUAGE: ORAL LANGUAGE AND ACADEMIC PERFORMANCE

Components of Oral Language
Receptive and Expressive Language
Literacy Instruction for English Language Learners
Instruction for Language Development

THINKING WITH IMAGES: NONVERBAL LEARNING DISABILITIES

Characteristics
Interventions
Instruction Using Visual Imagery

THINKING WITH STRATEGIES: METACOGNITIVE AND EXECUTIVE PROCESSES

Instruction in Strategies
General Principles

CLASSROOM ADJUSTMENTS

Alter the Difficulty Level
Provide a Classroom Coach
Allow More Time and Practice
Consider Physical Classroom Arrangements
Provide More than One Grade
Base Grades on Individualized Education Program Goals
Provide Opportunities for Improvement

CONCLUSION

APPENDIX A: ADDITIONAL STRATEGIES FOR TEST TAKING

APPENDIX B: INSTRUCTIONAL ACCOMMODATIONS SURVEY

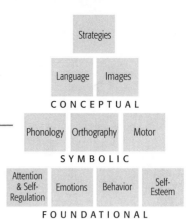

Strategies

Language | Images

CONCEPTUAL

Phonology | Orthography | Motor

SYMBOLIC

Attention & Self-Regulation | Emotions | Behavior | Self-Esteem

FOUNDATIONAL

CHAPTER 10

THINKING WITH LANGUAGE, IMAGES, AND STRATEGIES

with Ann M. Richards

With the passage of the No Child Left Behind Act of 2001 (PL 107-110) and its emphasis on academic content, many teachers have shifted the focus of their teaching from a developmental model to a primary focus on academic skill development. For the many students who struggle in school, this shift in instructional goals can leave them even further behind. Because of the diverse characteristics of students who struggle with aspects of learning, the range of instructional interventions that are needed can be vast. Some of these students are good at decoding but have difficulty understanding the overall meaning of what they read. Some have typical oral language abilities but struggle with tasks involving spatial organization. Others seem attentive and motivated but are unable to develop or revise their plans for completing homework and tests. These types of difficulties often signify that the student has a weakness in the conceptual building blocks. This chapter reviews the abilities related to thinking with language and images and using strategies.

THINKING WITH LANGUAGE: ORAL LANGUAGE AND ACADEMIC PERFORMANCE

> *Like the sea, talk is the environment that first*
> *incubates and then nurtures our development.*
> (Rubin, 1990, p. 3)

The sea is a complex system of different ecological microcosms that come together to form one vast body of water. Oral language in this metaphor can then be considered one of the essential microcosms or building blocks for literacy-based academics. Considerable research has documented that students who demonstrate difficulties in acquiring oral language often struggle to master the skills associated with reading (e.g., Dickinson, Anastasopoulos, McCabe, Peisner-Feinberg, & Poe, 2003; Dickinson & McCabe, 2001; McArthur, Hogben, Edwards, Heath, & Mengler, 2000; Mengler, Hogben, Michie, & Bishop, 2005; NICHD Early Child Care Research Network, 2005; Share & Leikin, 2004; Storch & Whitehurst, 2002). Students with weaknesses in oral language can exhibit difficulties in understanding what they read or what is said to them and in formulating oral and written responses. Essentially, a student's reading comprehension will be no stronger than his or her comprehension of oral language (Fletcher et al., 2007).

Within the school environment, students may fail to understand the information that teachers are conveying. They may miss important points when the teacher is lecturing, or when they are asked to comprehend assignments and test questions, they may misinterpret the meaning. These difficulties can inhibit students' abilities to comprehend what is read, solve problems, and monitor their social and academic environments.

When John was in eighth grade, he had been given a homework assignment to write an essay about a short story read in class. John had difficulty with understanding the story, so the special education teacher paraphrased and summarized the main events. She then attempted to explain the essay questions so that John could select the one he would attempt. After 40 minutes, John asked, "By the way, what is an essay?" His special education teacher then reviewed a standard process and structure for an essay: Begin with an introductory paragraph, add several supporting paragraphs to develop the topic introduced in the first paragraph, and summarize or draw conclusions in an ending paragraph. John then replied, "Oh, I thought she meant the letters *SA*." No wonder John had not been concerned that the assignment was due the following day!

Components of Oral Language

The following abilities are components of oral language: phonology, morphology, syntax, semantics, and pragmatics. *Phonology* refers to the sound system of a language. From birth to 4 years of age, children master sounds that are relevant to their native language (Ingram, 1986). Difficulties with the development of phonological awareness affect later success in reading. Chapter 7 provides a more comprehensive discussion of the difficulties associated with phonology.

Morphology refers to the meaning units of language. Just as a phoneme refers to the smallest unit of sound, a morpheme refers to the smallest unit of meaning. For example, the word *boys* is composed of two morphemes, the meaning unit *boy* and the plural marker *s*. An individual's understanding of the individual units of meaning can also influence his or her vocabulary, reading, and spelling development. For example, understanding that past tense is typically spelled with the letters *-ed* can guide the student to spell the word *jumped* correctly, even though the word sounds like it ends with a /t/.

Syntax refers to the underlying structure of language and the rules that guide word order. Students who have difficulties in the area of syntax often struggle to produce complex sentences in both oral and written exchanges. They may have difficulty formulating questions and using the correct verb tense when speaking.

Semantics refers to knowledge of word meanings. Difficulties in this area often affect a student's ability to comprehend information. John did not understand the meaning of the word *essay* and, consequently, he constructed his own interpretation of the task based on the phonological features of the letters *SA*.

Pragmatics refers to the social aspects of language and the varied use of language in different social contexts. Students with pragmatic language disorders may fail to alter their language use on the basis of the situation and the listener. As a result, they may speak to the school principal in the same tone and manner as they would to a peer on the playground (e.g., "Hey, man, what's happening?"). Young children may also have difficulty adjusting to the more formal pragmatic language used in classrooms. For example, when Katy was in kindergarten, her teacher asked her, "Katy, can you pass the glue to Pablo?" Katy responded by stating, "No, I don't have time." Although the teacher made her request in a question format, Katy did not comprehend that the request actually was a statement of an action that an authority figure was asking her to complete.

The first components of oral language are acquired in infancy. By the time many children are 9 months old, they understand that certain sounds represent words and that words represent objects, experiences, and feelings (Myklebust, 1965). Gradually, oral language develops as children learn to apply words to describe objects, experiences, and feelings. Children also begin to learn the rules of syntax by conversing with others. For example, a child might say to his mother, "Give blocks," to which his mother might respond, "Would you like me to give you the blocks?" Through an expansion of the original request, the mother has modeled to the child how language is used. In order to develop their abilities, children need to have practice using language for various tasks. Oral language provides the structure through which children interpret, organize, and store information about the world. Children with weaknesses in oral language tend to struggle with language-based, higher level academic tasks, such as reading comprehension, written expression, and math problem solving.

Receptive and Expressive Language

Oral language abilities provide the foundation for success in tasks involving comprehension, problem solving, and self-monitoring. For each of these tasks, students must have strong receptive and expressive oral language abilities. Receptive oral language refers to an individual's ability to understand what is being said. The major skill needed for success in this area is listening. Listening requires that students receive and interpret correctly the message that is being conveyed. Dickinson and McCabe (2001) found that students' receptive language skills affected their comprehension of written material to a greater degree in seventh grade than in kindergarten, indicating the increasing complexity of language tasks as well as the need to teach these skills at an early age.

Expressive oral language relates to an individual's ability to retrieve ideas and vocabulary and express these thoughts in an appropriate manner. The major ability needed for success in the area of expressive oral language is speaking. Speaking requires students to develop intent to speak, formulate what they are going to say, and finally produce the appropriate words and sentences. Deficiencies in the use of expressive language in preschool children have been found to predict subsequent academic difficulties (e.g., Dickinson et al., 2003; Dickinson & McCabe, 2001; NICHD Early Child Care Research Network, 2005; Share & Leikin, 2004; Storch & Whitehurst, 2002). Some students have adequate receptive language but poor expressive language. They understand what is said to them but have trouble responding orally. Other students, such as Katy, have poor receptive and expressive language.

When children are in school, teachers expect them to be able to follow verbal instructions, lectures, and guidelines. Teachers also expect students to respond to academic exchanges using a certain vocabulary and structure. For students with difficulties in listening and limited experience in formal oral exchanges, the ability to follow through on a given verbal direction can be a challenge. Poor receptive language can result in lower grades, gaps in a knowledge base, and the inability to work effectively with others. Social interactions can also be affected by difficulties with listening to and understanding language. As children grow older and become employed, poor receptive oral language abilities can hinder vocational success and lower job performance.

John has a part-time job after school at McBurgers. One afternoon, his supervisor stated, "Pull out the french fries after the timer goes off." Not understanding when he was supposed to remove the fries, he began wrapping hamburgers. When the timer went off, he did not remove the french fries. Smoke started to flow from the deep frier. John's supervi-

309

sor quickly pulled the french fries out of the oil and promptly informed John, "You've got to follow directions if you want to keep your job here."

Expressive language skills are needed consistently throughout school and in the work environment. Students are expected to give oral reports, engage in oral reading, and interact with their classmates on a daily basis. If a child's ability to tell stories or describe events is limited, performance in the areas of reading comprehension and written expression is affected (Catts, 1993; Roth & Speckman, 1994). When children have difficulties with acquiring and using language, academic performance is hindered (Bishop & Adams, 1990; Catts, 1993; Dickinson et al., 2003; Dickinson & McCabe, 2001; McArthur et al., 2000; Mengler et al., 2005; NICHD Early Child Care Research Network, 2005; Rissman, Curtiss, & Tallal, 1990; Roth & Speckman, 1994; Share & Leikin, 2004; Storch & Whitehurst, 2002).

Literacy Instruction for English Language Learners[1]

The importance of oral language proficiency is clearly demonstrated in the academic trajectory of students who are English language learners (ELLs); achievement of these learners lags behind that of English monolingual children (Lee, 2002). English language learners face a unique set of challenges, from navigating everyday conversations to understanding curriculum content in an unfamiliar language. According to the U.S. Department of Education, nearly 1 in 12 students in public schools in 2001–2002 received support services to learn English, making ELLs the fastest growing group in the school-age population of the United States (National Center for Educational Statistics [NCES], 2006). The largest growing segment of ELLs either emigrated to the United States before kindergarten or were born in the United States to immigrant parents. Although 70 percent of ELLs speak Spanish, the remaining 30 percent speak more than 400 different languages (NCES, 2006).

English language learners present a unique set of challenges to educators because of the central role played by academic language proficiency in the acquisition and assessment of content-area knowledge. Although ELLs vary in their academic outcomes and many thrive in U.S. schools, there is a significant proportion—some of whom have been formally designated as ELLs and are receiving support services for language development and some of whom have not been formally designated as ELLs—who struggle considerably in developing English proficiency and academic skills and meeting grade-level standards. For teachers, two major concerns exist regarding students who are ELLs: first, identifying what are effective evidence-based strategies and interventions for teaching academic skills and second, defining what is a reasonable rate for growth in English competency.

Researchers studying ELLs and academic achievement have begun to identify evidence-based strategies and interventions that are effective in teaching literacy skills to this population of learners. Crucial components of instruction for ELLs include decoding, comprehension, and oral language skills (August & Shanahan, 2006; Gentile, 2004; Graves, Gersten, & Haager, 2004). The need to focus on oral language skills when providing literacy instruction to ELLs cannot be overlooked. Gentile (2004) observed that instruction in literacy skills for ELLs without a corresponding emphasis on oral language development failed to yield positive results. Given that caveat, ELLs can meet with success when provided with effective intervention programs addressing all areas of oral language development.

As with their native English-speaking peers, ELLs can learn to decode words when provided with skilled, explicit instruction (Graves et al., 2004). Studies have

---

[1] This section was contributed by Annmarie Urso.

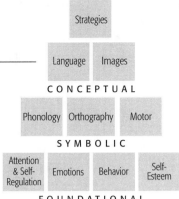

shown that when ELLs in kindergarten have received systematic instruction in phonological awareness, explicit instruction in phonics, opportunities for multiple reading experiences, and continual progress monitoring, their performance after 2 years has been comparable to their English-speaking peers (Lesaux & Siegel, 2003; Stuart, 1999).

Although learning to decode comes rather quickly to ELLs who receive skilled, systematic, and direct instruction, comprehending text is much more difficult and can be more challenging. Several factors contribute to the complexity of comprehension instruction for ELLs, including the ELL's native language literacy level, their oral language skills using academic language in English, and their oral language skills in conversational English. Many teachers are surprised to learn that good conversational English skills do not equate to the comprehension skills necessary for understanding academic language. Academic language, often referred to as Academic English, includes a student's capacity to read, write, and engage in extensive conversations about content-area subjects. Most ELLs lag well behind their peers in the oral language skills and content knowledge needed for proficiency in Academic English. For ELLs, the development of Academic English to the competency level of their English-speaking peers can take between 4 and 12 years, depending on whether the nonnative speaker of English had any schooling in their native language (Collier, 1995; Collier & Thomas, 1989; Cummins, 1989).

Vocabulary development is critical to the development of Academic English (August, Carlo, Dressler, & Snow, 2005). Native English speakers enter kindergarten with a vocabulary of 5,000–7,000 words, placing ELLs at a huge disadvantage compared with their native English-speaking peers (Hart & Risley, 1995). If ELLs have developed literacy in their own language, developing vocabulary in English involves learning the English vocabulary equivalent for a known concept. However, if ELLs have not developed literacy in their native language, they must learn both the concept and the vocabulary for each new word. The latter is a much more complex and time-consuming task for both ELLs and their teachers.

Researchers have found that through explicit, meaningful, and structured conversation and listening opportunities about academically important content, ELLs learn the words needed to engage in class discussions and the concepts needed to comprehend what they read in various content-area subjects. As with native English learners, memorizing word lists is inefficient and ineffective for learning vocabulary (Kauffman, 2007). The key to developing vocabulary concepts for ELLs is to provide meaningful, structured, and supported experiences adapted to the student's level of English development. Cooperative groupings, use of selected videos and media, as well as provision of enriching activities to support expository texts have been found to increase vocabulary development and comprehension (Carlo et al., 2004; Lesaux, 2006). When teaching reading comprehension skills, evidence-based strategies have been identified for struggling readers that can be especially helpful for ELLs. One of the most relevant and effective strategies is to teach the skills and strategies necessary for comprehension of text explicitly (Graves et al., 2004). For ELLs, particular focus on explicitly teaching the syntax of language and the text structure of expository, narrative, and hyper text (i.e., text that is read on a computer that has links and connections to other related information), with special attention paid to vocabulary development, has been shown to increase comprehension skills (August & Shanahan, 2006; Minskoff, 2005; National Reading Panel, 2000).

When ELLs have developed literacy skills in their first language in an academic setting for several years prior to entering English-speaking schools, researchers have found several distinct advantages. First, word reading, reading comprehension, and the use of reading strategies in English are strongly correlated to these skills in an ELL's first language (August & Shanahan, 2006). In addition, the early stages of spelling in English show the influence of the first language on the ELL's orthographic knowledge, as do aspects of their written expression (August & Shanahan, 2006).

Systematic progress monitoring also allows for appropriate levels of intervention and will ensure appropriate development of skills. The critical components of reading instruction for ELLs are 1) high quality, explicit instruction in phonemic awareness and decoding; 2) rich vocabulary development; 3) comprehension instruction using explicit and interactive teaching during all phases of reading; and 4) structured opportunities for oral language development, with a strong emphasis on daily oral language activities (Gentile, 2004; Graves et al., 2004; Kauffman, 2007). Extra time and instruction in literacy may be necessary to ensure an appropriate rate of Academic English achievement. Literacy instruction delivered by experienced, highly trained teachers must include several years of intensive, high-quality instruction with lots of practice and frequent assessment to identify students' strengths and weaknesses. In addition, awareness and development of the students' literacy skills in their native languages will enhance their English development (August & Shanahan, 2006). In summary, ELLs need skilled teachers who can deliver intensive and explicit reading instruction using evidence-based reading strategies and interventions in a supportive environment. This type of instruction will assist ELLs in becoming fluent in speaking, reading, and writing Academic English.

Instruction for Language Development

The acquisition of language occurs by both implicit and explicit instruction (Brabham & Villaume, 2002). Vygotsky (1978) explained that one important way in which language develops is through social interactions with more knowledgeable language users. Hall (1987) supported Vygotsky's theory but added that children developing language need to 1) be the major constructors of language, 2) construct language in conjunction with placing meaning to their world and print, and 3) use language as a function to clarify information about themselves and others. As teachers and students work together to attain educational goals, they must model the process of learning by talking about these processes as they perform tasks. Englert (1992) provided an analogy to explain the mutual and reciprocal contributions of the teacher and students. Think of a team practicing volleyball. The team works together to keep the ball in play. As they practice, the teacher, like any good volleyball coach, stands by, ready to assist and provide instruction when needed.

Modeling   Oral language forms the basis for understanding what is read, expressing ideas in writing, and solving mathematical story problems. Through discussions with students, teachers can model the kind of thinking that people do while reading and problem solving, thus building the conceptual block of language. What this means, quite simply, is that the teacher describes actions orally or the steps of a procedure while performing the activity. You may use visual cues and talk aloud while students watch and listen. Through modeling, students become more strategic in their approaches and assume increasing responsibility for task completion.

Expansion and Elaboration   Another way to help students increase their understanding is to describe the actions that the student is performing. Two simple techniques are expansion and elaboration. For expansion, extend the student's remark to a more complete and correct form. So if the child said, "I kept the book," you may remark, "Oh, you kept the book?" For elaboration, take the student's response, expand it to a correct form, and then add some

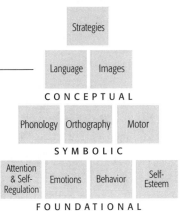

additional information. You may say, "I am glad you kept that book. I knew you would think it was an interesting story." These types of simple activities help students increase language abilities as well as word knowledge.

Paraphrasing   When students have trouble remembering what they hear, make sure that the students understand oral directions. Ask students to paraphrase, repeat, or explain instructions or ask students to repeat the questions they are being asked and rephrase the question in their own words before answering. Students may also ask questions and respond in different ways (e.g., read the information aloud, say it aloud, describe a visual image). Several techniques, outlined in the section on visual imagery, can help students learn how to form mental pictures.

Background Knowledge   One critical factor that influences oral expression, reading comprehension, and written expression is background knowledge, or what one already knows about a topic. When students do not understand what they hear or read or do not have much to write or say, it is usually because they have limited background knowledge about the topic. In other words, people understand most easily and write most fluently when the topics relate to or build on background and experiences. Cromley and Azevedo (2007) found that background knowledge and vocabulary made the strongest contributions to reading comprehension for students in ninth grade. They suggested that the most effective interventions for older students should focus on increasing academic vocabulary and background knowledge.

Both Katy and John have trouble understanding classroom instruction because many of the concepts are new and the vocabulary that is used is unfamiliar and difficult. The main reasons that they have trouble understanding are that they have limited vocabularies and lack the necessary background information to grasp the concepts presented.

John's high school biology teacher noted that John was highly motivated but did not retain the concepts that were presented in class and in the textbook. John had consequently failed the first three weekly biology examinations. John was also failing examinations in history. His history teacher, Dr. Mantell, commented that although John was attentive and participated actively in class, his oral answers to questions were often incorrect and, at times, not even related to the topic.

When asked to define words as part of a reading evaluation, John appeared to have tangential knowledge of some words, but he seemed confused about the exact meanings of words. For example, John said that *equator* was an antonym for *latitude*. When asked for a synonym for *zero*, he responded, "One million because it has lots of zeros." Responses to other questions further revealed his confusion and lack of information about basic concepts. When asked, "What is paper made from?" John replied, "Sodium." When asked, "Which country borders the United States on the north, and which country borders the United States on the south?" he answered, "Hawaii and England." For students such as John and Katy, the teacher should begin instruction by finding out what they already know about a topic and then relate the new information to the established concepts.

K-W-L Strategy   A simple strategy for helping students increase their knowledge is called the K-W-L strategy (Ogle, 1986). To begin, write three columns across the top of a piece of paper, as illustrated in Figure 10.1, and then help students complete the worksheet. In the first column, students brainstorm what

K What I Know	W What I Want to Learn	L What I Learned
Have students brain-storm and list any information that they already know about the topic.	Have students develop questions about what they want to learn about the topic.	Have students record what they have learned from reading and library research.

Figure 10.1. K-W-L sheet.

they already know about the topic (What I Know [K]). In the second column, after group discussions, students list questions about what they want to learn about the topic (What I <u>W</u>ant to Learn [W]). Students can then work in small groups to answer questions and record results in the third column (What I Learned [L]). For students with more limited abilities, a peer may help with notetaking.

After completing the worksheet, students may write a paragraph that summarizes what they have learned about the topic. K-W-L also provides the opportunity for the student to review and rehearse what has been learned. Katy completed a K-W-L sheet, presented in Figure 10.2, with a cooperative learning group in her fifth-grade classroom. The group was studying spiders.

K What we know	W What we want to find out	L What we learned
- Spiders have 8 legs - Spider have sharp teeth - - They climb in webs - Some spider bite people - Some can live under water - Some male spiders get killed	- Why do spider bite people? - Do all spider bite? - Why do spider have 8 eyes? - How many eggs do spiders lay? - Are spiders helpful to people? How? - Why do femal spiders kill the male spiders?	- To protect themselves - No - Not all have 8 eyes. - More then 100 eggs in a sack for sorten spiers) - They eat insects the plant we grew. - When there hungrey.

Figure 10.2. K-W-L on spiders.

Sampson (2002) suggested an adaptation to the K-W-L strategy that teaches students to support the statements they make with confirmed sources. She changed the first statement of the activity to read "What We Think We Know" followed by a column to confirm the idea in which students write down the correct information and another column to list the reference source. She then used the traditional "What I Want to Learn" and "What I Learned" columns but followed them with another column in which students would have to support what they learned with a source. Teachers reported that students benefited from this extension because it forced them to gather data from sources to support statements they had made.

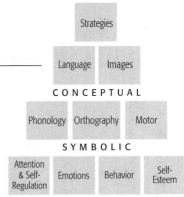

Vocabulary The breadth and depth of an individual's vocabulary can affect school success. Because vocabulary knowledge is needed for most academic tasks, teachers must remember that "vocabulary is acquired both incidentally through indirect exposure and intentionally through explicit instruction in specific words and word-learning strategies" (Diamond & Gutlohn, 2006, p. 1). Students with well-established vocabularies tend to speak, read, and write more effectively.

Findings from a review of 27 studies investigating the effects of vocabulary instruction with students with learning disabilities (LD) continue to substantiate that methods employing the direct teaching of vocabulary are effective and that systematic practice of word meanings is critical to vocabulary acquisition and maintenance (Burns, Dean, & Foley, 2004; Jitendra, Edwards, Sacks, & Jacobsen, 2004). In addition, explicit teaching of word meanings within the context of shared storybook reading is effective for young children with reading difficulties (Coyne, Simmons, & Kame'enui, 2004) and is the most powerful way to help children develop new vocabulary (Stahl & Stahl, 2004). Read books aloud several times to children and combine the reading with an explanation of 8–10 new vocabulary words (Biemiller, 2004). Coyne, McCoach, and Kapp (2007) found that extended instruction that provided review of the target words in varied and meaningful contexts resulted in more complete knowledge of word meanings for students in kindergarten than simply providing definitions during story reading. They concluded that extended, direct vocabulary instruction can increase vocabulary knowledge. In contrast, for older students with LD, methods such as looking up words in a dictionary and writing definitions or using context clues to determine a word's meaning are ineffective (Bryant, Goodwin, Bryant, & Higgins, 2003).

Students with LD as well as ELLs require multiple exposures to words to master word meaning. In addition to the need for more practice, a growing consensus exists regarding other elements of effective vocabulary instruction. In a review of four effective vocabulary programs, Foorman, Seals, Anthony, and Pollard-Durodola (2003) found that the programs were consistent on the following instructional principles: 1) introduction of approximately 3 words per day, or no more than 12 to 15 words per week; 2) selection of words that could be extended derivationally and conceptually through discussion; 3) location and discussion of words in engaging text; and 4) provision of contextualized definitions with practice opportunities in new and multiple contexts. In addition, words should be taught in a sequence with an attempt to determine which words should be learned next. The words to target for struggling readers are usually the ones that some children of that grade level know but others do not (Biemiller, 2005). Vocabulary instruction should focus on words that students will see or read often and will be useful (McKeown & Beck, 2004). Thus, the vocabulary words being taught need to be of appropriate complexity (Stahl & Stahl, 2004).

Graves (2000) outlined four components of an effective vocabulary program with accompanying procedures that can help students increase vocabulary.

1. Encourage students to engage in wide or expanded independent reading to expand word knowledge.

   • Check first to see if students can define the new word by reading it in context (i.e., by reading the rest of the sentence or paragraph). This strategy can reduce the amount of time they spend looking up words. If they cannot define the word, looking it up in the dictionary or asking someone else are better strategies than skipping the word.

2. Provide instruction in specific words to enhance comprehension of texts containing those words.

   • Ask the students to select a word, relate it to other information, check the definition, write the definition, and use the word in a written sentence. Grouping words by similar meaning for practice can enhance recall.

3. Provide instruction in independent word-learning strategies.

   • Encourage students to write down and define unfamiliar words in a small notebook, inside the covers of their notebooks, or on the reverse side of the page when they first encounter them.

4. Encourage the development of word consciousness and word-play activities to motivate and enhance learning.

   • Encourage students to practice using new words in conversations and assignments, to listen for new words when watching television, and to play with words by doing crosswords and other word puzzles. Practice with using words increases the likelihood that students will retain word meanings. Katy's fifth-grade teacher, Ms. McGrew, would log onto http://www.puzzlemaker.com. This web site enables teachers to create word puzzles for students using any words they select.

As students progress through school, the vocabulary in classes becomes increasingly specialized. Some students benefit from direct instruction on the use of common prefixes and suffixes and the study of word origins. Students can also study the various derivations of words to increase their understanding of how common morphemes, prefixes, and suffixes alter word meaning. This type of instruction can be enhanced with a graphic organizer. Ms. McGrew, Katy's teacher, would place a word in the center of the map, such as the word *friend*, and then have the students brainstorm all of the words they could think of that are formed using this root. Figure 10.3 illustrates the completed class graphic.

Many texts have glossaries; when they do not, students can make a list of words with easy-to-understand definitions. John found that dictionaries sometimes offered definitions that were more confusing than helpful. He found that a glossary in an ability-appropriate text with a good index was far more useful. Many teachers post words on signs in their rooms to help reinforce new or important vocabulary words or phrases. Building a word wall around a specific content area is also useful for helping students increase their vocabulary. Modeling the use of different strategies in the classroom on a regular basis helps students learn to apply them.

Students can also use technology to expand vocabulary. Students can use the Franklin Speaking Language Master™ (see Additional Resources) or a software program that provides pronunciations and definitions orally. A reading pen such as the Quicktionary Reading Pen and other reading pens provide definitions of scanned words. (See Additional Resources.)

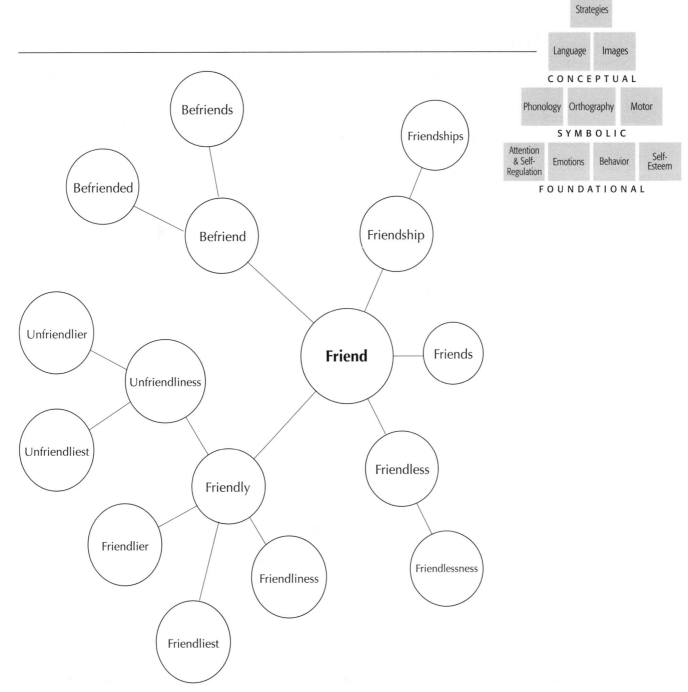

Figure 10.3. Map for derivations of the word *friend*.

Adequate time and attention must be devoted to helping students such as Katy and John increase their word knowledge through multiple exposures to words and systematic and intensive instruction. Without this type of instruction, gaps in vocabulary knowledge will continue throughout elementary school, leaving students at greater risk for continued problems with reading comprehension and written expression as they progress through school.

Higher Level Questioning Skills Some students need help developing the use of higher level questioning skills. As students progress in school, a greater emphasis is placed on assignments that require analytical and critical thinking. Asking questions presents an opportunity for active engagement with the material. As a result, more effective learning occurs. John found that it helped him to ask and try to answer questions in a variety of situations, such as taking notes from a text, writing a research paper, or studying a chapter in his math textbook. Model how to ask questions during class discussions.

Dr. Mantell, John's history teacher, encouraged students to recall related facts from several sources, express an opinion and give reasons, summarize what they had learned so far, predict the consequences of certain actions, and organize information in new ways. During class discussions, she asked the following types of questions:

- How are the ideas related to one another?

- How do they relate to what you already know?

- What is the main idea of _____?

- What if _____?

- How does it affect _____?

- What is the meaning of _____?

- Why is _____ important?

- Explain why _____.

- Explain how _____.

- How does this relate to what you've learned before?

- What conclusions can you draw?

- What is the difference between _____ and _____?

- How are _____ and _____ similar?

- How would you use _____?

- What are the strengths and weaknesses of _____?

- What is the best choice and why?

By using these types of questions, Dr. Mantell created an interactive classroom in which students are encouraged to discuss, clarify, compare, expand on, and review ideas.

THINKING WITH IMAGES: NONVERBAL LEARNING DISABILITIES

Although much of the emphasis in the field of LD has been placed on students who struggle with the acquisition and use of spoken and written language, a smaller subset of students show symptoms that are characteristic of what have been referred to as *nonverbal learning disabilities* (NVLD). Although the characteristics of students with NVLD do not fit neatly into any one block of the building blocks model, two major characteristics are poor spatial organization and inattention to visual details, abilities related to generating and using visual images.

Characteristics

Many students with NVLD are poorly organized and appear unfocused. Although they may be described as inattentive and distractible, these observed

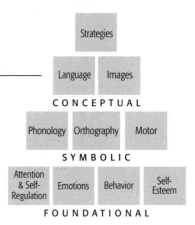

behaviors result from a reduced capacity for self-directed behavior rather than from attention-deficit/hyperactivity disorder (ADHD) (Fletcher, Taylor, Levin, & Satz, 1995). A student with NVLD has strengths in word decoding, spelling, and rote memory but encounters extreme difficulty with reading comprehension, arithmetic, and mathematical problem solving (Fletcher, 1985; Gathercole & Pickering, 2000; Miller, 2004; Rourke, 1995). Students often exhibit social difficulties, become overwhelmed by interacting with people, and have extreme difficulties in dealing with novel and complex materials. In addition, these students have difficulty acquiring new skills, particularly motor skills.

Because a student with NVLD presents early strengths in the development of general declarative knowledge and vocabulary, identification of these problems tends to occur in later grades. As the student moves through school, tasks that require higher level spatial-analytic abilities, such as those involved in mathematical problem solving, present increasing difficulty. Students with NVLD also lack skill in reading and responding to nonverbal communications due to their visual foundation (Most & Greenbank, 2000). Because a large proportion of the communication in an average conversation is nonverbal in nature, a student with NVLD may miss important information about what is being communicated and may be unsure of how to respond (Rothenberg, 1998). Students with Asperger syndrome often struggle with the same issues, and recent research suggests that NVLD may fall within the spectrum of autism disorders (Miller, 2004; National Research Council, 2001; Rourke et al., 2002).

Stephanie, a fourth-grade student, was often alone at lunchtime and recess. When she tried to engage her peers, she stood too close to them and asked in too loud of a voice if they would play with her. In the classroom, she often blurted out inappropriate answers. When she attempted to use a compass to draw a circle for her math assignment, she could not coordinate the series of movements. When she read aloud in class, she decoded words with ease but then had trouble responding to questions. Her responses often revealed poor comprehension and lack of attention to critical details. For example, when asked, "Why did the children go into the cave?" she responded, "What cave?" Stephanie's teacher, Ms. Richards, noticed that she was much more successful when ideas and concepts were presented to her sequentially within small groups of information and when she was provided with opportunities for repeated practice.

Interventions

In general, students with NVLD benefit when interventions are highly concrete and as verbal as possible. Help a student with NVLD feel in control of the present academic environment before introducing new information or skills. Methods should be highly structured and systematic and should provide external guidance. Expectations may need to be simplified, broken down, or modified. Establishing consistent expectations between home and school or from class to class is often beneficial and involves collaboration with family members and colleagues. Stephanie had difficulties with generalization, and she had trouble recognizing which skills she should apply in new situations. Her performance improved when her teacher reviewed previous steps before introducing new information or processes.

Students with NVLD benefit from consistency and predictability, which helps them avoid being overwhelmed or confused. Thus, relatively static learning environments can be helpful to them. These students often require more time when processing information that requires visual imagery (Cornoldi, Rigoni, Tressoldi, & Vio, 1999). Verbal clarifications can help students make meaningful connections among ideas (Foss, 1991; Vacca, 2001). For example, Ms. Richards found that Stephanie was confused by the time line about ancient Egypt. Once she had explained why the period of time indicated by B.C.E. (before the Common Era) decreased in years as time had passed, Stephanie was able to interpret the time line successfully.

Students with NVLD have difficulty with reading social cues, so they may misinterpret the actions of classmates and teachers. Direct teaching of cause-and-effect relationships for specific circumstances is helpful. Because verbal ability is typically considered a strength, teaching students how to use self-talk to reinforce routines or procedures can help them complete simple and complex tasks. Rourke (1995) recommended using a "part-to-whole" verbal teaching approach in which information is presented in a logical sequence. In this approach, the teacher helps students complete difficult tasks by encouraging them to proceed one step at a time, paying attention to details.

Ms. Richards taught Stephanie the following strategy to employ when she was approaching novel tasks. When Stephanie started to work, she first asked herself, "What does the teacher want me to do?" If she could not come up with this answer, she asked other students who were seated nearby. Stephanie then found a partner and worked out the steps to take to complete the task. Stephanie made an outline of the steps by placing picture cards that had been supplied to her on an outline. After she gained understanding of what was being asked and the steps she must take, Stephanie asked herself the question, "What do I need to accomplish this task?" She gathered the materials that she needed to complete the task and brought them into the working area. When Stephanie was unsure about a step, she first attempted to obtain clarification from a peer. If that failed, she proceeded to ask the teacher for clarification.

Both students with oral language impairments and students with NVLD can benefit from using visually based techniques to support learning.

Instruction Using Visual Imagery

Several techniques can be used to help students learn to structure information visually. When providing instruction in tasks that require visual imagery, create drawings, webs, or maps. Encourage students to try to create mental images of the information presented. Translating information into visual formats can help students such as John, Katy, and Stephanie store and retrieve important information.

Visualization   An easy way to encourage students to think with images is to help them learn to visualize words, settings, or scenes. Consider the expression "A picture is worth a thousand words." When students are shown pictures, it helps them expand their understanding. When students learn to form mental scenes, it enhances their expression.

When students in Stephanie's class were asked to write a story about traveling to the moon, Ms. Richards asked Stephanie to close her eyes and imagine she was in a spaceship on her way to the moon. She then asked Stephanie to tell her everything that she could see. Ms. Richards then wrote down Stephanie's observations so that Stephanie would be able to integrate the ideas into her writing assignment. She also asked Stephanie questions to help her expand information about the pictured scene.

320

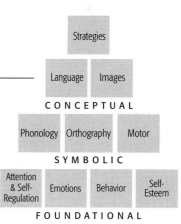

Specialized vocabularies are part of most domains of study.

For biology class, John was attempting to learn the terms *mitosis* and *meiosis.* He was having difficulty with grasping that in mitosis, when a cell reproduces, it creates two genetically identical daughter cells. In meiosis, the cell divides into four gametes, each of which possesses half the number of chromosomes in the original cell. John's teacher provided two diagrams in which the stages were laid out in a circle, in order to emphasize that the processes occur in a cycle. John's task was to fill in the names of the stages. Once John accomplished this, his teacher had John put this information into a hierarchy format so that he could see how his text described the process. To reinforce the information, the teacher then had John use materials—a sheet of paper as the cell; rubber bands for membranes; string for spindle fibers; and pennies, dimes, and quarters for chromosomes—so that he could create a visual display of the processes. John increased his understanding of the concepts by using materials that he could manipulate and by seeing the stages laid out in a visual sequence. He was able to pass the quiz and move on to the next biology lesson.

Many students do not view the diagrams, charts, graphs, and illustrations included in their texts as important pieces of information, or they do not know how to use them. Helping students understand how to interpret these illustrations can improve comprehension.

Ms. McGrew asked her students to develop posters for a section of her science class in which they were studying nutrition. Because Katy avoided the graphs and diagrams in her book (they look too much like math to her), she lacked important information, and, consequently, she failed to understand the assignment. Ms. McGrew asked Katy what aspect of nutrition interested her the most. Katy said that she often saw her mother making decisions about what to buy at the grocery store by reading information on labels, but she didn't know what it meant. Ms. McGrew used this example to develop Katy's understanding. She had her bring in labels from three brands of cereal and then assisted her in making a bar graph that compared the differences in amounts of vitamins, sugar, calories, fiber, and grams of fat visually through the use of color and proportion. Katy learned that a bar graph is a way to make comparisons, and she found out that her favorite cereal contained the most sugar and was the least nutritious. A few days later, she used her new knowledge to ask a question about a bar graph in her text.

Key-Word Method   Some methods that are designed to help students recall vocabulary focus on the creation of visual images. These methods can help students recall more difficult terminology, such as new words to be learned for a math, science, or history class. Mastropieri (1988) described the key-word method, which involves tying new words to visual images to help students recall word meanings and learn new vocabulary. Three steps are used in the key-word method: recoding, relating, and retrieving. For recoding, students change the new vocabulary word into a known word, the key word that has a similar sound and is easily pictured. For relating, students associate the key word with the definition of the new vocabulary word through a mental image or a sentence. For retrieving, students think of the key word, remember the association, and then retrieve the definition. Research findings indicate that the key-word mnemonic strategy can both increase vocabulary knowledge and facilitate recall of words over time (Jitendra et al., 2004).

To use the key-word method, begin by defining and discussing the meaning of the new word with students. Next, discuss with the students various options for a key word and then make a picture of the definition doing something with the key word. The key word may be a rhyming word or a word that evokes specific visual imagery. Students then study what they have imagined until they can recall the definition. For example, the special education teacher was trying to help Katy learn the meaning of the word *apex*. Katy created an image of a gorilla standing on a spot marked with the letter *X* on top of a mountain. When she was asked to produce the definition, this image came easily to mind. This strategy can also be used to develop mnemonic devices to assist students in remembering specific information.

Graphic Organizers   Graphic organizers provide a visual representation of main ideas or concepts. Together with the student, develop an idea framework in which information is organized to depict important relationships. Graphic organizers may take the form of maps, time lines, diagrams, pictures, flowcharts, pyramids, or webs.

Graphic organizers can be used for several different purposes. When teachers use graphic organizers as instructional tools in presenting new information to their classes, they often find that the graphic organizer helps them to formulate, clarify, and evaluate instructional objectives. When used in small-group discussions in class, students can be asked to analyze and visualize the relationships of key concepts. Students can generate their own graphic organizers after they read a selection. Because they are more actively engaged with the material, students who use postreading organizers learn more. Graphic organizers can also be helpful when students write papers, serving as a method for organizing information that is then developed into text.

Mapping   One simple procedure for organizing information in a visual display is called mapping or webbing. This procedure focuses on using the images block to enhance memory and understanding. Maps or webs are graphic organizers that help children develop and organize their thoughts. Picture a spider web. Think of how all of the threads connect and seem intertwined. Similar to a web, graphic organizers show connections. The visual display depicts the important ideas and the relationships among ideas. The illustrations of these relationships help students link together the information. Consequently, their understanding and ability to recall information improve.

Mapping techniques work well for visual learners because visual memory reinforces the learning of information. Mapping requires the use of both hemispheres of the brain. Information is linked together or chunked. Relationships among pieces of information, particularly between facts and ideas, are developed. Mapping strategies do not require neat handwriting or presentation to be effective and can be used in conjunction with other note-taking techniques. Buzan (1991) described a variety of ways in which the concept of mapping can be applied.

Adaptation of the K-W-L Strategy   An adaptation of the K-W-L strategy, described earlier in the chapter, adds mapping and summarization (Carr & Ogle, 1987). To add the mapping component, children categorize the information listed under L. The topic forms the center of the map. For example, because Katy was learning about spiders, she wrote *spiders* in the center of the map. Lines are then added to show the relationships between the main topic and the facts that are gathered.

Students then use the map to create a summary. The center of the map becomes the title of the essay, and each category is used as the topic for a new paragraph. Supporting details are then added to expand or explain the topic further. After practice with this procedure, some students are able to omit the

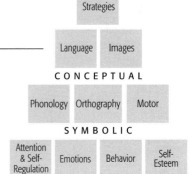

mapping step and write their summaries directly from the K-W-L worksheet. The adapted K-W-L strategy using mapping helps students acquire, relate, and learn concepts; increase vocabulary; and discuss important points and key words.

Brainstorming Another use of mapping is as a brainstorming strategy that lets students rapidly produce and order a large number of ideas. Each idea is organized by placing it next to related ones. This creative visual process begins with a central word or concept that is placed at the center of the page or screen; then, approximately 5–10 main ideas that relate to that concept are added. As materials become more detailed and supporting ideas are articulated, several more words that relate to any of the first words are added. The use of shapes, such as circles, squares, and rectangles, along with symbols, such as arrows and equal signs, becomes the visual means to designate relationships among concepts. In this way, an exponential number of related ideas can be produced quickly. Students may place a page horizontally or use large sheets of paper for this process. Some students learn to use index cards for each subset of information. Students can follow these steps to create a map:

1. Write the topic in the middle of the page, and draw a circle around it.

2. Draw a line outward from the circle, and write a related main idea or word on it.

3. Place a border or shape around the new information.

4. Add branches, each with an idea or fact, generally becoming more specific in detail.

5. Draw branching lines out from these facts, and keep adding relevant information.

6. Personalize the map by adding pictures and symbols and by creating acronyms. (Illogical and humorous associations are sometimes effective ways to remember information.)

7. Use key words when possible. Key words, usually nouns or verbs, can represent summarized ideas, resulting in fewer words to write and remember.

8. Look for repetitions and for more accurate linking words. Add numbers if there is a sequence or hierarchy to the information.

9. Use colored pencils or pens, using one color for main ideas, another color for supporting ideas, and another color for details.

Maps can also be linked. One map can identify the five main ideas in a chapter and the student can then create five individual maps, one for each idea. As a study strategy, students can try to reproduce the map from memory or arrange the same information in a different format. Students can post maps on the wall and embellish them with illustrations (in addition to using color).

Mapping can also facilitate active listening. During class discussions or lectures, help students identify a key idea or concept, which is then recorded in the center of the page. Ask the students to attempt to include each related idea. When discussions or presentations are not sequential, students may use mapping to isolate the key points that each speaker is adding to the discussions. Students can add the connections that were made among the points later. Taking the time to rearrange and review the map is a process that helps reinforce the important points of the discussion and helps clarify thinking and reduce the time needed to study. Some students prefer to make their maps after hearing the entire lecture or discussion in order to synthesize and review the information. Another effective strategy is to pair students together to create a map.

To create maps when reading text, ask a student to read the passage to be mapped, select the most important idea, and write it in the center of the page. As the student rereads the passage, he or she can identify key concepts and rank them in order of importance. The student can then arrange the concepts on the page, link the concepts by drawing circles and lines among them, and review the maps to determine if additional information needs to be added. By placing concepts on 3″ × 5″ cards or sticky notes, concepts can be rearranged easily. Students can also use the mapping technique for writing a paper. Students can take the notes that they have made (on either 3″ × 5″ index cards or on sticky notes) and place them in an order that structures the paper. Each card can then be expanded into a sentence or paragraph.

Figure 10.4 is an example of a mind map that John developed in his class on free enterprise. John's teacher assigned a chapter to be read and indicated that students should be prepared to join in a discussion about the reading the next day. The chapter was about marketing strategies and looked specifically at the advantages of selling to individuals versus

Figure 10.4. John's mind map.

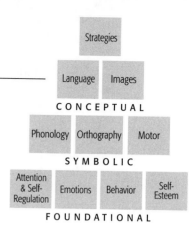

selling to the mass market. John read the chapter and began to sort out the information. He decided that although the author seemed to him to be talking about marketing, the content was more about how one decides to sell something. Because this seemed to John to be the main focus of the chapter, he placed it in the middle of his map. When he thought about what he had just read, it occurred to him that the author was talking about selling to a mass market, which seemed large, and about selling to people more directly, which is interpersonal. He added two nodes, or branches, one on each side of the first, to indicate this distinction. He also knew he needed a bit more information in order to keep this in focus, so he added the cue that mass marketing means that a large audience gets the same message or sales pitch. The author emphasized several points about mass marketing, so John wrote down short phrases he felt he could remember in order to summarize each of them. He then found that the author had used the same approach when writing about interpersonal marketing, so he added brief summaries to his map about those also.

John thought about what his teacher would ask them to discuss and decided that the topic would most likely be the advantages and disadvantages of each form of marketing. He noted that there were three advantages to selling to the mass market. He also recognized that there were three disadvantages. Because John was doing his map on the software program Inspiration® (see Additional Resources), he was able to rearrange the placement of these points easily so that the advantages were above his main concept and the negatives were below the main concept. (Placing concepts on index cards would provide the student with an alternate way to accomplish the same goal.) As John was thinking about where the connections should be placed, he also added arrows to show the connections he thought he saw; he then began to realize that what was an advantage of one type of marketing strategy was not an advantage in the other marketing strategy. (For example, quick feedback is an advantage when using an interpersonal marketing strategy but is not possible when using a mass-market strategy.) John figured out that the really important point he was supposed to learn is that it is hard to decide which marketing strategy to use because there is no clear choice.

Creating the map helped John take charge of his learning. He had to focus on key concepts, select supporting details, compare and contrast information, and make decisions about what was and was not important. The week before, after reading a chapter, he had forgotten what he had read and was uncomfortable going into class. This week, he felt he had a much better grasp of the reading assignment because the information was now easier to recall. The map represented a summary of his reading, and he knew that if he forgot a point, he could review the map and refresh his memory quickly.

Spatial Outlining   Spatial outlining is another type of graphic organizer that can help a student learn how to take notes when a teacher talks quickly or when the class discussion or lecture seems to jump around. This procedure helps the learner determine how ideas and concepts are related. John's special education teacher taught him to use spatial outlining by following these steps:

1. Turn standard notebook paper sideways (11″ × 8.5″) to allow a wider space for recording ideas and separating concepts from details and examples.

2. Divide each page into three columns: a very narrow one on the left for very general topic words; a medium column in the middle for more specific subpoints; and the widest column on the right for facts, details, and examples.

3. Decide which of the three columns each piece of information fits into and record it there. Leave plenty of white space for connecting ideas

later. Use pauses in the discussion or presentation to draw arrows and other signals in order to remember which pieces go together.

4. Review the outline, connecting the general topics with the subpoints and details in order to identify any missing information and to determine ideas that need clarification.

Additional applications of graphic organizers are included in Chapter 11.

THINKING WITH STRATEGIES: METACOGNITIVE AND EXECUTIVE PROCESSES

The building block of strategies is at the top of the Building Blocks model. This block is the most important because the abilities involved integrate language, reasoning, planning, self-monitoring, and self-evaluation. Evidence-based processing interventions tend to focus on higher level cognitive processes, such as working memory and executive functioning (Dehn, 2006). Most students can be successful in school if they learn how to be organized, reflective, and strategic. Unfortunately, many students with LD have a limited repertoire of strategies and fail to monitor their academic performance (Montague, 2007).

Metacognition is the ability to think about one's own thinking. It is a capacity to adjust how one learns and what skills and strategies are needed to complete changing academic demands (Zimmerman, 1986). Weaknesses in metacognition appear to affect the development and use of strategies adversely and to impede progress in academic tasks (Montague, 1997). Students who struggle in school often do not employ useful learning strategies. When students do not learn to use metacognitive strategies, their ability to complete tasks decreases. Students who are unable to choose the appropriate strategy to complete a task may be described as having deficient executive processing skills. Competency in metacognitive strategies has been found to be a strong predictor of academic success for students with LD at the college level, further validating the need for such skills (Ruban, 2000; Smitely, 2001).

Executive processing is the portion of metacognition that relates to a student's ability to choose a strategy that will assist in problem-solving activities. Estimating memory capacity for specific tasks, predicting accuracy on a memory task, allotting appropriate time to study, and deciding when one has studied enough are all parts of executive processing (Deshler, Ellis, & Lenz, 1996; Keeler & Swanson, 2001; Swanson & Siegel, 2001). Students must be able to recognize when the strategy they have chosen to solve a problem is ineffective so that they may alter their approach.

Students who lack problem-solving strategies generally need explicit instruction in specific cognitive strategies (e.g., visualization, verbal rehearsal, paraphrasing, summarizing, estimating). Meaningful strategy instruction can occur only when the learner is developmentally ready. Students need to have the prerequisite skills necessary to employ a strategy. Students must also be reminded that strategies are flexible and can be adapted to fit different learning environments. Strategy instruction is a long-term project and not a quick fix to cure significant learning problems.

Instruction in Strategies

Students who struggle with conceptual development need to be taught how to use organized, efficient strategies for solving problems. Although some students with LD use a range of study strategies successfully, many students who struggle do not employ functional learning strategies (Lerner & Kline, 2005). Too often they have not learned to use strategies flexibly or do not know how to choose strategies that are appropriate to the demands of the task. These students tend to have difficulty with many of the tasks that are essential for successful participation in most classes, such as taking effective notes or preparing for and taking tests. Many of the strategies described in the next sections have several common elements:

- Teaching students to become active learners
- Helping students evaluate the effectiveness of a strategy
- Determining ways to modify the strategy for use in different settings

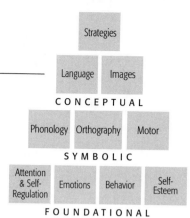

General Principles

Regardless of whether a strategy is designed primarily to enhance reading comprehension, written expression, or math problem-solving ability, several general principles apply (Meltzer, Roditi, & Stein, 1998):

- Teach strategies in the context of the curriculum.
- Teach different strategies so students can choose among strategies.
- Provide a balance between instruction in strategies and skills.
- Encourage students to understand their own learning styles.
- Show children how to adapt strategies as needed.

As students such as Katy, Stephanie, and John learn strategies, they should be encouraged to submit the first drafts of their outlines, notes, or graphic organizers for review and feedback.

Think-Alouds   Similar to the modeling techniques described earlier in this chapter, think-alouds can be used to explain to students which metacognitive and executive processes are effective when performing a skill, completing a task, or solving a problem (Davey, 1983). Think-alouds are a way for teachers to model how they think and learn. Davey (1983) listed the five major uses of think-alouds:

1. Making predictions or showing students how to develop a hypothesis
2. Describing visual images
3. Sharing an analogy or showing how prior knowledge applies
4. Verbalizing confusing points or demonstrating how to monitor understanding
5. Demonstrating repair strategies

When using think-alouds, develop guidelines for students' participation within the activity. The instruction should focus on the purpose, the relevant vocabulary, the organization, and the key points to observe (Good & Brophy, 1994). Guided instruction allows students to begin to think about what they are doing and what they can learn from it. After a presentation is done, ask students to discuss what they learned and to summarize the key points. You may also want to ask certain students to restate parts of the presentation for further rehearsal and review of concepts. Additional examples of the application of think-alouds for writing instruction are provided in Chapter 11.

Self-Regulated Strategy Development   Another procedure for promoting self-monitoring and regulation is self-regulated strategy development (SRSD) (Graham & Harris, 1999; Graham & Harris, 2005). Using SRSD, students learn a task-specific strategy along with self-regulating strategies, such as goal

327

setting, self-monitoring, and self-instruction. The following six instructional stages help students master task-specific strategies:

1. Help students develop the background knowledge they need to use the strategy.

2. Demonstrate how the strategy is used.

3. Let students observe the strategy in use.

4. Have students memorize the steps of the strategy.

5. Have students practice the strategy with teacher support.

6. Have students apply the strategy independently.

An application of this strategy to writing is described in Chapter 11.

Mnemonics The word *mnemonic* means memory aid. By using mnemonics, many students can improve their recall of related knowledge. One example is Kids Prefer Cheese Over Fried Green Spinach, which stands for the order of taxonomy in biology: kingdom, phylum, class, order, family, genus, and species. Many learning strategies use first-letter mnemonics. With these strategies, each letter reminds the student of the next step. Mnemonics aid students in forming associations that do not exist naturally in the content (Eggen & Kauchak, 1992). By forming these associations, students are able to store information in their long-term memory and retrieve it later in an efficient manner. When teaching students to use mnemonics, include the following steps (Alsopp, 1999):

1. Model when to use the mnemonic (i.e., its purpose).

2. Model what each part of the mnemonic stands for.

3. Model how to attach the information that the mnemonic represents to previously learned knowledge.

4. Provide students with cue cards associated with mnemonics to place at their desks.

5. Put up posters of mnemonics used on classroom walls.

6. Use rapid-fire verbal rehearsal to help students remember mnemonics.

For rapid-fire verbal rehearsal, the teacher moves quickly from student to student, asking which steps are represented by the varying letters.

Cognitive Behavior Modification Cognitive behavior modification (CBM) is based on the belief that perceptions influence behaviors; therefore, by changing a student's perceptions, his or her behavior can be altered (Meichenbaum, 1977, 1983). CBM combines aspects of behavior modification with monitoring instruction, evaluation, and verbalization. Change in behavior results from a change in thought processes. Common characteristics of CBM interventions include strategy steps, modeling, self-regulation, verbalization, and reflective thinking. The following general guidelines (Meichenbaum, 1977, 1983) help students be active participants in learning:

1. Analyze the target behavior.

2. Determine the strategies the student already uses (if any).

3. Select strategy steps that are as similar as possible to the strategy steps used by good problem solvers.

Strategies

Language | Images

CONCEPTUAL

Phonology | Orthography | Motor

SYMBOLIC

Attention & Self-Regulation | Emotions | Behavior | Self-Esteem

FOUNDATIONAL

4. Work with the student in developing the strategy steps.

5. Teach the prerequisite skills.

6. Teach the strategy steps using modeling, self-instruction, and self-regulation.

7. Provide explicit feedback.

8. Teach strategy generalization.

9. Help the student maintain the strategy.

Many students with LD require more repetition, more practice, and more reminders than their peers to learn a strategy.

Note-Taking Techniques As students progress through school, they need to develop an efficient method for notetaking. When reviewing pages of John's class notes, Dr. Mantell noted that John did not have a strategy for writing down important information presented during class lectures. He had trouble trying to decide what was important and what was unimportant, so he wrote down anything he could remember. As he tried to write everything down in class, he would often find that he did not understand what the teacher was saying.

As a first step for notetaking, check the student's understanding and use of note-taking systems. Notetaking involves listening, memory, writing, and reviewing information. Different note-taking abilities are needed before, during, and after information is presented. Before a lecture begins, students need to be ready to listen both physically (e.g., sitting up straight) and mentally, and they need to be familiar with the subject matter and vocabulary. During the lecture, students need to be able to pay attention, distinguish important and unimportant information, paraphrase the information given, and highlight key words and concepts within their notes. Some students need direct instruction in order to develop note-taking strategies to use in different situations. For instance, a student may need to learn how to identify key words and use abbreviations when taking notes. The use of an inexpensive laptop computer can make the process of taking notes more efficient. After the notes are taken, students must also be able to review, edit, and study the content of the notes. Several specific techniques for notetaking are described in the next sections.

Cornell or 1/4–3/4 Method The Cornell method for taking notes in lectures or discussions (Pauk, 1993) uses two columns that divide the page. The first column can be approximately one quarter to one third of the page, and the second column can be approximately two thirds to three fourths of the page. In this method, students write the name of the class, the date, the topic, and the readings being covered at the top of the page. In the first column, they write review or study questions, comments, questions to follow up on later, and topics expected or announced to be on upcoming examinations. In the second column, students write notes taken during class. Notes may take any form that works well, including formal outlines, bulleted lists, diagrams, and mind maps. The second column is also used to include details added during after-class review. A variation is to leave a half-page blank at the beginning or at the end of the notes for each session. The student uses this space later to create a summary.

Three-Column Method Use of a three-column method can further assist students in developing an organized system for taking notes (Saski, Swicegood, & Carter, 1983). Old information is recorded in the first column, and new information is recorded in the second. Students write questions about the material in the third column. (See Table 10.1). Another way to set up a three-column note-taking system

Table 10.1. First example of three-column notetaking

Column 1	Column 2	Column 3
Old information	New information	Questions
Should be 2" wide	Should be 5" wide	Should be 1" wide
	Basic note-taking column	Questions or comments about notes that should be elaborated on or that are important for future assignments

is to put basic ideas in the first column, background information in the second, and questions in the third. An example of this format is presented in Table 10.2.

AWARE Method   The AWARE method of notetaking was developed to help students remember all of the skills associated with notetaking (Suritsky & Hughes, 1993). This strategy teaches students to identify important information presented in a lecture. The steps involved in the AWARE method are presented in Table 10.3.

Dr. Mantell, John's history teacher, modeled the use of this strategy for her students. John could immediately see how this method would help him improve his note-taking skills. He also realized the importance of allotting a brief period of time each day for reviewing his notes.

Students who have difficulty with organization are also likely to have difficulty locating their notes later. John uses a separate notebook or folder for each subject; Stephanie likes having one notebook with sections for each subject.

When Ms. McGrew introduced note-taking skills to students, she modeled proper techniques by showing students an outline on a projector that was also provided as a handout. She demonstrated to students what they should be writing in their notes and what speakers may do to stress important information. For example, she explained that when teachers move closer to the class, the information is usually important. When teachers move away and lower their voices, the information is often less important. Other ways that teachers can assist students in notetaking include the following:

1. Alter the rate at which material is presented during a lecture

2. Provide visual aids

3. Provide verbal and nonverbal lecture cues

4. Use advance and post organizers

5. Insert questions into the lecture (Deshler et al., 1996)

When teachers incorporate each of these ideas, students can become more effective in their note-taking skills.

Time Management Strategies   Time management can be a problem for any student, but effective time management skills are especially critical for secondary

Table 10.2. Second example of three-column notetaking

Column 1	Column 2	Column 3
Basic ideas	Background information	Questions
Basic note-taking column, stress on information for tests, reports, and so on	Related or interesting information	Questions or comments about notes that should be elaborated on or that are important for future assignments

Table 10.3.   The steps for the AWARE method of notetaking

Step 1	**A**rrange to take notes	Arrive early
		Take a seat near the front or center
		Obtain a pen and notebook
		Make note of the date
Step 2	**W**rite quickly	Indent minor points
		Record some words without vowels
Step 3	**A**pply cues	Attend to accent and organizational verbal cues
		Record cued lecture ideas
		Make a checkmark before cued ideas
Step 4	**R**eview notes as soon as possible	
Step 5	**E**dit notes	Add information you forgot to record
		Add personal details
		Supplement notes with details from readings

Source: Suritsky & Hughes (1993).

students with LD or ADHD. These students may need extra time for completing reading and writing assignments, learning material from class notes, preparing for examinations, arranging for support services, scheduling appointments with instructors or tutors, and taking breaks to maintain focus during study sessions. Some students have problems with concepts of time (e.g., difficulty with being able to tell whether an impromptu conversation lasts 10 minutes or an hour, trouble estimating how long it will take to complete an activity). Setting priorities requires an additional set of skills. In addition, elementary school programs typically provide much more structure than is found in the high school environment, so secondary students have to take more responsibility for making decisions about how to manage their time themselves. The following strategies are recommended for students who need help learning to manage their time efficiently. Students should try a technique that appeals to them and then adopt it or modify it as needed. If the strategy seems ineffective, students can then discard it in favor of an alternative approach. The first step is determining an approach that works for the individual student.

How Hours Are Spent   Everyone has the same amount of time available—168 hours per week. Although much of that time is spent sleeping, an analysis of how the waking hours are spent may help students use their time more efficiently. Keeping a log of their activities for a week can help students develop an overview of how their time is spent.

John complained that he was spending all of his time at school or working on homework. His special education teacher encouraged him to keep a log of his activities. After completing his record, John and his teacher looked at it for patterns: how much time was spent in class; on entertainment and recreation; and on studying, sleeping, waiting, running errands, meeting family responsibilities, sending instant messages, or engaging in extracurricular activities. His teacher asked John to identify which areas require more time and which areas consume more time than necessary. The teacher then asked John to make a plan for the next week in which he would indicate when he intended to do certain things: attend class, study, meet with tutors, meet with study groups and instructors, do chores, see friends, send messages, watch television, play video games, and so forth. Throughout the next week, John recorded what he actually did. At the end of that week, the log was compared with the plan. John discovered that he had spent more time playing video games and sending instant messages to his friends than he thought that he would. He decided that the following week, he would spend less time on the computer and more time studying.

331

Students need to learn to use time-management tools, including daily planners, weekly schedules (a master list with recurring events recorded on it can be copied to save time), a monthly schedule, and a summary of major assignments. They need to be taught how to record information for each class systematically. John also found that he accomplished more when he developed a daily to-do list in the front of his daily planner. He also put the list on a dry-erase board in his bedroom.

Making Lists   Adults learn to write daily lists of what they hope to accomplish during a day or a week. Students can also make daily to-do lists that they carry with them. Younger students or students with writing difficulties can be asked to compose their lists aloud while someone else records what they describe. The list can be created the night before in the daily planner, on a piece of notebook paper, or on an index card; it can even be kept on a pocket cassette player. Once the list has been made, the student can number the tasks in order of priority. Students can add to the list as they realize that other tasks need to be done. Students also need to step back and look at the items on their lists that they do not accomplish. If the tasks are important, the student may need to work on strategies to accomplish more; if items aren't important, they should be removed from the list. Both Stephanie and Katy got more done in the classroom when tasks were explained and then written down in a series of steps. When they checked off completed items, they felt a sense of accomplishment.

Using Time Efficiently   As students progress through school, they need to take increased responsibility for using their time efficiently. A good study environment and a routine to make the most efficient use of study time become increasingly important; students, and sometimes their parents, can often use assistance in figuring out ways to minimize problems. At home, distractions can be avoided by hanging a "Do not disturb" sign on the door; turning off the television, computer, or stereo; and limiting telephone calls or video games to certain times. Teachers can encourage students to do the following:

- Develop specific agreements with their families about study time.

- Study the hardest or least interesting subject during their prime time. Prime time varies from student to student; more often than not, daylight hours are best.

- Include time for exercise, study breaks, and rewards. As students become older and homework assignments increase, they need to plan frequent breaks.

- Break term projects and big assignments into manageable, logical subgoals, and plot target completion dates on a time line and in a daily planner. Some students need assistance in determining the steps they need to take; others may have difficulty estimating the time they should allot. Assist the student in a review of how the project developed, identifying those steps they did well and those that need further attention.

- Take advantage of brief periods of time by having index cards with vocabulary or concepts on them.

Some students need a greater amount of time to complete their homework assignments. In the lower grades, a teacher often has a good sense of the effort that a project or assignment requires and how the child copes. Once students reach the point at which they have classes with several instructors, it can be hard to know the effect of multiple assignments. Asking students at the beginning of the school

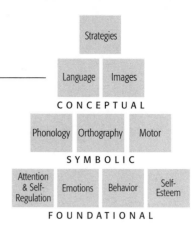

year about how they approach their assignments and what kind of time is required can help reduce the possibility of future homework problems.

Managing Procrastination If students find themselves continually procrastinating, the following suggestions may help. Encourage students to do the following:

- Write down what is important about the task.

- Make large tasks manageable by breaking them into subgoals. Model this behavior routinely in the classroom.

- Tell others what they will do by a certain date and then have others check to see if they have met their goals.

- Earn a reward only when goals (or subgoals) are accomplished.

- Reschedule tasks that get postponed.

- Resist postponing important tasks. Identify one specific subgoal that can be accomplished; completing small steps can create the motivation to move forward with the larger task.

Getting Organized Students can work on setting goals or establishing priorities by doing the following:

- Identify specific and realistic long-term and short-term goals. These should be used to provide structure for each class.

- Determine a plan to help attain goals by looking at the specific actions that need to be taken for each class, looking at what has worked in the past, and setting aside time each week to monitor progress.

Teach students to develop systems for organization that will help them retrieve information when they need it. Helpful strategies include the use of index cards or colored sticky notes, taking all notes in one notebook or on a computer, or placing all materials in labeled envelopes or file folders.

Organizing Materials Students with LD and ADHD often have difficulty with organizing materials for class. Although the selection of notebooks and folders is usually a matter of personal preference, a single-subject, spiral notebook for each class that is color-coordinated with folders is an efficient way to organize. For classes in which many handouts are distributed, students may prefer a loose-leaf notebook. They may divide notebooks into sections chronologically, by topic, or by component (e.g., class notes, notes on readings, handouts, maps). Notes may be taken in a spiral notebook with perforations for neat removal after class to be filed in the loose-leaf notebook. A plastic zipper pencil case can be used for items such as pencils, disks, concept cards, or highlighters; inside pockets of loose-leaf notebooks are handy for storing frequently used items such as the syllabus. When using a loose-leaf notebook, all papers should be three-hole punched and put into the notebook in a logical place, and index dividers should be used and labeled appropriately. Help students learn to keep their backpacks, book bags, and so forth neat and organized and encourage students to get into the habit of keeping certain items, such as their daily planner, calculator, and pens and pencils, in certain pockets of the backpack. Another good habit for students to learn is to check their backpacks or desks at the end of every day for items that need to be filed or thrown out. John found that if he cleaned out the papers, organized his homework, and packed his backpack the night before, it saved time and reduced stress in the morning.

Most students benefit from the use of a clutter-free study area. Students can organize materials by class. Everyday materials, such as a hole punch, dictionary, index cards, highlighters, and an assignment calendar, can be arranged in a convenient place. John found that by using and labeling folders and then keeping them in a plastic box, he could locate the materials for each class more easily. In addition, an area that is regularly identified for study often prompts or encourages the student to adopt behaviors that facilitate his or her studying.

Test-Taking Strategies Students such as Katy and John find test taking frustrating. Their problems with language, in addition to problems with providing correct responses, often prevent them from understanding the tasks that they are expected to perform. They are also less likely to employ appropriate strategies in preparing for tests and are therefore more likely to develop test anxiety as a result of previous negative experiences.

Test-taking strategies can be grouped into two categories: 1) strategies for preparing for the examination and 2) strategies for taking the examination. Test taking is a way for teachers to evaluate knowledge; and students' performances depend not only on how hard they study and what they know but how strategic they are in their approaches to tests. Davis, Sirotowitz, and Parker (1996) provided an extensive set of test-taking strategies. Appendix A contains a list of additional test-taking strategies.

Preparing Attending class regularly, keeping current with assignments, using appropriate support (e.g., peer tutors, study groups, study guides), meeting with teachers, and making arrangements for appropriate accommodations (e.g., recorded textbooks, in-class notetakers, extended time for tests, alternative testing site, alternative formats) set the stage for successful test taking. When a student is able to anticipate what the test will be like (i.e., what the format of the test will be, how much time will be allotted for the test, what material will be covered, and what types of answers the teacher expects), these skills become the basis for an effective study plan.

Dr. Mantell helped John plan backward from the date of the test for his history class. They talked about how much time would be needed to prepare for the test, and they considered how important the test was. They then used this information to formulate a study plan and timetable. John used his calendar and daily planner to record the steps of test preparation. Dr. Mantell shared a practice examination with the students in the class that was written in the same format. This helped John anticipate what types of questions would be on the test.

Two weeks before the test, John worked on bringing his assignments up to date. He then reviewed readings (e.g., annotations, notes, highlighted passages) and class notes and began to practice with study aids. Dr. Mantell encouraged him to ask questions and request clarification of information he found difficult. John made a point of identifying what had been emphasized in class and in his notes and identified key concepts and important details.

One week before the test, John wrote practice questions in the format of the test (i.e., multiple choice, matching, short answer, essay) and answered the practice test items. He outlined responses to essay questions, used flashcards for material that needed to be memorized, and made condensed study notes based on study materials. He also checked the end of his chapter units for sample questions. During the week of the test, John reviewed annotated and highlighted readings, notes, and handouts and made several crit-

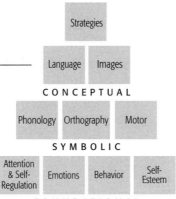

ical concept cards (i.e., he reduced study notes to index cards). The day before the test, John reviewed his notes, reading material, and concept cards. Dr. Mantell also recognized that John sometimes had problems with understanding how to frame his responses. By helping him understand key words often used in questions (e.g., *describe, discuss, analyze, outline, explain, illustrate, contrast*), John was able to improve the quality of his written responses.

When it was time to take his history test, John made sure that he had the materials he needed. He looked over the entire test and determined how much time he needed for each part before starting. For this test, John jotted down several dates he thought he might be asked about and quickly sketched out a mind map he didn't want to forget. He also made sure to underline important words in each of the questions. Then he did the shortest, easiest part of the test first. He saved the essay question for last because the objective questions would serve as warm-up exercises. He tried looking for information in subsequent test questions that he could use to answer other test items. He put a mark in the margin of the test page by questions that he wanted to come back to if he had enough time.

When John got his test results back, he had a B, two letter grades higher than on his last examination. Dr. Mantell asked him to look at which part of the test had the best score, and they talked about the strategies he had used and how they had helped. They also discussed what John had found difficult and looked carefully at his mistakes. Although John had responded to two questions quite well, he had misread instructions on one question. It was apparent that he had not yet grasped an important concept. They then discussed ways to use this information when it was time for John to prepare for his next test. Fortunately, John is highly motivated and wants to do well in his history class. He also has an extremely supportive teacher who understands John's difficulties with learning and is willing to take time to help John improve his study and test-taking skills.

Reducing Test Anxiety Most people experience some level of anxiety when taking tests. Given the nature of LD, students with a history of learning difficulties may be more vulnerable to test anxiety because of past failures. In addition, external distracters (e.g., noise, lighting, movement) and internal distracters (e.g., negative thoughts; bodily sensations such as tense muscles, increased heart rate, shallow breathing) can contribute to an already elevated level of anxiety.

In general, anxiety results from a sense of loss of control. Students need to understand that what is being tested is their knowledge, not their self-worth. John noted that sometimes even when he felt well prepared, his mind would go totally blank when the test was placed in front of him. Several strategies, in addition to adequate preparation, can help students such as John reduce their anxiety.

Simple breathing and relaxation exercises (e.g., taking several deep breaths) can help students regain focus. Sitting up straight gives the body the message that it is time to be in a state of readiness; slouching tends to confirm that one should feel bad. Using a pen or pencil to underline or circle key words in directions or in a question begins to shift the focus away from how the body is reacting. Covering questions with a blank piece of paper or with an arm can help keep the focus on the question at hand. Students can also practice positive self-talk. Johnson (1997) described several positive statements that a student might practice, such as

- I can feel anxious and think at the same time.

- This is only anxiety. I've been through this before, and I can wait it out.

- Everything is going to be okay.

- I can do well on this test even though I feel afraid. (Or even, I think I can try this one question.)

- Take it slowly, one step at a time.

- Lots of people feel this way when they take tests; I'm not the only one.

- All I can do is my best.

CLASSROOM ADJUSTMENTS

Students with difficulties with language and reasoning often require specific adjustments in the curriculum to succeed. They may need a different set of instructional materials, simplified assignments, or shortened assignments. When selecting accommodations, teachers should check with students to ascertain whether they think that the adjustment would be beneficial. Students of any age do not like to feel that they differ significantly from peers, so sometimes it is necessary to make an accommodation available to all students. The form in Appendix B is a survey to use with students to help determine and discuss appropriate accommodations. If a student can read the survey, he or she may complete it independently. If not, the teacher can conduct the survey as an oral interview.

Alter the Difficulty Level

Students with difficulties in language and reasoning often need the difficulty level of the assignments to be adjusted so that reading, writing, and problem-solving activities are geared to match their levels of oral language competence. Again, this does not mean that the assignments are not challenging but rather that they are at an appropriate instructional level. Vygotsky (1978) described a concept that he referred to as the zone of proximal development. This zone represents the gap between present performance levels and the level of learning that may be obtained when the student is paired with more knowledgeable others, such as adults or more capable peers. Good instruction, therefore, is provided at the upper bounds of an individual's knowledge when teachers and students work together to construct new knowledge (Englert, 1992).

Provide a Classroom Coach

Vygotsky (1978) also stressed the importance of social interaction as a means for expanding understanding. A student with weaknesses in oral language may not understand classroom instructions or may need more guidance to interpret assignments. A simple way to resolve this difficulty is to find a peer who is willing and able to clarify class instructions as needed. Katy knew that she could ask Stacy for clarification of instructions. Stacy was able to paraphrase the information and help Katy understand what she was supposed to do. Katy also knew that she could call Stacy at night when she needed clarifications about homework assignments.

Allow More Time and Practice

As a general rule, students with weaknesses in language and reasoning often need more time than other students to process responses to questions. Attempt to break down and simplify information and tasks and encourage students to begin their response to oral questions by restating the question in their own words. Students such as Katy and John need many opportunities for repetition, rehearsal, practice, and feedback. They need to practice specific strategies and use the strategies in various settings. Whenever possible, demonstrate and discuss connections among concepts and do not let the textbook control the content delivered to the student.

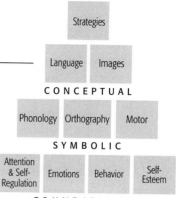

In other words, students must master concepts before moving on to new sets of information. It is far better for the students to complete several chapters successfully than to flounder through an entire book without ever grasping any of the ideas and concepts presented.

Consider Physical Classroom Arrangements

Some students benefit from sitting near the instructor or away from distracting noises such as air conditioners and heating systems or doors that open and close frequently. The most effective seats for listening are often described as being in the "T" of the classroom. The front row forms the top of the T and the center row, the line. John found it was easier for him to pay attention if his seat was close to where the teacher lectured.

Provide More than One Grade

Students with learning difficulties often feel discouraged when a paper is returned with a low grade and lots of corrections or comments. Provide feedback in ways that allow students to see the progress they have made as well as what they need to continue to work on. Positive feedback can help keep students motivated. Separate grades for content and presentation help students see the progress they are making while they struggle with difficulties such as poor spelling and punctuation. A grade can also be based on the amount of improvement from pretest to posttest. A student who went from 70% to 90% would receive the same grade as the student who went from 10% to 30%.

Base Grades on Individualized Education Program Goals

Some students need to have their grades based on accomplishment of their individualized education program (IEP) goals. Because of weaknesses in language and reasoning, they cannot be expected to accomplish the same tasks at the same rate as other students. The IEP is written to formulate appropriate goals and objectives on the basis of the learner's needs and characteristics. This does not mean that the curriculum is compromised but rather that the goals set for each student are realistic, challenging, and yet possible to achieve.

Provide Opportunities for Improvement

Classes in which students get what they perceive as only one chance to get it right can quickly become overwhelming. Motivation to improve can quickly be undermined. Devise assignments that can be developed in stages or that students can resubmit, in whole or part, to get additional feedback and points.

CONCLUSION

To succeed in school, students need to possess a range of strategies that they can apply in varied settings. Instruction in strategies is an ongoing endeavor that varies according to the tasks students are asked to perform and the goals they are expected to meet. Modeling, demonstrations, and explanations are valuable approaches that help students increase their oral language abilities and acquire an understanding of strategic approaches to learning. Active engagement in applying strategies such as those described in this chapter enables students to take control of their learning, resulting in increased motivation and learning. Incorporating a variety of graphic organizers and visual supports can help students envision relationships among concepts and improve recall of information. Students also benefit from time spent teaching them how to study, how to take lecture notes, and how to prepare for examinations.

One fact is clear: Students with weaknesses in language, visual imagery, and reasoning need to have teachers who establish realistic expectations and set clear educational goals. Teachers must attempt to adjust explanations to the level of the student's understanding. This does not mean lowered expectations; it means formulating a program that is challenging but possible for the student to learn and succeed. As Vygotsky (1978) noted, good instruction is one step above a student's present performance level. With proper, carefully designed instruction, students such as Katy, Stephanie, and John can become more strategic and successful in their learning.

ADDITIONAL STRATEGIES FOR TEST TAKING

This appendix outlines some ways in which students can improve their test-taking skills. Students can often improve their grades and test performance simply by paying attention to accuracy in recording answers and developing explicit strategies for answering different kinds of test questions.

RECORDING ANSWERS

Tests that require the use of a bubble sheet to record answers can be particularly problematic for students with some kinds of LD, such as visual-spatial or handwriting difficulties. Students who have difficulty with lining up numbers to solve math problems or copying information from a chalkboard are also likely to have difficulty with transferring the response from the test to the sheet. Recording the answers directly in the text booklet allows a student to demonstrate command of the subject without being penalized for copying errors. If this is not possible, urge the student to

- Check to be sure that the number on the answer sheet coincides with the number of the test item in the test booklet. Recheck when turning a page and when moving to a new row or column on the answer sheet.

- Consider completing the test by recording answers on the test pages and then transposing answers to the answer sheet

PIRATES Test-Taking Strategy

The PIRATES test-taking strategy (Hughes, Schumaker, Deshler, & Mercer, 1988) was developed to help students in middle and high school improve performance on objective tests. The steps included in the PIRATES strategy are outlined in Table 10A.1.

TEST FORMATS

Although some students seem to understand how to address test questions, other students need to develop overt strategies and practice step-by-step approaches that they can apply when trying to respond to test questions.

Multiple-Choice Questions

The following suggestions are helpful for students to keep in mind while answering multiple-choice questions:

Table 10 A.1. The steps for the PIRATES test-taking strategy

Step 1	**P**repare to succeed	Put your name and PIRATES on the test Allot time and order to sections Say affirmations Start within 2 minutes
Step 2	**I**nspect the instructions	Read instructions carefully Underline what to do and where to respond Notice special requirements
Step 3	**R**ead, remember, reduce	
Step 4	**A**nswer or abandon	
Step 5	**T**urn back	
Step 6	**E**stimate	Avoid absolutes Choose the longest or most detailed choice Eliminate similar choices
Step 7	**S**urvey	Review the answers before handing it in

Source: Hughes, Schumaker, Deshler, & Mercer (1988).

- Read the stem of the question, and predict what answer should follow.

- Read the stem with each choice.

- Read each answer choice and try to eliminate obviously incorrect or impossible options. If writing on the test is permitted, cross out incorrect options to help focus on the right response. Eliminating obviously incorrect options can help significantly if you are unsure about the answer. For a question that has four options, if you eliminate two options, the possibility of guessing the right answer is 50%.

- Code the question to make it easier to go back to later if you are uncertain of the correct response and watch for information in subsequent test items that may help answer the question.

- Reread the test question with the option that has been chosen. Subvocalizing the answer can help you make sure that it sounds correct and can help you read exactly what is there.

- Be sure that the answer sounds right grammatically.

- Watch out for phrases such as "All of the following except... ."

- When answering a question stated in the negative, try stating it in the positive first and consider the answers. Then select the best answer after re-reading the question in the negative.

- Ask for clarification if a question seems ambiguous. If clarification is not an option, select the best answer and briefly indicate why that answer seems best, perhaps adding a note that indicates that the question was difficult to understand.

Fill-in-the-Blank Questions

The following suggestions are helpful to keep in mind while answering fill-in-the-blank questions:

- Try to predict what is being asked and how the question should be answered while reading it.

- Write enough to let the instructor know that you understand the concept even if you cannot provide the specific response.

- Search for information in other test items that may help with fill-in-the-blank questions.

Matching

The following suggestions are helpful to keep in mind while answering matching questions:

- Check directions to determine if answers may be used more than once.
- Try to determine what would be an appropriate answer before looking at the options.

True/False Questions

The following suggestions are helpful to keep in mind while answering true/false questions:

- Read each statement carefully.
- Beware of words such as *always, never, all,* and *none*; these words frequently are used in statements that are false.

Short Answer

The following suggestions are helpful to keep in mind while answering short-answer questions:

- Read each question carefully.
- Be brief but complete.
- Make sure the response answers the question asked.
- If you are unsure, use information from the rest of the test to help jog your memory or confirm your answers.

Essay Tests

The following suggestions are helpful to keep in mind while answering essay questions:

- Read directions carefully. Do all questions require an answer? If not, how many need to be answered?
- Read each question carefully.
- Outline a response. If time runs out, partial credit might be given for the information in the outline.
- Be sure to respond to all parts of the question.
- Start with the strongest point. Be clear and concise.
- Get to the point relatively quickly and avoid adding irrelevant information.
- Be familiar with key essay words. (For specific suggestions, see Ellis [1994].)

INSTRUCTIONAL ACCOMMODATIONS SURVEY

Instructional Accommodations Survey

Student _____   Teacher _____

Directions: Indicate how much you think you would benefit from the following changes if your teachers would provide them for you. There are no wrong answers. Fill in your responses.

	Would help	Unsure	Would not help
Tests			
1. Having extra time to complete tests	☐	☐	☐
2. Answering test questions orally rather than in writing	☐	☐	☐
3. Having multiple-choice questions instead of essay questions	☐	☐	☐
4. Having essay questions instead of multiple-choice questions	☐	☐	☐
5. Taking tests in a quiet place	☐	☐	☐
6. Using a word processor on test	☐	☐	☐
7. Using a calculator on math tests	☐	☐	☐
8. Marking answers on tests rather than on bubble sheets	☐	☐	☐
9. Having short quizzes on smaller portions of a unit	☐	☐	☐
Class Projects and Assignments			
1. Having fewer problems to complete	☐	☐	☐
2. Having extra time to complete class assignments	☐	☐	☐
3. Having a proofreader to check written work	☐	☐	☐
4. Having textbooks on tape for in-class reading	☐	☐	☐
5. Reading textbooks or stories with a peer	☐	☐	☐
6. Substituting oral presentations for written projects	☐	☐	☐
7. Meeting more frequently with your teacher	☐	☐	☐

(continued)

(continued)

	Would help	Unsure	Would not help
Homework			
1. Having smaller amounts of home-work	☐	☐	☐
2. Having textbooks on tape for assigned readings	☐	☐	☐
3. Dictating papers rather than writing them	☐	☐	☐
4. Doing extra credit projects to raise grade	☐	☐	☐
5. Having someone to call about home-work assignments	☐	☐	☐
Environment			
1. Sitting in front of the room	☐	☐	☐
2. Sitting near the board	☐	☐	☐
3. Sitting close to the teacher	☐	☐	☐
4. Working on assignments with a small group	☐	☐	☐

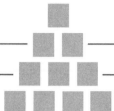

CHAPTER 11 OUTLINE

READING COMPREHENSION AND WRITTEN EXPRESSION: TEXT STRUCTURE

Narrative Text Structure: Story Grammar
Expository Text Structure

READING COMPREHENSION STRATEGIES

RAP
Reciprocal Teaching
Collaborative Strategic Reading
SQ3R
ReQuest Procedure
Multipass
PORPE

WRITTEN LANGUAGE STRATEGIES

Components of Writing
Self-Regulated Strategy Development
Cognitive Strategy in Writing Program
Essays

MATH PROBLEM SOLVING

Mathematical Knowledge
Instructional Concerns
Instructional Format
Instructional Sequence
Language and Mathematics
Story or Word Problem Strategies
Cue Cards
Effective Strategy Instruction
Effective Teaching Strategies for Advanced Math Courses
Software Selection and Math Instruction

CONCLUSION

APPENDIX: SYNONYMS FOR WORDS THAT CHILDREN USE COMMONLY IN WRITING

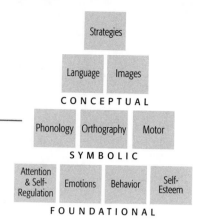

INSTRUCTION IN READING COMPREHENSION, WRITTEN EXPRESSION, AND MATH PROBLEM SOLVING

with Ann M. Richards

Our abilities to understand what we read and to express our ideas in writing are based on several factors: fluent reading and writing, background knowledge, vocabulary, and interest. Ideally, students should be able to read a chapter in a book and then paraphrase the information using their own words. John, one of the students described earlier in this book, struggled with the concepts presented in his content-area textbooks because of limited knowledge. He had trouble answering test questions based on the information presented. For John, summarizing what he had read seemed impossible because he had trouble distinguishing important from unimportant information. Fortunately, strategies exist that can help students such as John understand and recall information from text and express their ideas in writing.

READING COMPREHENSION AND WRITTEN EXPRESSION: TEXT STRUCTURE

The ability to understand what is read and the ability to organize longer pieces of writing do not just happen (Vogel & Moran, 1982). Students need to be taught how to increase their understanding, organize their thoughts, and structure their writing. In addition, comprehension of text often improves if students understand how texts are structured. Explicit instruction in text structure strategies helps students increase their knowledge and use of text structure and improves the cohesion and organization of their compositions (Lienemann, Graham, Leader-Janssen, & Reid, 2006; Williams, 2005; Williams, Hall, & Lauer, 2004). Two basic types of text structure exist: narrative and expository. *Narrative text* refers to fictional stories, whereas *expository text* refers to nonfictional passages.

Narrative Text Structure: Story Grammar

An effective way to help students increase understanding of narrative text and improve narrative writing is to teach them how to use story grammar. *Story grammar* simply refers to the underlying structure of a story. Story grammar instruction can be used as a prereading or prewriting strategy or as a postreading activity.

As noted previously, many children do not realize that comprehension requires attention, effort, and monitoring.

Shannon, one of Katy's classmates in fifth grade, wrote the story, presented in Figure 11.1, about a "qwen." After she had written her first draft, Katy was assigned as a peer editor to read her story and make suggestions for revision. Katy told Shannon that she thought her story was just fine but reminded her that she was supposed to write along the line at the left side. Shannon then added in the arrows. Shannon did not describe the character of Tammy in much detail, other than that she was "pretty" and had "pretty shoes." Direct instruction in story grammar can help students such as Katy and Shannon improve their narrative writing skills.

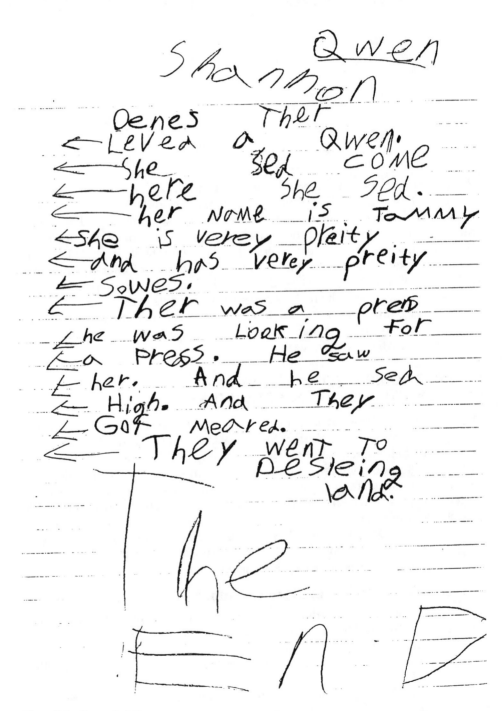

Figure 11.1. Shannon's story.

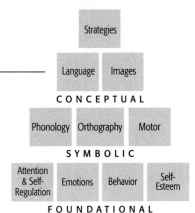

Simple Story Grammars Students may be introduced to the concept of story grammar as early as kindergarten or first grade. When first discussing story grammar, tell students that every story has three parts: a beginning, a middle, and an end. Then draw three circles and connect them with arrows to illustrate this sequence. To practice this concept, review a common fairy tale or fable, such as *The Tortoise and the Hare,* and ask the students, "What happened at the beginning? The middle? The end?" The students can then retell the main events of the fable in their own words.

Story Grammar Components By second or third grade, more detailed story grammars can be introduced, including the following general elements:

1. *The setting:* Where and when does the story take place?

2. *The main characters:* Who is the story about?

3. *The problem:* What happens to the main character?

4. *The solution:* What does the main character do to solve the problem?

5. *The ending:* How is the story resolved?

As students increase their knowledge about story grammar, more complex elements can be introduced. Ms. Moore, John's English teacher, used the following seven categories of story elements (Montague & Graves, 1993; Stein & Glenn, 1979):

1. *Major setting:* The main character is introduced.

2. *Minor setting:* The time and place of the story are described.

3. *Initiating event:* The atmosphere is changed and the main character responds.

4. *Internal response:* The characters' thoughts, ideas, emotions, and intentions are noted.

5. *Attempt:* The main character's goal-related actions are represented.

6. *Direct consequence:* The attainment of the goal is noted; if the goal is not attained, the changes resulting from the attempt are noted.

7. *Reaction:* The main character's thoughts and feelings in regard to the outcome are specified, along with the effect of the outcome on the character.

Thinking about these categories improved John's comprehension of short stories.

When asking students to recall a story that they have read or when helping them prepare to write a story, use story grammar to guide points for the discussion. Students may be provided with a list of elements to include in their story. Graves and Montague (1991) found that use of story grammar cue cards or a check-off system for story parts improved the quality of the stories written by students with learning disabilities (LD). Figure 11.2 presents a sample cue card.

Character Development In addition to strategies to assist with organization, some students benefit from instruction in character development. The following questions help students expand their descriptions of the physical appearance, the speech and actions, and the thoughts and emotions of the main characters (Leavell & Ioannides, 1993):

1. *Physical appearance:* What does the person look like?

2. *Speech and actions:* What does the person say? What does the person do?

☐	Describe the main characters.
☐	Describe the setting.
☐	Explain how a problem develops.
☐	Explain how the characters attempt to solve the problem.
☐	Describe how the characters feel.
☐	Create an ending.

Figure 11.2. Sample cue card.

3. *Thoughts and emotions:* What does the character think about? What emotions does the person display? How does the character feel about the outcome?

Before using this strategy, read two paragraphs to students: one in which the main character has been developed fully and another in which only minimal information is given. Students can be encouraged to discuss the differences between the two paragraphs and to note how detailed descriptions can help readers increase their understanding of the appearance and feelings of characters.

Story Maps Graphic organizers can also help students pay attention to relevant information and to understand the elements of a story. The ability to understand these details can help them to plan a story prior to writing. Story maps provide a structure in which to record and organize elements of a story. These simple steps can be used to create a map:

1. Have students brainstorm ideas.

2. Help them organize the ideas on the map and then subcategorize these ideas under characters, setting, problem, and ending.

3. Help students incorporate the information on the map into a story.

4. As skill increases, encourage students to take more responsibility for developing and organizing their own maps.

Story maps can also help students with a particular aspect of story grammar. By using story mapping to teach story grammar, teachers assist students in identifying story grammar elements when reading narrative texts (Boulineau, Fore, Hagan-Burke, & Burke, 2004). John was reading a novel for his English class that involved many characters. He was having trouble remembering the relationships among the characters. To help organize and remember the characters, John constructed a character map. He wrote each character's name in a circle, drew lines between characters with a relationship, and then wrote the relationship on the line, such as "sisters." Whenever he needed clarification, he consulted the map.

Questioning Initially, some students will require increased structure to incorporate elements of story grammar into their writing. Prior to writing, ask students to answer specific questions pertaining to the setting, problem, and ending.

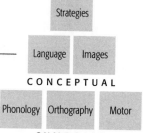

Setting

Characters

Who is the main character?
Who are the other characters?
What do you know about these characters?
What do they look like?
What do they act like?
What do they do?
How do they feel about what is happening?
What emotions do they display?
How are the characters alike? How do they differ?

Time

When does the story occur?
What is the time of year?

Place

Where does the story occur?
What is the place like?

The Problem

What is the main problem?
Are there other, minor problems?
How does the main character plan to solve the problem?
How do other characters respond to the problem?

The Solution

How is the problem resolved?
How does the story end?
How do the characters feel at the end?

STATE the Story Some students benefit from having a mnemonic to help them remember the steps of strategies more easily. One example is STATE the Story (Goldstein & Mather, 1998):

Setting (Who? What? Where? When?)
Trouble (What is the trouble or problem?)
Action (What happens?)
Turning point (What is done to resolve the problem?)
End (How does the story end?)

As students are reviewing a story or planning to write a story, encourage them to answer each of these elements. These steps can be written on the board or students can keep cue cards on their desks.

STORE the Story Another example of a first-letter mnemonic strategy is STORE the Story (Schlegel & Bos, 1986):

Setting (Who? What? Where? When?)
Trouble (What is the trouble or problem?)
Order of action (What happens?)
Resolution (What is done to solve the problem?)
End (How does the story end?)

To introduce the strategy, discuss the meaning of the verb *to store* (e.g., save, hold, keep for a while, put away) and explain to the students that the purpose of the strategy is to help them understand and remember (i.e., store) any story that they read by recognizing and recalling each part or to help them organize the components of a story prior to writing.

STORE the Story

Name _____ Date _____

Title _____

SETTING

   Who _____

   _____

   Where _____

   When _____

TROUBLE _____

   _____

   _____

ORDER
   OF ACTION   1. _____

                       2. _____

                       3. _____

                       4. _____

RESOLUTION   _____

   _____

   _____

ENDING   _____

   _____

Figure 11.3.   Sample cue sheet for the STORE strategy.

Using the STORE format, guide the students to create a group story. Then brainstorm ideas for the story and fill in the STORE cue sheet, crossing out ideas and adding others until satisfied. Students next read over the cue sheet to make sure that all parts make sense and fit in relation to other parts. When students need additional support, provide them with certain elements of the story or have them work with peers to complete the cue sheet. Figure 11.3 provides a sample cue sheet for using the STORE strategy.

C-SPACE   The mnemonic C-SPACE (MacArthur, Schwartz, & Graham, 1991) may be used as a prewriting strategy. Prior to writing, ask the students to think about 1) who will read the story and 2) what kind of story he or she wants to write. Next, the student takes notes on the story, using the following mnemonic:

C Who is the *character?*
S What is the *setting?*
P What is the *problem* or *purpose?*
A What *action* occurs?
C What is the *conclusion?*
E What is the *emotion* of the character?

As the final step, have students write stories by expanding on their notes.

W-W-W, What = 2, How = 2 Strategy A similar mnemonic strategy, W-W-W, What = 2, How = 2 (Graham & Harris, 1989), may be used as a prewriting strategy. Prior to writing, students answer the following questions:

1. *Who* is the main character? *Who* else is in the story?

2. *When* does the story take place?

3. *Where* does the story take place?

4. *What* does the main character do?

5. *What* happens when he or she tries to do it?

6. *How* does the story end?

7. *How* does the main character feel?

This strategy may be used with a picture stimulus as a basis for writing. Before a student attempts to use the self-instructional strategy, model and demonstrate it while thinking out loud using these steps:

1. Instruct students to look at the picture.

2. Tell students to use their imaginations.

3. Have students write down the story-part reminder (W-W-W, What = 2, How = 2).

4. Have students write down ideas for each part.

5. Have students write their stories.

6. Have students read their stories as a group activity.

7. Have the group discuss which elements of the stories are missing and how and where they can be added.

8. Have students add the missing elements.

Provide guidance until students can compose stories independently using the strategy.

Expository Text Structure

Although instruction in story narratives is often an appropriate place to begin with young readers and writers, specific instruction in expository structures is needed at all levels (Englert & Mariage, 1991). Expository text differs from narrative text in that it is written to represent the relationship between ideas; it is not simply a telling of a sequence of events. Students must acquire several different types of expository styles to succeed in higher grades (Westby, 1994). This is because many expository texts differ in their structure (e.g., definition and example, description, compare and contrast) and often, in fact, combine two or more different structures. Beginning in first grade, students can be taught to write simple expository paragraphs about animals, insects, food, and so forth.

A three-phase study by Williams (2005) explored the effects of explicitly teaching a text structure program to second-grade at-risk readers. The following components and key elements of a successful text structure program were identified: 1) instruction in clue words; 2) trade book reading and discussion to supplement expository sources (i.e. encyclopedias, text books); 3) vocabulary development; 4) reading and analysis of target paragraphs focusing on compare–contrast structure; 5) graphic organizers; 6) compare–contrast strategy questions; g) written summaries with a paragraph frame as support; and 7) review of vocabulary and the strategies at the end of each lesson. The results suggested that when provided with highly structured and explicit instruction that focuses on text structure, children at risk for reading failure show gains in comprehension, including the ability to transfer what they have learned to novel texts.

In later grades, different text structures can form the basis for instruction in paragraph and essay writing. Using a student's writing, model the process and provide positive and corrective feedback (Moran, 1988). Whichever strategies are employed, the structures and processes of writing need to be made apparent to students (Englert & Mariage, 1991). Stewart (1992) provided the following general guidelines for teaching specific writing skills, including text structure organization.

1. Provide direct instruction in writing by modeling and teaching writing strategies.

2. Emphasize high-level skills that focus on content and organization.

3. Control the task difficulty by isolating target objectives.

4. Teach students to use text structure to plan, generate, and monitor their writing.

5. Teach students to plan, implement, and monitor their use of strategies.

6. Integrate writing instruction with the curriculum.

Summarization   One method for integrating a reading comprehension and writing strategy is to have students ask two questions after reading a paragraph: 1) who or what was the paragraph about, and 2) what was happening in the paragraph (Malone & Mastropieri, 1992). Place a blank line after each paragraph and have students write a summary sentence for each paragraph. Have the steps written on a self-monitoring card so that students can check their application of the strategy.

When Katy was reading a chapter in her content-area textbooks, her teacher had her place a sticky note by the side of each paragraph. After reading each paragraph, Katy would then write a summary sentence on the note. She then moved all of her sentences in order onto a page in her notebook and used them to guide her writing. Using this technique, she was able to write a complete summary of the chapter events. This summary then served as a study guide for quizzes.

READING COMPREHENSION STRATEGIES

The National Reading Panel (2000) found that students' text comprehension improved when teachers demonstrated and then had students apply varied strategies, such as answering and generating questions and summarizing what was read. Several easy-to-use examples of research-based strategies are described in the following sections. The purposes of these strategies are to help students recognize the important information, formulate and answer questions, and

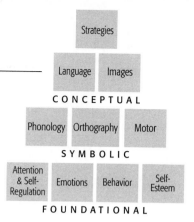

increase their abilities to explain and discuss what they have read. Instruction in these strategies can help students improve their understanding and increase their retention of important information. Several of these strategies use a first-letter mnemonic. These types of strategies can help students remember the various steps of a task.

RAP

As an upper-elementary school student, Katy benefited from a simple paraphrasing strategy developed by researchers at the University of Kansas (Schumaker, Denton, & Deshler, 1984). The acronym RAP represents three steps:

Read the paragraph.
Ask: What were the main ideas and details in this paragraph?
Put the main ideas into your own words.

By using this strategy for each paragraph, Katy became actively involved and increased her understanding of the material. By attempting to transform the text into her own words, she was able to monitor her level of understanding.

Reciprocal Teaching

The reciprocal teaching procedure (Palinscar & Brown, 1986) can be used with small groups within general education classrooms. This procedure includes the following four skills: questioning, summarizing, clarifying, and predicting. The first two skills, questioning and summarizing, help students learn to identify and paraphrase the most important information in the text. To begin, students may read a paragraph or passage together. After the passage is completed, they generate questions together about what has been read and then summarize the content in a sentence or two. For clarifying, students discuss any difficult or hard-to-understand sections and review the meaning of any new vocabulary. For the final skill, students predict what will happen in the next passage. The process of making predictions helps students link background knowledge with the new information. As students practice these procedures, they can take more responsibility for developing questions, summarizing the content, and making predictions about the next section. Activities involving self-questioning and comprehension monitoring promote active involvement with the reading process.

Collaborative Strategic Reading

Collaborative strategic reading (CSR) is an intensive classroom or group-based reading comprehension strategy designed to be used with expository text (Vaughn & Klingner, 1999). CSR works best when implemented within an elementary or high school class structure so that students use it over time and with a series of instructors. CSR integrates four specific reading comprehension strategies to teach students how to become active, effective readers. Successful implementation requires that teachers model the strategies, provide ongoing examples and opportunities, and guide and provide feedback over an extended period of time. The steps are summarized in the following sections.

Step 1: Preview The first step, previewing, develops students' interest in what they are reading, activates background knowledge, and encourages students to make predictions about what they will read. To review the concept of previewing, use a discussion such as one about movie previews to illustrate ways in which the viewer begins to develop expectations and interest in the upcoming movie. Once students understand the concept, model the tasks of previewing: Read the title; look at any pictures, graphs, or diagrams; read the headings and try to anticipate what they mean; look for key words (e.g., words that are underlined, italicized, in bold, or set off); and read the first and last paragraphs. As a final task, the student predicts what he or she thinks will be learned from the reading. After this procedure has been demonstrated, have the class practice the preview step several times over the next few days, providing feedback and support.

Step 2: Click and Clunk   In the second step, students learn to monitor their reading, determining what they already know and what causes difficulty. A *click* occurs when the reader identifies something he or she knows (it clicks because it makes sense). A *clunk* is a word or point that the student does not understand. For this step, model clicks and clunks and then ask students to write down their own clunks after reading a short assignment. Once students learn to recognize clunks, demonstrate strategies to address them. Strategies might include use of a glossary or a dictionary, rereading, discussion with a peer, and so forth. Ask students to identify the strategy they use to address the clunk so that they learn which strategies work best in which situations.

Step 3: Get the Gist   For the third step, ask each student to summarize the main idea of a paragraph in 10–12 words and then ask students to discuss and offer different versions. Ask students to provide evidence to support their summary and to exclude unnecessary details. Have students vote on which summary is best. After making their choices, they must also explain why.

Step 4: Wrap-Up   During wrap-up, the students review the reading and what has been learned by asking and responding to questions. Depending on the age group, provide question stems, such as

> How would you compare and contrast… ?
> How were they the same or different?
> How would you interpret… ?

Eventually, students should be encouraged to write their own questions. To improve students' abilities to ask higher level questions, you may assign values to questions. A $10 question is one in which the answer is located in the text and requires a short response; a $20 question is located in the text but requires more than two or three words to answer; a $30 question is found in the text but, in order to respond, students need to reread the text and compose an answer based on the reading; and a $40 question requires inference and generalization. Students have to integrate responses with previous knowledge and experience. Questions can be generated by each group and placed on one side of color-coded index cards; answers can be placed on the reverse side. These cards can be used for review, as the basis for questions on future tests, and as a resource for students to learn to ask good questions. The cards can also be used in a game in which members of one group quiz members of other groups.

To make the collaborative groups successful, students from a variety of reading levels (including both a good and poor reader) need to be present in each group, and at least one student member should have leadership skills. Assign the following roles:

- The Leader, who focuses the group on using the four strategies

- The Clunk expert, who reminds the group of strategies for figuring out a clunk

- The Gist expert, who reminds the group about steps to use to figure out the main idea

- The Announcer, who calls on students to read or share an idea and who reports back to the entire class

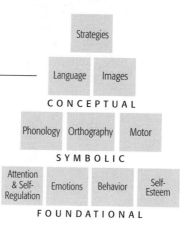

Reports may be written and submitted by the group or individually. As a final recommendation, students can keep a CSR Learning Log, modeled after the K-W-L strategy described in Chapter 10.

SQ3R

The **S**urvey, **Q**uestion, **R**ead, **R**ecite, and **R**eview (SQ3R; Robinson, 1970) strategy is best used when reading textbooks and articles. The steps help a student learn how to study the material and increase concentration. SQ3R is most useful for secondary students such as John who have trouble learning the information presented in textbook chapters. For increased structure and active involvement with the reading material, a student may both recite and write responses to questions. A modified SQ3R procedure is presented as follows.

Step 1: Have a Purpose for Reading   When a student does not understand why a reading has been assigned or why a text is important, problems often arise. Some classes are based on a developmental model that requires students to learn the previous material thoroughly before proceeding with the subsequent reading. In other subjects, the goal may be to introduce students to the breadth and scope of materials that are used rather than to expect students to master all of the details. Students who perceive reading requirements as something they have been told to do are likely to have difficulty motivating themselves to read. In contrast, students who understand the purpose of the reading assignment within the context of the class are more likely to complete the assignment. Initially, you can assist by making explicit the purpose behind the reading.

Step 2: Survey the Text   In this step, the reader becomes familiar with the organization and general content of the material to be read. As John uses this strategy, he follows these steps:

- Notes the author, title, and publication date

- Reads the preface or foreword (the preface often contains the author's explanation of his or her purpose in writing the text)

- Previews the table of contents

- Scans the book and reads any chapter summaries

- Takes note of the kinds of illustrative materials included, such as maps, charts, graphs, diagrams, and pictures

- Looks to see if the text contains an index (i.e., topics and page locations), an appendix (i.e., supplementary material such as tables or maps), a glossary (i.e., definitions of specific terms), or references and a bibliography (i.e., credits for other authors and their works and suggested additional readings)

- Reads headings if the material contains them (a list of headings in sequence almost always forms an outline of the main ideas; the text gives the supporting details)

- Reads the first and the last sentence of each paragraph in order to grasp the general idea of the chapter or article

Although a thorough survey of a textbook may take as much as a half hour, the survey reduces time spent reading later because students can identify sections that are more important to read than others.

Step 3: Ask Questions   As John surveys his text, he asks questions about what he is reading so that he stays actively engaged in the reading process. He is able to follow these steps:

- Turn each heading into a question by using words such as *who, what, when,* and *where.* Higher level questions (i.e., questions using words such as *how, why, explain, discuss, criticize, compare* and *contrast*) foster more abstract thinking.

- Use the questions asked to set a purpose for reading, which, in turn, increases motivation and understanding. Asking questions can take up to 15 minutes per chapter; trying to answer the questions should be delayed until later. Some readers benefit from listing their questions in order to refer to them as they read.

Step 4: Read the Selection, and Recite Important Information   Good readers spend more time on important sections. As an example, good readers may spend 80% of the time allotted for reading on the 20% of the text that they find important or difficult to understand (Robinson, 1993). During this step, students should keep in mind the questions that they formulated earlier. If the assignment is long, students can divide it into segments and respond to their questions as they finish each segment. If the reading is particularly difficult or the content is unfamiliar, students may need to proceed on a paragraph-by-paragraph basis. Short breaks, with preplanned limits, may allow students to continue with renewed concentration. After finishing reading, students may ask the questions orally and respond in complete sentences. As noted previously, some students may want to write their answers in order to maximize recall.

Step 5: Review the Selection   Because most forgetting occurs within the first 24 hours, setting aside time for review daily can save a lot of study time later on. John found that if he attempted to explain the reading to a friend or classmate, his understanding and retention of the material improved. Older students can be encouraged to form study groups so that this type of review and rehearsal can occur on a regular basis.

ReQuest Procedure

The **re**ciprocal **quest**ioning procedure (ReQuest) is designed for older students who have more advanced reading skills (Manzo, 1969, 1985). The purposes of this simple but effective procedure are to help students 1) set their own goals for reading and 2) learn how to ask and answer questions while they read. Before beginning, discuss with the student the purpose for reading the selection, then model how to ask questions. These questions may require factual recall, recognition, evaluation, or critical thinking.

Read the first sentence of a passage silently with the student. Close your book, and the have the student ask as many questions as he or she can. Have the student close his or her book, and then ask as many questions as you can. Continue this process sentence by sentence until the student can provide a reasonable prediction of what is going to happen next in the rest of the selection. At this point, tell the student to finish the passage to see whether the prediction is correct.

When Katy was first introduced to this strategy, she had trouble formulating questions. She would just say that she could not think of anything to ask. Her teacher then adjusted the level of the instructional material. She taught Katy how to paraphrase what she was reading and then how to take that content and ask simple questions.

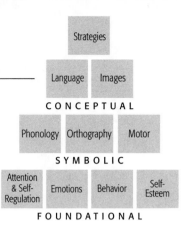

Multipass

Another example of a textbook study strategy designed for secondary students is Multipass, an adaptation of SQ3R. This strategy improves comprehension of content-area textbooks (Schumaker, Deshler, Alley, Warner, & Denton, 1982). Explain the steps and rationale and then demonstrate the strategy by thinking aloud. Students verbally rehearse the strategy. By using the three steps, the student never reads the passage in its entirety.

Step 1: Survey   The student surveys the textbook by reading the chapter title, introductory paragraph, table of contents (in order to understand the relationship of the chapter to others in the text), subtitles, illustrations, diagrams, and summary paragraphs. The student then paraphrases all the information gained from the first pass through the reading.

Step 2: Size Up   In the second step, the student sizes up by reading the questions at the end of the chapter and checking off those for which he or she already knows the answer. The student then looks through the text for headings and parts of the text that are in italics, bold, or colored print to identify cues. The student turns each of these cues into a question and skims the text for an answer. At the end of the chapter, the student paraphrases all remembered facts and ideas.

Step 3: Sort Out   The student sorts out by reading the questions at the end of the chapter again and marking those questions that he or she can answer immediately. If a question cannot be answered, the student attempts to locate the answer by skimming the text.

PORPE

PORPE (Simpson & Stahl, 1987) is an approach for studying textbook materials in which the reader creates and answers essay questions. John found that this strategy was particularly useful for preparing to take an in-class essay test on the assigned reading. Although time consuming, PORPE is an excellent strategy to use when a student needs to develop mastery of the content. The five steps include the following:

Step 1: Predict   After reading a chapter or section, John predicts possible essay questions from the information contained in the text by constructing questions using key words such as *explain, discuss, criticize, compare,* and *contrast.*

Step 2: Organize   John organizes, summarizes, and synthesizes the key points in each chapter in his own words. Then he outlines answers to the questions.

Step 3: Rehearse   As he reads, John rehearses by reciting aloud the information and asking himself questions to check for retention. This stage helps the reader place the key ideas, examples, and overall organization in long-term memory. This step is repeated over the next couple of days.

Step 4: Practice   John practices by attempting to answer the questions from memory. Students can sketch an outline or talk through an answer but need to make sure to include enough information.

Step 5: Evaluate   John evaluates his work by asking if there are enough concrete examples and if his answers are complete, accurate, and appropriate.

To check a student's knowledge of strategies, ask a student questions (Reid, 1988), such as the following:

- What is the most important reason for reading this material? Why does your teacher want you to read this material?

- Who is the best reader in the class (or in your group)? What makes this person a good reader?

- How good are you at reading this material? How do you know?

- What would be the best way to remember information in this reading?

- What would be the best way to find answers in this book?

- What is the hardest part about answering questions like the ones in this book?

WRITTEN LANGUAGE STRATEGIES

Several easy-to-use examples of strategies for writing are described in the next section. The purposes of these strategies are to help students formulate and write different types of texts. Instruction in these strategies can help students improve their understanding and increase their retention of important information. As with other strategies, several of these techniques use a first-letter mnemonic. These types of strategies can help students remember the various steps involved in a task.

Components of Writing

Although the actual process of writing does not follow discrete steps, the components involved include brainstorming or getting ideas, outlining and planning, writing a draft, revising the ideas, and editing or proofreading. Often, after writing a first draft, the student has to go back to brainstorming to come up with additional ideas. A student may also return to outlining or rethinking the organizational format of a paper during revision. As increasing numbers of students are writing on computers using word processing programs, the process of writing becomes even more recursive as one easily moves back and forth among drafting, revising, brainstorming, and editing. John found that he could start on a paper by entering in all of his ideas. By cutting and pasting, he could then easily rearrange his thoughts into a more comprehensive sequence.

Brainstorming Students should be encouraged to talk with people who can help clarify their assignments. Classmates, teaching assistants, teachers, and librarians can offer useful information and help identify sources. Procedures such as the K-W-L strategy described in Chapter 10 are useful at this stage. Some students find it helpful to use a tape recorder to collect or test ideas and to play the tape back to assess how good the ideas sound. Students can also play the tape to ensure that everything they want to include in the paper is there. John found that it was helpful to go on walking brainstorms during which he would take a tape recorder and record his ideas about one section of the paper while walking in one direction and then plan the second section on his return.

Outlining Prior to writing, students need to have a sense of how their paper will be organized. Some students benefit from looking at a model paper to see how it is structured. Practice with highlighting or outlining a model can help students identify the component parts as well as the organization. Software programs such as Inspiration® and Kidspiration® (for younger students; see Additional Resources) assist students in using techniques such as semantic webbing and mind maps and then changing these graphic organizers into outlines. With one push of a key, the student can move between maps and traditional linear outlines. It also helps to talk about the paper's organization with someone else. Paying close attention to

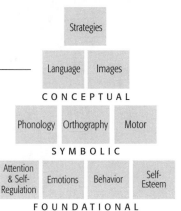

questions the listener asks can help the student identify the questions that need to be addressed in the paper. Some students like to write down the main thesis and list the subjects for each paragraph or section prior to writing.

Some writing assignments require the use of specialized vocabulary. Prior to writing, a student can make a vocabulary list of key words. The student might type key words in an extra large font so that they will be easier to check for spelling or usage.

Composing When writing the first draft, a student should be encouraged to focus on one section at a time because the sections can be reordered easily. The student may leave white space to separate parts of the paper and to make it easier to review. When reviewing the organization, the student may highlight the topic sentence (by using italics, underlining, bold print, or large font) in each paragraph. This helps emphasize the topic focus of each paragraph and is helpful if the sequence of thoughts needs to be rearranged. Another option is to give each section or paragraph a title; repeating the titles may help the writer to stay focused. At the end of the writing process, the student eliminates the highlighting. If the student is having particular difficulty with one section, it often helps to talk aloud. Many times people are able to say something more simply and directly than when they attempt to write it. Using a tape recorder can help a student remember what he or she has just said. Ryan was writing his first draft of a commercial. He decided he would try to sell someone a car. Before writing, he jotted down a few ideas and the names of his favorite cars: Mazda, Balboa, and Ferrari. He thought about the way people pay for cars and wrote, "check, credit cards, or cash." Figure 11.4 depicts his first draft.

Revising When a student is revising a paper, encourage him or her to read topic sentences aloud. This provides a summary of the paper. The student should

Figure 11.4. Ryan's commercial.

also check the transitions between paragraphs. If the sentences do not fit together, either the organization or the content needs more work. The student may also have someone else read his or her paper. If both the reader and the writer have a copy, the writer can make notes while the reader is reading. If the reader has trouble or hesitates, the student should make a note to check for coherence or usage errors. (Spelling and punctuation can also make a reader hesitate.) These errors should be corrected during the editing stage.

Students who have a limited vocabulary can be encouraged to take the time to vary their word usage or use more varied language by using a strategy in which they receive additional points when they use "$5 words." When Katy would write first drafts of papers, she would repeat the same words and same ideas over and over again. In her journal, she wrote, "Today when I got up, I was happy. I was happy today because we were going to have a party, and I will be happy. I was happy. I looked at the board. It said 'journal.' I was happy." Katy needs to have someone help her develop her ideas prior to writing and to help her select and use more varied vocabulary. The appendix at the end of this chapter presents a list of words that children use commonly in their writing with some possible synonyms. A peer could help Katy consider alternative words to use when revising drafts.

Another strategy that is successful in encouraging students to make revisions that are more substantial and meaningful is based on peer response. One student reads the paper (the writer) to another student (the editor), who also reads along. The editor responds by telling the writer two or three positive things about the writing. The editor then looks at the paper and indicates if certain places are not clear or if there are places where more information should be added. The writer then revises the paper, and the process is reversed, with the other student reading his or her paper. Initially, monitor the exchange among students until they have learned how to give both positive as well as constructive feedback.

Editing and Proofreading For editing, students can create a checklist of editing tasks (e.g., using spell check, checking for proper annotation of quotes, adding page numbers, eliminating highlighting). Students can check off each task as it is completed. John learned to keep a manual nearby that reminded him of specific rules that he found problematic, such as using quotation marks or citing quotations. He also made a list of common spelling errors in the back of his notebook.

In some cases, students find it easier to catch errors by reading sentences aloud starting at the end of the paper. This makes it easier to focus on the mechanics of the paper rather than the content. Students can start with the last sentence and work backward.

Revision and editing should be separated, not combined in one step. Students should review for content first, then for organization, then for transitions, and, finally, when it is time to create the final draft, for spelling, capitalization, and punctuation. Teachers who separate their comments on content from their comments about written presentation often help students develop a clearer sense of the problems they need to address. Chapter 9 provides specific suggestions for helping students with basic writing skills.

Some students benefit from a process approach to both narrative and expository structures that emphasizes writing and revising. Try using the following procedure, adapted from Wong, Wong, Darlington, and Jones (1991):

1. Teach students that writing is a process involving planning, generating sentences, and revising.

2. Discuss with students the relevance of planning in real-life situations.

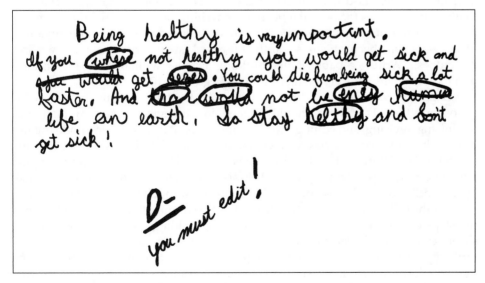

3. Elicit from students why planning is useful in writing (i.e., to direct them toward a topic and to clarify their writing goals).

4. Select a strategy for the specific essay type: narrative, reportive, or compare and contrast.

5. Model the planning strategy.

6. Have students take turns thinking aloud their essay plans.

7. Have students write a first draft.

8. Read the draft and ask for clarification of unclear sentences using an interactive teaching style, ensuring that the student understands why a sentence is unclear.

9. Have each student clarify and expand on sentences deemed unclear.

10. Work with the student to improve the clarity of the essay.

11. Explain how the revised sentences are better.

12. Repeat Steps 8–11 as often as necessary.

13. Have the student rewrite the essay.

14. When message clarity has been attained, work with the student at correcting spelling and grammatical errors.

15. Have the student write the final draft.

Students who struggle with basic writing skills need feedback prior to making edits. A child who spells the word *any* as *eney* cannot find the word in a dictionary and cannot use a spell checker. When Ryan was in third grade, he wrote a first draft of an expository paragraph about the importance of being healthy, presented in Figure 11.5. His only feedback was a failing grade and a comment that he must edit.

POWER Some students need assistance in understanding the stages of the writing process and have to be guided through the process. In her classroom, Katy would often start writing before she had spent time developing and organizing ideas. To help students such as Katy remember that writing is a process that requires planning, Englert, Raphael, Anderson, Anthony, and Stevens (1991) developed the acronym POWER to represent the following steps:

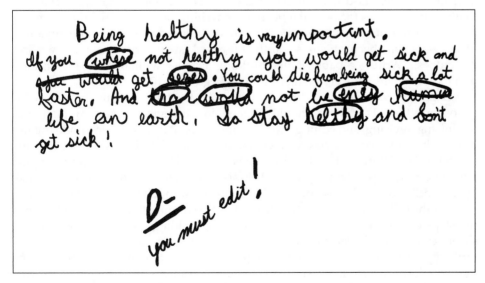

Figure 11.5. Ryan's first draft.

Plan
Organize
Write
Edit
Revise

Self-Regulated Strategy Development

Self-Regulated Strategy Development (Graham & Harris, 1999) can be employed to help a student to plan and organize writing. Use of this approach improves the quality of writing and a student's ability to plan and revise what he or she is going to say. To begin, schedule a conference with the student to discuss his or her current approach to writing. The student then learns three steps:

1. Think about who will read this (the audience) and why you are writing it.

2. Plan what to say (i.e., generate ideas and plan organization).

3. Write and say more (i.e., continue to improve the piece).

Follow up by describing the planning and writing strategy appropriate to the type of writing assignment (e.g., opinion piece, compare and contrast) and discussing the concept of progress monitoring (i.e., the steps to use to complete work). The student should be taught to count and graph elements that should be addressed in the assignment as one way to monitor his or her progress.

With this approach, also discuss with the student or the class the importance of what people say to themselves while working. Teach the students two positive statements to use while they are working. Model appropriate strategies, such as planning, reviewing, and self-evaluation.

Cognitive Strategy in Writing Program

To become members of the literacy community, students need to learn to talk about literacy (Englert, 1992). The Cognitive Strategy in Writing (CSIW) program (Englert, 1990; Englert & Raphael, 1989) emphasizes the dialogic and social nature of writing (Englert, 1992). Students must be able to convey ideas in a conventional format to a distant audience (Kozulin, 2003). This approach has been particularly successful for upper-elementary and middle school students with writing difficulties. When used with adolescents with LD, Hallenbeck (1996, 2002) found that having students focus on the purpose of writing, as well as the brainstorming and expansion of ideas, improved students' abilities to generate and organize ideas. As Hallenbeck (1996) so aptly observed about students with writing difficulties, "Writing a paper is like building a house without a blueprint; they don't know where they are going or how to begin" (p. 107).

Englert (1992) described three principles for teaching students how to write expository text: 1) writers should engage in strategies related to planning, organizing, revising, and editing text; 2) writers benefit from teachers modeling the inner talk and thinking involved in effective writing; and 3) writers need to learn about the social nature of writing by collaborating with each other and writing for authentic purposes. The program emphasizes teacher modeling through think-alouds and student rehearsal of modeled strategies through the use of think sheets.

For the CSIW think-alouds, describe aloud your inner thinking by verbalizing the steps of a strategy, asking questions, and providing answers. Various think sheets can be used that contain a set of self-questions intended to guide the writing process until the strategies and questions are internalized. The purpose of these think sheets is to make strategies visible to students and provide them with a vocabulary for talking about writing (Englert, 1992). The sheets guide students

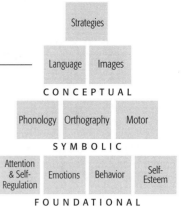

in strategy use as they engage in text construction and monitoring activities and can be adapted to meet particular writing assignments.

Englert and Raphael (1989) described several types of think sheets. The plan think sheet includes a series of prompts that help the writer focus on the audience. Questions may include

Who am I writing for?
Why am I writing this?
What do I already know about the topic?
How can I organize my ideas?

The organize think sheet presents a series of text structure questions, such as

What is being explained?
What materials are needed?
What are the steps?
What do you do first, second, third, fourth?

The self-edit think sheet has the writer rate performance on the questions included in the plan think sheet. The writer places a star by his or her favorite parts of the paper and question marks by parts that seem unclear. A peer editor then completes an editor think sheet. The author and editor then talk about ways to make the paper better.

Katy's compositions improved dramatically when she was given a series of think sheets to guide her writing. The provision of a series of questions helped her learn how to self-monitor and self-regulate. Prior to writing, Katy learned how to select a topic, identify her audience, brainstorm ideas, and then organize her ideas. In addition, the use of two software programs, Co:Writer®Solo and Write:Outloud®, provided additional support and helped her concentrate more fully on expressing her ideas (see Additional Resources). In high school, John found that using the software program *Draft Builder®* (see Additional Resources) provided him with a strategic approach to planning, organizing, and drafting essays and research projects.

Cohesion   Cohesion refers to the organization and unity of the text. Writers use various strategies and techniques to help readers understand their messages. Cohesive ties are words that signal the organization of text and provide transitions that show how a previous clause or statement is related to another. Explicit instruction in the use of cohesive ties helps students learn to organize and integrate concepts in writing. This instruction is aimed at helping students connect the sentences and paragraphs within their compositions by using words that signify a variety of types of relationships. Wallach and Miller (1988) described several types of cohesive ties:

1. Additive (*and, also, in addition*)

2. Amplification (*furthermore, moreover*)

3. Adversative (*but, however, in contrast, nevertheless*)

4. Causal (*if/then, because, due to, as a result*)

5. Conclusion (*therefore, accordingly, consequently*)

6. Temporal (*after, meanwhile, whenever, previously*)

7. Spatial (*next to, between, in front of, adjacent to*)

8. Continuative (*after all, again, finally, another*)

9. Likeness (*likewise, similarly*)

10. Example (*for example, as an illustration*)

11. Restatement (*in other words, that is, in summary*)

12. Exception (*except, barring, beside, excluding*)

Katy was able to organize a sequential paragraph about the steps involved in brushing her teeth by introducing the four sentences with the words *first, next, then,* and *finally.* At first, her teacher had her fold her paper into four squares and then write a linking word in the upper left corner of each square. Katy drew a picture of four steps and then wrote a sentence to describe each step.

Paragraphs Many strategies can be used to help students improve their skills in collecting and organizing the factual information that they wish to include in paragraphs, essays, or reports. In general, students benefit from formal instruction that presents organizational models and includes practice writing in a variety of modes (Vogel & Moran, 1982). As with other areas of achievement related to the conceptual blocks, students benefit from strategies that provide direct instruction and teacher modeling. For example, Wallace and Bott (1989) found that use of a metacognitive text structure strategy that involved completing a paragraph planning guide improved student skill in paragraph writing.

A key to teaching paragraph writing is to help students learn how to subordinate. As noted, John had trouble distinguishing main ideas from details. His English teacher demonstrated how to write a topic sentence for a paragraph and then how to support this sentence with details. She then showed John how to link paragraphs together to form an essay. She also spent time teaching the class how to turn essay questions on examinations into topic sentences.

Statement pie is one easy-to-use strategy for helping students develop expository paragraphs (Englert & Lichter, 1982; Hanau, 1974). In this strategy, *statement* refers to a topic statement, and *pie* refers to the details, which may be categorized as follows:

Proofs
Information
Examples

Wallace and Bott (1989) described the following adaptation:

1. Give students a completed paragraph guide as a model of the strategy.

2. Explain the meaning of *statement* and *pie.*

3. Model the detection and generation of pies.

4. Give students a statement.

5. Have students verbally generate appropriate pies using the following guide:

   Statement: topic statement
   Pie: a detail related to the topic statement
   Pie: another detail related to the topic statement
   Pie: another detail related to the topic statement

6. Give immediate feedback in regard to the appropriateness of each pie.

7. Give students another topic sentence in an area that is age appropriate and in which students have background knowledge.

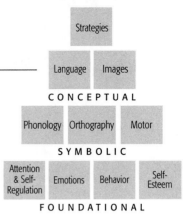

8. Have students generate and write appropriate pies to be used as paragraph planning guides on the given topic.

9. Give immediate feedback in regard to the appropriateness of each pie.

Use the following steps for outlining statements and pies in expository paragraphs:

1. Model the outlining of statements and pies in chosen expository paragraphs.

2. Give students paragraphs for guided practice.

3. Circle the statements, and underline the pies.

4. Write the statements and pies in a planning guide.

Use the following steps for writing paragraphs:

1. Model paragraph writing by

   • Selecting a topic

   • Writing a paragraph planning guide

   • Using the guide to construct sentences

   • Forming the sentences into a paragraph

   • Emphasizing key words and cohesive ties (e.g., *first, next, afterward, finally*)

2. Have students choose a topic from a list you have generated.

3. Have students generate statement–pie paragraph planning guides.

4. Have students write a paragraph.

5. Provide immediate feedback with regard to the appropriateness of the pies.

When he was in seventh grade, Samuel's English teacher was attempting to teach the class how to write descriptive paragraphs. She first had the class read sample paragraphs and then asked them to write a paragraph that was similar to the model. Figure 11.6 presents Samuel's first draft. He selected the topic "Monday has been very boring." Notice the teacher's feedback and grade. What Samuel needed as a writer was increased modeling and support, not a failing grade and a recommendation for a more interesting topic.

Essays

As students are learning to write paragraphs, they can be taught how to link the paragraphs together to form an essay.

Kerrigan's Method Kerrigan (1979) described a comprehensive procedure for teaching students how to write essays with the following six steps for theme organization and composition writing.

1. Have the student write a sentence in which a person or an object is/was something or does/did something. The sentence must follow seven rules:

   • Create a sentence about which you can say something more.

   • Concentrate on what the person or object does.

   • Be specific—what exactly did the person or object do?

367

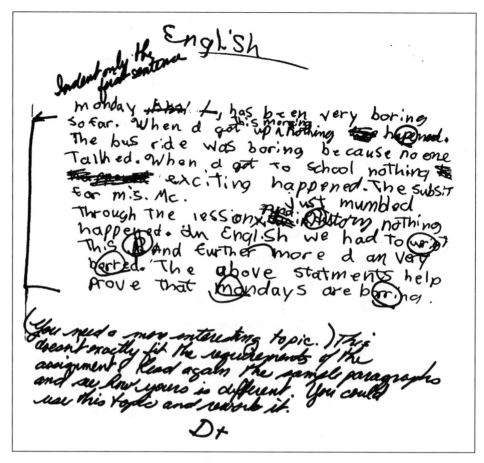

Figure 11.6. Samuel's first draft.

- Keep the sentence short until you become proficient.

- Keep the sentence as a statement, not a question or command.

- Ensure you have only one statement.

- Do not use a descriptive or narrative sentence.

2. Have the student write three sentences about the original sentence. Encourage the student to use simple, declarative sentences that give information clearly and directly about the original sentence. The information given must pertain to the whole of the original sentence and not to only a piece of it. Help the student provide more specific information rather than repeating the same idea in different words.

3. Ask the student to write four or five sentences about each of the three sentences in Step 2.

4. The sentences in Step 3 must be specific and concrete. Encourage the student to go into detail and use examples. Specify that the goal is to give more information about what has already been introduced, thus there must be no new ideas. Sharing short anecdotal stories with the student can be effective during the fourth stage.

   At this point, help the student review the content to ensure that the subject has not changed and that the central idea or theme is obvious from the first paragraph. Have the student focus on being understood by

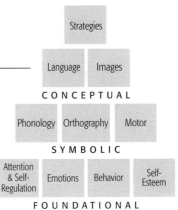

the prospective audience. Encourage the student to use vocabulary that is pertinent to the audience and to concentrate on making the theme clear, real, and convincing.

5. Have the student insert a clear, explicit reference to the theme of the preceding paragraph in the first sentence of the following paragraphs.

6. Have the student work to ensure that every sentence is connected with the previous sentence and makes a clear reference to it.

Use of Kerrigan's (1979) six steps to writing ensures that the whole theme is thoroughly connected. This method can help students like John to organize their ideas within a meaningful framework.

Visual displays posted in the classroom can also remind students of what information they should include as they write a paragraph, essay, or report. Ryan's teacher, Mr. Steen, created a poster in his room using the image of a dinosaur to remind the students of the elements of essays. He explained that the head represented the introduction; the body was supported by the facts and details, represented by the legs; and the tail served as a reminder that every good essay has a clear-cut ending. Figure 11.7 shows the visual mnemonic that he used. Ms. McGrew used a similar visual display, Ms. Edith Essay. Her head represented the introduction and her body was the main part of the text. The legs and arms were topic sentences for the paragraphs.

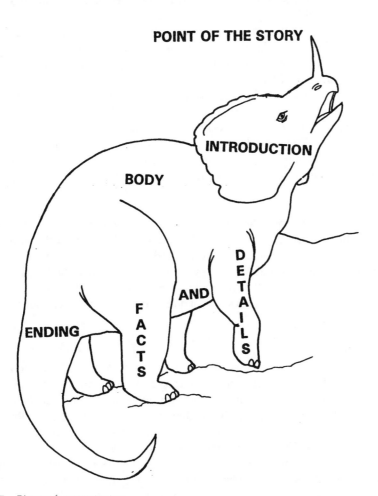

Figure 11.7. Dinosaur for essay structure.

Research As students progress through school, they are required to work more independently and are asked to present work with a greater scope or depth than has previously been required. To begin, assess a student's abilities to engage in independent research. Students with learning difficulties may need to practice the steps required for effective research before being able to work independently, or they may need to have the steps simplified or repeated over a period of time.

Some students find that conducting research on the computer is exciting; others find it frustrating and difficult. Poor spelling skills can prevent entering a correctly spelled item in a key word search. Trouble identifying specific words to narrow a search can frustrate those with poor word retrieval skills. When a topic is too broad or general, students may find that their search results in hundreds of sites or articles and quit working in frustration. As with other areas of academic performance, students need explicit instruction and practice in using the Internet to retrieve information for a report.

MATH PROBLEM SOLVING

As with reading comprehension and written expression, multiple factors can affect a student's ability to solve math problems effectively. In fact, Geary (2004) found that the estimated prevalence of math LD is equal to the 5 to 8 percent of reported reading disabilities in school-age children. Oral language abilities play a key role in math problem solving, as does the ability to move between verbal and spatial representations. Working memory allows students to store numbers while calculating problems, whereas long-term memory provides the ability to retrieve facts (Swanson & Jerman, 2006); therefore, problems in either domain can affect computational success. Poor planning processes, slow execution rates, and deficient reading skills are also common problems for students with math difficulties. Students who lack awareness of the skills, strategies, and resources that are needed to perform a task and who fail to use self-regulatory mechanisms to perform a task will undoubtedly have difficulty with mathematics (Montague & van Garderen, 2008; Swanson & Jerman, 2006; Swanson & Saez, 2003; Wong, Harris, Graham, & Butler, 2003). Similar to reading comprehension and written language, success in mathematics is dependent largely on background knowledge, symbolic facility, and the use of strategies.

John's limited acquired knowledge also affected his ability to solve mathematical problems. When John was asked the question, "If a foot-long ruler were divided into six equal parts, how long would each part be?" he responded, "One tenth." He did not know that a foot was composed of 12 inches. When he was asked the question, "If three people each have $4, how much money do they have all together?" he responded, "Between $13 and $14." John did not understand that this type of question has one correct response and does not require estimation.

Because of the complexity of mathematics, different students demonstrate problems with different applications. To explore the areas in which a student has particular difficulty, conduct a one-to-one math interview. Consider the full range of mathematical abilities, such as the student's ability to make predictions on the basis of patterns, to sort, to measure, to organize space, and to follow steps in completing problems. This is important because students need to know multiple concepts and show competence in a variety of skills to be successful across different mathematical domains (e.g., algebra, geometry) (Montague, 2007). Also check to see what strategies the student currently employs (e.g., Does the student talk to

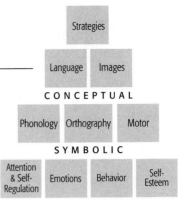

him- or herself, draw pictures to help understand problems, ask for clarifications, check his or her answers, or estimate an answer before solving a problem?). Attempt to discover the student's problem-solving strengths as well as weaknesses.

Mathematical Knowledge

While conducting the above assessments, teachers must be aware of the three types of knowledge students need to be successful in mathematics: declarative, procedural, and conceptual. For students to be successful in developing math competence and literacy, all three types are imperative (Hasselbring, Lott, & Zydney, 2005). *Declarative knowledge* refers to a student's abilities in the area of factual knowledge, or the information that students retrieve from memory without hesitation (Miller & Hudson, 2007). Examples of this knowledge are 6 + 4 = 10 and the fact that a square is a four-sided polygon with equal-length sides that meet at right angles. *Procedural knowledge* is the understanding of rules, algorithms, and procedures used to solve various mathematical tasks. Examples of this knowledge are the order of operations and knowledge of the sequential steps used to solve long division or algebraic expressions. *Conceptual knowledge* is an overarching piece that represents a student's knowledge and understanding of the meaning of how declarative and procedural knowledge work together to solve mathematical equations.

As with reading, students need to be provided with enough instructional examples and opportunities for practice. Several examples can be provided to define a given concept in order to help students develop accurate conceptualizations. For example, both Katy and John struggled with the concept of estimation. To help them improve this ability, their teachers provided examples from real-life situations (e.g., show how long it will take, what is the actual approximate temperature) and varied the language that was used (e.g., *between, approximately, about, close to*) in each example. Teachers can continue to model each step of the problem-solving sequence until students acquire the skill and then provide adequate practice so that they retain the skill.

Katy didn't look for patterns or meaning when she did math problems, and she was often puzzled when other students seemed to solve problems easily. Her teacher noted that Katy tried to memorize everything, as if remembering the response was the only way she could get the right answer. Many times the answers that she wrote were not even close to the correct solution. Katy's teacher was trying to find ways to ensure that Katy understood the procedures and was not just trying to imitate them.

Instructional Concerns

Over the last two decades, mathematics education has been undergoing reform because of low student performance on standardized math exams (Maccini, Mulcahy, & Wilson, 2007). In response to concerns, the National Council of Teachers of Mathematics (NCTM, 2000) developed standards that emphasize conceptual understanding, mathematical reasoning, and real-world applications for problem-solving skills. Because of the self-regulated nature of the activities that adhere to these standards, students with LD have struggled to succeed with these curricular changes (Woodward, 2006). The National Assessment of Educational Progress (NAEP, 2003) reported that 71% of students with disabilities compared with 27% of students without disabilities score below the basic level on mathematics performance assessments.

According to Jones, Wilson, and Bhojwani (1997), teachers tend to direct their instruction, in terms of the difficulty of the material, to students of higher achievement. Many students, particularly at the secondary level, do not have the skills needed to meet the demands of a traditional curriculum (Miller, 1996). To involve students with lower achievement, teachers should strive to

- Maintain a lively pace of instruction
- Obtain frequent active responses from all students
- Monitor individual students' attention and accuracy
- Provide feedback and positive reinforcement for correct responses
- Offer corrective feedback for errors

Achievement will be highest when all five of these principles are part of the instruction. In addition, explicit teaching of basic mathematical skills is more effective for students with disabilities than reform-based instructional practices (Kroesbergen & Van Luit, 2003).

Instructional Format

An effective format for a session in math instruction is to 1) begin with a short period of review of previously covered materials; 2) follow with teacher-directed instruction of the concept of the day and guided practice, and then and provide feedback; and 3) conclude with independent practice with corrective feedback; Students need enough time for instruction as well as for practice. In many classrooms, students' difficulties are compounded by long stretches of independent practice in which they receive little feedback prior to completion of the assignment. In addition to providing ongoing feedback, one successful variation is to engage students in small-group practice in which students can ask questions and check answers. Thus, essential teaching practices include advance organizers, communication of lesson objectives, teacher demonstration, guided practice, independent practice, and maintenance checks (Miller & Hudson, 2007).

Another example of a problem-solving format a teacher can use is to provide a 10-minute working period in which students work on solving problems, then a 5-minute period of teacher-guided self-reflection, and then another 10-minute working period (Naglieri & Gottling, 1995). During the self-reflection period, students can think about how they tried to solve the problems and then comment on what they did well and what they could do to improve their performance. Students can answer questions such as

- What did you notice about the strategies you used to solve the problem?
- How did you solve this problem?
- I noticed you had some trouble with_____. What did you do?
- What could you do to get more problems right?

The task of the instructor is to encourage students to verbalize the strategies they could use and explain why they might use those strategies. When using this exercise, place the emphasis on the strategies students are using rather than the number of correct answers they have (Naglieri & Gottling, 1995).

Students become discouraged when they receive problem sets or tests back with marks indicating they have answered questions incorrectly but with no other feedback. In a short period of time, they may come to feel that they have no control over doing math problems and lose the incentive to try. Rather than viewing problems as correct or incorrect, reinforce students by providing positive feedback on the steps of the problem that have been done correctly. Varied reinforcement strategies can also reduce the need for constant help (Miller & Mercer, 1997).

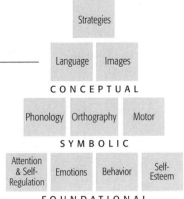

Within class sessions, teachers may present problems in four modes: active construction or manipulation of objects, fixed visual displays, oral statements, and written or symbolic presentations. The student's response may also be presented using one of the four options: active construction or manipulation of objects, identification of a visual display from a range of alternative displays, an oral statement, or a written or symbolic statement. In some instances, you may present the problem in one mode and ask the student to respond in the same mode. In other instances, you may ask the student to respond in an alternate mode from the one you used to present the problem. Students who have the opportunity to work with varied response presentations and options are more likely to generalize skills than students who spend the greatest proportion of their time writing responses to problems in workbooks (Jones et al., 1997).

Just as with reading and writing, explicit instruction for students with math disabilities results in more predictable and functional achievement (Kroesbergen & Van Luit, 2003; Swanson & Hosykn, 2001). Teachers need to plan and structure the learning experience, emphasizing mastery of concepts and skills and providing students with time to master those skills. In their book, *Guiding Children's Learning of Mathematics* (11th ed.), Kennedy, Tipps, and Johnson (2007) described many mathematical techniques and experiences that emphasize the teacher's role as a guide to children's learning. The book includes many practical resources and interesting activities to use with children in pre-school through sixth grade. The text focuses on both the conceptual and procedural aspects of teaching and learning mathematics with specific information about what teachers need to know, as well as the learning objectives for students.

Although the use of basal materials for classroom instruction in the area of mathematics is a successful strategy for some students, it is problematic for students with LD. Most textbooks rely on a spiraling approach to teaching math skills, in which numerous skills are introduced rapidly and reintroduced at different levels. Opportunities for mastery of individual concepts or for adequate practice and review are limited. Other concerns include inadequately sequenced problems and a lack of strategy instruction. Students who move through a math textbook without understanding concepts continue to experience failure. For students who struggle with mathematical concepts, prerequisite skills need to be introduced and practiced for several days (or even weeks). Review needs to be distributed over time so that students do not forget the concepts they are learning. For example, when Katy was asked to point to the shape that was a triangle, she responded that the class was not doing that kind of problem anymore.

When only those problems presented in texts or workbooks are used, difficulty with generalization of processes can occur. The worksheets provided by publishers often fail to provide opportunities for enough practice to achieve mastery. Adequate sampling of a range of real-life examples needs to be given for students to avoid limited or erroneous understanding of the concept (Jones et al., 1997). As an example, Jones and colleagues described the way in which students are often taught to understand fractions as lesser parts of one whole (e.g., 1/4, 1/3). Because some fractions are greater than the whole (e.g., 9/8), the original presentation limits students' understanding of computation with fractions and, as a result, can affect their problem-solving skills.

Instructional Sequence

When he was in fifth grade, John had memorized many multiplication facts but did not understand the basic process of multiplication. If he forgot the solution, he could not come up with the answer in another way. He also could not check to see if his answers were reasonable.

As a general rule for teaching mathematical concepts to a student, teachers should follow a sequence that goes from concrete (objects) to semiconcrete (drawings or representations) to abstract (numbers), which is commonly referred to as a concrete-representation-abstract (CRA) or concrete-semiconcrete-abstract (CSA) teaching sequence (Maccini et al., 2007; Mercer, 1992; Miller, 1996; Miller & Hudson, 2007). With this progression, students such as Katy and John develop mental representations of the meaning of numbers and as a result, improve their ability to think with images.

Concrete In this beginning stage of understanding, children see and manipulate objects to solve problems. To count from 1 to 10, for example, students would move and count 10 objects. To add, students would put together two or more groups and then count the total number. To subtract, students would remove a specified number of objects from the group. The basic purpose of working with manipulatives is to help students form mental images of the processes and an understanding of what numbers represent. In other words, by learning to perform problems with concrete objects, students understand how numbers (abstractions) relate to the objects. Sometimes, however, children do not fully grasp the connection between the use of manipulatives and math facts.

Students can also use an act-it-out strategy to simulate a story or word problem (Kennedy & Tipps, 2000). Provide simple story problems and have children act out the problems using real props as other students observe the acting out. Kennedy and Tipps suggested that younger students act out experiences such as "buying" items at a classroom store in order to solve math problems. Older students can simulate a microeconomics society by buying and selling products. Some problems may require several steps. Kennedy and Tipps described the use of the classic handshake problem: A basketball team has a meeting with five players attending. If each player shakes hands with each of the other players, how many handshakes occur among players at the meeting? As they act out the handshakes, students must determine a way to systematically record the number of handshakes.

Manipulatives can be used in many different ways when providing math instruction at all levels. The National Library of Virtual Manipulatives http://nlvm.usu.edu/en/nav/vlibrary.html provides a library of web-based and interac-tive manipulatives and concept tutorials at all levels for teachers' use. Even secondary-level students can benefit from the use of manipulatives (Allsopp, 1999; Allsopp, Kyger, & Lovin, 2007; Cass, Cates, Smith, & Jackson, 2003). Allsopp suggested a variety of manipulatives to use when teaching concepts at the concrete level:

- *Angles:* protractors, compasses, geoboards, rulers, tangrams, pattern blocks

- *Area:* geoboards, color tiles, base 10 blocks, decimal squares, cubes, tangrams, pattern blocks, rulers, fraction models

- *Volume:* capacity containers, cubes, geometric solids

- *Probability:* spinners, number cubes, fraction models, color tiles, cubes

- *Ratio/proportion:* color tile cubes, Cuisenaire rods, tangrams, pattern blocks

- *Polynomials:* algebra tiles, base 10 materials

- *Symmetry:* geoboards, pattern blocks, tangrams, cubes, attribute blocks

John's geometry teacher incorporated manipulatives into his daily schedule. Before working with geometric shapes on paper, the teacher made sure that students understood con-

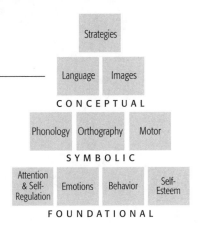

cepts such as points, corners, edges, sides, roundness, flatness, solids, stacks, and rolls. When these terms were understood, more difficult terms such as *faces* and *vertices* were easier to understand. He also used *tangrams,* a puzzle game with seven pieces, and *geoboards,* pegboards that come in various shapes and sizes, to improve spatial pattern recognition and spatial coordination. By using string or rubber bands or by drawing lines around the pegs or pins on the grid on a geoboard, students create shapes. For one assignment, the teacher asked students to make as many quadrilateral shapes as they could using the geoboard and then to count the number of parallel lines in each shape. Students recorded their answers on paper that had dots to represent the pegs in order to have a permanent record of what they had done.

A geoboard also works well as a manipulative for teaching the Pythagorean theorem. This type of instruction helps students learn to think with images and to relate concepts to visual representations, critical skills for increasing conceptual understanding.

Allsopp and colleagues (2007) caution, however, that teachers should not assume that students understand the same underlying mathematical ideas as teachers do when using manipulatives. Just because a student has a visual representation of something does not mean that he or she is getting the principle behind it. Be careful to continue to teach the ideas as they are using the manipulatives. Once students have demonstrated mastery of concepts with manipulatives, instruction can move to activities at the semiconcrete stage.

Semiconcrete or Representational In this stage, a student is shown that tallies or pictures can be drawn to represent objects. Teachers may help students develop understanding at the semiconcrete level by representing physical objects with dots, lines, sticks, or pictures. Students may be shown how to use popsicle sticks to represent each member of a set with a tally. This type of procedure encourages students to focus on the number properties of sets rather than other characteristics of the objects, such as color or size. The basic purpose of this level is to help students make associations between visual pictures and symbolic processes. Using manipulatives and pictorial representations is particularly beneficial for helping students with LD develop conceptual knowledge (Miller & Hudson, 2007).

Children with difficulties with either the symbolic or conceptual blocks need a lot of experience at the concrete and semiconcrete levels before they can use numbers meaningfully. When John was in third grade, he still counted on his fingers when solving simple addition and subtraction problems. His teacher showed him how to draw lines to add or subtract so that he did not have to rely on his fingers. For students with memory problems, working with manipulatives and pictorial representations improves their ability to retain what they are learning. When memory fails, recall of pictorial information may help them rediscover needed information.

Abstract At the abstract level, students learn to solve problems by using numbers. Some students memorize formulas or steps in a sequence without understanding the concepts behind them; when this is the case, they are unable to apply the information to different problems. Other children are asked to use numbers to solve problems when they really do not understand the meaning of numbers. Their first experience with numbers is at the abstract level rather than at the concrete level. Use of the CRA or CSA sequence ensures that concepts are taught to students with both three-dimensional (manipulatives) and two-dimensional representations (pictures) (Miller & Hudson, 2007).

In first grade, Katy's teacher showed the class the number *4* and said, "This is the number four." Although she had learned to count by rote from 1 to 20, Katy did not understand that the number 4 represented four objects. To her, numbers were no different than letters of the alphabet. In fact, sometimes when she was writing, she would create a word that was composed of letters and numbers. Before engaging in problems with numbers at the abstract level, Katy needed to go back to the concrete and then semiconcrete stages to learn that numbers represent a set of objects. Once she mastered this concept, she was ready to solve problems using numbers.

Language and Mathematics

Students who struggle to develop mathematical concepts require careful instruction. In considering the various strategies and methods used to teach mathematics, it is important to consider the ways in which comprehension of language may affect the learning process. Students who experience problems with language are likely to have difficulty with mathematics. Like Katy, they may be more likely to rely on memorization of facts and procedures rather than to develop a solid understanding of mathematical concepts and applications.

As with strategies for improving reading comprehension, students need opportunities to discuss, clarify, and state what is being learned. In addition, students need explicit instruction in the language of mathematics, which includes signs, symbols, and terms as well as the vocabulary used to express mathematical ideas. A teacher has two main roles: interpreting the language of mathematics and clarifying the student's attempts to use the language of mathematics.

Students who have difficulty using language need to try out possible answers to word problems (Tobias, 1993). All word problems contain assumptions. Asking students to talk through their approach helps them to identify incorrect assumptions. In a situation described previously, Katy was asked how many half of four trees would be. Katy envisioned that the trees would be cut in half horizontally, not separated into two groups. Her misunderstanding is based on an incorrect assumption. To correct this assumption, a teacher could have Katy practice this same type of problem using manipulatives.

When students do not have a strong language base, explanations need to be simple, accurate, and concise. Give the explanation just once, provide the student with the opportunity to think about the explanation, and encourage the student to ask meaningful questions.

Language skills are also needed to recall and use the many steps and rules involved in math. Some students, although they may have memorized terms and signs, fail to understand how meanings change in different contexts. For instance, a student who associates the word *multiply* with the idea of becoming larger may not grasp the concept that numbers become smaller when multiplying fractions. Tobias (1993) described the confusion of the student who understands the minus sign in subtraction and then tries to apply the same meaning to the interpretation of negative numbers.

Although so-called key words often appear in problems and may be relevant to the solution, they may not be relevant to the process of solving the problem. For example, a student may believe that the phrase "How many in all" means that the problem is asking them to add. Clearly, problems can be written so that the phrase signifies another process. Unfortunately, many students with poor math concepts may rely more on key words instead of attempting to understand the more critical information presented in the problem. They then have difficulty with solving problems that do not use key words or that use key words in ways that are irrelevant to the solution (Cawley, Miller, & School, 1987; Jones et al., 1997).

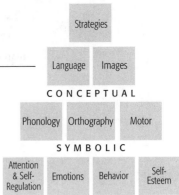

Story or Word Problem Strategies

When students work on story or word problems, they draw on two critical skills: comprehension and translation. Students need to understand what is being asked (to interpret the goal of the problem), and they need to be able to represent that information by planning and executing a solution. Polloway and Patton (1993) noted that students with math disabilities improve their problem-solving abilities through teacher-directed activities that include several key stages: 1) having the student read the problem carefully, 2) helping the student focus on significant information, 3) involving students in stating a solution, 4) developing strategies for solving the problem, and 5) performing the necessary calculations. To assist students who experience difficulty and require explicit instruction both in representing the problem and in solving it, Maccini (1998) developed the acronym STAR.

> **S** = Search the word problem
> **T** = Translate the words into an equation in picture form
> **A** = Answer the problem
> **R** = Review the solution

This strategy can be helpful for students such as John who recognize the value of strategies when attempting to solve word problems.

John began by employing the first step (**S** = Search the word problem). While searching the problem, he asked himself, "What facts do I know?" and "What do I need to find?" Once these questions were answered, John then wrote down the facts. In the second step (**T** = Translate the words into an equation in picture form), John attempted to do the following:

- *Choose the variable and identify the operations.* Translate the English terms into mathematical or algebraic terms, being careful to check the sequence in which the information needs to be conveyed. John used a chart of terms and their symbols that he had developed from his notes in order to double-check his translation.

- *Represent the equation using a drawing and concrete manipulatives.* Make a simple drawing of the problem in order to make it more meaningful or create a table of information, leaving blank spaces for any unknown information. Teach students to use as few unknowns as possible because a separate equation has to be developed to solve each unknown.

In the third step (**A** = Answer the problem), John answered the problem using cues and a work mat. He then performed the fourth step (**R** = Review the Solution) and reread the problem while asking, "Does the answer make sense?" and "Why?" to make a final check of his answer.

When John's algebra teacher talked to John's history teacher, he learned that John understood the value of using preorganizers and postorganizers when studying for tests and when writing papers. Because the first two steps in the STAR procedure represent pre-organizers and the last two steps represent postorganizers, the algebra teacher could help John see the value of working problems through on a step-by-step basis rather than guessing at the answer.

Through modeling and guided practice, students can learn how to plan what they need to do to solve problems. Students can be asked to solve different types of problems and obtain solutions depending on the type of question asked. Examples of different math problems include the following (Mather & Jaffe, 2002):

- Decide which operations to use. (For example, Harry weighed 250 pounds. He weighed 72 more pounds than James. How much did James weigh?)

- Make a table, graph, or chart of the information provided. (For example, Hansel and Gretel went to the witch's house every day except Sunday. On Mondays and Thursdays, Hansel went twice. On Wednesday, Gretel went in the morning, at noon, and once after Hansel was in bed. Who traveled to the witch's house more times in a month?)

- Make a drawing of the information provided. (For example, Mehitabel planted a square garden with 12 garlic plants on each side to keep the snails away. How many garlic plants did she plant?)

- Make inferences and logical deductions. (For example, the Carsons went to Jack-in-the-Bag and spent $20.75 for lunch. An adult meal costs $4.95 and lunch for a child costs $2.95. How many people are in the family? How many of them are children?)

Cue Cards

As students are learning a new algorithm (i.e., a set of rules for solving a kind of problem in a finite number of steps), they are likely to benefit from having an index card that lists several sequenced steps to follow when solving story problems. A sample card could list 1) read and reread the problem, 2) draw or mentally picture what is happening, 3) restate what is being asked, 4) choose the operation or operations, and 5) compute and check the answer. Another example of steps to write on an index card would be 1) read the problem, 2) reread the problem to determine what is known, 3) identify the question that is being asked, 4) identify the operation or operations to use, 5) use objects or drawings to solve the problem, 6) write the problem, and 7) write the solution.

As a final step in problem solving, students should check to make sure that their answer makes sense. Training students to estimate and evaluate their answers allows them to gain experience in testing their assumptions and in understanding when various processes are appropriate and when they are not. Another way to help students internalize important concepts is to ask them to explain the problem in their own words, try and explain it by putting it into a teacher's words, and, as a final step, translate the problem into mathematical language. Because students do not often get to see that even accomplished mathematicians often try several solutions, they need active modeling of the process.

John was having trouble understanding the meaning of place value when numbers included decimals. He thought that longer numbers would always be the bigger numbers. Therefore, he stated that 12.008 was larger than 12.8. John needed to review the concept of place value and the meaning of numbers containing fractions. As discussed in Chapter 10, teachers need to help students resolve conceptual difficulties by using manipulatives, drawings, and think-alouds.

Effective Strategy Instruction

As with reading and writing, students who have difficulties with mathematics may require additional time for processing and learning skills and can benefit from self-questioning strategies, guided practice, and modeling. These strategies often focus on assisting students in developing and using systematic procedures to solve problems, finding the key that is appropriate for the kind of problem that is being solved, and helping students identify the necessary and unnecessary details within problems. Students who learn to be active and successful participants in their learning perceive themselves as competent problem solvers (Jones et al., 1997). Teachers can aid students by writing out basic processes and

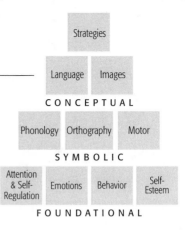

the necessary steps to procedures, drawing diagrams, and rewording problems in language closer to the student's own. Teachers can also create a variety of instructional techniques as they sequence tasks carefully. Miller (1996) presented the following sequence for mastery of word problems:

Word problems with single words or phrases

Word problems with sentences; numbers still aligned vertically

Word problems in a traditional paragraph format

Word problems without extraneous information

Word problems with extraneous information

Students create their own word problems (p. 357)

For students such as Ben, difficulties with reading and spelling can also affect math performance. Figure 11.8 presents several story problems Ben wrote when he was in third grade. Students were asked to write problems for peers to solve. After writing the problems, Ben drew illustrations. When he passed his problems to Marcos, Marcos replied, "I can't read these." Ben understands how to create and solve story problems, but other students cannot read his writing. In addition, Ben has trouble reading the chapters presented in the math textbook. Cawley and Miller (1986) advised the following:

If problem solving is truly the goal, obstacles to problem solving must be removed. A child who cannot solve problems because he or she cannot read the problems is not involved in problem solving but is involved in reading. (p. 47)

As with instruction in reading comprehension and written expression, effective mathematics instruction involves teacher modeling, demonstrations, and student rehearsal. When introducing new concepts and skills, perform the task while talking and then ask the student to perform the task as he or she talks it through. Describe and model how to solve the math problem several times using both visual and auditory cues (Allsopp, 1999). Then move from a teacher think-aloud (i.e., the teacher asks and then answers a question) to a teacher–student think-aloud (i.e., the teacher asks a question and then students help provide the answer). Students can then begin to help frame questions.

John's algebra teacher used this procedure, adapted from Allsopp (1999), to demonstrate how to solve two-variable math equations. He wrote the following equation on the board: $2a + 3b = 20$. He then stated, "I see that I have the letter a in this problem. What does the letter a stand for? I know that a letter stands for an unknown variable. I also know that when a letter is next to a number that it means multiplication. Now I also see that I have the letter b. Who can tell me what the b stands for in this problem?" A student answered, "Another unknown variable." The teacher said, "That's right, and who can tell me what it means when a letter is next to a number?" Another student answered, "It means to multiply." These types of think-alouds make the steps involved in problem solving apparent.

Students sometimes fail to understand that math is unlike other subjects. In most subjects, students learn content by starting with general concepts and then learn more specific information. In math, they need to start with very specific information that they then need to generalize. In teaching math problem solving, students need to learn information and then how to apply the information.

Some students have trouble understanding story problems. These students tend to make judgments about how to solve the problem on the basis of surface structure (i.e., the words or situation in the problem) rather than on an

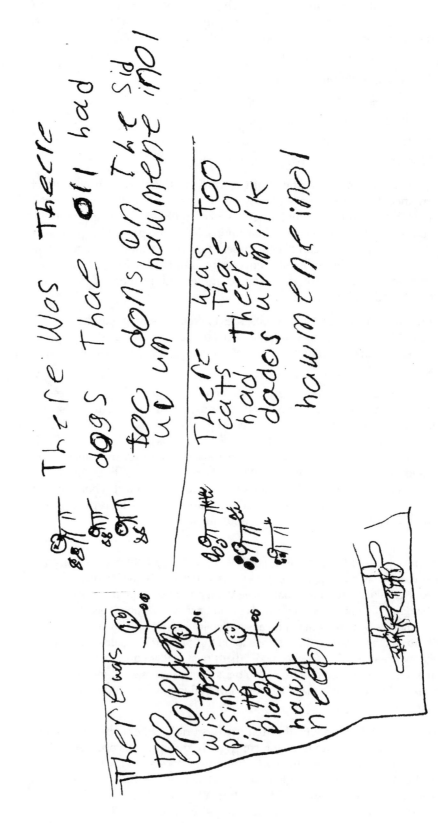

Thre Was Thecre
dogs that ol[l] had
too dons on The sid
uv um haumene ino!

Thel was too
cats that ol
had thele ol
dados uvmilk
haumene ino!

Thele uds
Too plecece
wis ther
plsus
in The
bloele
haunt
ne co!

Figure 11.8. Ben's story problems.

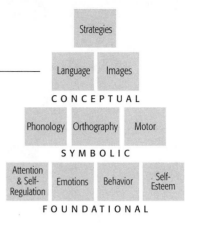

Strategies

Language | Images

CONCEPTUAL

Phonology | Orthography | Motor

SYMBOLIC

Attention & Self-Regulation | Emotions | Behavior | Self-Esteem

FOUNDATIONAL

understanding of the mathematical structure of the problem (Hutchinson, 1993). Instruction is most effective when it focuses on mathematical structure.

In class, present clear, straightforward examples and have students take notes. Students can then explain the steps in their own words. Then present problems to be solved in which the rules or principles that the students need to remember are clearly illustrated. Students can state the rule, principle, or formula that will be used to solve the problem. Once students know how to solve the problem, present problems that differ or vary by one step. As time goes on, the sequence or types of problems assigned can be varied but students should continue to state the rule or principle they must follow prior to attempting to solve it. Fuchs, Fuchs, and Hollenbeck (2007) suggested that teachers can change problems in the following four ways—referred to as *transfer features*—without altering their structure and the solution: a different look, different vocabulary or use of an unfamiliar key word, a different or additional question, and an irrelevant number or information. Students can work with problems classifying how a feature has changed.

Hutchinson (1993) described ways to present problems at three levels of difficulty. Introduce a problem (e.g., relational, proportional, a two-equation problem) and practice it in its simplest form. Once the student has demonstrated mastery, alter the problem by maintaining the mathematical structure of the problem and changing its surface structure or story line (i.e., a near-transfer problem). Once mastery is achieved, present students with problems in which the story line of the problem is maintained but an additional step is added (i.e., a far-transfer problem). Hutchinson provided the following example of a proportional problem at each of the three levels.

> *Problem:* On a map a distance of 2 centimeters (cm) represents 120 kilometers (km). What distance is represented on this map by 4 cm?
>
> *Near-Transfer Problem:* The ratio of the mass of the big box to the mass of the little box is 3:2. If the mass of the big box is 42 pounds, find the mass of the small box.
>
> *Far-Transfer Problem:* Emma's family is walking to raise money. For every 14 km that Emma walks, her brother walks 10 km, and her father walks 2 km. Emma's father walks 18 km. Find the distance walked by Emma and her brother. (p. 38)

Because of his past difficulties with acquiring mathematical concepts, John frequently felt like giving up before he even attempted to solve a problem. Fortunately, his teacher took an active role and employed multisensory approaches. In class, he used colored highlighters to emphasize key terms, operations, symbols, and numbers, and he drew visual breaks between each step. He had his students talk about the problem by having them say the numbers aloud as they wrote them, recite formulas, and put problems into their own words. He encouraged students to

- Read a problem twice before attempting to solve it

- Look for key terminology or essential features

- Eliminate unnecessary details and ask how the problem can be rephrased

- Consider what this problem reminds them of (do they see similar patterns in other problems they have done?)

- Use a variation of the K-W-L (Know-Want-Learned) strategy described in Chapter 9. Have students ask themselves, "What do I already know? What do I want to find out? What relates the two?"

- Determine principles and relationships involved, and determine the strategy to use to arrive at a solution
- Make a guess about what the result or answer would be
- Do each step on paper, not mentally
- Use summary sheets
- Check results
- Pay attention to special cases
- Explore alternative solutions

This step-by-step approach allowed both John and his teacher to determine where he encountered difficulty. Although John initially needed to have his teacher model the steps a number of times, he knew that he was making progress in solving math problems.

A think-aloud strategy that encourages a student to describe how he or she approaches a set of problems in a homework assignment or on a quiz or test can help the student see the value inherent in using a strategic approach. Naglieri and Gottling (1995) found that some students start with random strategies, setting themselves up to encounter frustration.

John initially failed to understand when he was taking an algebra test that it was to his advantage to go through and solve the easier problems first rather than spending too much time on just one problem. In addition, John would not check his answers before handing in his test. The teacher asked him to use a think-aloud approach in describing how he solved the assigned problems. At that point, John came to understand that his low grade was as much a result of carelessness as it was a lack of knowledge. On his next test, he made the effort to solve the easiest problems first and to check his responses. His score improved several points.

For other students, a think-aloud strategy helps them to recognize that they have a number of strategies or techniques already available to them. Montague (2003) recommended that teachers assist students in learning to

- Read the problem for understanding
- Paraphrase the problem into their own words
- Visualize the problem
- Hypothesize a way to solve the problem
- Estimate the answer
- Compute the answer
- Check the answer

Effective Teaching Strategies for Advanced Math Courses

As special educators work with students with LD, it is important to provide balanced instruction across mathematics standards (i.e., numbers and operations, algebra, geometry, measurement, data analysis, and probability) (Miller & Hudson, 2007). Adolescents with LD can be taught to solve more complex problems than their teachers generally expect as long as they are provided with guided instruction and sufficient opportunity to solve problems (Jones et al., 1997). Despite significant problems with computation, some students understand mathematical concepts quite well and succeed in math courses at the

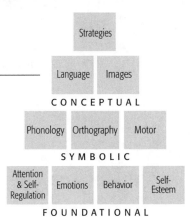

secondary level. Students need to make a persistent effort at strengthening their computational weaknesses and developing their self-monitoring skills. Teach students the full range of upper-level math concepts, including more complex equations and applications.

For algebra instruction, the most effective teachers engage in modeling, provide guided practice activities, and check students' responses (Maccini, McNaughton, & Ruhl, 1999). Maccini and colleagues recommended that instructors employ the following principles to help students with LD succeed in higher level mathematics courses:

Before beginning instruction

- Administer a daily quiz of previously learned skills.
- Give a general orientation to introduce the strategy; explain the rationale for self-questioning strategies.

During instruction

- Provide a clear and precise presentation of the skill or concept with a range of examples and nonexamples.
- Make use of manipulatives and computer-assisted instruction when possible.
- Teach students self-questioning strategies.
- Provide guided practice, reinforcing instruction with structured worksheets.
- Provide feedback and reinforcement by offering opportunities for monitoring students' level of understanding and providing corrective and positive reinforcement.

Maccini and colleagues (1999) also recommended requiring a level of mastery, using set criteria, providing independent practice, and assessing students frequently using a variety of measures, such as oral and written responses. The following types of self-questioning strategies can be taught to help students learn how to represent algebra word problems (Hutchinson, 1993):

- Have I read and understood each sentence? Are there any words whose meaning I need to ask?
- Have I understood the whole picture of the problem?
- Have I written down my representation of the problem on my worksheet (e.g., goals, unknowns, knowns, type of problem, equation)?
- What should I look for in a new problem to see if it is the same kind of problem?

For solving algebra word problems

- Have I written an equation?
- Have I expanded the terms?
- Have I written out the steps of my solution on the worksheet (e.g., collected like terms, isolated unknowns, solved for unknowns, checked my answer with the goal, highlighted my answer)?
- What should I look for in a new problem to see if it is the same kind of problem?

383

In a recent review of effective math interventions for secondary students, Maccini and colleagues (2007) concluded that student performance can be improved through the use of 1) effective teaching principles, 2) a CRA sequence in teaching, 3) methods to teach the structure of word problems, 4) peer-mediated instruction for basic skills, and 5) videodisks that provided contextualized instruction in problem solving.

Software Selection and Math Instruction

Students who use appropriate technology persist longer, enjoy learning more, and make gains in math performance (Babbitt & Miller, 1997). Babbitt and Miller outlined a variety of ways to use hypermedia to improve math problem solving. Babbitt (2000) recommended the following principles for using mathematical software.

- Choose programs that minimize the clutter on the screen; too much stimuli is a problem and often distracts from the math concept being presented.

- Match the procedures used in the software with those being taught in class. If there are differences, take the time to point them out to students.

- Choose software that can be modified to meet students' needs. Some students thrive on timed responses; others find the time limits frustrating. Students also vary with regard to their need for feedback or breaks. Also check to see if the software provides helpful feedback or if it limits the number of wrong answers for a single problem.

- Watch for increments between levels. Software programs often have jumps that are too large for students who are having difficulty. Choose software that has built-in instructional aids or that simulates real-life solutions and has good record-keeping capabilities A variety of software programs, ranging in content from basic math skills to advanced algebra, are available from Riverdeep (http://www.riverdeep.com). The Destination Math® series, which focuses on real-word mathematics, provides instruction in basic skills, math reasoning, conceptual understanding, and problem solving. Many software programs allow the teacher to create calculations or word problems while controlling the number of problems on the page, the type size, the graphics, and so forth.

CONCLUSION

Students with weaknesses in reading comprehension, written expression, and math problem solving benefit from specific explicit instruction to develop conceptual, procedural, and declarative knowledge as well as the use of strategies. These strategies are taught most effectively when coupled with discussion, modeling, practice, rehearsal, and application of the strategies to differing contexts. When students such as John and Katy are actively involved in their learning and practice using strategies in the context of academic subjects, their understanding of concepts and relationships improves. Although they are still likely to need adaptations within class settings and adjustments in the difficulty of assignments, repeated opportunities to engage in the problem-solving activities of understanding and producing text, as well as solving mathematical problems, can increase their knowledge and academic success.

SYNONYMS FOR WORDS THAT CHILDREN USE COMMONLY IN WRITING

Amazing: astonishing, astounding, dazzling, extraordinary, fabulous, fantastic, impressive, superb, unbelievable, wonderful

Anger: aggravate, agitate, annoy, arouse, displease, enrage, exasperate, incense, inflame, infuriate, irritate, madden

Angry: annoyed, exasperated, furious, indignant, inflamed, infuriated, irritated, mad, peeved, raging, vexed, wrathful

Answer: acknowledge, reply, respond, retort

Ask: beckon, demand, inquire, interrogate, invite, query, question, quiz, request, solicit, summon

Awful: base, contemptible, direful, distasteful, dreadful, grotesque, nasty, repulsive, terrible, unpleasant

Bad: contemptible, corrupt, criminal, dangerous, dark, deplorable, depraved, despicable, disgusting, dismal, evil, execrable, foul, ghastly, grisly, gruesome, heinous, horrid, immoral, insidious, malevolent, malicious, nasty, nefarious, noxious, putrid, rank, reprehensible, rotten, sinful, sinister, villainous, wicked

Beautiful: alluring, attractive, captivating, charming, comely, dazzling, delicate, engaging, enthralling, enticing, fascinating, glamorous, glowing, gorgeous, handsome, heavenly, lovely, pretty, radiant, ravishing, resplendent, sparkling, splendid, stunning

Begin: actuate, commence, embark, initiate, instigate, introduce, launch, open, originate, start

Big: capacious, colossal, elephantine, enormous, expansive, extensive, gargantuan, gigantic, huge, immense, large, mammoth, massive, robust, titanic, vast

Brave: audacious, bold, chivalric, courageous, daring, dashing, dauntless, fearless, gallant, heroic, plucky, valiant, valorous

Break: atomize, crack, demolish, destroy, fracture, pulverize, rupture, shatter, smash, splinter, wreck

Bright: colorful, gleaming, incandescent, intellectual, luminous, radiant, shimmering, shining, smart, sparkling, vivid

Calm: aloof, collected, composed, detached, level-headed, mild, peaceful, quiet, serene, smooth, still, tranquil, unexcited, unruffled

Come: advance, approach, arrive, near, reach

Cool: chilly, cold, frigid, frosty, icy, wintry

Crooked: bent, curved, hooked, twisted, zigzag

Cry: bawl, bellow, roar, scream, shout, sob, wail, weep, yell, yowl

Cut: carve, chop, cleave, crop, gash, lop, nick, prick, reduce, sever, slash, slice, slit

Dangerous: hazardous, perilous, risky, uncertain, unsafe

Dark: black, dim, dismal, dusky, gloomy, murky, sad, shaded, shadowy, sunless, unlit

Decide: choose, determine, resolve, settle

Definite: certain, clear, determined, distinct, obvious, positive, sure

Delicious: appetizing, delectable, delightful, enjoyable, exquisite, luscious, palatable, savory, scrumptious

Describe: characterize, narrate, picture, portray, record, recount, relate, report, represent

Destroy: demolish, end, extinguish, kill, raze, ruin, slay, waste

Difference: contrast, disagreement, dissimilarity, incompatibility, inequality

Do: accomplish, achieve, attain, carry out, conclude, effect, enact, execute, finish

Dull: boring, dead, dreary, dumb, expressionless, humdrum, insensible, lifeless, listless, monotonous, plain, slow, stupid, tedious, tiresome, tiring, unimaginative, uninteresting, wearisome

Eager: enthusiastic, fervent, interested, involved, keen

End: cease, close, conclude, discontinue, finish, halt, stop, terminate

Enjoy: appreciate, bask in, be pleased, delight in, devour, indulge in, like, luxuriate in, relish, savor

Explain: account for, clarify, define, elaborate, interpret, justify

Fair: honest, impartial, just, objective, unbiased, unprejudiced

Fall: descend, drop, plunge, topple, tumble

False: counterfeit, deceptive, erroneous, fake, fallacious, fraudulent, groundless, spurious, unfounded, untrue

Famous: celebrated, distinguished, eminent, famed, illustrious, noted, notorious, renowned, well-known

Fast: expeditiously, fleet, hastily, hasty, lickety-split, like a flash, mercurial, posthaste, quick, quickly, rapid, rapidly, snappily, snappy, speedily, speedy, swift, swiftly

Fat: bulky, burly, chubby, corpulent, obese, overweight, paunchy, portly, pudgy, rotund, stout, tubby

Fear: alarm, anxiety, apprehension, awe, dismay, dread, fright, horror, panic, scare, terror

Fly: coast, cruise, flee, flit, glide, hover, sail, skim, soar, waft, wing

Funny: amusing, comic, comical, droll, humorous, laughable, silly

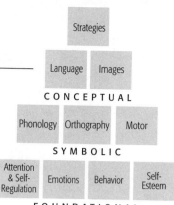

Get: accept, accumulate, acquire, bag, catch, collect, come by, derive, earn, fetch, find, gain, gather, glean, net, obtain, pick up, procure, reap, regain, salvage, score, secure, win

Go: depart, disappear, fade, move, proceed, recede, travel

Good: agreeable, apt, capable, edifying, excellent, fine, first-rate, friendly, generous, gracious, grand, honorable, kindly, marvelous, obedient, obliging, pleasant, pleasurable, proper, qualified, reliable, respectable, satisfactory, sterling, suitable, suited, superb, superior, top-notch, trustworthy, well-behaved, wonderful

Great: considerable, distinguished, grand, mighty, much, noteworthy, powerful, remarkable, worthy

Gross: coarse, crude, extreme, grievous, improper, indecent, low, obscene, outrageous, rude, shameful, uncouth, vulgar

Happy: blissful, cheerful, contented, delighted, ecstatic, elated, gay, glad, gratified, joyful, jubilant, overjoyed, pleased, satisfied, tickled

Hate: abhor, abominate, despise, detest, disapprove, disfavor, dislike, loathe

Have: absorb, acquire, bear, beget, believe, contain, enjoy, fill, gain, hold, maintain, occupy, own, possess

Help: abet, aid, assist, attend, back, befriend, benefit, encourage, relieve, serve, succor, support, wait on

Hide: camouflage, cloak, conceal, cover, mask, screen, shroud, veil

Hurry: accelerate, bustle, hasten, race, run, rush, speed, urge

Hurt: afflict, damage, distress, harm, injure, pain, wound

Idea: belief, concept, conception, notion, opinion, plan, thought, understanding, view

Important: considerable, critical, distinguished, essential, famous, indispensable, necessary, notable, primary, principal, significant, valuable, vital, well-known

Interesting: absorbing, animated, appealing, arresting, attractive, bewitching, bright, captivating, challenging, consuming, curious, enchanting, engaging, engrossing, entertaining, enthralling, exciting, fascinating, gripping, inspiring, intelligent, intriguing, inviting, involving, keen, lively, moving, piquant, provocative, racy, sharp, spellbinding, spicy, spirited, tantalizing, thought-provoking, titillating

Keep: hold, maintain, preserve, retain, support, sustain, withhold

Kill: abolish, assassinate, cancel, destroy, execute, murder, slay

Lazy: idle, inactive, indolent, slothful, sluggish

Little: cramped, diminutive, dinky, exiguous, itsy-bitsy, limited, microscopic, miniature, minute, petite, puny, runt, shrimp, slight, small, tiny

Look: behold, contemplate, discover, examine, explore, eye, gape, gawk, gaze, glance, glimpse, inspect, leer, notice, observe, ogle, peek, peep, peer, perceive, peruse, recognize, scrutinize, search for, see, seek, sight, spy, stare, study, survey, view, watch, witness

Love: admire, adore, appreciate, care for, cherish, esteem, fancy, like, savor, treasure, worship

Make: accomplish, acquire, beget, build, compose, construct, create, design, develop, do, earn, effect, execute, fabricate, form, gain, get, invent, manufacture, obtain, originate, perform, produce

Mark: brand, designate, effect, heed, impress, imprint, label, note, notice, price, sign, stamp, tag, ticket, trace

Mischievous: impish, naughty, playful, prankish, roguish, sportive, waggish

Move: accelerate, amble, bolt, bound, breeze, budge, chase, coast, crawl, creep, dart, dash, dawdle, drag, fling, flow, gallop, glide, go, hasten, high-tail, hobble, hotfoot, hump, hurry, inch, jog, journey, lag, lope, lumber, lunge, meander, mosey, pace, paddle, perambulate, plod, plug, poke, prance, promenade, race, ride, roam, run, rush, sail, saunter, scamper, scoot, scramble, scurry, scuttle, shuffle, skedaddle, slide, slip, slither, slouch, spin, sprint, stagger, stir, straggle, streak, stride, stump, swagger, tear, toddle, trail, traipse, travel, trek, trip, trot, trudge, waddle, walk, wander, whisk, wobble

Moody: changeable, fretful, glum, irritable, mopish, morose, peevish, short-tempered, spiteful, sulky, sullen, temperamental, testy, touchy

Neat: clean, dapper, desirable, elegant, orderly, shapely, shipshape, smart, spruce, super, tidy, trim, well-kept, well-organized

New: current, fresh, modern, novel, original, recent, unusual

Old: aged, ancient, archaic, broken-down, conventional, customary, dilapidated, extinct, faded, feeble, former, frail, mature, musty, obsolete, old-fashioned, outmoded, passé, primitive, ragged, stale, traditional, used, venerable, veteran, weak, worn

Part: allotment, fraction, fragment, piece, portion, sect, share

Place: area, dwelling, location, plot, position, region, residence, set, site, situation, space, spot, state, station, status

Plan: arrangement, blueprint, contrivance, design, device, diagram, draw, intention, map, method, plot, procedure, scheme, way

Popular: accepted, approved, celebrated, common, current, favorite, well-liked

Predicament: dilemma, jam, pickle, plight, problem, quandary, scrape, spot

Put: achieve, assign, attach, build, do, effect, establish, keep, place, save, set, set aside

Quiet: calm, mute, peaceful, restful, silent, soundless, still, tranquil

Right: accurate, apt, correct, factual, fair, good, honest, just, lawful, legal, moral, proper, suitable, true, upright

Run: dash, elope, escape, flee, hasten, hurry, race, rush, speed, sprint

Say/tell: advise, affirm, allege, announce, articulate, assert, assure, bellow, bid, boom, command, contend, converse, convey, declare, deliver, deny, dispute, direct, disclose, divulge, drawl, enlighten, exclaim, explain, express, grunt, hiss, impart, inform, insist, instruct, issue, jabber, lisp, mumble, mutter, narrate, negate, notify, order, philosophize, pronounce, protest, recount, relate, remark, reveal, roar, scream, screech, shriek, sigh, sing, snarl, snort, speak, squawk, stammer, state, stutter, suppose, swear, teach, thunder, train, utter, verbalize, voice, vow, whine, whisper, yell, yelp

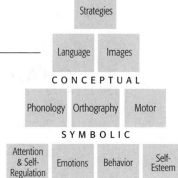

Scared: afraid, alarmed, apprehensive, disquieted, disturbed, fearful, frightened, haunted, horrified, insecure, jumpy, panicked, paralyzed, petrified, shocked, shrinking, shy, skittish, stunned, stupefied, terrified, terrorized, timid, timorous, tremulous, troubled, unnerved, vexed, worried

Show: demonstrate, display, exhibit, explain, expose, indicate, note, point to, present, prove, reveal

Slow: behind, gradual, late, leisurely, slack, tedious, unhurried

Stop: cease, conclude, discontinue, end, finish, halt, pause, quit

Story: account, anecdote, chronicle, epic, fable, legend, memoir, myth, narrative, record, sage, tale, yarn

Strange: curious, exclusive, irregular, odd, outlandish, peculiar, queer, uncommon, unfamiliar, unique, unusual, weird

Take: acquire, assume, bewitch, buy, capture, catch, choose, consume, engage, grasp, hold, lift, occupy, pick, prefer, purchase, recall, remove, retract, rob, seize, select, steal, win

Tell: advise, bid, command, declare, disclose, divulge, explain, expose, inform, narrate, order, recount, relate, repeat, reveal, show, uncover

Think: assume, believe, consider, contemplate, deem, judge, meditate, reflect

Trouble: anguish, anxiety, concern, danger, difficulty, disaster, distress, effort, exertion, grief, inconvenience, misfortune, pain, peril, worry, wretchedness

True: accurate, actual, dependable, exact, genuine, loyal, precise, proper, real, right, sincere, staunch, steady, trusty, valid

Ugly: evil, frightening, frightful, ghastly, grisly, gross, gruesome, hideous, homely, horrible, horrid, monstrous, plain, repugnant, repulsive, shocking, terrifying, unpleasant, unsightly

Unhappy: dejected, depressed, discouraged, dismal, downhearted, gloomy, glum, heartbroken, melancholy, miserable, poor, sad, sorrowful, uncomfortable, unfortunate, wretched

Use: consume, employ, exercise, exhaust, expend, spend

Wrong: erroneous, improper, inaccurate, inappropriate, incorrect, mistaken, unsuitable

CHAPTER 12 OUTLINE

THE CHANGING ROLE OF EDUCATION

WHAT TEACHERS WANT FROM STUDENTS

WHAT STUDENTS NEED FROM TEACHERS

ESSENTIAL GUIDELINES

CONCLUSION

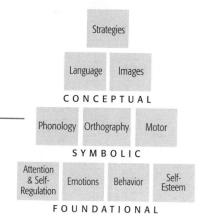

THE CLASSROOM ENVIRONMENT AS A MICROCOSM OF THE WORLD

The secret of education lies in respecting the pupil.
—Ralph Waldo Emerson

A teacher affects eternity.
—Henry Brooks Adams

It has been 10 years since the day in the life of Harper Unified School District described in the first chapter of this book. As time passes, students and teachers change, but the educational process of preparing children for their future continues. Teachers continue to be apprehensive for the students who have learning disabilities (LD) and behavior problems. What effect do those teachers have on their students? What strategies truly make a difference? Are educational plans, additional time spent in one-to-one instruction, specialized tutoring, and counseling effective?

For the children described in Chapter 1, life has changed. As a second grader, Andy struggled with fine and gross motor skills. Similar to the children in educator Rick Lavoie's (1994) description, Andy was the last one picked on the playground and sometimes the first one picked on. Now, 10 years later, as a graduating senior, Andy has been accepted to a 4-year college. His handwriting is still hard to read. In fact, he describes it as "chicken scratchings," but he has become proficient on the keyboard and still loves to draw. He has also learned to play the piano and spends much of his free time practicing with a local band. Andy still experiences problems with coordination, but years of karate have helped him with balance and muscle tone. As he leaves high school, Andy is happy and on the road to a successful academic career.

Ryan was the fourth grader with limited reading skills. He felt "dumb" because of his difficulty with reading and the need to receive support services in the resource room. As school progressed, Ryan's reading skills and self-confidence had improved, but he continued to struggle with reading and writing even as he graduated. He required accommodations in complex academic subjects. Ryan is about to complete a 2-year community college program in computer science. He has good friends and has not experienced any significant psychological problems. After he graduates, he plans to enter the work force as a computer programmer.

During high school, Stephanie, the fourth-grade girl with nonverbal learning disabilities, continued to have few friends and had a hard time working in groups. In spite of these difficulties, Stephanie graduated a year ago and has taken a job as a semiconductor assembler. Stephanie is enjoying the job because of its repetitive nature. Since she has started working at the company, she has made a few friends and has joined a bowling league. Her manager at the plant states, "Stephanie is a hard worker, but I have come to realize that I need to show her how to do things step by step. She needs to repeat things several times before she catches on. Once Stephanie can perform the task, she works diligently to do what is asked of her." Also, because of the patience of her manager, Stephanie can now complete three different jobs on the assembly line.

Ten years ago, Katy was finishing fifth grade. Although she possessed good rote skills, Katy struggled when attempting to learn new concepts and vocabulary throughout school. In high school, she received resource services to provide support for complex classes, such as history and science. During her senior year in high school, Katy decided to become a hair stylist. After graduating from high school, she attended beauty school for 6 months and earned her license. Katy now works for a local hairdresser and has developed a good clientele.

As a fifth grader, Anthony was depressed and increasingly isolated from family and friends. Because of this, Anthony was referred to the school psychologist for evaluation. During a visit with Anthony's mother, the school psychologist learned that many of Anthony's relatives and Anthony's father suffered from depression. Anthony was placed in therapy with a community-based psychologist and soon after began taking an antidepressant medication. Anthony still takes medication for depression and periodically visits his psychologist. Though still prone to bouts of unhappiness, Anthony is finishing his third year of college, and is planning to become an accountant.

Mark was the fifth-grade student whom Ms. Perry wished she could adopt. He had good abilities, but his home life was chaotic and inconsistent. Mark's mother eventually moved out of state, taking all of her children. Despite Mark's chaotic life, he continued to do well in school, and his school success provided an island of competence. He joined the track team in high school and was one of the school's top two runners. The combination of his good grades, achievement in track, and financial need enabled Mark to obtain a full scholarship to a 4-year college. Now a college junior, Mark rarely visits his family. He has pledged a fraternity and, through his friendships, developed an extended family. He is successful in school and would like to be a teacher.

Jeremy was the boy who was diagnosed with attention-deficit/hyperactivity disorder. His grades were marked by inconsistencies in middle school. Within the same class, he had As, Cs, and Fs, depending on the type of task. In high school, he attended an alternative school that provided students with more structure and support. During these years, Jeremy became an avid skier and spent weekends working for the ski patrol. Although Jeremy plans to go to college some day, he is currently working on the ski patrol in the winter and doing construction work in the summer.

Mr. Arnold was concerned about Maria as she finished sixth grade. Despite extended instruction in sixth grade, Maria continued to demonstrate problems with aspects of spelling, writing, and reading. Maria had an accommodation plan in high school that allowed her to have extended time on all tasks and tests requiring reading and writing. With these accommodations, she was able to stay on the honor roll. After graduating from high school, she applied to a 4-year college with an outstanding program in special education focusing on LD. She was accepted and received tutorial support and is now completing her junior year. On her application to the LD program, she was asked to write a personal statement describing how her LD has affected her school career (see Figure 12.1). Maria will succeed: She understands her learning problems, can explain how these problems affected her school performance, and recognizes how these experiences have shaped her personality.

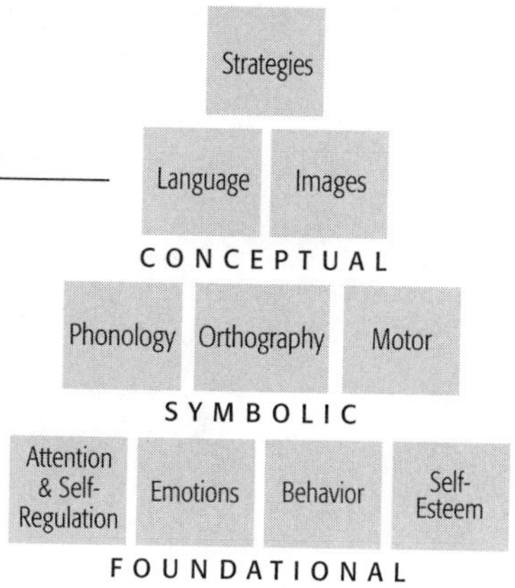

Samuel was the sixth-grade student who appeared to be in trouble for something every day. Despite support at school and through community resources, Samuel continued

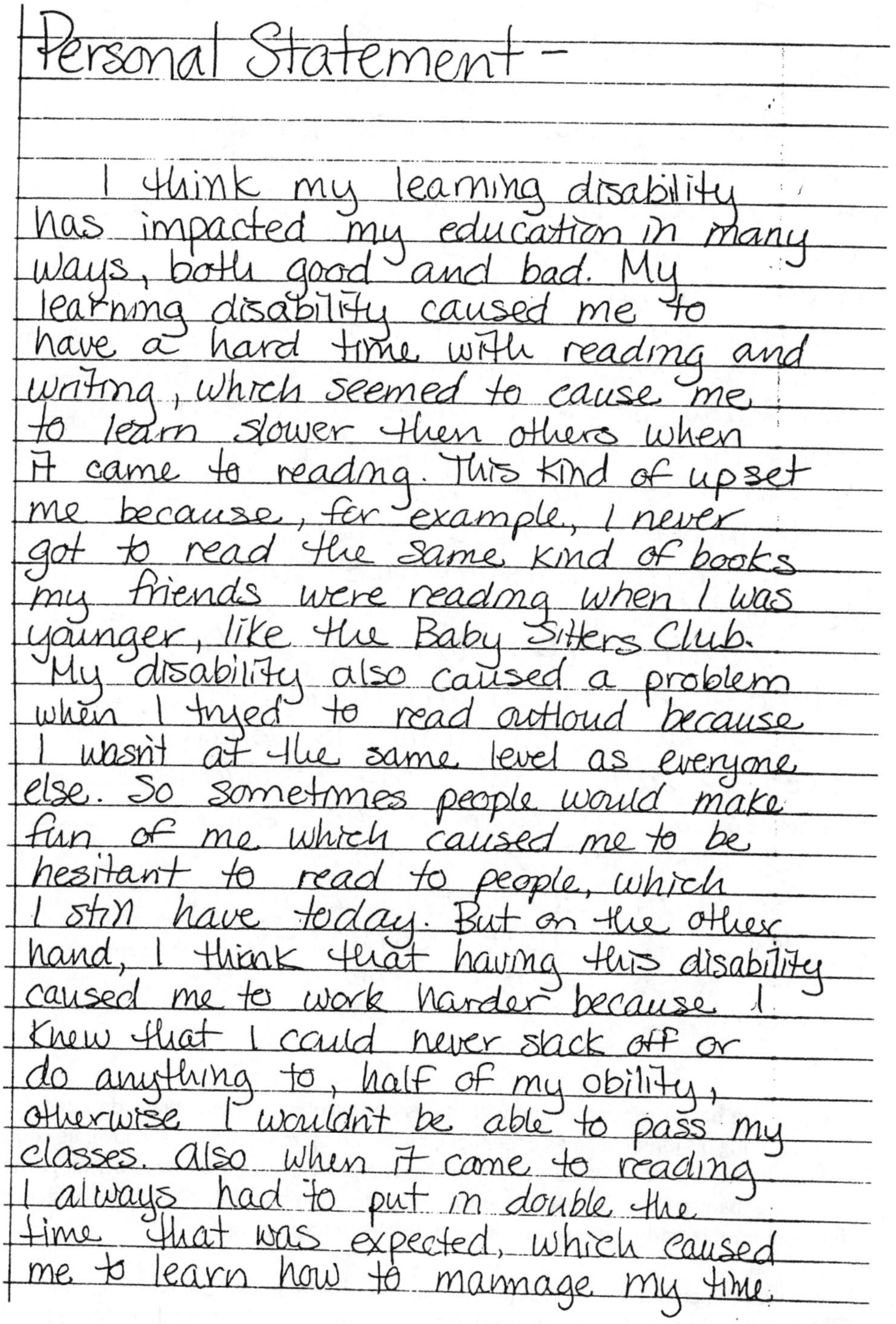

Strategies

Language   Images

CONCEPTUAL

Phonology   Orthography   Motor

SYMBOLIC

Attention & Self-Regulation   Emotions   Behavior   Self-Esteem

FOUNDATIONAL

Personal Statement –

I think my learning disability has impacted my education in many ways, both good and bad. My learning disability caused me to have a hard time with reading and writing, which seemed to cause me to learn slower then others when it came to reading. This kind of upset me because, for example, I never got to read the same kind of books my friends were reading when I was younger, like the Baby Sitters Club. My disability also caused a problem when I tryed to read outloud because I wasn't at the same level as everyone else. So sometimes people would make fun of me which caused me to be hesitant to read to people, which I still have today. But on the other hand, I think that having this disability caused me to work harder because I knew that I could never slack off or do anything to, half of my ability, otherwise I wouldn't be able to pass my classes. Also when it came to reading I always had to put in double the time that was expected, which caused me to learn how to mammage my time.

(continued)

Figure 12.1. Maria's personal statement for her application to her college's program on learning disabilities.

393

Figure 12.1. *(continued)*

too. I also think that having this disability made me more assertive. and confident in myself. Because I always had to standup for myself to other kids, when they made fun of me, and to my instructers by asking them for more time. or more help with something. This made me realize that if I needed something I had to be the one to say it, and that you aren't going to lose anything by asking, you just gain. I find that even today some of my friend will need something or will have a problem and they are to afraid to talk to their teachers about it. But with myself, I have always had really great relationships with my teachers and always keep in comunication with them at all times, telling them how I am doing and hrw I think everything is going, good or bad. I think my disability played a big part in this. So as you can see my disability has effected my education and life, but I feel like I have learned from it and that it make me a better persen.

to struggle. He began experimenting with drugs and alcohol and eventually dropped out of school during his junior year. As a teenager, he ended up repeatedly in the juvenile court for status offenses and received several felony charges for drug possession. Though he works doing manual labor, he rarely keeps a job longer than a month. Samuel is constantly in financial trouble and continues to abuse both alcohol and drugs.

Ben was the eighth-grade student who was a talented athlete but would rather walk over hot coals than write. He received resource support throughout high school and improved his writing immensely. After leaving high school, he spent 2 years in the Air Force. He is now a tennis professional at a local country club and has developed a well-

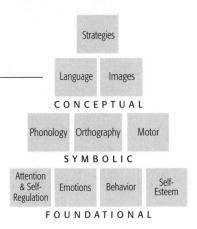

known tennis academy for children. Although he e-mails friends on a regular basis, he still does not like to write and spends little time reading or writing.

John, as a junior 10 years ago, was an enthusiastic student who had poor study skills and difficulty grasping concepts. John attempted several courses at the local community college but struggled with the content. He decided to forego college for a while and take a job working with a friend who owned a furniture store. He has now worked successfully at the store for 5 years. John is presently in his mid-20s. He and his wife have two children and have just bought their first home.

Are these the typical outcomes for students with histories of emotional, behavior, and academic problems at school? As a microcosm of the world, do school problems predict future lives? For some students, it would appear to be so. Yet for others, struggling in school does not appear to be a life sentence or a particularly negative predictor that one's adult life will be unfulfilled or disrupted. If success is defined as personal and vocational satisfaction, all but one of these students had a successful transition into adult life. It is unknown whether this group represents a better outcome than most because no large-scale studies have explored the outcomes of the 15%–20% of students struggling at school. The available data, however, suggest that these students do not succeed at anywhere near the rate of the general population (for a review, see Goldstein, 1995; Goldstein & Brooks, 2007).

Most educational personnel understand that certain characteristics place children at risk in school, and these characteristics decrease their chances for future success. Although the majority of school problems cannot be resolved quickly or cured easily, the first step in helping is to possess a working model to understand these problems. By focusing on strengths first and foremost and recognizing weaknesses in learning abilities, teachers can develop appropriate expectations and interventions. Understanding a student's unique disposition, support system, characteristics, and abilities empowers adults to create positive change and make a difference in an individual's life.

THE CHANGING ROLE OF EDUCATION

By the very nature of their work, teachers are futurists. They are entrusted with the important, though at times underappreciated, job of preparing children for successful adulthoods. Growth of formal education in the United States came about as a means of socializing a diverse group of immigrants. Teachers were entrusted with instilling not only academic information but also a set of values and ideals consistent with the culture. Today, however, the teaching of social and cultural values appears to no longer be of paramount importance for teachers (Goldstein & Brooks, 2007). Instead, parents look to teachers primarily to convey academic information to their children. In the early grades, parents expect teachers to teach basic skills and, in the later grades, to help children acquire complex information about the world around them. But is this all society demands of teachers and the educational system at this time? What has replaced teachers' primary charge of socializing culturally diverse immigrants? What is it that society and culture require from the educational system beyond imparting academic knowledge to students? Certainly, at the very least, society expects the educational system, including the postsecondary school system, to prepare students to enter the work force, a work force that has become technologically and intellectually more demanding and complex. It is no longer enough for a student to be the holder of many facts. One has to learn to think, reason, judge, and cope with complex information.

The secondary role that the schools and teachers have been given is to prepare children who are at risk. Students such as Andy, Ryan, Stephanie, Katy, Mark, Jeremy, Maria, Anthony, Ben, Samuel, and John can no longer afford to simply leave school because they are academically unsuccessful and still expect success in adult life. Teachers are increasingly required to help prepare those at greatest risk for successful transition into adult life. This is what society wants from schools and teachers. Society expects educators to be futurists: to gaze into the proverbial crystal ball, identify those students at risk, and then, through their expertise, reduce that risk.

WHAT TEACHERS WANT FROM STUDENTS

Teachers want successful students. In the classroom, students who are at risk demonstrate inappropriate behavior, participate less than students who are not at risk in academically engaged time, struggle with academic success, and often develop very different relationships with their teachers (Skiba, McLeskey, Waldron, & Grizzle, 1993). In response, teachers engage in an increased variety and frequency of behavior and educational management strategies. In 1983, Walker and Rankin suggested eight student qualities that predict classroom success. These qualities are still relevant today.

1. The ability to follow teacher directions consistently

2. The ability to follow classroom rules without the need for extensive teacher supervision

3. The ability to complete all or the majority of schoolwork without extensive teacher support

4. The ability to follow group rules and norms in all school situations

5. The ability to follow social rules while interacting with classmates without extensive teacher support

6. The ability and willingness to follow teacher instructions and assignment directions without significant assistance

7. Flexibility, or the ability to adjust to changes during the educational day

8. The capacity to respond to conventional classroom management techniques and to not stand apart from others behaviorally, academically, or socially

In one aspect or another, the students described in this text struggled to meet most of the teachers' attributes for becoming and being a successful student. Often, in a frustrating cycle, students' inabilities to be successful shape the nature and quality of the interactions they have with their teachers, which further shapes students' mindsets about school and their capabilities. A successful student then appears to be one who does not experience a learning or developmental problem; is neither depressed, anxious, nor experiencing significant life adjustment problems; resides in a stable family; does not experience problems with temperament resulting in an excessive activity level, inattention, or impulsivity; and does not exhibit disruptive behavior problems.

Unfortunately, successful students are viewed as those who do not possess liabilities that interfere with school performance. Of paramount importance for helping children who struggle in school is adoption of a new vision of what it means to be a successful student. Despite his struggles with motor development, Andy found success in music and other academic areas. If success is defined as

Strategies

Language   Images

CONCEPTUAL

Phonology   Orthography   Motor

SYMBOLIC

Attention & Self-Regulation   Emotions   Behavior   Self-Esteem

FOUNDATIONAL

entering adult life and finding a comfortable niche, Ryan and Katy too were successful, although they continued to struggle with reading. Even Mark, the boy who struggled because of problems in the home environment, managed to find an island of competence in his life. Thus, school success comes in many shapes and forms. The definition of a successful student must begin with an understanding of what students need from teachers. This definition must begin with the belief that all children can be successful at school.

WHAT STUDENTS NEED FROM TEACHERS

What do students need from teachers to experience success in school? First and foremost, students need empathic teachers who possess a reasoned and reasonable understanding of how children learn, feel, and behave. Teachers must be charismatic adults in the lives of children for whom school is unrewarding. Students need effective teachers capable of exuding an aura of authority and affection. Effective teachers 1) focus on academic goals, 2) carefully set instructional goals and materials, 3) structure and plan learning activities, 4) involve students in the learning process, 5) closely monitor students' progress, and 6) provide frequent feedback on progress and accomplishments (Goldstein & Brooks, 2007). They are capable of organizing and maintaining the classroom learning environment to maximize time spent engaged in productive activity and to minimize time lost during transitions or disruptions. Effective teachers are proactive and work to avoid problems rather than respond to them. They can develop a workable set of classroom rules; respond consistently and quickly to inappropriate behavior; do not take students' misbehaviors personally; and have at their disposal a repertoire of behavioral and educational strategies to help every student succeed. Most important, they know how to help every child feel competent, accepted, respected, and important in the process.

Students require teachers who are capable of developing clear rules and consequences for following or breaking them, who are prepared for class lessons, and who understand the learning characteristics of their students and provide appropriate instructions. They also need teachers who emphasize success rather than failure; who model appropriate behavior; and who communicate with students in positive, sensitive, and assertive ways. Students with learning and behavior difficulties benefit from teachers who communicate high expectations for student efforts and accomplishments while providing a supportive classroom environment. These teachers foster student success and use the power of success as effective motivators. They incorporate different types of approaches in teaching and allow adequate time for learning to take place through practice and application of skills. In discussing the experiences of adults with histories of LD, Reiff, Gerber, and Ginsberg (1993) stated that in many cases adults found innovative ways to teach themselves. In other words, the student's ability to learn was always present, but the teacher's knowledge of how to teach was lacking.

In 1991, Walker and Shea described effective teachers as authentic teachers. Their description focused on the personal traits that teachers as human beings bring with them into the classroom that foster successful students. These traits are perhaps most needed by students who are at risk. Authentic teachers choose their vocation and know why they make this choice. They accept children for the individuals they are rather than trying to make them someone they are not. They possess a workable model about how children learn, think, and feel. They are willing to examine their own behavior critically, learn new skills, and make changes as needed. They are patient, flexible, consistent, and supportive. The ideal teacher sounds very much like the ideal spouse, friend, or boss. Effective teachers can honestly respond that they would enjoy being a student in their own class. Perhaps the golden rule for being an effective teacher and meeting students' needs is striving to be a good human being.

ESSENTIAL GUIDELINES

Effective teachers follow these essential guidelines:

- *Want to teach:* If teachers do not enjoy being in classrooms, they should seek other professions. Models, guidelines, knowledge, or management strategies will not fill the void of an unfulfilling vocation.

- *Respect all students:* This chapter began with a quote by Emerson who stated that the secret of education lies not in strategy or technique but in respecting the student. If teachers set out to fix students, to shape, chip, or otherwise force them into their own preconceived notions of success, and convey to students that who they are is not good enough, then these students will not be successful in the classroom.

- *Work from a model:* One of every five children in the classroom experiences some type of foundational, processing, or thinking problem. Many experience multiple problems that impair their abilities to be successful in the traditional way at school. Teachers should begin with a model or framework for seeing the world through the eyes of these students to understand how to help them.

- *Understand the forces that shape student outcomes:* Effective teachers recognize that student, setting, teacher, and strategy are all variables that affect classroom behavior and student functioning. Modifying any one of these can successfully change outcomes.

- *Accept the fact that children think:* There is no doubt that behavior is shaped, developed, maintained, and modified on the basis of consequences. It is also equally important, however, to recognize that the methods and means by which children interpret, process, think, and talk to themselves about their experiences affect their self-esteem, their relationships with adults and other students, and their behavior. Effective teachers take the time to understand how students think and feel about their lives.

- *Focus on the work:* In the fabled children's classic *Stuart Little*, E.B. White (1945/1999) described how Stuart would maintain discipline: "Do you think you can maintain discipline?" asked the Superintendent. "Of course I can," replied Stuart. "I'll make the work interesting and the discipline will take care of itself" (pp. 86–87). When classroom work and activities are interesting, stimulating, and enjoyable, children become active participants in the educational process. Such participation is incompatible with classroom misbehavior and a lack of motivation.

- *Remember that schools cannot fix family problems:* Children who experience classroom problems are more likely than other children to come from families that experience increased stress and other impediments to successful family functioning. Effective teachers understand and accept that children come to the classroom with an outside history that significantly affects their functioning. By understanding and accepting this history, teachers can make school a safe haven and an important place for many children.

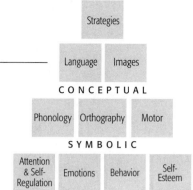

- *Recognize the importance of friends:* Socialization is a powerful force, not only for shaping children's current happiness but also as a predictive force in shaping a positive future. All students need to have opportunities to socialize and to have peers with whom to socialize.

- *Keep learning and growing:* As with any other skill, teaching is learned by trial and error, success and failure. Teachers must be honest and avoid being defensive when more experienced teachers provide guidance or advice. Take advantage of the knowledge of others. Knowledge about the brain's role in learning, emotions, and behavior continues to grow at an exponential pace. The more teachers learn, the more effective they become in developing strategies to help students experience success. The commitment to teach is also a commitment to a lifelong process of continued learning to maintain excellence in education.

Effective teachers help students develop the capacity to confront and overcome the various challenges that they will encounter in academic environments. To confront these challenges, a student must 1) understand his or her strengths and weaknesses, 2) acknowledge and confront his or her academic challenges, 3) want to succeed, and 4) set achievable goals (Gerber & Ginsberg, 1990). In other words, success depends on the individual's resilience, persistence, and motivation to accomplish goals. Successful students have a solid understanding and acceptance of their strengths and weaknesses and are persistent, motivated, hardworking, and goal-oriented. Perhaps most important, students who succeed develop a supportive environment that includes friends and family as well as their teachers: They find people who believe in their learning abilities.

CONCLUSION

Education is the legacy educators provide to our children and the gateway to their successful future. The future lies in their hands. Unlike snakes and salmon that never need to meet their mothers or bear cubs and primates that require only a few years with adults before they can survive alone, children need to be nurtured throughout their school years. The message in this text is that when a child struggles in school, teachers must first understand and determine the underlying factors contributing to learning, behavior, or emotional problems. When children misbehave, their reasons may not be readily apparent. When a child fails or refuses to complete work, it is rarely due to poor motivation. As discussed within the text, the classroom behavior, emotional, and learning problems of children can be placed within a triangular framework reflecting foundational abilities, symbolic processing abilities, and conceptual abilities. This model offers a bridge between scientific research and educational practice. The model is designed to increase understanding of the reasons why students struggle and, more importantly, the ways educators can help them, not just today but throughout their entire lives.

Students who struggle with school can succeed when they possess the persistence and resilience of Maria. As she described in her personal statement, one major factor contributing to her success was that she knew she could count on her teachers. As a result of their support, she believed her struggles helped her to become a better, more understanding person. As noted by Dr. Haim G. Ginott (1972) in the following poem that he wrote as a young teacher, teachers are the decisive element.

> I have come to a frightening conclusion.
>
> I am the decisive element in the classroom.

It is my personal approach that creates the climate.

It is my daily mood that makes the weather.

As a teacher, I possess tremendous power to make a child's life miserable or joyous.

I can be a tool of torture or an instrument of inspiration.

I can humiliate or humor, hurt or heal.

In all situations, it is my response that decides whether a crisis will be escalated or de-escalated, and a child humanized or dehumanized. (p. 13)

ADDITIONAL RESOURCES

READING

Alphabetic Phonics
Cox, A.R.
Educators Publishing Service
Post Office Box 9031
Cambridge, Massachusetts 02139
(800) 435-7728
Fax: (888) 440-2665
e-mail: customer_service@epsbooks
.com
http://www.epsbooks.com

Benchmark Phonetic Connections
(BuildUp Phonics, BuildUp Phonics
Readers)
Benchmark Education Company
629 Fifth Avenue
Pelham, New Jersey 10803
(877) 236-2465
Fax: (877) 732-8273
e-mail: info@benchmarkeducation.com
http://www.benchmarkeducation.com

Concept Phonics
Fischer, P.E.
Oxton House Publishers
Post Office Box 209
Farmington, Maine 04938
(800) 539-READ
Fax: (207) 779-0623
e-mail: info@oxtonhouse.com
http://www.oxtonhouse.com

Corrective Reading Decoding
SRA/McGraw-Hill
220 East Danieldale Road
Desoto, Texas 75115
(888) SRA-4543
Fax: (972) 228-1982
e-mail: SRAWebRequest@mcgraw-hill
.com
http://www.sraonline.com

**Discover Intensive Phonics
for Yourself**
Reading Horizons
60 North Cutler Drive
North Salt Lake, Utah 84054
(800) 333-0054
Fax: (801) 295-7088
e-mail: info@readinghorizons.com
http://www.readinghorizons.com

Earobics Literacy Launch®
Cognitive Concepts, Inc.
Post Office Box 1363
Evanston, Illinois 60204
(888) 328-8199
Fax: (847) 328-5965
e-mail: support@earobics.com
http://www.earobics.com

**Easy Lessons for Teaching
Word Families**
Lynch, J.
Scholastic Books
2931 East McCarty Street
Jefferson City, Missouri 65102
(800) 724-6527
e-mail through an online form at
http://scholastic.custhelp.com/
cgi-bin/scholastic.cfg/php/enduser/
ask.php
http://www.scholastic.com

Edmark Reading Program
PRO-ED, Inc.
8700 Shoal Creek Boulevard
Austin, Texas 78757
(800) 897-3202
e-mail: info@proedinc.com
http://www.proedinc.com

EPS Phonics Plus
EPS Phonics Plus Readers
Educators Publishing Service
Post Office Box 9031
Cambridge, Massachusetts 02139
(800) 435-7728
Fax: (888) 440-2665
e-mail: customer_service@epsbooks
.com
http://www.epsbooks.com

Explode the Code
Hall, N.M.
Educators Publishing Service
Post Office Box 9031
Cambridge, Massachusetts 02139
(800) 435-7728
Fax: (888) 440-2665
e-mail: customer_service@epsbooks
.com
http://www.epsbooks.com

EZ2 Read Decodable Bundle
Nicholson, B.
3524 Ridgeview Drive
El Dorado Hills, California 95762
(888) 521-4080
e-mail: gnicholson@ez2read.com
http://www.ez2read.com

Fast ForWord
Scientific Learning
300 Frank H. Ogawa Plaza
Suite 600
Oakland, California 94612-2040
(888) 665-9707
Fax: (510) 444-3580
e-mail: customerservice@scilearn.com
http://www.scilearn.com

Fluency First
Rasinski, T., and Padak, N.
Wright Group/McGraw-Hill
220 East Danieldale Road
DeSoto, Texas 75115
(800) 648-2970
Fax: (800) 593-4418
e-mail: mmh_cs@mcgraw-hill.com
http://www.wrightgroup.com

Flyleaf Publishing
(Decodable Books K–3)
Post Office Box 287
Lyme, New Hampshire 03768
(800) 449-7006
e-mail: comments@flyleafpublishing
.com
http://www.flyleafpublishing.com

Fundations®
Wilson, B.
Wilson Language Training
47 Old Webster Road
Oxford, Massachusetts 01540
(508) 368-2399
Fax: (508) 368-2300
e-mail: info@WilsonLanguage.com
http://www.WilsonLanguage.com

Glass Analysis for Decoding Only
Glass, G.G., and Glass, E.W.
Easier to Learn, Inc.
Post Office Box 259
Blue Point, New York 11715
(631) 475-7693 (telephone and fax)
e-mail through an online form at
http://www.glassanalysis.com/
contact.html
http://www.glassanalysis.com

Great Leaps Reading
Campbell, K.U.
Diarmuid, Inc.
Post Office Box 357580
Gainesville, Florida 32635
(877) 475-3277
Fax: (352) 384-3883
e-mail: info@greatleaps.com
http://www.greatleaps.com

Herman Method™
Herman, R.
Sopris West
4093 Specialty Place
Longmont, Colorado 80504
(800) 547-6747
Fax: (888) 819-7767
e-mail: customerservice@sopriswest
.com
http://www.sopriswest.com

1000 Instant Words: The Most Common Words for Teaching Reading, Writing, and Spelling
Fry, E.
Teacher Created Materials
5301 Oceanus Drive
Huntington Beach, California 92649
(800) 858-7339
Fax: (714) 230-7070
e-mail: customerservice@teacher-createdmaterials.com
http://www.teachercreatedmaterials.com

Introducing Word Families through Literature
Coldwell, J.
Carson-Dellosa Publishing Company, Inc.
Post Office Box 35665
Greensboro, North Carolina 27425
(336) 632-0084
(800) 321-0943
Fax: (336) 632-0087
e-mail through an online form at
http://www.carsondellosa.com/cd2/Forms/custservicemail.aspx
http://www.carson-dellosa.com

Ladders to Literacy: A Kindergarten Activity Book, Second Edition
O'Conner, R.E., Notari-Syverson, A., and Vadasy, P.F.
Paul H. Brookes Publishing Company
Post Office Box 10624
Baltimore, Maryland 21285
(800) 638-3775
Fax: (410) 337-8539
e-mail: custserv@brookespublishing.com
http://www.brookespublishing.com

Language! The Comprehensive Literacy Curriculum, Second Edition
Greene, J.F.
Sopris West
4093 Specialty Place
Longmont, Colorado 80504
(800) 547-6747
Fax: (888) 819-7767
e-mail: customerservice@sopriswest.com
http://www.sopriswest.com

Language Essentials for Teachers of Reading and Spelling (LETRS)
Moats, L.
Sopris West
4093 Specialty Place
Longmont, Colorado 80504
(800) 547-6747
Fax: (888) 819-7767
e-mail: customerservice@sopriswest.com
http://www.sopriswest.com

Let's Go Read!® 1: An Island Adventure®
Let's Go Read!® 2: An Ocean Adventure®
Edmark
Riverdeep Inc., A Limited Liability Company
100 Pine Street, Suite 1900
San Francisco, California 94111
(415) 659-2000
Fax: (415) 659-2020
e-mail: info@riverdeep.net
http://www.edmark.com

Lexia Early Reading v3.0+
Lexia Primary Reading v1.0+
Lexia Learning Systems, Inc.
  (Lexia Early Reading,
  Lexia Primary Reading)
  200 Baker Avenue, Extension
  Concord, Massachusetts 01742
  (800) 435-3942
  Fax: (781) 259-1349
  e-mail: info@lexialearning.com
  http://www.lexialearning.com

Lindamood Phoneme Sequencing
  Program for Reading, Spelling,
  and Speech (LiPS)
  Lindamood, P.C., and Lindamood, P.D.
  PRO-ED Inc.
  8700 Shoal Creek Boulevard
  Austin, Texas 78757
  (800) 897-3202
  Fax: (800) 397-7633
  e-mail: info@proedinc.com
  http://www.proedinc.com

Magnetic and Overhead
  Onsets and Rimes
  Teaching Resource Center
  Post Office Box 82777
  San Diego, California 92138
  (800) 833-3389
  Fax: (800) 972-7722
  e-mail: customer.service@trcabc.com
  http://www.trcabc.com

Making Words
Making Big Words
  Cunningham, P.M., and Hall, D.P.
  School Specialty Publishing
  Post Office Box 141487
  Grand Rapids, Michigan 49514
  (800) 417-3261
  Fax: (888) 203-9361
  e-mail: cpg_custserv@schoolspecialty
  .com
  http://www.schoolspecialtypublishing
  .com/

Megawords: Multisyllabic Words
  for Reading, Spelling, and Vocabulary
  Johnson, K., and Bayrd, P.
  Educators Publishing Service
  Post Office Box 9031
  Cambridge, Massachusetts 02139
  (800) 435-7728
  Fax: (888) 440-2665
  e-mail: customer_service@epsbooks
  .com
  http://www.epsbooks.com

Neuhaus Education Center
Practices for Developing Accuracy
  and Fluency (with CD-ROM)
Reading Readiness Kit
Scientific Spelling Manual
  4433 Bissonnet
  Bellaire, Texas 77401
  (713) 664-7676
  Fax: (713) 664-4744
  e-mail: info@neuhaus.org
  http://www.neuhaus.org

Open Court Phonics Kits
Open Court Reading Series
  Archer, A., Flood, J., Lapp, D., and
  Lungren, L.
  SRA/McGraw-Hill
  220 East Danieldale Road
  Desoto, Texas 75115
  (888) SRA-4543
  Fax: (972) 228-1982
  e-mail: SRAWebRequest@mcgraw-hill
  .com
  http://www.sraonline.com

Orton-Gillingham
  Institute for Multi-Sensory Education
  1000 S. Old Woodward, Suite 105
  Birmingham, Michigan 48009
  (800) 646-9788
  Fax: (248) 646-4585
  e-mail: imse@orton-gillingham.com
  http://www.orton-gillingham.com

Patterns for Success in Reading and Spelling
Henry, M.K., and Redding, N.C.
PRO-ED Inc.
8700 Shoal Creek Boulevard
Austin, Texas 78757
(800) 897-3202
Fax: (800) 297-7633
e-mail through an online form at
http://www.proedinc.com/customer/
contactUs.aspx
http://www.proedinc.com

Phonemic Awareness in Young Children
Adams, M., Foorman, B., Lundberg, I., and Beeler, T.
Paul H. Brookes Publishing Company
Post Office Box 10624
Baltimore, Maryland 21285
(800) 638-3775
Fax: (410) 337-8539
e-mail: custserv@brookespublishing.com
http://www.brookespublishing.com

Phonic Reading Lessons
Kirk, S.A., Kirk, W., Minskoff, E., Mather, N., & Roberts, R.
Academic Therapy Publications
20 Commercial Boulevard
Novato, California 94949
(800) 422-7249
Fax: (888) 287-9975
e-mail: sales@academictherapy.com
http://www.academictherapy.com

Phonics and Spelling through Phoneme-Grapheme Mapping
Grace, K.E.S.
Sopris West
4093 Specialty Place
Longmont, Colorado 80504
(800) 547-6747
Fax: (888) 819-7767
e-mail: customerservice@sopriswest.com
http://www.sopriswest.com

Phonics from A to Z: A Practical Guide (2nd Edition)
Blevins, W.
Scholastic Books
2931 East McCarty Street
Jefferson City, Missouri 65102
(800) 724-6527
e-mail through an online form at
http://scholastic.custhelp.com/
cgi-bin/scholastic.cfg/php/enduser/
ask.php
http://www.scholastic.com

Phonics Q: The Complete Cueing System
Herzog, P.
Post Office Box 22825
Seattle, Washington 98122
(206) 325-7989
Fax: (206) 325-5066
e-mail: info@phonicsq.com
http://www.phonicsq.com

Phonological Awareness Kit
Primary (Grades K–3), Intermediate (Grades 3–9)
Robertson, C., and Salter, W.
LinguiSystems, Inc.
3100 4th Avenue
East Moline, Illinois 61244
(800) 776-4332
Fax: (800) 577-4555
e-mail: service@linguisystems.com
http://www.linguisystems.com

Project Read
Greene, V.E., and Enfield, M.L.
Language Circle Enterprises, Inc.
1620 West 98th Street
Suite 130
Bloomington, Minnesota 55431
(800) 450-0343
Fax: (952) 884-6787
e-mail: languagecircle@projectread.com
http://www.projectread.com

Read 180
Hasselbring, T.
Scholastic Books
2931 East McCarty Street
Jefferson City, Missouri 65101
(800) 724-6527
(877) 234-READ
e-mail through an online form at
http://scholastic.custhelp.com/
cgi-bin/scholastic.cfg/php/enduser/
ask.php
http://www.scholastic.com

Retrieval, Automaticity, Vocabulary, Elaboration, and Orthography (RAVE-O)
Center for Reading and Language Research
Miller Hall
Tufts University
Medford, Massachusetts 02155
(617) 627-3815
Fax: (617) 627-3827
e-mail: UITSC@tufts.edu
http://ase.tufts.edu/crlr/raveo.html

Read Naturally
Ihnot, C.
750 S. Plaza Drive #100
Saint Paul, Minnesota 55120
(800) 788-4085
(612) 452-4085
Fax: (651) 452-9204
e-mail: READNAT@aol.com
http://www.readnaturally.com

Read Well
Sprick, M.
Sopris West
4093 Specialty Place
Longmont, Colorado 80504
(800) 547-6747
Fax: (888) 819-7767
e-mail: customerservice@sopriswest
.com
http://www.sopriswest.com

Read, Write, & Type Learning System (CD-ROM)
Wordy Qwerty
Talking Fingers, Inc.
830 Rincon Way
San Rafael, California 94901
(800) 674-9126
e-mail: contact@talkingfingers.com
http://www.talkingfingers.com

Readinga-z.com: The Online Reading Program
LearningPage
1840 E. River Road, Suite #320
Tucson, Arizona 85718-5834
(866) 889-3729
Fax: (520) 327-9934
e-mail: razsupport@readinga-z.com
http://www.readinga-z.com

The Reading Lesson
Levin, M., and Langton, C.
Mountcastle Company
One Annabel Lane, Suite 214
San Ramon, California 94593
(925) 830-8655
Fax: (925) 476-1525
e-mail: mntcastle@earthlink.net
http://www.readinglesson.com

Reading Mastery Classic II, 2002 Edition
SRA/McGraw-Hill
220 East Danieldale Road
Desoto, TX 75115-2490
(888) SRA-4543
Fax: (972) 228-1982
custserv@mcgraw-hill.com
http://www.sraonline.com

Reading Milestones
PRO-ED, Inc.
8700 Shoal Creek Boulevard
Austin, Texas 78757-6897
(800) 897-3202
e-mail: info@proedinc.com
http://www.proedinc.com

Reading Reflex
McGuinness, C., and McGuinness, G.
The Free Press
1230 Avenue of the Americas
New York, New York 10020
(800) 732-3868
http://www.SimonSays.com

Recipe for Reading: New Century Edition
Traub, N., and Bloom, F.
Educators Publishing Service
Post Office Box 9031
Cambridge, Massachusetts 02139-9031
(800) 435-7728
Fax: (888) 440-2665
e-mail: customer_service@epsbooks
.com
http://www.epsbooks.com

Rewards
Archer, A.L., Gleason, M.M., and Vachon, V.
Sopris West
4093 Specialty Place
Longmont, Colorado 80504
(800) 547-6747
Fax: (888) 819-7767
e-mail: customerservice@sopriswest
.com
http://www.sopriswest.com

Road to the Code: A Phonological Awareness Program for Young Children
Blachman, B., Ball, E.W., Black, R., and Tangel, D.M.
Paul H. Brookes Publishing Company
Post Office Box 10624
Baltimore, Maryland 21285
(800) 638-3775
Fax: (410) 337-8539
e-mail: custserv@brookespublishing
.com
http://www.brookespublishing.com

Scott Foresman Early Reading Intervention
Simmons, D.C., and Kame'enui, E.J.
Pearson Scott Foresman
Post Office Box 2500
145 Mount Zion Road
Lebanon, Indiana 46052
(800) 552-2259
e-mail: K12CS@custhelp.com
pearson.com
http://www.scottforesman.com

Simon Sounds It Out
Don Johnston, Inc.
26799 West Commerce Drive
Volo, Illinois 60073
(800) 999-4660
Fax: (847) 740-7326
e-mail: info@donjohnston.com
http://www.donjohnston.com

Six-Minute Solution: A Reading Fluency Program
Adams, G., and Brown, S.
Sopris West
4093 Specialty Place
Longmont, Colorado 80504
(800) 547-6747
Fax: (888) 819-7767
e-mail: customerservice@sopriswest
.com
http://www.sopriswest.com

Slingerland®
Slingerland Institute for Literacy
One Bellevue Center
411 108th Avenue NE
Bellevue, Washington 98004
(425) 453-1190
Fax: (425) 635-7762
e-mail: mail@slingerland.org
http://www.slingerland.org

Soliloquy Reading Assistant (CD-ROM)
Soliloquy Learning
100 Fifth Avenue
Suite #410
Waltham, Massachusetts 02451
(877) 235-6036
Fax: (781) 547-6039
e-mail: slsupport@soliloquylearning
.com
http://www.soliloquylearning.com

Sonday System
Winsor Learning, Inc.
1620 West Seventh Street
St. Paul, Minnesota 55102
(800) 321-7585
Fax: (651) 222-3969
e-mail through an online form at
http:// www.winsorlearning.com/
contactus/
http://www.readabc.com

Sound Partners
*Vadasy, P.,Wayne, S., O'Connor,
R., Jenkins, J., Pool, K., Firebaugh,
M., and Peyton, J.*
Sopris West
4093 Specialty Place
Longmont, Colorado 80504
(800) 547-6747
Fax: (888) 819-7767
e-mail: customerservice@sopriswest
.com
http://www.sopriswest.com

**Sounds Abound: Listening, Rhyming,
and Reading**
Sounds Abound Interactive Software
Catts, H., and Olsen, T.
LinguiSystems, Inc.
3100 4th Avenue
East Moline, Illinois 61244
(800) 776-4332
Fax: (800) 577-4555
e-mail: service@linguisystems
.com
http://www.linguisystems.com

**Sounds Abound Program: Teaching
Phonological Awareness in the
Classroom**
Lenchner, O., and Podhajski, B.
LinguiSystems, Inc.
3100 4th Avenue
East Moline, IL 61244
(800) 776-4332
Fax: (800) 577-4555
http://www.linguisystems.com

Sounds Great
Wright Group/McGraw-Hill
220 East Danieldale Road
DeSoto, Texas 75115
(800) 648-2970
Fax: (800) 593-4418
e-mail: mmh_cs@mcgraw-hill.com
http://www.wrightgroup.com

Spalding: The Writing Road to Reading
Spalding Education International
2814 West Bell Road, Suite 1405
Phoenix, Arizona 85053
(602) 866-7801
Fax: (602) 866-7488
e-mail: staff@spalding.org
http://www.spalding.org

**Specialized Program Individualizing
Reading Excellence (S.P.I.R.E.)**
Clark-Edmands, S.
Educators Publishing Service
Post Office Box 9031
Cambridge, Massachusetts 02139
(800) 225-5750
(800) 435-7728
Fax: (888) 440-2665
http://www.epsbooks.com

Story Grammar Marker
MindWing Concepts, Inc
Scibelli Enterprise Center
One Federal Street
Springfield Enterprise Center
Springfield, Massachusetts 01105
(888) 228-9746
http://www.mindwingconcepts.com

Teacher-Directed PALS: Paths to Achieving Literacy Success
Mathes, P., Allor, J.H., Allen, S.H., and Torgesen, J.K.
Sopris West
4093 Specialty Place
Longmont, Colorado 80504
(800) 547-6747
Fax: (888) 819-7767
e-mail: customerservice@sopriswest.com
http://www.sopriswest.com

WatchWord
Lacey, K., and Baird, W.
Sopris West
4093 Specialty Place
Longmont, Colorado 80504
(800) 547-6747
Fax: (888) 819-7767
e-mail: customerservice@sopriswest.com
http://www.sopriswest.com

Wilson Fluency/Basic™
Wilson, B.
Wilson Language Training
47 Old Webster Road
Oxford, Massachusetts 01540
(508) 368-2399
Fax: (508) 368-2300
e-mail: info@wilsonlanguage.com
http://www.wilsonlanguage.com

Wilson Reading System®
Wilson, B.
Wilson Language Training
47 Old Webster Road
Oxford, Massachusetts 01540
(508) 368-2399
Fax: (508) 368-2300
e-mail: info@wilsonlanguage.com
http://www.wilsonlanguage.com

Word Journeys: Assessment-Guided Phonics, Spelling, and Vocabulary Instruction
Ganske, K.
Guilford Press
72 Spring Street
New York, New York 10012
(800) 365-7006
Fax: (212) 966-6708
e-mail: info@guilford.com
http://www.guilford.com

Words
Henry, M.K.
PRO-ED Inc.
8700 Shoal Creek Boulevard
Austin, Texas 78757
(800) 897-3202
Fax: (800) 297-7633
e-mail: info@proedinc.com
http://www.proedinc.com

Wright Skills Decodable Books
Wright Group/McGraw-Hill
19201 120th Avenue
Bothell, Washington 98011
(800) 523-2371
Fax: (800) 543-7323
http://www.wrightgroup.com

Zoo-Phonics
20950 Ferretti Road
Groveland, California 95321
(800) 622-8104
Fax: (209) 962-4320
http://www.zoo-phonics.com

SPELLING AND VOCABULARY

Saxon Phonics and Spelling
Saxon Phonics Intervention
Saxon Publishers
Harcourt Achieve
Customer Service 5th Floor
6277 Sea Harbor Drive
Orlando, Florida 32887
(800) 284-7019
Fax: (866) 378-2249
saxonpublishers.harcourtachieve.com

Scholastic Spelling
Moats, L., and Foorman, B.
Scholastic Books
2931 East McCarty Street
Jefferson City, Missouri 65102
(800) 724-6527
http://www.scholastic.com

Sitton Spelling Sourcebook Series
Sitton, R.
Egger Publishing, Inc.
Post Office Box 12248
Scottsdale, Arizona 85267
(888) 937-7355
e-mail: rsitton@sittonspelling.com
Free Overview Video Package: contact
(888) 937-7355
http://www.sittonspelling.com

Spellography

Rosow, B., and Moats, L.C.
Sopris West
4093 Specialty Place
Longmont, Colorado 80504
(800) 547-6747
Fax: (888) 819-7767
e-mail: customerservice@sopriswest
.com
http://www.sopriswest.com

Words Their Way: Word Study for Phonics, Vocabulary, and Spelling Instruction (4th ed.)

Bear, D.R., Invernizzi, M., Templeton, S., and Johnston, F.
Pearson Education, Inc.
Upper Saddle River, New Jersey
07458

Customer Support:
145 S. Mount Zion Road
Post Office Box 2500
Lebanon, Indiana 46052
(800) 321-3106
Fax: (800) 393-3156
http://www.pearsonschool.com

WRITTEN LANGUAGE AND GRAPHIC ORGANIZERS

Co-Writer® Solo

Don Johnston, Inc.
26799 West Commerce Drive
Volo, Illinois 60073
(800) 999-4660
Fax: (847) 740-7326
e-mail: info@donjohnston.com
http://www.donjohnston.com

Draft Builder®

Don Johnston, Inc.
26799 West Commerce Drive
Volo, IL 60073
(800) 999-4660
Fax: (847) 740-7326
e-mail: info@donjohnston.com
http://www.donjohnston.com

Inspiration®
Kidspiration®

Inspiration Software, Inc.
9400 SW Beaverton-Hillsdale Highway
Suite 300
Beaverton, Oregon 97005
(800) 877-4292
Fax: (503) 297-4676
e-mail: CustomerService@inspiration
.com
http://www.inspiration.com

Write: Outloud®

Don Johnston, Inc.
26799 West Commerce Drive
Volo, Illinois 60073
(800) 999-4660
Fax: (847) 740-7326
e-mail: info@donjohnston.com
http://www.donjohnston.com

HANDWRITING RESOURCES

Fonts4Teachers

Downhill Publishing
36 Clover Street
Newark, New Jersey 07105
(800) 203-0612
Fax: (310) 325-1108
e-mail: info@fonts4teachers.com
http://www.fonts4teachers.com

Pencil Grip

Post Office Box 67096
Los Angeles, California 90067
(888) 736-4747 (PEN-GRIP)
Fax: (310) 788-0644
e-mail: info@thepencilgrip.com

Start Write: Handwriting Software
The Handwriting Worksheet Wizard™

Startwrite Inc.
80 South Redwood Road, Suite 215
North Salt Lake, UT 84054
(801) 936-7779 (local & international)
(888) 974-8322
Fax: (801) 936-7777
e-mail through an online form at:
http://www.startwrite.com/contact
.php
http://www.startwrite.com

ASSISTIVE TECHNOLOGY

Books on Tape
A Division of Random House, Inc.
Attn: Customer Service
400 Hahn
Westminster, Maryland 21157
e-mail through an online form at:
http://www.booksontape.com/
contacts.cfm
http://www.booksontape.com

Dragon NaturallySpeaking
Nuance
1 Wayside Road
Burlington, Massachusetts 01803
(781) 565-5000
Fax: (781) 565-5001
e-mail through an online form at:
http://support.nuance.com/
customerservice/email/
http://www.nuance.com

Franklin Speaking Language Master
Franklin Electronic Publishers
One Franklin Plaza
Burlington, New Jersey 08016
800-266-5626
Fax: (609) 239-5948
e-mail: service@franklin.com
http://www.franklin.com

Quicktionary Reading Pen
WizCom Technologies Inc.
234 Littleton Road, Suite 1B
Westford, Massachusetts 01886
(888) 777-0552 x104
Fax: (978) 727-0032
e-mail: support@readingpen
.com
http://www.readingpen.com

Reading Pen
Ventura Educational Systems
Post Office Box 1622
Arroyo Grande, CA 93421
(800) 336-1022
Fax: (800) 493-7380
e-mail: sales@venturaes.com
http://www.venturaes.com

Recorded Books, LLC
270 Skipjack Road
Prince Frederick, Maryland 20678
(800) 638-1304
Fax: 410-535-5499
e-mail: customerservice@recorded
books.com
http://www.recordedbooks.com

Recording for the Blind & Dyslexic
National Headquarters
20 Roszel Road
Princeton, New Jersey 08540
(866) 732-3585
(800) 221-4792
e-mail: custserv@rfbd.org
http://www.rfbd.org

SpeakQ™
Quillsoft Ltd.
2416 Queen Street East
Toronto, Ontario M1N 1A2
CANADA
(866) 629-6737
(416) 698-0111
Fax: (416) 698-1555
e-mail: sales@quillsoft.ca
http://www.wordq.com

MATHEMATICS

Great Leaps Math Program
Great Leaps Oral Calculation Program
Diarmuid, Inc.
Post Office Box 357580
Gainesville, Florida 32635
(877) 475-3277
Fax: (352) 384-3883
e-mail: info@greatleaps.com
http://www.greatleaps.com

Math Their Way (K–2)
Mathematics…A Way of Thinking (3–6)
Baretta-Lorton, R.
Center for Innovation in Education, Inc.
Post Office Box 2070
Saratoga, California 95070
(800) 395-6088
(408) 367-4628
Fax: (408) 868-0347
e-mail: mathawayofthink@center
http://www.center.edu

411

Multiplication Rap CD + Tape
Pace, Inc.
7803 Pickering Street
Kalamazoo, Michigan 49022
http://www.TeachersParadise.com

Times Tables the Fun Way
Addition the Fun Way
City Creek Press, Inc.
Post Office Box 8415
Minneapolis, Minnesota 55408
(800) 585-6059
Fax: (877) 286-1163
http://www.citycreek.com

TouchMath
Bullock, J.
Innovative Learning Concepts, Inc.
6760 Corporate Drive
Colorado Springs, Colorado 80919
(800) 888-9191
Fax: (719) 593-2446
http://www.touchmath.com

Two Plus Two Is Not Five
Greenwalk, S.
Longevity Publishing LLC
10179 Pinewood Avenue
Englewood, Colorado 80111
(720) 489-7243
Fax: (267) 590-2320
e-mail: info@longevitypublishing.com
http://www.longevitypublishing.com

WEB SITES AND PROFESSIONAL ORGANIZATIONS[1]

WEB SITES

Association for Direct Instruction
This web site is devoted to Direct Instruction (DI). The site contains video clips of procedures, movie clips of DI lessons, articles, and other support services for teachers who use DI.
http://www.adihome.org

Center for Applied Special Technology
The Center for Applied Special Technology develops innovative, technology-based educational resources and strategies based on the principles of Universal Design for Learning (UDL). The products resource page contains interactive UDL lesson design tools and an online tool called Book Builder, which enables educators to develop their own digital books to support reading instruction for children ages 3–10. Teachers can create, edit, and save universally designed texts that support diverse learners.
e-mail: cast@cast.org
http://www.cast.org

Florida Center for Reading Research
The Florida Center for Reading Research (FCRR) web site contains a wealth of information on reading for teachers, reading coaches, administrators, parents, and researchers. Videos, presentations, interviews, recommended readings, webcasts, and reviews of evidenced-based reading programs and interventions are especially helpful. The FCRR webcast page also provides a video podcast for teachers on the sounds of standard English.
e-mail: fcrr@fcrr.org
http://www.fcrr.org

Hand Made Math Manipulatives Instruction
http://mason.gmu.edu/~mmankus/Handson/manipulatives.htm
This site provides manipulatives and instructions that can be printed out for ease of use. Manipulatives include pattern blocks; rhombus, trapezoid, and hexagon cutouts; and base-five and base-ten blocks, among others.

Intervention Central
Intervention Central provides a collection of free tools and resources for differentiating instruction, monitoring progress, academic assessment, and behavioral interventions. The site is maintained by Jim Wright, a school psychologist in Syracuse, New York.
e-mail: subscribe through an online form at web site below.
http://www.interventioncentral.org

---

[1] Web sites compiled by Annmarie Urso

LD Online

LD Online is a service of WETA, a public broadcasting station in Washington, DC. This web site provides comprehensive information on learning disabilities and general special education services for parents, teachers, and other professionals.

e-mail: Contact is through an online form at http://ldonline.org/sitecontact

http://ldonline.org

Learning Toolbox

This web site, developed by the College of Education at James Madison University, contains tools and resources to assist secondary and postsecondary students who have LD and ADHD. The web site provides strategies for test taking, studying, notetaking, problem solving, and remembering information. The toolbox has three access areas—one for parents explaining the strategies children may be using and how to help support them at home; one for teachers outlining the steps for selecting and teaching the strategies; and, last, one for the students that helps them select and use an appropriate strategy.

e-mail: through an online form at

http://coe.jmu.edu/Learningtoolbox/contactus.html

http://coe.jmu.edu/Learningtoolbox/

National Assistive Technology Research Institute

This web site provides a clearinghouse for the latest assistive technology information and resources.

e-mail: natri@coe.uky.edu

http://natri.uky.edu

National Center for Culturally Responsive Educational Systems

The National Center for Culturally Responsive Educational Systems is a project funded by the U.S. Department of Education's Special Education Programs. This program provides technical assistance and professional development to close the achievement gap between students from culturally and linguistically diverse backgrounds and their peers and reduce inappropriate referrals to special education. This web site provides downloads of professional development modules, tools, products, and position papers.

e-mail: Elizabeth.Kozleski@asu.edu

http://www.nccrest.org

National Center on Student Progress Monitoring

To meet the challenges of implementing effective progress monitoring, the Office of Special Education Programs (OSEP) funded the National Center on Student Progress Monitoring. Housed at the American Institutes for Research, and working in conjunction with researchers from Vanderbilt University, this is a national technical assistance and dissemination center dedicated to the implementation of scientifically based student progress monitoring. This web site provides tools for use by teachers, information for parents, and a library of resources on progress monitoring.

e-mail: studentprogress@air.org

http://www.studentprogress.org

National Dissemination Center for Children with Disabilities

The National Dissemination Center for Children with Disabilities is a national center for resources on disabilities. Information about disabilities, links to web sites of national organizations devoted to various disabilities, and research-based information on educational topics are available on this site.

e-mail: nichcy@aed.org

http://www.nichcy.org

National Library of Virtual Manipulatives

This web site, filled with virtual manipulatives, including bar charts, base ten materials, counting chips, and more, was developed with support from the National Science Foundation by a team of mathematicians, math educators, and instructional designers.

http://nlvm.usu.edu/en/nav/vlibrary.html

National Research Center on Learning Disabilities

This web site contains downloads, publications, presentations, and resources focusing on LD determination procedures and response to intervention.
e-mail: nrcld@ku.edu.
http://www.nrcld.org

Read, Write, Think

The Read, Write, Think web site is a partnership between the International Reading Association, the National Council of Teachers of English, and the Verizon Foundation. This site provides access to high-quality practices and resources in reading and language arts instruction through free, Internet-based content. Lesson plans, standards, web resources, and student materials are available for download.
e-mail: is through an online form at http://www.readwritethink.org/contact.html
http://www.readwritethink.org

Schwab Learning

This web site provides an online guide of resources and information for parents of children with learning difficulties, including information on behavior, social skills, LD, ADHD, assistive technology, helping children with homework, and various other topics concerning families.
Media Inquiries: marketing@schwablearning.org otherwise contact through online feedback form at http://www.schwablearning.org/feedback.aspx
http://www.schwablearning.org

Southwest Educational Development Laboratory

The Southwest Educational Development Laboratory is a private, nonprofit education, research, development, and dissemination corporation that creates and provides research-based products and services to improve teaching and learning. This valuable web site provides a searchable research database of early reading assessment tools, an electronic library of resources on various education topics, short papers on different reading focus areas in downloadable pdf format suitable for parents and practitioners, and a research-based cognitive reading framework.
e-mail: info@sedl.org
http://www.sedl.org

Special Connections

This web site contains a compilation of ideas and materials funded through OSEP and coordinated through the University of Kansas. Four main areas of focus include instruction, assessment, behavior plans, and collaboration. Each module provides tools for implementing specific practices, case study materials, references, and resources related to each practice.
http://www.specialconnections.ku.edu

Special Education Resources on the Internet

Special Education Resources on the Internet is a collection of Internet-accessible resources of interest to individuals working in special education or related fields. This site is frequently modified and updated to remain current and accurate.
e-mail: webmaster@seriweb.com
http://www.seriweb.com

TeachingLD

This web site is provided by the Division for Learning Disabilities of the Council for Exceptional Children, which is the largest international professional organization focused on LD. This site features current practice alerts and expected rates of progress on curriculum-based measures for students.
e-mail: Subscribe through online form at http://www.dldcec.org/contact/default.htm
http://www.dldcec.org

Vaughn Gross Center for Reading and Language Arts, University of Texas at Austin

This web site has a materials download section with free booklets, videos, and professional development guides appropriate for pre-K–secondary teachers as

well as ELL, ESL, and special education teachers. This web site also highlights research being conducted at the center.
e-mail: info@texasreading.org
http://www.texasreading.org

What Works Clearinghouse
This web site was established in 2002 by the U.S. Department of Education's Insti-tute of Education Sciences to provide educators, policymakers, researchers, and the public with a central and trusted source of scientific evidence of what works in education.
e-mail: Contact through online form at http://ies.ed.gov/ncee/wwc/help/webmail/
http://www.w-w-c.org

REFERENCES

Aaron, P.G. (1997). The impending demise of the discrepancy formula. *Review of Educational Research, 67*, 461–502.

Aaron, P.G., & Simurdak, J. (1991). Reading disorders: Their nature and diagnosis. In J.E. Obrzut & G.W. Hynd (Eds.), *Neuropsychological foundations of learning disabilities: A handbook of issues, methods, and practice* (pp. 549–571). San Diego: Academic Press.

Abramowitz, A.J., & O'Leary, S.G. (1991). Behavior interventions for the classroom: Implications for students with ADHD. *School Psychology Review, 20*, 220–234.

Abramowitz, A.J., O'Leary, S.G., & Futtersak, M.W. (1988). The relative impact of long and short reprimands on children's off-task behavior in the classroom. *Behavior Therapy, 19*, 243–247.

Accardo, P.J., Blondis, T.J., & Whitman, B.Y. (1990). Disorders of attention and activity level in a referral population. *Pediatrics, 85*, 426–431.

Achenbach, T.M., Conners, C.K., Quay, H.C., Verhulst, F.C., & Howell, C.T. (1989). Replication of empirically derived syndromes as a basis for taxonomy of child/adolescent psycho-pathology. *Journal of Abnormal Child Psychology, 17*, 299–320.

Achenbach, T.M., & Edelbrock, C. (1981). Behavioral problems and competencies reported by parents of normal and disturbed children aged 4 through 16. *Monographs of the Society for Research and Child Development, 46* (Serial No. 188).

Achenbach, T.M., & Edelbrock, C. (1991). *Manual for the Child Behavior Checklist and 1991 Profile.* Burlington, VT: University of Vermont Press, Department of Psychiatry.

Achenbach, T.M., McConaughy, S.H., & Howell, C.T. (1987). Child/adolescent behavioral and emotional problems. Implications of cross-informant correlations for situational specificity. *Psychological Bulletin, 101*, 213–232.

Acker, M.M., & O'Leary, S.G. (1988). Effects of consistent and inconsistent feedback on inappropriate child behavior. *Behavior Therapy, 19*, 619–624.

Ackerman, P.T., Dykman, R.A., & Peters, J.E. (1977). Teenage status of hyperactive and nonhyperactive learning disabled boys. *American Journal of Orthopsychiatry, 47*, 577–596.

Adams, M.J. (1990). *Beginning to read: Thinking and learning about print.* Cambridge, MA: The MIT Press.

Adams, M.J., Foorman, B.R., Lundberg, I., & Beeler, T. (1998). *Phonemic awareness in young children: A classroom curriculum.* Baltimore: Paul H. Brookes Publishing Co.

Adelman, H., & Taylor, L. (1983). Enhancing motivation for overcoming learning and behavior problems. *Journal of Learning Disabilities, 16*, 384–392.

Adelman, H., & Taylor, L. (1990). Intrinsic motivation and school misbehavior: Some intervention implications. *Journal of Learning Disabilities, 23*, 541–550.

Albano, A.M., & Kendall, P.C. (2002). Cognitive behavioral therapy for children and adolescents with anxiety disorders: Clinical research advances. *International Review of Psychiatry, 14*, 129–134.

Allen, L. (1998). An integrated strategies approach: Making word identification instruction work for beginning readers. *Reading Teacher, 52*, 254–268.

Allsopp, D.H. (1999). Using modeling, manipulatives, and mnemonics with eighth-grade math students. *Teaching Exceptional Children, 32*(2), 74–81.

Allsopp, D.H., Kyger, M.M., & Lovin, L.H. (2007). *Teaching mathematics meaningfully: Solutions for reaching struggling learners.* Baltimore: Paul H. Brookes Publishing Co.

Alvarez, M.C. (1983). Sustained timed writing as an aid to fluency and creativity. *Teaching Exceptional Children, 15*, 160–162.

American Psychiatric Association. (1994). *Diagnostic and statistical manual of mental disorders* (4th ed.). Washington, DC: Author.

American Psychiatric Association. (2000). *Diagnostic and statistical manual of mental disorders* (4th ed., text rev.). Washington, DC: Author.

Anastopoulos, A.D., Barkley, R.A., & Shelton, T. (1994). The history and diagnosis of attention-deficit/hyperactivity disorder. *Therapeutic Care and Education, 3*, 96–110.

Anderson, H.H., & Brewer, J.E. (1946). Studies of teachers' classroom personalities: II. Effects of teachers' dominative and integrative contacts on children's classroom behavior. *Applied Psychological Monographs, 8*.

Anderson, J.C., Williams, S., McGee, R., & Silva, P.A. (1987). DSM-III disorders in preadolescent children. Prevalence in a large sample from the general population. *Archives of General Psychiatry, 44*, 69–76.

Anderson, L.M. (1985). What are students doing when they do all that seatwork? In C.W. Fisher & D.C. Berliner (Eds.), *Perspectives on instructional time* (pp. 187–211). New York: Longman.

Anderson, V.L., Levinsohn, E.M., Barker, W., & Kiewra, K.R. (1999). The effects of meditation on teacher perceived occupational stress, state and trade anxiety and burnout. *School Psychology Quarterly, 14*, 3–25.

Angold, A., Costello, E.J., & Erklani, A. (1999). Comorbidity. *Journal of Child Psychology and Psychiatry, 40,* 57–87.

Angold, A., Egger, H., Erklani, A., & Keeler, G. (2005). *Prevalence and comorbidity of psychiatric disorders in preschoolers attending a large pediatric service.* Unpublished manuscript.

Anthony, J.L., & Francis, D.J. (2005). Development of phonological awareness. *Current Directions in Psychological Science, 14,* 255–259.

Apel, K., & Swank, L.K. (1999). Second chances: Improving decoding skills in the older student. *Language, Speech, and Hearing Services in Schools, 30,* 231–242.

Archer, A.L., Gleason, M.M., & Vachon, V. (2000). *Reading excellence: Word attack and rate development strategies.* Longmont, CO: Sopris West.

Artiles, A.J., Rueda, R., Salazar, J.J., & Higareda, I. (2005). Within-group diversity in minority disproportionate representation: English language learners in urban school districts. *Exceptional Children, 71,* 283–300.

Asarnow, J.R., Jaycox, L.H., & Tompson, M.C. (2001). Depression in youth: Psychosocial interventions. *Journal of Clinical Child Psychology, 30,* 33–47.

Ashman, A.F., & Conway, R.N.F. (1997). *An introduction to cognitive education: Theory and application.* London: Routledge.

Athanasiou, M.S., Geil, M., Hazel, C.E., & Copeland, E.P. (2002). A look inside school-based consultation: A qualitative study of the beliefs and practices of school psychologists and teachers. *School Psychology Quarterly, 17,* 258–298.

Attie, I., Brooks-Gunn, J., & Petersen, A.C. (1990). The emergence of eating problems: A developmental perspective. In M. Lewis & S. Miller (Eds.), *Handbook of developmental psychopathology* (pp. 409–420). New York: Kluwer Academic/Plenum Publishers.

August, D., Carlo, M., Dressler, C., & Snow, C. (2005). The critical role of vocabulary development for English language learners. *Learning Disabilities Research & Practice, 20,* 50–57.

August, D., & Shanahan, T. (Eds.). (2006). *Developing literacy in second-language learners: Report of the National Literacy Panel on language-minority children and youth.* London: Routledge.

Babbitt, B.C. (2000). 10 tips for software selection for math instruction (LD Online Reprint). *The CDA Gram, 34*(2), 11–12.

Babbitt, B.C., & Miller, S.P. (1997). Using hypermedia to improve the mathematics problem-solving skills of students with learning disabilities. In K. Higgins & R. Boone (Eds.), *Technology for students with learning disabilities* (pp. 91–108). Austin, TX: PRO-ED.

Baddeley, A.D. (1986). *Working memory.* New York: Oxford University Press.

Badian, N.A. (1997). Dyslexia and the double deficit hypothesis. *Annals of Dyslexia, 47,* 69–87.

Badian, N.A. (1998). A validation of the role of preschool phonological and orthographic skills in the prediction of reading. *Journal of Learning Disabilities, 31,* 472–481.

Bagwell, C.L., Molina, D.S., Pelham, W.E., & Hoza, B. (2001). ADHD and problems in peer relations: Predictions from childhood to adolescence. *Journal of the American Academy of Child and Adolescent Psychiatry, 40,* 1285–1299.

Bailet, L.L. (1991). Beginning spelling. In A.M. Bain, L.L. Bailet, & L.C. Moats (Eds.), *Written language disorders: Theory into practice* (pp. 1–21). Austin, TX: PRO-ED.

Baker, L., & Brown, A. (1980). *Metacognitive skills and reading* (Tech. Rep. No. 188). Urbana: University of Illinois, Center for the Study of Reading.

Baker, L., & Cantwell, D.P. (1987). A prospective psychiatric follow-up of children with speech/language disorders. *Journal of the American Academy of Child and Adolescent Psychiatry, 26,* 546–553.

Baker, L., & Cantwell, D.P. (1992). Attention deficit disorder and speech/language disorders. *Comprehensive Mental Health Care, 2,* 3–16.

Bakker, D.J. (1972). *Temporal order in disturbed reading: Developmental and neuropsychological aspects in normal and reading-retarded children.* Rotterdam, Netherlands: Rotterdam University Press.

Bakker, D.J. (1979). Hemisphere differences and reading strategies: Two dyslexias? *Bulletin of the Orton Society, 29,* 84–100.

Bakker, D.J. (1980). Hemisphere-specific dyslexia models. In R.N. Malatesha & L.C. Hastlage (Eds.), *Lateralization of language in the child* (pp. 310–351). Amsterdam, Netherlands: Swets & Zeitlinger.

Bakker, D.J. (1992). Neuropsychological classification and treatment of dyslexia. *Journal of Learning Disabilities, 25,* 102–109.

Bakker, D.J., & Vinke, J. (1985). Effects of hemisphere-specific stimulation on brain activity and reading in dyslexics. *Journal of Clinical and Experimental Neuropsychology, 7,* 505–525.

Ball, S. (1995). Anxiety and test performance. In C.D. Spielberger & P.R. Vagg (Eds.), *Test anxiety: Theory, assessment, and treatment* (pp. 3–14). Washington, DC: Taylor & Francis.

Balthazor, M.J., Wagner, R.K., & Pelham, W.E. (1991). The specificity of the effects of stimulant medication on classroom learning-related measures of cognitive processing for attention deficit disorder children. *Journal of Abnormal Child Psychology, 19,* 35–52.

Bandura, A. (1969). *Principles of behavior modification.* New York: Holt, Rinehart & Winston.

Bannatyne, A. (1971). *Language, reading and learning disabilities.* Springfield, IL: Charles C Thomas.

Barbe, W.B., Lucas, V.H., Wasylyk, T.M., Hackney, C.S., & Braun, L.A. (1987). *Zaner-Bloser handwriting: Book 1. Basic skills and application.* Columbus, OH: Zaner-Bloser.

Barkley, R.A. (1981). *Hyperactive children: A handbook for diagnosis and treatment.* New York: Guilford Press.

Barkley, R.A. (1990). *Attention deficit hyperactivity disorder: A handbook for diagnosis and treatment.* New York: Guilford Press.

Barkley, R.A. (1994). What to look for in a school for a child with ADHD. *The ADHD Report, 2* (3), 1–3.

Barkley, R.A. (1995). ADHD and I.Q. *The ADHD Report, 3*(2), 1–3.

Barkley, R.A. (1997a). *The nature of self-control.* New York: Guilford Press.

Barkley, R.A. (1997b). *Defiant children: A clinician's manual for assessment and parent training* (2nd ed.). New York: Guilford Press.

Barkley, R.A. (2005). *Attention deficit hyperactivity disorder* (3rd ed.). New York: Guilford Press.

Barkley, R.A., Fischer, M., Edelbrock, C.S., & Smallish, L. (1990). The adolescent outcome of hyperactive children diagnosed by research criteria: I. An eight-year prospective follow-up study. *Journal of the American Academy of Child and Adolescent Psychiatry, 29,* 546–557.

Barkley, R.A., & Gordon, M. (2002). Research on comorbidity, adaptive functioning and cognitive impairments in adults with ADHD: Implications for a clinical practice. In S. Goldstein & A. Teeter Ellison (Eds.), *Clinician's guide to adult ADHD: Assessment and intervention* (pp. 46–73). New York: Academic Press.

Barkley, R.A., McMurray, M.B., Edelbrock, C.S., & Robbins, K. (1990). Side effects of methylphenidate in children with attention deficit hyperactivity disorder: A systemic placebo-controlled evaluation. *Pediatrics, 86,* 184–192.

Barkley, R.A., & Murphy, K.R. (2006). Identifying new symptoms for diagnosing ADHD in adulthood. *The ADHD Report, 14*(4), 7–11.

Barlow, D.H. (2002). *Anxiety and its disorders: The nature and treatment of anxiety and panic* (2nd ed.). New York: Guilford Press.

Barrett, P.M. (2004). *FRIENDS for Life group leaders' manual for children.* Bowen Hills, Queensland: Australian Academic Press Pty Ltd.

Barrett, P.M. (2005). *FRIENDS for Life group leaders' manual for youth.* Bowen Hills, Queensland: Australian Academic Press.

Barrett, P.M., Duffy, A.L., Dadds, M.R., & Rapee, R.M. (2001). Cognitive-behavioral treatment of anxiety disorders in children: Long-term (6-year) follow-up. *Journal of Consulting and Clinical Psychology, 69,* 135–141.

Barrett, P.M., & Turner, C. (2001). Prevention of anxiety symptoms in primary school children: Preliminary results from a universal school-based trial. *British Journal of Clinical Psychology, 40,* 399–410.

Barrett, P.M., Webster, H., & Turner, C. (2003). *Introduction to FRIENDS: A program for enhancing life skills promoting psychological resilience.* Bowen Hills, Queensland: Australian Academic Press Pty. Ltd.

Barrios, B.A., & Hartmann, D.P. (1988). Fears and anxieties. In E.J. Mash & L.J. Terdal (Eds.), *Behavioral assessment of disorders* (2nd ed., pp. 196–262). New York: Guilford Press.

Barron, A.P., & Earls, F. (1984). The relation of temperament and social factors to behavior problems in three-year-old children. *Journal of Child Psychology and Psychiatry, 25,* 23–33.

Bateman, B. (1992). Learning disabilities: The changing landscape. *Journal of Learning Disabilities, 25,* 29–36.

Baydala, L., Sherman, J., Rasmussen, C., Wikman, E., & Janzen, H. (2006). ADHD characteristics in Canadian Aboriginal children. *Journal of Attention Disorders, 9,* 642–647.

Bean, A.W., & Roberts, M.W. (1981). The effect of time-out release contingencies on changes in child non-compliance. *Journal of Abnormal Child Psychology, 9,* 95–105.

Bear, G.G. (1990). Models and techniques that focus on prevention. In A. Thomas & J. Grimes (Ed.), *Best practices in school psychology* (p. 652). Silver Spring, MD: National Association of School Psychologists.

Beidel, D.C. (1991). Social phobia and overanxious disorder in school age children. *Journal of the American Academy of Child and Adolescent Psychiatry, 30,* 545–552.

Belfiore, P.J., Grskovic, J.A., Murphy, A., & Zentall, S.S. (1996). The effects of antecedent color on reading for students with learning disabilities and co-occurring attention-deficit/hyperactivity disorder. *Journal of Learning Disabilities, 29,* 432–438.

Bender, W.N. (1997). *Understanding ADHD: A practical guide for teachers and parents.* Englewood Cliffs, NJ: Prentice Hall.

Bener, A., Al Qahtani, R., & Abdelaal, I. (2006). The prevalence of ADHD among primary school children in an Arabian society. *Journal of Attention Disorders, 10*(1), 77–82.

Berk, L.E., & Landau, S. (1993). Private speech of learning disabled and normally achieving children in classroom academic and laboratory contexts. *Child Development, 64,* 556–571.

Berliner, D.C. (1988). The half-full glass: A review of research on teaching. In E.L. Meyen, G.V. Vergason, & R.J. Whelan (Eds.), *Effective instructional strategies for exceptional children* (pp. 37–56). Denver, CO: Love Publishing.

Berninger, V.W. (1996). *Reading and writing acquisition: A developmental neuropsychological perspective.* Boulder, CO: Westview Press.

Berninger, V.W., & Abbott, R.D. (1994). Redefining learning disabilities: Moving beyond aptitude–achievement discrepancies to failure to respond to validated treatment protocols. In G.R. Lyon (Ed.), *Frames of reference for the assessment of learning disabilities: New views on measurement issues* (pp. 163–183). Baltimore: Paul H. Brookes Publishing Co.

Berninger, V., & Amtmann, D. (2003). Preventing written expression disabilities through early and continuing assessment and intervention for handwriting and/or spelling problems: Research into practice. In H.L. Swanson, K. Harris, & S. Graham (Eds.), *Handbook of research on learning disabilities* (pp. 345–363). New York: Guilford Press.

Berninger, V.W., Mizokawa, D., & Bragg, R. (1991). Theory-based diagnosis and remediation of writing disabilities. *Journal of School Psychology, 29*, 57–97.

Berninger, V., Rutberg, J., Abbott, R., Garcia, N., Anderson-Youngstrom, M., Brooks, A., et al. (2006). Tier 1 and Tier 2 early intervention for handwriting and composing. *Journal of School Psychology, 44*, 3–30.

Berninger, V.W., Vaughan, K., Abbott, R.D., Brooks, A., Begay, K., Curtin, G., et al. (2000). Language-based spelling instruction: Teaching children to make multiple connections between spoken and written words. *Learning Disability Quarterly, 23*, 117–135.

Bernstein, G.A., Layne, A.E., Egan, E.A., & Tennison, D.M. (2005). School-based interventions for anxious children. *Journal of American Academy of Child and Adolescent Psychiatry, 44*, 1118–1127.

Betts, E.A. (1946). *Foundations of reading instruction.* New York: American Book.

Biederman, J., Faraone, S.V., Mick, E., & Lelon, E. (1995). Psychiatric comorbidity among referred juveniles with major depression: Fact or artifact? *Journal of the American Academy of Child and Adolescent Psychiatry, 34*, 579–590.

Biederman, J., Faraone, S.V., Mick, E., Williamson, B.A., Wilens, T.E., Spencer, T.J., et al. (1999). Clinical correlates of ADHD in females. *Journal of the American Academy of Child and Adolescent Psychiatry, 38*, 966–975.

Biederman, J., Faraone, S.V., Milberger, S., Curtiss, S., Chen, L., Marrs, A., et al. (1996). Predictors of persistence and remissions of ADHD in adolescence: Results from a 4-year prospective follow-up study. *American Journal of Child and Adolescent Psychiatry, 35*, 343–351.

Biederman, J., Faraone, S.V., Milberger, S., Jetton, J.G., Chen, L., Mick, E., et al. (1996). Is childhood oppositional defiant disorder a precursor to adolescent conduct disorder? Findings from a 4-year follow-up study of children with ADHD. *Journal of the American Academy of Child and Adolescent Psychiatry, 35*, 1193–1204.

Biederman, J., Monuteaux, M., Mick, E., Spencer, T., Wilens, T., Silva, J., et al. (2006). Young adult outcome of attention deficit hyperactivity disorder: A controlled 10-year follow-up study. *Psychological Medicine, 36*, 167–179.

Biederman, J., Munir, K., Knee, D., Amermentano, M., Autor, S., Waternaux, C., et al. (1987). High rate of affective disorder in probands with attention deficit disorder in their relatives: A controlled family study. *American Journal of Psychiatry, 144*, 330–333.

Biemiller, A. (2004). Teaching vocabulary in the primary grades. In J.F. Baumann & E.J. Kame'enui (Eds.), *Vocabulary instruction: Research to practice* (pp. 28–40). New York: Guilford Press.

Biemiller, A. (2005, July). *Teaching vocabulary in the primary and upper elementary grades.* Paper presented at the meeting of the International Dyslexia Association's Special Conference, Research to Practice, Advances in Reading and Literacy, Washington, DC.

Birsh, J.R. (Ed.). (2005). *Multisensory teaching of basic language skills* (2nd ed.). Baltimore: Paul H. Brookes Publishing Co.

Bishop, D.V.M., & Adams, C. (1990). A prospective study of the relationship between specific language impairment, phonological disorders and reading retardation. *Journal of Child Psychology and Psychiatry, 31*, 1027–1050.

Blachman, B.A. (1994). Early literacy acquisition: The role of phonological awareness. In G.P. Wallach & K.G. Butler (Eds.), *Language learning disabilities in school-age children and adolescents* (pp. 253–274). New York: Merrill.

Blachman, B.A., Ball, E.W., Black, R., & Tangel, D.M. (2000). *Road to the code: A phonological awareness program for young children.* Baltimore: Paul H. Brookes Publishing Co.

Blachman, B.A., & Tangel, D.M. (2008). *Road to reading: A program for preventing & remediating reading difficulties.* Baltimore: Paul H. Brookes Publishing Co.

Blick, D.W., & Test, D.W. (1987). Effects of self-recording on high-school students' on-task behavior. *Learning Disability Quarterly, 10*, 203–213.

Block, J.H. (1977). Hyperactivity: A cultural perspective. *Journal of Learning Disabilities, 10*, 236–240.

Boder, E. (1973). Developmental dyslexia: A diagnostic approach based on three atypical reading patterns. *Developmental Medicine and Child Neurology, 15*, 663–687.

Boulineau, T., Fore, C., III, Hagan-Burke, S., & Burke, M.D. (2004). Use of story-mapping to increase the story-grammar text comprehension of elementary students with learning disabilities. *Learning Disabilities Quarterly, 27*, 105–121.

Bowen, R.C., Oxford, D.R., & Boyle, M.H. (1990). The prevalence of overanxious disorder and separation anxiety disorder: Results from the Ontario Child Health Study. *Journal of the American Academy of Child & Adolescent Psychiatry, 29*, 753–758.

Bowers, P.G., Sunseth, K., & Golden, J. (1999). The route between rapid naming and reading progress. *Scientific Studies of Reading, 3*, 31–53.

Bowers, P.G., & Wolf, M. (1993). Theoretical links between naming speed, precise timing mechanisms, and orthographic skill in dyslexia. *Reading and Writing: An Interdisciplinary Journal, 5,* 69–85.

Bowley, B., & Walther, E. (1992). Attention deficit disorders and the role of the elementary school counselor. *Elementary School Guidance and Counseling, 27,* 39–46.

Brabham, E., & Villaume, S. (2002). Vocabulary instruction: Concerns and visions. *Reading Teacher, 55,* 264–267.

Braswell, L., & Bloomquist, M.L. (1991). *Cognitive-behavioral therapy with ADHD children: Child, family and school interventions* (p. 210). New York: Guilford Press.

Breen, M.J., & Barkley, R.A. (1988). Child psychopathology and parenting stress in girls and boys having attention deficit hyperactivity disorder with hyperactivity. *Journal of Pediatric Psychology, 13,* 265–280.

Breier, A., Charney, D.S., & Heninger, G.R. (1984). Major depression in patients wtih agoraphobia and panic disorder. *Archives of General Psychiatry, 41,* 1129–1135.

Brendtro, L.K., Brokenleg, M., & Van Bockern, S. (1990). *Reclaiming youth at risk: Our hope for the future.* Bloomington, IN: National Educational Service.

Brent, D.A., Perper, J.A., Moritz, G., Allman, C., Friend, A., Roth, C., et al. (1993). Psychiatric risk factors for adolescent suicide: A case-controlled study. *Journal of the American Academy of Child and Adolescent Psychiatry, 32,* 521–529.

Brigham, T.A., Graubard, P.S., & Stans, A. (1972). Analysis of the effects of sequential reinforcement contingencies on aspects of composition. *Journal of Applied Behavior Analysis, 5,* 421–429.

Broca, P. (1861). Nouvelle observation d'aphemia produite par une lésion de la moitié posterieure des deuxième et troisième circonvolutions frontales [The novel observation of aphasia produced by a lesion in the second and third posterior frontal convolution]. *Bulletin de la Société Anatomie, 6,* 398–407.

Brooks, A., Vaughan, K., & Berninger, V. (1999). Tutorial interventions for writing difficulties: Comparison of transcription and text generation processes. *Learning Disability Quarterly, 23,* 183–190.

Brooks, R. (1991). *The self-esteem teacher.* Circle Pines, MN: American Guidance Service.

Brooks, R., & Goldstein, S. (2001). *Raising resilient children: Fostering strength, hope, and optimism in your child.* New York: Contemporary Books.

Brooks, R.B. (1999a). Creating a positive school climate: Strategies for fostering self-esteem, motivation, and resilience. In J. Cohen (Ed.), *Educating hearts and minds: Social emotional learning and the passage into adolescence* (pp. 61–73). New York: Teachers College Press.

Brooks, R.B. (1999b). Fostering resilience in exceptional children: The search for islands of competence. In V. Schwean & D. Saklofske

(Eds.), *Handbook of psychosocial characteristics of exceptional children* (pp. 563–586). New York: Kluwer Academic/Plenum Publishers.

Brooks, R.B. (2002). Creating nurturing classroom environments: Fostering hope and resilience as an antidote to violence. In S. Brock, P. Lazarus, & S. Jimerson (Eds.), *Best practices in school crisis prevention and intervention* (pp. 67–93). Bethesda, MD: NASP Publications.

Brooks, R.B. (2004). To touch the hearts and minds of students with learning disabilities: The power of mindsets and expectations. *Learning Disabilities: A Contemporary Journal, 2,* 9-18.

Brophy, J., & Good, T.L. (1986). Teacher behavior and student achievement. In M.C. Wittrock (Ed.), *Handbook of research on teaching* (3rd ed., pp. 311–361). New York: Macmillan.

Brown, A.L., & Palinscar, A.S. (1982). Inducing strategic learning from texts by means of informed self-control training. *Topics in Learning and Learning Disabilities, 2,* 1–18.

Bruck, M. (1993). Component spelling skills of college students with childhood diagnoses of dyslexia. *Learning Disability Quarterly, 16,* 171–184.

Brunsdon, R., Coltheart, M., & Nickels, L. (2005). Treatment of irregular word spelling in developmental surface dysgraphia. *Cognitive Neuropsychology, 22,* 213–251.

Bryan, T., & Nelson, C. (1994). Doing homework: Perspectives of elementary and junior high school students. *Journal of Learning Disabilities, 27,* 488–499.

Bryant, D.P., Goodwin, M., Bryant, B.R., & Higgins, K. (2003). Vocabulary instruction for students with learning disabilities. *Learning Disability Quarterly, 26,* 117–128.

Buchoff, R. (1990). Attention deficit disorder: Help for the classroom teacher. *Childhood Education, 67,* 86–90.

Bugental, D.B., Lyon, J.E., Lin, E.K., McGrath, E.P., & Binbela, A. (1999). Children tune out in response to the ambiguous communication style of powerless adults. *Child Development, 70,* 214–230.

Bullock, J. (1991). *TouchMath, The touchpoint approach for teaching basic math computation* (4th ed.). Colorado Springs, CO: Innovative Learning Concepts.

Burcham, B., Carlson, L., & Milich, R. (1993). Promising school-based practices for students with attention deficit disorder: Issues in the education of children with attentional deficit disorder (special issue). *Exceptional Children, 60,* 174–180.

Burchard, J.D., & Barrera, F. (1972). An analysis of time-out and response cost in a programmed environment. *Journal of Applied Behavioral Analysis, 5,* 271–282.

Burns, M.K., Dean, V.J., & Foley, S. (2004). Preteaching unknown key words with incremental rehearsal to improve reading fluency and comprehension with children identified as reading disabled. *Journal of School Psychology, 42,* 303–314.

Busch, B. (1993). Attention deficits: Current concepts, controversies, management and approaches to classroom instruction. *Annals of Dyslexia, 43,* 5–26.

Bushell, D. (1973). *Classroom behavior.* Englewood Cliffs, NJ: Prentice Hall.

Buzan, T. (1991). *Use both sides of your brain.* New York: Dutton.

Calfee, R.C. (1998). Phonics and phonemes: Learning to decode and spell in a literature-based program. In J.L. Metsala & L.C. Ehri (Eds.), *Word recognition in beginning literacy* (pp. 315–340). Mahwah, NJ: Lawrence Erlbaum Associates.

Calfee, R.C., Lindamood, P., & Lindamood, C. (1973). Acoustic–phonic skills in reading: Kindergarten through twelfth grade. *Journal of Educational Psychology, 64,* 293–298.

Campbell, K.U. (1998). *Great leaps reading program.* (4th ed.). Gainesville, FL: Diarmuid.

Campbell, K.U. (2005). *Great leaps reading program: Grades 3–5.* Gainesville, FL: Diarmuid.

Campbell, S.B., Endman, M.W., & Bernfeld, G. (1977). A 3-year follow-up of hyperactive preschoolers into elementary school. *Journal of Child Psychology and Psychiatry, 18,* 239–249.

Canino, F.J. (1981). Learned-helplessness theory: Implications for research in learning disabilities. *Journal of Special Education, 15,* 471–484.

Cantwell, D.P., & Baker, L. (1985). Psychiatric and learning disorders in children with speech and language disorders: A descriptive analysis. *Advances in Learning and Behavioral Disabilities, 4,* 29–47.

Cantwell, D.P., & Baker, L. (1991). Association between attention-deficit/hyperactivity disorder and learning disorders. *Journal of Learning Disabilities, 24,* 88–95.

Cantwell, D.P., Baker, L., & Mattison, R. (1981). Prevalence, type, and correlates of psychiatric disorder in 200 children with communication disorder. *Journal of Developmental and Behavioral Pediatrics, 2,* 131–136.

Caravolas, M., Snowling, M., & Hulme, C. (1999, April). *Emergent spelling: Initial skills and concurrent predictors.* Paper presented at the annual meeting of the Society for the Scientific Study of Reading, Montreal, Quebec, Canada.

Carbo, M. (1989). *How to record books for maximum reading gains.* New York: National Reading Styles Institute.

Carey, W.B. (1970). A simplified method for measuring infant temperament. *Journal of Pediatrics, 77,* 188–194.

Carlisle, J.F. (1993). Selecting approaches to vocabulary instruction for the reading disabled. *Learning Disabilities Research & Practice, 8,* 97–105.

Carlisle, J.F., & Rice, M.S. (2002). *Improving reading comprehension: Research-based principles and practices.* Timonium, MD: York Press.

Carlo, M.S., August, D., McLaughlin, B., Snow, C., Dressler, C., Lippman, D.N., et al. (2004). Closing the gap: Addressing the vocabulary needs of English-language learners in bilingual and mainstream classrooms. *Reading Research Quarterly, 39,* 118–215.

Carnine, D.W., Silbert, J., Kame'enui, E.J., & Tarver, S.G. (2004). *Direct instruction reading* (4th ed.). Upper Saddle River, NJ: Pearson.

Carr, E., & Ogle, D. (1987). K-W-L Plus: A strategy for comprehension and summarization. *Journal of Reading, 30,* 626–631.

Carreker, S. (2005). Teaching reading: Accurate decoding and fluency. In J.R. Birsh (Ed.), *Multisensory teaching of basic language skills* (2nd ed., pp. 141–182). Baltimore: Paul H. Brookes Publishing Co.

Carroll, J.B. (1993). *Human cognitive abilities: A survey of factor-analytic studies.* New York: Cambridge University Press.

Carver, R.P. (1990). *Reading rate: A review of research and theory.* San Diego: Academic Press.

Cass, M., Cates, D., Smith, M., & Jackson, C. (2003). Effects of manipulative instruction on solving area and perimeter problems by students with learning disabilities. *Learning Disabilities Research & Practice, 18,* 112–120.

Castellanos, F.X., Giedd, J.N., Marsh, W.L., Hamburger, S.D., Vaituzis, A.C., Dickstein, D.P., et al. (1996). Quantitative brain magnetic resonance imaging in attention-deficit hyperactivity disorder. *Archives of General Psychiatry, 53,* 607–616.

Castles, A., & Coltheart, M. (1993). Varieties of developmental dyslexia. *Cognition, 47,* 149–180.

Catts, H.W. (1993). The relationship between speech-language impairments and reading disabilities. *Journal of Speech and Hearing Research, 36,* 948–958.

Cawley, J.F., & Miller, J.H. (1986). Selected views on metacognition, arithmetic problem solving, and learning disabilities. *Learning Disabilities Focus, 2*(1), 36–48.

Cawley, J.F., Miller, J.H., & School, B.A. (1987). A brief inquiry of arithmetic word-problem-solving among learning disabled secondary students. *Learning Disabilities Focus, 2*(2), 87–93.

Chambless, D.L., & Ollendick, T.H. (2001). Empirically supported psychological interventions: Controversies and evidence. *Annual Review of Psychology, 52,* 685–716.

Chard, D.J., & Dickson, S.V. (1999). Phonological awareness: Instructional and assessment guidelines. *Intervention in School and Clinic, 34,* 261–270.

Chard, D.J., & Osborn, J. (1999a). Phonics and word recognition instruction in early reading programs: Guidelines for accessibility. *Learning Disabilities Research & Practice, 14,* 107–117.

Chard, D.J., & Osborn, J. (1999b). Word recognition instruction: Paving the road to successful reading. *Intervention, 34,* 271–277.

Chess, S., & Thomas, A. (1986). *Temperament in clinical practice*. New York: Guilford Press.

Clark, D.B., & Uhry, J.K. (1995). *Dyslexia: Theory and practice of remedial instruction* (2nd ed.). Timonium, MD: York Press.

Clark, L., & Elliott, S. (1988). The influence of treatment strength information on knowledgeable teachers' pre-treatment evaluations of social skills training methods. *Professional School Psychology, 3*, 241–251.

Cohen, J. (2006). Social, emotional, ethical, and academic education: Creating a climate for learning, participation in democracy, and well-being. *Harvard Educational Review, 76*, 201–237.

Cohen, L.S., & Biederman, J. (1988). Further evidence for an association between affective disorders and anxiety disorders: Review and case reports. *Journal of Clinical Psychiatry, 49*, 313–316.

Cohen, M.J., Sullivan, S., Minde, K.K., Novak, C., & Helwig, C. (1981). Evaluation of the relative effectiveness of methylphenidate and cognitive behavior modification in the treatment of kindergarten-aged hyperactive children. *Journal of Abnormal Child Psychology, 9*, 43–54.

Cohen, N.J., Davine, M., & Meloche-Kelly, M. (1989). Prevalence of unsuspected language disorders in a child psychiatric population. *Journal of the American Academy of Child and Adolescent Psychiatry, 28*, 107–111.

Collier, V.P. (1995). Acquiring a second language for school. *Directions in Language & Education National Clearinghouse for Bilingual Education, 1*(4). Retrieved May 1, 2007, from http://www.ncbe.gwu.edu/ncbepubs/directions/04.htm

Collier, V.P., & Thomas, W.P. (1989). How quickly can immigrants become proficient in school English? *Journal of Educational Issues of Language Minority Students, 5*, 26–38.

Coltheart, M. (1978). Lexical access in simple reading tasks. In G. Underwood (Ed.), *Strategies of information processing* (pp. 151–216). San Diego: Academic Press.

Conradt, J., & Essau, C.A. (2003, July). *Feasibility and efficacy of the FRIENDS program for the prevention of anxiety in children*. Paper presented at the 24th International Conference: Stress and Anxiety Research Society, Lisbon, Portugal.

Cooper, H., & Nye, B. (1994). Homework for students with learning disabilities: The implications of research for policy and practice. *Journal of Learning Disabilities, 27*, 470–479.

Corcos, E., & Willows, D.M. (1993). The processing of orthographic information. In D.M. Willows, R.S. Kruk, & E. Corcos (Eds.), *Visual processes in reading and reading disabilities* (pp. 163–190). Mahwah, NJ: Lawrence Erlbaum Associates.

Corkin, S. (1974). Serial-ordering deficits in inferior readers. *Neuropsychologia, 12*, 347–354.

Cornoldi, C., Rigoni, F., Tressoldi, P.E., & Vio, C. (1999). Imagery deficits in nonverbal learning disabilities. *Journal of Learning Disabilities, 32*, 48–58.

Costello, E.J., Erklani, A., & Angold, A. (2006). Is there an epidemic of child or adolescent depression? *Journal of Child Psychology & Psychiatry, 47*, 1263–1271.

Coyne, M.D., McCoach, B.D., & Kapp, S. (2007). Vocabulary intervention for kindergarten students: Comparing extended instruction to embedded instruction and incidental exposure. *Learning Disability Quarterly, 30*, 74–88.

Coyne, M.D., Simmons, D.C., & Kame'enui, E.J. (2004). Vocabulary instruction for young children at risk of experiencing reading difficulties: Teaching word meanings during shared storybook readings. In J.F. Baumann & E.J. Kame'enui (Eds.), *Vocabulary instruction: Research to practice* (pp. 41–58). New York: Guilford Press.

Critchley, M. (1964). *Developmental dyslexia*. Westport, CT: Heinemann.

Cromley, J.G., & Azevedo, R. (2007). Testing and refining the direct and inferential mediation model of reading comprehension. *Journal of Educational Psychology, 99*, 311–325.

Cruickshank, W.M. (1977). Least-restrictive placement: Administrative wishful thinking. *Journal of Learning Disabilities, 10*, 193–194.

Cummins, J. (1989). *Empowering minority students*. Sacramento, CA: California Association for Bilingual Education.

Cunningham, A.E., & Stanovich, K.E. (1998). The impact of print exposure on word recognition. In J.L. Metsala & L.C. Ehri (Eds.), *Word recognition in beginning literacy* (pp. 235–262). Mahwah, NJ: Lawrence Erlbaum Associates.

Cunningham, A.E., Stanovich, K.E., & Wilson, M.R. (1990). Cognitive variation in adult college students differing in reading ability. In T.H. Carr & B.A. Levy (Eds.), *Reading and its development: Component skills approaches* (pp. 129–159). San Diego: Academic Press.

Cunningham, P.M., & Cunningham, J.W. (1992). Making words: Enhancing the invented spelling–decoding connection. *Reading Teacher, 46*, 106–115.

Cunningham, P.M., & Hall, D.P. (1994). *Making words: Multilevel, hands-on, developmentally appropriate spelling and phonics activities*. Torrance, CA: Frank Schaffer.

Cunningham, P.M., Hall, D.P., & Cunningham, J.W. (2000). *Guided reading: The Four-Blocks way*. Greensboro, NC: Carson-Dellosa Publishing.

Curwin, R.L., & Mendler, A.N. (1988). *Discipline with dignity*. Reston, VA: Association for Supervision and Curriculum Development.

Curwin, R.L., & Mendler, A.N. (1997). Beyond obedience: A discipline model for the long term. *Reaching Today's Youth, 1*, 21–23.

Cutting, L.E., & Denckla, M.B. (2003). Attention: Relationships between attention-deficit hyperactivity disorder and learning disabilities. In H.L. Swanson, K.R. Harris, & S. Graham (Eds.), *Handbook of learning disabilities* (pp. 125–139). New York: Guilford Press.

Daigneault, S., Braun, C.M.J., & Whitaker, H.A. (1992). An empirical test of two opposing theoretical models of prefrontal function. *Brain and Cognition, 19*, 48–71.

Danziger, S., & Danziger, S. (1993). Child poverty and public policy: Toward a comprehensive anti-poverty agenda. *Daedelus, 122*, 57–84.

Das, J.P. (1980). Planning: Theoretical considerations and empirical evidence. *Psychological Research* (W. Germany), *41*, 141–151.

Das, J.P., Kar, B.C., & Parrila, R.K. (1996). *Cognitive planning: The psychological basis of intelligent behavior.* Thousand Oaks, CA: Sage Publications.

Das, J.P., Naglieri, J.A., & Kirby, J.R. (1994). *Assessment of cognitive processes.* Needham Heights, MA: Allyn & Bacon.

Davey, B. (1983). Think-aloud: Modeling the cognitive processes for reading comprehension. *Journal of Reading, 27*, 44–47.

Davis, L., Sirotowitz, S., & Parker, H.D. (1996). *Study strategies made easy: A practical plan for school success.* Plantation, FL: Specialty Press.

Deci, E.L., & Flaste, R. (1995). *Why we do what we do: Understanding self-motivation.* New York: Penguin Books.

DeFries, J.C., Olson, R.K., Pennington, B.F., & Smith, S.D. (1991). The Colorado Reading Project: An update. In D.D. Duane & D.B. Gray (Eds.), *The reading brain: The biological basis of dyslexia* (pp. 53–87). Timonium, MD: York Press.

Dehn, M.J. (2006). *Essentials of processing assessment.* New York: Wiley.

de la Paz, S. (1999). Composing via dictation and speech recognition systems: Compensatory technology for students with learning disabilities. *Learning Disability Quarterly, 22*, 173–182.

Denckla, M.B. (1972). Clinical syndromes in learning disabilities: The case for splitting versus lumping. *Journal of Learning Disabilities, 5*, 401–406.

Denckla, M.B. (1979). Childhood learning disabilities. In K.M. Heilman & E. Valenstein (Eds.), *Clinical neuropsychology* (pp. 535–573). New York: Oxford University Press.

Denckla, M.B., & Cutting, L.E. (1999). History and significance of rapid automatized naming. *Annals of Dyslexia, 49*, 29–42.

Denckla, M.B., & Rudel, R. (1974). Rapid automatized naming of pictured objects, colors, letters and numbers by normal children. *Cortex, 10*, 186–202.

Deshler, D.D., Ellis, E.S., & Lenz, B.K. (1996). *Teaching adolescents with learning disabilities: Strategies and methods* (2nd ed.). Denver, CO: Love Publishing.

Diamond, L., & Gutlohn, L. (2006). *Teaching vocabulary.* Retrieved December 13, 2006, from http://www.ldonline.org/article/9943

Dickinson, D.K., Anastasopoulos, L., McCabe, A., Peisner-Feinberg, E.S., & Poe, M.D. (2003). The comprehensive language approach to early literacy: The interrelationships among, vocabulary, phonological sensitivity, and print knowledge among preschool-aged children. *Journal of Educational Psychology, 95*, 465–481.

Dickinson, D.K., & McCabe, A. (2001). Bringing it all together: The multiple origins, skills and environmental supports of early literacy. *Learning Disabilities Research & Practice, 16*, 186–202.

Dickstein, D.P., Garvey, M., Pradella, A.G., Greenstein, D.K., Sharp, W.S., Castellanos, F.X., et al. (2005). Neurologic examination of abnormalities in children with bipolar disorder or ADHD. *Biological Psychiatry, 58*, 517–524.

Diller, L. (1998). *Running on Ritalin.* New York: Bantam.

Diller, L.N. (2006a). Science, ethics and the psychosocial treatment of ADHD: Editorial. *Journal of Attention Disorders, 9*, 571–574.

Diller, L.N. (2006b). *Last normal child.* Westport, CT: Greenwood Publishing Group.

Doehring, D.G. (1968). *Patterns of impairment in specific reading disability.* Bloomington, IN: University Press.

Dolch, E.W. (1939). *A manual for remedial reading.* Champaign, IL: Garrard Press.

Douglas, V.I. (1972). Stop, look and listen: The problem of sustained attention and impulse control in hyperactive and normal children. *Canadian Journal of Behavioral Science, 4*, 259–282.

Douglas, V.I. (1983). Attentional and cognitive problems. In M. Rutter (Ed.), *Developmental neuropsychiatry* (pp. 280–329). New York: Guilford Press.

Douglas, V.I. (1985). The response of ADD children to reinforcement: Theoretical and clinical implications. In L.N. Bloomingdale (Ed.), *Attention deficit disorder: Identification, course and rationale* (pp. 87–99). Jamaica, NY: Spectrum.

Douglas, V.I., Barr, R.G., O'Neil, M.E., & Britton, B.G. (1986). Short-term effects of methylphenidate on the cognitive, learning, and academic performance of children with attention deficit disorder in the laboratory and classroom. *Journal of Child Psychology and Psychiatry, 27*, 191–211.

Douglas, V.I., & Parry, P.A. (1983). Effects of reward on delayed reaction time task performance of hyperactive children. *Journal of Abnormal Child Psychology, 11*, 313–326.

Douglas, V.I., & Peters, K.G. (1979). Toward a clear definition of the attentional deficit of hyperactive children. In G.A. Hale & M. Lewis (Eds.), *Attention and the development of cognitive skills* (pp. 41–62). New York: Kluwer Academic/Plenum Publishers.

Douglass, B. (1984). Variation on a theme: Writing with the LD adolescent. *Academic Therapy, 19,* 361–363.

Downing, J. (1973). *Comparative reading: Cross national studies of behavior and processes in reading and writing.* New York: Macmillan.

Dunlap, G., & Kern, L. (1996). Modifying instructional activities to promote desirable behavior: A conceptual and practical framework. *School Psychology Quarterly, 11,* 297–312.

Dunlap, G., Kern-Dunlap, L., Clarke, S., & Robbins, F.R. (1991). Functional assessment, curricular revision, and severe behavior problems. *Journal of Applied Behavior Analysis, 24,* 387–397.

DuPaul, G.J. (1991). Attention-deficit hyperactivity disorder: Classroom intervention strategies. *School Psychology International, 12,* 85–94.

DuPaul, G.J., Guevremont, D.C., & Barkley, R.A. (1992). Behavioral treatment of attention-deficit/hyperactivity disorder in the classroom. The use of the attention training systems. Treatment of children with attention-deficit/hyperactivity disorder (ADHD) (Special issue). *Behavior Modification, 16,* 204–225.

DuPaul, G.J., & Henningson, P.N. (1993). Peer tutoring effects on the classroom performance of children with ADHD. *School Psychology Review, 22,* 134–143.

DuPaul, G.J., & Rapport, M.D. (1993). Does methylphenidate normalize the classroom performance of children with attention deficit disorder? *Journal of the American Academy of Child and Adolescent Psychiatry, 32,* 190–198.

DuPaul, G.J., & Stoner, G.D. (2003). *ADHD in the schools* (2nd ed.). New York: Guilford Press.

Edelbrock, C., Rende, R., Plomin, R., & Thompson, L.A. (1995). A twin study of competence and problem behavior in childhood and early adolescence. *Journal of Child Psychology and Psychiatry, 36,* 775–785.

Edelen-Smith, P.J. (1997). How now brown cow: Phoneme awareness activities for collaborative classrooms. *Intervention in School and Clinic, 33,* 103–111.

Education for All Handicapped Children Act of 1975, PL 94-142, 20 U.S.C. §§ 1400 *et seq.*

Eggen, P.D., & Kauchak, D. (1992). *Educational psychology: Classroom connections.* New York: Macmillan.

Ehri, L.C. (1986). Sources of difficulty in learning to read and spell. In M.L. Wolraich & D. Routh (Eds.), *Advances in developmental and behavioral pediatrics* (pp. 121–195). Greenwich, CT: JAI Press.

Ehri, L.C. (1989). The development of spelling knowledge and its role in reading acquisition and reading disability. *Journal of Learning Disabilities, 22,* 356–365.

Ehri, L.C. (1994). Development of the ability to read words: Update. In R. Ruddell, M. Ruddell, & H. Singer (Eds.), *Theoretical models and processes of reading* (4th ed., pp. 323–358). Newark, DE: International Reading Association.

Ehri, L.C. (1997). Learning to read and learning to spell are one and the same, almost. In C.A. Perfetti, L. Rieben, & M. Fayol (Eds.), *Learning to spell: Research, theory, and practice across languages* (pp. 237–270). Mahwah, NJ: Lawrence Erlbaum Associates.

Ehri, L.C. (1998). Grapheme–phoneme knowledge is essential for learning to read words in English. In J.L. Metsala & L.C. Ehri (Eds.), *Word recognition in beginning literacy* (pp. 3–40). Mahwah, NJ: Lawrence Erlbaum Associates.

Ehri, L.C. (2000). Learning to read and learning to spell: Two sides of a coin. *Topics in Language Disorders, 20*(3), 19–36.

Ehri, L.C. (2005). Learning to read words: Theory, findings, and issues. *Scientific Studies of Reading, 9,* 167–188.

Ehri, L.C. (2006). Alphabetics instruction helps students learn to read. In R.M. Joshi & P.G. Aaron (Eds.), *Handbook of orthography and literacy* (pp. 649–677). Mahwah, NJ: Lawrence Erlbaum Associates.

Elia, J., Borcherding, B.G., Rapoport, J.L., & Keysor, C.S. (1991). Methylphenidate and dextroamphetamine treatments of hyperactivity: Are there true nonresponders? *Psychiatry Research, 36*(2), 141–155.

Elias, M.J., Zins, J.E., Graczyk, P.A., & Weissberg, R.B. (2003). Implementation, sustainability and scaling up of social, emotional and academic innovations in public schools. *School Psychology Review, 32,* 303–319.

Elkonin, D.B. (1973). U.S.S.R. In J. Downing (Ed.), *Comparative reading: Cross national studies of behavior and processes in reading and writing* (pp. 551–579). New York: Macmillan.

Ellis, A.W. (1985). The cognitive neuropsychology of developmental (and acquired) dyslexia: A critical survey. *Cognitive Neuropsychology, 2,* 169–205.

Ellis, E.S. (1994). An instructional model for integrating content-area instruction with cognitive strategy instruction. *Reading and Writing Quarterly: Overcoming Learning Difficulties, 1,* 63–90.

Englert, C.S. (1990). Unraveling the mysteries of writing through strategy instruction. In T.E. Scruggs & B.Y.L. Wong (Eds.), *Intervention research in learning disabilities* (pp. 186–223). New York: Springer-Verlag.

Englert, C.S. (1992). Writing instruction from a sociocultural perspective: The holistic, dialogic, and social enterprise of writing. *Journal of Learning Disabilities, 25,* 153–172.

Englert, C.S., Hiebert, E.H., & Stewart, S.R. (1985). Spelling unfamiliar words by an analogy strategy. *Journal of Special Education, 19*, 291–306.

Englert, C.S., & Lichter, A. (1982). Using statement-pie to teach reading and writing skills. *Teaching Exceptional Children, 14*(5), 164–170.

Englert, C.S., & Mariage, T.V. (1991). Shared understandings: Structuring the writing experience through dialogue. *Journal of Learning Disabilities, 24*, 330–342.

Englert, C.S., & Raphael, T.E. (1989). Developing successful writers through cognitive strategy instruction. In J. Brophy (Ed.), *Advances in research on teaching* (Vol. 1, pp. 105–151). Greenwich, CT: JAI Press.

Englert, C.S., Raphael, T.E., Anderson, L.M., Anthony, H.M., & Stevens, D.D. (1991). Making strategies and self-talk visible: Writing instruction in regular and special education classrooms. *American Educational Research Journal, 23*, 337–372.

Ernst, M., Cohen, R.M., Liebenauer, L.L., Jons, P.H., & Zametkin, A.J. (1997). Cerebral glucose metabolism in adolescent girls with attention-deficit/hyperactivity disorder. *Journal of the American Academy of Child and Adolescent Psychiatry, 36*, 1399–1406.

Essau, C.A., Conradt, J., & Petermann, F. (2000). Course and outcome of anxiety disorders in adolescents. *Journal of Anxiety Disorders, 16*, 67–82.

Evans, E.B., Beardslee, W., Biederman, J., Brent, D., Charney, D., Coyle, J., et al. (2005). Depression and bipolar disorder. In D.L. Evans, E.B. Foa, R.E. Gur, H. Hendin, C.P. O'Brien, M.E.P. Seligman, et al. (Eds.), *What we know and what we don't know: A research agenda for improving the mental health of our youth* (pp. 161–182). New York: Oxford University Press.

Evans, J.J., Floyd, R.G., McGrew, K.S., & Leforgee, M.H. (2002). The relations between measures of Cattell-Horn-Carroll (CHC) cognitive abilities and reading achievement during childhood and adolescence, *School Psychology Review, 31*, 246–262.

Faraone, S.V., & Biederman, J. (2005). What is the prevalence of adult ADHD? *Journal of Attention Disorders, 9*, 384–391.

Faraone, S.V., Biederman, J., & Mick, E. (2006). The age dependent decline of ADHD: A meta-analysis of follow-up studies. *Psychological Medicine, 36*, 159–165.

Faraone, S.V., Perlis, R.H., Doyle, A.E., Smoller, J.W., Goralnick, J.J., Holmgren, M.A., et al. (2005). Advancing the Neuroscience of ADHD: Molecular genetics of attention-deficit/hyperactivity disorder. *Biological Psychiatry, 57*, 1313–1323.

Favell, J.E. (1977). *The power of positive reinforcement: A handbook of behavior modification.* Springfield, IL: Charles C Thomas.

Fay, J., Cline, F.W., & Sornson, B. (2005). *Meeting the challenge.* Golden, CO: Love and Logic Institute.

Feldman, R.A., Caplinger, T.E., & Wodarski, J.S. (1983). *The St. Louis conundrum: The effective treatment of antisocial youths.* Englewood Cliffs, NJ: Prentice Hall.

Felton, R.H. (1993). Effects of instruction on the decoding skills of children with phonological-processing problems. *Journal of Learning Disabilities, 26*, 583–589.

Felton, R.H., & Wood, F.B. (1989). Cognitive deficits in reading disability and attention deficit disorder. *Journal of Learning Disabilities, 22*, 3–13.

Felton, R.H., & Wood, F.B. (1992). A reading level match study of nonword reading skills in poor readers with varying IQ. *Journal of Learning Disabilities, 25*, 318–326.

Fergusson, D.M., & Horwood, L.J. (1993). The structure, stability and correlations of the trait components of conduct disorder, attention deficit and anxiety/withdrawal reports. *Journal of Child Psychology and Psychiatry and Allied Disciplines, 34*, 749–766.

Fernald, G.M. (1943). *Remedial techniques in basic school subjects.* New York: McGraw-Hill.

Fifer, F.L. (1986). Effective classroom management. *Academic Therapy, 21*, 401–410.

Fischer, C.W., Berliner, D.C., Filby, N.N., Marliave, R.S., Cahen, L.S., & Dishaw, M.M. (1980). Teaching behaviors, academic learning time and student achievement: An overview. In C. Denham & A. Liberman (Eds.), *Time and learning* (pp. 187–202). Washington, DC: National Institute of Education.

Fischer, P. (1999). Getting up to speed. *Perspectives (The International Dyslexia Foundation), 25*(2), 12–13.

Fisher, S.E., Francks, C., McCracken, J.T., McGough, J.J., Marlow, A.J., MacPhie, L., et al. (2002). A genomewide scan for loci involved in ADHD. *American Journal of Human Genetics, 70*, 1183–1196.

Fletcher, J.M. (1985). Memory for verbal and nonverbal stimuli in learning disability subgroups: Analysis by selective reminding. *Journal of Experimental Child Psychology, 40*, 244–259.

Fletcher, J.M., Francis, D.J., Shaywitz, S.E., Lyon, G.R., Foorman, B.R., Stuebing, K.K., et al. (1998). Intelligence testing and the discrepancy model for children with learning disabilities. *Learning Disabilities Research & Practice, 13*, 186–203.

Fletcher, J.M., Lyon, G.R., Fuchs, L.S., & Barnes, M.A. (2007). *Learning disabilities: From identification to intervention.* New York: Guilford Press.

Fletcher, J.M., Taylor, H.G., Levin, H.S., & Satz, P. (1995). Neuropsychological and intellectual assessment of children. In H. Kaplan & B. Sadock (Eds.), *Comprehensive textbook of psychiatry* (pp. 581–601). Baltimore: Williams & Wilkins.

Floyd, R.G., Evans, J.J., & McGrew, K.S. (2003). Relations between measures of Cattell-Horn-Carroll (CHC) cognitive abilities and mathematics achievement across the school-age years. *Psychology in the Schools, 60*, 155–171.

Foa, E.B., Costello, E.J., Franklin, M., Kagan, J., Kendall, P., Klein, R., et al. (2005). Anxiety Disorders. In D.L. Evans, E.B. Foa, R.E. Gur, H. Hendin, C.P. O'Brien, M.E.P. Seligman, et al. (Eds.), *What we know and what we don't know: A research agenda for improving the mental health of our youth* (pp. 161–182). New York: Oxford University Press.

Foorman, B.R. (2007). Primary prevention in classroom reading instruction. *Teaching Exceptional Children, 39*(5), 24–30.

Foorman, B.R., Seals, L.M., Anthony, J., & Pollard-Durodola, S. (2003). A vocabulary enrichment program for third and fourth grade African-American students: Description, implementation, and impact. In B.R. Foorman (Ed.), *Preventing and remediating reading difficulties: Bringing science to scale* (pp. 419–441). Timonium, MD: York Press.

Forehand, R., & McMahon, R. (1981). *Helping the non-compliant child.* New York: Guilford Press.

Forehand, R., & Scarboro, M.E. (1975). An analysis of children's oppositional behavior. *Journal of Abnormal Child Psychology, 3,* 27–31.

Foss, J.M. (1991). Nonverbal learning disabilities and remedial interventions. *Annals of Dyslexia, 41,* 128–140.

Fountas, I.C., & Pinnell, G.S. (1999). *Matching books to readers: Using leveled books in guided reading, K–3.* Westport, CT: William Heinemann.

Francis, G., Last, C.G., & Strauss, C.C. (1987). Expression of separation anxiety disorder: The roles of age and gender. *Child Psychiatry and Human Development, 18,* 82–89.

Frankenberger, W., & Fronzaglio, K. (1991). A review of states' criteria and procedures for identifying children with learning disabilities. *Journal of Learning Disabilities, 24,* 495–500.

Freebody, P., & Byrne, B. (1988). Word-reading strategies in elementary school children: Relations to comprehension, reading time, and phonemic awareness. *Reading Research Quarterly, 23,* 441–453.

Fry, E.B. (1977). *Elementary reading instruction.* New York: McGraw-Hill Book Company.

Fuchs, D., & Deshler, D.D. (2007). What we need to know about responsiveness to intervention (and shouldn't be afraid to ask). *Learning Disabilities Research & Practice, 22,* 129–136.

Fuchs, D., Fuchs, L.S., & Fernstrom, P. (1993). A conservative approach to special education reform: Mainstreaming through transenvironmental programming and curriculum-based measurement. *American Educational Research Journal, 30,* 149–177.

Fuchs, D., Mock, D., Morgan, P.L., & Young, C.L. (2003). Responsiveness-to-intervention: Definitions, evidence, and implications for the learning disabilities construct. *Learning Disabilities Research & Practice, 18,* 157–171.

Fuchs, L.S., Fuchs, D., & Hollenbeck, K.N. (2007). Extending responsiveness to intervention to mathematics at first and third grades. *Learning Disabilities Research & Practice, 22,* 13–24.

Fuchs, L.S., Hamlett, C.L., & Powell, S.R. (2003). *Math Flash* [Computer software]. (Available from: L.S. Fuchs, 328 Peabody, Vanderbilt University, Nashville, TN 37203).

Fuchs, L.S., & Vaughn, S.R. (2005). Response-to-intervention as a framework for the identification of learning disabilities. *Trainer's Forum: Periodical of the Trainers of School Psychologists, 25*(1), 12–19.

Fuster, J.M. (1989). A theory of prefrontal functions: The prefrontal cortex and the temporal organization of behavior. In J.M. Fuster (Ed.), *The prefrontal cortex: Anatomy, physiology, and neuropsychology of the frontal lobe* (pp. 1–32). New York: Raven Press.

Futtersak, M.W., O'Leary, S.G., & Abramowitz, A.J. (1989). *The effects of consistently and increasingly strong reprimands in the classroom.* Unpublished manuscript.

Gardner, F.E.M. (1992). Parent–child interaction and conduct disorder. *Educational Psychology Review, 4,* 135–163.

Gaskins, I.W. (1998). A beginning literacy program for at-risk and delayed readers. In J.L. Metsala & L.C. Ehri (Eds.), *Word recognition in beginning literacy* (pp. 209–232). Mahwah, NJ: Lawrence Erlbaum Associates.

Gathercole, S.E., & Pickering, S.J. (2000). Working memory deficits in children with low achievements in the national curriculum at 7 years of age. *British Journal of Educational Psychology, 70,* 177–194.

Geary, D.C. (2003). Learning disabilities in arithmetic: Problem-solving differences and cognitive deficits. In H.L. Swanson, K.R. Harris, & S. Graham (Eds.), *Handbook of learning disabilities* (pp. 199–212). New York: Guilford Press.

Geary, D.C. (2004). Mathematics and learning disabilities. *Journal of Learning Disabilities, 37,* 4–15.

Gentile, L. (2004). *The oracy instructional guide.* Carlsbad, CA: Dominie Press, Inc.

Gentry, J.R. (1982). An analysis of developmental spelling in GYNS AT WRK. *Reading Teacher, 36,* 192–200.

Gentry, J.R. (1984). Developmental aspects of learning to spell. *Academic Therapy, 20,* 11–19.

Gentry, J.R. (1987). *Spel ... is a four-letter word.* Westport, CT: Heinemann.

Gerber, A. (1993). *Language-related learning disabilities: Their nature and treatment.* Baltimore: Paul H. Brookes Publishing Co.

Gerber, P.J., & Ginsberg, R.J. (1990). *Identifying alterable patterns of success in highly successful adults with learning disabilities.* Washington, DC: Office of Special Education and Rehabilitation Services.

Geschwind, N. (1982). Why Orton was right. *Annals of Dyslexia, 32,* 13–30.

Gettinger, M. (1990). Best practices in increasing academic learning time. In T.R.

Kratochwill, S.N. Elliott, & P.C. Rotto (Eds.), *Best practices in school psychology* (pp. 565–592). Silver Spring, MD: National Association of School Psychologists.

Gillingham, A., & Stillman, B.W. (1973). *Remedial training for children with specific disability in reading, spelling, and penmanship.* Cambridge, MA: Educators Publishing Service.

Ginott, H. (1972). *Teacher and child.* New York: Avon Books.

Gittelman, R. (1984). Anxiety disorders in childhood. *Psychiatric Update, 3,* 410–418.

Glasgow, K.L., Dornbusch, S.M., Troyer, L., Steinberg, L., & Ritter, P.L. (1997). Parenting styles, adolescents' attributions, and educational outcomes in nine heterogeneous high schools. *Child Development, 68,* 507–529.

Glass, G.G. (1973). *Teaching decoding as separate from reading.* New York: Adelphi University.

Glasser, W. (1965). *Reality therapy.* New York: Harper & Row.

Glasser, W. (1997). A new look at school failure and school success. *Phi Delta Kappan, 78,* 596–602.

Glenn, P., & Hurley, S. (1993). Preventing spelling disabilities. *Child Language, Teaching, and Therapy, 9,* 1–12.

Glow, R.A., & Glow, P.H. (1980). Peer and self-rating: Children's perception of behavior relevant to hyperkinetic impulse disorder. *Journal of Abnormal Psychology, 8,* 471–490.

Goldberg, E. (2001). *The executive brain: Frontal lobes in the civilized mind.* New York: Oxford University Press.

Goldstein, S. (1995). *Understanding and managing children's classroom behavior.* New York: Wiley.

Goldstein, S. (1997). *Managing attention deficit disorder and learning disabilities in late adolescence and adulthood: A guide for practitioners.* New York: Guilford Press.

Goldstein, S. (1999). Attention-deficit/hyperactivity disorder. In C.R. Reynolds & S. Goldstein (Eds.), *Handbook of neurodevelopmental and genetic disorders* (pp. 154–184). New York: Guilford Press.

Goldstein, S. (2006). Is ADHD a growth industry? *Journal of Attention Disorders, 9,* 461–464.

Goldstein, S., & Brooks, R. (Eds.). (2005). *Handbook of resilience in children.* New York: Springer.

Goldstein, S., & Brooks, R. (2007). *Understanding and managing children's classroom behavior: Creating sustainable, resilient schools* (2nd ed.). New York: Wiley.

Goldstein, S., & Goldstein, M. (1990). *Managing attention deficit disorder in children: A guide for practitioners.* New York: Wiley.

Goldstein, S., & Goldstein, M. (1991). *It's just attention disorder: User's manual* (p. 64). Salt Lake City, Utah: Neurology, Learning, and Behavior Center.

Goldstein, S., & Goldstein, M. (1992). *Hyperactivity: Why won't my child pay attention?* New York: Wiley.

Goldstein, S., & Goldstein, M. (1998). *Understanding and managing attention-deficit/hyperactivity disorder in children: A guide for practitioners* (2nd ed.). New York: Wiley.

Goldstein, S., & Gordon, M. (2003). Gender issues and ADHD: Sorting fact from fiction. *The ADHD Report, 11*(4), 7–16.

Goldstein, S., & Jones, C.B. (1998). Managing and educating children with ADHD. In S. Goldstein & M. Goldstein (Eds.), *Understanding and managing attention-deficit/hyperactivity disorder in children: A guide for practitioners* (2nd ed., pp. 545–591). New York: Wiley.

Goldstein, S., & Mather, N. (1998). *Overcoming underachieving: An action guide for helping your child succeed in school.* New York: Wiley.

Goldstein, S., & Naglieri, J.A. (2006). The role of intellectual processes in the DSM-V diagnosis of ADHD: Editorial. *Journal of Attention Disorders, 10*(1), 3–8.

Goldstein, S., & Teeter-Ellison, A. (2002). *Clinician's guide to Adult ADHD: Assessment and intervention.* New York: Academic Press.

Good, T.L., & Brophy, J.E. (1994). *Looking in classrooms* (6th ed.). New York: Harper-Collins.

Good, T.L., & Grouws, D. (1977). Teaching effects: A process-product study in fourth grade mathematics classrooms. *Journal of Teacher Education, 28,* 49–54.

Goodman, G., & Poillion, M.J. (1992). ADD: Acronym for any dysfunction or difficulty. *Journal of Special Education, 26,* 37–56.

Goodwin, R.D., & Gotlieb, I.H. (2004). Panic attacks and psychopathology among youth. *Acta Psychiatrica Scandinavika, 109,* 216–221.

Goonan, B. (2003). Overcoming test anxiety: Giving students the ability to show what they know. In J.E. Wall & G.R. Walz (Eds.), *Measuring up: Assessment issues for teachers, counselors, & administrators* (pp. 257–272). Washington DC: Office of Educational Research and Improvement, U.S. Department of Education.

Gordon, M., Thomason, D., Cooper, S., & Ivers, C.L. (1991). Nonmedical treatment of ADHD/hyperactivity: The attention training system. *Journal of School Psychology, 29,* 151–159.

Gordon, S.D., & Davidson, N. (1981). Behavioral parent training. In N. German & L. Kriskern (Eds.), *Handbook of family therapy* (pp. 236–251). New York: Brunner/Mazel.

Goswami, U. (2006). Orthography, phonology, and reading development: A cross-linguistic perspective. In R.M. Joshi & P.G. Aaron (Eds.), *Handbook of orthography and literacy* (pp. 463–480). Mahwah, NJ: Lawrence Erlbaum Associates.

Goulandris, N.K., & Snowling, M. (1991). Visual memory deficits: A plausible cause of developmental dyslexia? Evidence from a single case study. *Cognitive Neuropsychology, 8,* 127–154.

Grace, K.E.S. (2007). *Phonics and spelling through phoneme-grapheme mapping.* Longmont, CO: Sopris West.

Graham, S. (1983). The effect of self-instructional procedures on LD students' handwriting performance. *Learning Disability Quarterly, 6*, 231–234.

Graham, S. (1999). Handwriting and spelling instruction for students with learning disabilities: A review. *Learning Disability Quarterly, 22*, 78–98.

Graham, S., Berninger, V., Weintraub, N., & Schafer, W. (1997). The development of handwriting speed and legibility in grades 1 through 9. *Journal of Educational Research, 92*, 42–52.

Graham, S., & Harris, K.R. (1989). Components analysis of cognitive strategy instruction: Effects on learning disabled students' compositions and self-efficacy. *Journal of Educational Psychology, 81*, 353–361.

Graham, S., & Harris, K.R. (1999). Assessment and intervention in overcoming writing difficulties: An illustration from the Self-Regulated Strategy Development model. *Learning, Speech, and Hearing Services in Schools, 30*, 255–264.

Graham, S., & Harris, K. (2005). *Writing better: Effective strategies for teaching students with learning difficulties.* Baltimore: Paul H. Brookes Publishing Company.

Graham, S., & Madan, A.J. (1981). Teaching letter formation. *Academic Therapy, 16*, 389–396.

Graham, S., & Miller, L. (1980). Handwriting research and practice: A unified approach. *Focus on Exceptional Children, 13*(2), 1–16.

Graham, S., Weintraub, N., & Berninger, V. (1998). The relationship between handwriting style and speed and legibility. *Journal of Educational Research, 91*, 290–296.

Graves, A., & Montague, M. (1991). Using story grammar cueing to improve the writing of students with learning disabilities. *Learning Disabilities Research & Practice, 6*, 246–250.

Graves, A.W., Gersten, R., & Haager, D. (2004). Literacy instruction in multiple-language first-grade classrooms: Linking student outcomes to observed instructional practice. *Learning Disabilities Research & Practice, 19*, 262–272.

Graves, F. (2000). A vocabulary program to complement and bolster a middle-grade comprehension program. In B.M. Taylor, M.F. Graves, and P. Van Den Broek (Eds.), *Reading for meaning: Fostering comprehension in the middle grades* (pp. 116–135). New York: Teachers College Press.

Greene, G. (1999). Mnemonic multiplication fact instruction for students with learning disabilities. *Learning Disabilities Research & Practice, 14*, 141–148.

Greene, J.F. (2005). *LANGUAGE! The comprehensive literacy curriculum* (2nd ed.). Longmont, CO: Sopris West.

Greene, R. (1993). Hidden factors affecting the education success of ADHD students. *The ADHD Report, 2*, 8–9.

Greenhill, L.L., & Osman, B.B. (1991). *Ritalin: Theory and patient management.* Larchmont, NY: Mary Ann Liebert.

Grossen, B. (1997). *Thirty years of research: What we now know about how children learn to read.* Santa Cruz, CA: Center for the Future of Teaching & Learning.

Guevremont, D.C., DuPaul, G.J., & Barkley, R.A. (1993). Behavioral assessment of attention deficit hyperactivity disorder. In J.L. Matson (Ed.), *Handbook of hyperactivity in children* (pp. 150–168). Boston: Allyn & Bacon.

Haenlein, M., & Caul, W.F. (1987). Attention deficit disorder with hyperactivity: A specific hypothesis of reward dysfunction. *Journal of the American Academy of Child and Adolescent Psychiatry, 26*, 356–362.

Hagerman, R. (1991). Organic causes of ADHD. *ADD-VANCE, 3*, 4–6.

Hale, J.B., & Fiorello, A.A. (2004). *School neuropsychology: A practitioner's handbook.* New York: Guilford Press.

Hall, B.W., Hines, C.V., Bacon, T.P., & Koulianos, G.M. (1992, April). *Attributions that teachers hold to account for student success and failure and their relationship to teaching level and teacher efficacy beliefs.* Paper presented at the annual meeting of the American Educational Research Association, San Francisco.

Hall, N. (1987). *The emergence of literacy.* Portsmouth, NH: Heinemann.

Hallahan, D. (2007). Learning disabilities: Whatever happened to intensive instruction? *LDA Newsbriefs, 42*(1), 1, 3–5, 24.

Hallahan, D.P., & Sapona, R. (1983). Self-monitoring of attention with learning-disabled children: Past research and current issues. *Journal of Learning Disabilities, 16*, 616–620.

Hallenbeck, M.J. (1996). The cognitive strategy in writing: Welcome relief for adolescents with learning disabilities. *Learning Disabilities Research & Practice, 11*, 107–119.

Hallenbeck, M.J. (2002). Taking charge: Adolescents with learning disabilities assume responsibility for their own writing. *Learning Disability Quarterly, 25*, 227–246.

Hamlet, C.C., Axelrod, S., & Kuerschner, S. (1984). Eye contact as an antecedent to compliant behavior. *Journal of Applied Behavior Analysis, 17*, 553–557.

Hammill, D.D., Leigh, E., McNutt, G., & Larsen, S. (1981). A new definition of learning disabilities. *Learning Disability Quarterly, 4*, 336–342.

Hamstra-Bletz, L., & Blote, A.W. (1993). A longitudinal study on dysgraphic handwriting in primary school. *Journal of Learning Disabilities, 26*, 689–699.

Hanau, L. (1974). *The study game: How to play and win with statement-pie.* New York: Barnes & Noble.

Harnadek, M.C.S., & Rourke, B.P. (1994). Principal identifying features of the syndrome of nonverbal learning disabilities in children. *Journal of Learning Disabilities, 23*, 108–113.

Harrier, L.K., & DeOrnellas, K. (2005). Performance of children diagnosed with ADHD on selected planning and reconstitution tests. *Applied Neuropsychology, 12*, 106–119.

Hart, B., & Risley, T.R. (1995). *Meaningful differences in the everyday experience of young American children.* Baltimore: Paul H. Brookes Publishing Co.

Hart, E.L., Lahey, B.B., Loeber, R., Applegate, B., & Frick, P. (1995). Developmental change in attention deficit hyperactivity disorder in boys: A four-year longitudinal study. *Journal of Abnormal Child Psychology, 23*, 729–749.

Hasbrouck, J., & Tindal, G. (2005). *Oral reading fluency data.* Behavioral Research and Teaching. Eugene, OR: University of Oregon.

Hasselbring, T.S., Lott, A.C., & Zydney, J.M. (2005). *Technology-supported instruction for students with disabilities: Two decades of research and development.* Washington, DC: American Institutes for Research. Available at http://www.cited.org

Hayes, S.C., & Nelson, R.O. (1983). Similar reactivity produced by external cues and self-monitoring. *Behavior Modification, 7*, 193–196.

Hechtman, L. (1991). Resilience and vulnerability in long term outcome of attention deficit hyperactivity disorder. *Canadian Journal of Psychiatry, 36*, 415–421.

Heckelman, R.G. (1969). A neurological-impress method of remedial-reading instruction. *Academic Therapy, 4*, 277–282.

Heckelman, R.G. (1986). N.I.M. revisited. *Academic Therapy, 21*, 411–420.

Henderson, E.H. (1990). *Teaching spelling* (2nd ed.). Boston: Houghton Mifflin.

Hinshaw, S. (1992). Academic underachievement, attention deficits, and aggression: Comorbidity and implications for intervention. *Journal of Consulting and Clinical Psychology, 60*, 893–903.

Hinshelwood, J. (1895). Word-blindness and visual memory. *Lancet, 2*, 1564–1570.

Hinshelwood, J. (1902). *Congenital word-blindness with reports of two cases.* London: John Bale, Sons & Danielsson, Ltd.

Hinshelwood, J. (1917). *Congenital word-blindness.* London: Lewis.

Hobbs, N. (1966). Helping the disturbing child: Psychological and ecological strategies. *American Psychologist, 21*, 1105–1115.

Hobbs, S.A., Forehand, R., & Murray, R.G. (1978). Effects of various durations of time-out on the non-compliance and disruptive behavior of children. *Journal of Behavior Therapy and Experimental Psychiatry, 6*, 256–257.

Hohman, L.B. (1922). Post-encephalitic behavior disorders in children. *Johns Hopkins Hospital Bulletin, 33*, 372–375.

Horn, J.L., & Cattell, R.B. (1966). Refinement and test of the theory of fluid and crystallized intelligence. *Journal of Educational Psychology, 57*, 253–270.

Houten, R.V., Morrison, E., Jarvis, R., & MacDonald, M. (1974). The effects of explicit timing and feedback on compositional response rate in elementary school children. *Journal of Applied Behavior Analysis, 7*, 547–555.

Hughes, C.A., Schumaker, J., Deshler, D., & Mercer, C. (1988). *The test-taking strategy.* Lawrence, KS: Edge Enterprises.

Hughes, J., & Kwok, O. (2007). Influence of student–teacher and parent–teacher relationships on lower achieving readers' engagement and achievement in the primary grades. *Journal of Educational Psychology, 99*, 39–51.

Hulme, C. (1981). *Reading retardation and multisensory teaching.* London: Routledge & Kegan Paul.

Hundert, J. (1976). The effectiveness of reinforcement, response cost, and mixed programs on classroom behaviors. *Journal of Applied Behavior Analysis, 9*, 107.

Hurray, G. (1993). *A spelling dictionary for beginning writers.* Cambridge, MA: Educators Publishing Service.

Hutchinson, N.L. (1993). Effects of cognitive strategy instruction on algebra problem solving of adolescents with learning disabilities. *Learning Disability Quarterly, 16*, 34–50.

Hynd, G.W., Hern, K.L., Novey, E.S., & Eliopulos, D. (1993). Attention-deficit/hyperactivity disorder and asymmetry of the caudate nucleus. *Journal of Child Neurology, 8*, 339–347.

Individuals with Disabilities Education Act (IDEA) Amendments of 1997, PL 105-17, 20 U.S.C. §§ 1400 *et seq.*

Individuals with Disabilities Education Improvement Act (IDEA) of 2004, PL 108-446, 20 U. S. C. §§ 1400 *et seq.*

Ingalls, S.I. (1991). *Levels of processing related to learning disability and disability characteristics.* Unpublished manuscript.

Ingersoll, B., & Goldstein, S. (1993). *Attention deficit disorder and learning disabilities: Myths, realities and controversial treatments.* New York: Doubleday.

Ingersoll, B.D., & Goldstein, S. (1995). *Attention deficit disorder and learning disabilities: Realities, myths and controversial treatments.* New York: Doubleday.

Ingram, D. (1986). Phonological development: Production. In P. Fletcher & M. Garman (Eds.), *Language and acquisition* (pp. 223–239). Cambridge: Cambridge University Press.

Interagency Committee on Learning Disabilities. (1987). *Learning disabilities: A report to Congress.* Bethesda, MD: National Institutes of Health.

Isaacson, S.L. (1989). Role of secretary vs. author in resolving the conflict in writing instruction. *Learning Disability Quarterly, 12*, 200–217.

Iseman, J.S. (2005). *A cognitive instructional approach to improving math calculation of chil-*

dren with ADHD: Application of the PASS theory. Unpublished doctoral dissertation, George Mason University, Fairfax County, VA.

Iwata, B.A., & Bailey, J.S. (1974). Reward versus cost token systems: An analysis of the effects on students and teachers. *Journal of Applied Behavioral Analysis, 7,* 567–576.

Jacobson, R.H., Lahey, B.B., & Strauss, C.C. (1983). Correlates of depressed mood in normal children. *Journal of Abnormal Child Psychology, 11,* 29–40.

Jensen, P.S. (2000). Pediatric psychopharmacology in the United States: Issues and challenges in the diagnosis and treatment of attention-deficit/hyperactivity disorder. In L.L. Greenhill & B.B. Osman (Eds.), *Ritalin: Theory and practice* (2nd ed., pp. 1–3). Larchmont, NY: Mary Ann Liebert.

Jensen, P.S., & Cooper, J.R. (2004). *Attention deficit hyperactivity disorder: State of the science.* Kingston, NJ: Civic Research Institute.

Jensen, P.S., Kettle, L., Roper, M.T., Sloan, M.T., Dulcan, M.K., Hoven, C., et al. (1999). Are stimulants overprescribed? Treatment of ADHD in four U.S. communities. *Journal of the American Academy of Child and Adolescent Psychiatry, 38,* 797–804.

Jiron, C., Sherrill, R., & Chiodo, A. (1995, November). *Is ADHD being overdiagnosed?* Paper presented at the National Academy of Neuropsychology, San Francisco.

Jitendra, A.K., Edwards, L.L., Sacks, G., & Jacobsen, L.A. (2004). What research says about vocabulary instruction for students with learning disabilities. *Exceptional Children, 70,* 299–322.

Joffe, R., Dobson, K., Fine, S., Marriage, K., & Haley, G. (1990). Social problem solving in depressed, conduct disordered and normal adolescents. *Journal of Abnormal Child Psychology, 18,* 565–575.

Johnson, D.J. (1995). An overview of learning disabilities: Psychoeducational perspectives. *Journal of Child Neurology, 10*(1), 2–5.

Johnson, D.J., & Myklebust, H.R. (1971). *Learning disabilities: Educational principles and practices* (2nd ed.). New York: Grune & Stratton.

Johnson, L.V., & Bany, M.A. (1970). *Classroom management: Theory and skill training.* New York: Macmillan.

Johnson, S. (1997). *Taking the anxiety out of taking tests: A step-by-step guide.* Oakland, CA: New Harbinger Publications.

Jones, C.B. (1989, November/December). Managing the difficult child. *Family Day Caring,* 6–7.

Jones, C.B. (1991). *Sourcebook on attention disorders: A management guide for early childhood professionals and parents.* Tucson, AZ: Communication Skill Builders.

Jones, C.B. (1994). *Attention deficit disorder: Strategies for school-age children.* Tucson, AZ: Communication Skill Builders.

Jones, E.D., Wilson, R., & Bhojwani, S. (1997). Mathematics instruction for secondary students with learning disabilities. *Journal of Learning Disabilities, 30,* 151–163.

Joshi, R.M., Hoien, T., Feng, X., Chengappa, R., & Boulware-Gooden, R. (2006). Learning to spell by ear and by eye: A cross-linguistic comparison. In R.M. Joshi & P.G. Aaron (Eds.), *Handbook of orthography and literacy* (pp. 569–577). Mahwah, NJ: Lawrence Erlbaum Associates.

Kail, R., Hall, L.K., & Caskey, B.J. (1999). Processing speed, exposure to print, and naming speed. *Applied Psycholinguistics, 20,* 303–314.

Kame'enui, E.J. (1993). Diverse learners and the tyranny of time: Don't fix blame; fix the leaky roof. *The Reading Teacher, 46,* 376–383.

Kaplan, L. (1970). *Mental health and education.* New York: Harper & Row.

Kashdan, T.B., & Herbert, J.D. (2001). Social anxiety disorder in childhood and adolescence: Current status and future directions. *Clinical Child and Family Psychology Review, 4,* 37–62.

Katz, M. (1994, May). From challenged childhood to achieving adulthood: Studies in resilience. *CH.A.D.D.E.R.,* 8–11.

Katz, M. (1997). *Playing a poor hand well.* New York: W.W. Norton.

Kauffman, D. (2007). *What's different about teaching reading to students learning English?* Washington, DC: Center for Applied Linguistics.

Kauffman, J.M. (2005). *Characteristics of emotional and behavioral disorders of children and youth* (8th ed.). Upper Saddle River, NJ: Pearson.

Kauffman, J.M., & Wong, K.L.H. (1991). Effective teachers of students with behavioral disorders: Are generic teaching skills enough? *Behavioral Disorders, 16,* 225–237.

Kaufman, A.S., & Kaufman, N.L. (2004). *Kaufman Assessment Battery for Children—Second Edition.* Circle Pines, MN: American Guidance Service.

Kavale, K.A. (2005). Identifying specific learning disability: Is responsiveness to intervention the answer? *Journal of Learning Disabilities, 38,* 553–562.

Kavale, K.A., Kaufman, A.S., Naglieri, J.A., & Hale, J. (2005). Changing procedures for identifying learning disabilities: The danger of poorly supported ideas. *The School Psychologist, 59,* 16–25.

Kavanagh, J.F. (1988, October). *New federal biological definition of learning and attentional disorders.* Speech given at the 15th Annual Conference of the New York branch of the Orton Society.

Kazdin, A.E. (1982). The token economy: A decade later. *Journal of Applied Behavior Analysis, 15,* 331–346.

Kazdin, A.E. (1987a). *Conduct disorders in childhood and adolescence.* Newbury Park, CA: Sage Publications.

Kazdin, A.E. (1987b). Treatment of antisocial behavior in children: Current status and future directions. *Psychological Bulletin, 102,* 187–203.

Kazdin, A.E. (2000). *Behavior modification in applied settings* (6th ed.). Belmont, CA: Wadsworth Publishing.

Kazdin, A.E. (2003). Psychotherapy for children and adolescents. *Annual Review of Psychology, 54,* 253–276.

Kazdin, A.E., Sherick, R.B., Esveldt-Dawson, K., & Rancurello, M.D. (1985). Non-verbal behavior and childhood depression. *Journal of the American Academy of Child Psychiatry, 24,* 303–309.

Kearney, C.A., & Albano, A.M. (2004). The functional profiles of school refusal behavior. *Behavior Modification, 28,* 147–161.

Kearney, C.A., & Silverman,W.K. (1996). The evolution and reconciliation of taxonomic strategies for school refusal behavior. *Clinical Psychology: Science and Practice, 3,* 339–354.

Keeler, C.E., & Swanson, H.L. (2001). Does strategy knowledge influence working memory in children with mathematical disabilities? *Journal of Learning Disabilities, 34,* 418–434.

Keller, C.E., & Sutton, J.P. (1991). Specific mathematics disorders. In J.E. Obrzut & G.W. Hynd (Eds.), *Neuropsychological foundations of learning disabilities: A handbook of issues, methods, and practice* (pp. 549–571). San Diego: Academic Press.

Kendall, P.C., Hudson, J.L., Choudhury, M., Webb, A., & Pimentel, S. (2005). Cognitive behavioral treatment for childhood anxiety disorders. In E.D. Hibbs & P.S. Jensen (Eds.), *Psychosocial treatments for child and adolescent disorders: Empirically based strategies for clinical practice* (2nd ed., pp. 47–73). Washington, DC: American Psychological Association.

Kendall, P.C., Stark, K., & Adam, T. (1990). Cognitive distortion or cognitive deficit in childhood depression. *Journal of Abnormal Child Psychology, 18,* 255–270.

Kendall, P.C., & Watson, D. (1989). *Anxiety and depression: Distinctive and overlapping features.* New York: Academic Press.

Kennedy, L.M., & Tipps, S.J. (2000). *Guiding children's learning of mathematics* (9th ed.). Belmont, CA: Wadsworth/Thomson Learning.

Kennedy, L.M., Tipps, S., & Johnson, A. (2007). *Guiding children's learning of mathematics* (11th ed.). Belmont, CA: Wadsworth/Thomson Learning.

Keogh, B. (2003). *Temperament in the classroom: Understanding individual differences.* Baltimore: Paul H. Brookes Publishing.

Kerrigan, W.J. (1979). *Writing to the point: Six basic steps* (2nd ed.). New York: Harcourt Brace Jovanovich.

Kessler, R.C., Berglund, P., Demler, O., Jin, R., & Walters, E.E. (2006). Lifetime prevalence and age-of-onset distributions of DSM-IV disorders in the national comorbidity survey replication. *Archives of General Psychiatry, 62,* 593–602.

King, N.J., Heyne, D., Tonge, B.J., Gullone, E., & Ollendick, T.H. (2001). School refusal: Categorical diagnoses, functional analysis, and treatment planning. *Clinical Psychology and Psychotherapy, 8,* 352–360.

King, N.J., Muris, P., & Ollendick, T.H. (2005). Childhood fears and phobias: Assessment and treatment. *Child and Adolescent Mental Health, 10,* 50–56.

Kirk, S.A. (1962). *Educating exceptional children.* Boston: Houghton Mifflin.

Kirk, S.A., & Bateman, B. (1962/1963). Diagnosis and remediation of learning disabilities. *Exceptional Children, 29,* 73–78.

Kirk, S.A., Kirk, W.D., Minskoff, E.H., Mather, N., & Roberts, R. (2007). *Phonic reading lessons: Skills.* Novato, CA: Academic Therapy.

Kirk, S.A., McCarthy, J.J., & Kirk, W. (1968). *Examiner's manual: Illinois Test of Psycholinguistic Abilities* (Rev. ed.). Urbana: University of Illinois Press.

Kiser, L.J., Ackerman, B.J., Brown, E., Edwards, N.B., McGolgan, E., Pugh, R., et al. (1988). Post traumatic stress disorder in young children: A reaction to purported sexual abuse. *Journal of the American Academy of Child and Adolescent Psychiatry, 27,* 645–649.

Klingner, J., Sorrells, A.M., & Barrera, M.T. (2007). Considerations when implementing response to intervention with culturally and linguistically diverse students. In D. Haager, J. Klingner, & S. Vaughn (Eds.), *Evidence-based reading practices for response to intervention* (pp. 223–244). Baltimore: Paul H. Brookes Publishing Co.

Klingner, J.K., Vaughn, S., Hughes, M.T., Schumm, J.S., & Elbaum, B. (1998). Outcomes for students with and without learning disabilities in inclusive classrooms. *Learning Disabilities Research & Practice, 13,* 153–161.

Kollins, S.H., Lane, S.D., & Shapiro, S.K. (1997). Experimental analysis of childhood psychopathology: A laboratory analysis of the behavior of children diagnosed with ADHD. *Psychological Record, 47,* 25–44.

Korhonen, T.T. (1991). Neuropsychological stability and prognosis of subgroups of children with learning disabilities. *Journal of Learning Disabilities, 24,* 48–57.

Kosc, L. (1974). Developmental dyscalculia. *Journal of Learning Disabilities, 7,* 164–167.

Kovacs, M. (1983). *The children's depression inventory: A self-rated depression scale for school aged youngsters.* Unpublished manuscript, University of Pittsburgh.

Kovacs, M., Paulauskas, S., Gatsonis, C., & Richards, C. (1988). Depressive disorders in childhood: III. A longitudinal study of comorbidity with a risk for conduct disorders. *Journal of Affective Disorders, 15,* 205–217.

Kozulin, A. (2003). Psychological tools and mediated learning. In A. Kozulin, B. Gindis,

V. S. Ageyev, & S. M. Miller (Eds), *Vygotsky's educational theory in cultural context* (pp. 15–38). New York: Cambridge University Press.

Kreidler, W.J. (1984). *Creative conflict resolution*. Glenview, IL: Scott Foresman.

Kroesbergen, E.H., & Van Luit, J.E.H. (2003). Mathematics interventions for children with special educational needs. *Remedial and Special Education, 24*, 97–114.

Kroese, J.M., Hynd, G.W., Knight, D.F., Hiemenz, J.R., & Hall, J. (2000). Clinical appraisal of spelling ability and its relationship to phonemic awareness (blending, segmenting, elision, and reversal), phonological memory, and reading in reading disabled, ADHD, and normal children. *Reading and Writing: An Interdisciplinary Journal, 13*, 105–131.

Kunsch, C.A., Jitendra, A.K., & Sood, S. (2007). The effects of peer-mediated instruction in mathematics for students with learning problems: A research synthesis. *Learning Disabilities Research & Practice, 22*, 1–12.

Kussmaul, A. (1877a). Disturbances of speech. In H. von Ziemssen (Ed.) & J.A. McCreery (Trans.), *Cyclopedia of the practice of medicine* (p. 595). New York: William Wood.

Kussmaul, A. (1877b). Die Storungen der Sprache. Ziemssen's Handbuch d. Speciellen *Pathologie u. therapie, 12*, 1–300.

Lahey, B.B., Applegate, B., McBurnett, K., Biederman, J., Greenhill, L., Hynd, G., et al. (1994). DSM-IV field trial for attention-deficit/hyperactivity disorder in children and adolescents. *American Journal of Psychiatry, 151*, 1673–1685.

Lahey, B.B., Frick, P.J., Loeber, R., Tannenbaum, B.A., Van Horn, Y., & Christ, M.A.G. (1990). *Oppositional and conduct disorder: I. A meta-analytic review*. Unpublished manuscript. University of Georgia–Athens.

Lahey, B.B., Pelham, W.E., Loney, J., Lee, S., & Willcutt, E. (2005). Instability of the DSM-IV subtypes of ADHD from preschool through elementary school. *Archives of General Psychiatry, 62*, 896–902.

Lang, P.J. (1968). Fear reduction and fear behavior: Problems in treating a construct. In J.M. Shlien (Ed.), *Research in psychotherapy* (Vol. 3, pp. 90–102). Washington, DC: American Psychological Association.

Larsen, S.C. (1987). *Assessing the writing abilities and instructional needs of students*. Austin, TX: PRO-ED.

Last, C.G. (1989). Anxiety disorders of childhood or adolescence. In C.G. Last & M. Hersen (Eds.), *Handbook of child psychiatric diagnosis* (pp. 145–173). New York: Wiley.

Last, C.G., Hanson, C., & Franco, N. (1997). Anxious children in adulthood: A prospective study of adjustment. *Journal of the American Academy of Child and Adolescent Psychiatry, 36*, 645–652.

Last, C.G., Hersen, M., Kazdin, A.E, Finkelstein, R., & Strauss, C.C. (1987). Comparison of DSM-III separation anxiety and overanxious disorders: Demographic characteristics and patterns of comorbidity. *Journal of the American Academy of Child and Adolescent Psychiatry, 26*, 527–531.

Lavoie, R. (1994). *Last one picked, first one picked on* [Videotape]. (Available from PBS Video, P.O. Box 279, Melbourne, FL 32902 [800] 752–9727)

Layne, A.E., Bernstein, G.A., & March, J.S. (2006). Teacher awareness of anxiety symptoms in children. *Child Psychiatry and Human Development, 36*, 383–392.

Learning Disabilities Roundtable. (2005, February). *Comments and recommendations on regulatory issues under the Individuals with Disabilities Education Improvement Act of 2004, Public Law 108-446*. Retrieved January 15, 2007, from http://www.ncld.org/advocacy/pdf/2004LDRoundtableRecs.pdf

Leavell, A., & Ioannides, A. (1993, Summer). Using character development to improve story writing. *Teaching Exceptional Children (Special Edition)*, 41–45.

Lee, J. (2002). Racial and ethnic achievement gap trends: Reversing the progress towards equity. *Educational Researcher, 32*, 3–12.

Leitchman, H.M. (1993). *Attention deficit disorder subgroups: ADD outcome matrix*. Boston: Wediko Children's Services.

Leitenberg, H., & Callahan, E.J. (1973). Reinforcement practice and reductions of different kinds of fears in adults and children. *Behaviour Research & Therapy, 11*, 19–30.

Lerner, B. (1996). Self-esteem and excellence: The choice and the paradox. *American Educator, 20*, 14–19.

Lerner, J.W., & Kline, F. (2005). *Learning disabilities and related disorders: Characteristics and teaching strategies* (10th ed.). Boston: Houghton Mifflin.

Lerner, J.W., & Lowenthal, B. (1992). Attention deficit disorders: New responsibilities for the special educator. *Learning Disabilities, 4*, 1–8.

Lesaux, N.K. (2006). Building a consensus: Future directions for research on English language learners at risk for learning difficulties. *Teachers College Record, 108*, 2406–2438.

Lesaux, N.K., & Siegel, L.S. (2003). The development of reading in children who speak English as a second language. *Developmental Psychology, 39*, 1005–1019.

Levine, M. (1987). *Developmental variations and learning disorders*. Cambridge, MA: Educators Publishing Service.

Levine, M. (1990). *Keeping a head in school*. Cambridge, MA: Educators Publishing Service.

Levine, M.D. (2002). *A mind at a time*. New York: Simon & Schuster.

Liaupsin, C., Umbreit, J., Ferro, J.B., Urso, A., & Upreti, G. (2006). Improving academic engagement through systematic, function-based intervention. *Education and Treatment of Children, 29,* 573–592.

Liberman, I.Y. (1973). Segmentation of the spoken word and reading acquisition. *Bulletin of the Orton Society, 23,* 65–77.

Liberman, I.Y., & Shankweiler, D. (1985). Phonology and the problems of learning to read and write. *Remedial and Special Education, 6,* 8–17.

Liberman, I.Y., Shankweiler, D., & Liberman, A.M. (1989). The alphabetic principle and learning to read. In D. Shankweiler & I.Y. Liberman (Eds.), *Phonology and reading disability: Solving the reading puzzle* (pp. 1–33). Ann Arbor: University of Michigan Press.

Licht, B.G. (1983). Cognitive-motivational factors that contribute to the achievement of learning disabled children. *Journal of Learning Disabilities, 16,* 483–490.

Lieberman, L.M. (1992). Preserving special education . . . for those who need it. In W. Stainback & S. Stainback (Eds.), *Controversial issues confronting special education* (pp. 29–43). Boston: Allyn & Bacon.

Liebowitz, M.R., Gorman, J.M., Fyer, A.J., & Klein, D.F. (1985). Social phobia: Review of a neglected disorder. *Archives of General Psychiatry, 42,* 729–736.

Lienemann, T.O., Graham, S., Leader-Janssen, B., & Reid, R. (2006). Improving the writing performance of struggling writers in second grade. *Journal of Special Education, 40(2),* 66–78.

Lindamood, C.H., & Lindamood, P.C. (1998). *Lindamood phoneme sequencing program (LiPS) for reading, spelling, and speech.* Austin, TX: PRO-ED.

Lipka, O., Lesaux, N.K., & Siegel, L.S. (2006). Retrospective analyses of the reading development of grade 4 students with reading disabilities: Risk status and profiles over 5 years. *Journal of Learning Disabilities, 39,* 364–378.

Livingston, R., Lawson, L., & Jones, J.G. (1993). Predictors of self-reported psychopathology in children abused repeatedly by a parent. *Journal of the American Academy of Child and Adolescent Psychiatry, 5,* 948–953.

Lloyd, J.W., Landrum, T.J., & Hallahan, D.P. (1991). Self-monitoring applications for classroom intervention. In H.M Walker, M.R. Shinn & G. Stoner (Eds.), *Interventions for achievement and behavior problems* (pp. 310-311). Silver Spring, MD: National Association of School Psychologists.

Loeber, R. (1985). Patterns and development of antisocial child behavior. *Annals of Child Development, 2,* 77–116.

Loeber, R., Lahey, B.B., & Thomas, C. (1991). Diagnostic conundrum of oppositional defiant disorder and conduct disorder. *Journal of Abnormal Child Psychology, 100,* 379–390.

Lomas, B., & Gartside, P. (1999). ADHD in adult psychiatric outpatients. *Psychiatric Services, 5,* 705.

Loney, J., Kramer, J., & Milich, R. (1981). The hyperkinetic child grown up: Predictors of symptoms, delinquency and achievement at follow-up. In K.D. Gadow & J. Loney (Eds.), *Psychosocial aspects of drug treatment for hyperactivity* (pp. 181–211). Boulder, CO: Westview Press.

Lovett, M.W. (1987). A developmental approach to reading disability: Accuracy and speed criteria of normal and deficient reading skill. *Child Development, 58,* 234–260.

Lovett, M.W., Lacerenza, I., & Borden, S.I. (2000). Putting struggling readers on the PHAST track: A program to integrate phonological and strategy-based remedial reading instruction and maximize outcomes. *Journal of Learning Disabilities, 33,* 458–476.

Lowry-Webster, H.M., Barrett, P.M., & Dadds, M.R. (2001). A universal prevention trial of anxiety and depressive symptomatology in childhood: Preliminary data from an Australian study. *Behaviour Change, 18,* 36–50.

Lowry-Webster, H., Barrett, P., & Locke, S. (2003). A universal prevention trial of anxiety symptomatology during childhood: Results at one-year follow-up. *Behaviour Change, 20,* 25–43.

Luby, J., Heffelfinger, A., Mrakotsky, C., Hessler, M., Brown, K., & Hildebrand, T. (2002). Preschool major depressive disorder: Preliminary validation for developmentally modified DSM-IV criteria. *Journal of American Academy of Child and Adolescent Psychiatry, 41,* 928–937.

Luria, A.R. (1966). *Human brain and psychological processes.* New York: Harper and Row.

Luria, A.R. (1973). The origin and cerebral organization of man's conscious action. In S.G. Sapir and A.C. Nitzburg (Eds.), *Children with learning problems* (pp. 109–130). New York: Brunner/Mazel.

Luria, A.R. (1980). *Higher cortical functions in man* (2nd ed.). New York: Basic Books.

Lynch, J. (1998). *Easy lessons for teaching word families.* New York: Scholastic.

Lyon, G.R. (1995). Toward a definition of dyslexia. *Annals of Dyslexia, 45,* 3–27.

Lyon, G.R., Shaywitz, S.E., & Shaywitz, B.A. (2003). A definition of dyslexia. *Annals of Dyslexia, 53,* 1-14.

Lyon, G.R., & Watson, B. (1981). Empirically derived subgroups of learning disabled readers: Diagnostic characteristics. *Journal of Learning Disabilities, 14,* 256–261.

MacArthur, C.A., Schwartz, S.S., & Graham, S. (1991). A model for writing instruction: Integrating word processing and strategy instruction into a process approach to writing. *Learning Disabilities Practice, 6,* 230–236.

Maccini, P. (1998). *Effects of an instructional strategy incorporating concrete problem representation on the introductory algebra performance of secondary students with learning disabilities.* Unpublished dissertation, The Pennsylvania State University, University Park, PA.

Maccini, P., McNaughton, D., & Ruhl, K.L. (1999). Algebra instruction for students with learning disabilities: Implications from a research review. *Learning Disability Quarterly, 22*, 113–119.

Maccini, P., Mulcahy, C.A., & Wilson, M.G. (2007). A follow-up of mathematics interventions for secondary students with learning disabilities. *Learning Disabilities Research & Practice, 22*, 58–74.

Madsen, C.H., Becker, W.C., & Thomas, D.R. (1968). Rules, praise and ignoring: Elements of elementary classroom control. *Journal of Applied Behavior Analysis, 1*, 139–150.

Malone, L.D., & Mastropieri, M.A. (1992). Reading comprehension instruction: Summarization and self-monitoring training for students with learning disabilities. *Teaching Exceptional Children, 58*, 270–279.

Manis, F.R., Seidenberg, M.S., & Doi, L.M. (1999). See Dick RAN: Rapid naming and the longitudinal prediction of reading subskills in first and second graders. *Scientific Studies of Reading, 3*, 129–157.

Manis, F.R., Seidenberg, M.S., Doi, L.M., McBride-Chang, C., & Petersen, A. (1996). On the bases of two subtypes of development [sic] dyslexia. *Cognition, 58*, 157–195.

Mann, V.A. (2003). Language processes: Keys to reading disability. In H.L. Swanson, K.R. Harris, & S. Graham (Eds.), *Handbook of learning disabilities* (pp. 213–228). New York: Guilford Press.

Mannuzza, S., Klein, R.G., Bonagura, N., Malloy, P., Giampino, T.L., & Addalli, K.A. (1991). Hyperactive boys almost grown up: V. Replication of psychiatric status. *Archives of General Psychiatry, 48*, 77–83.

Manzo, A.V. (1969). The ReQuest procedure. *Journal of Reading, 13*, 123–126.

Manzo, A.V. (1985). Expansion modules for the ReQuest, CAT, GRP, and REAP reading/study procedures. *Journal of Reading, 28*, 498–502.

Marks, I.M. (1969). *Fears and phobias.* New York: Academic Press.

Marshall, J.C., & Newcombe, F. (1978). Patterns of paralexia: A psycholinguistic approach. *Journal of Psycholinguistic Research, 2*, 178–199.

Martin, R. (2005). The future of learning disabilities as federal laws change again. *Learning Disability Quarterly, 28*, 144–146.

Marton, P., Connolly, J., Kutcher, S., & Cornblum, M. (1993). Cognitive social skills and social self-appraisal in depressed adolescents. *Journal of the American Academy of Child and Adolescent Psychiatry, 32*, 739–744.

Marx, E., & Schulze, C. (1991). Interpersonal problem-solving in depressed students. *Journal of Clinical Psychology, 47*, 361–367.

Mastropieri, M.A. (1988). Using the keyword method. *Teaching Exceptional Children, 20*(2), 4–8.

Mastropieri, M.A., Leinart, A., & Scruggs, T.E. (1999). Strategies to increase reading fluency. *Intervention in School and Clinic, 34*, 278–283.

Mather, N. (1991). *An instructional guide to the Woodcock-Johnson Psycho-Educational Battery–Revised.* New York: Wiley.

Mather, N., Bos, C., Podhajski, B., Babur, N., & Rhein, D. (2000). *Screening of early reading processes.* Unpublished manuscript, University of Arizona–Tucson.

Mather, N., & Goldstein, S. (2001). *Learning disabilities and challenging behaviors: A guide to intervention and classroom management.* Baltimore: Paul H. Brookes Publishing Co.

Mather, N., & Gregg, N. (2006). Specific learning disabilities: Clarifying, not eliminating, a construct. *Professional Psychology, 37*, 99-106.

Mather, N., & Healey, W.C. (1990). Deposing aptitude–achievement discrepancy as the imperial criterion for learning disabilities. *Learning Disabilities: A Multidisciplinary Journal, 1*, 40–48.

Mather, N., & Jaffe, L. (2002). *Woodcock-Johnson III: Recommendations, reports, and strategies.* New York: Wiley.

Mather, N., & Kaufman, N. (2006). It's about the *what,* the *how well,* and the *why. Psychology in the Schools, 43*, 747–752.

Mather, N., & Roberts, R. (1995). *Informal assessment and instruction in written language: A practitioner's guide for students with learning disabilities.* New York: Wiley.

Mathers, M.E. (2006). Aspects of language in children with ADHD: Applying functional analyses to explore language use. *Journal of Attention Disorders, 9*, 523–533.

Mathes, P.G., & Fuchs, L.S. (1993). Peer-mediated reading instruction in special education resource rooms. *Learning Disabilities Research & Practice, 8*, 233–243.

Matson, J.L. (1989). *Treating depression in children and adolescents.* New York: Pergamon Press.

Mattis, S., French, J.H., & Rapin, I. (1975). Dyslexia in children and young adults: Three independent neuropsychological syndromes. *Developmental Medicine and Child Neurology, 17*, 150–163.

Mattison, R.E., & Bagnato, J. (1987). Empirical measurement of overanxious disorder in boys 8 to 12 years old. *Journal of the American Academy of Child and Adolescent Psychiatry, 26*, 536–540.

Maurer, A. (1965). What children fear. *Journal of Genetic Psychology, 106*, 265–277.

McArthur, G.M., Hogben, J.H., Edwards, V.T., Heath, S.M., & Mengler, E.D. (2000). On the "specifics" of specific reading disability and specific language impairment. *Journal of Child Psychology and Psychiatry, 41*, 869–874.

McCardle, P., Scarborough, H.S., & Catts, H.W. (2001). Predicting, explaining, and preventing children's reading difficulties. *Learning Disabilities Research & Practice, 16*, 230–239.

McCarney, S.B., & Cummins, K.K. (1988). *The pre-referral intervention manual: The most* common learning and behavior problems encountered in the educational environment. Columbia, MO: Hawthorne Educational Services.

McConville, D.W., & Cornell, D.G. (2003). Aggressive attitudes predict aggressive behavior in middle school students. *Journal of Emotional and Behavioral Disorders, 11,* 179–187.

McCoy, K.M., & Prehm, H.J. (1987). *Teaching mainstreamed students: Methods and techniques.* Denver, CO: Love Publishing.

McDaniel, T. (1980). Corporal punishment and teacher liability: Questions teachers ask. *Clearing House, 54,* 10–13.

McGee, R., & Share, D.L. (1988). Attention deficit hyperactivity disorder and academic failure: Which comes first and what should be treated? *Journal of the American Academy of Child and Adolescent Psychiatry, 27,* 251–259.

McGee, R., Silva, P.A., & Williams, S. (1984). Background characteristics of aggressive, hyperactive, and aggressive-hyperactive boys. *Journal of the American Academy of Child and Adolescent Psychiatry, 23,* 280–284.

McGee, R., & Stanton, W.R. (1990). Parent reports of disability among 13-year-olds with DSM-III disorders. *Journal of Child Psychology and Psychiatry and Allied Disciplines, 31,* 793–801.

McGrew, K.S. (2005). The Cattell-Horn-Carroll (CHC) theory of cognitive abilities: Past, present and future. In D. Flanagan, & P. Harrison (Eds.), *Contemporary intellectual assessment: Theories, tests, and issues* (2nd ed., pp.136–202). New York: Guilford Press.

McGrew, K.S., & Knopik, S.N. (1993). The relationship between the WJ-R *Gf-Gc* cognitive clusters and writing achievement across the life span. *School Psychology Review, 22,* 687–695.

McGuinness, C., & McGuinness, G. (1998). *Reading reflex: The foolproof phono-graphix method for teaching your child to read.* New York: The Free Press.

McKeown, M.G., & Beck, I.L. (2004). Direct and rich vocabulary instruction. In J.F. Baumann & E.J. Kame'enui (Eds.), *Vocabulary instruction: Research to practice* (pp. 13–27). New York: Guilford Press.

McLeer, S.V., Deblinger, E., Atkins, M.S., Foa, E.B., & Ralphe, D.L. (1988). Post traumatic stress disorder in sexually abused children. *Journal of the American Academy of Child and Adolescent Psychiatry, 27,* 650–654.

McNamara, J.J. (1972). Hyperactivity in the apartment bound child. *Clinical Pediatrics, 11,* 371–372.

Medco Health Solutions. (2005). ADHD medication use growing faster among adults than children. *New Research.* Retrieved December 2, 2005, from http://www.medco.com

Meese, R.L. (1994). *Teaching learners with mild disabilities: Integrating research and practice.* Pacific Grove, CA: Brooks/Cole.

Mehrabian, A., & Ferris, S.R. (1967). Inference of attitudes from nonverbal communication in two channels. *Journal of Consulting Psychology, 31,* 248.

Meichenbaum, D. (1977). *Cognitive-behavior modification: An integrative approach.* New York: Kluwer Academic/Plenum Publishers.

Meichenbaum, D. (1983). *Teaching thinking: A cognitive-behavioral approach.* Austin, TX: PRO-ED.

Meichenbaum, D. (1986). *Metacognitive methods of instruction: Current status and future prospects.* New York: Hawthorne Press.

Meichenbaum, D. (1990). Cognitive perspective on teaching self-regulation. *American Journal on Mental Retardation, 94,* 367–368.

Meltzer, L.J. (1994). Assessment of learning disabilities: The challenge of evaluating the cognitive strategies and processes underlying learning. In G.R. Lyon (Ed.), *Frames of reference for the assessment of learning disabilities: New views on measurement issues* (pp. 571–606). Baltimore: Paul H. Brookes Publishing Co.

Meltzer, L.J., Roditi, B., & Stein, J. (1998). Strategy instruction: The heartbeat of successful inclusion. *Perspectives (The International Dyslexia Foundation), 24*(3), 10–13.

Mendler, A.N. (1992). *What do I do when...? How to achieve discipline with dignity in the classroom.* Bloomington, IN: National Educational Service.

Mengler, E.D., Hogben, J.H., Michie, P., & Bishop, D. (2005). Poor frequency discrimination is related to oral language disorder in children: A psychoacoustic study. *Dyslexia, 11,* 155–173.

Menzies, R.G., & Clark, J.C. (1993). The etiology of childhood water phobia. *Behaviour Research & Therapy, 31,* 499–501.

Mercer, C.D. (1992). *Students with learning disabilities* (4th ed.). New York: Macmillan.

Mercer, C.D. (1995, March). *Perspectives on the future of learning disabilities: The main thing is to keep the main thing the main thing.* Paper presented at the Learning Disabilities Association of America International Conference, Orlando, FL.

Mercer, C.D., & Campbell, K.U. (1998). *Great Leaps reading program.* Gainesville, FL: Diarmuid.

Mercer, C.D., Campbell, K.U., Miller, M.D., Mercer, K.D., & Lane, H.B. (2000). Effects of a reading fluency intervention for middle schoolers with specific learning disabilities. *Learning Disabilities Research & Practice, 15,* 179–189.

Mercugliano, M., Power, T.J., & Blum, N.J. (1999). *The clinician's practical guide to attention-deficit/hyperactivity disorder.* Baltimore: Paul H. Brookes Publishing Co.

Merrell, K.W. (2002). Social-emotional intervention in schools: Current status, progress, and promise. *School Psychology Review, 31,* 143–147.

Meyer, M.S., & Felton, R.H. (1999). Repeated reading to enhance fluency: Old approaches and new directions. *Annals of Dyslexia, 49*, 283–306.

Meyer, M.S., Wood, F.B., Hart, L.A., & Felton, R.H. (1998). Selective predictive value of rapid automatized naming in poor readers. *Journal of Learning Disabilities, 31*, 106–117.

Milich, R., Ballentine, A.C., & Lynam, D.R. (2001). ADHD/combined type and ADHD predominantly inattentive type are distinct and unrelated disorders. *Clinical Psychology: Science and Practice, 8*, 463–488.

Milich, R., & Loney, J. (1979). The role of hyperactive and aggressive symptomatology in predicting adolescent outcome among hyperactive children. *Journal of Pediatric Psychology, 4*, 93–112.

Miller, C.J., Miller, S.R., Bloom, J.S., Jones, J., Lindstrom, W., Craggs, J., et al. (2006). Testing the double-deficit hypothesis in an adult sample. *Annals of Dyslexia, 56*, 83–102.

Miller, K. (2004). When Asperger's syndrome and a nonverbal learning disability look alike. *Pediatrics, 114*, 1458–1463.

Miller, L.C. (1983). Fears and anxieties in children. In C.E. Walker and M.C. Roberts (Eds.), *Handbook of clinical child psychology* (pp. 337–380). New York: Wiley.

Miller, P.M. (1972). The use of visual imagery and muscle relaxation in the counterconditioning of a phobic child: A case study. *Journal of Nervous and Mental Disease, 154*, 457–460.

Miller, S.P. (1996). Perspectives on mathematics instruction. In D.D. Deshler, E.S. Ellis, & B.K. Lenz (Eds.), *Teaching adolescents with learning disabilities* (2nd ed., pp. 313–367). Denver, CO: Love Publishing.

Miller, S.P., & Hudson, P.J. (2007). Using evidence-based practices to build mathematics competence related to conceptual, procedural, and declarative knowledge. *Learning Disabilities Research & Practice, 22*, 47–57.

Miller, S.P., & Mercer, C.D. (1997). Educational aspects of mathematics disabilities. *Journal of Learning Disabilities, 30*, 47–56.

Minskoff, E. (2005). *Teaching reading to struggling learners*. Baltimore: Paul H. Brookes Publishing Co.

Moats, L.C. (1991). Spelling disability in adolescents and adults. In A.M. Bain, L.L. Bailet, & L.C. Moats (Eds.), *Written language disorders: Theory into practice* (pp. 23–42). Austin, TX: PRO-ED.

Moats, L.C. (1995). *Spelling: Development, disability, and instruction*. Timonium, MD: York Press.

Moats, L.C. (2000). *Speech to print: Language essentials for teachers*. Baltimore: Paul H. Brookes Publishing Co.

Monroe, M. (1932). *Children who cannot read*. Chicago: University of Chicago Press.

Monroe, M., & Backus, B. (1937). *Remedial reading: A monograph in character education*. Boston: Houghton Mifflin.

Montague, M. (1997). Cognitive strategy instruction in mathematics for students with learning disabilities. *Journal of Learning Disabilities, 30*, 164–177.

Montague, M. (2003). *Solve it! A mathematical problem solving instructional program*. Reston, VA: Exceptional Innovations.

Montague, M. (2007). Self-regulation and mathematics instruction. *Learning Disabilities Research & Practice, 22*, 75–83.

Montague, M., & Graves, A. (1993). Improving students' story writing. *Teaching Exceptional Children, 25*(4), 36–37.

Montague, M., & van Garderen, D. (2008). Effective mathematics instruction. In R. Morris & N. Mather (Eds.), *Evidence-based interventions for students with learning and behavioral challenges* (pp. 236-257). New York: Routledge.

Moran, M.R. (1988). Reading and writing disorders in the learning disabled student. In N.J. Lass, L.V. McReynolds, J.L. Northern, & D.E. Yoder (Eds.), *Handbook of speech–language pathology and audiology* (pp. 835–857). Philadelphia: Brian C. Decker.

Morgan, D.P., & Jenson, W.R. (1988). *Teaching behaviorally disordered students: Preferred practices*. New York: Macmillan.

Morgan, W.P. (Nov. 7, 1896). Word blindness. *British Medical Journal, 1378*, 98.

Morris, R., Blashfield, R.K., & Satz, P. (1986). Developmental classification of reading-disabled children. *Journal of Clinical and Experimental Neuropsychology, 8*, 371–392.

Morris, R.D., Stuebing, K.K., Fletcher, J.M., Shaywitz, S., Lyon, G.R., Shankweiler, D.P., et al. (1998). Subtypes of reading disability: Variability around a phonological core. *Journal of Educational Psychology, 90*, 347–373.

Morris, R.J., & Kratochwill, T.R. (1983). *Treating children's fears and phobias: A behavioral approach*. Elmsford, NY: Pergamon Press.

Morris, R.J., Kratochwill,T.R., Schoenfield,G., & Auster, E.R. (in press). Childhood fears, phobias, and related anxieties. In R.J. Morris & T.R. Kratochwill (Eds.), *The practice of childhood therapy* (4th ed.). Mahwah, NJ: Lawrence Erlbaum & Associates.

Most, R., & Greenbank, A. (2000). Auditory, visual, and auditory-visual perception of emotions by adolescents with and without learning disabilities. *Learning Disabilities Research & Practice, 15*, 171–178.

Muenke, M. (2006). *The genetics of ADHD*. Presentation at the 19th annual meeting of Children and Adults with Attention Deficit Hyperactivity Disorder (CHADD), Chicago.

Muris, P., & Mayer, B. (2000). Early treatment of anxiety disorders in children. *Gedrag & Gezondheid: Tijdschrift voor Psychologie & Gezondheid, 28*, 235–242.

Muris, P., Merckelbach, H., deJong, P.J., & Ollendick, T.H. (2002). The etiology of specific fears and phobias in children: A critique of the non-associative account. *Behaviour Research & Therapy, 40,* 185–196.

Myklebust, H.R. (1965). *Development and disorders of written language* (Vol. 1). New York: Grune & Stratton.

Naglieri, J.A., & Das, J.P. (1997). Intelligence revised. In R. Dillon (Ed.), *Handbook on testing* (pp. 136–163). Westport, CT: Greenwood Press.

Naglieri, J.A., & Das, J.P. (2007). Planning, attention, simultaneous, successive (PASS) theory: A revision of the concept of intelligence. In D.P. Flanagan and P.L. Harrison (Eds.). *Contemporary intelligence assessment* (2nd Ed.) (pp. 136–182). New York: Guilford Press.

Naglieri, J., Goldstein, S., Iseman, J.S., & Schwebach, A. (2003). Performance of children with attention deficit hyperactivity disorder and anxiety/depression on the WISC-III and Cognitive Assessment System (CAS). *Journal of Educational Assessment, 21,* 32–42.

Naglieri, J.A., & Gottling, S.H. (1995). Mathematics instruction and learning disabilities. *Psychological Reports, 76,* 1343–1354.

Naglieri, J.A., & Gottling, S.H. (1997). Mathematics instruction in PASS cognitive processes: An intervention study. *Journal of Learning Disabilities, 30,* 513–520.

Naglieri, J.A., & Pickering, E.B. (2003). *Helping children learn: Intervention handouts for use in school and at home.* Baltimore: Paul H. Brookes Publishing Co.

Naglieri, J.A., Salter, C.J., & Edwards, G.H. (2004). Assessment of ADHD and Reading Disabilities Using the PASS Theory and Cognitive Assessment System. *Journal of Psychoeducational Assessment. 22,* 93–105.

National Advisory Committee on Handicapped Children. (1968, January 31). *Special education for handicapped children: First annual report.* Washington, DC: U.S. Department of Health, Education, and Welfare.

National Assessment of Educational Progress. (2003). *NAEP 2002 mathematics report card for the nation and states.* Princeton, NJ: Educational Testing Service.

National Center for Educational Statistics. (2006). *Public elementary/secondary school universe survey 2001–2002 and local education agency universe survey 2001–2002.* Washington, DC: U.S. Department of Education.

National Council of Teachers of Mathematics. (2000). *Principles and NCTM standards for school mathematics.* Reston, VA: Author.

National Joint Committee on Learning Disabilities. (2005). Responsiveness to intervention and learning disabilities. *Learning Disability Quarterly, 28,* 249–260.

National Reading Panel. (2000). *Report of the National Reading Panel. Teaching children to read: An evidence-based assessment of the scientific research literature on reading and its implications for reading instructions* (NIH Publication No. 00-4769). Washington, DC: U.S. Government Printing Office.

National Research Council, Committee on Education Intervention for Children with Autism, Division of Behavioral and Social Sciences Education. (2001). *Educating children with autism.* Washington, DC: National Academies Press.

Nelson, N.W., & Van Meter, A.M. (2006). The writing lab approach for building language, literacy, and communication abilities. In R.J. McCauley & M.E. Fey (Eds.), *Treatment of language disorders in children* (pp. 383–422). Baltimore: Paul H. Brookes Publishing Co.

Newby, R.F., Recht, D.R., & Caldwell, J.A. (1993). Validation of a clinical method for the diagnosis of two subtypes of dyslexia. *Journal of Psychoeducational Assessment, 11,* 72–83.

Newcomer, P.L. (2003). *Understanding and teaching emotionally disturbed children and adolescents* (3rd ed.). Austin, TX: PRO-ED.

NICHD Early Child Care Research Network. (2005). Pathways to reading: The role of oral language in the transition to reading. *Developmental Psychology, 41,* 428–442.

Nicholls, J.G., McKenzie, M., & Shufro, J. (1994). Schoolwork, homework, life's work: The experience of students with and without learning disabilities. *Journal of Learning Disabilities, 27,* 562–569.

Nigg, J.T., & Hinshaw, S.P. (1998). Parent personality traits and psychopathology associated with anti-social behaviors in childhood ADHD. *Journal of Child Psychology and Psychiatry, 39,* 145–159.

No Child Left Behind Act of 2001, PL 107-110, 115 Stat. 1425, 20 U.S.C. §§ 6301 *et seq.*

Norvell, N., & Towle, P.O. (1986). Self-reported depression and observable conduct problems in children. *Journal of Clinical Child Psychology, 15,* 228–232.

Novick, B.Z., & Arnold, M.M. (1988). *Fundamentals of clinical child neuropsychology.* New York: Grune & Stratton.

O'Connor, R.E., & Jenkins, J.R. (1999). Prediction of reading disabilities in kindergarten and first grade. *Scientific Studies of Reading, 3,* 159–197.

Ogle, D.M. (1986). K-W-L: A teaching model that develops active reading of expository text. *Reading Teacher, 39,* 564–570.

O'Leary, K.D., & O'Leary, S.G. (1977). *Classroom management: The successful use of behavior modification* (2nd ed.). Elmsford, NY: Pergamon Press.

Ollendick, T.H., King, N.J., & Frary, R.B. (1989). Fears in children and adolescents: Reliability and generalization ability across gender, age and nationality. *Behavior Research Therapy, 27,* 19–26.

Ollendick, T.H., King, N.J., & Muris, P. (2002). Fears and phobias in children: Phenomenology, epidemiology, and aetiology. *Child and Adolescent Mental Health, 7,* 98–106.

Ollendick, T.H., Matson, J.L., & Helsel, W.J. (1985). Fears in children and adolescents: Normative data. *Behavior Research and Therapy, 23,* 465–467.

Ollendick, T.H., Yang, B., King, N.J., Dong, Q., & Akande, A. (1996). Fears in American, Australian, Chinese, and Nigerian children and adolescents: A cross-cultural study. *Journal of Child Psychology and Psychiatry, 37,* 213–220.

Orton, J. (1966). The Orton-Gillingham approach. In J. Money (Ed.), *The disabled reader: Education of the dyslexic child* (pp. 119–145). Baltimore: Johns Hopkins University Press.

Orton, S.T. (1925). Word-blindness in school children. *Archives of Neurology and Psychiatry, 14,* 581–615.

Orton, S.T. (1937). *Reading, writing, and speech problems in children.* New York: W.W. Norton.

Osgood, C.E. (1957). Motivational dynamics of language behavior. In M.R. Jones (Ed.), *Nebraska symposium on motivation* (pp. 348–424). Lincoln: University of Nebraska Press.

Paine, S.C., Radicchi, J., Rosellini, L.C., Deutchman, L., & Darch, C.B. (1983). *Structuring your classroom for academic success.* Champaign, IL: Research Press.

Palinscar, A.S., & Brown, A.L. (1986). Interactive teaching to promote independent learning from text. *Reading Teacher, 39,* 771–777.

Pancheri, C., & Prater, M.A. (1999, March/April). What teachers and parents should know about Ritalin. *Teaching Exceptional Children,* 20–26.

Paolito, A.W. (1999). Clinical validation of the Cognitive Assessment System for children with ADHD. *The ADHD Report, 1,* 1–5.

Parker, R.N. (1992). *The ADD hyperactivity handbook for schools.* Plantation, FL: ADD Warehouse.

Patrick, H., Ryan, A.M., & Kaplan, A. (2007). Early adolescents' perceptions of the classroom social environment, motivational beliefs, and engagement. *Journal of Educational Psychology, 99,* 83–98.

Patterson, G.R. (1982). *Coercive family process.* Eugene, OR: Castalia Press.

Patterson, G.R. (1986). Performance models for antisocial boys. *American Psychologist, 41,* 432–444.

Pauk, W. (1993). *How to study in college.* Boston: Houghton Mifflin.

Pelham, W.E. (1986). The effects of psychostimulant drugs on learning and academic achievement in children with attention-deficit disorders and learning disabilities. In J.K. Torgesen & B.Y.L. Wong (Eds.), *Psychological and educational perspectives on learning disabilities* (pp. 333–364). San Diego: Academic Press.

Pelham, W.E., & Bender, M.E. (1982). Peer relationships in hyperactive children. In K.D. Gadow & I. Bialer (Eds.), *Advances in learning and behavioral disabilities* (Vol. 1, pp. 365–436). Greenwich, CT: JAI Press.

Pelham,W.E., Gnagy, E.M., Greenslade, K.E., & Milich, R. (1992). Teacher ratings of DSM-III-R symptoms for the disruptive behavior disorders. *Journal of the American Academy of Child and Adolescent Psychiatry, 31,* 210–218.

Pelham, W.E., & Milich, R. (1984). Peer relations of children with hyperactivity/attention deficit disorder. *Journal of Learning Disabilities, 17,* 560–568.

Pennington, B.F. (1991). *Diagnosing learning disorders: A neuropsychological framework.* New York: Guilford Press.

Perfetti, C.A. (1992). The representation problem in reading acquisition. In P.B. Gough, L.C. Ehri, & R. Treiman (Eds.), *Reading acquisition* (pp. 145–174). Mahwah, NJ: Lawrence Erlbaum Associates.

Perfetti, C.A., Marron, M.A., & Foltz, P.W. (1996). Sources of comprehension failure: Theoretical perspectives and case studies. In C. Cornoldi & J. Oakhill (Eds.), *Reading comprehension difficulties: Processes and intervention* (pp.137–165). Mahwah, NJ: Lawrence Erlbaum Associates.

Peterson, A.C., Compas, B.E., Brooks-Gunn, J., Stemmler, M., Ey, S., & Grant, K.E. (1993). Depression in adolescence. *American Psychologist, 48,* 155–164.

Peterson, K.C., Prout, M.F., & Schwarz, R.A. (1991). *Post-traumatic stress disorder: A clinician's guide.* New York: Kluwer Academic/Plenum Publishers.

Petrauskas, R., & Rourke, B.P. (1979). Identification of subgroups of retarded readers: A neuropsychological multivariate approach. *Journal of Clinical Neuropsychology, 1,* 17–37.

Pfiffner, L.J., & O'Leary, S.G. (1993). School-based psychological treatments. In J.L. Matson (Ed.), *Handbook of hyperactivity in children* (pp. 234–255). Boston: Allyn & Bacon.

Pfiffner, L.J., O'Leary, S.G., Rosen, L.A., & Sanderson, W.C., Jr. (1985). A comparison of the effects of continuous and intermittent response cost and reprimands in the classroom. *Journal of Clinical Child Psychology, 14,* 348–352.

Phillips, G.W. (1983). Learning the conservation concept: A metaanalysis (Doctoral dissertation, University of Kentucky). *Dissertation Abstracts International, 44,* 1990B. (University Microfilms No. 83-22983).

Pierrehumbert, B., Bader, M., Thévoz, S., Kinal, A., & Halfon, O. (2006). Hyperactivity and attention problems in a Swiss sample of school-aged children: Effects of school achievement. *Journal of Attention Disorders, 10*(1), 65–76.

Pinnell, G.S., & Fountas, I.C. (1998). *Word matters: Teaching phonics and spelling in the reading/writing classroom.* Westport, CT: William Heinemann.

Platzman, K.A., Stoy, M.R., Brown, R.T., Coles, C.D., Smith, I.E., & Falek, A. (1992). Review of observational methods in attention deficit hyperactivity disorder (ADHD):

Implications for diagnosis. *School Psychology Quarterly, 7,* 155–177.

Pliszka, S.R. (1992). Comorbidity of attention-deficit hyperactivity disorder and overanxious disorder. *Journal of the American Academy of Child and Adolescent Psychiatry, 31,* 197–203.

Polloway, E.A., Epstein, M.H., Bursuck, W.D., Madhavi, J., & Cumblad, C. (1994). Homework practices of general education teachers. *Journal of Learning Disabilities, 27,* 500–509.

Polloway, E.A., Epstein, M.H., & Foley, R. (1992). A comparison of the homework problems of students with learning disabilities and non-handicapped students. *Learning Disabilities: Research & Practice, 7,* 203–209.

Polloway, E.A., & Patton, J.R. (1993). *Strategies for teaching learners with special needs* (5th ed.). New York: Merrill.

Poznanski, E.O. (1982). The clinical phenomenology of childhood depression. *American Journal of Orthopsychiatry, 52,* 308–313.

Puig-Antich, J., & Rabinovich, H. (1986). Relationship between affective and anxiety disorders in childhood. In R. Gittelman (Ed.), *Anxiety disorders of childhood* (pp. 220–247). New York: Guilford Press.

Pynoos, R.S., Frederick, C., Nader, K., Arroyo, W., Steinberg, A., Eth, S., et al. (1987). Life threat and post-traumatic stress in school-age children. *Archives of General Psychiatry, 44,* 1057–1063.

Rack, J.P., Snowling, M.J., & Olson, R.K. (1992). The nonword reading deficit in developmental dyslexia: A review. *Reading Research Quarterly, 27*(1), 28–53.

Rapport, M.D. (1987). *The attention training system.* DeWitt, NY: Gordon Systems.

Rapport, M.D. (1989). The classroom functioning and treatment of children with ADHD: Facts and fictions. *CH.A.D.D.E.R., 3,* 4–5.

Rapport, M.D., Murphy, H.A., & Bailey, J.S. (1982). Ritalin vs. response cost in the control of hyperactive children: A within-subject comparison. *Journal of Applied Behavior Analysis, 15,* 205–216.

Read, C. (1971). Pre-school children's knowledge of English phonology. *Harvard Educational Review, 41*(1), 1–34.

Redd, W.H., Morris, E.K., & Martin, J.A. (1975). Effects of positive and negative adult–child interactions on children's social preferences. *Journal of Experimental Child Psychology, 19,* 153–164.

Rehabilitation Act Amendments of 1992, PL 102–569, 29 U.S.C. §§ *et seq.*

Reid, D.K. (1988). *Teaching the learning disabled: A cognitive developmental approach.* Boston: Allyn & Bacon.

Reid, R., Maag, J.W., & Vasa, S.F. (1994). Attention deficit hyperactivity disorder as a disability category: A critique. *Exceptional Children, 60,* 198–214.

Reiff, H.B., Gerber, P.J., & Ginsberg, R. (1993). Definitions of learning disabilities from adults with learning disabilities: The insiders' perspectives. *Learning Disability Quarterly, 16,* 114–125.

Reitsma, P. (1989). Orthographic memory and learning to read. In P.G. Aaron & R.M. Joshi (Eds.), *Reading and writing disorders in different orthographic systems* (pp. 51–73). New York: Kluwer Academic/Plenum Publishers.

Rhode, G., Jenson, W.R., & Reavis, H.K. (1992). *The tough kid book: Practical classroom management strategies.* Longmont, CO: Sopris West.

Richards, M.H., Boxer, A.M., Petersen, A.C., & Albrecht, R. (1990). Relation of weight to body in pubertal boys and girls from two communities. *Developmental Psychology, 26,* 313–321.

Richardson, E., & DiBenedetto, B. (1996). Identifying dyslexic students. In L.R. Putnam (Ed.), *How to become a better reading teacher: Strategies for assessment and intervention* (pp. 53–63). Englewood Cliffs, NJ: Prentice Hall.

Richardson, E., Kupietz, S., & Maitinsky, S. (1986). What is the role of academic intervention in the treatment of hyperactive children with reading disorders? *Journal of Children in Contemporary Society, 19,* 153–167.

Richardson, S.O. (1992). Historical perspectives on dyslexia. *Journal of Learning Disabilities, 25,* 40–47.

Rief, S. (1993). *How to reach and teach ADD/ADHD children.* West Nyack, NY: The Center for Applied Research in Education.

Rissman, M., Curtiss, S. & Tallal, P. (1990) School placement outcomes of young language-impaired children. *Journal of Speech-Language Pathology & Audiology, 14*(2), 49–58.

Ritter, B. (1968). The group desensitization of children's snake phobias using vicarious and contact desensitization procedures. *Behaviour Research & Therapy, 6,* 1–6.

Roberts, M.W. (1982). *Surviving with your adolescent who has attention deficit disorder.* In Proceedings of the Fourth Annual C.H.A.D.D. Conference: Pathways to progress [Cassette Recording]. Chicago, IL: CASET Associates.

Roberts, R., & Mather, N. (2007). *Phonic reading lessons: Practice.* Novato, CA: Academic Therapy.

Robinson, A. (1993). *What smart students know.* New York: Crown Paperbacks.

Robinson, F.P. (1970). *Effective study* (5th ed.). New York: HarperCollins.

Robinson, P.W., Newby, T.J., & Ganzell, S.L. (1981). A token system for a class of underachieving children. *Journal of Applied Behavior Analysis, 14,* 307–315.

Roffman, A.J. (2000). *Meeting the challenge of learning disabilities in adulthood.* Baltimore: Paul H. Brookes Publishing Co.

Rose, T.L. (1984). The effects of two prepractice procedures on oral reading. *Journal of Learning Disabilities, 17,* 544–548.

Rose, T.L., & Sherry, L. (1984). Relative effects of two previewing procedures on LD adolescents' oral reading performance. *Learning Disability Quarterly, 7,* 39–44.

Rosen, L.A., O'Leary, S.G., Joyce, S.A., Conway, G., & Pfiffner, L.J. (1984). The importance of prudent negative consequences for maintaining the appropriate behavior of hyperactive children. *Journal of Abnormal Child Psychology, 12,* 581–604.

Rosenberg, M.S. (1989). The effects of daily homework assignments on the acquisition of basic skills by students with learning disabilities. *Journal of Learning Disabilities, 22,* 314–323.

Rosenshine, B., & Stevens, R. (1986). Teaching functions. In M.D. Wittrock (Ed.), *Handbook of research on teaching* (3rd ed., pp. 167–216). New York: Macmillan.

Roth, F.P., & Speckman, N.J. (1994). Oral story production in adults with learning disabilities. In R.L. Bloom, L.K. DeSanti, & J.S. Ehrlich (Eds.), *Discourse analysis and applications: Studies in adult clinical populations* (pp. 131–148). Mahwah, NJ: Lawrence Erlbaum Associates.

Rothenberg, S. (1998). Nonverbal learning disabilities and social functioning: How can we help? *The Journal of the Learning Disabilities Association of Massachusetts, 8*(4), 10.

Rourke, B., Ahmad, S., Collins, D., Hayman-Abello, B., Hayman-Abello, S., & Warriner, E. (2002). Child clinical/pediatric neuropsychology: Some recent advances. *Annual Reviews of Psychology, 53,* 309–339.

Rourke, B.P. (1989). *Nonverbal learning disabilities: The syndrome and the model.* New York: Guilford Press.

Rourke, B.P. (1995). *Syndrome of nonverbal learning disabilities: Neurodevelopmental manifestations.* New York: Guilford Press.

Routh, D.K. (1978). Hyperactivity. In P.R. Magrab (Ed.), *Psychological management of pediatric problems* (Vol. 2, pp. 71–98). Baltimore: University Park Press.

Ruban, L.M. (2000). Patterns of self-regulated learning and academic achievement among university students with and without learning disabilities. (Doctoral dissertation, University of Connecticut, 2000). *Dissertation Abstracts International, 61,* 1296.

Rubin, D.L. (1990). *Perspectives on talking and learning.* Urbana, IL: National Council of Teachers of English.

Rueda, R., & Windmueller, M.P. (2006). English language learners, LD, and overrepresentation: A multiple-level analysis. *Journal of Learning Disabilities, 39,* 99–107.

Rumsey, I., & Ballard, K.D. (1985). Teaching self-management strategies for independent story writing to children with classroom behavior difficulties. *Educational Psychology, 5,* 147–157.

Rutter, M. (1978). Prevalence and types of dyslexia. In A.L. Benton & D. Pearl (Eds.), *Dyslexia: An appraisal of current knowledge* (pp. 3–28). New York: Oxford University Press.

Rutter, M. (1980). School influences on children's behavior and development. *Pediatrics, 65,* 208–220.

Rutter, M. (1985). Resilience in the face of adversity: Protective factors and resistance to psychiatric disorder. *British Journal of Psychiatry, 147,* 598–611.

Rutter, M. (1987). Psychosocial resilience and protective mechanisms. *American Journal of Orthopsychiatry, 57,* 316–331.

Rutter, M., Maughan, B., Mortimore, P., & Ouston, J. (1979). *Fifteen thousand hours: Secondary schools and their effect on children.* London: Open Books.

Safer, D.J., Zito, J.M., & Fine, E.M. (1996). Increased methylphenidate usage for attention deficit disorder in the 1990s. *Pediatrics, 98,* 1084–1088.

Sampson, M.B. (2002). Confirming a K-W-L: Considering the source. *Reading Teacher, 55,* 528–532.

Samuels, S.J. (1979). The method of repeated readings. *Reading Teacher, 32,* 403–408.

Sanderson, A. (1999). Voice recognition software: A panacea for dyslexic learners or a frustrating hindrance? *Dyslexia, 5,* 113–122.

Saski, J., Swicegood, P., & Carter, J. (1983). Note taking formats for learning disabled adolescents. *Learning Disability Quarterly, 6,* 265–272.

Satterfield, J.H., Hoppe, C.M., & Schell, A.M. (1982). A perspective study of delinquency in 110 adolescent boys with attention deficit disorder and 88 normal adolescent boys. *American Journal of Psychiatry, 139,* 795–798.

Satz, P., & Morris, R. (1981). Learning disability subtypes: A review. In F.J. Pirozzolo & M.C. Wittrock (Eds.), *Neuropsychological and cognitive processes in reading* (pp. 109–141). New York: Academic Press.

Sawyer, D.J. (1987). *Test of Awareness of Language Segments.* Austin, TX: PRO-ED.

Scarboro, M.E., & Forehand, R. (1975). Effects of two types of response contingent time out on compliance and oppositional behavior of children. *Journal of Experimental Child Psychology, 19,* 252–264.

Scarborough, H.S. (1991). Antecedents to reading disability: Preschool language development and literacy experiences of children from dyslexic families. In B.F. Pennington (Ed.), *Reading disabilities: Genetic and neurological influences* (pp. 31–45). New York: Kluwer Academic/Plenum Publishers.

Scheuermann, B., Jacobs, W.R., McCall, C., & Knies, W.C. (1994). The personal spelling dictionary: An adaptive approach to reducing the spelling hurdle in written language. *Intervention in School and Clinic, 29,* 292–299.

Schlegel, M., & Bos, C.S. (1986). *STORE the story: Fiction/fantasy reading comprehension and writing strategy.* University of Arizona, Department of Special Education and Rehabilitation, Tucson. Unpublished manuscript.

Schleifer, M., Weiss, G., Cohen, N.J., Elman, M., Cvejic, H., & Kruger, E. (1975). Hyperactivity in preschoolers and the effect of methylphenidate. *American Journal of Orthopsychiatry, 45,* 35–50.

Schneider, W., & Shiffrin, R.M. (1977). Controlled and automatic human information processing: Detection, search, and attention. *Psychological Review, 84,* 1–66.

Schoenfield, G., & Morris, R.J. (2008). Childhood fears and related anxieties. In R. Morris & N. Mather (Eds.), *Evidence-based interventions for students with learning and behavioral challenges* (pp. 79-102). New York: Routledge.

Scholnick, E.K. (1995, Fall). Knowing and constructing plans. *SRCD Newsletter,* 1–3.

Schumaker, J.B., Denton, P.H., & Deshler, D.D. (1984). *The paraphrasing strategy learning strategies curriculum.* Lawrence: University of Kansas.

Schumaker, J.B., Deshler, D.D., Alley, G.R., Warner, M.M., & Denton, P.H. (1982). MULTIPASS: A learning strategy for improving reading comprehension. *Learning Disability Quarterly, 5,* 295–304.

Schwean, V.L., Parkinson, M., Francis, G., & Lee, F. (1993). Educating the ADHD child: Debunking the myths (Special Issue). *Canadian Journal of School Psychology, 9,* 37–52.

Scott, C.M. (2000). Principles and methods of spelling instruction: Applications for poor spellers. *Topics in Language Disorders, 20*(3), 66–82.

Seabaugh, G.O., & Schumaker, J.B. (1981). *The effects of self-regulation training on academic productivity of LD and NLD adolescents* (Research Report No. 37). Lawrence: University of Kansas.

Segal, J. (1988). Teachers have enormous power in affecting a child's self-esteem. *Brown University Child Behavior and Development Newsletter, 4,* 1–3.

Semrud-Clikeman, M. (1996). Neuropsychological evidence for subtypes in developmental dyslexia. In L.R. Putnam (Ed.), *How to become a better reading teacher: Strategies for assessment and intervention* (pp. 43–52). Englewood Cliffs, NJ: Prentice Hall.

Semrud-Clikeman, M. (2005). Neuropsychological aspects for evaluating learning disabilities. *Journal of Learning Disabilities, 38,* 563–568.

Semrud-Clikeman, M., & Hynd, G.W. (1991). Specific nonverbal and social-skills deficits in children with LD. In J.E. Obrzut & G.W. Hynd (Eds.), *Neuropsychological foundations of learning disabilities: A handbook of issues, methods, and practice* (pp. 603–629). San Diego: Academic Press.

Seymour, P.H., & Evans, H.M. (1999). Foundation-level dyslexia: Assessment and treatment. *Journal of Learning Disabilities, 32,* 394–405.

Share, D.L., & Leikin, M. (2004). Language impairment at school entry and later reading disability: Connections at lexical versus supralexical levels of reading. *Scientific Studies of Reading, 8*(1), 87–110.

Shaywitz, S. (2003). *Overcoming dyslexia: A new and complete science-based program for reading problems at any level.* New York: Alfred A. Knopf.

Shaywitz, S.E., & Shaywitz, B.A. (2003). Neurobiological indices of dyslexia. In H.L. Swanson, K.R. Harris, & S. Graham (Eds.), *Handbook of learning disabilities* (pp. 514–531). New York: Guilford Press.

Shea, T.M., & Bauer, A.M. (1987). *Teaching children and youth with behavior disorders* (2nd ed.). Englewood Cliffs, NJ: Prentice Hall.

Shear, K., Jin, R., Ruscio, A.M., Walters, E.E., & Kessler, R.C. (2006). Prevalence and correlates of estimated DSM-IV child and adult separation anxiety disorder in the National Comorbidity Survey Replication. *American Journal of Psychiatry, 163,* 1074–1083.

Sheslow, D.V., Bondy, A.S., & Nelson, R.O. (1983). A comparison of graduated exposure, verbal coping skills and their combination in the treatment of children's fear of the dark. *Child and Family Behavior Therapy, 4,* 33–45.

Shure, M. (1994). *Raising a thinking child.* New York: Holt, Rinehart, & Winston.

Shure, M., & Aberson, A. (2005). Enhancing the process of resilience through effective thinking. In S. Goldstein & R. Brooks (Eds.), *Handbook of resilience* (pp. 373-396). New York: Academic Press.

Silver, A.A., & Hagin, R.A. (1990). *Disorders of learning in childhood.* New York: Wiley.

Silverman, W.K., & Nelles, W.B. (1990). Simple phobia in childhood. In M. Hersen & C.G. Last (Eds.), *Handbook of child and adult psychopathology: A longitudinal perspective* (pp. 89–103). Elmsford, NY: Pergamon Press.

Simpson, M.L., & Stahl, N.A. (1987). PORPE: A comprehensive study strategy using self-assigned writing. *Journal of College Reading and Learning, 20,* 51–57.

Simpson, R.G., & Buckhalt, J.A. (1990). A non-formula discrepancy model to identify learning disabilities. *School Psychology International, 11,* 273–279.

Sitton, R.A., & Forest, R.G. (1994). *QuickWord.* North Billerica, MA: Curriculum Associates.

Skiba, R.J., McLeskey, J., Waldron, N.L., & Grizzle, K. (1993). The context of failure in the primary grades: Risk factors in low and high referral rate classrooms. *School Psychology Quarterly, 8,* 81–98.

Slingerland, B.H. (1981). *A multisensory approach to language arts for specific language disability children: A guide for primary teachers* (Book 3). Cambridge, MA: Educators Publishing Service.

Smitely, B.L. (2001). *Factors predicting academic adjustment among college students with learning disabilities.* Unpublished doctoral dissertation, University of Miami.

Smith, C.R. (1997, February). *A hierarchy for assessing and remediating phonemic segmentation difficulties*. Paper presented at the Learning Disabilities Association International Conference, Chicago.

Smith, J.M., & Smith, D. (1966). *Child management: A program for parents*. Ann Arbor, MI: Ann Arbor Publishers.

Solomon, R.W., & Wahler, R.G. (1973). Peer reinforcement control of classroom problem behavior. *Journal of Applied Behavior Analysis, 6*, 49–56.

Soodak, L.C., & Podell, D.M. (1994). Teachers' thinking about difficult-to-teach students. *Journal of Educational Research, 88*, 44–51.

Spalding, R.B., & Spalding, W.T. (1990). *The writing road to reading* (4th ed.). New York: William Morrow.

Spear-Swerling, L., & Sternberg, R.J. (1996). *Off track: When poor readers become "learning disabled."* Boulder, CO: Westview Press.

Speece, D.I. (2005). Hitting the moving target known as reading development: Some thoughts on screening first-grade children for secondary interventions. *Journal of Learning Disabilities, 38*, 437–493.

Sprick, M., Howard, L., & Fidanque, A. (1998). *Read well*. Longmont, CO: Sopris West.

Spring, C., Yellin, A.M., & Greenberg, L.M. (1976). Effects of imipramine and methylphenidate on perceptual-motor performance of hyperactive children. *Perceptual and Motor Skills, 43*, 459–470.

Stahl, S.A., & Stahl, K.A.D. (2004). Word wizards all! Teaching word meanings in preschool and primary education. In J.F. Baumann & E.J. Kame'enui (Eds.), *Vocabulary instruction: Research to practice* (pp. 59–78). New York: Guilford Press.

Stanovich, K.E. (1982a). Individual differences in the cognitive processes of reading: I. Word decoding. *Journal of Learning Disabilities, 15*, 485–493.

Stanovich, K.E. (1982b). Individual differences in the cognitive processes of reading: II. Text-level processes. *Journal of Learning Disabilities, 15*, 549–554.

Stanovich, K.E. (1991). Conceptual and empirical problems with discrepancy definitions of reading disability. *Learning Disability Quarterly, 14*, 269–280.

Stanovich, K.E. (1994). Are discrepancy-based definitions of dyslexia empirically defensible? In K.P. van den Bos, L.S. Siegel, D.J. Bakker, & D.L. Share (Eds.), *Current directions in dyslexia research* (pp. 15–30). Lisse, Netherlands: Swets & Zeitlinger.

Stanovich, K.E. (1999). The sociopsychometrics of learning disabilities. *Journal of Learning Disabilities, 32*, 350–361.

Stanovich, K.E. (2005). The future of a mistake: Will discrepancy measurement continue to make learning disabilities a pseudoscience? *Learning Disability Quarterly, 28*, 103–106.

Stanovich, K.E., Siegel, L.S., & Gottardo, A. (1997). Converging evidence for phonological and surface subtypes of reading disability. *Journal of Educational Psychology, 89*, 114–127.

Stark, K.D., Livingston, R.B., Laurent, J.L., & Cardenas, B. (1993). *Childhood depression: Relationship to academic achievement and scholastic performance*. Unpublished manuscript.

Stein, M. (1997). We have tried everything and nothing works: Family-centered pediatrics and clinical problem solving. *Journal of Developmental and Behavioral Pediatrics, 18*, 114–119.

Stein, N., & Glenn, C.G. (1979). An analysis of story comprehension in elementary school children. In R.O. Freedle (Ed.), *New directions in discourse processes* (Vol. 2, pp. 53–120). Norwood, NJ: Ablex.

Stern, C., & Stern, M. (1971). *Children discover arithmetic: An introduction to structural arithmetic*. New York: HarperCollins.

Stern, M.B. (2005). Multisensory mathematics instruction. In J.R. Birsh (Ed.), *Multisensory teaching of basic language skills* (2nd ed., pp. 457–479). Baltimore: Paul H. Brookes Publishing Co.

Stewart, S.R. (1992). Development of written language proficiency: Methods for teaching text structure. In C.S. Simon (Ed.), *Communication skills and classroom success* (pp. 419–432). Eau Claire, WI: Thinking Publications.

Stokes, T.R., & Baer, D.M. (1977). An implicit technology of generalization. *Journal of Applied Behavior Analysis, 10*, 349–367.

Stoner, G., & Carey, S.P. (1992). Serving students diagnosed with ADD: Avoiding deficits in professional attention. *School Psychology Quarterly, 7*, 302–307.

Storch, S.A., & Whitehurst, G.J. (2002). Oral language and code-related precursors to reading: Evidence from a longitudinal structural model. *Developmental Psychology, 38*, 934–937.

Stormont, M. (1998). Family factors associated with externalizing disorders and preschools. *Journal of Early Intervention, 21*, 232–251.

Stott, D.H. (1981). Behavior disturbance and failure to learn: A study of cause and effect. *Educational Research, 23*, 163–172.

Strang, J.D., & Rourke, B.P. (1985). Arithmetic disability subtypes: The neuropsychological significance of specific arithmetical impairment in childhood. In B.P. Rourke (Ed.), *Neuropsychology of learning disabilities: Essentials of subtype analysis* (pp. 167–183). New York: Guilford Press.

Strauss, A.A., & Lehtinen, L.E. (1947). *The psychopathology and education of the brain-injured child* (Vol. 1). New York: Grune & Stratton.

Strauss, C.C., Lease, C.A., Last, C.G., & Francis, G. (1988). Overanxious disorder: An examination of developmental differences. *Journal of Abnormal Child Psychology, 16*, 433–443.

Strickland, G. (1998). *Bad teachers*. New York: Pocket Books.

Strother, D.B. (1984). Another look at time-on-task. *Phi Delta Kappan, 66*, 714–717.

Struthers, J.P., Bartlamay, H., Dell, S., & McLaughlin, T.F. (1994). An analysis of the Add-A-Word spelling program and public posting across three categories of children with special needs. *Reading Improvement, 31*, 28–36.

Stuart, M. (1999). Getting ready for reading: Early phoneme awareness and phonics teaching improves reading and spelling in inner-city second language learners. *British Journal of Educational Psychology, 69*, 587–605.

Sullivan, M.A., & O'Leary, S.G. (1990). Maintenance following reward and cost token programs. *Behavior Therapy, 21*, 139–149.

Sulzer-Azaroff, B., & Mayer, G.R. (1991). *Behavior analysis for lasting change*. New York: Holt, Rinehart & Winston.

Suritsky, S.K., & Hughes, C.A. (1993). *Note taking strategy training for college students with learning disabilities*. Unpublished manuscript, Pennsylvania State University, University Park.

Swanson, H.L., & Hoskyn, M. (1998). Experimental intervention research on students with learning disabilities: A meta-analysis of treatment outcomes. *Review of Educational Research, 68*, 277–321.

Swanson, H.L., & Hoskyn, M. (2001). A meta-analysis of intervention research for adolescent students with learning disabilities. *Learning Disabilities Research & Practice, 16*, 109–119.

Swanson, H.L., & Jerman, O. (2006). Math disabilities: A selective meta-analysis of the literature. *Review of Educational Research, 76*, 249–274.

Swanson, H.L., & Saez, L. (2003). Memory difficulties in children and adults with learning disabilities. In H.L. Swanson, K.R. Harris, & S. Graham (Eds.), *Handbook of learning disabilities* (pp. 182–198). New York: Guilford Press.

Swanson, H.L., & Siegel, L. (2001). Learning disabilities as a working memory deficit. *Issues in Education, 7*, 1–48.

Swanson, J.M., Cantwell, D., Lerner, M., McBurnett, K., & Hanna, G. (1991). Effects of stimulant medication on learning in children with ADHD. *Journal of Learning Disabilities, 24*, 219–230.

Sylvester, C., Hyde, T.S., & Reichsler, R.J. (1987). The diagnostic interview for children and personality inventory for children in studies of children at risk for anxiety disorders or depression. *Journal of the American Academy of Child and Adolescent Psychiatry, 26*, 668–675.

Tangel, D.M., & Blachman, B.A. (1992). Effect of phoneme awareness instruction on kindergarten children's invented spelling. *Journal of Reading Behavior, 24*, 233–261.

Tarver-Behring, S., Barkley, R.A., & Karlsson, J. (1985). The mother–child interactions of hyperactive boys and their normal siblings. *American Journal of Orthopsychiatry, 355*, 202–209.

Temple, E., Poldrack, R.A., Salidis, J., Deutsch, G.K., Tallal, P., Merzenich, M.M., et al. (2001). Disrupted neural responses to phonological and orthographic processing in dyslexic children: An fMRI study. *NeuroReport, 12*, 299–307.

Templeton, S. (2004). The vocabulary–spelling connection: Orthographic development and morphological knowledge at the intermediate grades and beyond. In J.F. Baumann & E.J. Kame'enui (Eds.), *Vocabulary instruction: Research to practice* (pp. 118–138). New York: Guilford Press.

Tenenbaum, H.R., & Ruck, M.D. (2007). Are teachers' expectations different for racial minority than for European American students? A meta-analysis. *Journal of Educational Psychology, 99*, 253–273.

Terestman, N. (1980). Mood quality and intensity in nursery school children as predictors of behavior disorder. *American Journal of Orthopsychiatry, 50*, 125–138.

Tesiny, E.P., Lefkowitz, M.M., & Gordon, W.H. (1980). Childhood depression, locus of control, and school achievement. *Journal of Educational Psychology, 72*, 506–510.

Thomas, A., & Chess, S. (1977). *Temperament and development*. Levittown, PA: Brunner/Mazel Publishing.

Thomas, D.R., Becker, W.C., & Armstrong, M. (1968). Production and elimination of disruptive classroom behavior by systematically varying teachers' behavior. *Journal of Applied Behavior Analysis, 1*, 35–45.

Thomsen, K. (2002). *Building resilient students*. Thousand Oaks, CA: Corwin Press.

Thurber, D.N. (1983). Write on! With continuous stroke point. *Academic Therapy, 18*, 389–395.

Tobias, S. (1993). *Overcoming math anxiety*. New York: W.W. Norton.

Torgesen, J.K. (1992). Learning disabilities: Historical and conceptual issues. In B.Y.L. Wong (Ed.), *Learning about learning disabilities* (pp. 3–38). San Diego: Academic Press.

Torgesen, J.K. (1993). Variations on theory in learning disabilities. In G.R. Lyon, D.B. Gray, J.F. Kavanagh, & N.A. Krasnegor (Eds.), *Better understanding learning disabilities: New views from research and their implications for education and public policies* (pp. 153–170). Baltimore: Paul H. Brookes Publishing Co.

Torgesen, J.K. (1994). Issues in the assessment of executive function: An information-processing perspective. In G.R. Lyon (Ed.), *Frames of reference for the assessment of learning disabilities: New views on measurement issues* (pp. 143–162). Baltimore: Paul H. Brookes Publishing Co.

Torgesen, J.K., Alexander, A.W., Wagner, R.K., Rashotte, C.A., Voeller, K., Conway, T., et al. (2001). Intensive remedial instruction for children with severe reading disabilities: Immediate and long-term outcomes from two instructional approaches. *Journal of Learning Disabilities, 34,* 33–58.

Torgesen, J.K., & Burgess, S.R. (1998). Consistency of reading-related phonological processes throughout early childhood: Evidence from longitudinal-correlational and instructional studies. In J.L. Metsala & L.C. Ehri (Eds.), *Word recognition in beginning literacy* (pp. 161–188). Mahwah, NJ: Lawrence Erlbaum Associates.

Treiman, R. (1998). Why spelling? The benefits of incorporating spelling into beginning reading instruction. In J.L. Metsala & L.C. Ehri (Eds.), *Word recognition in beginning literacy* (pp. 289–313). Mahwah, NJ: Lawrence Erlbaum Associates.

Treiman, R., & Bourassa, D.C. (2000). The development of spelling skill. *Topics in Language Disorders, 20*(3), 1–18.

Trueman, D. (1984). What are the characteristics of school phobic children? *Psychological Reports, 5,* 191–202.

Tsovili, T.D. (2004). The relationship between language teachers' attitudes and the state-trait anxiety of adolescents with dyslexia. *Journal of Research in Reading, 27,* 69–86.

Turner, B.G., Beidel, D.C., Hughes, S., & Turner, M.W. (1993). Text anxiety in African American school children. *School Psychology Quarterly, 8,* 140–152.

U.S. Bureau of the Census (2005). http://factfinder.census.gov/home/saff/nain.html?_ling5en

Vaal, J.J. (1973). Applying contingency contracting to school phobia: A case study. *Journal of Behavior Therapy and Experimental Psychiatry, 4,* 371–373.

Vacca, D.M. (2001). Confronting the puzzle of nonverbal learning disabilities. *Educational Leadership, 59*(3), 26–32.

Van Hauten, R., Nau, P., MacKenzie-Keating, S., Sameoto, D., & Colavecchia, B. (1982). An analysis of some variables influencing the effectiveness of reprimands. *Journal of Applied Behavior Analysis, 15,* 65–83.

Vaughn, S., & Klingner, J.K. (1999). Teaching reading comprehension through collaborative strategic reading. *Intervention in School and Clinic, 34,* 284–292.

Vellutino, F.R. (1979). *Dyslexia: Theory and research.* Cambridge, MA: The MIT Press.

Vellutino, F.R., & Scanlon, D.M. (1987). Phonological coding, phonological awareness, and reading ability: Evidence from a longitudinal and experimental study. *Merrill Palmer Quarterly, 33,* 321–363.

Vellutino, F.R., Scanlon, D.M., & Tanzman, M.S. (1994). Components of reading ability: Issues and problems in operationalizing word identification, phonological coding, and orthographics coding. In G.R. Lyon (Ed.), *Frames of reference for the assessment of learning disabilities: New views on measurement issues* (pp. 279–332). Baltimore: Paul H. Brookes Publishing Co.

Voeller, K.S. (1991). Towards a neurobiologic nosology of attention deficit hyperactivity disorder. *Journal of Child Neurology, 6,* S2–S8.

Vogel, S., & Moran, M.R. (1982). Written language disorders in learning disabled college students: A preliminary report. In W. Cruickshank & J. Lerner (Eds.), *The Best of ACLD 1981: Vol 3. Coming of age* (pp. 211–225). Syracuse, NY: Syracuse University Press.

Vygotsky, L.S. (1978). *Mind in society.* Cambridge, MA: Harvard University Press.

Wagner, R.K., & Torgesen, J.K. (1987). The nature of phonological processing and its causal role in the acquisition of reading skills. *Psychological Bulletin, 101,* 192–212.

Wagner, R.K., Torgesen, J.K., Laughon, P., Simmons, K., & Rashotte, C.A. (1993). The development of young readers' phonological processing abilities. *Journal of Educational Psychology, 85,* 1–20.

Walker, H.M., & Rankin, R. (1983). Assessing the behavioral expectations and demands of less restrictive settings. *School Psychology Review, 12,* 274–284.

Walker, H.M., & Walker, J.E. (1991). *Coping with non-compliance in the classroom.* Austin, TX: PRO-ED.

Walker, J., & Shea, T.M. (1990). *Behavior management: A practical approach for educators.* (4th ed.). Upper Saddle River, NJ: Pearson Education.

Wallace, G.W., & Bott, D.A. (1989). Statement-pie: A strategy to improve the paragraph writing skills of adolescents with learning disabilities. *Journal of Learning Disabilities, 22,* 541–543, 553.

Wallach, G.P., & Miller, L. (1988). *Language intervention and academic success.* New York: Little, Brown.

Wechsler, D. (1991). *Wechsler Intelligence Scale for Children* (3rd ed.). San Antonio, TX: The Psychological Corporation.

Weinberg, W., & Rehmet, A. (1983). Childhood affective disorder and school problems. In D.P. Cantwell & G.A. Carlson (Eds.), *Affective disorders in childhood and adolescence: An update* (pp. 109–128). Jamaica, NY: Spectrum.

Weiner, B. (1974). *Achievement motivation and attribution theory.* Morristown, NJ: General Learning Press.

Weiner, S. (1994). Four first graders' descriptions of how they spell. *Elementary School Journal, 94,* 315–332.

Weinstein, C.S. (1979). The physical environment of the school. *Review of Educational Research, 49,* 577–610.

Weintraub, N., & Graham, S. (1998). Writing legibly and quickly: A study of children's ability to adjust their handwriting to meet common classroom demands. *Learning Disabilities Research & Practice, 13*, 146–152.

Weintraub, S., & Mesulum, M.M. (1983). Developmental learning disabilities of the right hemisphere. *Archives of Neurology, 40*, 463–468.

Weiss, G., & Hechtman, L. (1979). The hyperactive child syndrome. *Science, 205*, 1348–1354.

Weiss, G., & Hechtman, L. (1993). *Hyperactive children grown up: ADHD in children, adolescents, and adults* (2nd ed.). New York: Guilford Press.

Weist, M.D. (2003). Commentary: Promoting paradigmatic change in child and adolescent mental health and schools. *School Psychology Review, 32*, 336–341.

Wellington, T.M., Semrud-Clikeman, M., Gregory, A.L., Murphy, J.M., & Lancaster, J.L. (2006). Magnetic resonance imaging volumetric analysis of the putamen in children with ADHD: Combined type versus control. *Journal of Attention Disorders, 10*, 171–180.

Wender, P.H. (1979). The concept of adult minimal brain dysfunction. In L. Bellak (Ed.), *Psychiatric aspects of minimal brain dysfunction in adults* (pp. 97–115). New York: Grune & Stratton.

Werner, E.E. (1993). Risk, resilience, and recovery: Perspectives from the Kauai longitudinal study. *Development and Psychopathology, 5*, 503–515.

Werner, E.E. (1994). Overcoming the odds. *Developmental and Behavioral Pediatrics, 15*, 131–136.

Werner, E.E., & Smith, R.S. (1992). *Overcoming the odds: High risk children from birth to adulthood.* Ithaca, NY: Cornell University Press.

West, R.P., & Sloan, H.N. (1986). Teacher presentation rate and point delivery rate. *Behavior Modification, 10*, 267–286.

Westby, C.E. (1994). The effects of culture on genre, structure, and style of oral and written texts. In G.P. Wallach & K.G. Butler (Eds.), *Language learning disabilities in school-age children and adolescents* (pp. 180–218). New York: Merrill.

Westman, J.C. (1996). Concepts of dyslexia. In L.R. Putnam (Ed.), *How to become a better reading teacher: Strategies for assessment and intervention* (pp. 65–73). Upper Saddle River, NJ: Prentice Hall.

Whalen, C.K., & Henker, B. (1991). Therapies for hyperactive children: Comparisons, combinations, and compromises. *Journal of Consulting and Clinical Psychology, 59*, 126–137.

Whalen, C.K., Henker, B., Collins, B., McAuliffe, S., & Vaux, A. (1979). Peer interaction in a structured communication task: Comparisons of normal and hyperactive boys and of methylphenidate (Ritalin) and placebo effects. *Child Development, 50*, 388–401.

Wheldall, K., & Lam, Y.Y. (1987). Rows versus tables: The effects of two classroom seating arrangements on classroom disruption rate, on-task behavior and teacher behavior in three special school classes. *Educational Psychology: An International Journal of Experimental Educational Psychology, 7*, 303–312.

White, E.B. (1999). *Stuart Little.* New York: HarperCollins Publishers. (Original work published 1945).

White, M.A. (1975). Natural rates of teacher approval and disapproval in the classroom. *Journal of Applied Behavioral Analysis, 8*, 367–372.

Wigfield, A., & Meece, J.L. (1988). Math anxiety in elementary and secondary school students. *Journal of Educational Psychology, 80*, 210–216.

Wilde, S. (1997). *What's a schwa sound anyway?* Westport, CT: William Heinemann.

Williams, J.P. (2005). Instruction in reading comprehension for primary-grade students: A focus on text structure. *Journal of Special Education, 39*(1), 6–18.

Willams, J.P., Hall, K.M., & Lauer, K.D. (2004). Teaching expository text structure to young at-risk learners: Building the basics of comprehension instruction. *Exceptionality, 12*(3), 129–144.

Willows, D.M., Kruk, R.S., & Corcos, E. (Eds.). (1993). *Visual processes in reading and reading disabilities.* Mahwah, NJ: Lawrence Erlbaum Associates.

Willows, D.M., & Terepocki, M. (1993). The relation of reversal errors to reading disabilities. In D.M. Willows, R.S. Kruk, & E. Corcos (Eds.), *Visual processes in reading and reading disabilities* (pp. 31–56). Mahwah, NJ: Lawrence Erlbaum Associates.

Wilson, B. (2004). *Wilson Reading/System®, instructor manual* (3rd ed.). Oxford, MA: Wilson Language Training.

Wilson Language Training. (2002). *Fundations™.* Oxford, MA: Wilson Language Training.

Wilson Language Training. (2006). *Wilson Fluency/Basic.* Oxford, MA: Wilson Language Training.

Wittchen, H.U., Stein M.B., & Kessler, R.C. (1999). Social fears and social phobia in a community sample of adolescents and young adults: Prevalence, risk factors and comorbidity. *Psychological Medicine, 29*, 309–323.

Wolf, M. (1999). What time may tell: Towards a new conceptualization of developmental dyslexia. *Annals of Dyslexia, 49*, 3–28.

Wolf, M., & Bowers, P.G. (1999). The double-deficit hypothesis for the developmental dyslexias. *Journal of Educational Psychology, 91*, 415–438.

Wolf, M., & Denckla, M.B. (2006). *Rapid Automatized Naming and Rapid Alternating Stimulus tests.* Austin, TX: PRO-ED.

Wolf, M., Miller, L., & Donnelly, K. (2000). Retrieval, automaticity, vocabulary, elaboration, orthography (RAVE-O): A comprehensive fluency-based reading intervention program. *Journal of Learning Disabilities, 33*, 322–324.

Wolf, M., O'Brien, B., Donnelly Adams, K., Joffe, T., Jeffrey, J., Lovett, M., et al. (2003). Working for time: Reflections on naming speed, reading fluency, and intervention. In B. Foorman (Ed.), *Preventing and remediating reading difficulties: Bringing science to scale* (pp. 355–379). Timonium, MD: York Press.

Wolf, M., & Segal, D. (1999). Retrieval rate, accuracy, and vocabulary elaboration (RAVE) in reading-impaired children: A pilot intervention program. *Dyslexia, 5*, 1–27.

Wolfson, J., Fields, J.H., & Rose, S.A. (1987). Symptoms, temperament, resiliency and control in anxiety disordered preschool children. *Journal of the American Academy of Child and Adolescent Psychiatry, 26*, 16–22.

Wong, B.Y.L. (1986). A cognitive approach to spelling. *Exceptional Children, 53*, 169–173.

Wong, B.Y.L., Harris, K.R., Graham, S., & Butler, D. (2003). Cognitive strategies instruction research in learning disabilities. In H.L. Swanson, K.R. Harris, & S. Graham (Eds.), *Handbook of learning disabilities* (pp. 383–402). New York: Guilford Press.

Wong, B.Y.L., Wong, R., Darlington, D., & Jones, W. (1991). Interactive teaching: An effective way to teach revision skills to adolescents with learning disabilities. *Learning Disabilities Research & Practice, 6*, 117–127.

Woodcock, R.W., McGrew, K.S., & Mather, N. (2001). *Woodcock-Johnson III Tests of Cognitive Ability*. Itasca, IL: Riverside.

Woodward, J. (2006). Making reform-based mathematics work for academically low-achieving middle school students. In M. Montague & A. Jitendra (Eds.), *Teaching mathematics to middle school students with learning difficulties* (pp. 29–50). New York: Guilford Press.

Wylie, R., & Durrell, D. (1970). Teaching vowels through phonograms. *Elementary English, 47*, 787–791.

Zabel, R.H. (1987). Preparation of teachers for behaviorally disordered students: A review of literature. In M.C. Wang, M.C. Reynolds, & H.J. Walberg (Eds.), *Handbook of special education: Research and practice* (Vol. 2). New York: Pergamon Press.

Zagar, R., & Bowers, N. (1983). The effect of time of day on problem solving and classroom behavior. *Psychology in the Schools, 20*, 337–345.

Zahn-Waxler, C., Schmitz, S., Fulker, D., Robinson, J., & Ende, R. (1996). Behavior problems in five-year-old monozygotic and dizygotic twins: Genetic and environmental influences, patterns of regulation and internationalization of control. *Developmental Psychopathology, 8*, 103–122.

Zametkin, A.J., & Rapoport, J.L. (1987). Neurobiology of attention-deficit disorder with hyperactivity: Where have we come in 50 years? *Journal of the American Academy of Child and Adolescent Psychiatry, 36*, 676–686.

Zentall, S.S. (1984). Context effects in the behavioral ratings of hyperactivity. *Journal of Abnormal Child Psychology, 12*, 345–352.

Zentall, S.S. (1988). Production deficiencies in elicited language but not in the spontaneous verbalizations of hyperactive children. *Exceptional Children, 60*, 143–153.

Zentall, S.S. (1989). Attentional cuing and spelling tasks for hyperactive and comparison regular classroom children. *Journal of Special Education, 23*, 83–93.

Zentall, S.S. (1995). Modifying classroom tasks and environments. In S. Goldstein (Ed.), *Understanding and managing children's classroom behavior* (pp. 356–374). New York: Wiley.

Zentall, S.S. (2005). *ADHD and education: Foundations, characteristics, methods and collaboration*. Upper Saddle River, NJ: Prentice Hall.

Zentall, S.S. (2006). *ADHD and education: Foundations, characteristics, methods, and collaborations*. New York: Merrill Publishers.

Zentall, S.S., & Goldstein, S. (1999). *Seven steps to homework success*. Plantation, FL: Specialty Press.

Zentall, S.S., & Kruczek, T. (1988). The attraction of color for active attention-problem children. *Journal of Abnormal Child Psychology, 15*, 519–536.

Zigmond, N. (2004). Searching for the most effective service delivery model for students with learning disabilities. In H.L. Swanson, K.R. Harris, & S. Graham (Eds.), *Handbook of learning disabilities* (pp. 110–122). New York: Guilford Press.

Zigmond, N., Jenkins, J., Fuchs, L., Deno, S., Fuchs, D., Baker, J.N., et al. (1995). Special education in restructured schools: Findings from three multi-year studies. *Phi Delta Kappan, 76*, 531–540.

Zimmerman, B.J. (1986). Becoming a self-regulated learner: Which are the key subprocesses? *Contemporary Educational Psychology, 11*, 307–313.

Zirkel, P.A. (1992). A checklist for determining legal eligibility of ADD/ADHD students. *Special Educator, 8*, 93–97.

INDEX

Page numbers followed by *f* indicate figures; those followed by *t* indicate tables.